# Intellectual Property Law and Access to Medicines



The history of patent harmonization is a story of dynamic actors, whose interactions with established structures shaped the patent regime. From the inception of the trade regime to include intellectual property (IP) rights to the present, this book documents the role of different sets of actors – states, transnational business corporations, or civil society groups – and their influence on the structures – such as national and international agreements, organizations, and private entities – that have caused changes to healthcare and access to medication. Presenting the debates over patents, trade, and the Agreement on Trade-Related Aspects of Intellectual Property Rights (TRIPS Agreement), as it galvanized non-state and nonbusiness actors, the book highlights how an alternative framing and understanding of pharmaceutical patent rights emerged: as a public issue, instead of a trade or IP issue. The book thus offers an important analysis of the legal and political dynamics through which the contest for access to lifesaving medication has been, and will continue to be, fought.

In addition to academics working in the areas of international law, development, and public health, this book will also be of interest to policy makers, state actors, and others with relevant concerns working in nongovernmental and international organizations.

**Srividhya Ragavan** is a Professor of Law and Director of the India Program at Texas A&M University School of Law, Texas, United States.

**Amaka Vanni** is an Assistant Professor at School of Law, University of Leeds, United Kingdom.

Part of the
LAW, DEVELOPMENT AND GLOBALIZATION
series

Series editors
Julio Faundez, *University of Warwick, UK*
Adriaan Bedner, *University of Leiden, The Netherlands*

For information about the series and details of previous and forthcoming titles, see https://www.routledge.com/Law-Development-and-Globalization/book-series/CAV30

A GlassHouse book

# Intellectual Property Law and Access to Medicines

## TRIPS Agreement, Health, and Pharmaceuticals

**Edited by Srividhya Ragavan and Amaka Vanni**

Routledge
Taylor & Francis Group
a GlassHouse Book

First published 2021
by Routledge
2 Park Square, Milton Park, Abingdon, Oxon OX14 4RN

and by Routledge
605 Third Avenue, New York, NY 10158

A GlassHouse book

*Routledge is an imprint of the Taylor & Francis Group, an informa business*



*British Library Cataloguing-in-Publication Data*
A catalogue record for this book is available from the British Library

*Library of Congress Cataloging-in-Publication Data*
Names: Ragavan, Srividhya, editor. | Vanni, Amaka, editor.
Title: Intellectual property law and access to medicine: TRIPS Agreement, health, and pharmaceuticals/edited by Srividhya Ragavan and Amaka Vanni. Description: Milton Park, Abingdon, Oxon; New York, NY: Routledge, 2021. | Series: Law, development and globalization | Includes bibliographical references and index.
Identifiers: LCCN 2020056692 (print) | LCCN 2020056693 (ebook) | ISBN 9780367436384 (hardback) | ISBN 9781003176602 (ebook)
Subjects: LCSH: Drugs–Patents. | Drug accessibility–Law and legislation. | Foreign trade regulation–Health aspects. | Agreement on Trade-Related Aspects of Intellectual Property Rights (1994 April 15) | Patents (International law)
Classification: LCC K1519.D78 I58 2021 (print) | LCC K1519.D78 (ebook) | DDC 346.04/86–dc23
LC record available at https://lccn.loc.gov/2020056692
LC ebook record available at https://lccn.loc.gov/2020056693

ISBN: 978-0-367-43638-4 (hbk)
ISBN: 978-1-032-00970-4 (pbk)
ISBN: 978-1-003-17660-2 (ebk)

Typeset in Galliard
by KnowledgeWorks Global Ltd.

To our beloved parents, families and friends

# Contents

# Preface

The globe that existed at the start of the book ceased to exist at the time we completed it. The globe which enabled Amaka, from Nigeria and Sri, from Texas to meet in Washington, DC had been "masked" by an incredible virus unleashing its prowess. COVID-19 snuck on a globe drunk on trade and a specific ideology of intellectual property (IP), which ultimately created a new class defined only by their ability to access health care! Except, of course, the United States, which after refusing meaningful scientific data, bravely fought the virus – unmasked – in a manner reminiscent of a true maverick fighting without armory.

As India and South Africa appealed to the Trade-Related Aspects of Intellectual Property Rights (TRIPS) Council seeking a waiver from the patent provisions, COVID-19 completed the process of personifying the flaws of the New Trading Order. Hopefully, COVID-19 represents an opportunity in a world order where the flourish of the trade regime will lie in acknowledging its flaws and failings to form a cohesive coalition for a new beginning.

# Acknowledgements

The Society of International Economic Law (SIEL) Global Conference was held in Washington, DC in 2018. That year, the conference was bustling with activity. I was excited to be at the 2018 SIEL Global Conference to which I had gone to receive the first SIEL/Hart Prize for Early Career Scholar in International Economic Law. At the conference, a friend introduced me to Professor Srividhya Ragavan, Texas A&M School of Law, who was there for a day to make a presentation on mapping three generations of access to medicines. I had cited Sri Ragavan's book several times in my PhD thesis and, hence was excited to meet Sri in person. Our meeting at SIEL was brief but we laughed about how legal discourse had excluded critical actors involved in the debate. As with most things in life, this conversation laid the foundation for further deliberations and incubated the idea of three generations of access to medication into an edited book project.

The beginnings of our work together were tumultuous. We lived in different continents, in completely different time zones, but most importantly, living in Dubai, I lacked access to WhatsApp calls, which remains to be Sri's lifeline to the world. To me, it sounded like the inability to make WhatsApp calls was the final nail on the coffin, shutting down our dream project. Neither of us fully recall what revived the project, but it did, thankfully.

We began the project as academics committed to the cause of access, not to philosophical greatness of an ideology; our commitment to use policy as a tool to generate real change that touches the lives of others. Thus, this project has contributions from academics, trade, and intellectual property (IP) experts alongside the voice of activists, each offering diverse perspectives and analyses on the Trade-Related Aspects of Intellectual Property Rights (TRIPS) Agreement, right to health, and access to medicines. The myriad issues explored in this book, as we have seen, address distinct shifts and rupture within the medicines access debates and global pharmaceutical patent regime. In focusing on issues affecting trade and the IP system, the chapters in this book have each delved into substantive legal issues, realistic impediments and concerns, and the politics and law of the global pharmaceutical patent regime. The biggest takeaway for us is the privilege of knowing and connecting with each of our authors and their work. Their knowledge and commitment to the cause has been our fuel to complete it in a timely manner.

As we present this book, Sri and I have often reminisced about how both of our lives unfolded simultaneously. We both felt excitement over different things that connected us with the idea of enabling access – me over a documentary, and Sri, over a blog. We both moved from our respective locations to new homes, new lives. My young son learnt to walk as we finished our chapter together without WhatsApp! I lost a dear family member even as Sri struggled with the realities of ill-health of a dear family member. I adjusted to a new job. I have worked from Nigeria, the United Kingdom, and Dubai, many times connecting after my family was fast asleep. Sri has worked from the United States and India, oftentimes late into the middle of the night. Yawning five times every three seconds over Zoom was a common feature for both of us!

By the time Sri and I presented this book to the publisher, even more unique realities had unfolded. COVID-19 had unfurled itself and engulfed the globe, "Zoom"ing it into a new reality! If anything, COVID-19 further stressed the importance of public health, of access and the reality that the global discourse on innovation has become disconnected with the cause for which it began – human lives! As coeditors, we believe the true success of this project will be realized when many of the questions raised in this book become redundant with the universal availability of access to medication.

Both of us co-editors have benefited from the guidance and inputs of a number of colleagues and friends. We want to acknowledge Texas A&M University for the PESCA Grant. Personally, both of us want to thank our families, parents, and in-laws – every page is symbolic of the contributions of our families to our lives.

# Notes on Contributors

## The Editors

**Dr. Srividhya Ragavan** is a Professor of Law at Texas A&M University School of Law where she is the Director of the India Program. She is the author of *Patent and Trade Disparities in Developing Countries* (2012), and coeditor (with Irene Calboli) of *Diversity in Intellectual Property – Identities, Interests, and Intersections* (2016).

**Dr. Amaka Vanni** is an Assistant Professor of Law at the School of Law, University of Leeds, United Kingdom. She is the author of the award-winning book *Patent Games in The Global South: Pharmaceutical Patent Law-Making in Brazil, India and Nigeria* (2020). She received a BA (honors) from Keele University and LLM and PhD degrees in International Economic Law from the University of Warwick, United Kingdom.

## The Contributors

**Brook K. Baker** is a Professor, Northeastern University. School of Law, Honorary Research Fellow – University of KwaZulu Natal, Senior Policy Analyst – Health GAP (Global Access Project).

**Swaraj Paul Barooah** is an independent consultant on IP policy. He has observed and analyzed the Access to Knowledge and Access to Medicines movements in India as well as globally for more than a decade as an online analyst and subsequently as editor in chief of SpicyIP (https://spicyip.com/). He was also formerly Policy Director at the Centre for Internet and Society (CIS), India, as well as the Project Manager for the 4th Global Congress on IP and the Public Interest (New Delhi, 2015).

**Dr. Jorge Antonio Zepeda Bermudez** is a medical doctor with a master's degree in Communicable Diseases (Tropical Medicine) and a PhD in Public Health. He is currently a Senior Researcher and Head of the NAF. He was the Executive Director for UNITAID and later became the Vice President for Health Production and Innovation at Fiocruz.

**Dr. Gabriela Costa Chaves** holds master's and PhD degrees in Public Health focused on pharmaceutical policies. Dr. Gabriela Costa Chaves holds master's and PhD degrees in Public Health (ENSP/Fiocruz) focused on pharmaceutical policies. In 2013, she joined the Department of Medicines Policy and Pharmaceutical Services (NAF) at ENSP/Fiocruz as a researcher. She has worked for several civil society and non-for-profit organizations.

**Jeremy de Beer** is Law Professor at the University of Ottawa's Faculty of Law and Member of the Centre for Law, Technology, and Society. He is also a cofounding director of the Open African Innovation Research network, Senior Fellow at the Centre for International Governance Innovation, and Senior Research Associate at the University of Cape Town's IP Unit. As a practicing lawyer, he has argued more than a dozen cases before the Supreme Court of Canada, advised businesses and law firms large and small, and consulted for agencies from national governments, global think tanks, and the United Nations.

**Felipe de Carvalho Borges da Fonseca** is a Journalist, Member of GTPI-Rebrip since 2011, and acting coordinator since 2012. He holds a Master's degree in International Political Economy from the Institute of Economics (PEPI/IE/UFRJ), Federal University of Rio de Janeiro, Rio de Janeiro, Brazil.

**Graham Dutfield** is a Professor of International Governance, School of Law, University of Leeds.

**Teo Firpo** is a Researcher for the Innovation Growth Lab (IGL) for Nesta in London, England.

**Gaëlle Groux** holds a BSc in Biomedical and Political Science from Western University and a joint Juris Doctor and Master of International Affairs at the University of Ottawa and Carleton University, respectively. She has worked with both the Open African Innovation Research (OpenAIR) Network and Universities Allied for Essential Medicines (UAEM) on intellectual property issues for many years. She is a published author in both immunology and law journals and has presented her work at numerous international conferences.

**Anand Grover** is a Senior Advocate practicing in the Supreme Court of India and is the Director of the Lawyers Collective. He and his team in the Lawyers Collective represented the Cancer Patients Aid Association in the Novartis case from the beginning in the Patent Controller Office to the end in the Supreme Court. Mr. Grover is a pioneer in the field of HIV and has handled several hundred HIV-related litigations in India. He was the UN Special Rapporteur on the right of everyone to the enjoyment of the highest attainable standard of physical and mental health from 2008 to 2014.

**Dr. Anthony C. K. Kakooza**'s research and academic interests are primarily on Intellectual Property law aspects related to Traditional Knowledge and

Folklore (Traditional Cultural Expressions). He is an Associate Professor of Law at Uganda Christian University as well as an Adjunct Professor of Law at the University of Illinois in Urbana-Champaign and has served as a Visiting Professor at the Cornell University Law School in New York as well as Masaryk University, Brno, Czech Republic.

**Dr. Burcu Kilic** is a Research Director, Access to Medicines Program, Public Citizen. Dr. Kilic is a scholar, lawyer, and advocate with over a decade of experience working in social justice movements, as well as building and leading international campaigns. She has researched and written extensively on intellectual property, innovation, and trade and provided technical advice and assistance in numerous countries in Asia, Latin America, Europe, and Africa on access to medicines. She completed her PhD at Queen Mary, University of London, holds LLM degrees in Intellectual Property Law from Queen Mary, University of London, and Information Technology Law from Stockholm University. She obtained her law degree with distinction from Ankara University.

**Van Anh Le** holds a PhD in Intellectual Property (IP) Law from the University of Bangor, United Kingdom. She gained her LLB in International Law in Ho Chi Minh University of Law (Vietnam) and completed the LLM in International Commercial and Business Law in Bangor. She is currently a Teaching Fellow at the University of Warwick, United Kingdom. Prior to taking up this post, she worked at Durham University. Her areas of expertise include patent law, access to medicine, and general IP policies in developing countries. Before embarking on academic career, Van Anh completed the Legal Practice Course in Vietnam and worked for a couple of years as a tax consultant in the private sector (Ernst and Young).

**Doris Estelle Long** is Professor Emeritus of Law, Former Director of the Center for Intellectual Property, Privacy and Information Security Law, UIC John Marshall Law School; President, Doris Long Consulting; Screenwriter/ Producer, VeraKen Productions.

**Bryan Mercurio** is the Simon FS Li Professor of Law at the Chinese University of Hong Kong (CUHK). Professor Mercurio is coauthor of one of the most widely used casebooks on WTO law and coeditor of the leading collection on bilateral and regional trade agreements. Prior to relocating to Hong Kong, Professor Mercurio taught at the Faculty of Law at the University of New South Wales, worked in government, and practiced international trade, intellectual property, and commercial law in the United States and Australia.

**Michael S. Mireles** is a Professor at the University of the Pacific, McGeorge School of Law in Sacramento, California.

**Emily Michiko Morris** is an Associate Professor and David L. Brennan Endowed Chair in Law at the University of Akron School of Law. She was previously a Visiting Associate Professor and Director of International and Non-J.D. Programs at Penn State Dickinson Law.

**Sergio Napolitano** is an expert in IP, competition and trade. He is currently General Counsel and External Relations Director at Medicines for Europe, the European association representing the generic and biosimilar medicines industry. In 2018, he was nominated in a list of the 50 most influential people worldwide in IP law, policy, and business. Before joining Medicines for Europe, Sergio Napolitano worked in the Directorate General for External Policies of the European Parliament as part of the Secretariat of the Committee on International Trade (INTA). In 2012, he authored a Report of the European Parliament on "The Role of the Congress in Shaping the US Trade Policy". He previously worked at the Permanent Representation of Italy to the EU on multilateral, plurilateral, and bilateral trade negotiations, EU investment policy, and IPR. Sergio Napolitano is qualified for mediator certification in most American states. He holds a degree in Law from the University of Naples Suor Orsola Benincasa, an Erasmus Diploma at the Université Paris-Sorbonne, and an LLM on EU and European Public Law from the University College of London (UCL).

**Caroline B. Ncube** is a Professor of Law and the DST/NRF SARChl Research Chair in Intellectual Property, Innovation and Development, University of Cape Town. She holds a PhD from the University of Cape Town, an LLB degree from the University of Zimbabwe, and an LLM from the University of Cambridge. She is a Fellow of the Cambridge Commonwealth Society and a Shell Centenary Fund Scholar. She is an Associate Member of the Centre of Law, Technology and Society at the University of Ottawa.

**Emmanuel Kolawole Oke** is a Lecturer in International Intellectual Property Law at Edinburgh Law School, University of Edinburgh. He has LLB and LLM degrees from the University of Lagos. He also has an LLM degree in Intellectual Property and Technology Law from the National University of Singapore. He obtained his PhD from University College Cork, Ireland. His research explores the interface between intellectual property and other branches of international law such as international trade law, international investment law, international taxation law, and international human rights law.

**Dr. Maria Auxiliadora Oliveira** is a medical doctor with a master's degree in Communicable Diseases and a PhD in Sociology of Technological Innovation and Industrial Engineering. She has been a staff member at the ENSP/Fiocruz since 1978. She was the head of the NAF, where she is currently a Senior Researcher. She has also been a consultant to the Public Health, Innovation and Public Health (PHI) of the World Health Organization.

**J. Janewa Osei-Tutu** is an Associate Professor of Law, Florida International University College of Law.

**Michael Palmedo** is a Post Doctoral Research Fellow at American University's Program on Information Justice and Intellectual Property. His chapter in this book is from research he conducted through the Shamnad Basheer IP/Trade Fellowship at the Texas A&M University School of Law.

**Dr. Susan Isiko Štrba** combines teaching and research with providing policy and legislative advice and technical training to governments, intergovernmental organizations, and civil society. She focuses mainly on human rights, intellectual property, trade and development. She has also published numerous journal articles in the field of human rights, trade, intellectual property, and development. She currently researches the interface of technology, intellectual property, and the African Continental Free Trade Area.

**Shirin Syed** is a Research and Teaching Scholar, Department of Law, KBC North Maharashtra University, India.

**Marcela Fogaça Vieira** is a Human Rights Lawyer, Member of GTPI-Rebrip since 2005 and was acting as coordinator from 2012 to 2016. She is the project coordinator of the knowledge network for innovation and Access to Medicines, Global Health Centre.

**Pedro Villardi** is an Internationalist, Member of GTPI-Rebrip since 2009, and coordinator since 2012.

**Peter K. Yu** is Regents Professor of Law and Communication and Director of the Center for Law and Intellectual Property at Texas A&M University. Peter Yu he previously held the Kern Family Chair in Intellectual Property Law at Drake University Law School and was Wenlan Scholar Chair Professor at Zhongnan University of Economics and Law in Wuhan, China.

# Introduction
# Access to Medicines and TRIPS Agreement: A Mapping of the Tradescape

*Srividhya Ragavan and Amaka Vanni*

## Introduction

The onset of the COVID-19 pandemic happened on an unassuming globe then focused on breaking barriers to trade. Although the structures of international trade have undergone systemic changes over the years, the expansion of the concept of property to include intellectual property (IP) rights has remained significant and impactful. Much of the global impact from the expansion of the concept of property rights is owed to trade prescriptions relating to patenting of lifesaving medications which largely resulted in the morphing of patents into a luxury creating barriers to access lifesaving medications. The disconnect of IP rights, primarily patents, from innovation as well as the end objective of public benefit had begun much before the onset of the COVID-19 pandemic. In reality, the COVID-19 pandemic precipitated and exacerbated an existing but largely ignored issue of the effects of poor public health on global productivity and, consequently, trade. Notably, when COVID-19 pandemic crept to engulf the world, one nation at a time, global efforts to protect public health was largely viewed as a barrier to trade. It is unclear if that has changed now. What has become clear is that the COVID-19 pandemic, in affecting every facet of life and every nation, showcased how unprepared the world was, and continues to be, in handling dangerous and unusual diseases. As the disruptive force of the virus continues to tear through families and national economies, it threatens the foundations and ideologies over which international laws and norms that have governed pharmaceutical patents and regulatory protections have been built. The COVID-19 pandemic has unleashed unprecedented challenges to health care in general and has forced the globe to reckon with how international treaties dealing with IP have, in fact, been an impediment for medicines access resulting in drug shortages, high prices, and has dissociated drug development with innovation.

As COVID-19 continues to ravage into 2021, the unpreparedness and consequential failures is a natural outcome of not heeding to years of warning from health activists to be prepared for such an eventuality. Today, the focus on creating a COVID-19 vaccine is mired with questions about protection, price, and access involving different sets of actors. Even though this book was conceived in the pre-COVID era, it remains relevant in the post-COVID era in performing the important function of documenting the role of different sets of actors and their influence on the structures – such as national and international agreements, organizations, and private entities – that have caused changes to health care, and access to medication, and how these (in)actions led us to where we are today.

## Historiography of the Pre-COVID Globe

This juncture in history is appropriate for analyzing the trajectory of the global struggles to access to medication. In fact, the year 2020 marks the 25th anniversary of the TRIPS Agreement and thus presents an opportune moment for critical appraisal from diverse perspectives. The term "TRIPS Agreement" denotes the Agreement on Trade-Related Aspects of Intellectual Property Rights[1] (TRIPS Agreement) which is the most wide-ranging and influential multilateral treaty to date in the field of IP. Sweeping in scope, it established a global minimum standard for the protection of IP. For many developing countries, however, the TRIPS Agreement prescribed a higher standard than previously allowed in their national laws such as longer terms, broader rights, and fewer exceptions to the scope of rights. While innovation and trade remained the larger objective, the World Trade Organization's (WTO) global patent prescription largely created a privileged societal class with access to lifesaving medication, distinguishing them from those excluded from access to available medications. Patent protection as mandated by the TRIPS Agreement, the distinctive feature that caused the morphing of lifesaving medication into a luxury, has remained an integral part of the discussion on access to medication. Hence, this decade witnessed an elevated interest over the role of patents in the context of pharmaceutical innovation and its effect on access to medication.

Historically, the past 25 years of TRIPS have been marked by debates between those that want to limit the Agreement's scope with those that crave to expand it. The HIV/AIDS crisis of the late 1990s and early noughties underscored the limitations of the TRIPS Agreement leading to the Doha Declaration on the TRIPS Agreement and Public Health (Doha Declaration), which epitomizes an attempt to ameliorate these limitations.[2] The emerging economies of Brazil, India, Russia, and China – which initially approached the TRIPS negotiation as weaker participants and importers of patented technology[3] – have graduated

1 *See* Agreement on Trade-Related Aspects of Intellectual Property Rights, Apr. 15, 1994, Marrakesh Agreement Establishing the World Trade Organization, Annex C, 1869 U.N.T.S. 299, I.L.M. 1197 (1994) [hereinafter TRIPS Agreement].

2 World Trade Organization, Ministerial Declaration of 14 November 2001, WTO Doc. WT/MIN(01)/DEC/1, 41 ILM 746 (2002) [hereinafter Doha Declaration].

3 Frederick M. Abbott et al., Emerging Markets and the World Patent Order 5 (2014).

into key participants of the trade regime and on discussions on the scope of the TRIPS Agreement.

Meanwhile, goaded by a quest for expanding private property rights, the US and the European Union (EU) fervently sought to expand the scope of and encourage patents. The fetish for encouraging patents notwithstanding, inflated prices within the US and the EU, made lifesaving medication inaccessible for patients while simultaneously increasing health-care spending as a percentage of the Gross Domestic Product (GDP). Meanwhile, multilateral, plurilateral, and mega-regional trade agreements have ratcheted up the standards of IP protection beyond those stipulated by the TRIPS Agreement. In all, the TRIPS Agreement exacerbated the access to lifesaving pharmaceuticals into a global concern from what was essentially a poor country issue.

Amidst this, the year 2020 also represents a confluence of factors that has elevated the imminence of the access debate in the context of the TRIPS Agreement. Notably, the WTO slipped into an existential crisis – a whining US, crying foul at all trading partners while creating protectionism locally in the name of "America First"; stalemate in the WTO's Dispute Settlement Body; an inflow of talent capital that merged national borders but raised social issues; a realization within the developed world that *free trade ain't free* but represents competition from hitherto unknown quarters of the world-increasing global trade tensions, disrupting traditional theories of innovation. The most influential factor though was COVID-19. As the coronavirus gripped the globe, the WTO in crisis forcibly reconciled the power of public health to increase or impede trade even as the World Health Oraganization (WHO) faced its own existential crisis when the US threatened to defund it.

At this juncture in history, even without the pandemic unfurled, patents had lost its sheen and was being perceived, however unfairly, as *the* woe affecting pricing and as a tool thwarting access to lifesaving medication. While the effect of pharmaceutical pricing remains a significant question in the United States (US), pricing and other policies remain subjects of a larger access to medication debate globally.[4] Over time, it is true that patents have evolved into a strategic business tool, which, in turn, resulted in a slow but steady downgrading from

4 In 2016, as the debate on price of pharmaceuticals became an important election issue in the United States, the fact that patents contribute to such an increase in price came into the limelight. For example, in January 2016, the US News reported that 50 Democratic members of the House, led by Rep. Lloyd Doggett, D-Texas, urged government agencies to consider diluting or diminishing the exclusive rights over patents on pharmaceuticals. *See* Kimberley Leonard, *Can the Government Already Control Drug Prices*, US News (Jan. 11, 2016), http://www.usnews.com/news/articles/2016/01/11/congressional-democrats-urge-nih-to-act-on-drug-prices. Similarly, in 2016, Sen. Bernie Sanders and Rep. Elijah Cummings sought more information about the price increases for *Iclusig*, a drug used to treat chronic myeloid leukemia which was priced at $199,000 for a year's worth of treatment. *See Sanders, Cummings Send Letter on ARIAD's Staggering Price Increases* (Oct. 20, 2016), https://bit.ly/2ETma5B.

its touted position of being the unique economic prescription to kick-start innovation. As such, the rhetoric of innovation, which long served as a platform to nestle patents, was being challenged within many countries and in many industries. From the US, the traditional flag holder unfurling the benefits of patents, to developing countries such as India, which is a relatively newer graduate of the trade regime, the role of patents has become a subject for scrutiny.[5] Consequently, transnational civil society networks have continued to play key roles in reframing the narrative surrounding patents.

The above background makes the analysis in the book appropriate and timely. The analysis would complement the current paradigm shift with preference to a realistic approach to enable access to medication over an ideologically normative and inflexible approach. An inclusive approach rather than an exclusive solution can result in sustainable access to medicines. The analysis below provides a backdrop by classifying the struggles for access to medication discussions into generational questions, using the various chapters to weave three eras of medicine access struggles into the dialogue.

## The *Tradescape*: An Analysis of Structures and Actors

The tumultuous *tradescape,* which references the landscape of the trade regime, provides the background and hopes to outline a historiographic mapping of the struggles of diverse actors for access to medicine rupturing established global structures over three generations. The historiographic mapping traces the changes in the patent discourse terrain by analyzing the metamorphosis of IP ideology, particularly patents. In doing so, this book captures the different sets of actors such as states, transnational business corporations, civil society groups, and the (re)framing of patent discourses within and among these actors.

Our intergenerational analyses of the legal issues surrounding the access to medicine question provide an insight into the *structures* within which the actors have operated along with the dynamic relationship between *structures and actors.* The term *structure*, as used in this book, refers to the economic system within which various actors operate. The influence of structures over the behavior of actors and, in turn, the influence exerted by actors over structures eventually caused generational shifts in the debate on the role of patents, trade, and access to medication. The book examines the influences over established global protocols, national and international agreements, and state and non-state entities. In doing so, we acknowledge that the history of patent harmonization discourse is a story of dynamic actors, whose interactions with established structures continue to shape the global patent regime.

5 *See, e.g.*, Srividhya Ragavan, *Of the Inequals of Uruguay,* 274 MARQ. INTELL. PROP. L. REV. 10 (2006) (on India's process patent regime and its graduation into the TRIPS patent regime).

### *Patents and the Global Neoliberal Economy Synthesis*

The mercantile economic system of 18th-century Europe enabled competitive advantage by embracing patents to incentivize innovation.[6] Importantly, the norms that nation-states have exerted – and will continue to exert – influences policies that results in international structures in the form of treatises and institutions. Thus, the 18th-century structures were instrumental in kick-starting transnational commerce that inspired international regimes such as the Paris Convention for the Protection of Industrial Property.[7] However, the beginnings of the contemporary structures can be attributed to the deepening of the neoliberal ideal, which led to the uneasy marriage of IP with trade, generating a new set of actors (for example, corporations), whose actions have had historical impact.

The expansion of the neoliberal trading system increased the value of information and knowledge, which, in turn, proportionally increased the value of IP and vice versa.[8] Soon, higher IP standards became the preferred norm for developed nations to gain competitive advantage in the international market. It precipitated a renewed structure in the form of the WTO with a propensity to move toward stronger enforcement and with more vested interests to propel IP into a newer *avatar* armed with the trade enforcement mechanism, which devalued humane influences. Susan Sell, in explaining the influence these neoliberal structures exert on actors along with the development of highly protectionist global IP standards, notes that "structures help to identify the significant agents in any particular context and also shapes preferences."[9]

6 Edward C. Walterscheid, *The Early Evolution of the United States Patent Law: Antecedents (Part II)*, 76 J. PAT. &TRADEMARK OFF. SOC'Y, 852 (1994) [hereinafter Walterscheid Part II]; Thomas M. Mesbesher, *The Role of History in Comparative Patent Law*, 78 J. PAT. &TRADEMARK OFF. SOC'Y 594, 602 (1996).

7 Paris Convention for the Protection of Industrial Property, Mar. 20, 1883, as revised at the Stockholm Revision Conference, July 14, 1967, 828 U.N.T.S. 305 [hereinafter Paris Convention]. In particular, the Great Exhibition of 1851, which promised to "unify the industrial products of all civilised peoples on earth in a comparative display" necessitated an overarching transnational structure monitored by an international organization as a means to reduce imitation. This and subsequent patent congresses formed parts of the drafts of Paris Convention eventually paving the way for international IP regulatory structures such as the WIPO, the weak enforcement of which precipitated the move to a different structure with stronger enforcement mechanism. *See* Margrit Seckelmann, *From the Paris Convention (1883) to the TRIPS Agreement (1994): The History of the International Patent Agreements as a History of Propertisation?*, 14 J. DER JURISTISCHEN ZEITGESCHICHTE 51, 59 (2013); JOHN BRAITHWAITE & PETER DRAHOS, GLOBAL BUSINESS REGULATION 56 (2004).

8 BRAITHWAITE & DRAHOS, *supra* note 7, at 61, noting that transnational business corporations wanted the ability to locate their production anywhere in the world but have the assurance that their IP will be protected. They pushed the IP regime to be part of a multilateral trade agreement to ensure global coverage.

9 SUSAN K. SELL, PRIVATE POWER, PUBLIC LAW 5 (2003).

These structures, she adds, "alert us to whose preferences are likely to matter, not just in the domestic context, but in the international arenas."[10] In this respect, the neoliberal structure in the US, propelled by competitive markets, economic expansionism, and monopolistic accumulation, became a motivation for economic coercion that enabled private sector actors to pursue extensive IP protections. Importantly, it underscores how law (in this case, IP and international trade law) is deeply implicated in the construction of a neoliberal global political economy.[11]

The emergence of private sector actors who successfully fostered international support characterizes a distinctive aspect of the contemporary trade regime, which naturally strengthened global protection of IP.[12] The distinguishing feature is that powerful nation-states, particularly the US, incorporated the interests of monopolistic transnational corporations to allow public international law to work in a manner that achieves the ends of private corporations, albeit in the name of global trade benefits.[13] However, the consequential emergence of public interest-minded non-state actors resulted in a pushback along the lines of fairer pricing, wider access to, and availability of essential medicines. The emergence of these actors and their impact on the structures resulted in a generational shift, causing the maturation of developing countries – once importers of IP – into informed players invigorating the debate on private versus public. It brought a fresh set of talent capital that has astounded the trade regime. All of the non-state actors, which include civil society, patient groups, and nations, on the development spectrum engaged in an unsynchronized challenge to existing structures. In focusing on the participation of these actors and the challenges they posed to the neoliberal capitalist structures, the book underscores the dynamics between the various players to define, particularly how they have altered, the political landscape over which the fight for access to affordable life-saving medication will continue.

The book is unique in presenting the debates over the impact of patents, trade, and the TRIPS Agreement on access to medicine and how they galvanized non-state and nonbusiness actors, such as nongovernmental organizations and civil society groups, the roles of which have been exceptional in the last two decades. The book highlights how the presence of non-state actors "diffused the

10 *Id.*

11 Jedediah S. Britton-Purdy et al., *Building a Law-and-Political-Economy Framework: Beyond the Twentieth-Century Synthesis*, Columbia Public Law Research Paper No. 14-657 (Mar. 2, 2020), Yale L. J. (forthcoming).

12 Braithwaite & Drahos, *supra* note 7, at 61; Susan K. Sell, *Intellectual Property Protection and Antitrust in the Developing World: Crisis, Coercion, and Choice*, 49 Int'l Org. 315–49, 320 (1995).

13 *See generally* Keith Aoki, *Neocolonialism, Anticommons Property, and Biopiracy in the (Not-So-Brave) New World Order of International Intellectual Property Protection*, 6 Ind. J. Global Legal Stud. 11, 13 (1998), who notes the use of international law by the United States to enforce its system of property rights.

leverage of asymmetries of power based on political and market forces alone."[14] Importantly, the actors have proffered an alternative framing and understanding of pharmaceutical patent "right" as a public issue as opposed to trade or IP issue. In summary, the book presents how both *structures* and *actors* shift conceptions of the role of IP rights (IPRs) and underscore the emergent controversies over access to medication.

## Mapping the Historiography of the International Patent System

In the historiography of the evolution of patents, early influences of nation-states as important actors played a critical role in motivating the creation of the multilateral trade system that currently impacts access to medication issues. Historically, actions of nation-states were influenced by social and economic factors that resulted in the evolution of patent laws specifically fashioned to nurture national development. For example, patents were used as a tool for innovation and to retain immigration in Venice, the earliest state where patents originated.[15] Similarly, patents were introduced to attract foreigners and support domestic industrialization in Britain, another important state actor, by "stimulating the local production of both raw materials and a wide variety of manufactured goods previously imported from abroad."[16] In the US, patent provisions were introduced to promote science and technology.[17] Arguably, in their earliest instance, patents were disconnected with the ideals of global trade but meant to foster local industrialization and as part of an effort to further national objectives.[18] Thus, early patent regimes embraced a developmental approach to achieve national economic self-sufficiency.

Just as local economic realities dictated early patent development, bad economic times disfavored patents. In fact, patent development in the West has been remarkably acquiescent to symmetrical social and economic influence. For example, the end of the 1860s – which coincided with the beginning of economic depression in Europe and North America – saw a growing anti-patent

14 John Agada et al., *Globalization of Intellectual Property Rights: Implications of the TRIPS Agreement for Access to HIV/AIDS drugs in Africa*, 46 Proc. Am. Soc. Inf. Sci. Technol. 1–11, 9 (2009).

15 Skilled artisans and artists were granted two-year monopoly rights, while tax breaks were granted to skilled workers by the city-state. The Venetian system influenced patent evolution in Europe.

16 Walterscheid Part II, *supra* note 6, at 879.

17 In the United States, as in Venice and England, the general sentiment was to establish a patent regime that would result in national economic benefits. Thus, patent policies were historically meant to achieve national objectives and were instituted with an appreciation of the importance of addressing welfare considerations.

18 Srividhya Ragavan, Patent and Trade Disparities in Developing Countries 17 (2012).

feeling in the West.[19] Thus, the consequent economic depression and political upheavals by the financial crisis in 1873 were credited as key factors in the dissatisfaction toward patents.[20] This dissatisfaction grew, according to Ragavan, because patented products become accessible to even fewer people than during normal economic times.[21] There was also dissatisfaction against patents in European countries such as the Netherlands and Germany.[22] For instance, Marks Langs notes that the economic recession in Germany created uncertainty among politicians and fueled anti-patent sentiments among proponents of free trade.[23] Similarly, in the Netherlands, Eric Schiff asserts that as "free trade movement was gaining momentum in the country, patents came to be seen as a form of protectionism and impediment to trade."[24] Thus, even in countries where patents were seen as beneficial to domestic development, lack of access to what was considered a privilege necessitated a restraint in their use. Whenever the patent regime was considered as not achieving its aim of producing public benefit, it arguably led to a general anti-patent perception. Interestingly, the access to medication discourse of the last two decades, and significant developments in the pharmaceutical and bioscience fields in developed countries, has resulted in a reemergence of the dissatisfaction toward patents.

## *Rise of Multilateralism: From Paris Convention to TRIPS Agreement*

From nation-states, multilateral organizations represent another set of actors contributing to the global patent evolution. Indeed, multilateralization resulted in a system wherein global objectives of the trade regime gained priority over national objectives. Local national realities were consequently relegated to tertiary consideration. Historically, the first strides toward multilateralism began in 1883 when the Paris Convention was ratified. The goal of this first multilateral agreement was to enhance IP protection in foreign jurisdictions by replacing the fragmented reciprocal arrangements among European powers.[25]

19 *Id.* at 20.

20 Ragavan, *supra* note 18, at 20.

21 *Id.* at 27.

22 Eric Schiff, Industrialization Without National Patents: The Netherlands, 1869–1912; Switzerland, 1850–1907, 19 (1971); Petra Moser, *Patents and Innovation: Evidence from Economic History*, 27 J. Econ. Perspect. 26 (2013).

23 Markus Lang, *The Anti-Patent Movement Revisited: Institutional Change and Cognitive Frames in Nineteenth-Century Germany*, SSRN Electronic J. 7 (2010).

24 Schiff, *supra* note 22, at 26.

25 The original signatories were Belgium, Portugal, France, Guatemala, Italy, the Netherlands, San Salvador, Serbia, Spain, and Switzerland. The United States joined the Convention in 1887. Ecuador, El Salvador, and Guatemala later withdrew from the Convention in 1886, 1887, and 1895, respectively. Ulf Anderfelt, International Patent-Legislation and Developing Countries 69 (1971).

The Paris Convention allowed flexibility in its interpretation in national laws as long as such interpretation applied to both nationals and foreigners and did not contravene any provisions of the Convention.[26] This legislative freedom created heterogeneous global patent rules wherein countries adopted different standards of industrial property protection.[27] Even though the Paris Convention was seen by many, including legal scholars[28] and developing countries, as favorable to developed countries, it was still regarded by certain countries, such as the US, as insufficient.[29] This was because it did not have any enforcement mechanism and its provisions were flouted by many countries. It eventually resulted in the creation of the World Intellectual Property Organization (WIPO) in 1967, which helped to further promote worldwide awareness of IPRs.[30] Even though the principle of national treatment still applied, developed countries were concerned about insufficient IP protection and enforcement in developing countries.[31] These concerns as well as the structure of the WIPO, particularly weak enforcement mechanisms, compelled a move toward stronger enforcement structures.

### *The Birth of Generics and New Actors*

The growth of multilateral IP systems coincided with the growth of generic drugs industries in some developing countries such as India and Brazil. At that time, reducing a high rate of poverty and eradicating epidemic diseases burden

26 Paris Convention, *supra* note 7, at art. 15.

27 In Switzerland and Spain, for example, chemical products were not patentable, while France and Italy did not grant patent to pharmaceutical substances. *See* Surendra J. Patel, *Intellectual Property Rights in the Uruguay Round: A Disaster for the South?*, 24 Econ. Political Wkly. 980 (1989).

28 Patel, *supra* note 27, at 982–83; *see generally* Rajeev Dhavan et al., *Conquest by Patent: The Paris Convention Revisited*, 32 J. Ind. L. Instt. 140–45 (1990); Edith Penrose, *International Patenting and the Less-Developed Countries*, 83 Econ. J., 768 (1973); Constantine Vaitsos, *Patents Revisited: Their Function in Developing Countries*, 9 J. Dev. Stud. 71,–97 (1972).

29 Brazil was the first country to table discontentment with provisions of the Paris Convention in 1961 and was followed by similar proposals from Bolivia and Argentina. *See* Andrea Koury Menescal, *Changing WIPO's Ways? The 2004 Development Agenda in Historical Perspective*, 8 J. World Intellect. Prop. 761–96, 764–66 (2005); *see also* Peter K. Yu, *Tale of Two Development Agendas*, 35 Ohio N. U. L. Rev. 65 (2009); Patel, *supra* note 27, at 983.

30 The WIPO emerged from the United International Bureaux for the Protection of Intellectual Property (BIRPI), which itself was formed by the merged Paris Convention and the 1886 Berne Union for the Protection of Literary and Artistic Works (Berne Convention) under a single secretariat in 1893. See Christopher May, *The Pre-History and Establishment of the WIPO*, 1 WIPO J. 16–26 (2009); Debora J. Halbert, *The World Intellectual Property Organization: Past, Present and Future*, 54 The Copyright Society of the USA (2007).

31 The principle of national treatment allows countries to extend to foreign nationals the same rights and legal privileges enjoyed by their own nationals. *See* Paris Convention, art 2.

became an integral part of government's national development objectives.[32] India had the highest priced drugs in the world, and in response, it amended its patent laws in line with its national goals and enacted the Indian Patent Act 1970.[33] The enactment abolished product patents for pharmaceuticals and agrochemicals and only allowed process patents.[34] India also signed an Agreement with the United Nations Children's Fund to locally manufacture penicillin and other antibiotics, which resulted in the establishment of the Hindustan Antibiotics Limited in 1954 to produce low-cost generic drugs.[35] In Brazil, similar domestic reforms were implemented to ensure availability of reasonably priced drugs. Brazil's Law Number 7.903/1945 removed product patent protection for medicines, food and chemicals.[36] In 1969 and 1971, respectively, two new amendments enabled Brazil to domestically manufacture pharmaceuticals.[37]

The law reforms in India and Brazil resulted in the establishment of an indigenous pharmaceutical industry, which helped control public health expenditure. For example, within a decade of reforming its patent law, the Indian generic drug sector grew to be one of the biggest GDP generators for the country.[38] By 1991, domestic firms accounted for 70 percent of the bulk drugs production and 80 percent of formulations.[39] Similarly in Brazil, the 10 largest national pharmaceutical companies increased their market share by 10 percent within a decade

32 *See* RAGAVAN, *supra* note 18, at 32; *see generally* AMAKA VANNI, PATENT GAMES IN THE GLOBAL SOUTH: PHARMACEUTICAL PATENT LAWMAKING IN BRAZIL, INDIA AND NIGERIA 70–71 (2020).

33 *See* Justice N. Rajagopala Ayyangar, *Report on the Revision of the Patents Law*, Sept. 1959 citing the United States Senate Committee Kefauver Committee Report headed by Senator Estes Kefauver. The Ayyangar Report laid the foundation for the Indian patent regime, particularly for its analysis of the adaptability of foreign patent regimes and policy options to address India's national needs. *See also* Patents Act 1970, 27 India A.I.R. Manual 450, § 84 (1979).

34 *Id.* § 5.

35 RAGAVAN, *supra* note 18, at 35.

36 Law No 7.903/1945; *see also* Bruno Salama & Daniel Benoliel, *Pharmaceutical Patent Bargains: The Brazilian Experience*, 18 CARDOZO J. INT'L &COMP. L. 633, 639–40 (2010); VANNI, *supra* note 32, ch. 4 focuses on Brazil's intersection of the HIV/AIDS program and pharmaceutical patent regime to trace the development of socially conscious patent and pharmaceutical policies; Christopher S. Mayer, *The Brazilian Pharmaceutical Industry Goes Walking from Ipanema to Prosperity: Will the New Intellectual Property Law Spur Domestic Investment?*, 12 TEMP. INT'L &COMP. L. J. 37 (1998).

37 Law Number 1.005/1971 in 1969 removed food, chemical, and pharmaceutical substances, materials, products, and medicines from the list of patentable materials, while Law Number 5.772/71 in 1971 prohibited the patenting of processes for food, chemicals, and medicines. *See* VANNI, *supra* note 32, at 71.

38 While only two indigenous companies were among the top 10 firms in terms of retail sales in 1970, by 1996, this rose to six, and by 2001, it was up to eight. *See* VANNI, *supra* note 32, at 72.

39 Jean Lanjouw, *The Introduction of Pharmaceutical Product Patents in India: "Heartless Exploitation of the Poor and Suffering"?* (Nat'l Bureau of Econ. Rsch., Working Paper No. 6366, 1998).

after the removal of patent products.[40] Peter Drahos, in analyzing this growth, notes that generics drug manufacturers posed a viable threat to the Western pharmaceutical companies that had dominated the international pharmaceutical industry.[41] Feeling the loss of access to developing country markets, Western pharmaceutical cartels lobbied their national governments to secure higher patent standards away from WIPO through a forum where the large pharmaceuticals players could secure a global IP standard. In light of these concerns and pressures from IP industries, the US moved the issue of IP discussion to the General Agreement on Tariffs and Trade (GATT) – a forum in which it was the single most influential player.[42]

The birth of generics and their success in catering to medicine access not only contributed to more economic productivity by addressing treatment but also leveled the playing field. This shifted the globe into its next era of access to medication. The foundational pillars of this new era rested on pharmaceutical companies' fear of the generic industry. Previously, and using patents as a tool, pharmaceutical companies had created a new class-based society divided by their ability to access medication. However, the introduction of generics into the market resulted in re-scrambling the class-based access-to-medication system. The fear of transnational pharmaceutical corporations resulting from the emergence of generic industries located in developing countries consequently caused a pushback affecting medicine access.

## An Uneasy Marriage of Trade and IP

The pushback from the pharmaceutical industry propelled a proliferation of international norm-setting activities creating new structural mechanisms to achieve harmonization of laws. In the territory of international norm setting, harmonization created legal equality into a system that naturally comprised of unequal parties with huge variation in economic and bargaining parities.[43]

40 Gary Gereffi, The Pharmaceutical Industry and Dependency in the Third World 229 (1983). The Brazilian government enacted policies to attract investments for the creation of a chemical industry to produce specialized chemicals, active pharmaceutical ingredients (APIs), and their intermediates in order to reduce dependency on imported APIs for pharmaceutical and chemical production. *See* Vanni, *supra* note 32, at 73.

41 Peter Drahos, *Developing Countries and International Intellectual Property Standard-Setting*, 5 J. World Intellect. Prop. 765–89, 768 (2005).

42 Laurence Helfer calls the process of moving international law-making and standard setting from one forum to another as "regime shifting," where state and non-state actors alike shift law-making from one international venue to another. *See* Laurence R. Helfer, *Regime Shifting: The TRIPs Agreement and New Dynamics of International Intellectual Property Lawmaking*, 29 Yale J. Int'l. L. 1, 2 (2004); *see generally* Ha-Joon Chang, *Intellectual Property Rights and Economic Development: Historical Lessons and Emerging Issues*, 2 J. Human Dev. Capab. 287–309 (2001); Sell, *supra* note 9, at 13; Sell, *supra* note 12, at 327, 332; Drahos, *supra* note 41, at 769.

43 Ragavan, *supra* note 18, at 140.

Meanwhile, much had changed in the 110 years between the Paris Convention in 1883 and the signing of the TRIPS Agreement in 1994. In 1948, the GATT was created to regulate world trade by reducing tariff, minimizing trade barriers, and boosting economic recovery after the devastation of the Second World War. However, a weak dispute settlement mechanism cited as the reason for a limited global trade expansion, in turn triggered calls from various countries, mostly the US, for a more powerful and comprehensive organization.[44] The result was the conception of the WTO, distinguished by its ability to create credible threats and enforce disputes between sovereign members. The ability to enforce disputes through trade sanction was one of the salient features of the TRIPS Agreement, the other being the setting of mandatory minimum standards of protection.[45] The ability to enforce disputes materialized in the form of a dispute resolution mechanism to adjudicate cases of violation of WTO agreements.[46] The enforcement mechanism of the WTO addressed one of the main criticisms that the developed nations had leveled against previous international IP regimes. According to Braithwaite and Drahos, one of the US complaints against WIPO (in addition to the voting rules) was the lack of enforcement of IP.[47] Thus, the dispute settlement mechanism is a direct response to address a lack of credible surveillance in WIPO Conventions and further strengthened the liaison between trade and IP laws in unprecedented ways.

At the Uruguay Round meetings, the US and the European Economic Community (EEC) linked IP issues to the larger international trade framework to ameliorate the Paris Convention deficiency in harmonizing global IP rules.[48]

44 Peter Drahos, *Global Property Rights in Information: The story of TRIPS at the GATT*, 13 Prometheus 6–19, 12 (1995).

45 TRIPS Agreement, Article 27 includes in the definition of patentable subject matter both pharmaceutical products and process and introduces the concept of non-discrimination in all fields of technology for patent application.

46 TRIPS Agreement, *supra* note 1, at Articles 63 and 64. Article 64 of the TRIPS Agreement provides for dispute settlement through Articles 22 and 23 of the General Agreement on Tariffs and Trade (GATT); *see also* Understanding on Rules and Procedures Governing the Settlement of Disputes, Apr. 15, 1994, Annex. 2, Legal Instruments—Results of the Uruguay Round, 33 I.L.M, 1125, 1226, 1244 [hereinafter DSU]. Article 6 of the DSU provides for the establishment of a panel at the instance of the complaining party, which is the Dispute Settlement Body. Over the years, various countries have initiated and/or completed dispute settlement procedures relating to the provisions of the TRIPS Agreement. *See* DS50: India – Patent Protection for Pharmaceutical and Agricultural Chemical Products (1996); DS114: Canada – Patent Protection of Pharmaceutical Products (2000); DS170: Canada – Term of Patent Protection (2001); DS199: Brazil – Measures Affecting Patent Protection (2001); *see generally* Matthew Kennedy, WTO Dispute Settlement and the TRIPS Agreement: Applying Intellectual Property Standards in a Trade Law Framework (2016).

47 Braithwaite & Drahos, *supra* note 7, at 566.

48 A. Jane Bradley, *Intellectual Property Rights, Investment, and Trade in Services in the Uruguay Round: Laying the Foundations*, 23 Stan. J. Int'l L. 59 (1987).

Commentators agree that the move by the US and EEC to include IP as part of the GATT regime created an environment conducive for developed countries to use access to their markets as a bargaining chip.[49] It resulted in establishing a higher standard of IP in the form of minimum benchmarks along with a much-needed enforcement mechanism. Drahos, in analyzing the IP negotiations, notes that the US and the EEC used the threat of denying market access as a means to build the consensus required to shape the content of the TRIPS Agreement text.[50] Further, the nature of cross-negotiations at the GATT allowed for countries to leverage losses in one area into a concession in another. For example, developing countries hoped for elimination or minimization of barriers in agricultural trade as an important trade-off, which never truly materialized. In the end, developed countries were able to push through higher levels of IP in the form of the TRIPS Agreement text. TRIPS proponents believed that the ability of the WTO to generate threats and the enforcement of retaliatory mechanisms compelled sovereign obedience. As shall be seen, it is the signing of the TRIPS Agreement that precipitated the generational debates on medicine access.

Now, 25 years later, a fault line can be traced in the TRIPS regime between developed and developing nations at the interface of IP and access to medication. The structural paradigm of trade and the TRIPS Agreement invigorated the next set of actors, particularly invested developing countries and committed civil societies. For developing countries and civil society groups aligned with the views of developing countries, the TRIPS Agreement mirrored the interests of global corporate actors in developed countries. As a result, it reflected the specific view of IP as uniquely promoted by Western countries, aligned with their transnational corporations and divorced from the harsh realities that plagued the rest of the world. This fault line, as the chapters in the book highlight, weaves a common thread between diverse issues such as definitions of inventiveness, use of compulsory license (CL), patent examination processes, treatment of public health objectives, and legitimate domestic policy on patent law.

### *HIV/AIDS Crisis and the Limitations of the TRIPS Agreement*

As the world globalized and harmonized internationally, one key event showcased the disparities and limitations of the TRIPS Agreement in the context of access to medicine. Widely known as the HIV/AIDS crisis, this issue precipitated the struggle for access to medication. The widespread occurrence of specific diseases associated with an HIV infection that raged through the world in the late 1980s and 1990s, killing millions of people, changed the ground realities. The devastation on the lives of people located in mostly poorer countries

49 Drahos, *supra* note 41, at 769; *see also* Sell, *supra* note 9, ch. 4; Susan K. Sell, *TRIPS: Fifteen Years Later*, 18 J. Intell. Prop. L. 4 (2011).

50 Drahos, *supra* note 38, at 774.

as a result of the lack of access to antiretroviral medicines emphasized the limitations of the TRIPS Agreement.[51] By 2001–20 years after the first HIV/AIDS diagnosis and with more than 2.5 million deaths from AIDS, with the prospect of a profound effect on the productivity of nation-states – the TRIPS Agreement faced an existential crisis.[52]

Unsurprisingly, when the Indian generic drug manufacturer Cipla announced it would sell triple-drug therapy for $350 per patient per year to Médecins Sans Frontières (MSF) and directly to poor nations, several major pharmaceuticals lowered prices.[53] This prompted the then United Nations Secretary-General Kofi Anan to reaffirm that HIV/AIDS constituted a national security threat and a public health crisis.[54] The HIV/AIDS crisis not only showcased the inflexibility of the TRIPS Agreement but also challenged its structural establishment. The implications of the TRIPS Agreement on public health and the Cipla announcement mobilized support like never before from global non-state actors such as transnational civil society groups and health activists.[55] This phenomenon remains unique to date and the book captures that as part of the global transitions of the medicines access debate. In the US, for instance, groups such as the Consumer Project on Technology (CPTech, now Knowledge Ecology International, or KEI) rallied against the impact of the TRIPS Agreement on drug prices. Medicine access activists such as MSF and the Working Group on Intellectual Property (GTPI), the positions of which are captured in the book, initiated campaigns linking the effect of patents on availability and access to medication.[56] In support, multilateral agencies such as the WIPO and the World Health Organization (WHO), and institutions such as the United Nations Commission on Human Rights raised concerns regarding the impact of the TRIPS Agreement on access to medicine and the resulting implications for health and human rights.[57] Simultaneously, at national levels, various events resulted in amplifying the access to medication

51 Vanni, *supra* note 32, at 22; *see also* Ethan B. Kapstein & Joshua W. Busby, AIDS Drugs For All 55 (2013).

52 2007 World Health Organization HIV/AIDS Update Presentation, http://www.who.int/hiv/facts/2007_epiupdate_report_fullpresentation_en.ppt. According to the WHO, about 35 million people have died from the epidemic from 1988 to 2018. *See Why the HIV Epidemic Is Not Over*, World Health Org., https://www.who.int/hiv-aids/latest-news-and-events/why-the-hiv-epidemic-is-not-over.

53 *Indian Company Offers to Supply AIDS Drugs at Low Cost in Africa*, N.Y. Times, https://www.nytimes.com/2001/02/07/world/indian-company-offers-to-supply-aids-drugs-at-low-cost-in-africa.html?module=inline.

54 *Secretary-General Proposes Global Fund for Fight Against HIV/AIDS and Other Infectious Diseases at African Leaders Summit*, UN, https://www.un.org/press/en/2001/SGSM7779R1.doc.htm.

55 *See generally* Brook Baker, *infra* Part III, Chapter 15.

56 Vanni, *supra* note 32, at 97–99. See *generally* Felipe de Carvalho Borges da Fonseca et al., *infra* Part III, Chapter 16.

57 Office of the High Commissioner for Human Rights, *Human Rights and Trade* (2003), https://www2.ohchr.org/english/issues/globalization/trade/docs/5WTOMinisterial-Cancun.pdf.

debate. For example, 41 pharmaceutical companies in South Africa plus the South African Pharmaceutical Manufacturers' Association filed a lawsuit against the national government for including TRIPS flexibilities into domestic law to increase the affordability and accessibility of medicines. The vocal mobilization of civil society and the media attention from the lawsuit forced pharmaceutical companies to withdraw the suit, thus allowing for the amendment. The consequential alliances of developing countries with civil society activists dominated the efforts to make the global IP regime more equitable.

Importantly, two limitations of the TRIPS Agreement came to the fore. First, the inability of the TRIPS Agreement to address practical difficulties of poorer countries to access medicines by manufacturing generic versions of expensive medications. Second, even if flexibilities were incorporated, a realization that there were countries that lacked adequate manufacturing capacity and that the TRIPS Agreement prevented them from importing generic medications from countries such as India, which had the capacity to manufacture these medications. In response to the first concern, the WTO General Council adopted the Doha Declaration in 2001.[58] The Doha Declaration recognized the gravity of health issues facing many countries and emphasized the autonomy of states to implement and interpret the TRIPS Agreement in a manner supportive of public health.[59] To address the issue of countries without manufacturing abilities, the WTO General Council adopted Article 31*bis* in August 2003, paving the way for importation of low-cost medicines from countries with manufacturing capacity.[60] The amendments also allowed any member country, either acting individually or as a regional grouping, to grant CLs with a view of exporting pharmaceutical products to countries with insufficient or no manufacturing capacities.[61]

Recent developments buoyed by the pharmaceutical industry lobby in developed nations pushed back via trade and investment agreements, resulting in an array of bilateral and plurilateral agreements which became a choice mechanism for building extensive TRIPS-plus IP protection. Thus, trade agreements such as the Trans-Pacific Partnership (TPP) and the proposed Regional Comprehensive Economic Partnership have pushed the bar for higher IP standards. With that, a new set of tools to enhance private property rights emerged. Data exclusivity, patent/marketing approval linkage, third-party dispute settlement, and reduced use of flexibilities are all exemplars of the contemporary issues.[62] The emergence of newer issues, structures, and actors propelled a new era with a new set of regulatory compliance standards.

58 Doha Declaration, *supra* note 2.

59 *Id.*

60 Decision on the Implementation of Paragraph 6 of the Doha Declaration on the TRIPS Agreement and Public Health; *see also* Doha WTO Ministerial 2001: Ministerial Declarations and Decisions, WTO Doc. WT/MIN(01)/17 (Nov. 20, 2001), http://www.wto.org/english/thewto_e/minist_e/min01_e/mindecl_implementation_e.htm.

61 *Id.*

62 See *generally* Burcu Kilic, *infra* Part I, Chapter 5.

## Recent Developments and Emerging Issues

The next generation in the drug debate surprisingly involved developed countries where a steady increase in the price of pharmaceuticals over a decade caused health-care costs to skyrocket, raising questions with implications beyond patents. Interestingly, pharmaceutical companies are facing growing condemnation against the background of soaring drug prices, causing governments to become constituencies acting for the cause of making either medication or health care accessible to citizens. For example, the UK's National Institute for Health and Care Excellence recommended against the use of *trastuzumab emtansine* (brand name *Kadcyla*) in the National Health Service because of its high price, even though it recognized the efficacy of the drug to treat breast cancer.[63] Similarly, when patient-led campaign organization Just Treatment criticized the price of cystic fibrosis drug *Orkambi* manufactured by Vertex Pharmaceuticals, the NHS entered into price negotiations to reduce the cost.[64] In the Netherlands, hospitals started making their own generic versions of expensive medicines to ensure availability of expensive drugs.[65] In France, Médecins du Monde filed a challenge at the European Patent Office against Gilead's *Sovaldi* – used to treat hepatitis C – challenging the cost and patent validity of the drug.[66] The US has been exceptional, where several issues have been raised on the question of pharmaceutical pricing, health-care access, patents, secondary patents, data exclusivity, and more. The practice of inflating the price of off-patent drugs, such as in the case of *Humalog* – a brand of insulin manufactured by Eli Lilly whose patent had expired 75 years ago and whose price nearly tripled between 2002 and 2013 and doubled again since then – raised concerns even among supporters of the Pharmaceutical Research and Manufacturers of America. The biggest game changers were American senators and members of Congress – who evangelized to sympathizers for reducing health-care costs – who became critical of the exorbitant cost of pharmaceuticals.[67]

63 *Kadcyla too expensive for routine funding on NHS*, NICE (2016), https://www. nice.org.uk/news/article/kadcyla-too-expensive-for-routine-funding-on-nhs.

64 *The Global Battle over High Drug Prices*, The Economist, https://www.economist.com/business/2019/05/21/the-global-battle-over-high-drug-prices.

65 *Dutch Join Backlash at Expensive Drugs by Making Their Own*, Reuters, https://www.reuters.com/article/us-netherlands-pharmaceuticals-insight/dutch-join-backlash-at-expensive-drugs-by-making-their-own-idUSKCN1QP0M4.

66 *Concerns over High-Priced Medicines Back in the European Parliament*, POLITICO, https://www.politico.eu/article/concerns-over-high-priced-medicines-back-in-the-european-parliament/.

67 *Patents Under Debate as Pharma Executives Face US Senate Committee*, Intellectual Property Watch, https://www.ip-watch.org/2019/02/27/patents-debate-pharma-executives-face-us-senate-committee/; *It's Time for Pharmaceutical Companies to Have Their Tobacco Moment*, N.Y. Times, https://www.nytimes.com/2019/02/24/opinion/drug-prices-congress.html.

Particularly in the US, and generally in the West, the evolution of health care into a privilege has proportionally seen an increase in discontentment and considerable challenges against all structural barriers that work to overprotect private capital at a huge public cost. Thus, beginning with the subject of patents and its correlation to innovation, several issues have brought the health-care access debate to the forefront by raising concerns about secondary patents, the regulatory issues relating to patents, market and data exclusivities, patent linkage, and more, each of which is dealt with in the book.[68] For example, secondary patenting – the practice of filing patents that are minor variants of the parent compound – leads to evergreening by creating a stack of patents, such that the innovator can exercise monopoly even after the first of several stacked patents expires.[69,70] Such stacking effectively extends monopoly that unfairly delays the entry of generics to the market and raises costs for governments and patients as a result. Secondary patents have been challenged because, while they can increase the number of patents, they do not necessarily reflect the presence of innovation.[71] A report by the advocacy group Initiative for Medicines, Access & Knowledge (I-MAK) discussed that pharmaceutical companies file hundreds of patent applications that are used to extend their patent term beyond the 20 years of protection intended under international patent law.[72] This effectively blocks competition, keeps cheaper versions of medicines off the market, and makes medicines harder to access on account of high drug prices. In effect, the world is witnessing a global shift in the access-patent discourse. Previously considered a problem for low-income countries, the issue is a global barrier to public health and trade.

Like secondary patents, the issue of data exclusivity can also work in tandem with the patent regime to add another level of protection. Data exclusivity refers to the practice of protecting clinical trial data submitted to a regulatory body to prove the safety, quality, and efficacy of a new drug.[73] In practical terms,

68 Adam Jaffe & Josh Lerner, Innovation and Its Discontents 78 (2004).

69 *See generally* Amy Kapczynski, *The Right to Medicines in Age of Neoliberalism*, 10 Humanity J. (Apr. 26, 2019), http://humanityjournal.org/issue10-1/the-right-to-medicines-in-an-age-of-neoliberalism/; Hannah Brennan et al., *A Prescription for Excessive Drug Pricing: Leveraging Government Patent Use for Health*, 18 Yale J. Law Technol. 280 (2017); Bhaven N. Sampat & Kenneth C. Shadlen, *Secondary Pharmaceutical Patenting: A Global Perspective*, 46.3 Res. Policy 693–707 (2017); C. Scott Hemphill & Bhaven N. Sampat, *Evergreening, Patent Challenges, and Effective Market Life in Pharmaceuticals*, 31.2 J. Health Econ. 327–39 (2012).

70 Srividhya Ragavan, *Drugs, Drugs Everywhere but Just Not for the Poor*, 8 WIPO J. 41–53 (2016).

71 Feroz Ali et al., Pharmaceutical Patent Grants in India: How our Safeguards Against Ever-greening Have Failed, and Why the System must be Reformed 18 (2018).

72 Initiative for Medicines, Access & Knowledge (I-MAK), Overpatented, Overpriced: How Excessive Pharmaceutical Patenting is Extending Monopolies and Driving up Drug Prices 2 (2018).

73 *See generally* Srividhya Ragavan, *The Significance of the Data Exclusivity and Its Impact on Generic Drugs*, 1.1 J. Intell. Prop. Stud. 131–41 (2017); Srividhya Ragavan, *Data Exclusivity: A Tool to Sustain Market Monopoly*, 8.2 *Jindal Global L. Rev.* 241 (2017).

this prohibits the dissemination of clinical trial data to a third party (usually, a generic company), thereby preventing the generic company from relying on the data for its own drug approval. For instance, the US Affordable Health Care for America Act in 2009 extended a 12-year exclusivity period for biologics.[74] When patents are awarded for 20 years, whether the safety data and related information should be independently protected remains an important question. It is more complicated in cases where the underlying patent is found invalid, resulting in the clinical trial data alone preventing a generic drug company from releasing a cheaper version until the data protection period is over, thereby virtually allowing the holder of the invalid patent to monopolize the market for the duration when data protection prevails.

Data exclusivity can also affect the use of CL by requiring the generic manufacturer to seek the patent holder's approval to use the test data separately for marketing approval. In the EU, for instance, depending on whether the originator drug is a chemical or biologic, a generic may not be marketed between 10 and 12 years after the grant of the initial market authorization for the originator product.[75] This forces a generic company to duplicate the clinical trial, the cost of which will be passed on to consumers. The issue of data exclusivity, especially as required under Article 39 of the TRIPS Agreement, has been contentious among legal scholars and commentators. For example, Daniel Gervais reads data exclusivity as a mandate in the TRIPS requirement to protect against unfair commercial use.[76] Carlos Correa, on the other hand, argue that the language of Article 39 falls short of what could be recognized as data exclusivity, and that the US position is inconsistent with the TRIPS Agreement.[77] Similarly, Ellen T'Hoen believe that the TRIPS Agreement does not oblige countries to confer exclusive rights over data related to marketing approval to the originator company.[78] This book presents these challenges and issues that implicate data exclusivity, patents, and their effect on access to medication.

In addition, patent linkage has grown in recent times to pose as a barrier to medicine access. According to Ragavan, patent linkage, which is the tying-in of patent information with data exclusivity, requires the regulatory body to

74 Affordable Health Care for America Act, 155 Cong. Rec. H12623, 12784 (Nov. 7, 2009). *See also* Srividhya Ragavan, *The (Re)Newed Barrier to Access to Medication: Data Exclusivity*, 51 Akron L. Rev. 1186 (2017).

75 I-MAK, *supra* note 72, at 3.

76 Daniel Gervais, The TRIPS Agreement: Drafting History and Analysis 545 (4th ed. 2012).

77 Carlos Correa, Trade Related Aspects of Intellectual Property Rights: A Commentary on the TRIPS Agreement 367 (2007). *See also* Carlos Correa, *Unfair Competition Under the TRIPS Agreement: Protection of Data Submitted for the Registration of Pharmaceuticals,* 3 Chi. J. Int'l L. 69, 72–73 (2002).

78 Ellen F. M. 't Hoen et al., *Data Exclusivity Exceptions and Compulsory Licensing to Promote Generic Medicines in the European Union: A Proposal for Greater Coherence in European Pharmaceutical Legislation*, 10 J. Pharm. Policy Pract. 2 (2017).

verify if a generic application relates to a patented product. Thus, a government body essentially performs the role of a gatekeeper of private property. This adds another layer of administrative approval, thus operating to further delay the entry of generics.[79] Patent linkage has far-reaching effects due to its widening scope and geographical coverage via free trade agreements (FTAs) and mega-regional agreements. By delaying the entry of generics into markets, patent linkage allows the high prices of originator medicines to remain unrestrained.[80] It is essentially an additional layer that shields the originator pharmaceutical company from generic competitors. As Kyung-Bok asserts, patent linkage facilitates innovator pharmaceutical companies to obtain a *de facto* injunction against a generic drug company.[81] Such injunctions can delay generic applications for up to 30 months, unless noninfringement or invalidity is established earlier, either by court judgment or patent expiry, during the 30 months.[82]

## Overview of the Book: Examining Three Generations of Access to Medicines Debate

The preceding section provides a background of how the TRIPS Agreement can impact public health through trade and productivity. Indeed, the signing of the TRIPS Agreement marks the beginning of a generational debate to access medication. The chapters in the book expand on this conceptual genealogy to delineate the historical trajectory of what we, the editors, consider a rendition of the three generations of global struggles with access to medication presented under the title **Access to Medicines and TRIPS Agreement: A Mapping of the Tradescape.**

The section below provides an overview of the chapters discussed in the book.

Part I titled **International Norm Setting and Patent Metamorphosis: First Generation** shows the institutions and actors involved in the metamorphosis of pharmaceutical patents, both at the international and domestic levels. We call it first generation because it details key episodes in the pharmaceutical patent trajectory to tease out how the "story and dialogue" changed and the new fault lines that have been drawn leading to a notable divergence between IPRs in the pharmaceutical industry and those in any other industry. Consisting of seven chapters, Part I offers an insight into the transformation of pharmaceutical patents and access to medicine interests in respective forums, notably the WTO (*Chapter 1*), the WHO (*Chapter 2*), the EU and the generic drugs industry (*Chapter 3*), FTAs

79 Ragavan, *supra* note 74, at 1163–96; Texas A&M University School of Law Legal Studies Research Paper No. 18–19, 1192.

80 Kyung-Bok Son et al., *Moderating the Impact of Patent Linkage on Access to Medicines: Lessons from Variations in South Korea, Australia, Canada, and the United States*, 14 Glob. Health 3 (2018).

81 *Id.*

82 *Id.*

(*Chapter 4*), a case study of the TPP and the US-Mexico-Canada Agreement (*Chapter 5*), the African Union (*Chapter 6*), and on the Bayh-Dole Act and the litigation of US government–funded patent in Europe and Japan (*Chapter 7*). The critical observation of the chapters within this section is the confluence of various actors and institutions in the development, framing, and reframing of pharmaceutical patent laws, which has led to the steady ratcheting up of standards and norms in a manner that has made access to medication a luxury.

Following this, Part II titled **State Action and Access to Medicines Debate: Second Generation** captures the role of state actors and their engagements as part of an emerging and changing global pattern. We call it second generation because it looks at how countries adapted to the globalization of patents and how their domestic patent law activities changed and continue to change the global narrative on public health and access to medicine. The seven chapters in Part II offer insights into the operation and variations of pharmaceutical patent norms in select countries. In doing so, the chapters capture the ground realities as well as policies employed by national governments to improve access. The detailed accounts include a discussion of how industrial and related policies were used to encourage local production and technology transfer in select countries such as in Brazil (*Chapter 8*); the introduction and employment of innovative policies to aid the development of the domestic economy and technology originating in China (*Chapter 9*); the influence of IP provisions in preferential trade agreements (PTAs) in Canada which have had varying impact on domestic subregions and subpopulations (*Chapter 10*); analyses of the landmark Novartis case in India (*Chapter 11*) and the "pharmagate" crisis in South Africa, and the effect of these domestic legal disputes on generic pharmaceutical manufacturing landscape and medicine access in both countries, respectively (*Chapter 12*); the role of government in using CLs and their fallout on public health discourse in Thailand (*Chapter 13*); and the unilateral norm-setting actions of the US using the Office of the US Trade Representative Special 301 Reports (*Chapter 14*). The national studies highlight two important aspects. First, they underscore how a number of emerging markets have risen to challenge existing ideologies on global patent framework and, second, how the legal system – including policy makers and the judiciary – play a key role in the interpretation of laws, which can be critical in driving the discourse and dialogue on patent reform and access to medication debates.

Part III of this volume titled **Global Patterns and Emerging Issues: Third Generation** highlights new changes and challengers to the existing framework. Here, focus is on the participation of civil society that brought patent law into the field of activism, the role of the private sector to mobilize the access to medicine issue, and the emergence of new issues which triggered a simultaneous convergence *and* divergence of regulatory standards. We call it third generation because it captures the state of "flux" due to advances in technology and new threats to global health, which pose new challenges to an already complex system of IP. Analyses in this section include the role of civil society in reframing the narratives surrounding patents and in strengthening the network of civil society participation (*Chapter 15*); the firsthand experience of GTPI, a grass-root civil society and patient group in Brazil, in vocalizing access to medicine advocacy and mobilization efforts in Brazil and in other countries (*Chapter 16*); and the responsibility of the private sector as regards right to health and access to affordable medicines (*Chapter 17*). Within Part III, the last five chapters look at other elements in the evolving global scene that are relevant to the discussions on the TRIPS Agreement and access to medicine. The various issues include the relationship between IPRs and competition law (*Chapter 18*); the distinct world of pharmaceutical patents due to the convergence of various domestic regulatory frameworks and actors (*Chapter 19*); discussions on the barriers engendering the creation of effective competitive regulatory mechanisms for controlling pharmaceutical prices (*Chapter 20*); how pharmaceutical companies use trademark laws to manipulate consumers to control markets beyond the life of patents (*Chapter 21*); the practice of Traditional Medical Knowledge (TMK) and pushback from the pharmaceutical industry to marginalize TMK (*Chapter 22*); and how the digital divide can affect access to medicine by exacerbating the inequality in medicine access and availability (*Chapter 23*).

## COVID-19 and Access to Medicines: Concluding Lessons

If there is a disruptive force that helped reckon with generations of struggle and acknowledge the significance of public health to economic prosperity and trade, it is COVID-19. The pandemic unfurled into the globe quietly but emphatically – stopping trade and economic activity. For a while, by giving *Remdesivir* an orphan drug status out of turn, the US seemed to struggle to reconcile the idiocy of its IP ideology even as New York State was being halted to an economic stop by COVID-19. In all, the pandemic has raised questions on the viability of the current IP system to foster trade, the role of pharmaceutical innovation, the importance of transfer of technological knowledge, and, generally, the imminence of access to medicine. It has also forced the globe to address the issue of research and development of new treatments for infectious diseases and readiness for future pandemics. The concluding chapter looks at the COVID-19 pandemic and access to medication debate (*Chapter 24*). In revisiting the pharmaceutical patent landscape, it examines how the current IP framework has ceased to be a model for delivering products critically needed to respond to global health emergencies.

In presenting conceptual and policy problems affecting poor nations, as well as the contemporary but comparable health-care access issues of developed countries, the book's distinguishing feature is the diversity of issues discussed. By examining the role of civil society groups, patient organizations, regulatory bodies, and government officials in developed and developing nations and their impact on the various legal structures within which they operate, we believe the book will provide a unique insight into the global debate on patents and access to medication discourse. As scholars committed to the cause, we hope that the theme covered in this book will reverberate globally.

# Part I

# International Norm Setting and Patent Metamorphosis

## First Generation

# 1 World Trade Organization

## A Barrier to Global Public Health?

*Srividhya Ragavan*

## Introduction

"The World Health Organization Draws Flak for Coronavirus Response," read the headline of the Wall Street Journal on February 12, 2020.[1] The global struggle with the coronavirus pandemic has highlighted two things: first, the importance of medication; second, the need to access health care and medication. With tens of thousands of individuals infected with COVID-19, and a death toll spreading into almost all countries, the International Health Regulations Emergency Committee of the World Health Organization (WHO) declared this virus a "public health emergency of international concern." Disruptive global epidemics – such as the AIDS, ebola, and SARS – have time and again raised the issue of global response and preparedness to pandemics.[2] While the WHO continues to be at the center of the debate, the role of the World Trade Organization (WTO) remains crucial in proactively preventing or addressing epidemics and pandemics.[3] The harmonized trading system of the WTO was built on an underlying assumption that egalitarian access to health is a barrier to trade and that disparate access to health was the solution to innovation. Considering that a public health crisis in one part of the world can affect global trade in unimaginable ways, protecting public health has become the threshold to protect global trade.

In the face of a global pandemic, access to health care and medication is the one paradigm that can alleviate many global concerns, including those involving and relating to trade such as employment, travel, and more. Lack of medications – either from lack of availability of medication or lack of access – can catapult a

1 Jeremy Page & Betsy McKay, *The World Health Organization Draws Flak for Coronavirus Response*, WALL ST. J. (Feb. 12, 2020), https://on.wsj.com/35e3V5x.

2 Brendan Murray, *Slump in Global Goods Trade to Deepen with Coronavirus, WTO Says*, BLOOMBERG (Feb. 17, 2020), https://bloom.bg/2Z8OAPK.

3 *See generally* Ana Swanson, *Global Trade Sputters, Leaving Too Much Here, Too Little There*, N.Y. TIMES (Apr. 10, 2020), https://www.nytimes.com/2020/04/10/business/economy/global-trade-shortages-coronavirus.html.

possible national public health issue into an international global health crisis. In turn, a global health crisis can affect several industries in ways otherwise unimaginable. Hence, there is a need for balance between innovation and access. The role of the WTO as the gatekeeper for eliminating trade barriers while preserving access to health-care remains important in taking a strategic leadership position for health-related matters. If global productivity is affected due to lack of access to available medication, global trade suffers as a consequence. Despite this reality, the WTO has remained normative and divorced from the real impact of local realities on larger health issues. Its stature as a global organization notwithstanding, the WTO has shown a remarkable tendency to succumb to unrealistic rhetoric and pressures from corporate interests and powerful countries that have shown susceptibility to pandering by powerful trade lobbies. Consequently, the WTO has been irrelevant in ensuring access to medication as a means to strengthen productivity and global trade.[4]

Indeed, the WTO's failure to balance innovation with access has caused, contributed to, and affected access to medications. The actions of the WTO have actively contributed to morphing access to lifesaving medications into a luxury by creating an elite global class of people with access to health care and medication or, *mediclass*. While the WTO's emphasis on patents on lifesaving medications played a role in innovation, it largely facilitated corporations from disengaging with issues that raise public policy, public health, and right to life concerns – both by commissions and omissions that denied access to lifesaving medications.

This chapter outlines seven specific ways in which the WTO has, through its actions, inactions, and/or prescriptions, detrimentally affected access to medicines. Hence, it outlines how the WTO's myopic actions resulted in trade becoming a barrier to public health, and in turn, to trade itself. The chapter emphasizes that minimizing barriers to access medications and health is the lifeline to minimizing barriers to trade. It is imperative to control the pandemic as the first step to rejuvenate trade. This pandemic has raised questions on preserving public health, and on innovation implicating the role of intellectual property (IP) in trade in this area. Despite the impact of the public health crisis on trade, the WTO largely remained silent during the COVID pandemic until a waiver was sought without addressing how Trade Related Aspects of Intellectual Property Rights (TRIPS) provisions on innovation is a barrier to health and thus, indirectly to trade. In highlighting the ways in which the WTO has been a barrier to the protection of public health, the hope is that the trade regime of the future will promote rather than prevent countries from instituting measures critical to improving global public health, which in turn is the lifeline to improving productivity and trade.

4 Srividhya Ragavan & Brian Manning, *The Dispute Settlement Process of the WTO: A Normative Structure to Achieve Utilitarian Objectives*, 79 UMKC L. Rev. 1, 22 (2010).

## It Began with the Original Draft

When the WTO was established, the TRIPS Agreement mandated that countries provide product patent protection as part of the required minimum standards.[5] At that time, developing countries vociferously pointed to local realities to highlight that the TRIPS Agreement would be detrimental to accessing lifesaving medication in poorer members. Moreover, poorer countries criticized the TRIPS Agreement for not considering their resource restraints before enforcing the establishment of the patent regime. The main criticism against the TRIPS Agreement was that the harmonization effort did not provide for – nor did it factor in – issues of national import. Weaving adequate flexibility to allow countries at different stages of economic growth to balance between "incentives to create and the benefits of free competition" was an important aspect that the TRIPS agenda overlooked.[6] The overwhelming reality was that the ***minimum standards*** set forth in the TRIPS Agreement represented a maximalist approach.[7]

Particularly, the TRIPS Agreement's approach to access to medication was criticized for not taking the objectives and principles of the Agreement into account. Article 7 of the TRIPS Agreement outlines objectives stating that the enforcement of intellectual property mechanisms should promote technological innovation and transfer of technology in a manner mutually advantageous to the social and economic welfare of the users.[8] On a plain reading, Article 7 emphasizes the welfare paradigm by asserting that the international obligations of protection and enforcement of IP rights should contribute to the national, social, and economic welfare of members. The outlined objectives have been criticized for the primacy they lend to IP protection, and for not providing members with adequate flexibility to address national issues.[9] The principles under which the objectives of Article 7 work are outlined in Article 8.[10] Entitled *Principles,* Article 8 recognizes members' rights to adopt public interest or public health measures, provided they are consistent with the TRIPS provisions.[11] Thus, Article 8 recognizes limitations on private rights under some circumstances. This article can also be viewed

5 TRIPS: Agreement on Trade Related Aspects of Intellectual Property Rights, Apr. 15, 1994, Marrakesh Agreement Establishing the World Trade Organization, Annex 1C, 1869 U.N.T.S. 299, 33 I.L.M. 1197 (1994) [hereinafter TRIPS Agreement], art. 27.

6 TRIPS Agreement, *supra* note 5.

7 Jerome H. Reichman, *Enforcing the Enforcement Procedures of the TRIPS Agreement*, 37 Va. J. Int'l L. 335, 337–39 (1997).

8 TRIPS Agreement, art. 7, *supra* note 5.

9 *Id. See, e.g., The Doha Round*, http://www.wto.org/english/tratop_e/dda_e/dda_e.htm (last visited June 11, 2011).

10 *Id.* at art. 8.

11 *Id.*

as limiting the policy-making rights of member states in a public health or public interest exigency.[12] Operationally, the assertion of Article 7 to balance members' rights with obligations notwithstanding, the TRIPS Agreement was more effective in encouraging fulfillment of obligations than in enabling members to achieve public policy and national developmental goals. Consequently, the WTO faced considerable push-back, most significantly from health activists, patient groups, and nongovernmental organizations (NGOs), on the grounds that the innovation agenda did not address the question of providing global access to lifesaving drugs.[13] Thus, the WTO draft did not give preference to access to medication.

## WTO's Elitist Attitude Toward Epidemics

The establishment of minimum standards, with maximalist approach toward IP protection, characterized an inadequacy of the TRIPS Agreement in catering to issues such as balancing innovation with access to lifesaving medicines. For instance, during the early 1990s, the HIV/AIDS epidemic was ravaging the world at an unprecedented rate, particularly in developing countries. The patented medication, which cost \$15,000–\$20,000 per patient per year, remained inaccessible to many HIV/AIDS patients who needed antiretroviral drugs (ARVs) to survive.[14]

Africa was affected the most; thus, the impact of the high price of ARVs was felt more starkly there. Only one in thousand patients living with HIV had access to AIDS treatment at that time.[15] Highlighting the extent of the epidemic, in 1996, South Africa requested the United States (US) to allow access to the medication at an affordable price commensurate with its per capita income.[16]

12 TRIPS Agreement, *supra* note 5, at art. 8(1).

13 Ellen't Hoen, The Global Politics of Pharmaceutical Monopoly Power 22, 78 (2009); *see also*, Germán Velasquez & Pascale Boulet, *Globalization and Access to Drugs: The Implications of the WTO/TRIPS Agreement*, Health Economic and Drugs DAP Series No. 007, 25 (1998), http://apps.who.int/medicinedocs/en/d/Jwhozip35e/3.7.1.html; *see also* Robert Weissman, *The Strange Trips: The Pharmaceutical Industry Drive to Harmonize Global Intellectual Property Rules, and the Remaining WTO Legal Alternatives Available to Third World Countries*, 17 Univ. Pa. J. Int. Law 1069 (1996), https://scholarship.law.upenn.edu/jil/vol17/iss4/2.

14 Carmen Perez-Casas et al., *Accessing ARVs: Untangling the Web of Antiretroviral Price Reductions*, 10 (2001), https://msfaccess.org/sites/default/files/MSF_assets/HIV_AIDS/Docs/AIDS_report_UTW1_ENG_2001.pdf; *see also*, Ellen 't Hoen *et al.*, *Driving a Decade of Change: HIV/AIDS, Patents and Access to Medicines for All*, 14 J. Int. AIDS Soc. 1, 15 (2011).

15 Barton Gellman, *An Unequal Calculus of Life and Death; As Millions Perished in Pandemic, Firms Debated Access to Drugs; Players in the Debate Over Drug Availability and Pricing*, Washington Post (Dec. 27, 2000), at A1.

16 Helene Cooper *et al.*, *AIDS Epidemic Puts Drug Firms in a Vise: Treatment vs. Profits*, Wall St. J. (Mar. 2, 2001), https://www.wsj.com/articles/SB983487988418159849.

The US treated the issue as a routine noncompliance of the TRIPS Agreement; the then US Trade Representative, Mr. Papovich, asked South Africa to either comply with the TRIPS Agreement or, alternately, face trade sanctions.[17] South Africa could not afford trade sanctions, which could lead to further economic misery. Therefore, South Africa passed the Medicines and Related Substances Act Amendment of 1997 to statutorily implement negotiated TRIPS flexibilities.[18] Under the statute, a deteriorating public health condition vested the health minister with the right to import or compulsorily license patents.[19] Condemning the health minister's "sweeping authority," the US denied South Africa permission to export under the generalized system of preference scheme.[20] Meanwhile, the Pharmaceutical Manufacturers' Association of South Africa (PMA) filed a suit against the South African government to suspend the Medicines Act.[21] The situation exacerbated when an update of public health conditions in 1999 revealed that one in five South Africans was AIDS infected.[22]

17 *Id.*

18 *See* South Africa Statutory Instrument 1997 Act No. 59 (2002) (as amended) [hereinafter Medicines Act]. The 1997 legislation amended the South African Medicines and Related Substances Control Act No. 101 of 1965.

19 Medicines Act at § 15(c), which reads: "The Minister may prescribe conditions for the supply of more affordable medicines in certain circumstances so as to protect the health of the public and in particular may, notwithstanding anything to the contrary contained in the Patents Act 1978 (Act No. 57 of 1978), determine that the rights with regard to any medicine under a patent granted in the Republic shall not extend to acts in respect of such medicine which has been put onto the market by the owner of the medicine or with his or her consent." While Medicines Act § 22C(1)(a) states "The Director-General may on application in the prescribed manner and on payment of the prescribed fee, issue to a medical practitioner, dentist, practitioner, nurse or other person registered under the Health Professions Act, 1974, a license to compound and dispense medicines, on the prescribed conditions."

20 Naomi A. Bass, *Compulsory Licensing and the South African Medicine Act of 1997: Violation or Compliance of the Trade-Related Aspects of Intellectual Property Rights Agreement*, 34 GEO. WASH. INT'L L. REV. 191, 211–12 (2002). Pretoria had requested additional benefits under the generalized system of preference scheme. The scheme allows poor countries to export products to the United States at reduced duties.

21 *See* Patrick Marc, *Compulsory Licensing and the South African Medicine Act of 1997: Violation or Compliance of the Trade-Related Aspects of Intellectual Property Rights Agreement*, 21 N.Y.L. SCH. J. INT'L & COMP. L. 109, 121 (2001) (highlighting America's opposition to attempts by South Africa to legislate compulsory licensing provisions). The PMA in South Africa represents the pharmaceutical manufacturers of the developed nations.

22 South Africa accounted for a total of 26 million of the world's 36 million HIV-affected patients. Seven countries in southern Africa reported that 20 percent of the adults were infected with HIV. Botswana accounted for the highest percentage of the disease with 35.8 percent infected adults. *See* Sara M. Ford, *Compulsory Licensing Provisions Under the TRIPS Agreement: Balancing Pills and Patents*, 15 AM. U. INT'L L. REV. 941, 951 (2000); *see also Patent Protection and Access to HIV/AIDS Pharmaceuticals in Sub-Saharan Africa*, INTERNATIONAL INTELLECTUAL PROPERTY INSTITUTE, 55–90 (2000); *see generally* Liz McGregor, *Botswana Battles Against Extinction*, THE GUARDIAN (July 8, 2002), http://www.guardian.co.uk/aids/story/0,7369,751263,00.html.

It caused President Clinton to issue an Executive Order to promote access to HIV/AIDS medicines and extended the South African policy to all poor countries.[23]

Unlike South Africa, Thailand's efforts to amend the 1979 patent legislation to facilitate generic drugs is discussed in the chapter authored by Van Anh Le.[24] In 1992, Thailand had extended patent protection to pharmaceuticals and increased the patent term to 20 years.[25] Just like in South Africa, the US threatened sanctions unless amendments were introduced to the Thai patent legislation.[26] However, under trade pressure from the US[27] in 1999, Thailand abolished compulsory licensing and the local-working requirement.[28] These patent-friendly amendments resulted in an increase in AIDS infection with decreasing availability of medication.[29] By 2000, about 3 percent of the Thai population were reportedly infected with AIDS. The situation caused the Office of the US Trade Representative (USTR) to reverse course pledging to not raise further objections "provided the compulsory license is issued in a manner fully consistent with the WTO/TRIPS Agreement."[30]

The precedents established by South Africa and Thailand resulted in Brazil amending its patent legislation of 1969 to comply with the TRIPS Agreement by introducing compulsory licensing flexibilities to preserve public health.[31]

23 Exec. Order No. 13155, 3 C.F.R. 268–70 (2000) prohibiting the US from taking "[a]ctions pursuant to section 301(b) of the Trade Act of 1974 with respect to any law or policy in beneficiary sub-Saharan African countries that promotes access to HIV/AIDS pharmaceuticals or medical technologies and that provides adequate and effective IP protection consistent with the TRIPS Agreement." *See also* Rosalyn S. Park, *The International Drug Industry: What the Future Holds for South Africa's HIV/AIDS Patients*, 11 Minn. J. Global Trade 125, 138 (2002).

24 *See generally* Van Anh, Part II, chapter 13; *see also* Rosemary Sweeney, *The U.S. Push for Worldwide Patents Protection for Drugs Meets the AIDS Crisis in Thailand: A Devastating Collision*, 9 Pac. Rim L. & Pol'y J. 445, 446 (2000).

25 *See* Thailand Statutory Instruments, Thai (amended) Patent Act (No. 2) B.E. 2535 (1992), as amended.

26 *See* Sweeney, *supra* note 24, at 446–48. The amended Thai patent legislation retained the authority to issue compulsory licenses (CLs) of patented goods not locally manufactured. A Pharmaceutical Patent Board was created with the power to compulsorily license patents in a public health crisis, to control prices, and to seek pricing and cost information on drugs. The patent amendment did not protect existing products patented in other countries but not marketed in Thailand.

27 *Id.* at 461. In 1997, Thailand suffered a severe economic crisis, increasing its reliance on American exports.

28 *See* Thailand Statutory Instruments, Thai (amended) Patent Act (No. 3) B.E. 2542 (1999). The amended law abolished the Pharmaceutical Review Board. Importation of patented products by the patentee was deemed as working the patent locally; *see generally* Susannah Markandya, *Timeline of Trade Disputes Involving Thailand and Access to Medicines* (July 23, 2001), http://www.cptech.org/ip/health/c/thailand/thailand.html.

29 Sweeney, *supra* note 24, at 446.

30 Markandya, *supra* note 28.

31 Brazil Industrial Property Law No. 9, 279 of May 14, 1996 (effective May 1997).

Meanwhile, spending $303 million per annum on a single ARV pushed Brazil to its economic limit.[32] When Roche Inc., after six months of negotiations, refused to discount the price of ARVs, Brazil threatened to compulsorily license them.[33] The background of the tremendous success of the AIDS drug distribution program forced the US to drop its claims against Brazil in the WTO.[34] Consequently, Roche and Merck negotiated with Brazil to reduce the cost of the AIDS drugs by 70 percent.[35] The WTO did not have the jurisdiction to interfere directly. But, just like with the COVID-19 pandemic, the WTO chose to stick with the normative questions on trade, if and when presented to it. The WTO's silence and inability to acknowledge the barriers that its agreement create to public health – and in turn, to global trade – weakened its stature. Further, the extent of unilateral interference and pressure by the US reiterated the susceptibility and disadvantages of the unequal bargaining parities of members. It weakened the rhetoric for a multilateral forum. Furthermore, the WTO's inability to work with the WHO to clarify whether and how countries can utilize flexibilities to safeguard public health, considering the fact that patents increasingly impede medicine access, has impacted the WTO's reputation negatively.

32 Melody Petersen & Larry Rohter, *Maker Agrees to Cut Price of Two AIDS Drugs in Brazil*, N.Y. Times (Mar. 31, 2001), http://www.nytimes.com/2001/03/31/health/31AIDS.html?ex=1051934400&en=f9e3ca8f7ee0983c&ei=5070; *see also* Mario Osava, *Government to Violate Patents on AIDS Drugs*, Inter-Press Service (Aug. 23, 2001).

33 *See* Miriam Jordan, *Brazil to Break Patents on AIDS Medication Nelfinavir*, Wall St. J. (Aug. 23, 2001), at A1 (detailing that Brazil requested Roche, Inc. to reduce the cost of the AIDS cocktail drugs, *nelfavir* and *viracept*. Roche Inc. refused to consider anything more than a 13 percent reduction in price. Brazilian officials announced that the patent in nelfinavir would be compulsorily licensed for local manufacture of generic versions unless the price was reduced; *see also Ministry of Health Announces Compulsory Licensing of Nelfinavir Patent* (Aug. 22, 2001), http://www.cptech.org/ip/health/c/brazil/nelf08222001.html; *see also* Amaka Vanni, Patent Games In The Global South: Pharmaceutical Patent Law-Making in Brazil, India and Nigeria 90–94 (2020) (discussing HIV/AIDS medicines and the politics of CL in Brazil).

34 Helene Cooper, *U.S. Drops WTO Claims Against Brazilian Patent Law*, Wall St. J. (June 27, 2001), at B7.

35 Jennifer L. Rich, *Roche Reaches Accord on Drug with Brazil*, N.Y. Times (Sept. 1, 2001), http://www.nytimes.com/2001/09/01/business/worldbusiness/01DRUG.html?-searchpv=day03; *see also* Paulo Rebelo, *Brazil Targets Another AIDS Drug*, Wired News (Aug. 29, 2001), http://www.wired.com/news/politics/0,1283,46353,00.html; *see generally Roche Surprised by Authorities Declaration* (Aug. 23, 2001), http://www.cptech.org/ip/health/c/brazil/. Brazil provided the AIDS "cocktail" medications free for its citizens and thus reduced the national AIDS mortality rate from 10,592 in 1995 to 1700 in 2001. To ensure supplies of the drugs to 100,000 HIV/AIDS patients, Brazil manufactures seven of the 12 medications at a local company – *Farmanguinhos*; *see* Gustavo Capdevila & Mario Osava, *US Drops Brazil Patents Case*, I. P. S. News Agency (June 26, 2002), http://www.ipsnews.net/2001/06/trade-us-drops-brazil-patents-case-paves-way-for-low-cost-drugs/.

## Flexibility Gone Awry

The AIDS crisis showcased economic and social challenges of poorer nations. Soon, developing nations sought a "broad and balanced" program within the TRIPS Agreement.[36]

In June 2001, a special session of the TRIPS Council heard the views of over 40 countries on issues relating to IP and access to medicine, and identified key elements relating to safeguarding public health.[37] Meanwhile, the US had to address a domestic anthrax scare in 2001.[38] Responding to a relatively small but increased number of patients contracting anthrax from unknown sources, the US Department of Health and Human Services (HHS) immediately sought a workable solution to access medication and determined that compulsorily licensing the anthrax medication, *ciprofloxin*, was the most viable solution. HHS approached the patent owner, Bayer AG Corporation to lower its selling price![39] This reaction of the HHS destroyed the credibility of the US argument that compulsory licensing of pharmaceuticals was an undesirable option to address public health crises.[40] Consequently, the anthrax issue facilitated concessions to developing nations at the Doha Round of the WTO, which allowed members to derogate from patent rights to prioritize public health issues.[41] The resulting Doha Declaration on the TRIPS Agreement and Public Health 2001 (Doha Declaration) encouraged members capable of manufacturing generic drugs, such as India and Brazil, to tackle prevailing or potential public health needs by locally manufacturing generic medications.[42] Unfortunately, this solution could not help least developed states with no capacity to manufacture generic drugs. Basically, Article 31(f) of the TRIPS Agreement required compulsorily licensed medication to predominantly supply the domestic market of the member authorizing such use.[43] Thus, the WTO's flexibilities continued to remain ineffective in some countries even after the Doha Declaration was ratified.[44]

36 *See* Helene Cooper & Geoff Winestock, *Poor Nations Win Gains in Global Trade Deal as U.S. Compromises*, Wall St. J. (Nov. 15, 2001), at A1 (discussing issues raised by the Indian Commerce and Industry Minister in the WTO session at Qatar).

37 TRIPS Agreement, *supra* note 5; *TRIPS and Public Health*, Third World Network, http://www.twnside.org.sg/title/twr131e.htm (last visited Mar. 29, 2005); *see also* James Thuo Gathii, *The Legal Status of the Doha Declaration on TRIPS and Public Health Under the Vienna Convention on the Law of Treaties*, 15 Harv. J. L. & Tech. 291, 295–98 (2002).

38 Cecilia Oh, *Developing Countries Call for Action on TRIPS at Doha WTO Ministerial Conference*, Third World Network, http://www.twnside.org.sg/title/twr131d.htm (last visited June 12, 2011).

39 Divya Murthy, *The Future of Compulsory Licensing: Deciphering the Doha Declaration on the TRIPS Agreement and Public Health*, 17(12) Am. U. Int'l L. Rev. 1299, 1302 (2002).

40 *Id.*

41 *Id.*

42 World Trade Organization, Ministerial Declaration of 14 November 2001, WTO Doc. WT/MIN(01)/DEC/1, 41 ILM 746 (2002) [hereinafter Doha Declaration].

43 TRIPS Agreement, *supra* note 5, at art. 31(f).

44 *Id.*

The issues arising from the operation of Article 31(f) were later partly addressed by Article 31*bis* of the TRIPS Agreement – allowing export of generics for a limited purpose – was adopted in 2006.[45]

This was the first glimpse post the WTO's establishment on how trade would be affected if public health was left unprotected. The trade regime on the health and medication issues miscalculated this reality for over 25 years! The ideological affinity over the patents and innovation rhetoric erased any semblance of realism; instead, it induced a normative reading of the WTO texts which would ultimately blindside the globe into COVID-19. Realistic issues of local import were brushed aside as mere poor-country sob stories to help ignore the importance of health for robust trade, representing yet another lost opportunity for the WTO.

## WTO Reducing the Line Between Domestic and Market Access Issues

The WTO's agreements distinguish between domestic regulations and market access restrictions.[46] Domestic regulations are internal national regulations. Market access restrictions are customs and other regulations that affect access to the market by third countries, thus acting as trade barriers. The agreements prohibit members from creating market access restrictions that discriminate unfairly against imports, but provide extensive regulatory autonomy for domestic regulations.[47] In any given dispute, the role of the WTO's Dispute Settlement Body (DSB) is to determine whether a market access restriction exists in the member state in question.[48] While general wisdom favors the removal of all market access restrictions, justifiable exceptions can be found in almost any country for several

45 *See* General Council, *Implementation of the Paragraph 6 of the Doha Declaration on the TRIPS Agreement and Public Health*, WTO Doc. WT/L/540 (Aug. 30, 2003).

46 Joost Pauwelyn, *Rien Ne Va Plus? Distinguishing Domestic Regulation from Market Access in GATT and GATS* 132 Duke Law School, Legal Studies Paper No. 85, http://ssrn.com/abstract=638303.

47 *Id.* at 32.

48 Understanding on Rules and Procedures Governing the Settlement of Disputes, Apr. 15, 1994, Annex 2, Legal Instruments—Results of the Uruguay Round, 1869 U.N.T.S. 401 [hereinafter DSU], art. 1. Article 3(4) specifies that "[r]ecommendations or rulings made by the DSB shall be aimed at achieving a satisfactory settlement... in accordance with the rights and obligations under this Understanding and under the covered agreements." *Id.* at art. 3(4). Further, Article 3(7) highlights that "the first objective of the dispute settlement mechanism is usually to secure the withdrawal of the measures concerned if these are found to be inconsistent with the provisions of any of the covered agreements." *Id.* at art. 3(7). Thus, the DSU does not concern itself with the larger question of the effect of a market access restriction on domestic issues; *see also* Marie-Christine Lebret & Arlène Alpha, *Factsheet 4—The Application of Rules: Cotton*, GRET, http://www.gret.org/publications/ouvrages/infoomc/en/F04en.html (last visited July 14, 2010) (highlighting that the DSB's role is limited to enforcing existing rules).

reasons: political, social, and/or market-oriented. Further, a blanket recommendation from a global body or the DSB to remove the market access restriction – without fully appreciating the broader national, regional, or even global effects of such removal – would be myopic and could create economic and social imbalance within a country.

Member governments of the WTO have a larger task to accomplish for national markets. Member governments' resources are limited, in the sense that they demand allocation toward conflicting or directly competing social, economic, and welfare-oriented goals. For instance, should a country prioritize providing patent protection to allow foreign investment in the future, or should it take care of an existing public health crisis by providing generic drugs? States have been traditionally allowed to act as they see fit on issues relating to the political and social heart of their sovereignty, like health-care issues.[49] For member nations, trade regulations represent one part, albeit important, of the paradigm of socio-economic issues that need resolution. Acknowledging this approach, the WTO treaty envisages sovereign latitude for countries to address issues of national import to resolve complex local issues that each country faces – issues that can interfere with trade obligations.[50]

The DSB's role would be more realistic if it considers the likely effects of a market access restriction by weighing it alongside the cost to international trade *as well as to the member*. Instead, the DSB has tended to have a normative approach. For example, in 1994, when India attained WTO membership, the TRIPS Agreement provided a transitional period until January 1, 2005 to move toward the product patent regime.[51] During this transitional period, Article 70(8) of the TRIPS Agreement required members to establish a transitional "mailbox" mechanism, i.e., to establish a means to file patent applications that would be considered for patent protection after the transition in 2005.[52] By virtue of Article 70(9), members were required to provide exclusive marketing rights (EMR) to patent applications in the mailbox.[53] Thus, patent applications filed by transitioning members would enjoy EMR provided two conditions were met: first, an application has been filed in another member state and, second, the application matured into an actual patent.[54]

When India became a TRIPS Agreement signatory, the President of India promulgated the Patents (Amendment) Ordinance 1995[55] for accepting mailbox

49 Pauwelyn, *supra* note 46, at 135.

50 *Id.* at 133.

51 TRIPS Agreement, *supra* note 5, at art. 65.

52 *Id.* at art 70(8).

53 *Id.*

54 *Id.* at art 70(9).

55 *See* Patents (Amendment) Ordinance, 2004, No. 7, https://spicyip.com/wp-content/uploads/2020/02/2004-patent-ordinance-later-rejected.pdf [hereinafter Patents Ordinance]; *see also* India Const. art. 123, § 1 (which authorizes the President to legislate when parliament is not in session when the President deems necessary to take immediate action).

applications for agricultural and chemical product inventions. The Ordinance detailed application procedures, scope, and enforcement of rights of EMR.[56] When the Ordinance expired, the Parliament was not in session; hence the Indian government attempted to meet India's TRIPS obligations by issuing administrative orders[57] instructing the Patent Office to receive patent applications for pharmaceutical, agricultural, and chemical products.[58] Thus, from January 1, 1995 to February 15, 1997, India received and stored 1339 applications under the administrative scheme.[59] As of late September 1997, no applicant requested an EMR.[60] In July 1996, the US requested consultations with India pursuant to Article 4 of the Dispute Settlement Understanding (DSU), read with Article 64 of the TRIPS Agreement, claiming that India was in breach of its TRIPS obligations for not statutorily offering the mailbox mechanism.[61] When consultations failed, the US requested that a dispute panel be established to review the claim.[62] The panel determined that India violated Article 70(8) of the TRIPS Agreement in not establishing a statutory means to establish a mailbox mechanism.[63] India was also found to have violated Article 70(9) of the TRIPS Agreement in not creating a statutory mechanism to grant EMR.[64]

For instance, when India appealed the panel's decision, the Appellate Body (AB) determined that the TRIPS Agreement would be interpreted based on the legitimate expectations of the parties at the time of signing the treaty.[65] This interpretation does not comport with an objective-based interpretation of treaty, as required under the Vienna Convention.[66] Thus, the AB held that legitimate expectations of parties to a treaty were reflected in the treaty language, leaving the interpreter to examine the words of the treaty *alone* to determine the intentions of the parties.[67] Traditionally, international agreements are not interpreted like statutes, which are construed more strictly to defer to the views of the legislature. International agreements are not enforcement mechanisms, but instruments that memorialize

56 *See* Patents Ordinance, *supra* note 55.

57 Robert Pechman, *Seeking Multilateral Protection for Intellectual Property: The United States "TRIPS" over Special 301*, 7 Minn. J. Global Trade 179, 196 (1998) (discussing that the United States subjected countries with inadequate protection of IP rights to special 301 trade sanctions).

58 *See* Panel Report, *India—Patent Protection for Pharmaceutical and Agricultural Chemical Products*, WTO Doc. WT/DS50/R (Sept. 5, 1997) [hereinafter Panel Report India], paras. 2.3 and 2.5.

59 *Id.* at para 7.4.

60 *Id.* at para 7.5.

61 *Id.* at para 1.1.

62 *Id.*

63 *Id.* at para 8.1.

64 *Id.*

65 *See* Notification of an Appeal, *India-Patent Protection for Pharmaceutical and Agricultural Chemical Products*, WTO Doc. WT/DS50/6 (Oct. 16, 1997).

66 *Id.* § 55. *See also* Vienna Convention on the Law of Treaties, art. 26, May 23, 1969, 1155 U.N.T.S. 331, 8 I.L.M. 679.

67 *Id.* at para 45.

collective sovereign intentions. The intentions of parties with respect to international agreements and obligations are generally amenable to local needs and political and economic situations; therefore, a more flexible and broader construction is warranted. Unfortunately, a strict constructionist, textualist, and non-traditionalist approach would be an imperfect treatment of substantive issues. But the AB used a strict normative constructionist approach of Article 70(8)[68] of the TRIPS Agreement to determine that India failed to establish a legally sound transitional mailbox mechanism.[69]

In all, the DSB of the WTO failed to accept India's position that the scheme was legitimate under the jurisprudence developed by Indian courts![70] Instead, like the panel,[71] the AB required precedents explicitly showing that a court would uphold the validity of administrative actions and refused to defer to a nation's interpretation of its own legislation to hold that India violated the TRIPS Agreement.[72]

The normative approach did not consider local issues and disregarded important national ramifications. Even assuming trade improved as a consequence of the patent regime, the ensuing development would not be sustainable, which has proved to be true over time in several developing countries.

## WTO's Inability to Address Unilateral Actions

The WTO has been criticized for not curtailing countries with higher bargaining parity, such as the US, from taking actions that amount to an overreach in that it forces TRIPS-plus trade terms that are detrimental to countries with lower bargaining parity. For example, in February 2020, the US-India Memorandum of Understanding on Intellectual Property Rights – for the exchange of knowledge and training of officials working in offices undertaking IP management in India – presented serious concerns.[73] The employees of US Patent and Trademark Office training Indian patent office personnel on the Indian statute – which incorporates more TRIPS flexibilities than the US – is an appalling proposition.[74]

68 *Id. at para* 56.

69 *Id. at para* 58.

70 India offered case laws in support of its assertion. India cited the two Supreme Court cases to confirm the Indian position that its reliance on an administrative practice regarding the handling of pharmaceutical and agricultural chemical product patent applications is not unconstitutional; *see* State of Haryana v. Mahendra Singh & Others, AIR 1988 SC 1681; *see also* Union of India v. H.R. Patankar & Ors., AIR 1984 SC 1587 (holding that statutory rules cannot be amended by Executive instructions but "if the rules are silent" on any particular point Government can fill up the gaps by issuing executive instructions, in conformity with the existing rules); *see generally*, India Const. art 73, §1(a).

71 *See* Panel Report India, *supra* note 58, at para. 7.37.

72 *Id.*

73 Joe Mathew, *Civil Society Groups Oppose India-US MoU on Intellectual Property Rights*, Business Today (Feb. 22, 2020), https://www.businesstoday.in/.

74 Letter from Malini Aisola, IP-HEALTH, on Concerns regarding proposed US-India MoU on Intellectual Property Rights (Feb. 22, 2020).

Similarly, the Special 301 reporting system is a caricature of overreach. Traditionally, the USTR, which forms a part of the executive office of the President of the US, oversees the enforcement of US trade policy, including IP policy. As part of that role, USTR annually lists countries – the Special 301 list – for taking sovereign actions that USTR believes detrimentally affects US trade. Thus, when India reduced drug prices to protect cancer patients, it featured in the USTR's Special 301 list for derogating from IP provisions of TRIPS. The Special 301 process is best defined as an overreach mechanism statutorily supported under the Trade Act, 1974 of the US.[75] Ultimately, the USTR is an American administrative body specifically charged to examine issues from a myopic and limited perspective of US trade from which vantage they summon sovereign nations to defend their trade positions, with little regard to local realities that necessitate sovereign decisions. Consequently, USTR takes upon itself the righteous role of citing countries for lack of patent protection, even when the nation uses negotiated flexibilities to prevent slipping into a public health crisis. USTR's zealous enforcement mechanism requires it to submit an annual report to both the House and Senate, with a unique and often, unrealistic focus describing enforcement actions that "have to be taken" against other sovereigns to protect US trade.

Considering the above, questionable unilateral interference is normal for the US. Thus, when patentee Bayer AG marketed *soranafib tosylate* as *Nexavar* at approximately $5000 per month in India,[76] a price that was nearly five times higher than the median annual income in India, the US' visceral reaction followed the issuance of a compulsory license (CL) for the drug in India.[77] Notably, on August 2, 2013, the pharmaceutical industry's lobbying efforts translated into a request from the chairman of the US Senate Committee on Finance and the House Committee on Ways and Means to the US International Trade Commission to institute an investigation on India's trade practices,[78] using powers under Section 1332(g) of the Tariff Act of 1930.[79] The Special 301 Report of USTR, on which India is usually featured, specifically identified the Bayer

75 Trade Act of 1974, Pub. L. No. 93-618, sec 182, 88 Stat. 1978, 2041 (1975) (codified as 19 U.S.C § 2242 (2000)) and the Trade Facilitation and Trade Enforcement Act of 2015, 19 U.S.C. § 2242 [hereinafter TFTEA].

76 Michael Palmedo, *Graphics on U.S. Pharmaceutical Exports to India, Patents, the Compulsory License, and Prices*, INFOJUSTICE.ORG (Feb. 19, 2014), http://infojustice.org/archives/32249; *see also India Grants First Compulsory License to Generic Drug Producer*, ICTSD.ORG (Mar. 14, 2012), http://www.ictsd.org/bridges-news/bridges/news/india-grants-first-compulsory-license-to-generic-drug-producer; *see also Bayer v. Natco*, M.P. Nos. 74–76 of 2012 and M.P. No. 108 of 2012.

77 Srividhya Ragavan, *Patients Win over Patents*, THE HINDU (Mar. 7, 2013), https://www.thehindu.com/opinion/op-ed/patients-win-over-patents/article4482469.ece.

78 International Trade Commission Investigation, Notice for Investigation No. 332–543 (Aug. 29, 2013) (on issues relating to trade, investment, and industrial policies in India, with particular reference to its effects on the United States economy and United States jobs).

79 19 U.S.C. § 1332(g).

decision as "concerning," in the 2012 and 2013 reports! This, from the US which professes to value judicial independence. India was cited as a consequence of the Bayer decision in the Special 301 reports even as late as in 2020.[80]

In fact, the US established a similar pattern of response in Colombia following the release of Resolution 2475 of 2016 on June 17, 2016.[81] The Resolution issued a compulsory license to lower the price of *imatinib*, a leukemia drug marketed as *Glivec*, the patentee of which was Novartis AG.[82] At that time, the cost of 400 mg of *Glivec* in Colombia amounted to $15,000 per patient per year and represented nearly twice the average annual income of Colombians.[83]

The US response to Colombia was predictable. In May 2016, USTR, citing Resolution 2475, indicated that funds intended for a peace accord with Paz Colombia could be at risk.[84] USTR's response caused the House Democrats to express serious concern over USTR's actions.[85] The letter,

80 79 Fed. Reg. 421 (Jan. 3, 2014); *see also* Office of the U.S. Trade Rep., Special 301 Report (2012, 2013), https://www.ustr.gov.

81 Andrew Goldman, *Colombia Issues Public Interest Declaration to Lower Price of Glivec*, Keionline.org (June 15, 2016), https://www.keionline.org/23119; Ministry of Health and Social Protection Resolution No. 2475 of June 14, 2016, https://www.minsalud.gov.co/Normatividad_Nuevo/Resoluci%C3%B3n%202475%20de%202016.pdf (last visited Oct. 31, 2016).

82 *See generally* Ministro de Salud y Protección Social, *Solicitud de una declaración de interés público en el acceso al medicamento imatinib bajo condiciones de competencia*, Minsalud, https://www.minsalud.gov.co/sites/rid/Lists/BibliotecaDigital/RIDE/VS/MET/Solicitud-de-una-declaracion-en-el-acceso-al-medicamento-IMATINIB.pdf (last visited Oct. 31, 2016).

83 Andrew Goldman, *Background FAQ on Glivec (imatinib) Compulsory License in Colombia*, Keionline.org, https://www.keionline.org/book/background-faq-on-glivec-imatinib-compulsory-license-in-colombia (last visited Oct. 31, 2016).

84 WOLA, *Excerpts from the August 24 Announcement of a Final Peace Accord between the Colombian Government and the FARC: The Joint Communiqué*, colombiapeace.org, https://colombiapeace.org/excerpts-from-the-august-24-announcement-of-a-final-peace-accord-between-the-colombian-government-and-the-farc/ (last visited Oct. 31, 2016). The conflict with FARC ended after more than 50 years. Unfortunately, Paz-Columbia was never implemented because the deal was rejected in a referendum; *see* Sibylla Brodzinsky, *Colombia Referendum: Voters Reject Peace Deal with FARC Guerrillas*, The Guardian (Oct. 3, 2016), https://www.theguardian.com/world/2016/oct/02/colombia-referendum-rejects-peace-deal-with-farc; *see* Stephanie Burgos, *Does Colombia Really Have to Choose Between Poverty and Public Health*, Oxfamaerica.org (May 23, 2016), http://politicsofpoverty.oxfamamerica.org/2016/05/does-colombia-really-have-to-choose-between-peace-and-public-health/.

85 Andrew Goldman, *15 House Dems Press USTR to Clarify Position on Compulsory Licensing of Cancer Drug Patent in Colombia*, Keionline.org (May 26, 2016), https://www.keionline.org/23097; *see* Zach Carter, *Colombia Fears U.S. May Reject Peace Plan to Protect Pharma Profits*, The Huffington. Post (May 11, 2016), http://www.huffingtonpost.com/entry/colombiagleevec_us_5733d4ece4b077d4d6f224ee; Carolyn Y. Johnson and Karen DeYoung, *Dispute with Swiss Drug Maker Has Colombian Officials Worried about U.S. Peace Funding*, Washington Post (May 18, 2016), https://www.washingtonpost.com/business/economy/dispute-with-swiss-drugmaker-has-colombian-officials-worried-about-us-peace-funding/2016/05/18/6f1903ee-1c5e-11e6-8c7b-6931e66333e7_story.html.

addressed to then US Trade Representative Ambassador Michael Forman, asserted that the US would detract from its obligations as a signatory to the TRIPS Agreement and the Doha Declaration, which expressly authorize the use of such licenses for the situation for which it was used by Colombia. This narrative underscores the lack of legitimacy of US involvement in another country's sovereign actions taken expressly in the public interest or to protect public health, such as the compulsory licensing of pharmaceuticals.

## Preserving Bargaining (Im)parities?

WTO membership entails that all disputes be resolved through the multilateral dispute system of the WTO, using the DSB's process.[86] After the US gained membership to the WTO, the Uruguay Round Agreements Act of 1994 was passed as the implementing legislation.[87] But, the US Congress failed to repeal Section 301 of the Trade Act of 1974 – which unilaterally authorizes USTR to identify and pursue countries perceived as denying adequate and effective protection of IPRs or fair and equitable market access to US industries or entities that rely on IP protection.[88] Consequently, the European Union (EU) claimed that "by imposing specific, strict time limits within which unilateral determinations must be made and trade sanctions must be taken, Sections 306 and 305 of the Trade Act of 1974 violated the US commitment to the WTO to resolve multilateral disputes through the DSB process.[89] Based on this, the EU requested consultation as required under the DSU with the US.[90]

The failure of consultations resulted in a panel being established to determine whether the Special 301 program violated the US obligations under Article 23(1) and (2) of the DSU in the dispute *United States Sections 301–310*.[91] The panel opined that the statutory language of Section 304 constituted a serious threat to multilateral dispute resolution. Nevertheless, a "Statement of Administrative Action (SAA)" from the US administrative authorities, the panel held, alleviated the concerns.[92] The SAA was treated as an "authoritative expression" by the US on

86 *See* DSU, *supra* note 48.

87 Omnibus Trade and Competitiveness Act of 1988.

88 TFTEA, *supra* note 75, at §182 of the Trade Act of 1974.

89 Panel Report, US—Section 301–310 of the Trade Act of 1974, WTO Doc. WT/DS152/R (Dec. 22, 1999) [hereinafter Section 301 Dispute], paras. 1.3 and 1.4.

90 *See* DSU, *supra* note 48. Article 6 of the DSU provides for the establishment of a panel at the instance of the complaining party, which is the Dispute Settlement Body; *see also* European Communities request for the establishment of a panel pursuant to Article 6 of the DSU (WTO Doc. WT/DS152/11).

91 Section 301 Dispute, *supra* note 89, at para 4.8. The EU asserted that its own WTO implementation mechanism, being Trade Barriers Regulation, Council Regulation (EC) No. 3286/94, Dec. 22, 1994, conformed in letter and spirit with Article 23 of the DSU.

92 Statement of Administrative Action, reprinted in H.R. Doc. No. 103–316, at 1029 (US Exhibit 11), ch. B, subch. 2, littera b (enforcement of United States rights), 364.

the subject of reconciling its domestic laws with the country's international trade obligations.[93]

The SAA was effectively a pledge by the US that USTR will (a) invoke the DSU dispute settlement procedures, as required under current law, and (b) base any Section 301 determination of violation or denial of US rights under a relevant WTO agreement on a panel or AB findings adopted by the DSB.[94] Considering the SAA, the panel held that Special 301–310 provisions did not violate US international trade obligations, provided the US did not repudiate its SAA undertakings. However, the panel noted that even a *mere threat of trade sanction* could be perceived as a threat to the WTO. The panel report added that threat alone can enable a member to exert undue leverage and can "disrupt the very stability and equilibrium which multilateral dispute resolution was meant to foster and consequently establish, namely equal protection of both large and small, powerful and less powerful members through the consistent application of a set of rules and procedures."[95]

In stark contrast to WTO's deference to the SAA, the DSB (panel and AB), in the *India-Mailbox* dispute, refused to accept India's rationale wherein administrative orders are treated as legally tenable tools to implement certain aspects of the statute in question.[96] It justifies the criticism that the WTO's DSB has consistently failed to appreciate local realities that impede IP implementation and has thus, preserved bargaining inequities.[97] DSB's tendency is to ignore domestic realities and rationale in determining perceived derogations of international obligations.[98] Deference to domestic lawmakers' wisdom has been difficult to generate at the WTO, particularly the DSB, when the wisdom is from a developing country.

Instead, the DSB panel's exceptional deference to the SAA undertakings of a powerful member implies that the system has merely worked to reinforce the balance of power inequities. The DSU has been consistently criticized for lacking important paradigms required to appreciate the complexities involved in establishing an IP regime.[99] The DSU's inability to appreciate local realities and over-reliance on WTO negotiating history – when the balance of powers was even more skewed than in current times – are all internal barriers that have impeded the WTO from achieving the spirit of the overall objectives.[100]

93 *Id.*

94 *Id.* at 365–66.

95 Section 301 Dispute, *supra* note 89, at para. 7.89.

96 *See* Panel Report India, *supra* note 58; *see also* Appellate Body Report, *India—Patent Protection for Pharmaceutical and Agricultural Chemical Products*, WTO Doc. WT/DS50/AB/R (Dec. 19, 1997).

97 *Id.*

98 *See* Srividhya Ragavan, Patents and Trade Disparities in Developing Countries 366 (2012).

99 Thomas Cottier, *The Agreement on Trade-Related Aspects of Intellectual Property Rights*, *in* 1 The World Trade Organization: Legal and Political Analysis 1063 (P.F.J. Macrory *et al.* ed., 2005).

100 *Id.*

## Spinning Alone and in an Unrealistic Zone

The WTO's trade and health agenda should be couched within the "broader societal interests and especially development-oriented concerns" outlined in Article 7 of the TRIPS Agreement.[101] Other international organizations such as the World Intellectual Property Organization (WIPO) – and now, the WHO in the post-COVID scenario – have all embarked more seriously on cooperating on the public health sphere.[102] For instance, WIPO's recent IP and Development Agenda outlines in Agenda 45 that IP enforcement should be contextualized within developmental concerns stated in Article 7 of the TRIPS Agreement.[103] The WIPO agendas define larger public interest concerns and implicate the work of the UN, WTO, and WHO.[104] The WTO should work with international organizations such as WIPO, UN, and WHO on issues that converge for global organizations.

The lack of a formal platform for institutional involvement and intervention creates functional issues. Issues emanating from the WTO's trade regime – such as IP and access to lifesaving medications – are converging platforms. Like the WIPO, the WHO's objectives for trade and health diplomacy include a commitment to support national health initiatives by increasing global negotiation capabilities to enable collective action to address health challenges. Similarly, the UN Report on Access to Medicines also calls for WTO members to "commit at the highest political levels, to the letter and spirit of the Doha Declaration" and promote the use of TRIPS flexibilities.[105]

Formal cooperation between global organizations seems to be the way forward. The WTO typically cites the DSB's periodic consultation with WIPO. For instance, in *China – Measures Affecting the Protection and Enforcement of Intellectual Property Rights*,[106] WIPO, in responding to the DSB panel's request, submitted factual information from the official records of various diplomatic conferences regarding the interpretation of Articles 5(1), 5(2), and 17 of the Berne Convention.[107] But these are exceptions that are limited to seeking factual

101 TRIPS Agreement, art.7, *supra* note 5.

102 Convention Establishing the World Intellectual Property Organization, July 14, 1967, 21 U.S.T. 1770, 1772–73, 828 U.N.T.S. 3, 11, 13 [hereinafter WIPO Convention], http://www.wipo.int; *see also The World Health Organization*, World Health Org. (2016), www.who.int.

103 *Id.* at Agenda 45.

104 *Id.*

105 *See* U.N. Secretary-General, *Report of the United Nations Secretary-General's High-Level Panel on Access To Medicines* (Sept. 2016), https://static1.squarespace.com/static/562094dee4b0d00c1a3ef761/t/57d9c6ebf5e231b2f02cd3d4/1473890031320/UNSG+HLP+Report+FINAL+12+Sept+2016.pdf.

106 Panel Report, China—Measures Affecting the Protection and Enforcement of Intellectual Property Rights, WTO Doc. WT/DS362/R (Jan. 26, 2009).

107 *Id.* at 4; *see also* Berne Convention for the Protection of Literary and Artistic Works, 25 U.S.T. 1341, 828 U.N.T.S. 221, 223 (Sept. 9, 1886, rev. July 24, 1971).

information, rather than working toward a cooperative solution. Further, DSBs have traditionally provided limited deference to WIPO even where it has sought input.[108] In the *United States* – Section 211 *Omnibus Appropriations Act of 1998*, for instance, the AB's report mentions the Director-General of WIPO's response to a request for information by the DSU panel, noting that "the Panel did not discuss this. However, the Panel seems to have taken [a different] view."[109] Also, WIPO has limited powers to intervene in the DSB process unless input is specifically requested. Although, an *amicus* brief can be filed, the DSU's obligation is limited to accepting *amicus* briefs and thus, they have limited value.[110] Thus, a platform for institutional involvement of international organizations is needed.

WIPO's Development Milestone in 2007 provided an opportunity to be involved in the development and public health-related matters.[111] It was hoped that WIPO [or, perhaps, the WHO] would evolve as a negotiator for developing nations to work with the WTO and restore WIPO's relatively weak image in the post-WTO era. The Committee on Development and Intellectual Property, established by the WIPO General Assembly in 2008, has the objective of implementing the Development Agenda recommendations.[112] The Development Agenda set the right tenor for WIPO to work on issues relating to development in the IP context, although much progress has not yet been made.[113]

The coronavirus pandemic is proof that unrelated global systems and larger global trade can collapse from pandemics and epidemics. Therefore, the need for innovation balanced with access is the next global agenda. The goal should be to intensify cooperation of global organizations on IP related issues, an ideal already memorialized under Agenda 40.[114]

108 *See, e.g.*, United States—Section 211 Omnibus Appropriations Act of 1998, United States, WTO Doc. WT/DS176/AB/R, WT/DS176; *see also* United States—Section 211 Omnibus Appropriations Act of 1998, United States, Report of the Appellate Body; *see also* China—Measures Affecting the Protection and Enforcement of Intellectual Property Rights, WTO Doc. WT/DS362/R (Jan. 26, 2009); *see also* European Communities—Protection of Trademarks and Geographical Indications for Agricultural Products and Foodstuffs, WTO Doc. WT/DS174, WT/DS290; *see* Thomas Cottier & Marina Foltea, *Global Governance in Intellectual Property Protection: Does the Decision-making Forum Matter?*, 3 W.I.P.O.J. 2, 139, 158 (2012).

109 Appellate Body Report, United States—Section 211 Omnibus Appropriations Act of 1998, WTO Doc. WT/DS176/AB/R (Jan. 2, 2002), para. 189.

110 *See, e.g.*, Appellate Body Report, Mexico—Tax Measures on Soft Drinks and Other Beverages, WTO Doc. WT/DS308/AB/R (adopted Mar. 24, 2006).

111 *See Development Agenda for WIPO*, World Intell. Prop. Org., http://www.wipo.int/ip-development/en/agenda/ (last visited Sept. 26, 2019).

112 *See* Committee on Development and Intellectual Property, World Intell. Prop. Org., http://www.wipo.int/policy/en/cdip/ (last visited Sept. 26, 2019).

113 *The 45 Adopted Recommendations Under the WIPO Development Agenda*, World Intell. Prop. Org. (adopted 2007), http://www.wipo.int/ip-development/en/agenda/recommendations.html.

114 *Id.* at Agenda 40.

## Conclusion: Even a Pandemic Has Kept the WTO Elitist and Out of Touch

While innovation is an important mandate, the IP regime's imbalances at the WTO have failed to account for local realities, largely contributing to a crisis in global access to medication. While the TRIPS Agreement's deficiencies and its disengagement with realities are important aspects, WTO's inaction – and its singular focus on trade dissociated with local realities – has mired the organization since inception. Meanwhile, the rhetoric of innovation has not helped innovation nor helped establish the patent regime as a vehicle for innovation. In fact, the patent regime has transformed into a barrier to innovation and access to medicine, profoundly impacting the WTO negatively to a point of rendering it irrelevant.

# 2 World Health Organization

## Contributions to Access to Health and TRIPS Agreement Discourse

*Susan Isiko Štrba*

## Introduction

Since the entry into force of the Agreement on Trade-Related Aspects of Intellectual Property Rights (TRIPS Agreement), the World Health Organization (WHO) has, at the request of the World Health Assembly (WHA), addressed the impact of trade agreements and intellectual property (IP) protection on public health and access to medicines or health products.[1] Nevertheless, WHO work in this respect is more publicly visible after the WHO was admitted as an observer at the World Trade Organization (WTO) TRIPS Council in 2000. The Global Strategy and Plan of Action on Public Health, Innovation, and Intellectual Property (GSPOA-PHI),[2] together with various resolutions, constitute the mandate of WHO work on IP rights (IPR) and access to health products. In September 2006, the WHO Secretariat was established to facilitate the work of the Intergovernmental Working Group on PHI. In May 2008, the WHA adopted Resolution WHA61.21 on the GSPOA-PHI. Most of the recent work of the WHO on IP and access to medical products centers on implementing the GSPOA-PHI.

The PHI Team, located in the Department of Essential Medicines and Health Products, is primarily responsible for the interface between public health, innovation, research, transfer of technology, and IP. The key activities of the PHI Team include the (1) development of policy guidance and provision of technical assistance on management and application of IP to promote needs

1 According to the WHO, the term "health products" is understood to include vaccines, diagnostics, and medicines in accordance with Resolution WHA59.24.2. *See Global Strategy and Plan of Action on Public Health, Innovation and Intellectual Property*, World Health Org., 1, 3 n. 1 (2011), https://www.who.int/phi/publications/Global_Strategy_Plan_Action.pdf [hereinafter *Global Strategy and Plan of Action*]. In this chapter, we use "health products" instead of "access to medicines," so as to capture the different products which could be affected by intellectual property but were not the focus of debate until recently.

2 Global Strategy and Plan of Action, Resolution WHA61.21, 61st World Health Assembly (2008), http://www.wpro.who.int/health_research/wha61_21_global_strategy_poa_health_innovation_may2008.pdf [hereinafter *GSPOA-PHI*].

based innovation and access to patent protected essential medicines and health products; (2) facilitation of technology transfer to, and building capacity in, developing countries for the manufacturing of strategically selected health products to improve access; and (3) facilitation of monitoring and evaluation of the GSPOA-PHI to provide evidence for its impact and direction.[3]

The WHO performs its work on IPR and public health by (1) providing, upon request, technical support to member states on public health aspects of IP and trade policies; (2) conducting training and capacity building on the health impact of trade agreements and the management and application of IP for public health; (3) researching the relationship of innovation, IP, and access to medical products; and (4) facilitating access to patent information.[4] The WHO closely collaborates with other relevant international and regional organizations, such as the WTO and the World Intellectual Property Organization (WIPO),[5] in an effort to fulfill its mandate.

This chapter examines the contribution of the WHO to access to health products in relation to the TRIPS Agreement or IPR. It captures the actions and inactions of the WHO so as to delineate its contributions to change in the access to medicines discourse since the coming into force of the TRIPS Agreement. The mandate of the WHO to deal with IP and access to medicines will be discussed, as well as the WHO policy perspectives on health products and how they relate to IP. The chapter also analyzes parts of the GSPOA-PHI to demonstrate the extent to which it has promoted access to medicines. It also outlines recent developments and highlights WHO action and contribution, with some examples of specific activities undertaken by the WHO to promote access to medicines in response to its various resolutions.

Some clarification on the structure of WHO and use of terms in this chapter is necessary. The WHA is the decision-making body of the WHO. It is attended by delegations from all member states and focuses on a specific health agenda prepared by the Executive Board (EB). The main functions of the WHA are the determination of the WHO's policies, appointment of the Director-General, supervision of financial policies, and review and approval of the proposed program budget. The WHA is held annually in Geneva, Switzerland.[6]

The EB is composed of 34 technically qualified members elected for three-year terms. It prepares the draft agenda and resolutions for the WHA. The annual EB meeting is usually held in January when the members agree upon the agenda for the WHA and the resolutions to be considered by it. A second shorter meeting of the EB takes place in May as a follow-up to the WHA. The

3 *Public Health, Innovation, Intellectual Property, and Trade*, World Health Org., https://www.who.int/phi/about/en/ (last visited June 11, 2019) [hereinafter *PHI*].

4 *Id.*

5 *Id.*

6 *World Health Assembly*, World Health Org., https://www.who.int/about/governance/world-health-assembly (last visited May 17, 2019).

main functions of the EB are the implementation of the WHA's decisions and policies, provision of advice, and general facilitation of its work.[7]

The WHO Secretariat is the managing body of the decisions of the WHA. The WHA, EB, and WHO Secretariat form the WHO. In this chapter, unless expressly indicated, the term WHO is used to refer to all three entities.

## WHO Mandate on Intellectual Property and Access to Medical Products

Current activities of the WHO on public health, IP, and trade are mainly aimed at capacity building, research, information sharing, and technical and policy support to member states. This work is guided by the relevant parts of the GSPOA-PHI and relevant WHA resolutions.

The 49th WHA in May 1996 was the first forum in which the potential impact of globalization and trade were discussed in the WHO. The WHA adopted the Revised Medicine Strategy resolution to be incorporated into the WHO medicines policy, which included gathering "information on the impact of the World Trade Organization on national policies for essential medicines."[8] Therefore, the WHO adopted an action plan to (1) identify WTO agreements related to access to essential medicines and pharmaceutical policies, with subsequent notification to member states of their existence; (2) study the implications of globalization on innovation, development, production, trade, and prices of medicines, to identify possible negative effects that the TRIPS Agreement and/or other trade agreements have on access to essential medicines; and (3) notify member states on the need to adopt measures to protect public health.[9]

The WHO Action Program on Essential Drugs published a monograph (or "Red Book," as it was popularly called) on the implications of the TRIPS Agreement on access to medicines.[10] The monograph aimed at informing health policy professionals with limited or no legal background on the potential impact of the TRIPS Agreement on public health and pharmaceutical policy.[11] While the monograph was well received by a number of countries and civil society, the Pharmaceutical Research and Manufacturers of America and the United States

7 *Executive Board*, World Health Org., https://www.who.int/about/governance/executive-board (last visited May 17, 2019).

8 Revised Drug Strategy, Resolution WHA49.14, 49th World Health Assembly (1996), https://www.who.int/phi/WHA49.14.pdf.

9 Intellectual Property in the Context of the wto trips Agreement: Challenges for Public Health, 10 (Jorge A. Z. Bermudez & Maria Auxiliadora Oliveira eds., 2004) [hereinafter Intellectual Property].

10 Germán Velásquez & Pascale Boulet, *Globalization and Access to Drugs: Implications of the WTO/TRIPS Agreement* (1999), https://apps.who.int/medicinedocs/pdf/whozip35e/whozip35e.pdf.

11 Intellectual Property, *supra* note 9, at 81–97.

criticized it as being unbalanced. The monograph was revised, with the input of the WTO. This sent a warning to the WHO on how much it can interfere with WTO work while trying to promote access to medicines.

Meanwhile, there was also controversy surrounding the revision of the WHA Resolution on the Revised Drug Strategy (Resolution WHA52.19),[12] which would strengthen the WHO's mandate to monitor international trade agreements. In January 1998, the WHO EB passed a draft resolution[13] on the Revised Drug Strategy which urged member states to "ensure that public health rather than commercial interests have primacy in pharmaceutical and health policies and to review their options under the Agreement on Trade Related Aspects of Intellectual Property Rights to safeguard access to essential drugs."[14] The draft resolution requested the WHO Director-General to "assist Member States to analyse the pharmaceutical and public health implications of agreements overseen by the World Trade Organization and to develop appropriate policies and regulatory measures."[15] This draft resolution was prompted by concerns of EB members, including Canada, Egypt, and Zimbabwe, on the potential impact of WTO agreements on access to medicines.[16]

In May 1998, this resolution was submitted to the 51st WHA for consideration. It met with considerable opposition from a few member states. Furthermore, some opposed the operative paragraph instructing the WHO to examine the TRIPS Agreement, arguing that the WHO was not the competent authority to interpret trade agreements. This amounted to an attempt to declare trade agreements as untouchable by non-trade organizations. A compromise text was adopted at the WHA52 in 1999.[17]

The Revised Drug Strategy marks the start of the WHO's major work on access to medicines. Under its mandate, together with Resolution WHA54.11 on the WHO Medicines Strategy[18] and Resolution WHA56.27 on IPR, innovation, and public health,[19] the WHO cooperates with member states,

12 Revised Drug Strategy, Resolution WHA52.19 (May 24, 1999), http://apps.who.int/medicinedocs/documents/s21344en/s21344en.pdf.

13 The Executive Board, ***Revised Drug Strategy***, World Health Org. (Jan. 27, 1998), http://apps.who.int/gb/archive/pdf_files/EB101/pdfangl/angr24.pdf.

14 *Id.* para. 1(2).

15 *Id.* para. 2(6).

16 *Id.* (It is notable that developed countries like Canada supported the proposal on access to medicines.)

17 Germán Velásquez et al., ***The Debate on Intellectual Property Rights and Public Health***, in Intellectual Property in the Context of the WTO TRIPS Agreement: Challenges for Public Health, 81–97, 86 (Jorge A. Z. Bermudez & Maria Auxiliadora Oliveira eds., 2004).

18 WHO Medicines Strategy, Resolution WHA54.11, 54th World Health Assembly (May 21, 2001), http://apps.who.int/gb/archive/pdf_files/WHA54/ea54r11.pdf.

19 Intellectual Property Rights, Innovation and Public Health, Resolution WHA56.27, 56th World Health Assembly (May 28, 2003), http://apps.who.int/gb/archive/pdf_files/WHA56/ea56r27.pdf.

at their request, and with other international organizations to (1) assist member states to develop pharmaceutical and health policies and regulatory measures to maximize the positive and mitigate the negative impact of international, regional, and bilateral trade agreements; (2) monitor, analyze, study, and report on existing and future pharmaceutical and health implications of international trade agreements; and (3) collect data and proposals from the different actors involved and produce an analysis of IPR, innovation, and public health, including the question of funding and incentive mechanisms for the creation of new medicines and other products against diseases that disproportionately affect developing countries. Subsequent resolutions have been directed at breaking these general areas of work into more specific areas of technical cooperation.

One of the objectives of the WHO Medicines Strategy is the improvement of access to essential medicines. To this end, the WHO supports countries in their effort to use public health safeguards in international, regional, and bilateral trade agreements.[20] In 2003, the WHO openly expressed its "concerns about the current patent protection system, especially as regards access to medicines in developing countries" and urged member states to adapt national legislation to fully utilize the flexibilities contained in the TRIPS Agreement. Reinforcing the Medicines Strategy, Resolution WHA57.14 (2004) urged member states, as a matter of priority, to encourage bilateral trade agreements to take into account the flexibilities contained in the TRIPS Agreement and recognized by the Doha Declaration on the TRIPS Agreement and Public Health (Doha Declaration).[21]

Resolution WHA59.26 urges member states to "continue to develop capacity at national level to track and analyse the potential opportunities and challenges of trade and trade agreements for health-sector performance and health outcomes."[22] It requests the WHO to "respond to Member States' requests for support of their efforts to build the capacity to understand the implications of international trade and trade agreements may have on health."[23] This resolution is deemed to strengthen the WHO's mandate on issues related to trade agreements, IPR, and public health, and further endorses the WHO's multiagency approach in technical cooperation, which emphasizes working with and training trade, health, and patent officials on

20 *WHO Medicines Strategy Countries at the Core (2004–2007)*, World Health Org., https://apps.who.int/iris/bitstream/handle/10665/68514/WHO_EDM_2004.2.pdf?sequence=1&isAllowed=y (last visited Dec. 11, 2019).

21 Scaling Up Treatment and Care Within a Coordinated and Comprehensive Response to HIV/AIDS, Resolution WHA57.14, para. 2(6), 57th World Health Assembly (May 22, 2004), https://apps.who.int/iris/bitstream/handle/10665/20139/A57_R14-en.pdf?sequence=1&isAllowed=y (last visited Dec. 11, 2019).

22 World Health Organization, *Resolution and Decisions Annexes*, 59th World Health Assembly, WHA59/2006/REC/1, 37, ¶ 1.5 (May 22–27, 2006).

23 *Id.* ¶ 2.2.

trade and IP issues.[24] Various WHO policy actions attempt to support these resolutions.

## WHO Policy Perspectives on Access to Health Products

The WHO policy perspectives place public health and access to medicines as priorities over economic objectives, in line with the basic requirements of the Doha Declaration.[25] The Doha Declaration affirmed that the TRIPS Agreement "can and should be interpreted in a manner supportive of WTO Members' rights to protect public health and, in particular, to promote access to medicines for all."[26] A WHO publication maps out some of the options and their implications for public health.[27] The WHO seeks to provide technical assistance and country support to member states to promote implementation of the TRIPS Agreement in a way that is consistent with the protection of public health and promotion of access to medicines. The WHO seeks to achieve these policy objectives through different activities as will be demonstrated below.

Paragraph 6 of the Doha Declaration instructed the TRIPS Council to find an expeditious solution to the problem faced by WTO members with insufficient or no pharmaceutical manufacturing capacity of effectively using the TRIPS Agreement's compulsory licensing provisions.[28] A decision was adopted on August 30, 2003 (Paragraph 6 Decision) for the implementation of this paragraph.[29] The WHO has been committed to assisting member states in making effective use of the Paragraph 6 system (or article 31*bis*) of the TRIPS Agreement to permit the export of pharmaceutical products manufactured under compulsory license (CL).

The WHO provides useful guidance on how to use TRIPS flexibilities to promote access to medicines by enunciating and assessing the Doha Declaration. In its guide on the production and export of generic medicines, the WHO

24 Council for Trade-Related Aspects of Intellectual Property Rights, *Technical Cooperation Activities: Information from Other Intergovernmental Organizations* ¶ 2, WTO Doc. IP/C/W/478/Add.4 (Oct. 23, 2006), http://www10.who.int/phi/WHO_Comm_TRIPS_implementation_activities_W478A4_2006.pdf [hereinafter *Technical Cooperation Activities 478*].

25 World Trade Organization, *Declaration on the TRIPS Agreement and Public Health*, Ministerial Conference, Fourth Session, Doha, November 9–14, 2001, WTO Doc. WT/MIN(01)/DEC/2 (Nov. 14, 2001) [hereinafter *Doha Declaration*].

26 *Id.* ¶ 4.

27 Carlos M. Correa, *Implications of the Doha Declaration on the TRIPS Agreement and Public Health*, World Health Org. (2002), https://apps.who.int/medicinedocs/pdf/s2301e/s2301e.pdf (last visited Dec. 10, 2019).

28 *Doha Declaration*, *supra* note 25.

29 General Council, *Implementation of Paragraph 6 of the Doha Declaration on the TRIPS Agreement and Public Health*, WTO Doc. WT/L/540 and Corr. 1 (Sept. 2, 2003), https://www.wto.org/english/tratop_e/trips_e/implem_para6_e.htm (last visited Dec. 10, 2019).

suggests that a public health-oriented interpretation and implementation of the provisions would be required to achieve access to medicines.[30] In some cases, it would also require changes to national laws.[31] For exporting countries, this would include provisions that permit the export of pharmaceutical products produced under CL, by explicitly stating that the supply of an export market is a possible ground for compulsory licensing. For countries wishing to import generic medicines, national laws should permit CLs for import and should include specific provisions for government use or public noncommercial use of patents, and the waiver of payment of remuneration or royalties to the patent holder. National laws should also not limit the implementation of the system to a restricted list of products or diseases, by incorporating a broad definition of pharmaceutical products for which the system can be used, and should include diagnostics, vaccines, and medical devices used for treatment within the definition.[32]

During the negotiation under Paragraph 6 of the Doha Declaration, the WHO's view was, and continues to be, that:

> [T]he guiding principle must be that patients in a country without or lacking domestic pharmaceutical production capacity should be no less protected by compulsory licensing provisions (or indeed other TRIPS safeguards) than those in countries capable of producing the product, nor should they face any greater procedural hurdles.[33]

In line with this, the WHO outlined the key factors necessary for effective implementation of the Paragraph 6 Decision: (1) rapid and effective response to public health needs; (2) equality of opportunities for countries in need, irrespective of the patent status of a drug in the importing country, and without regard to its membership in the WTO; (3) sustainability of quality supply at affordable prices; (4) facilitation of a multiplicity of potential suppliers, both from developed and developing countries, which can compete to drive prices down; and (5) provision of a wide range of pharmaceutical products to meet an array of health problems.[34]

30 World Health Organization, *Recommended Inn List 55 International Nonproprietary Names for Pharmaceutical Substances*, 20 WHO Drug Inf. 1, 22 (2006), https://www.who.int/medicines/publications/druginformation/WHO_DI_Vol20-1.pdf?ua=1 (last visited Dec. 10, 2019).

31 *Id.*

32 *Id.*

33 Statement by the representative of the World Health Organization at the WTO Council for TRIPS, Sept. 17, 2002, Geneva, quoted in Council for Trade-Related Aspects of Intellectual Property Rights, *Technical Cooperation Activities: Information From Other Intergovernmental Organizations* ¶ 2, WTO Doc. IP/C/W/424/Add.4 (Oct. 26, 2004), https://www.who.int/medicines/areas/policy/wto_tec_assistance/en/ (last visited Sept. 29, 2019) [hereinafter *Technical Cooperation Activities 424*].

34 *Id.*

Affordability of essential drugs is a public health priority of the WHO. It therefore considers the primacy of assessing the impact of IP on essential drugs, especially those still under patents. The WHO recognized equity pricing as a means to adapt prices to the purchasing power of governments and households. Equity pricing can be achieved through a combination of factors which may include voluntary licensing, compulsory licensing, and implementation of the Paragraph 6 Decision. Other WHO-supported measures to improve access to medicines include mechanisms to promote competition, such as price information and the application of safeguards contained in the TRIPS Agreement.[35] The WHO also cautions member states against TRIPS-plus activities such as free trade or investment agreements.[36]

Additionally, the WHO facilitates informed country approaches to health and trade by providing independent data and technical assistance to countries to address the health implications of trade issues at the national, subregional, and regional levels. The WHO's policy perspective is that countries are informed of all available options in the implementation of the TRIPS Agreement, the Doha Declaration, and the Paragraph 6 Decision. This is achieved mainly through (1) awareness raising and capacity building of policy makers on the health impact of international trade agreements to ensure effective participation in international and regional negotiations, and that developing country needs and interests are adequately taken into account; (2) review of national health, pharmaceutical, and IP policies, legislation, and practices to promote the incorporation of TRIPS safeguards in the national policy and legal framework; and (3) continued monitoring and analysis of the impact of trade agreements on public health and access to essential medicines, including the impact of new trends and developments at the regional and bilateral levels.[37]

35 *Id.* at 2. TRIPS safeguards or flexibilities include setting standards of patentability which reflect public health concerns, legislative provisions for compulsory licensing, parallel importation, exceptions to exclusive rights, implementation of the decisions of Paragraph 6, and other measures which promote generic competition, as well as the full use of the possibility to extend the transition period in accordance with Article 66.1 of the TRIPS Agreement.

36 For example, the WHO SEA Regional Office participated in a workshop on the "Use of TRIPS Flexibilities to Access to Affordable Antiretrovirals in Asia" in Bangkok from May 29–31, 2012. The workshop, addressed, *inter alia,* the possible impact of including rules that go beyond the TRIPS Agreement or TRIPS-plus rules. The workshop was co-organized by Asia Pacific Network of People Living with HIV, UNDP, and UNAIDS, in partnership with the International Treatment Preparedness Coalition, Médecins Sans Frontières, TREAT Asia, UNICEF, and the WHO, to improve knowledge of TRIPS flexibilities and legal options to facilitate access to antiretrovirals in Asia. *See* Council for Trade-Related Aspects of Intellectual Property Rights, *Technical Cooperation Activities: Information from other Intergovernmental Organizations: World Health Organization (WHO), Addendum* 1, 7, WTO Doc. IP/C/W/581/Add.2 (2012) [hereinafter *Technical Cooperation Activities 581*].

37 *Technical Cooperation Activities 424, supra* note 33, at 3.

The WHO's 2008 guide on the production and export of generic medicines under the TRIPS Agreement suggests that a public health–oriented interpretation and implementation is essential to achieving access to medicines.[38] The WHO continues to identify issues related to the implementation of the Doha Declaration, and to develop technical and policy guidance in the form of technical publications and briefing documents, in consultation with various experts and international organizations. In this regard, the WHO produces technical papers on current issues in the area of IP and public health.[39]

Furthermore, the WHO has, in collaboration with the Global Fund for the Fight against AIDS, Tuberculosis and Malaria, the Joint United Nations (UN) Programme on HIV and AIDS, the UN Development Programme (UNDP), and the UN Children's Fund, developed a guide for the application and granting of CLs and authorization of government use of pharmaceutical patents. The guide focuses on such grant and authorization in the context of the purchase and import of patent protected pharmaceutical products and provides general recommendations to governments, procurement agencies, and nongovernmental organizations on the modalities for the application of CLs and government use authorization.[40] More recently, the WHO collaborated with Colombia by writing a letter to Novartis indicating Colombia's right to issue a CL.[41]

## The Global Strategy and Plan of Action for Public Health, Innovation, and Intellectual Property

### *In General*

As mentioned earlier, the WHA adopted the GSPOA-PHI in 2008. It comprises 8 elements, 25 sub-elements, and 108 specific actions designed to set, prioritize, and promote research; foster and build innovation capacity; promote technology transfer and local production of medical products; promote the management and application of IPR to improve public health; improve access to medical products; mobilize resources for research and development (R&D) relevant to this area; and monitor and evaluate progress in all these areas.[42]

38 Carlos M. Correa, *Implementation of the WTO General Council Decision on Paragraph 6 of the Doha Declaration on the TRIPS Agreement and Public Health, WHO Health Economics and Drugs, Essential Drugs and Medicines Policy*, World Health Org. (2004), http://www.who.int/medicines/ (last visited Dec. 11, 2019).

39 *See, e.g.*, Carlos M. Correa, *Implication of the Doha Declaration on the TRIPS Agreement and Public Health*, Health Economics and Drugs Series, No. 012 (2002), https://apps.who.int/medicinedocs/en/d/Js2301e/ (last visited Dec. 14, 2019).

40 *Technical Cooperation Activities 424*, *supra* note 33, at 4.

41 Interview with Peter Beyer, Senior Advisor and Group Lead, *Intellectual Property and Public Health*, World Health Org. (July 16, 2019).

42 *Global Strategy and Plan of Action*, *supra* note 1, at 1 (emphasis added).

In relation to IP and access to health products, the GSPOA-PHI reiterates the Doha Declaration's[43] affirmation that the TRIPS Agreement can and should be interpreted and implemented in a manner supportive of the rights of WTO members to protect public health and, in particular, to promote access to medicines for all.[44] Elements 4 and 5 are particularly focused on access to health products.

### *On Transfer of Technology (Element 4)*

The GSPOA-PHI encourages supporting development cooperation, partnerships, and networks to build and improve transfer of technology, and reiterates article 7 of the TRIPS Agreement.[45] The actions envisaged under transfer of technology include supporting improved collaboration and coordination of technology transfer for health products, bearing in mind different levels of development. In particular, the GSPOA-PHI calls on stakeholders to continue to promote and encourage technology transfer to least developed country members of WTO consistent with article 66.2 of the TRIPS Agreement.[46] However, the WHO could promote technology transfer beyond the confines of the TRIPS Agreement. It would seem that the WHO is limited by the perception that it cannot provide trade advice to its members. The limitation is more pronounced when the WHO has to work in partnership with other institutions which manage the use of IP, in this case, the WTO.[47]

### *On the Application and Management of IP (Element 5)*

The GSPOA-PHI encourages and supports the application and management of IP in a manner that maximizes health-related innovation, especially to meet the R&D needs of developing countries; protects public health and promotes access to medicines for all; and explores and implements, where appropriate, possible incentive schemes for R&D.

It stresses the crucial need to strengthen innovation capacity as well as the capacity to manage and apply IP in developing countries, including full utilization of the flexibilities provided under the TRIPS Agreement and related instruments to protect public health. To this end, the GSPOA-PHI envisages supporting information sharing and capacity building in the application and

43 *Doha Declaration*, *supra* note 25.

44 *Global Strategy and Plan of Action*, *supra* note 1, at 4, ¶ 8.

45 Article 7 of TRIPS Agreement states: "the protection and enforcement of intellectual property rights should contribute to the promotion of technological innovation and to the transfer and dissemination of technology, to the mutual advantage of producers and users of technological knowledge and in a manner conducive to social and economic welfare, and to a balance of rights and obligations."

46 *GSPOA-PHI*, *supra* note 2, at 12.

47 We will discuss collaboration in more detail later.

management of IP with respect to health-related innovation and the promotion of public health in developing countries.[48]

The GSPOA-PHI seeks to strengthen education and training in the application and management of IP from a public health perspective, taking into account the provisions of the TRIPS Agreement, including flexibilities recognized by the Doha Declaration and other related WTO agreements.[49] The GSPOA-PHI further seeks to promote active and effective participation of health representatives in IP-related negotiations, where appropriate, in order that such negotiations also reflect public health needs.[50] It requests the WHO to provide appropriate technical support (including policy processes), in collaboration with other competent international organizations, to countries that intend to make use of the provisions of the TRIPS Agreement, including the flexibilities recognized by the Doha Declaration and other related WTO instruments, to promote access to pharmaceutical products.[51] Requiring appropriateness and collaboration with other competent international organizations might limit the freedom of the WHO to achieve public health interests in light of IP since "competent" organizations are interested in economic gains.

Under the GSPOA-PHI, the WHO is instructed to "play a strategic and central role in the relationship between public health and innovation and IP within its mandates (including those contained in relevant WHA resolutions), capacities and constitutional objectives, bearing in mind those of other relevant intergovernmental organizations."[52] In terms of collaboration with other intergovernmental organizations, Resolution WHA61.21 specifically requests the Director-General "to coordinate with other relevant international intergovernmental organizations, including WIPO, WTO and UNCTAD, to effectively implement the global strategy and plan of action."[53] More than 20 plans of action in the GSPOA-PHI name the WIPO, WTO, UN Conference on Trade and Development (UNCTAD), and other international organizations as stakeholders responsible for implementation.[54]

Since the admission of the WHO as an ad hoc observer to the TRIPS Council in 2000, it has submitted a number of communications summarizing its activities in the area of public health and IP.[55] This collaboration intensified after the

48 *GSPOA-PHI*, *supra* note 2, at 13.

49 *Id.* at 14, ¶ 5(1)(e).

50 *Id.* at 14, ¶ 5(1)(f).

51 *Id.* at 14, ¶ 5(2)

52 *Id.* ¶ 15.

53 *Id.*

54 World Health Organization, *Collaboration with WIPO and WTO*, World Health Org., https://www.who.int/phi/documents/background_ebreport/en/ (last visited June 15, 2019) [hereinafter *Collaboration with WIPO and WTO*].

55 *Overview on Technical Cooperation Programmes Relating to the Implementation of the TRIPS Agreement*, World Health Org., https://www.who.int/phi/wto_communications/en/ (last visited June 17, 2019).

adoption of the GSPOA-PHI, following which the Directors-General of the WHO, WIPO, and WTO met and discussed potential interagency collaboration to facilitate implementation of GSPOA-PHI actions that list the WHO, along with the WIPO or WTO, as stakeholders. The collaboration is aimed to make best use of available resources through closer coordination and to enable more effective program delivery through cooperation in the conduct of activities. The WHO, WIPO, and WTO have set up regular joint coordination meetings on all issues related to public health and IP, although the WHO often attends as an invited presenter.[56] The most recent of such collaboration meetings with the WIPO is the seminar on policies and practices for effective response to global health crises.[57] At the seminar, attended by the author, the WHO representative pointed out that the WHO encourages transparency and fairness in pricing. She emphasized that there is no need to innovate if the drugs cannot be used by the patients that need them. Yet on May 28, 2019, the WHO adopted a resolution on transparency,[58] which does not obligate pharmaceutical companies to be transparent regarding the prices of medicines. This resolution emphasizes the purely voluntary nature of disclosures for sensitive information on R&D and indicates the limits of the WHO's authority over the medicine industry. This might call into question the power of the WHO to manage economic issues or influence its members that are partial to strong protection of economic interests to promote access to medicines.

Collaboration with other institutions has also been pronounced in the WHO's work with the UNCTAD. Under the GSPOA-PHI, the UNCTAD was invited as a stakeholder to act on the issue of transfer of technology in the pharmaceutical area and the local production of health products in developing countries. In response, the UNCTAD, in cooperation with the German International Cooperation, implemented a project on "Access to High Quality and Affordable Medicines in Africa and South-East Asia," which focuses on the need to "provide coherence among domestic policies aimed at promoting local production of pharmaceutical products and access to medicines."[59]

56 Since 2010, there have been several workshops on IP and Public Health, organized mainly by WTO or WIPO and WHO participating as presenter. *See Public Health, Innovation, Intellectual Property and Trade*, World Health Org., https://www.who.int/phi/training/en/ (last visited June 20, 2019).

57 *Global Challenges Seminar on Urgent Innovation: Policies and Practices for Effective Response to Global Health Crises*, World Intellectual Prop. Org. (Apr. 16, 2019), https://www.wipo.int/meetings/en/details.jsp?meeting_id=51766 (last visited June 11, 2019).

58 *Improving the Transparency of Markets for Medicines, Vaccines, and Other Health Products*, Resolution WHA72.8, 72nd World Health Assembly (May 28, 2019), https://apps.who.int/gb/e/e_wha72.html#resolutions (last visited Dec. 14, 2019).

59 *Tool Box for Policy Coherence in Access to Medicines and Local Pharmaceutical Production*, UNCTAD (2017), https://unctad.org/en/pages/PublicationWebflyer.aspx?publicationid=1921 (last visited Dec. 12, 2019).

## *Implementation of the GSPOA-PHI*

The use of TRIPS flexibilities and the GSPOA-PHI by the WHO is a concern for several organizations. One example will suffice here. At the 72nd session of the WHA,[60] the Non-Aligned Movement (NAM) requested WHO members to implement the recommendations of the GSPOA-PHI to promote new thinking on innovation and access to medicines.[61] The NAM further encouraged member states to make full use of the flexibilities available under the TRIPS Agreement, including those recognized by the Doha Declaration and the Paragraph 6 Decision, to address the public health needs of developing countries.[62]

In a 2012 report to the WTO,[63] the WHO focused on activities aimed at the implementation of the GSPOA-PHI, including the provision of policy and technical guidance, transfer of technology and local production, training and enhancing capacity, and direct country support. For example, the Pan American Health Organization (PAHO) continued to systemize key information on national IP frameworks in the Americas. Based on conceptual mapping and the WHO Pharmaceutical Sector Country Profile,[64] indicators are defined and classified as basic or advanced according to the depth of information that they provide related to IPR management. The standardization of information across member states constitutes an important step toward a better understanding of IP frameworks from a public health perspective and can facilitate the implementation of related monitoring and evaluation mechanisms. The platform promotes and supports innovation, access to medicines, rational use, quality, and governance of the health technologies sector.[65]

## *Overall Program Review*

The Expert Panel reviewed the GSPOA-PHI program between March and September 2017 "to assess the continued relevance of the aims and objectives of

60 *72nd World Health Assembly, May 20–28, 2019*, World Health Org., https://www.who.int/about/governance/world-health-assembly/seventy-second-world-health-assembly (last visited Nov. 6, 2019).

61 Ministers of Health Non-Aligned Movement (NAM), Ministerial Declaration of 21 May 2019, *Universal Health Coverage: Leave No One Behind* ¶ 18 (2019).

62 *Id.* ¶ 19. (Including by adopting and applying rigorous definitions of invention and patents, adopting and applying legislation that facilitates the issuance of compulsory licenses and ensuring that bilateral and regional trade and investment agreements do not include provisions that may undermine the full use of TRIPS flexibilities for public health and encourage the provision of assistance to developing countries in this regard.)

63 *Technical Cooperation Activities 581, supra* note 36.

64 *Development of Country Profiles and Monitoring of the Pharmaceutical Situation in Countries*, World Health Org., http://www.who.int/medicines/areas/coordination/coordination_assessment/en/index.html (last visited June 21, 2019).

65 *Technical Cooperation Activities 581, supra* note 36; *see also Overview on Technical Cooperation Programmes Relating to the Implementation of the TRIPS Agreement*, World Health Org. (2012).

the GSPOA-PHI, its achievements and weaknesses, identify any remaining challenges and recommend a way forward until 2022."[66] The Expert Panel observed that although progress has been made in certain aspects of both innovation and access, many of the challenges that motivated the formulation of the GSPOA-PHI remain, and new challenges have emerged. These include a lack of new health products in areas of need, a lack of sustainable financing, the unaffordability of many new medicines, a lack of essential health products and inappropriate use, ineffective delivery and supply chain infrastructure, and the absence of robust regulatory frameworks and trained personnel, mainly but not exclusively in developing countries.[67]

The main issue concerning the GSPOA-PHI has been the lack of impact in implementation. The Expert Panel therefore made recommendations addressed to the WHO Secretariat and/or member states. The recommendations made concerning IP were slated for action between 2019 and 2022.

Under the strategy of promoting technology transfer,[68] the Expert Panel recommended that the WHO Secretariat work with the WTO Secretariat to identify how article 66(2) of the TRIPS Agreement could be implemented more effectively in relation to health technology transfer. The indicator for this action point will be a progress report on health technology transfer in the context of article 66(2) of the TRIPS Agreement by 2021.

The Expert Panel also made recommendations on how to manage IP to contribute to innovation and public health.[69] First, the WHO Secretariat, in collaboration with other international organizations working on IP, is to advocate for the development of national legislation to fully reflect the TRIPS flexibilities, including those recognized in the Doha Declaration and in articles 27, 30 (including the research exception and "Bolar" provision), 31, and 31*bis* of the TRIPS Agreement. The indicator for progress on this recommendation will be an interorganizational report on national legislation and patenting guidelines that include the TRIPS flexibilities by 2021. It is not clear what will happen if the WHO and WTO do not agree on the direction of the national legislation.

66 World Health Organization, Overall Programme Review of the Global Strategy and Plan of Action on Public Health, Innovation and Intellectual Property: Report of the Review Panel (Nov. 2017), https://www.who.int/medicines/areas/policy/overall-programme-review-global-strategy-phi/en/; *see also* World Health Organization, Global Strategy and Plan of Action on Public Health, Innovation and Intellectual Property: Report of the Director-General ¶ 5 (Jan. 26, 2018), http://apps.who.int/gb/ebwha/pdf_files/WHA71/A71_13-en.pdf (last visited June 20, 2019).

67 World Health Organization, Global Strategy and Plan of Action on Public Health, Innovation and Intellectual Property: Report of the Director-General, https://apps.who.int/iris/handle/10665/274044 (last visited June 20, 2019) (emphasis added).

68 *Id.* at 5.

69 *Id.* at 6.

Second, the WHO Secretariat, in collaboration with partners, is to promote the further development of and greater access to databases of patents and non-confidential license agreements for health products. The indicator for progress is monitoring of the coverage and use of existing and new databases of patent and license information.[70]

Third, member states and other funders, with WHO Secretariat support, are to strengthen the Medicines Patent Pool (MPP),[71] which may include support for the expansion of its portfolio to cover other diseases or technologies where the MPP model can have the most impact. The indicator for progress is the number of diseases and/or technologies covered by the MPP's portfolio and the amount of funding committed by new donors by 2020.[72] Much as the MPP database is still limited, the WHO is advancing in its effort to provide patent information.

Fourth, member states – when negotiating trade agreements – should take into account the impact on public health of adopting provisions that go beyond the requirements of the TRIPS Agreement. The indicator for progress is the assessment by 2022 of evidence that negotiators of new trade agreements have considered the public health impact of the adoption of such agreements. Several bilateral trade agreements which constrain access to medicines have been concluded with TRIPS-plus provisions. The work of the WHO is still useful when providing future technical assistance to countries which are not party to the TRIPS-plus agreements.

The WHO has provided technical support to member states on the public health aspects of IP and trade policies. It has also provided training and capacity building on the health impact of trade agreements and how to manage and apply IP for public health and facilitate access to patent information. The WHO Report on the Role of Local Production in Developing Countries highlights the importance of transparent and fair patent administration systems using the example of access to patent information.[73]

70 Most patent license information is owned by WIPO although the Medicines Patent Pool (MPP) owns some.

71 The MPP is a United Nations–backed public health organization working to increase access to, and facilitate the development of, lifesaving medicines for low- and middle-income countries.

72 *See* MedsPaL, www.medspal.org (last visited June 28, 2019) (showing how the MPP covers all medicines on the WHO Essential Medicines lists. Particularly important to access to patent information, the MPP MedsPal free database provides information on the patent and licensing status of patented medicines on the WHO list of essential medicines in low- and middle-income countries).

73 World Health Organization, The Role of Intellectual Property in Local Production in Developing Countries: Opportunities and Challenges (2016), https://www.who.int/phi/implementation/ip_trade/en/ (last visited Dec. 11, 2019).

## Some Recent Developments in the Effort to Promote Access to Medicines

### *Contribution to Access to Hepatitis C Treatment*

According to the WHO, approximately 71 million people are living with the chronic hepatitis C virus (HCV), millions are newly infected each year, and 399,000 people die from HCV-related complications annually.[74] Yet the global response to reduce the burden of HCV has been very limited until recently.[75] The available treatment was expensive, poorly tolerated, and had low cure rates, particularly for people living in lower middle–income countries.[76]

In 2016, the WHO published the first global report on access to HCV medicines.[77] The report provides the information that countries and health authorities need to identify the appropriate HCV treatment and procure such treatment at affordable prices. It demonstrates how barriers to treatment access can be overcome. It also provides information on the production of new HCV drugs and generic versions worldwide, including where such drugs are and are not registered and patented, and what opportunities countries have under license agreements that were signed by some companies. The report also includes the current pricing of all recommended direct acting antivirals (DAAs) worldwide, including those produced by generic companies.[78]

In 2018, the WHO published the second edition of the global report,[79] which reviewed the progress countries have made in expanding access to lifesaving DAAs, including their affordability.

As mentioned earlier, the WHO's technical cooperation is based on its mandate derived from the GSPOA-PHI and relevant resolutions. For example, Resolution WHA67.6[80] on the prevention, diagnosis, and treatment of viral hepatitis requested the Director-General "to work with national authorities, upon their request, to promote comprehensive, equitable access

74 *Hepatitis C*, World Health Org. (July 9, 2019), http://www.who.int/mediacentre/factsheets/fs164/en/ (last visited Dec. 11, 2019).

75 *Id.*

76 *Id.*

77 World Health Organization, Global Report on Access to Hepatitis C Treatment – Focus on Overcoming Barriers, WHO/HIV/2016.20 (Oct. 2016), https://www.who.int/hepatitis/publications/hep-c-access-report/en/ (last visited Dec. 11, 2019).

78 *Id.*

79 World Health Organization, Progress Report on Access to Hepatitis C Treatment: Focus on Overcoming Barriers in Low- and Middle-Income Countries (Mar. 2018), http://apps.who.int/iris/bitstream/handle/10665/260445/WHO-CDS-HIV-18.4-eng.pdf?sequence=1 (last visited Dec. 11, 2019).

80 Resolution on Viral Hepatitis, Resolution WHA67.6, 67th World Health Assembly (May 24, 2014).

to prevention, diagnosis and treatment for viral hepatitis" and "to assist Member States to ensure equitable access to quality, effective, affordable and safe hepatitis B and HCV treatments and diagnostics, in particular in developing countries."

Contributing to the implementation of this resolution was one of the main activities in the area of public health and IP in 2014.[81] During the 2014 World Hepatitis Day, the WHO Regional Office for South-East Asia (SEARO) made a presentation on "Access to Antivirals and Treatment" covering IP aspects.[82]

For countries to identify ways of increasing access to and improving affordability of new HCV medicines, they need clarity on the patent status of these medicines. To assess whether a medicine is patent protected in a certain country requires expert knowledge and access to specialized databases that are not easily available. Therefore, in response to the GSPOA-PHI's mandate,[83] the WHO Secretariat published an analysis of the patent situation of seven new hepatitis treatments. These patent working papers[84] identify the most relevant patents related to seven medicines and list the countries in which these patents have been filed and granted.[85]

### *Road Map for Access to Medicines, Vaccines, and Other Health Products (2019–2023)*

At its 71st session, the WHA requested the Director-General to develop a road map report in consultation with Member States, outlining the WHO's work on access to medicines and vaccines, including activities and deliverables from 2019 to 2023.[86] The draft road map was then noted in the WHA72.[87]

81 Council for Trade-Related Aspects of Intellectual Property Rights, *Technical Cooperation Activities: Information From Other Intergovernmental Organizations, (WHO), Addendum*, WTO Doc. IP/C/W/603/Add.1, 1 (Oct 17, 2014).

82 World Health Organization & Institute of Liver and Biliary Sciences, Towards a Comprehensive National Hepatitis Prevention and Control Programme, India: Report of the Technical Consultation: World Hepatitis Day 2014 (2015), http://www.searo.who.int/india/publications/technical_consultation_world_hepatitis-day2014.pdf (last visited Dec. 11, 2019).

83 *Global Strategy and Plan of Action*, *supra* note 1, element 5(1)(c).

84 *WHO Updates Patent Information on Treatments for Hepatitis C*, World Health Org., http://www.who.int/phi/implementation/ip_trade/ip_patent_landscapes/en/ (last visited June 20, 2019).

85 WTO, *infra* note 86, at 2.

86 *Addressing the Global Shortage of, and Access to, Medicines and Vaccines*, Resolution WHA71(8), 71st World Health Assembly (May 28, 2018), http://apps.who.int/gb/ebwha/pdf_files/WHA71/A71(8)-en.pdf (last visited June 28, 2019).

87 Access to Medicines and Vaccines: Report of the Director-General, 72nd World Health Assembly, WHO Doc. A72/17 Annex (Apr 4, 2019) [hereinafter Draft Roadmap].

Strategic area VII of the road map deals with the improvement of equitable access to health products. It is hoped that the road map will foster innovation and access to health products by implementing appropriate IP rules and management. Deliverables include (1) promotion of public health-oriented licensing agreements and transparency regarding the patent status of existing and new health technologies; (2) information on country experiences promoting public health approaches in the implementation of health-related provisions of the TRIPS Agreement and related agreements, including relevant TRIPS flexibilities and IP management; and (3) support for the expansion of the MPP to patented medicines included in the WHO treatment guidelines through identification of potential products for licensing.

The identified milestones for 2019 were the following: (1) updating the WHO, WIPO, and WTO 2012 trilateral study on promoting access to medical technologies and innovation; (2) updating the progress report on access to hepatitis C treatment; and (3) patent transparency for and promotion of all medicines on the WHO Model List of Essential Medicines and new ones on the WHO treatment guidelines to support efforts to strengthen countries' abilities to analyze the information contained in those databases, and to improve the quality of patents.[88]

Deliverables under this strategy of the road map include the (1) provision of technical support and capacity building, including policy processes and assistance to countries that intend to use of the TRIPS Agreement to promote access to pharmaceutical products, and (2) continued strengthening of the collaboration between the WHO, WIPO, and WTO, including to implement the road map, and with other relevant international organizations such as the UNCTAD and UNDP.[89] A predictable impact of the WHO's collaboration with organizations that promote IP is that such collaboration might render the WHO ineffective in promoting access to medicines vis-à-vis IP. However, the WHO maintains that participating in and attending meetings organized by the WTO allows it to present a health perspective to the participants.[90]

The road map does not add anything new to the GSPOA-PHI on IP and access to health products. However, there is more emphasis on collaboration with international organizations such as the WIPO and WTO, which are experts in IP and have an interest to promote it even at the cost of health. Regarding deliverables of the road map, the report on HCV or the trilateral study of the WHO, WIPO, and WTO on access to medical technologies have not yet been updated. The study was expected to have been updated by end of 2019 or early 2020 at the time of writing.[91]

88 *Id.* at 38.
89 *Id.* at 39.
90 Interview with Peter Beyer, *supra* note 41.
91 Email communication from WHO dated Jan. 16, 2019.

## Specific Activities to Promote Access to Medicines

### *Training and Enhancing Capacity*

Over the years, the WHO has been organizing regional, subregional, and national training workshops for developing country policy makers, with the aim of enhancing developing country capacity to ensure effective participation in trade negotiations, and ensuring that public health interests are adequately considered in national policy and legislation. The WHO encourages effective collaboration between health, trade, and patent agencies for informed and coherent decision-making on public health and IP issues. The WHO thus adopts multi-agency approaches in conducting briefings and training sessions for health, trade, and patent officials.

In March 2007, the WHO organized a two-week course on IP and public health, co-sponsored by the Ministry of Health of Argentina, PAHO, University of Buenos Aires, and UNDP, with the objective of increasing awareness of the importance of applying IP laws and policies in a manner consistent with public health.[92]

The WHO organized the regional workshop on local production of essential medicines, in collaboration with the WHO Regional Office for Africa (AFRO), to prepare a strategic framework of activities to strengthen local production capacities for essential medicines for the period of 2006–2010. The strategic framework covered national medicines policies, IPR, and trade-related issues.[93]

In November 2017, the World Conference on Access to Medical Products and International Laws for Trade and Health was held in New Delhi, India, with the main objective of exchanging knowledge and expanding understanding on contemporary issues in international trade laws, including research and innovation for access to medical products to achieve the Sustainable Development Goals (SDGs) 2030 Agenda. The themes addressed include access to medical products, and IPR and trade for SDGs in the context of such access.[94,95]

In 2012, the WHO SEARO supported a workshop on "Globalizing Asia: Health Law and Policy, Approaches, and Gaps" in Bangkok. The WHO contributed to the identification of possible domestic and regional legal and policy approaches that could serve as a basis for meeting international obligations in

92 Council for Trade-Related Aspects of Intellectual Property Rights, *Technical Cooperation Activities: Information From Other Intergovernmental Organizations* ¶ 19, WTO Doc. IP/C/W/516/Add.1 (Oct. 15, 2008).

93 *Technical Cooperation Activities 478*, *supra* note 24, at 19.

94 Council for Trade-Related Aspects of Intellectual Property Rights, *Technical Cooperation Activities: Information from Other Intergovernmental Organizations*, WTO Doc. IP/C/W/644/Rev.1/Add.2, 2 (Oct. 2, 2018), https://www.who.int/phi/WHO-communication2017.pdf?ua=1 (last visited June 27, 2019).

95 The executive summary and final report of the conference are available at https://1st.worldsdg2030.org/reports.aspx (last visited June 20, 2019).

the area of trade and IP, including the use of TRIPS flexibilities that may help protect public health.[96]

The WHO, together with partner organizations and WHO Regional Offices, organized subregional and regional training sessions for patent examiners on developing a public health perspective regarding examination of pharmaceutical patents. For example, a training session jointly organized with the WHO AFRO, UNDP, and the University of Cape Town was held in 2008 in South Africa to increase knowledge and understanding about the public health implications of IP.[97]

Recognizing that effective collaboration between health, trade, and patent agencies is essential for informed and coherent decision-making on public health and IP issues, the WHO continues to conduct briefings and training sessions for health, trade, and patent officials. These training sessions aim to enhance developing country capacity to ensure effective participation in trade negotiations and to ensure that public health interests are adequately taken into account in national policy and legislation.[98]

### *Policy and Technical Guidance*

The WHO identifies issues related to the TRIPS Agreement and the implementation of its article 31*bis* and provides practical and assessable policy guidance and technical advice through its publications. Availability of accurate and up-to-date information is crucial for effective decision-making on access to affordable medicines.

For example, the WHO SEARO collaborates with Ministries of Health to provide information on IPR, trade, and public health, with the objective of raising awareness regarding trade negotiation processes and their policy implications for access to all medical products for public health.[99]

96 *Technical Cooperation Activities 581*, *supra* note 36, at 6.

97 Council for Trade-Related Aspects of Intellectual Property Rights, *Technical Cooperation Activities: Information from Other Intergovernmental Organizations*, WTO Doc. IP/C/W/549/Add.4, 4–5 (Oct. 25, 2010), https://www.who.int/phi/WHO_Comm_TRIPS_implementation_activities_W549A4_2010.pdf?ua=1 (last visited June 20, 2019).

98 Council for Trade-Related Aspects of Intellectual Property Rights, *Technical Cooperation Activities: Information from Other Intergovernmental Organizations*, WTO Doc. IP/C/W/516Add.1, 4 (Oct. 15, 2008), https://www.who.int/phi/WHO_Comm_TRIPS_implementation_activities_W516A1_2008a.pdf?ua=1 (last visited June 20, 2019) [hereinafter *Tech Cooperation Activities*] (detailing how activities have included organizing meetings of experts on enabling legislation to facilitate an increase in access to essential medicines in July 2007 in West Africa, Accra. The workshop aimed at examining various policy and legislative tools available for reducing essential drug prices and taking advantage of the flexibilities of the TRIPS Agreement, including through an evaluation of existing capacity in the region for generic production of medicines).

99 Council for Trade-Related Aspects of Intellectual Property Rights, *Technical Cooperation Activities: Information from Other Intergovernmental Organizations*, WTO Doc. IP/C/W/633/Add.2, 3 (Oct. 2, 2017) https://www.who.int/phi/WHO-communication2017.pdf?ua=1.

The WHO, in collaboration with Professor Carlos Correa, published a guide for CLs and government use of pharmaceutical patents.[100] The guide focuses on the grant of CLs and government use authorization in the context of the purchase and import of patent-protected pharmaceutical products.

### *Direct Country Support*

As far back as 1999, the WHO has provided support to countries on request, such as briefings on TRIPS flexibilities and advice on the revision of national pharmaceutical legislation. For example, it has provided support to China, South Africa, Thailand, and the countries of the Association of Southeast Asian Nations and the Southern African Development Community.[101] The country support aimed at developing public health sensitive patent legislation and incorporating TRIPS flexibilities in domestic legislation.

In collaboration with the relevant international organizations, the WHO provides technical and policy support in framing national policies, laws, and regulations to favor application and management of IP in a manner that maximizes health-related innovation and promotes access to health products and services. For example, the WHO/PAHO provided technical assistance to Chile in May 2017 and El Salvador in August 2017 on the use of TRIPS flexibilities. The PAHO also finalized the conceptual framework for Central America and the Dominican Republic on IP and public health to have a clear vision of the existing legal framework of IP and how it could impact access to medical products. The WHO hopes that the framework will help the PAHO guide its technical cooperation on IP and public health in the subregion.[102]

In October 2017, upon request from the governments of Moldova and Ukraine, the WHO Europe organized a two-day training seminar for government officials from the two countries to explore legal options in increasing access to lower priced medicines. The seminar primarily focused on increasing access to essential medicines to treat HIV, HCV, and cancer. The dialogues highlighted the interplay between health, trade, and IP, with a focus on the potential impact of current trade agreements on people's access to medicines in Moldova and Ukraine.[103]

100 Carlos M. Correa & World Health Organization, *Guide for the Application and Granting of Compulsory Licenses and Authorization of Government Use of Pharmaceutical Patents* (2009), https://apps.who.int/iris/bitstream/handle/10665/70096/WHO_PHI_2009.1_eng.pdf?sequence=1&isAllowed=y.

101 Council for Trade-Related Aspects of Intellectual Property Rights, *Technical Cooperation Activities: Information from Other Intergovernmental Organizations*, WTO Doc. IP/C/W/202, 2 (Aug. 31, 2000), https://www.who.int/phi/WHO_Comm_TRIPS_implementation_activities_W202_2000.pdf?ua=1.

102 *Tech Cooperation Activities*, *supra* note 98, at 4.

103 *Id.*

In June 2018, the WHO, WTO, and WIPO jointly provided technical support to Georgia for the implementation of its amended patent law.[104]

### *Transfer of Technology and Local Production*

In 2016, the WHO, with the support of the European Commission, published a report on the role of IP in local production in developing countries as part of a wider project covering different aspects and challenges of local production and the conditions under which it may increase access to essential medicines. The report focuses on the role of IP in facilitating local production to ultimately improve access to medical products in low- and middle-income countries.[105]

The WHO also responded to a request received by Colombia during the WHA in 2016 on ensuring access to *imatinib*, a cancer treatment included in the WHO Essential Medicines List.[106]

## Conclusions

Since the TRIPS Agreement became effective, several institutions, including the WHO, have shown interest in shaping international IP rules to fit their mandates. Through a number of resolutions and strategies, the WHO has addressed the impact of international trade agreements and IP on access to medicines or health products. Specifically, it has guided members on how to use TRIPS flexibilities to promote public health through publications, regional and subregional workshops and meetings, as well as national interventions.

It is important to recall that most of the WHO members are also members of the WTO; thus, some members in the WHO protect their economic interests in the WTO, which leads to compromises as to courses of action. It is not surprising that several resolutions and strategies are seemingly not implemented.

In addition, collaboration with international organizations has advantages, such as not duplicating resources. But there is a risk of the WHO's efforts and views being overshadowed by those of organizations with enough resources to hold more frequent meetings on IP and have the WHO participate only as an invitee. Furthermore, there is a risk of censorship on what the WHO can do, by arguing lack of competence for the WHO to interpret trade agreements protecting and promoting IP.

104 *Id.*

105 Council for Trade-Related Aspects of Intellectual Property Rights, *Technical Cooperation Activities: Information from Other Intergovernmental Organizations*, WTO Doc. IP/C/W/614/Add.4, 2 (Oct. 24, 2016), https://www.who.int/phi/WHO_final_Report_W614A4.pdf?ua=1 (last visited June 28, 2019).

106 *Id.* at 4.

# 3 From TRIPS to Access to Medicines

## What's There in Between?

*Sergio Napolitano**

## Introduction

The compatibility of the Agreement on Trade-Related Aspects of Intellectual Property Rights (TRIPS Agreement) rules on intellectual property (IP) with the public health objective of access to medicines is a highly political and complex debate. This chapter attempts to define the elements of the TRIPS Agreement that have been having an impact, over the years, on the generic and biosimilar medicine sector and access to these medicines, both in developed and less developed countries. The analysis will start from an assessment of the underlying objectives of the TRIPS Agreement,[1] that is, the protection of IP rights (IPR) for incentivizing investments in innovative technologies. It will continue with a reflection of the way the text of the TRIPS Agreement counterbalances the mandated protection of patent rights in comparison with the actual practices of members of the World Trade Organization (WTO)[2] in applying these flexibilities in the context of trade negotiations. It will conclude with a description of the prominent role that competition, conceived in its broadest manner, can play to ensure effective and timely access to medicines for all. The analysis is completed with suggestions of a possible way forward focused on an equitable use of the TRIPS Agreement by WTO members in trade policy initiatives and preferential trade agreements, the application of IPR in more transparent and well-functioning IP systems, and an increasingly stronger use of competition law enforcement.

The key role of competition authorities is also defined in their stronger involvement in "policy-making" processes, as well as their oversight of the proper functioning and compatibility of the IP system with public health objectives, including timely generic and biosimilar medicine competition and

* The views and opinions expressed in this chapter are the author's own and do not necessarily represent the official policy or position of any people, institutions, or organizations that he may or may not have been associated with in his professional or personal capacity.

1 *See* TRIPS: Agreement on Trade-Related Aspects of Intellectual Property Rights, Apr. 15, 1994, Marrakesh Agreement Establishing the World Trade Organization, Annex C, 1869 U.N.T.S. 299, I.L.M. 1197 (1994) [hereinafter TRIPS Agreement].

2 *Id.* at arts. 8, 27, 30, 31, and 40.

subsequent patient access to these medicines. The analysis below does not aim to discuss in detail every single aspect of the TRIPS Agreement that has had an impact on access to medicines. It mainly focuses on the impact of certain IP elements of the TRIPS Agreement with a view to suggesting possible policy solutions.[3]

## Incentivizing Investments in Pharmaceutical Products

One of the purpose of the TRIPS Agreement, as stated in Article 7, is the incentivization of innovation.[4] Stimulating innovation, indeed, is generally the stated objective of all IPR provisions, which are embedded in bilateral, plurilateral, or multilateral agreements. The general rationale on which patents are based is that by providing for a certain period of actual exclusivity on the market, innovative companies are incentivized or stimulated to increase investments in research and development (R&D) and innovative medicinal products. The second part of Article 7 of the TRIPS Agreement focuses on how protection and enforcement of IPR need to be applied, that is, to the mutual advantage of both producers and users of the innovation, in a way that preserves social and economic welfare as well as a balance of rights and obligations;[5] the latter often becomes the most controversial element of the TRIPS Agreement, as argued later in this chapter.

The question of whether IPR are perfectly fit for incentivizing investments in R&D and innovation needs to be assessed by focusing on a two-fold analysis: first, whether IPR are always, necessarily, the best possible incentive to innovation; and second, whether other factors have been demonstrated to have driven actual investments in R&D and innovation in a certain territory. However,

3 This chapter does not discuss the impact of regulatory protections applied on the basis of the TRIPS Agreement despite not being actually mandated by the Agreement. However, it is worth mentioning that Article 39.3 of the TRIPS Agreement has been often used to justify the introduction of regulatory data or market exclusivities in trade agreements and in WTO members' legislation. However, Article 39.3 mandates the protection of the data submitted for the approval of a pharmaceutical product against disclosure and unfair commercial use (i.e. protection of confidential information). This is different from the objective of data exclusivity, which is to prevent regulatory agencies from relying on the data of the reference product for the approval of the generic medicine. As the generic medicine producer develops its own data to demonstrate bioequivalence, it needs no access to the protected data of the reference product. The objective of the data exclusivities as applied by the abovementioned WTO members is therefore not described in Article 39. TRIPS Agreement, *supra* note 1, at art. 39.

4 *Id.* at art. 7. The article states: "The protection and enforcement of intellectual property rights should contribute to the promotion of technological innovation and to the transfer and dissemination of technology, to the mutual advantage of producers and users of technological knowledge and in a manner conducive to social and economic welfare, and to a balance of rights and obligations."

5 *Id.* at art. 7.

investments in R&D and innovation are not the only important objectives when trying to achieve access to medicines more generally. Indeed, a third element to be considered is the extent of the prominence of incentivizing actual production of medicines, which is not, however, within the purposes of the TRIPS Agreement.

### *Incentives to R&D and Innovation in Pharma*

First, to assess the impact of the TRIPS Agreement on investments in innovation, one needs to consider whether IPR, and patents in particular – by providing for a minimum period of 20 years of exclusivity on the market – offer a significant reward for the patent holder's investments to develop a new chemical entity, and therefore an effective incentive. Whether the actual patent holder effectively made the invention or acquired it from another entity, or whether and in what cases the length of such monopolies is adequate for the innovator to recoup the investments are separate discussions that this chapter will not address. However, it seems certain and widely recognized that patents, by excluding direct potential competitors from markets where they are in place and enforceable, represent a strong commercial incentive, which *de facto* links the existence of a patent with its actual commercialization in the same territory. In this sense, patents indisputably represent a very strong and concrete incentive to investments in innovation.

The link between the existence of patents and investments in R&D and innovation in a given territory has never been clearly proved and demonstrated.[6] Such a link would only be hypothetically possible in a legislative system that linked the granting of a patent to conducting its R&D in the same territory. However, the compatibility of this with WTO rules would need to be considered. As a consequence, the abovementioned commercial element cannot be disregarded for patents to be considered a real incentive to R&D and innovation. Indeed, the equation is rather simple: the circumstance that a patent exists in certain countries stimulates investments in R&D and innovation, but not necessarily in countries where these patents exist. What the protection of innovation granted in a given market or territory actually incentivizes is the commercial launch of the innovative product in that market.

The recoupment of the investments made for R&D and innovation derives – in the vast majority of cases – from commercializing the innovative product in

6 It is shown in various studies that such a link is hard to be made. *See*, for instance: *Effects of Supplementary Protection Mechanisms for Pharmaceutical Products*, Technopolis Group (2018), sec. 6.1.2, https://www.technopolis-group.com/wp-content/uploads/2020/02/Effects-of-supplementary-protection-mechanisms-for-pharmaceutical-products.pdf; R.W. de Boer (Rens), *Supplementary Protection Certificate for Medicinal Products, An Assessment of European Regulation* 46 (2015), http://www.spcwaiver.com/files/Netherlands_SPC_assessment.pdf.

countries where prices can be higher and there is affordability to purchase or use such innovation, i.e. mainly developed countries. In Europe, for instance, in addition to the 20 years of patent protection covering innovative molecules, a company can request for a Supplementary Protection Certificate (SPC) – that extends the market exclusivity of a patented product by up to 5 years – in order to compensate for the actual monopoly loss between the patent filing and the attainment of the marketing authorization.[7] Even in Europe, many innovators choose not to apply for an SPC, or even launch certain innovative products in certain member states of the European Union (EU) where lower prices with limited possible profits are forecast, due to the limited budgetary resources in those countries. Therefore, when strong IPR standards are in place in more developed countries, it is hardly justifiable that lesser developed countries that can barely provide basic access to health care be encouraged to introduce and enforce strong IPR rules in their legislation. In lesser developed countries, these IPR rules prevent marketing of generic and biosimilar medicines during the protection period and limit access to more affordable medicines – without necessarily stimulating investments in R&D.

With the need to balance protection of IPR with access to medicines, it would be fair to conclude that the existence of strong IPR – mainly in countries that can afford long exclusivity periods for innovative and more expensive products – will certainly be a strong and sufficient incentive to invest in R&D and innovation. Extending exclusivities beyond certain limits (e.g., TRIPS or higher standards) in less developed countries would not bring huge economic benefits to innovative companies and simultaneously make it even harder for their national health-care systems to function properly and provide access to basic health care. A pivotal objective of any pharmaceutical policy, including IP-related ones, needs to be universal access to health care.

Bearing in mind that providing exclusive rights is not necessarily linked to the location of the investments in R&D and innovation, the second important element of this analysis is the assessment of the actual drivers of such investments. It is true that the promise of being granted long exclusive rights in some countries represents a significant incentive to invest in innovation, especially in the context of a very globalized industry like pharmaceuticals. However, it is solidly demonstrated that R&D investments in a certain specific region are driven by a combination of policies and factors not only or necessarily related to IPR; that is, tax, legal, or fiscal policies, as well as the level

7 An SPC is different from a patent in so far as it provides for an extension of the market exclusivity of a patented medicinal product, and is meant to cover only patents on active pharmaceutical ingredients (API). The extension of the market exclusivity specifically is given by the fact that an SPC can only be obtained if the product obtains a marketing authorization and if such marketing authorization is received more than 5 years after the patent filing. For these reasons, it is called "*sui generis* protection" in the EU. The (EC) 469/2009 of the European Parliament and of the Council of May 6, 2009, Concerning the Supplementary Protection Certificate for Medicinal Products, 2009 O.J. (L 152/1), art. 4.

of education, labor costs, public funds, and others.[8] Indeed, national governments have formulated several policies to stimulate R&D: industry-specific tax rates, investment tax credits or tax breaks, and R&D tax incentives. Studies of the Organization for Economic Cooperation and Development (OECD) show the possible benefits of these measures, maintaining that "depending on their design, tax incentives can increase private research spending by an amount equal to the loss in tax revenue on average."[9] R&D is also stimulated by incentivizing policies that strengthen confidence in the stability of the country's banking system.

The role of high education and human capital is also pivotal to stimulate R&D and innovation. Fiscal policies can support not only foreign direct investments but also higher education and an abundance of highly skilled graduates to stimulate knowledge and allow companies to remain competitive in the innovative sphere. In this respect, the OECD studies also note that "investment in the education and training of researchers and other highly skilled workers is a major factor in determining the contribution that scientific research can make to scientific progress and innovation."[10] The same is valid for public-private partnerships in joint research projects, which have the potential to "fill gaps in the science and innovation systems and increase the leverage of public support to business R&D through cost and risk sharing."[11]

Therefore, a multitude of policies stimulate investment or relocation of R&D in a certain country. That a strong IP system leads automatically to more innovation is contradicted even by empirical evidence, at least with regard to patents and pharmaceutical products. Indeed, Europe, for instance, has one of the strongest and certainly longest IPR and regulatory protection systems for pharmaceuticals. However, the majority of innovative products whose IP is registered in Europe derives from the United States (US), and in particular, from certain regions of the US where certain policies – unrelated to IPR – have been put in place. As shown in a study published by the European Commission on SPCs, "[a]lmost 44% of SPC applicants are US-based, while the EU has close

8 *See*, for instance: *Worldwide R&D Incentives Reference Guide 2018*, EY, https://www.ey.com/Publication/vwLUAssets/ey-2018-worldwide-rd-incentives-reference-guide/$-FILE/ey-2018-worldwide-rd-incentives-reference-guide.pdf; Chiara Criscuolo, *The Effect of R&D Tax Incentives on Location of R&D Investment*, ResearchGate, https://www.researchgate.net/publication/242590846_The_effect_of_RD_tax_incentives_on_location_of_RD_investment.

9 *Tax Incentives for Research and Development: Trends and Issues*, Science Technology and Industry, Organization for Econ. Co-Operation & Dev. 4 (2002), http://www.oecd.org/sti/inno/2498389.pdf.

10 Organization for Economic Co-Operation and Development, *Innovation and Growth: Rationale for an Innovation Strategy* 18 (2007), https://www.oecd.org/science/inno/39374789.pdf [hereinafter *Innovation and Growth*]. The report also notes that human capital is a key factor in the adoption of new technologies and the introduction of innovative practices.

11 *Id.* at 21.

to 30%."[12] Furthermore, competition is another fundamental factor stimulating investments and driving innovation aimed at producing breakthrough or incremental innovative products that differentiate them from those commercialized by other market players.[13]

Thus, it follows that a blind attempt to focus all efforts on strengthening exclusivity rights at all costs in order to stimulate R&D and innovation does not necessarily produce the stated objectives. Rather, it tends to drive investments mainly in developing products for which high profits can be expected – in an attempt to maximize exclusivities – rather than where real public health needs are. In fact, limiting competition through exclusivity rights may actually have the opposite effects of limiting innovation and increasing prices.[14]

## *Incentives to the Production of Medicines*

A holistic discussion about the TRIPS Agreement and incentives to invest in developing pharmaceutical products cannot disregard the importance of stimulating the actual manufacturing of medicines. Patents represent a commercial reward for investments in innovation. However, the powers vested by several acts – listed in Article 28 of the TRIPS Agreement – prevent competitors from taking various actions, including making generic or biosimilar versions of patented products in countries where patents exist, even for the purpose of exporting those generic and biosimilar medicines to countries where no IPR or other exclusivities exist or have expired.

One of the main issues for developing and less developed countries is the lack of a strong – or even basic – local pharmaceutical industry that develops and manufactures pharmaceutical products for its own people. If it is true that patent rights prevent manufacturers of generic and biosimilar medicines from producing their products where these rights exist, it is equally true that the

12 Margaret Kyle, *Economic Analysis of Supplementary Protection Certificates in Europe* 4, Eur. Comm'n (2017), https://ec.europa.eu/growth/industry/intellectual-property/patents/supplementary-protection-certificates_en.

13 In the context of biosimilar medicines in the US, for instance, the past Commissioner of the Food and Drug Administration (FDA) Commissioner Scott Gottlieb M.D. stressed that "[b]y enabling a path for competition from biosimilars, we also give innovators an added incentive to invest in further research that'll lead to the discovery of even better drugs that deliver additional benefits for patients." *Remarks from FDA Commissioner Scott Gottlieb, M.D., As Prepared for Delivery at the Brookings Institution on the Release of the FDA's Biosimilars Action Plan*, U.S. Food & Drug Admin., https://www.fda.gov/news-events/press-announcements/remarks-fda-commissioner-scott-gottlieb-md-prepared-delivery-brookings-institution-release-fdas (last visited July 2019) [hereinafter *Remarks from FDA Commissioner Scott Gottlieb*].

14 "[L]imited competition among suppliers may increase the cost of inputs and make products supplied less innovative. It may discourage innovation, or make it costly to develop it or to defend the associated intellectual property." *Innovation and Growth, supra* note 10, at 2.

introduction of exclusive rights in countries that need to develop a local manufacturing pharma industry does not stimulate investments in the production of medicines. On the contrary, it stimulates delocalization of manufacturing. In less developed countries where no IPR protection exists, IPR can certainly not be identified as a factor limiting local production, but surely its introduction would not support the creation of a local manufacturing industry.

At the same time, as discussed above, it is difficult to establish the correlation between the introduction of IPR and R&D investments and innovation in a given region. Indeed, IPR essentially provide an incentive to commercialize the innovation, rather than a direct incentive to invest in R&D in that territory. Paradoxically, the introduction of strong exclusivity rights in less developed countries has not incentivized innovative or even generic pharmaceutical industry to invest in those countries. On the contrary, the negative effects of a delayed entry of generic medicines would be strongly felt, not only in terms of access to medicines, but also in terms of budgetary impacts for governments. Meanwhile in developed countries, strong IPR have led, over the last two decades, to a shift of investments in manufacturing generic or biosimilar medicines and the related supply chain to countries with shorter exclusivity rights for innovative products. For instance, the active pharmaceutical ingredients (API) industry – where European countries were once world leaders – has developed relatively quickly in some Asian countries like China and India in the last two decades. This has contributed to developing manufacturing science high-skill jobs and, subsequently, economic growth in those regions.

The circumstance that leads to IPR having dissuasive effects – in terms of investments in the development and manufacturing of medicines, including all the related manufacturing and incremental innovation – has been demonstrated by the legislative changes in the EU in relation to the SPC, which makes the European IP protection the longest worldwide. Indeed, the length of the EU SPC has forced generic and biosimilar medicines producers – as well as API manufacturers – to invest in manufacturing their products outside of Europe to remain competitive vis-à-vis global competitors not only in countries with shorter IP protection but also in Europe as soon as IPR expire.

To avoid a massive migration of pharmaceutical manufacturing out of Europe, the EU's solution has been an amendment to the SPC legislation, i.e. the SPC manufacturing waiver. The SPC manufacturing waiver, which came into force in July 2019, allows generic and biosimilar producers to manufacture their products in Europe during the EU SPC protection period for two purposes: export to third countries during the EU SPC period, and entry into the EU markets immediately at SPC expiry.[15] This shows that patent rights – insofar as they prevent manufacturing of generic and biosimilar versions of the

15 *See Supplementary Protection Certificates for Pharmaceutical and Plant Protection Products*, Eur. Comm'n, https://ec.europa.eu/growth/industry/intellectual-property/patents/supplementary-protection-certificates_en (information on the SPC manufacturing waiver).

patented product – significantly impact business decisions regarding the location of manufacturing generic medicines and the creation or strengthening of a solid pharmaceutical manufacturing industry that is most needed in poorer countries.

The SPC manufacturing waiver demonstrates that incentives for manufacturing medicines – and in particular, generic and biosimilar medicines – can actually be compatible with IPR. Even in such a globalized sector, it responds to the need for a strong local pharmaceutical industry, ensuring continuity of supply and reducing risks of shortages of medicines while also preserving the exclusivity rights and broader incentives to invest in innovation and R&D.

Importantly, SPC rights are different from patent rights, and the TRIPS Agreement does not mandate any SPC or form of patent extension. Patent protection provides incentives that essentially materialize in the form of an exclusivity on the market, leading to an economic benefit for the patent holder to recoup investments and realize profits. Preventing manufacturing of the generic version of the medicine during the exclusivity right – even in the absence of a generic launch, which would indeed infringe the exclusivity granted by the patent – brings limited benefits to the patent holder but simultaneously produces significant limiting effects to the growth of the manufacturing industry.

In conclusion, the importance of incentivizing investments in actual manufacturing of medicines has increased over time and needs to be integrated or incorporated into IP policies. Considering the empirical evidence of the reasons why companies invest in R&D and innovation in certain countries rather than others, the narrative that IPR – and in particular, patents – are always the most important factor driving investments in R&D no longer seems to be true. Thus, rigid policies aimed at transposing strong IPR in any region of the world are outdated, and indeed, even against the spirit and the purposes of the TRIPS Agreement as well as the WTO objectives more generally. It seems fair to conclude that the TRIPS Agreement, or at least the policies deriving from it, may need some recalibration to reflect the evolution of the pharmaceutical industry, the developments of modern pharmaceutical policies, and the renovated need for universal access to health care.

## Equality v. Equity – The Political Debate

The TRIPS Agreement sets minimum standards of IP protection that WTO members need to implement in their legislation. However, in order to address public health and access to medicines issues in developing and less developed countries, the TRIPS Agreement includes some exceptions to these minimum standards. In particular, the exceptions – generally referred to as "flexibilities" – are related to specific elements such as research exceptions and the so-called *Bolar* provision, an outline of anticompetitive practices, or provisions relating to compulsory licenses. This reflects the differences, sometimes very significant, in the levels of economic development of the WTO members.

Such flexibilities are conceived as exceptional measures; in practice, they are generally used to the extent needed. However, the political discussions at the WTO between member countries that intend to extend such flexibilities and the more conservative ones are never-ending, showing a certain discontent on the part of the developing and less developed countries with some of the requirements of the TRIPS Agreement, particularly the impact such requirements have – and would continue to have – on their health-care systems.

This also reflects a lack of uniform commitment to the objectives of the TRIPS Agreement, stated in Article 7 that while the protection and enforcement of IPR have to contribute to the promotion of innovation and technology dissemination, they also have to promote/enable/encourage "social and economic welfare" and, very importantly, have to aim at a "balance of rights and obligations."[16]

Determining a balance of the rights and obligations is clearly the most controversial element within the membership of the WTO, and the effort to strike such a balance – especially in relation to the actual impact on public health of an international agreement that establishes private rights – is a political and even a moral duty of all the WTO members.

This is particularly required since the TRIPS Agreement is prescriptive about the introduction and enforcement of IPR. Article 2 of the agreement establishing the WTO, also called the "Marrakesh Agreement," outlines in paragraph 2 that the negotiated multilateral agreements, including the TRIPS Agreement, are "binding on all Members."[17] Since membership to the WTO is voluntary, abiding by the TRIPS rules is mandatory only if a country intends to remain or become a member of the WTO. However, in a globalized world – where industries have global presence and global activity where trade in goods or services regularly takes place between different countries – the political pressure to become or remain a member of the WTO is certainly very high. Therefore, the logical question is whether the political dynamics and the extremization of the positions between WTO members actually allow the striking of the balance highlighted in Article 7 of the TRIPS Agreement? Working toward a balance between rights and obligations among a diverse membership is a strong commitment of the WTO members. But is this stated objective realistic in light of the current disagreements in the TRIPS Council?

More often than not, the political commitment toward such a balance embedded in the legal text of the TRIPS Agreement is far from the actual dynamics in the context of bilateral or plurilateral negotiations for preferential trade agreements. Indeed, in trade negotiations aimed at bilateral or plurilateral trade agreements involving developed and less developed countries, it is very common

16 TRIPS Agreement, *supra* note 1, at art. 7.

17 WTO Agreement: Marrakesh Agreement Establishing the World Trade Organization, 9, Apr. 15, 1994, 1867 U.N.T.S. 154, 33 I.L.M. 1144 (1994), https://www.wto.org/english/docs_e/legal_e/04-wto.pdf.

to witness the former exerting significant pressure to introduce strong IP standards in the national legislation of the latter. In such negotiations, TRIPS or TRIPS-plus provisions are very often pushed and eventually included in the agreement, maybe in exchange for concessions completely unrelated to health, e.g. agricultural goods quota and others. Unless the less developed country strongly stands firm on its position against TRIPS-plus measures – which often leads to a freezing of the negotiations – such TRIPS-plus rules and other exclusivity provisions are included in the agreement.

Yet this trend does not always reflect the political commitment embedded in Article 7 of the TRIPS Agreement and the need for openness to flexibilities. The TRIPS Agreement seems to embed, even if subtly, a distinction between the concepts of equality and equity. The flexibilities in the TRIPS Agreement and the need for a balance of rights and obligations seem to derive from the assumption that equality of treatment would be unfair and unjust in certain cases; hence no equal treatment can be expected for different situations. Indeed, while the letter of the TRIPS Agreement states that different levels of development of the WTO members cannot be treated equally but rather in an equitable way, the spirit of this TRIPS equity should also be reflected in bilateral and plurilateral trade negotiations.

Similarly, the WTO, with its diverse membership, should tend toward an equitable application and enforcement of its provisions, in line with the Roman concept of *aequitas*, by which different cases have to be treated in different ways, with a level of flexibility that mirrors the level of differentiation.[18] While this flexible approach cannot be disregarded in negotiations at the multilateral level, even more, it can also not be completely neglected in bilateral and plurilateral negotiations. This is not only a political, but even a moral duty.

## Competition and the TRIPS Agreement

The stated objective of the WTO and the trade-related rules to be implemented by its member states are aimed at avoiding protectionist measures and distortion to international trade. The TRIPS Agreement, in particular, aspires to the "effective and adequate protection" of IPR. It is relevant to highlight that the preamble of the TRIPS Agreement also includes the desire "to ensure that measures and procedures to enforce intellectual property rights do not themselves become barriers to legitimate trade."[19] Therefore, the TRIPS Agreement

18 The Roman *aequitas* started being applied to the more rigid ancient Roman legal system, strongly based on a formal *ius civile*, when the Roman Empire expanded toward different regions and populations. The increasing cultural and traditional differences among people subject to Roman power required an increasing flexibility in the application and enforcement of the law, which started therefore to be based on treating different situations in different ways, that is, "equity."

19 TRIPS Agreement, *supra* note 1, at pmbl.

includes IP measures and balancing provisions by including flexibilities, while at the same time ensuring that IP rules do not hamper fair competition in a way that would constitute a barrier to legitimate trade.

Obviously, strong competition measures that counterbalance strong IPR limit the possibility for IP holders to use IP systems (very often legally) to artificially extend their exclusivities beyond the actual intention of the law. In fact, national IP laws are always subject to different – and often broader – interpretations and applications that may result in an artificial maximization of the protection or the so-called IP "evergreening." This may occur because the text of the law may be excessively vague or because multiple IP titles and other forms of market protection overlap. Competition law, however, has the purpose of ensuring that IP law is not abused and that once competition is supposed to take place on the market, no obstacle hinders it. Nonetheless, while IP measures in the TRIPS Agreement are clearly prescriptive, competition provisions are permissive only. Indeed, the agreement provides for several obligations ("shall") throughout the text, e.g. "patents shall be available for any inventions,"[20] "[a] patent shall confer"[21] certain exclusive rights, the patent protection "shall not end before the expiration of a period of twenty years"[22] from the filing date. Obligations are also related to the safeguards for patent holders, e.g. "[a]n opportunity for judicial review of any decision to revoke or forfeit a patent shall be available,"[23] "judicial authorities shall have the authority to order the defendant to prove" non-infringement of process patents and "[m]embers shall provide [...] that any identical product [...] be deemed to have been obtained by the patented process,"[24] as a "deterrent to infringement, the judicial authorities shall have the authority to order that goods that they have found to be infringing be, without compensation of any sort, disposed of outside the channels of commerce,"[25] and "[t]he judicial authorities shall have the authority to order the infringer to pay the right holder damages [...] to compensate for the injury" caused by the IP infringement.[26]

The only obligation to safeguard against abuses of enforcement procedures concerns "compensation for the injury suffered because of such abuse" in the form of indemnification.[27] However, in practice, it is extremely complicated for generic medicine companies to demonstrate the actual economic loss for a product not launched in the market because of such abuse. Nonetheless, the TRIPS Agreement does not contemplate the possibility of considering patent holders liable for the damages caused to the national health-care budgets due to the

20 TRIPS Agreement, *supra* note 1, at art. 27.
21 *Id.* at art. 28.
22 *Id.* at art. 33.
23 *Id.* at art. 32.
24 *Id.* at art. 34.
25 *Id.* at art. 46.
26 *Id.* at art. 45.
27 *Id.* at art. 48.

abuse of enforcement procedures or anticompetitive practices that ultimately delay the entry of generic medicines.

All the other safeguards related to possible anticompetitive practices or abuses of IP are in the form of a permission ("may") rather than an obligation.[28] Even paragraph 4 in the Doha Declaration of 2001 (Doha Declaration) clarifies the role of the TRIPS Agreement in the context of access to medicines, and specifies that the TRIPS flexibilities in paragraph 5 "does not oblige any specific legislative enactment."[29] Indeed, paragraph 4 of the Doha Declaration clarifies that the TRIPS Agreement does not prevent WTO members from acting to protect public health, which also represents a freedom to operate rather than an obligation to do it in determined cases. By providing exclusive private rights for innovative medicines, the TRIPS Agreement entails a limitation of competition in the market, leading to significant impacts on public health. Such impacts are positive, insofar as IPR stimulate investments in innovative medicines, and negative, due to the limitation of competition.

However, the clear direct impact of IP policies on public health shows their delicate nature, which deserves a reflection on the circumstance that the TRIPS Agreement's strong prescriptive IP rules establishing private rights are not counter-balanced by prescriptive competition rules aimed at ensuring the achievement of public economic and health benefits.

Competition has a dual pivotal role: first, when it comes to the enforcement of competition law, and second, in terms of the contribution that competition policies can make in informing IP and public health policies. The role of competition law and enforcement when implementing and enforcing IPR, recognized in the Trilateral Study by the WTO, World Intellectual Property Organization (WIPO), and the World Health Organization (WHO) focused on the intersection between public health, IP, and trade, and acknowledges that "[l]egal provisions on competition can be considered an integral part of rules on IP protection."[30] Indeed, competition law enforcement serves to correct or prevent anticompetitive behaviors that create unnecessary barriers to market entry of

28 For instance, "*[a]ppropriate measures . . . may be needed to prevent the abuse of intellectual property rights by right holders*" (art. 8), "*Members may exclude from patentability inventions*" to protect human health (art. 27); they "*may provide limited exceptions to the exclusive rights conferred by a patent*" (art. 30); in the context of compulsory licenses, "*[t] he need to correct anti-competitive practices may be taken into account in determining the amount of remuneration*" in the context of a compulsory license due to a practice determined judicially to be anti-competitive (art. 31). The control of anti-competitive practices in contractual licenses is also put under an obligation not to prevent, *i.e.*, a freedom to legislate members from specifying in their legislation what practices represent an abuse of IP rights with adverse effects on competition, adding that "*Member may adopt . . . appropriate measures to prevent or control such practices*" (art. 40).

29 World Health Organization et al., Promoting Access to Medical Technologies and Innovation: Intersections Between Public Health, Intellectual Property and Trade 73 (2013).

30 *Id.* at 76.

generic and biosimilar medicines. In different countries and regions, competition authorities have been tackling such behaviors, particularly those that either tend to maximize exclusivities beyond the genuine intention of the law – with anticompetitive effects on the market for potential competitors and reducing access and affordability of medicines – or to abuse the regulatory, pricing, and reimbursement systems to delay generic entry.

However, the role of competition policies – as opposed to the exclusive mere enforcement of competition law dictated by legal positivism – becomes increasingly prominent. The abovementioned Trilateral Study stresses the importance of competition policies "in providing 'checks and balances' to IPRs" and "in designing rules on IP protection."[31] Competition policies become even more vital for the well-functioning of legislative systems with very strong IP standards. It is fair to maintain that the stronger the IP systems, the stronger their competition rules and policies should be. Therefore, competition policies need to carefully consider and act on cases where certain practices, even if allowed by law, result in delaying competition beyond the intention of the legislation. It often happens that the legal use of IP systems can indeed produce anticompetitive effects, which eventually result in an abuse or misuse of the systems. For instance, in the US, past Food and Drug Administration Commissioner Scott Gottlieb was particularly focused on tackling anticompetitive practices deriving from a legal, but still wrongful, use of the system. He strongly underlined the need for "vibrant competition" from biosimilar medicines and commented that "patent thickets that are purely designed to deter the entry of approved biosimilars are spoiling this sort of competition." He also committed to ensuring that Risk Evaluation and Mitigation Strategies safety programs in the US would not be "used to delay competition from entering the market by refusing to sell the samples necessary for developing generic drugs."[32] Similarly, the European Commission in the final report of its pharmaceutical sector inquiry highlighted several practices put in place by patent holders, such as the practice of filing divisional patents to the European Patent Office to "extend the examination period of the patent office, as the examination of divisional applications continues even if the parent application is withdrawn or revoked, which, under certain conditions, can add to the legal uncertainty for generic companies," or again, the "common practice" of patent thickets with the objective to "delay or block the market entry of generic medicines," with the result that "individual medicines are protected by up to nearly 100 product-specific patent families, which can lead to up to 1,300 patents and/or pending patent applications across the [EU] Member States," with "the awareness by patent holders that some of their patents might not be strong." [33]

31 *Id.*

32 *Remarks from FDA Commissioner Scott Gottlieb*, *supra* note 13.

33 European Commission, Pharmaceutical Sector Inquiry: Final Report 2009 201 (2009), http://ec.europa.eu/competition/sectors/pharmaceuticals/inquiry/staff_working_paper_part1.pdf.

The proliferation of patents and the related exclusivity rights translates into a proliferation of litigation, which, according to the European Commission, "can also be an efficient means of creating obstacles for generic companies," and that "originator companies may consider ...[acquiring these patents] not so much on its merits, but rather as a signal to deter generic entrants."[34] All these examples clearly describe a legal but wrongful use of the IP system to achieve anticompetitive objectives. Such use of the IP system surely does not reflect the original intention of the provisions and principles embedded in the TRIPS Agreement and of the WTO member states. In light of the above, it seems clear that a holistic approach is needed while designing policies having an impact on public health – an approach reflecting a fair and fundamental balance between the protection of IP, effective competition, and the impact on health.

A very prominent role is played by the WHO, WTO, and WIPO in their joint work. Their trilateral cooperation, crystallized in a 2012 study, represents the perfect foundation and starting point for a greatly needed interplay between the policy initiatives put forward by the three institutions, which need to converge toward the same economic and societal objectives. Besides the pivotal contribution of the WHO in all the policies with implications on public health, a strong cooperation between the WTO and WIPO is also based on a 1995 Agreement between the two institutions, as well as stated in the preamble of the TRIPS Agreement.[35, 36] According to the above trilateral study, the WIPO has the extremely delicate task and responsibility of educating and providing advice to governments about the application of the TRIPS Agreement as well as its "legal, technical and economic implications."[37] It is therefore vital for the credibility and sustainability of the multilateral system that such trilateral cooperation be increasingly strengthened in the future, in order to allow member states to profit from the transparent policy initiatives that take into consideration not only the protection of IPR but also the strong need to protect and stimulate competition, for "the shared objective of universal coverage and better health outcomes for all."[38]

## Conclusions

The political debate around whether the TRIPS Agreement is suitable for protecting IPR while simultaneously allowing the achievement of public health objectives, including universal access to medicines, remains highly sensitive and delicate.

34 *Id.* at 201.

35 TRIPS Agreement, *supra* note 1.

36 *Id.* at 15 ("*Desiring to establish a mutually supportive relationship between the WTO and the World Intellectual Property Organization (referred to in this Agreement as "WIPO") as well as other relevant international organizations.*").

37 World Health Organization et al., *supra* note 29, at 71.

38 *Id.* at 8.

In an attempt to support national policies incentivizing investments in technological innovation, the TRIPS Agreement focuses on one of the many policy options that are fit for this purpose, namely, the protection and enforcement of IPR, including patent rights. While the TRIPS Agreement contributes to providing incentives to R&D and innovation, it does not include any effective incentive to actually produce pharmaceutical products. On the contrary, extending patent rights and regulatory exclusivities in national legislations does not stimulate pharmaceutical manufacturing in such countries, since the same patents prohibit manufacture of a generic or biosimilar version of a patented product – even if it is not marketed where the patent exists. The lack of local production of quality pharmaceutical products is one of the main causes of limited access to medicines in several less developed countries worldwide. While IPR cannot be considered the only factor contributing to this lacuna, its introduction or extension would certainly not support the creation of local manufacturing industries, and the reliance will always be on imported products.

A mature trade organization like the WTO needs to increasingly focus its efforts in constructive dialogs to stimulate the development of a strong pharmaceutical manufacturing industry throughout its membership by applying its rules, including the TRIPS Agreement, in an equitable way, and by stimulating its members to do the same in bilateral and plurilateral negotiations.

In light of the current political debates in different regions, especially in more developed countries, on ensuring the sustainability of health-care systems and universal access to health care, this seems to be the right moment for a genuine introspection on the objectives of the TRIPS Agreement, its achievements, and its impact on access to medicines. While IP laws in the pharmaceutical sector aim at incentivizing investments in R&D and innovation by providing private exclusive rights that guarantee significant economic returns, the public health objectives that the IP and pharmaceutical policies aim to achieve – including access to medicines – cannot fade into the background, as they are the ultimate purpose of any public policy aiming at producing societal benefits. Therefore, a very careful recalibration should be made among the different IP and related policies, namely, the protection of IPR, the proper functioning of the IP system, and competition laws and policies. While the protection of IPR is detailed in all its granularities in the TRIPS Agreement, the well-functioning of the actual IP systems in letter and spirit remains to be assessed country by country.

The hard task before policy makers is to assess the effective impact of the TRIPS Agreement over the last decades, on creating an important incentive to innovation by assessing, at the same time, the side effects of its system in terms of allowing effective and timely competition of generic and biosimilar medicines in WTO members' territories, as well as universal access to medicines more generally.

In conclusion, the following questions need thorough reflection: how do patent systems work in practice? Can we consider IP systems infallible? Are IP offices' granting procedures fully transparent and predictable? In light of several secondary patents, patent extensions, or SPCs litigated and often invalidated in courts, are these court decisions being monitored carefully? Do patent offices follow the life cycle of the IPR they grant and adjust their practices to the case law? Are there sophisticated systems for competition authorities to properly monitor and counterbalance IPR and their use every time it is necessary? Is the role of competition authorities fully integrated in the policy making process?

By mandating certain IP standards, the TRIPS Agreement presupposes functional and efficient national or regional systems managing the life cycle of IPR, from the transparency of procedures for the granting of patents to smooth non-abusive litigation of such patents; from a strong reflection on court decisions on patents to the subsequent consideration on the part of IP offices of such decisions when granting new patents; from a strong counterbalancing competition law to a broader constant monitoring of the compliance throughout the whole IP cycle with competition law and competition policies, including the cases of legal practices producing nonetheless anticompetitive effects. In fact, legal (mis)uses of IP systems leading to anticompetitive effects are extremely hard to sanction, but extremely detrimental to the public health system, and should constantly be under the scrutiny of competition authorities.

The TRIPS Agreement covers the above elements of a functioning IP system only in part, namely by mandating certain IP standards. However, accompanied by all the other fundamental components described above, these IP standards would become more widely acceptable, sustainable, and fully compatible with all public health priorities. A system establishing carefully designed IP rules cannot disregard how such rules are implemented and applied in daily practice; they should include equally carefully designed effective balancing of competition rules. The more sophisticated an IP system, the greater the need for sophisticated competition rules. This is pivotal for credible patent systems, especially considering the evolution of the pharmaceutical industry and the growth in specialty products that lead to an increasingly higher reliance on secondary patents and ad hoc exclusivities.

In the context of bilateral or plurilateral negotiations for preferential trade agreements, TRIPS standards usually represent a negotiating starting point. Developed countries tend to negotiate and apply political pressure to introduce IP provisions going beyond what is mandated by the TRIPS Agreement, known as TRIPS-plus provisions. In order to produce economic and public health benefits, a carefully recalibrated trade policy should pair provisions regarding IPR with TRIPS-plus competition rules, including, for instance, obligations to implement deterrents to misuses or abuses of IPR that result in delaying entry of generic and biosimilar medicine, or by establishing strengthened cooperation between the competition authorities of the trade partners.

The future sustainability of the WTO system in relation to the TRIPS Agreement will depend on whether WTO members are willing to put concrete political efforts toward a recalibration of IP policies via the inclusion of complementary strong competition rules and oversight. The role of the WHO and a strong focus on competition and timely access to medicines – in the context of the recently started trilateral cooperation between the WIPO, WTO, and WHO – could well become a game changer.

# 4 Free Trade Agreements

## Longer, Further, Deeper Impact on Pharmaceutical Patents

*Bryan Mercurio*

### Introduction

The state of pharmaceutical patents has changed massively since the creation of the World Trade Organization (WTO) and the advent of the Agreement on Trade-Related Aspects of Intellectual Property (TRIPS Agreement) in 1995.[1] As the editors of this volume recognize, the intervening 25 years have seen a slew of fundamental changes, not only in our perceptions of patents and access to medicines as it relates to the TRIPS Agreement, but also in our perceptions of the "international standard" and the obligations imposed by it. While some commentators decried the standards promulgated by the TRIPS Agreement,[2] little did they then realize that the pharmaceutical industry and a select group of powerful countries would push for even higher standards of protection in free trade agreements (FTAs) and other standalone treatises. With the massive success of this push, the 25 years since the TRIPS Agreement has been characterized by a shift towards intellectual property (IP) maximalism seeking longer periods, increased scope, depth, and levels of protection.

In some respects, the change is understandable as developing and bringing to market a successful pharmaceutical product is time-consuming and extraordinarily expensive. With failure rates far exceeding successes – less than 12% of all drugs entering clinical testing obtain marketing approval[3] – and with the nature

1 TRIPS: Agreement on Trade-Related Aspects of Intellectual Property Rights, Apr. 15, 1994, Marrakesh Agreement Establishing the World Trade Organization, Annex 1C, 1869 U.N.T.S. 299, 33 I.L.M. 1197 (1994) [hereinafter TRIPS Agreement].

2 *See* Commission on Intellectual Property Rights, *Integrating Intellectual Property Rights and Development Policy* (2002), http://www.iprcommission.org/graphic/documents/final_report.htm; Peter Drahos, *Developing Countries and International Intellectual Property Standard-Setting*, 5 J. WORLD INTELLECT. PROP. 765 (2002); SUSAN SELL, PRIVATE POWER, PUBLIC LAW: THE GLOBALIZATION OF INTELLECTUAL PROPERTY RIGHTS 121–62 (2003).

3 *See* Joseph A. DiMasi et al., *Innovation in the Pharmaceutical Industry: New Estimates of R&D Costs*, 47 J. HEALTH ECON. 20, 23 (2016) ("The overall probability of clinical success (i.e. the likelihood that a drug that enters clinical testing will eventually be approved) was estimated to be 11.83%. This success rate is substantially lower than the rate of 21.50% estimated for the previous study, but consistent with several recent studies of clinical success rates.").

of the patent application and marketing approval processes (meaning that, on average, 8–12 years of protection will have elapsed before a product even reaches the market),[4] the industry has understandably sought ways to guarantee a minimal period of monopoly sales in order to recoup costs and generate enough profit to encourage further creation of life-enhancing and lifesaving products. The TRIPS Agreement may not be the most efficient or effective framework to generate production of new pharmaceutical products, but it is essentially a closed agreement, and the issue of replacing it with an alternative framework is not on the agenda.[5] Thus, the pharmaceutical industry is left with lobbying governments to promote longer, further, and deeper levels of protection, while governments simultaneously struggle to balance the containment of health costs, reasonable access to medicines, and ever-increasing standards being negotiated into FTAs. There is little empirical data or evidence demonstrating the effects of the higher so-called TRIPS-plus levels of protection on countries, but clearly the costs outweigh the benefits to most recipient countries. What is also clear is that prior to accepting such provisions, most countries do not conduct – or even attempt – to quantify the costs, to tailor the provisions to meet their own needs and priorities, or to add safeguards that could limit the negative health outcomes. Yet there is a growing movement – ironically, primarily from high-income developed country parties – to "pullback" from the maximalist agenda and provide for flexibilities or safeguards into FTAs.

The next section of this chapter highlights the key TRIPS-plus provisions in FTAs negotiated by the United States (US) and European Union (EU) to prove the trend towards longer, further, and deeper pharmaceutical patent protection.[6] More specifically, this chapter primarily uses the texts of the Trans-Pacific Partnership (TPP, the name of the agreement prior to US withdrawal) and the EU–Canada Comprehensive Economic and Trade Agreement (CETA), as these agreements feature the typical provisions negotiated by the branded pharmaceutical industry's two leading proponents. These agreements have been selected as they not only illustrate the trend towards longer, further, and deeper levels of protection but are also the first agreements negotiated by the two trading powers which "pullback" from previous agreements, either through less onerous TRIPS-plus provisions or through inclusion of safeguards. In the interest of brevity, we will provide one example each of the three trends. The last section of this chapter offers concluding analysis.

4 Hiroko Yamane, Interpreting Trips: Globalization of Intellectual Property Rights and Access to Medicines 240 (2011).

5 This was evident by the reception in Geneva to my paper, Bryan Mercurio, *TRIPS and Innovation: A Necessary Reappraisal?* (2014), http://e15initiative.org/publications/trips-patents-and-innovation-a-necessary-reappraisal/.

6 See generally Michael Handler & Bryan Mercurio, *Intellectual Property*, *in* Bilateral and Regional Trade Agreements: Analysis and Commentary 324 (Simon Lester et al. eds., 2nd ed., 2016); see also Bryan Mercurio, Drugs, Patents and Policy: A Contextual Study of Hong Kong (2018).

## TRIPS-plus Provisions in FTAs: Longer, Further, and Deeper

### *Longer Period of Protection*

Given the unique marketing approval process for pharmaceutical products, the effective period of patent protection is not 20 years, but an average of 8–12 years.[7] The simplest method the industry uses to ensure a minimum period of protection for inventions is through patent term extensions. Both the US and EU provide for longer levels of protection than required in the TRIPS Agreement.

Article 33 of the TRIPS Agreement requires patents to be granted for at least 20 years from the date of filing. The TRIPS Agreement does not obligate or prohibit member countries from "compensating" patent holders for "unreasonable" delays in approving a patent. Likewise, the TRIPS Agreement does not obligate or prohibit members from adjusting protection for delays in the registration of a pharmaceutical product. Following the lead of the US, and often negotiating such extensions into FTAs, numerous countries now "compensate" pharmaceutical patent owners for any "unreasonable" delay caused by the patent office in assessing the application for a patent and by the national drug authority in examining an application for marketing approval. The US template in this regard allows patent protection extensions for (a) delay in the issuance of a patent, with the extension period linked to a certain time period following particular dates – i.e. where patent examination extends beyond five or four years from the date of the filing or three or two years after a request for an extension;[8] and (b) unreasonable curtailment of the patent term as a result of the marketing approval process, with the term "unreasonable" always left undefined.[9]

The manifestation of these obligations in domestic law differs between jurisdictions. In 2005, Australia operationalized the law in a fairly typical manner, with patent term extensions of up to five years available for certain patents relating to pharmaceutical substances following the Australia–US FTA; the pharmaceutical substance must be included in the Australian Register of Therapeutic Goods (ARTG), and at least five years must have passed between the date the patent application was filed and the date of first approval of any product

7 DiMasi et al., *supra* note 3, at 24–25.

8 *See, e.g.*, US–Singapore FTA (Article 16.7.7), AUSFTA (Article 17.9.8), US–Chile (Article 17.9.6); US–Morocco FTA (Article 15.9.7), US–Bahrain FTA (Article 14.8.6), and US–Oman FTA (Article 15.8.6(a)) referring to four and two years, respectively, while US–Colombia FTA (Article 16.9.6(b)), US–Peru TPA (Article 16.9.6(b)), and US–Panama TPA (Article 15.9.6(b)) refer to five and three years, respectively. The KORUS FTA (Article 18.8.6(a)) refers to four and three years, respectively.

9 *See, e.g.*, US–Singapore FTA (Article 18.8.4(a)), AUSFTA (Article 17.10.4), US–Chile FTA (Article 17.10.2); US–Morocco FTA (Article 15.10.3), CAFTA–DR–US (Article 15.10.2), US–Bahrain FTA (Article 14.8.6), US–Oman FTA (Article 15.8.6 (a)), and KORUS FTA (Article 18.8.6(b)).

containing the pharmaceutical substance.[10] In order to receive the extension, the patent owner must apply for an extension of term within six months of the grant of the patent, or six months from the first approval date and therefore first inclusion in the ARTG, whichever date is later.[11] The extension that will be granted is the time period from the filing date of the patent to the first regulatory approval date, less five years.[12] The extended term essentially provides the same level of protection to the patent owner as the normal term; however, the following activities do not constitute patent infringement: (a) exploitation of any form of the invention that is not a pharmaceutical substance; and (b) exploitation of pharmaceutical substances for non-therapeutic uses.[13]

The TPP operates along the same lines as the US template. Article 18.46 ("Patent Term Adjustment for Unreasonable Granting Authority Delays") of the TPP not only calls for each party to "make best efforts to process patent applications in an efficient and timely manner, with a view to avoiding unreasonable or unnecessary delays," but requires patent applicants or owners to request adjustment of the patent term as compensation for unreasonable or unnecessary delays by the patent office. Paragraph 4 defines an unreasonable delay as where the issuance of a patent occurs more than five years from the date of filing, or three years after a request for examination of the application has been made, whichever is longer. Like other US agreements, the patent term extension provision contains safeguards which exclude from the relevant timeframe those periods of time that (a) do not occur during the processing or examination of the patent application by the granting authority, (b) are not directly attributable to the granting authority, and (c) are attributable to the patent applicant.

Subsection C of Chapter 18 contains provisions relating solely to pharmaceutical products; Article 18.48 seeks to promote efficient and timely processing of applications for marketing approval and requires parties to establish a system to allow patent applicants to extend the patent term for "unreasonable curtailment of the effective patent term" due to regulatory approval for pharmaceutical products.[14] Like earlier US agreements, the TPP does not define

10 Patents Act 1990 (Cth) § 70(3). The first regulatory approval date is defined in § 70(5).

11 *Id.* § 71(2). This limitation is common among adoptees of patent term extension. For example, in Chile, a patent applicant has up to six months after the patent grants to request patent term adjustment, whereas in Peru, an applicant only has 30 days after the patent grants to request patent term adjustment (although Peru it should be noted that does not allow patent term adjustment for pharmaceutical products or any processes). See Article 51*bis* Chilean Law No. 19.039 on Industrial property (Consolidated Text of Jan. 26, 2007, approved by Decree-Law No. 3), http://www.wipo.int/edocs/lexdocs/laws/en/cl/cl046en.pdf; *The Patent Term Extension (PTE) and Patent Term Adjustment (PTA) in the Peruvian Legal Framework*, Barreda Moller (May 14, 2018), https://www.barreda-moller.com/en/noticia/the-patent-term-extension-pte-and-patent-term-adjustment-pta-in-the-peruvian-legal-framework.

12 *Id.* § 77.

13 *Id.* § 78.

14 Trans-Pacific Partnership, Feb. 4, 2016, art. 18.48(2) [hereinafter TPP].

"unreasonable curtailment" or set out minimum or maximum extension periods for regulatory delays.[15]

Similar to the US, the EU extends the life of patent protection by combining the patent and marketing approval process, without using subjective terms such as "unreasonable curtailment." Instead, the patent term extension is based solely on the time taken from the initial patent application to the obtainment of marketing approval. More specifically, Article 20.27 of the CETA states that each party shall provide a period of *sui generis* protection, i.e. the period which elapsed between the date on which the application for a patent was filed and the date of the first authorization to place the product on the market of that party as a pharmaceutical product, reduced by a period of five years. In essence, the EU approach allows a party to take five years to grant both patent protection and marketing approval for a pharmaceutical, above which the patent term will be effectively extended through a *sui generis* form of protection. Since Canada did not allow for patent term extensions prior to the CETA, the EU relaxed its usual approach of requiring the patent extension for a period of five years in its FTAs; instead, the CETA provides that the duration of the *sui generis* protection may not exceed a period of two to five years, to be established by each party.[16] Canada has opted to provide two-year additional protection, while the EU continues to provide five-year additional protection.[17] In accordance with Article 20.27.7(b), the additional protection can be reduced or withheld if the patent owner's failure to act resulted in "unjustified" delays in the regulatory approval process.

With these examples, it is clear that both the US and EU are attempting to ensure that delays to the patent or marketing approval process do not unreasonably reduce the monopoly sales period for a pharmaceutical product. While the extensions are not inherently unfair and, in many ways, seem reasonable, they do extend beyond what is obligated in the TRIPS Agreement. Adding extra years of protection to a patent may negatively impact public health in developing countries, which rely on the lower prices generated by generic competition to supply their populations with pharmaceutical products.

### *Further Levels of Protection*

FTAs almost always provide for further levels of protection beyond what is required by the TRIPS Agreement. The term "further" refers to provisions covered by or mentioned in the TRIPS Agreement, but where the FTA provides

15 *Id.* at art. 18.48(4) (the text also encourages that parties establish an expedited regulatory review process for pharmaceutical products).

16 EU agreements always provide five years protection. *See, e.g.*, EU–Korea FTA (Article 10.35.2); EU–Singapore FTA (Article 10.31).

17 Certificate of Supplementary Protection Regulations (2017), in conjunction with amendments to the Patent Act, https://laws-lois.justice.gc.ca/eng/regulations/SOR-2017-165/FullText.html.

for either more onerous obligations, or more comprehensive coverage or, alternatively, a reduction in available flexibilities and policy space. One key provision which illustrates further levels of protection utilized by both the US and EU is that of test data protection.

Test data generated by branded pharmaceutical companies is submitted as part of the marketing approval process for a new pharmaceutical product, and also used as evidence of prior marketing approval of the product in another territory. Article 39.3 in the TRIPS Agreement provides for protection against "unfair commercial use" of test data used to obtain marketing approval of pharmaceutical products, yet some countries maintain that the provision requires WTO Members to grant originators of test data with exclusive rights.[18] Instead, most governments and commentators argue that Article 39.3 provides members with considerable leeway in defining "unfair commercial use" and compliance merely involves prohibiting "dishonest" use of test data.[19]

Modern FTAs negotiated by the US and EU go further in seeking to protect the test data separate from – and in addition to – patent protection. Thus, data protection is not an extension of patent rights, but an autonomous right independent of patent rights. Most often, test data protection runs concurrently with and ends before the expiration of patent protection. However, if there is no patent over a pharmaceutical product, the patent gets invalidated, or if the patent term expires prior to the test data protection, the test data protection will still be in force and serve to prevent entry of a competitor product on the market until the period of data protection expires. Test data protection does not prohibit a generic or competitor company from conducting its own tests and generating its own data to use for marketing approval, but it is not attractive as it is expensive, time-consuming, and arguably unethical.[20]

Test data protection in FTAs can take one of two forms: test data exclusivity or market exclusivity. Test data exclusivity prevents the regulatory authority from accepting applications from generic applicants which rely on the test data until the exclusivity period ends, whereas market exclusivity prevents a subsequent generic applicant from relying on the data provided by the original applicant for a given period of time following the first registration. While both preclude the regulatory authority from granting marketing authorization for a set period of time, the latter is a stronger form of protection because it provides an additional period of de facto exclusivity equal to the time it takes the regulatory authority to consider the application and grant marketing approval.

US FTAs generally seek a five-year period of exclusivity for a new pharmaceutical product, in line with Article 18.50 of the TPP. In addition, the TPP requires parties to provide at least three-year marketing exclusivity for a previously

18 *See* MERCURIO, *supra* note 6, at 157.

19 *See* i.e. Carlos Maria Correa, *Unfair Competition Under the TRIPS Agreement: Protection of Data Submitted for the Registration of Pharmaceuticals*, 3 *Chicago J. Int. Law* 1, 69–85 (2002).

20 *Id.* at 159.

approved pharmaceutical product covering a new indication, new formulation, or new method of administration, and at least five-year marketing exclusivity for a party where a new pharmaceutical product contains a chemical entity not previously approved by that party.[21]

Moreover, the TPP contains a safeguard to public health not seen in the previous US FTAs; Article 18.50(3) explicitly provides that notwithstanding the test data protection provisions (as well as biologic protection found in Article 18.51):

> ... a Party may take measures to protect public health in accordance with: (a) the Declaration on TRIPS and Public Health; (b) any waiver of any provision of the TRIPS Agreement granted by WTO Members in accordance with the WTO Agreement to implement the Declaration on TRIPS and Public Health and that is in force between the Parties; or (c) any amendment of the TRIPS Agreement to implement the Declaration on TRIPS and Public Health that enters into force with respect to the Parties.[22]

The CETA is narrower than the TPP in that Article 20.29(1) only requires parties to protect undisclosed test data or other data necessary to determine whether the use of those products is safe and effective when approving the marketing of pharmaceutical products that utilize new chemical entities – as opposed to the broader "new pharmaceutical product" language used in the TPP – where the origination of such data involves considerable effort, "except where the disclosure is necessary to protect the public or unless steps are taken to ensure that the data are protected against unfair commercial use."[23]

In other respects, however, the CETA is more onerous than the TPP. More specifically, Article 20.29(2) provides for test data protection and exclusivity in that third parties (e.g. generic applicants) cannot rely on such data for a period of not less than six years from the date on which the party granted marketing approval to the originator of the data, and parties are prohibited from granting marketing approval to any applicant who relies on such data for a period of not less than eight years from the date on which the party granted marketing approval to the originator of the data.

21 TPP, *supra* note 14, at art. 18.50(2). *See also e.g.* US–Singapore FTA (Article 16.8.1); US–Oman FTA (Article 15.9.1); US–Bahrain FTA (Article 14.9.1), and CAFTA–DR–US (Article 15.10.1). Other US agreements confine data exclusivity protection to pharmaceutical products utilizing new chemical entities. This can be seen in the US–Chile FTA (Article 17.10.1), US–Morocco FTA (Article 15.10.1), and KORUS FTA (Article 18.9.1).

22 *Id.* at art. 18.50(3)(a)–(c).

23 Comprehensive Economic and Trade Agreement, Can.–E.U., Oct. 30, 2016, art. 20.29(1) [hereinafter CETA].

While the CETA does not contain any special provision or additional protection for biologic products, the TPP recognizes that there are additional costs associated with such products[24] and requires effective market protection through test data provisions for a period of at least eight years from the date of first marketing approval of a product that is – or contains – a biologic or, alternatively, parties must "deliver a comparable outcome in the market" through a combination of five years' test data protection and through other measures, in recognition that market circumstances also contribute to effective market protection.[25]

### *Deeper Levels of Protection*

FTAs often provide for deeper levels of protection than required in the TRIPS Agreement; here, deeper is coverage of an issue which is not addressed in the multilateral agreement. The most notable example in relation to pharmaceuticals is patent linkage, which in its purest form links marketing approval with the patent status of a pharmaceutical product.

In most countries, the granting of marketing approval for a pharmaceutical product is based solely on whether the product is safe and effective; its patent status is irrelevant. The patent status is entirely separate from whether a pharmaceutical product is approved for marketing and sale to the public. The separation of patent status and marketing approval is sensible, as the authorities granting patents and those granting marketing approval have very different areas of expertise and competence. Patent examiners assess and grant patents on the basis of whether the pharmaceutical at issue is novel and inventive and otherwise meets the criteria for a grant of patent in that jurisdiction, whereas national drug regulatory authorities simply assess whether the product at issue is safe and effective as a potential medical treatment. Thus, national drug regulatory authorities are not patent enforcers and are not concerned with the patent status of products they assess. Stated more bluntly, even the potential infringement of a patented product by the applicant generic manufacturer is extraneous and immaterial to decisions of domestic regulatory authorities.[26]

24 John A. Vernon et al., *Exploration of Potential Economics of Follow-On Biologics and Implications for Data Exclusivity Periods for Biologics*, 16 BUJ SCI. & TECHNOL. L. 55 (2009) (noting that biologics on average do not recover their R&D costs until 17 years after they begin being marketed and sold).

25 TPP, *supra* note 14, at art. 18.51(1).

26 *See* EUROPEAN COMMISSION, PHARMACEUTICAL SECTOR ENQUIRY: FINAL REPORT 315, ¶ 872 (2009) ("The task of marketing authorization bodies is to verify whether a medicinal product is safe, effective, and of good quality. Their main function is to ensure that the pharmaceutical products reaching the market are not harmful to public health. Other factors, such as the patent status of the product, should therefore not be taken into account when assessing the risk/benefit balance of a medicine.").

Where a patent holder believes its patent is being infringed, it has the responsibility of enforcing its rights by suing the alleged infringer to prevent further sales of the infringing product and recover damages. In some instances, the defendant will then raise a defence by challenging the validity of the patent. Though lengthy and costly, such litigation ensures the validity of a patent before enforcing the rights asserted by the inventor. The procedure is also logical, as IP rights are "private rights;" hence patent owners should be responsible for their enforcement.

Despite its existence in the US prior to the TRIPS Agreement, patent linkage is not mentioned in the agreement, meaning that it is not mandated or prohibited. Several US FTAs introduce provisions which prevent national drug regulatory authorities from granting marketing approval to generic versions of a drug that has been granted a patent in the jurisdiction, without the consent of the patent holder.[27] In this regard, the regulatory authority takes on the additional role as enforcer of a private right – a significant benefit to the patent owner. While patent linkage is technically prohibited in the EU and not negotiated into its agreements,[28] every US FTA contains a version of the TRIPS-plus provision.

Despite being prohibited in the EU, several member states maintain patent linkage. For instance, Hungary requires applicants to compulsorily sign a declaration stating they do not intend to infringe the patent to obtain approval.[29] Other member states only recently abandoned patent linkage.[30] It should also be noted that the EU does not actively seek to prohibit patent linkage in its FTAs. Article 20.28 – the only place where patent linkage is mentioned in the CETA – merely states that "[i]f a Party relies on 'patent linkage' mechanisms... it shall ensure that all litigants are afforded equivalent and effective rights of appeal."[31]

27 Bryan Mercurio, *Patent Linkage Regulations: The Importance of Context and of Balancing Competing Interests*, *in* Contemporary Issues in Pharmaceutical Patent Law: Setting the Framework and Exploring Policy Options 97–122 (Bryan Mercurio & Daria Kim eds., 2017).

28 *See*, European Union: European Parliament Regulation (EC) No. 726/2004 of the European Parliament and of the Council, Mar. 31, 2004, Article 81; *see also*, European Union: European Parliament Directive (EC) No. 2001/83 of the European Parliament and of the Council, Nov. 6, 2001, art. 126.

29 Article 7(3) of Decree 52/2005 of the Ministry of Health.

30 *See, e.g.*, Italy, Slovakia, and Portugal, respectively: Article 68(1bis) of the Code of Industrial Property (*Codice della proprietà industriale*) introduced with Article 38(2) of Law No. D.Lgs. n. 131 of Aug. 13, 2010, and repealed by Article 83(1) of Law No. D.Lgs. n. 1 of Jan. 24, 2012 as converted with amendments into Law No. 27 of Mar. 24, 2012; *Zákon o liekoch a zdravotníckych pomôckach a o zmene a doplnení niektorých zákonov*, Official Journal No. 362/2011, item 117, 3110; Official Journal of Dec. 12, 2011, 1st series No. 236, 5258.

31 CETA, *supra* note 23, at art. 20.28.

In contrast, the US seeks to use FTAs to expand its regime of patent linkage to other nations. Article 18.53 of the TPP provides parties with two options, as given below:

1 If a Party permits, as a condition of approving the marketing of a pharmaceutical product, persons, other than the person originally submitting the safety and efficacy information, to rely on evidence or information concerning the safety and efficacy of a product that was previously approved, such as evidence of prior marketing approval by the Party or in another territory, that Party shall provide:

   a a system to provide notice to a patent holder or to allow for a patent holder to be notified prior to the marketing of such a pharmaceutical product, which such other person is seeking to market that product during the term of an applicable patent claiming the approved product or its approved method of use;
   b adequate time and opportunity for such a patent holder to seek, prior to the marketing of an allegedly infringing product, available remedies in subparagraph (c); and
   c procedures, such as judicial or administrative proceedings, and expeditious remedies, such as preliminary injunctions or equivalent effective provisional measures, for the timely resolution of disputes concerning the validity or infringement of an applicable patent claiming an approved pharmaceutical product or its approved method of use.

2 As an alternative to paragraph 1, a Party shall instead adopt or maintain a system other than judicial proceedings that precludes, based upon patent-related information submitted to the marketing approval authority by a patent holder or the applicant for marketing approval, or based on direct coordination between the marketing approval authority and the patent office, the issuance of marketing approval to any third person seeking to market a pharmaceutical product subject to a patent claiming that product, unless by consent or acquiescence of the patent holder.[32]

Thus, the TPP allows parties to initiate a regime of patent linkage either by (a) requiring notice and adequate opportunity to seek remedies, including injunctive relief, while instituting provisional measures for the determination of validity or infringement of the patent; or (b) establishing the traditional form of patent linkage, whereby a regulatory authority is prohibited from issuing marketing approval to a generic version of the drug while a patent remains in force, except through consent or acquiescence of the patent owner. The option

32 TPP, *supra* note 14, at art. 18.53.

contained in the first paragraph makes the TPP slightly more permissive than the usual US patent linkage provision – which requires both notification and consent before the regulatory authority can grant marketing approval to a pharmaceutical product under patent. For example, the provision contained in Article 16.8.4 of the US–Singapore FTA reads:

b each Party shall make available an extension of the patent term to compensate the patent owner for unreasonable curtailment of the patent term as a result of the marketing approval process; and
c the Party shall not grant marketing approval to any third party prior to the expiration of the patent term, unless by consent or acquiescence of the patent owner.[33]

Again, under the TPP, a party need not adopt a traditional patent linkage model as long as that party requires notice to be given to the patent owner and ensures there is sufficient time and opportunity for a patent owner to seek a preliminary injunction and resolve the patent dispute prior to a generic pharmaceutical product entering the market.

Nevertheless, patent linkage remains a key tool for the branded pharmaceutical industry to delay access to generic drugs. However, in a notable pullback, the TPP provides that the agreement does not impede the rights and flexibilities of parties to take measures which would be consistent with the TRIPS Agreement and the Doha Declaration.[34] This link to the TRIPS Agreement and the Doha Declaration clears up a potential hole in previous US FTAs whereby the patent linkage provision, as well as the test data provision, could have potentially prohibited registration of a pharmaceutical product and impeded parties from issuing a compulsory license.

## Conclusion

This chapter has attempted to briefly track the development of international standards relating to pharmaceutical patents since the advent of the TRIPS Agreement. Far from representing the limits of protection, the TRIPS Agreement has come to be seen merely as a minimum standards agreement which members

33 *See, e.g.*, Article 16.8.4 of the US–Singapore FTA. For identical or similar wording, see AUSFTA (Article 17.10.5), CAFTA–DR–US (Article 15.10.2), and the US–Oman FTA (Article 15.9.4). The US–Morocco FTA contains a similar provision but may go further and limit applications to the regulatory authority during the patent term to those that are consistent with the research and testing exemption (commonly known as a "Bolar" provision) contained earlier in the FTA. On the other hand, the temporary-shift in US policy means that US PTAs with Peru, Colombia, and Panama do not contain the requirement that the country's regulatory agency withhold the approval of a generic drug until it can certify that no patent would be violated if marketing approval were granted for the generic. In the TPP negotiations, the US has reverted to its more traditional position.

34 TPP, *supra* note 14, at art. 18.6.

can alter to raise protection. Not content with doing so domestically, certain members have successfully exported versions of their domestic laws by including them as part of the IP or pharmaceutical chapter of FTAs. For over two decades, standards have risen and converged, with gains in one area being met with requests for still yet longer, further, or deeper levels of protection in the next negotiation. In some ways, this trend continued in the TPP and CETA, two recent negotiations led by the US and EU, respectively. However, these treaties differ from past treaties in one meaningful respect, as they provide for a slight pullback or additional safeguards which balance the interests of users and public interest with the pharmaceutical industry. These pullbacks and safeguards have not received much attention in literature but are important and perhaps harbingers of a larger and more sustained rebalancing in future agreements. Given the progression of FTAs, however, one cannot be too optimistic that the gains made in the TPP and CETA will be repeated, or that the push for longer, further, and deeper levels of protection will abruptly end. On the contrary, one can be certain that the industry will seek greater levels of protection and that some governments will listen, for better or worse.

# 5 From the TPP to USMCA

## A High-Powered Battle over Biologics

*Burcu Kilic*

### Introduction

The Transpacific Partnership Agreement (TPP) – supposed to be President Obama's signature economic project – covered roughly 12 percent of the world's population and 40 percent of the global Gross Domestic Product.[1] This largest global deal of the 21st century was to include various countries spanning different levels of development and social, economic, and political priorities: Australia, Brunei Darussalam, Chile, New Zealand, Peru, Singapore, Vietnam, Japan, Malaysia, Canada, and Mexico.

Pharmaceutical-related patent rules were at the center of TPP negotiations, as they have been for every recent United States (US) trade agreement since the North American Free Trade Agreement (NAFTA). Over the six-plus years of these negotiations, which began in 2009, many draft proposals were leaked. The US championed proposals expanding the scope of pharmaceutical patents, introducing new forms of pharmaceutical monopolies, and lengthening existing market exclusivities, thus impacting pharmaceutical prices and availability of generic medicines. When revealed, many of these proposals faced serious opposition. These extreme demands continue to face deep resistance, while the US continued to recommend the same measures through revised texts and proposals.[2]

The TPP negotiations over biologics were most contentious, and the last remaining potential deal-breakers until negotiations were finalized. The TPP was the first trade agreement to provide mandatory minimum exclusivity for biologics. Yet this provision was opposed by many – including public health advocates, US Congress members (thus contributing to a stalemate over the agreement's ratification), and ironically the pharmaceutical industry – which fiercely criticized the TPP as offering insufficient protection for biologics. President Trump's executive order upon assuming office in 2017 formally ended US participation in the TPP.

1 Brock R. Williams, Cong. Research Serv., R42344, Trans-Pacific Partnership (TPP) Countries: Comparative Trade and Economic Analysis 2 (2013).
2 Burcu Kilic, *Defending the Spirit of the DOHA Declaration in FTAs: Trans-Pacific Partnership and Access to Affordable Medicines*, 12 Loy. U. Chi. Int'l L. Rev. 23 (2014).

Soon after, the US started renegotiating the NAFTA with Canada and Mexico (the US-Mexico-Canada Agreement or USMCA). The TPP faced fierce criticism for its pharma-friendly patent provisions that put the health and well-being of people at risk. Yet the USMCA incorporated almost every TPP pharmaceutical-related patent provision, and even went beyond. A 10-year exclusivity period for biologics proved the US' persistence in standardizing longer exclusivity periods for biologics. However, resistance to the Office of the US Trade Representative (USTR) and wide opposition to pharmaceutical-related patent provisions prevented some harmful rules from being included in the TPP and USMCA.

Through analysis and advocacy, Public Citizen and its partners showcased the implications of the TPP for pharmaceutical access and innovation and helped countries oppose harmful pharmaceutical-related patent provisions. The technical insight and collaborative advocacy work with country partners nourished political resistance in TPP negotiating countries and created long negotiating delays. Conflicts erupting from access to medicines and high drug costs placed the TPP at the epicenter of the US presidential election discussions in 2016.

Trump's withdrawal from the TPP, though costly, was still a victory for the access to medicines supporters. It led to progressive discussions on high drug prices, affordability, and innovation models. More importantly, it started a new advocacy framework for the USMCA, causing a huge pushback to pharma-friendly patent provisions. While many USMCA provisions mirrored the TPP, the final USMCA text reflected a different balance of priorities, becoming the foundation for all future US trade agreements.

## Transpacific Partnership Agreement

The TPP is a "trade" deal, but ironically deals little with trade. Of the TPP's 30 chapters, only 5 address traditional trade issues. The rest focus on a wide variety of regulatory and legal issues – including intellectual property (IP), state-owned enterprises, financial services, e-commerce, investment, labor, pharmaceuticals, and more – that affect millions of people in the Pacific Rim. Significant concerns were raised about both process (secret negotiations with details kept from public view, creating a democratic deficit) and content (leaked chapters confirmed critics' worst fears of a corporate-friendly deal) of the agreement.[3]

The final text was formally published in November 2015 after a tough battle between the US and other TPP countries. Some provisions that most worried critics had been improved after years of negotiations. However, the final

3 Chris McCall, *Trans-Pacific Trade Pact Triggers Fears over Drug Prices*, 385 Lancet 9966 (2015).

TPP text still included provisions ultimately extending monopoly rights and undermining the efforts and commitments that parties had made (and will make) toward affordable health care and medicine, such as stringent patentability requirements.[4] The IP chapter thus remained the most controversial chapter of the TPP. It included far-reaching measures to lengthen, strengthen, and broaden patents and other pharmaceutical monopolies, such as patent provisions aimed to further delay access to generic medicines and to undermine public health flexibilities and safeguards embedded in the World Trade Organization's (WTO) Agreement on Trade-Related Aspects of Intellectual Property Rights (TRIPS Agreement).

The ensuing resistance to the US' proposed measures on patents and exclusivities has continued to endure well past the last round of TPP negotiations. Despite resistance from non-US parties, USTR successfully pressured other countries to accept many harmful rules highlighted by critics after numerous leaks. These rules include the following:

- **Secondary patents** creating new drug monopolies by expanding the scope of patent protection and requiring patents for minor variations on old medicines. The provision provides options for parties to grant patents on "new uses," "new methods," or "new processes" of using a known product. However, in practice, new uses, new methods, or new processes may all refer to second use claims, such as use of a medicine to treat disease Y. Accordingly, a Swiss-type claim[5] (a process *for use* rather than *use*) can satisfy this requirement very easily even though the parties exclude diagnostic, therapeutic, and surgical methods from patentability.[6]
- **Patent term extensions** lengthening drug monopolies by requiring countries to extend patent terms if review at the patent office or regulatory authority exceeds a certain period, even for low-quality patents that should not have been filed or granted.
- **Market exclusivity for small molecule drugs** extending commercial control over regulatory information by providing at least five years of exclusivity for information related to new products and either (a) three years of additional exclusivity for new uses, forms, and methods of using old drugs; or (b) five years of exclusivity for new combination products utilizing old compounds.

4 *WikiLeaks Publication of Complete, Final TPP Intellectual Property Text Confirms Pact Would Raise Costs, Put Medicines Out of Reach*, Public Citizen (Oct. 9, 2015), https://www.citizen.org/pressroom/pressroomredirect.cfm?ID=5662.

5 "The use of compound X for the preparation of a medicament for the treatment of condition Y." This type of claim is commonly referred to as a "Swiss-style" claim. This type of claims was originally approved by the Swiss Patent Office as a mechanism to allow for protection of a new therapeutic use of a known compound (i.e. second or further medical use), given prohibition of claims to methods of medical treatment.

6 Daniel Armstrong, *The Arguments of Law Policy and Practice Against Swiss-Type Patent Claims*, https://www.wgtn.ac.nz/__data/assets/pdf_file/0003/821703/Armstrong.pdf.

- **Patent linkage** facilitating patent abuse by requiring countries to condition marketing approval on patent status. Under patent linkage, even spurious patents may function as barriers, thus delaying generic drug registration.
- **Biologic exclusivity** delaying availability of affordable treatments for cancer and other cutting-edge biologic medicines by requiring at least five years of marketing exclusivity, possibly more if not supported by additional regulatory measures.

### *Organizing for Access at the TPP Negotiations*

The TPP raised the profile of access to medicines advocacy in trade politics. Public Citizen had a major role in exposing various secretive TPP negotiations for civil society groups worldwide. Combining technical expertise with advocacy, it built on its long-standing global relationships and became a primary confidant and source of timely analyses for negotiators, civil society organizations (CSOs), and academics from most negotiating countries.

Throughout the negotiations, Public Citizen experts published analyses drawing on detailed readings of TPP negotiating countries' laws, international rules, and academic literature, and set the standard for technical analyses – also translated in Spanish, Vietnamese, and Chinese – of the TPP IP rules.

Civil society partners, journalists, and negotiators have relied on Public Citizen's up-to-date online library of articles and analyses related to the TPP and access to medicines. In-depth legal knowledge analyses regarding how the US proposals would transform countries' laws (regarding patents, medical test data, and access to medicines) helped formulate coalition strategy on the TPP. The technical insight and collaborative advocacy work with country partners nourished political resistance in TPP negotiating countries.

Access to medicines advocates played a much larger role in CSO opposition than in any prior US-negotiated free trade agreement (FTA); consequently, access concerns benefited from much greater publicity. Indeed, the organized and systematic advocacy led to a wave of media coverage, helping win new unusual allies, and turning the tide of global debate against TRIPS-plus patent rules. Even the Vatican criticized anti-access provisions in trade agreements: "Among the most damaging concessions developing countries make in regional and bilateral agreements are those enhancing the monopolies on life-saving medicines, which reduce access and affordability."[7]

A slew of articles by the Washington Post, New York Times, and others drew critical public attention to the TPP and access to medicines, attention that "injected a moral dimension" into trade talks.[8] The final text of the TPP

7 Russ Britt, *Pope Aide Questions Big Pharma on Availability of Life-Saving Drugs*, MARKETWATCH (Dec. 6, 2013), https://www.marketwatch.com/story/pope-aide-questions-big-pharma-on-availability-of-lifesaving-drugs-1386342795.

8 *With Protections Set to Lapse on Advanced Drugs, U.S. Presses Strict Rules Overseas*, WASHINGTON POST, Mar. 14, 2014.

included major revisions to the original US-proposed terms and a few hard-won flexibilities that allowed TPP countries to retain their existing policy settings and enabled transition periods for developing country members.[9]

The controversy presented by the TPP patent rules was unprecedented, creating new prospects for systematic access to medicines advocacy in future. It led to a consumer movement against biologics exclusivity in US FTAs that could keep prices out of reach worldwide, particularly for developing countries.

## *Biologics Exclusivity – An Overview*

The most contentious battle in the TPP was over biologics. Biologics – also called biotherapeutics or biopharmaceuticals – are medical products consisting of a large complex molecule typically derived from living cells or organisms, which can include therapeutic proteins, DNA vaccines, monoclonal antibodies, and fusion proteins. These molecules – not usually found in allopathic medicines – are typically injected or infused in the bloodstream or on cell surfaces.[10] These characteristics differentiate biologics from traditional small molecule medicines that are typically manufactured through chemical synthesis and have a unique molecule subject to well-established analytical tests.[11]

According to the US Food and Drug Administration (FDA), biologics "may be used to treat a variety of medical conditions for which no other treatments are available."[12] These medicines have provided major advances for treating cancer and autoimmune diseases (including rheumatoid arthritis).[13] Their importance could further increase with technological advances on genes, traits, and proteins. While the generic version of a small molecule drug must be identical to the reference drug and have equivalent therapeutic functions, follow-on biologics are not required to have the same chemical and structural characteristics as their reference biologic product, as long as they achieve an equivalent therapeutic effect.[14]

9 *TPP Transition Periods: Bad Rules Coming Soon in a TPP Country Near You*, Public Citizen (Nov. 16, 2015), https://www.citizen.org/wp-content/uploads/tpp-transition-periods-november.pdf.

10 Thomas Morrow & Linda Hull Felcone, *Defining the Difference: What Makes Biologics Unique*, Biotechnology Healthcare, 28–29 (Sept. 2004), https://www.ncbi.nlm.nih.gov/pmc/articles/PMC3564302/pdf/bh0104024.pdf.

11 *Id.*

12 *See What are "Biologics" Questions and Answers*, U.S. Food and Drug Admin. (Feb. 2, 2018), https://www.fda.gov/about-fda/center-biologics-evaluation-and-research-cber/what-are-biologics-questions-and-answers.

13 Ameet Sarpatwari, et al., *Progress and Hurdles for Follow-on Biologics*, 372 N. Engl. J. Med. 25, 2380–82 (June 18, 2015); *see also* Siba P. Raychaudhuri & Smriti K. Raychaudhuri, *Biologics: Target-Specific Treatment of Systemic and Cutaneous Autoimmune Diseases*, 54 Indian J. Dermatol. 2, 100–09 (2009).

14 John S. MacNeil & Frank Douglas, *Challenges to Establishing a Regulatory Framework for Approving Follow-on Biologics: A Background Paper*, MIT Center for Biological Innovation (Nov. 14, 2007), http://cbi.mit.edu/wp-content/uploads/2011/04/FOB_macneil.pdf.

For this reason, they are not referred to as "generics." In other words, follow-on biologics (also called biosimilars) are therapeutic alternatives to approved biologic products, the data protection of which has expired.[15] Due to the inherent variability of biologic systems and manufacturing processes, biologics display a certain degree of variability (microheterogeneity) even between different batches of the same product.[16] Because of unavoidable differences in the manufacturing process, a biosimilar and its respective originator biologic product will not be entirely identical.[17] In contrast, a generic product can be chemically identical to its reference product.[18]

To encourage biosimilars to enter and compete with pioneer biologics, many countries created regulatory pathways for biosimilars, just as they did earlier for generic medicines. A biosimilar competitor usually introduces its product at a price 10–30 percent lower than the pioneer biologic product's price.[19] The licensing route for biosimilars is based on these principles: (a) biologics are not chemical drugs; (b) the generic approach is unlikely to be applicable to biologics; and (c) biosimilars are similar to the reference product in terms of safety, purity, and potency.[20]

### *Biologics Exclusivity in the US*

Regulatory exclusivity, distinct from patent protection,[21] includes data and market exclusivity and is granted by drug regulatory authorities. The FDA defines exclusivity as "exclusive marketing rights granted by the FDA upon approval of a drug and can run concurrently with a patent or not."[22] In fact, biologics'

15 Martina Weise, et al., *Biosimilars: What Clinicians Should Know*, 120 Blood 26, 5111 (2012).
16 *Id.*
17 *Id.*
18 David M. Dudzinski, *Reflections on Historical, Scientific, and Legal Issues Relevant to Designing Approval Pathways for Generic Versions of Recombinant Protein-Based Therapeutics and Monoclonal Antibodies,* 60 Food & Drug L. J. 143 (2005).
19 *Emerging Health Care Issues: Follow-on Biologic Drug Competition,* Fed. Trade Comm'n (June 2009), https://www.ftc.gov/sites/default/files/documents/reports/emerging-health-care-issues-follow-biologic-drug-competition-federal-trade-commission-report/p083901biologicsreport.pdf [hereinafter *Emerging Health Care Issues*].
20 Lawrence A. Kogan, *The U.S. Biologics Price Competition and Innovation Act of 2009 Triggers Public Debates, Regulatory/Policy Risks, and International Trade Concerns,* 6 Global Trade & Customs J. 513, 519 (2011).
21 *See* John R. Thomas, Cong. Research Serv., R42890, The Role of Patents and Regulatory Exclusivities in Pharmaceutical Innovation (2014) (noting that "patents and regulatory exclusivities are separate entitlements that are administered by different federal administrative agencies and that depend upon distinct criteria…").
22 *Patents and Exclusivity,* FDA/CDER SBIA Chronicles (May 19, 2015), http://www.fda.gov/downloads/Drugs/DevelopmentApprovalProcess/SmallBusinessAssistance/UCM447307.pdf.

exclusivity can be granted even when there is no patent, or after patents have expired.[23]

Recognizing the biologics market's complex nature, the US adopted the Biologics Price Competition and Innovation Act (BPCIA) in 2010 and created an abbreviated approval pathway for biological products demonstrated to be "highly similar" (biosimilars) to or "interchangeable" with FDA-approved biological products. The BPCIA provides brand manufacturers 12 years of exclusivity from the approval date of new biologic products.[24] This provision – providing 12 years of exclusivity – was buried inside the 20,000-page Patient Protection and Affordable Care Act (ACA). A robust debate to fix an appropriate exclusivity period, if any, was overshadowed by other controversial, and better known, aspects of the ACA.[25]

To grant marketing approval for a pharmaceutical product, drug regulatory authorities require pharmaceutical companies to submit data demonstrating the safety, quality, and efficacy of the product. However, regulatory market exclusivity prevents the FDA from approving competitors' applications for entering into the market during a period after the originator drug is licensed.[26] The US included a five-year exclusivity in the Hatch-Waxman Act[27] for new chemical drugs,[28] which established the approval pathway for generic drugs. The BPCIA extended exclusivity to 12 years for new biologic products.

Under the BPCIA, the FDA may not accept an application for a biosimilar product "until four years after the date on which the new biological reference product was first licensed."[29] Meanwhile, the FDA may not approve

23 *See Emerging Health Care Issues, supra* note 19, at vi (noting that "to the extent that there are new biologic molecules that cannot obtain patent protection, an exclusivity period may be warranted."); *see* Henry Grabowski, et al., *Data Exclusivity Periods and Next Generation Improvements to Innovator Biologics: Key Issues*, Duke U. Dept. of Econ. Working Paper, No. 2009–05 (2009) (noting that "data exclusivity provides additional protection to the innovator … to the extent that the patent is circumvented by a biosimilar, or that the remaining patent length is shorter than the data exclusivity period at the time of approval").

24 *See* 42 U.S.C. § 262; *Implementations of the Biologics Price Competition and Innovation Act of 2009*, Fed. Drug Admin (last updated Feb. 2, 2016), http://www.fda.gov/downloads/Drugs/GuidanceComplianceRegulatoryInformation/ucm216146.pdf.

25 Elizabeth Richardson, *Health Policy Brief: Biosimilars*, Health Affairs (Oct. 13, 2013), https://www.healthaffairs.org/do/10.1377/hpb20131010.6409/full/healthpolicybrief_100.pdf.

26 Vincent J. Roth, *Will FDA Data Exclusivity Make Biologic Patents Passe?*, 29 Santa Clara High Technol. L. J. 249 (2012).

27 Drug Price Competition and Patent Term Restoration (Hatch Waxman) Act (Pub. L. 98-417), 98 Stat. 1585 (codified as amended in scattered sections of 15, 21, 35, & 42 U. S. C.).

28 21 C.F.R. § 314.108.

29 42 U.S.C. § 262(k)(7)(B).

the application for the biosimilar product to enter the market "until twelve years after the date on which the reference product was first licensed."[30] Thus, during the first 4 years of the 12-year exclusivity period under the BPCIA, a licensed biologic product is granted both data exclusivity for its application and market exclusivity in relation to biosimilar applicants under the 42 U.S.C. § 262(k) pathway. Following the fourth year, a biosimilar applicant may rely on a reference biologic product's safety and efficacy data to file an application. Placing the biosimilar applicant's product on the market, however, will not be permitted until the reference biologic product's 12-year exclusivity period has elapsed.

### *Biologics Exclusivity in the TPP*

Ever since TPP negotiations began in 2009, pharmaceutical and biotech industries consistently demanded that the special 12-year exclusivity[31] period for biologics in US law be extended to all other countries party to the agreement.[32] USTR added a placeholder biologic exclusivity period (meaning this issue would be revisited later) in its initial TPP proposals.[33] USTR reportedly proposed 12 years of data exclusivity for biologics as part of a non-paper in 2013.[34] The 2014 leak of the IP chapter revealed that negotiators from participant countries disagreed on whether the agreement should contain a 12-, 8-, 5-, or 0-year exclusivity period.[35] Pharmaceutical industry lobbyists insisted that biologics needed 12 years of exclusivity in the TPP to recover investment in research and

30 42 U.S.C. § 262(k)(7)(A).

31 The Affordable Care Act requires 12 years of biologics exclusivity, which is 4 years data and 8 years market exclusivity. But the White House aims to reduce this period to 7 years and has pledged to consumers and federal programs the resultant savings in its recent annual budgets. Burcu Kilic & Peter Maybarduk, *What's New in the TPP Text?*, Public Citizen 10 (Nov. 13, 2013), https://www.citizen.org/wp-content/uploads/migration/whats_new_in_the_wikileaks_tpp_text-1.pdf.

32 *Members of Congress and Governors Backing PhRMA/BIO, Calling for 12 Years Data Protection for Biologic Drugs in TPP*, KEI (Sept. 6, 2012), https://www.keionline.org/21979.

33 *Chapter 18 Intellectual Property: Chapter Summary*, Office of U.S. Trade Rep., https://ustr.gov/sites/default/files/TPP-Chapter-Summary-Intellectual-Property.pdf (last visited Oct. 27, 2019); *supra* note 30 at art. QQ.E.16.

34 *In TPP, U.S. Floats 12-Year Data Period for Biologics, Flexibilities for Developing Countries*, Inside U.S. Trade (Nov. 29, 2013), http://insideepa.com/index.php?option=com_user&view=login &return=aHR0cDovL2luc2lkZWVwYS5jb20vMjAxMzExMjcyNDU0MzA2L1dUTy1EYWlseS1OZXdzL0RhaWx5LU5ld3MvaW4tdHBwLXVzLWZsb2F0cy0xMi15ZWFyLWRhdGEtcGVyaW9kLWZvci1iaW9sb2dpY3MtZmxleGliaWxpdGllcy1mb3ItZGV2ZWxvcGluZy1jb3VudHJpZXMvbWVudS1pZC05NDguaHRtbA.

35 *Updated Trans-Pacific Partnership Agreement (TPP)-The IP Chapter (second publication)*, Wikileaks, https://wikileaks.org/tpp-ip2/ (last visited Nov. 2, 2019).

development (R&D),[36] a perspective shared by few beyond the industry and its backers.[37]

Negotiators from other TPP countries were well aware that exclusivity would mean product monopolies, no generic or biosimilar competition, astronomical medicine prices, and treatment rationing. Among them, only the US was promoting 12 years of exclusivity for biologics. Japan, with the second largest pharmaceutical market in the TPP behind the US, provided eight years of market exclusivity for pharmaceutical products (without distinguishing between small molecule and biologic drugs). Australia, Chile, Malaysia, New Zealand, Peru, Singapore, and Vietnam provided five years of exclusivity. Brunei and Mexico provided no biologics exclusivity.

Eventually the US' proposed 12-year period was overruled and the negotiations centered around either a 5- or 8-year exclusivity period. Japan, often considered the US' prime ally in submitting and promoting pharma-favored provisions, proposed eight years of exclusivity, which became the more likely outcome. Though shorter than USTR's initial outlandish demand, it was not a true compromise. It would still have required major changes to three quarters of the TPP countries' laws; they were strongly opposed to such a change. Eight years of exclusivity was then considered a major victory for the brand-name industry but would be damaging to access to medicines across the region and to the future of medical innovation. Lengthy monopolies for biologics not only delay the entry of competitors with lower priced biosimilars, but also preclude new innovators from arising in a timely manner.[38] Innovation builds on prior knowledge, with progress measured by the next innovation, not the last.[39]

When TPP negotiators and trade ministers gathered in Maui in July 2015 for possibly the 31st round of negotiations, the TPP was close to completion, with only the most contentious issues left but still including biologics. By that time, TPP negotiators had already succeeded in pushing back against some of the most deleterious new rules being advanced by USTR. Yet an eight-year exclusivity period was still being presented as a middle course option. United under the leadership of Australia, a pact including New Zealand, Malaysia, Chile, Peru, and Brunei was formed to oppose this so-called middle course.

36 *See generally The Trans-Pacific Partnership and Innovation in the Bioeconomy: The Need for 12 Years of Data Protection for Biologics*, Bio Tech. Innovation Org., https://www.bio.org/sites/default/files/files/TPP%20White%20Paper%20_2_.pdf (last visited Nov. 5, 2019).

37 Burcu Kilic & Courtney Pine, *Inside Views: Decision Time on Biologics Exclusivity: Eight Years is No Compromise,* Intell. Prop. Watch (July 27, 2015), http://www.ip-watch.org/2015/07/27/decision-time-on-biologics-exclusivity-eight-years-is-no-compromise/.

38 Laurence J. Kotlikoff, *Stimulating Innovation in the Biologics Industry: A Balanced Approach to Marketing Exclusivity* 1, Teva U.S.A. Gov. Affairs (Sept. 2008), http://www.kotlikoff.net/sites/default/files/Kotlikoff_Innovation_in_Biologics21.pdf.

39 *Id.* at 4.

US trade officials found themselves attacked from both sides: the opposition pact led by Australia inside the negotiation room and the access to medicines advocates protesting outside. Hundreds of activists participated in a unified sounding of the *pū* (Hawaiian conch shell), setting a new world record that called for negotiators to "Stand Up Together."[40] The Maui protest was a product of a comprehensive campaign to transform US drug pricing – with grassroots, legislative, and agency components.

US trade officials hoped that the Maui meeting would be the final round, but talks broke down as they failed to resolve one of the only outstanding issues: the length of exclusivity for biologic drugs. Australian trade officials were clear that their negotiating mandate was to secure five years only; the Australian Parliament would strictly reject anything longer.[41] Standing alongside Australia were Chile, Malaysia, New Zealand, Peru, and Brunei, which opposed the industry and asserted they would accept nothing beyond five years.

The USTR initially accepted only eight years but later reconfigured it into five-plus-three years in order to get a deal. This creative proposal reportedly drew on Japanese law, which provided de facto exclusivity to pharmaceutical companies, preventing generic entry even after patent expiration in certain cases.[42]

This proposal would allow some countries to leave their data or marketing exclusivity laws technically intact with a five-year term of protection but allow countries to supplement with a three-year post-marketing surveillance (or pharmacovigilance) term that would also exclude competition. This mix of the US and Japanese systems was just a repackaging of the eight years strictly rejected by many negotiating countries.

The opposing TPP countries continued to insist for five years of exclusivity at the true final round in Atlanta in October 2015. The talks were extended thrice as negotiators struggled to reach a deal on exclusivity periods. As expected, biologics was one of the last issues to be agreed upon when the TPP negotiations concluded in Atlanta.

"Agreed" may be the wrong word, since in the early hours of the final day, the ministers actually agreed to disagree. Their solution was a dual system permitting countries to provide: (a) eight years of market exclusivity counting from the date the biologic is approved in the country concerned,[43] or (b) five years of market exclusivity counting from the date the biologic is approved in the country

40 *Record Breaking TPP Protest in Maui*, Citizen's Trade Campaign (CTC) (July 30, 2015), https://www.citizenstrade.org/ctc/blog/2015/07/30/record-breaking-tpp-protest-in-maui/.

41 Jonathan Weisman, *Patent Protection for Drugs Puts Pressure on U.S. in Trade Talks*, N.Y. Times (July 30, 2015), https://www.nytimes.com/2015/07/31/business/international/pacific-trade-deal-drugs-patent-protection.html.

42 *U.S., TPP Countries Scramble to Find Compromise on Biologics Data Exclusivity*, Inside U.S. Trade (July 31, 2015, 6:07 PM), https://insidetrade.com/daily-news/us-tpp-countries-scramble-find-compromise-biologics-data-exclusivity.

43 Transpacific Partnership Agreement, ch. 18, art. 18.51.1(a), Feb. 4, 2016.

concerned, combined with other measures to deliver a comparable market outcome to that of eight years.[44]

In reality, despite all the formulations and direct requests from President Obama to foreign leaders, the TPP delivered only a baseline of five years exclusivity, and US trade officials were forced to acquiesce. However, the provision recognized that "international and domestic regulation of new pharmaceutical products that are or contain a biologic is in a formative stage and that market circumstances may evolve over time."

Article 18.52: Biologics

1 With regard to protecting new biologics, a Party shall either:

   a with respect to the first marketing approval in a Party of a new pharmaceutical product that is or contains a biologic, provide effective market protection through the implementation of Article 18.50.1 (Protection of Undisclosed Test or Other Data) and Article 18.50.3, mutatis mutandis, for a period of at least eight years from the date of first marketing approval of that product in that Party; or, alternatively,
   b with respect to the first marketing approval in a Party of a new pharmaceutical product that is or contains a biologic, provide effective market protection: (i) through the implementation of Article 18.50.1 (Protection of Undisclosed Test or Other Data) and Article 18.50.3, mutatis mutandis, for a period of at least five years from the date of first marketing approval of that product in that Party.[45]

It required TPP parties to "consult after ten years, or as otherwise decided by the TPP commission, to review the period of exclusivity."[46]

At the closing press conference, Ambassa dor Michael Froman, USTR for the Obama administration, announced the outcome:

> On biologics, as you know, this is one of the most challenging issues in the negotiation. We've worked cooperatively with all of our TPP partners to

44 *Id.* at art. 18.51.1(b).

45 Article 18.52 of the TPP, Consolidated Text, (Oct. 5, 2015), https://wikileaks.org/tpp-ip3/WikiLeaks-TPP-IP-Chapter/WikiLeaks-TPP-IP-Chapter-051015.pdf.

46 "Recognizing that international and domestic regulation of new pharmaceutical products that are or contain a biologic is in a formative stage and that market circumstances may evolve over time, the Parties shall consult after 10 years, or as otherwise decided by the TPP Commission, to review the period of exclusivity provided in paragraph 1 and the scope of application provided in paragraph 2, with a view to providing effective incentives for the development of new pharmaceutical products that are or contain a biologic, as well as with a view to facilitating the timely availability of follow-on biosimilars, and to ensuring that the scope of application remains consistent with international developments regarding approval of additional categories of new pharmaceutical products that are or contain a biologic," article 18.52.3.

> secure a strong and balanced outcome that both incentivizes the development of these new lifesaving drugs, while ensuring access to these pioneering medicines and their availability. And this is the first trade agreement in history to ensure a minimum period of protection for biologics and in doing so will help set a regional model and will create an environment in which, through comparable treatment, there will be an effective period of protection to encourage both innovation and access.[47]

Biologics continued to cause the most conflict after the TPP concluded. The pharmaceutical industry was not happy with the outcome. The Biologics Industry Organization, calling the outcome "short sighted," argued that the TPP outcome may "chill global investment" and slow development of new biologics.[48] Similarly, the Pharmaceutical Research and Manufacturers of America (PhRMA) expressed disappointment, noting that 12 years of exclusivity was "not a random number, but the result of long debate in Congress." Industry officials said they were considering the possibility of opposing the deal outright.[49]

The issue also presented a major sticking point for key members of Congress. Senate Finance Committee Former Chairman Orrin Hatch, a long-standing supporter of a 12-year exclusivity period, emphasized "the TPP is too weak on IP protections particularly for biologics" and said, "the White House may need to renegotiate."[50] Some congressional Democrats raised concerns that the pact would drive up global drug costs and freeze cheaper generic drugs out of the market.[51]

The TPP compromise remained contentious. Although the TPP represented the first trade agreement with a binding provision specific to biologics, the vague wording largely maintained the status quo. It created a constructive ambiguity, leading to an ongoing conflict about the interpretation and implementation of the provision. Several TPP governments declared that the TPP provision did not require them to change their existing systems of five years of biologics

47 *Transcript of the Trans-Pacific Partnership Atlanta Ministerial Closing Press Conference*, Office of U.S. Trade Rep. (Oct. 5, 2015), https://ustr.gov/about-us/policy-offices/press-office/speechestranscripts/2015/october/transcript-trans-pacific.

48 *BIO Statement on Data Exclusivity Provisions Within the Trans-Pacific Partnership*, Biotechnology Innovation Org., https://www.bio.org/media/press-release/bio-statement-data-exclusivity-provisions-within-trans-pacific-partnership#.VhHs80Sv2nM.twitter (last visited Nov. 2, 2019).

49 Jim Zarroli, *TPP Negotiators Reached Agreement with Sticky Compromise on Biologics Drugs*, NPR (Oct. 8, 2015), https://www.npr.org/2015/10/08/446980186/tpp-negotiators-reached-agreement-with-sticky-compromise-on-biologics-drugs.

50 Sarah Karlin-Smith, *How TPP Helps Pharma*, Politico (Nov. 9, 2015), https://www.politico.com/tipsheets/prescription-pulse/2015/11/how-tpp-helps-pharma-211169.

51 Glenn Hess, *Trans-Pacific Trade Pact Faces Rocky Road*, Chem. Eng'g News (Feb. 29, 2016), https://cen.acs.org/articles/94/web/2016/02/Trans-Pacific-trade-pact-faces.html.

exclusivity.[52] While these countries have stated that they would not go beyond their current levels of protection, US officials reassured industry that the TPP "actually puts in place an effective standard of eight years among the TPP-member nations."[53]

The Obama administration submitted the agreement to Congress for an up-or-down vote. Many congressional Democrats pointed to overly generous biologic exclusivity as a main reason to oppose it. They emphasized that if ever the US proposed shortening its exclusivity period below eight years, it could be argued that doing so would be inconsistent with the TPP.[54]

The constructive ambiguity over biologics helped push the TPP into a turbulent election cycle, where it became a symbol of failed globalism and the loss of American jobs overseas caused by decades of bad deals. Upon assuming office, President Trump signed an executive order and formally ended US participation in the agreement. In the face of US withdrawal, the remaining TPP countries (the so-called TPP11) agreed on the outlines of the deal under a new name, the Comprehensive and Progressive Agreement for Trans-Pacific Partnership (CPTPP), and suspended some of the most egregious provisions, including the provision on biologics, until the US rejoins the TPP, should it decide to do so under a new administration.

The suspended controversial provisions from the TPP include:[55]

- Patentable Subject Matter – Article 18.37.2
- Patent Term Adjustment for Unreasonable Granting Authority Delays – Article 18.46
- Patent Term Adjustment for Unreasonable Curtailment – Article 18.48
- Protection of Undisclosed Test or Other Data – Article 18.50
- Biologics – Article 18.51

Without the US in the mix, the CPTPP's IP chapter is simpler but still controversial. It remains to be seen how the suspension of these provisions would be treated if the US does decide to rejoin the TPP.

52 *E.g.,* Australia: http://dfat.gov.au/trade/agreements/tpp/outcomes-documents/Pages/outcomes-biologics.aspx; *Transcript of the Trans-Pacific Partnership Atlanta Ministerial Closing Press Conference,* Office of U.S. Trade Rep. (Oct. 5, 2015), https://ustr.gov/about-us/policy-offices/press-office/speechestranscripts/2015/october/transcript-trans-pacific; *Trans-Pacific Partnership: Intellectual Property,* N.Z. Foreign Aff. & Trade, http://tpp.mfat.govt.nz/assets/docs/TPP_factsheet_Intellectual-Property.PDF; Singapore: https://www.politicopro.com/trade/story/2015/10/pro-trade-tppbiologics-behsudi-059493.

53 *Earnest Defends TPP Biologics Outcome, Rejects Hatch's Call for Renegotiation,* Inside U.S. Trade (Nov. 11, 2015, 12:56 PM), https://t.co/LVDAf7IKEs.

54 H. Comm. on Ways & Means Minority Staff Rep., 114th Cong. TPP Issue Analysis: Access to Medicines (2015).

55 *CPTPP Suspensions Explained,* Australian Government, Dep't Foreign Aff. & Trade, https://dfat.gov.au/trade/agreements/in-force/cptpp/outcomes-documents/Pages/cptpp-suspensions-explained.aspx (last visited Nov. 2, 2019).

## Unites States-Mexico-Canada Agreement

Shortly after withdrawing from the TPP, the Trump administration began to renegotiate the NAFTA. The text of the rebranded NAFTA – the USMCA – was finally released in November 2018, again after many months of secretive negotiations.

Better known as NAFTA 2.0, speculation ran rampant for months about the possible terms of an updated agreement between the three countries under the direction of the Trump administration. The final USMCA was simply an updated version of the nearly quarter decade-old NAFTA, yet with significant and harmful changes to the IP provisions, built on similar concepts promoted in other US trade agreements written since the original NAFTA was first enacted. The final text – closely mimicking the language and structure of the original US-proposed IP language in the TPP – incorporated almost all of the pharma-friendly patent-related provisions, many of which were suspended by the CPTPP countries.

Building on this TPP, NAFTA 2.0 provided 10 years of market exclusivity for biologics, counting from the date the biologic is approved in the country in question. This major change would negatively affect health budgets and access to medicines and further lock down the US into the same policies that contributed to making its medicine prices the world's highest, with even less hope for change. Several pharmaceutical-related patent provisions in NAFTA 2.0 had the potential to keep generics off-market, raise costs for North American countries, and contribute to treatment rationing. In June 2019, more than 100 members of Congress demanded the elimination of 10 years of biologics exclusivity. A letter sent to USTR Robert Lighthizer reads:

> Unless the USMCA text is amended, it would limit Congress's ability to adjust the biologics exclusivity period, instead locking the U.S. into policies that keep cancer and other drug prices high while exporting this model to Mexico, which has no additional exclusivity period for biologics, and to Canada, which has an eight-year period.[56]

In the last few years, high prescription drug prices became a dominant policy issue in the US and a primary concern for the Congress. The role of biologic drugs in rising prescription drug costs raised concerns among lawmakers on both sides of the aisle. In 2018, US spending on biologics totaled $182 billion and is expected to reach $319 billion by 2023.[57] Biosimilar competition can deliver significant discounts not only for the reference product, but for its entire associated product class. By enshrining at least 10 years of exclusivity, USMCA

56 Congress of the United States, to Robert E. Lighthizer, U.S. Trade Representative (July 11, 2019) (on file at https://www.citizen.org/wp-content/uploads/lighthizermeds.pdf).

57 *Global Use of Medicine in 2019 and Outlook to 2023*, IQVIA (Jan. 29, 2019), https://tinyurl.com/yxptt9c9.

undermined the US Congress's ability to reduce the exclusivity period and make biologic drugs more affordable.

The White House budget reports released during the Obama administration repeatedly suggested reducing the window of exclusivity from 12 to 7 years, which would save the federal government $11 billion over the next 10 years.[58] In 2016, a bipartisan group of congressmen sought to expedite the entry of lower cost biosimilar products by reducing the biologics exclusivity period to seven years.[59] In 2019, some members of Congress created legislation to cut the current term of 12 years to 5.[60]

A Federal Trade Commission (FTC) report conducted in 2009 concluded that innovative biologic products should not receive additional market exclusivity beyond the term of their patents, because the potential harm posed by such exclusivity period is that biotechnology companies will "direct scarce [R&D] dollars toward developing low-risk clinical and safety data for drug products with proven mechanisms of action, rather than toward new inventions to address unmet medical needs."[61] The main argument for a biologics exclusivity period of 12 years is "to compensate for the perceived failures of the patent system to reward, protect, and incentivize biologic drug innovation,"[62] according to the report. However, patent protection and market-based pricing are sufficient to incentivize biologic innovation. The FTC report concluded that, even after the entry of biosimilars, biologic drug manufacturers are likely to continue to earn substantial revenues and maintain their first-mover advantages by retaining 70–90 percent of their market share years after biosimilars have entered the market.[63]

Meanwhile, the reduction in spending would transfer savings to healthcare payers, providers, and patients.[64] Some economists called the exclusivity difference "entirely unwarranted and arbitrary."[65] More recently, a study published in *Nature Biotechnology* demonstrated that development times for

58 *See* Office of Mgmt. & Budget, Exec., Office of the President, Budget of the United States of America, Fiscal Year 2016 (2015). For the 2013, 2014, and 2015 budget proposals, see also, *President's Budget,* Office of Mgmt. & Budget, https://www.whitehouse.gov/omb/budget (last visited Nov. 3, 2019).

59 S.3094, 114th Cong. (2016).

60 H.R. Res. 3379, 116th Cong. 2019–2020.

61 Fed. Trade Comm'n, Emerging Health Care Issues: Follow-on Biologic Drug Competition: Federal Trade Commission Report, June 27, 2009.

62 *Id.* at 25.

63 *Id.* at 30.

64 Andrew W. Mulcahy, et al., *The Cost Savings Potential of Biosimilar Drugs in the United States*, Rand Corp. (2014), https://www.rand.org/content/dam/rand/pubs/perspectives/PE100/PE127/RAND_PE127.pdf.

65 Avik Roy, *Prescription Drug Prices: A Key Driver of Health Care Costs, House Committee on Oversight and Reform*, Found. Res. on Equal Opportunity (2019), https://docs.house.gov/meetings/GO/GO00/20190129/108817/HHRG-116-GO00-Wstate-RoyA-20190129.pdf.

biologics are the same – or possibly somewhat shorter – than those for small molecules:

> Although new laws are being considered by policymakers around the world to further expand market exclusivities for biologics, we found no evidence that developing biologic drugs was more time-intensive than developing traditional small-molecule drugs. In addition, biologic drugs appear to be associated with higher probabilities of success during clinical testing and regulatory approval than small molecule drugs. Policymakers should prioritize eliminating barriers to biosimilar competition and continue to monitor the potential impact of varying exclusivity protections on biologic versus small-molecule drug development.[66]

Eventually, the USMCA faced an uphill battle in the US Congress, with many members voicing opposition to the final text and calling for renegotiation of the pharmaceutical-related patent provisions – particularly the biologics exclusivity period – with a view to lowering drug prices. Once again, history repeated itself; biologics exclusivity became a leading issue of contention, an obstacle to bringing the USMCA for a vote. However, this time the Trump administration was willing to scrap pharma-friendly patent provisions, including biologics exclusivity, to win support for the deal from Democrats in Congress.[67]

## Conclusion

Although negotiators from several countries fought valiantly against much worse provisions, enshrining five years of exclusivity into the TPP was a major victory for the pharmaceutical industry. US trade negotiators expended a tremendous amount of national political capital for biologics exclusivity at the expense of other issues. Indeed, the TPP was the first trade agreement that provided mandatory minimum exclusivity for biologics. Yet it was also the first provision the TPP11 parties scrapped following US withdrawal. Even after suspending the most controversial pharmaceutical-related provisions, implementation of the CPTPP will still benefit US pharmaceutical and biotechnology companies in the remaining TPP countries.

The negotiations over biologics exclusivity significantly delayed the conclusion of President Obama's signature 21st-century hallmark global trade deal, leaving the decision in the hands of his successor, who, with a stroke of a pen, delivered on his campaign promise to formally withdraw. Yet US trade negotiators moved quickly to renegotiate the NAFTA (later rebranded as USMCA)

66 Reed F. Beal, et al., *Pre-Market Development Times for Biologic Versus Small-Molecule Drugs*, 37 Nat. Biotechnol. 708 (2019).

67 *Trump Administration Willing to Drop USMCA Pharma Provisions*, Financial Times (Dec. 3, 2019), https://www.ft.com/content/f5448be0-1652-11ea-9ee4-11f260415385.

instead. The USMCA closely tracked the structure and text of the TPP and took a step toward enshrining the long biologics exclusivity under US law here and across the globe. However, that step was not simply a step, but a leap. It created a wide-ranging debate at the US Congress about patents and regulatory exclusivities keeping drug prices artificially high, generic drugs off the market, and skyrocketing drug costs.

The final text of the USMCA approved by the Trump administration and House Democrats struck extended biologic exclusivity from the agreement completely, along with a few other pharma-friendly provisions on patent evergreening, regulatory exclusivity for new indications, and the hard linkage of regulatory approval and patent status.[68] Had those provisions remained, they would have made it more difficult for US lawmakers to legislate drug pricing reform policies.

The TPP started a new era for global access to medicines advocacy. Ten years of biologics exclusivity in the USMCA and its far-reaching implications for US drug pricing policies brought more US health groups into the trade fight. These groups worked together to inform and influence Congress, through office visits and letters, as well as by keeping the profile of the issue high with the public and maintaining pressure on Congress.

Pharmaceutical companies lost another battle on biologics after the TPP and the CPTPP. The USMCA proved that renewed focus on high drug prices in the US will make it difficult for lawmakers to include pharma-related patent provisions without public knowledge. The USMCA amendments were a result of a comprehensive campaign to transform US trade policy with fair trade advocates, access to medicines groups, and grassroots. Each resisted rule or policy inspired more price-lowering generic competition, better access to affordable medicines, and health system efficiency.

This progressive campaign created a new template for US trade deals under the Trump administration. The USMCA template still includes harmful TRIPS-plus provisions, which would delay generic competition and make drugs unaffordable in developing countries.

Trade agreements have a terrible record of promoting the interests of pharmaceutical companies against the ability of people in developing countries to access lifesaving affordable medicines. However, advocacy around drug prices and access to medicines in FTAs continues to inspire thought, action, and results. Fortunately, Public Citizen has a proven excellent record of foiling this aspect of US trade policy.

68 *Protocol of Amendment to the Agreement Between the United States Of America, The United Mexican States, And Canada*, Office of U.S. Trade Rep. (Dec. 10, 2019), https://ustr.gov/sites/default/files/files/agreements/FTA/USMCA/Protocol-of-Amendments-to-the-United-States-Mexico-Canada-Agreement.pdf.

# 6 African Union Continental Free Trade Area

## Opportunities for New Regional Discourse?

*J. Janewa Osei-Tutu*

### Introduction

The African Union (AU) has embarked on the important process of creating intellectual property (IP) law and policy for the African continent. As it stands, it is difficult to decipher a coherent approach to IP for the African continent and little has been written on the subject. However, as this chapter will illustrate, there are some common themes in AU documents that should help shape its Pan-African IP framework.

The AU, comprising fifty-five member states,[1] was officially launched in 2002 as a successor to the Organization of African Unity.[2] The AU was established to create an "integrated, prosperous, and peaceful Africa …."[3] Its fifty-five member states, comprising over one billion people, make up all the countries on the African continent.[4] As a Pan-African organization, the AU creates common policies for increased economic integration of the African continent. The AU's potential role in developing IP policy for Africa is significant. Since most African countries have been identified by the United Nations (UN) as "developing" and "least-developed," human development and human flourishing must be central to any successful Pan-African IP policies.

The AU Agenda 2063 sets out ambitious AU policies in a variety of areas.[5] The Agenda 2063 is described as the "shared framework for inclusive growth

1 *Member States*, African Union, https://au.int/en/member_states/countryprofiles2 (last visited June 11, 2020) ("The AU is made up of 55 Member States which represent all the countries on the African continent. AU Member States are divided into five geographic regions, which were defined by the OAU in 1976 (CM/Res.464QCXVI"). The following list shows "all members states grouped by region, in alphabetical order, and their date of joining the AU or its predecessor the OAU.") *Id.*

2 *About the African Union*, African Union, https://au.int/en/overview (last visited Aug. 22, 2020).

3 *AU in a Nutshell*, African Union, https://au.int/en/au-nutshell (last visited Oct. 23, 2016).

4 *Member States, supra* note 1.

5 *Agenda 2063: The Africa We Want*, African Union, https://au.int/en/agenda2063/overview (last visited June 11, 2020).

and sustainable development for Africa ...."[6] There are various AU documents that present policy statements regarding IP in the AU. In addition, the AU created an IP organization for the African continent and member states negotiated a continental free trade area that will contain IP provisions.

However, the AU has not yet articulated a clear vision of IP for its member states. Ideally, a Pan-African IP policy will account for human rights and promote human development on the African continent, while allowing AU member states sufficient flexibility to accommodate national differences. In particular, the health-related policy space that has been achieved under the international IP framework, as is evident through instruments such as the Doha Declaration on the TRIPS Agreement and Public Health (Doha Declaration),[7] should be preserved and expanded.

The AU has an opportunity to create a framework for Pan-African IP laws and policies that will benefit African nations and their citizens. While laws and standards may be developed in the future through the Protocol to the African Continental Trade Area or as part of the standard-setting work of the Pan-African Intellectual Property Organization (PAIPO), existing international IP obligations will largely shape what the AU and its member states can do legislatively. Due to international obligations, there are constraints in creating African-centered IP laws, but there is some flexibility to tailor IP policies to meet regional and national health and development objectives.[8]

This chapter begins with a brief introduction to existing international IP obligations. It then discusses the AU's IP policies as derived from AU policy statements and language from the statute of the PAIPO. Although the treaty establishing the PAIPO is not yet in force, it gives some indication of the potential AU approaches to IP. Finally, the chapter examines the African Continental Free Trade Area (AfCFTA) and identifies some possibilities for this agreement to create and implement development-oriented IP.

## Existing International IP Obligations

Most nations in the world are members of the World Trade Organization (WTO).[9] This means that, even if a nation is not a WTO member state, it will

6 *Agenda 2063, The Africa We Want, Background Note 01*, 2, African Union Commission (2015), https://au.int/sites/default/files/documents/33126-doc-01_background_note.pdf.

7 World Trade Organization, *Ministerial Declaration of 14 November 2001*, WTO Doc. WT/MIN(01)/DEC/1, 41 ILM 746 (2002) [hereinafter Doha Declaration].

8 Of course, these IP policies cannot run afoul of international obligations.

9 *See Members and Observers*, World Trade Org., https://www.wto.org/english/thewto_e/whatis_e/tif_e/org6_e.htm (last visited June 11, 2020) (detailing how the WTO has a total of 164 member states since July 2016. No additional states have joined since that time).

likely have some trading relationships with WTO member states and have to take the WTO rules into account. Since nearly all AU members are also members of the WTO,[10] any agreement on IP must be consistent with the IP obligations under the WTO. The WTO Agreement on Trade-Related Aspects of Intellectual Property Rights (TRIPS Agreement) creates obligatory minimum standards for IP protection.[11] Thus, the TRIPS Agreement obligations limit what member states can do with their national laws. For example, all WTO members must offer a minimum 20-year term of protection for patents,[12] provide patent protection for all fields of technology, including for pharmaceutical drugs.[13]

Developing and least developing countries were not required to immediately implement the TRIPS Agreement IP standards when the agreement came into force in 1995[14] but were initially given five and ten additional years before they had to revise their national laws to comply.[15] Even with the delayed period for implementation, several commentators observed that the harmonized standards were not appropriate for non-industrialized nations.[16] Indeed, in 2013, the least developed nations sought and obtained an additional delay for the implementation of some of the minimum IP standards under the TRIPS Agreement until July 2021.[17]

10 *Id.* (showing that not all AU member states are WTO member states. For instance, Algeria, Egypt, Ethiopia, Eritrea, Somalia, Sudan, and South Sudan were not WTO members at the time of writing).

11 TRIPS: Agreement on Trade-Related Aspects of Intellectual Property Rights, Apr. 15, 1994, Marrakesh Agreement Establishing the World Trade Organization, Annex 1C, 1869 U.N.T.S. 299, 33 I.L.M. 1197 (1994) [hereinafter TRIPS Agreement].

12 *Id.* at art. 33.

13 *Id.* at art. 27.1.

14 *See Final Act Embodying the Results of the Uruguay Round of Multilateral Trade Negotiations*, Apr. 15, 1994, 1867 U.N.T.S. 14, 33 I.L.M. 1143 (1994) [hereinafter Final Act] at art. 14 (as part of the Marrakesh agreements, the TRIPS Agreement came into force on January 1, 1995).

15 TRIPS Agreement, *supra* note 11, at art. 66.

16 *See* Peter K. Yu, *TRIPS and Its Discontents*, 10 Marquette. Intellect. Prop. L. Rev. 369, 379 (2006) (discussing developing countries dissatisfaction with the WTO and the TRIPS Agreement).

17 Council for Trade-Related Aspects of Intellectual Property Rights, *Extension of the Transition Period Under Article 66.1 for Least Developed Country Members*, WTO Doc. IP/C/64 (June 12, 2013) (The extension did not apply to most-favored nations, or national treatment obligations set out in Articles 3, 4, and 5 of the TRIPS Agreement. As paragraph 3 of the Decision notes, further extensions are possible.). "This Decision is without prejudice to the Decision of the Council for TRIPS of 27 June 2002 on 'Extension of the Transition Period under Article 66.1 of the TRIPS Agreement for Least-Developed Country Members for Certain Obligations with respect to Pharmaceutical Products' (IP/C/25), and to the right of least developed country Members to seek further extensions of the period provided for in paragraph 1 of Article 66 of the Agreement." *Id.*

High standards of IP protection are valuable for industrialized countries that export IP-protected goods to other nations. For example, according to a 2016 United States (US) government report, the US is a top producer of IP goods and its IP exports are valued at several hundred billion dollars.[18] However, at an earlier stage of development, the US and other countries had less stringent IP standards.[19] For many African countries, the internationally mandated IP standards in TRIPS are less beneficial to them because they do not typically produce and export significant amounts of IP-protected goods. For instance, as net consumers rather than producers of patented pharmaceutical goods, high standards of patent protection are often more costly than beneficial for African countries.[20] This is not to say that African nations do not benefit at all from IP. While they may not be strong in patent-related industries, African nations produce significant amounts of cultural works and

18 Justin Antonipillai, et al., *Intellectual Property and the U.S. Economy: 2016 Update*, iii, Econ. & Stats. Admin., U.S. Pat. & Trademark Off. (2016) https://www.uspto.gov/sites/default/files/documents/IPandtheUSEconomySept2016.pdf. This 2016 update is the latest publicly available United States government data and is the same information as cited in the IPEC February 2019 Annual Intellectual Property Report to Congress prepared by the Trump administration. *See also Annual Intellectual Property Report to Congress*, U.S. Intell. Prop. Enforcement Coordinator, (Feb. 2019), https://www.whitehouse.gov/wp-content/uploads/2019/02/IPEC-2018-Annual-Intellectual-Property-Report-to-Congress.pdf.

19 Amaka Vanni, *Patent Games in the Global South: Pharmaceutical Patent Law Making in Brazil, India and Nigeria*, 43–44 (2019) (discussing the hypocrisy of international IP and the TRIPS standards, "TWAIL also highlights the perceived hypocrisy and double standard apparent not only within the TRIPS Agreement but also in the politico-economic pressure that bears on Third World countries in the way they interpret their TRIPS Agreement obligations locally. The fact that many of today's advanced economies did not allow patents on chemical and pharmaceutical substances afforded them the opportunity to develop their pharmaceutical industries via imitation or otherwise. For example, chemical substances remained un-patentable until 1967 in West Germany, 1968 in the Nordic countries, 1976 in Japan, 1978 in Switzerland, and 1992 in Spain. Pharmaceutical products remained un-patentable until 1967 in West Germany and France, 1979 in Italy, and 1992 in Spain, while pharmaceutical products were also un-patentable in Canada into the 1990s. It was only when these countries began to achieve technological breakthroughs that their preference for weak IP laws changed and fueled the calls for a stronger global patent system. In other words, it was only when owners and manufacturers of innovations saw the considerable advantages in IP monopolistic potentials that states increased support for stronger international protection.").

20 *See* Naomi A. Bass, *Implications of the Trips Agreement for Developing Countries: Pharmaceutical Patent Laws in Brazil and South Africa in the 21st Century*, 34 Geo. Wash. Int'l L. Rev. 191, 204–06, 211–15 (2002); Marianne Buckley, *Looking Inward: Regional Parallel Trade as a Means of Bringing Affordable Drugs to Africa*, 41 Seton Hall. L. Rev. 625, 628 (2011); John A. Harrelson, *Trips, Pharmaceutical Patents, and the HIV/AIDS Crisis: Finding the Proper Balance Between Intellectual Property Rights and Compassion*, 7 Widener L. Symp. J. 175, 190 (2001); *See* Ellen T. H'oen, *TRIPS, Pharmaceutical Patents, and Access to Medicines: Seattle, Doha and Beyond*, 3 Chi. J. Int'l L. (2002).

products,[21] which means that copyrights, trademarks, and geographical indications could be beneficial, particularly if African nations export cultural works and products to other nations. Also, from a health perspective, effective trademark enforcement could help stem the trade in dangerous counterfeit medicines, for example.

In sum, the AU member states must comply with TRIPS standards. As briefly discussed, this can have both positive and negative effects. The next section attempts to decipher the AU approach to IP based on its publicly available documents and in light of AU linkages to the Sustainable Development Goals (SDGs) and human rights instruments.

## Ascertaining the Pan-African Approach to Intellectual Property

The AU does not have a specific IP policy for the continent. However, it has created policies that are related to IP, and it has also made statements that give an indication of its potential IP policies. Finally, the statute for the PAIPO is an additional source that can be used to discern the direction the AU might take as it develops its approach to IP for the African continent.

### *The AU Agenda and IP Strategy*

The AU 2063 Agenda has several continental frameworks, including the *Science, Technology and Innovation Strategy for Africa 2024*, the *Boosting Intra-African Trade*, and the *Accelerated Industrial Development for Africa*, among others.[22] The strategy that is most pertinent to its IP policy is the *Science, Technology and Innovation Strategy for Africa* (STISA).[23]

The STISA is part of a broad and ambitious agenda that has innovation and human development as its main goals.[24] It outlines the first ten years of the AU science technology and innovation strategy goals as part of the overall AU

21 *See* Boatema Boateng, *The Hand of the Ancestors: Time, Cultural Production, and Intellectual Property Law*, 47 Law & Soc'y Rev. 943, 943–51 (2013). *See also* Paul Kuruk, *Protecting Folklore Under Modern Intellectual Property Regimes: A Reappraisal of the Tensions between Individual and Communal Rights in Africa and the United States*, 48 Am. Univ. L. Rev. 769, 776–88 (1999); Sean Pager, *Accentuating the Positive: Building Capacity for Creative Industries into the Development Agenda for Global Intellectual Property Law*, 28 Am. Univ. Int'l L. Rev. 223, 263–70 (2012) (discussing copyright laws, infringement and Nigeria's Nollywood).

22 *AU an Overview of Agenda 2063*, 6, https://au.int/sites/default/files/documents/33126-doc-11_an_overview_of_agenda.pdf (last visited June 15, 2020).

23 *Science, Technology and Innovation Strategy for Africa 2024*, African Union Commission, https://au.int/sites/default/files/newsevents/workingdocuments/33178-wd-stisa-english_-_final.pdf [hereinafter STISA].

24 *Id.* at 10.

2063 Agenda.[25] The introductory paragraphs explain the AU Agenda 2063 as "underpinned by science, technology and innovation as multi-function tools and enablers for achieving continental development goals."[26] The AU Commission is responsible for providing policy leadership on the STISA.[27] The STISA envisions that the PAIPO,[28] which still requires additional signatures before it comes into force, would implement IP policy for the AU.[29]

The STISA is based on six priority areas that are relevant to the AU vision for the continent. These priority areas include eradicating hunger, preventing and controlling diseases, and wealth creation.[30] The pillars upon which the AU intends to develop its strategy are, among other things, building and upgrading research infrastructure, promoting innovation and entrepreneurship, and creating an enabling environment.[31] A thoughtful IP strategy will be essential to creating a strong foundation for African innovation and human development. For instance, because food security and prevention and control of diseases are essential to promoting health and well-being on the continent, one would expect the AU IP policy to reflect such considerations. Although the AU member states must maintain IP laws that are TRIPS-consistent, there is sufficient policy space to develop African-oriented policies that align with these AU priority areas.[32]

The STISA document appears to recognize classic Western approaches to IP but also acknowledges African traditional medicinal knowledge.[33] Strengthening IP rights (IPR) is among the "strategic objectives" listed under Section 2.2 of the STISA. Specifically, Section 2.2(d) states as an objective to "[p]rotect knowledge production (including inventions, and indigenous knowledge) by strengthening Intellectual Property... and regulatory regimes at all levels."[34] This is already distinct from the TRIPS Agreement, which makes no reference to traditional knowledge.

25 *Id.* ("STISA-2024 is the first of the ten-year incremental phasing strategies to respond to the demand for science, technology and innovation to impact across critical sectors such as agriculture, energy, environment, health, infrastructure development, mining, security and water among others.").

26 *Id.* at 8.

27 *Id.* at 35 ("The African Union Commission as the AU secretariat shall be responsible for providing political and policy leadership for implementation of this Strategy.").

28 See Section 3(d) for a discussion of the PAIPO.

29 STISA, *supra* note 23, at 36 ("PAIPO is in the process of being established to implement AU policy in the field of Intellectual property. It will ensure dissemination of patent information, provide technical and financial support to invention and innovation and promote protection and exploitation of research results.").

30 *Id.* at 10.

31 *Id.*

32 TRIPS Agreement, *supra* note 11, arts. 1.1, 7, and 8.

33 STISA, *supra* note 23, at 22 (recognizing the need "to promote research, invention and innovation in traditional medicine and strengthening local health ecosystems, taking into account the socio-cultural and environmental situation of the people.").

34 *Id.* at 25.

As it relates to health and IP, the AU may be signaling an intent to create some formal policies relating to the protection of traditional and indigenous knowledge. The World Intellectual Property Organization (WIPO) has been working for several years on a draft treaty to protect traditional knowledge but has yet to conclude any agreement.[35] Continent-wide recognition and protection for traditional knowledge would be an important step in the right direction, and it would not be without precedent. As will be discussed below, there are international agreements and recent trade agreements that recognize traditional knowledge, so regional recognition and protection for traditional knowledge would not be without precedent.[36]

In addition to protecting indigenous medicinal knowledge and cultural IP, African nations would benefit from IP policies that adequately protect IPR without sacrificing public health. Because Africa is not a monolith, the AU policies can be expected to account for differing levels of development and the particular needs of its member states. Of course, the AU policies will ultimately be implemented at a continental level and, most importantly, at the national level.[37] Ideally, this would result in African approaches rather than adopting Western approaches to IP that may not be suitable for the continent and that may not align with the "African shared values"[38] that the AU wishes to advance. Unfortunately, as will be discussed below, the draft PAIPO statute was criticized for doing just that: creating IP policies that make sense for a Western industrialized country but are of little benefit for African nations.[39]

Finally, as African nations work to achieve the Sustainable Development Goals (SDGs), the AU can be creative in ensuring that its IP policies recognize and prioritize human development. This is important because human development objectives, such as improving health outcomes, may be overlooked in international IP disputes to prioritize and to protect IPR.[40] As the next section explains,

35 *See First session of the Intergovernmental Committee on Intellectual Property and Genetic Resources, Traditional Knowledge and Folklore*, WIPO/GRTKF/IC/1, World Intell. Prop. Org. (2001), https://www.wipo.int/meetings/en/details.jsp?meeting_id=4295; *see also Decision of the Report on the Intergovernmental Committee on Intellectual Property and Genetic Resources, Traditional Knowledge and Folklore (IGC)*, World Intell. Prop. Org., https://www.wipo.int/export/sites/www/tk/en/igc/pdf/igc_mandate_2020-2021.pdf (The IGCGRTKF had it mandate renewed for 2020–2021 as negotiations continue).

36 *See* section on The AfCFTA and IP.

37 STISA, *supra* note 23, at 10 ("At the national level, Member States should incorporate this strategy into their National Development Plans. At regional level, Regional Economic Communities (RECs), regional research institutions, networks and partners should leverage the strategy in designing and coordinating initiatives. At continental level, the African Union Commission (AUC), NEPAD Agency and their partners should advocate and create awareness, mobilize necessary institutional, human and financial resources, track progress and monitor implementation.").

38 STISA, *supra* note 23, at 23.

39 *See* section on The Pan-African Intellectual Property Organization, *infra*.

40 *See* J. Janewa Osei-Tutu, *Human Development as a Core Objective of Global Intellectual Property Law*, 105 Ky. L. J. 1 (2016).

the SDGs are integral to the AU Agenda 2063 and should, therefore, be an important part of Pan-African IP policy.

### *The Sustainable Development Goals*

The AU strategy emphasizes sustainable socioeconomic growth, reducing poverty, achieving food security, promoting public health, and protecting the environment.[41] This is a model that envisions innovation and human development occurring together. If this framework is well executed, African countries could develop and implement IP policies that promote human flourishing as an integral part of the innovation model. The SDGs, which the AU links to its strategy, also support a human-centered IP model.

TheUN developed 17 SDGs that member states aim to achieve by the year 2030.[42] The SDGs replace the prior set of goals, the Millennium Development Goals, which were in place from 2000 to 2015.[43] The UN characterizes the SDGs as a "call for action for all countries – poor, rich, middle-income, to promote prosperity while protecting the planet …."[44] As this statement makes clear, sustainable development is essential for all countries.

The seventeen SDGs are (1) end poverty; (2) zero hunger; (3) good health and well-being; (4) quality education; (5) gender equality; (6) clean water and sanitation; (7) affordable and clean energy; (8) decent work and economic growth; (9) industry, innovation, and infrastructure; (10) reduced inequality; (11) sustainable cities; (12) responsible production and consumption; (13) climate action;

41 STISA, *supra* note 23, at 11.

42 Sustainable Development Goals, *17 Goals to Transform Our World*, United Nations Development Programme, https://www.un.org/sustainabledevelopment/ (last visited June 11, 2020) [hereinafter *17 Goals*].

43 Sustainable Development Goals, *Background on the Goals*, United Nations Development Programme, https://www.undp.org/content/undp/en/home/sustainable-development-goals/background.html (last visited June 11, 2020). ("The Sustainable Development Goals (SDGs) were born at the United Nations Conference on Sustainable Development in Rio de Janeiro in 2012. The objective was to produce a set of universal goals that meet the urgent environmental, political and economic challenges facing our world. The SDGs replace the Millennium Development Goals (MDGs), which started a global effort in 2000 to tackle the indignity of poverty. The MDGs established measurable, universally-agreed objectives for tackling extreme poverty and hunger, preventing deadly diseases, and expanding primary education to all children, among other development priorities. For 15 years, the MDGs drove progress in several important areas: reducing income poverty, providing much needed access to water and sanitation, driving down child mortality and drastically improving maternal health. They also kick-started a global movement for free primary education, inspiring countries to invest in their future generations. Most significantly, the MDGs made huge strides in combatting HIV/AIDS and other treatable diseases such as malaria and tuberculosis.").

44 *17 Goals*, *supra* note 42.

(14) life below water; (15) life on land; (16) peace, justice, and strong institutions; and (17) partnerships.[45]

These SDGs cover a wide range of topics and, at a glance, it is apparent that several of the SDGs can be supported by development-oriented IP policies. For example, patent rights may be implicated in the development of environmental technologies, health-related technologies, and medicines, as well as access to food and clean water. Copyrights can facilitate or hinder access to education, and the various forms of IP are relevant to industry, innovation and infrastructure, and wealth generation. These areas are all pertinent to African nations at their varying levels of development.

In its document on linkages with the SDGs, the AU Agenda 2063 maps the 20 AU Agenda goals onto the SDGs to show how they intersect. The AU goals that are most closely related to, or potentially affected by, IPR are AU Goals 1–4, and 16.[46] The AU identifies its Goals 1 through 4 as intersecting with SDGs 1–4, 8, 9, and 11. As it relates to health and well-being, the most pertinent are AU Goal 1 (quality of life), Goal 2 (education), and Goal 3 (health). Also pertinent is the AU Goal 16, which is "African cultural renaissance," and includes traditional cultural heritage, creative arts, and businesses as a priority.[47] In addition, the AU Goal 4, which can impact quality of life but will not be discussed here, is transformed economies.[48] I will focus this discussion on the AU Goals 1, 2, and 3 and the SDGs as they relate to IPR, human development, and health.

The first AU goal is a fairly broad one: "a high standard of living, quality of life and well-being for all citizens."[49] The same is true for the second goal, which is "well-educated citizens and [a] skills revolution underpinned by science, technology and innovation," and the third goal, which is "healthy and well-nourished citizens." These three AU goals – quality of life, education, and health – are interrelated.

As the access to medicines debate illustrates, IPR positively affect human health to the extent patents can incentivize the creation of new medicines that improve or save lives. On the other hand, patents can limit access to lifesaving medicines due to the potential effects on pricing.[50] Traditional

45 Sustainable Development Goals, *About the Sustainable Development Goals*, United Nations Development Programme, https://www.un.org/sustainabledevelopment/sustainable-development-goals/ (last visited June 11, 2020).

46 *Agenda 2063 Linkages with Sustainable Development Goals*, African Union, 1–2, https://www.un.org/en/africa/osaa/pdf/events/20160420/linkagesagenda2063sdg.pdf.

47 *Id.*

48 *Id.*

49 *Id.*

50 Cynthia M. Ho, *Should all Drugs be Patentable? A Comparative Perspective*, 17 Vand. J. Ent. L. 295, 305 (2015) ("Both of the requirements on patentability and disclosure are intended to ensure that the social harm of higher prices is limited to situations where society would most benefit, justifying the burden of a patent.").

medicinal knowledge, which may fall under AU Goal 16, could also be pertinent to improving health outcomes. Protecting effective traditional medicinal practices may also be a way to promote local innovation and reduce reliance on foreign medicines. Encouraging traditional knowledge as a form of localized IP could encourage the use and efficacy of traditional medicinal knowledge.

Education is relevant to health outcomes, and both education and health affect one's well-being.[51] Education improves people's lives by creating opportunities. As it relates to health, education can be essential in reducing and managing noncommunicable diseases, such as diabetes and asthma, as well as limiting the spread of communicable diseases.[52] For instance, the spread of diseases such as Ebola, swine flu, and other viral outbreaks was partially contained by educating the public about prevention.[53]

The AU Goals 1–3 (quality of life, health, and education) align with a number of SDGs. With a view to implementing the SDGs as part of its IP policy, the AU could be expected to emphasize a Pan-African IP policy that prioritizes human development and human flourishing.

As the next section outlines, respect for human rights, which enable human flourishing, is also integral to the broader AU agenda.

### *Human Rights*

The AU issued a statement relating to human rights, describing the advancement of human rights as a "core priority" for the AU.[54] In its statement, the AU

51 *See generally*, Robert A. Hahn & Benedict Truman, *Education Improves Public Health and Promotes Health Equity*, 45 Int'l J. Health Serv. 657–78 (May 19, 2015) ("We argue that education – the product and personal attribute acquired – is both a critical component of a person's health and a contributing cause of other elements of the person's concurrent and future health. Consistent with other definitions of health, a person who lacks basic elements of an education is not fully healthy.").

52 *Noncommunicable Diseases*, World Health Org., https://www.who.int/news-room/fact-sheets/detail/noncommunicable-diseases (last visited June 11, 2020) ("To lessen the impact of NCDs on individuals and society, a comprehensive approach is needed requiring all sectors, including health, finance, transport, education, agriculture, planning and others, to collaborate to reduce the risks associated with NCDs, and promote interventions to prevent and control them.").

53 *More than 300,000 People Reached with Awareness-Raising Campaign to Contain Deadly Ebola Outbreak in DRC*, UNICEF (June 5, 2018), https://www.unicef.org/press-releases/more-300000-people-reached-awareness-raising-campaign-contain-deadly-ebola-outbreak.

54 Addis Ababa, *Statement on the Launch of the Campaign in the Lead-up to the 70th Anniversary of the Universal Declaration of Human Rights*, AU (Dec. 10, 2017), https://au.int/ar/node/33466 ("The advancement of human and people's rights is a core priority of the African Union.").

acknowledges the role of the Universal Declaration of Human Rights (UDHR)[55] in shaping and inspiring the African Charter on Human and Peoples' Rights, which is one of the core African human rights instruments.[56]

The stated importance of human rights to the AU is also reflected in the AU founding instruments.[57] According to the founding documents, the AU aims to promote sustainable development, raise the standard of living, and encourage research in all fields, particularly science and technology. It also seeks to eradicate disease and promote good health on the African continent.[58]

Given the significance of human rights to the AU, it would be logical for human rights to shape the AU's approach to IPR. The AU Commission created a Human Rights Strategy for Africa,[59] which makes no reference to IP. This is not surprising, particularly since human rights and IP are not typically seen as related to one another. Still, scholars have proposed a human rights framework for IP, which can serve as a basis for IP policies that promote human rights.[60]

Importantly, Article 25 of the UDHR recognizes a human right to health, stating in part, "Everyone has the right to a standard of living adequate for the health and well-being of himself and of his family ...."[61] Similar language is found in Article 12 of the International Covenant on Economic Social and Cultural Rights (ICESCR), which recognizes "the right of everyone to the enjoyment of the highest attainable standard of physical and mental health."[62] The right to health includes the right to the prevention and control of diseases and promoting public health.[63] Related to the right to health is the right to food,

55 G.A. Res. 217 (III) A, *Universal Declaration of Human Rights* (Dec. 10, 1948) [hereinafter UDHR], art. 29.

56 *African (Banjul) Charter on Human and Peoples' Rights*, African Commission on Human and Peoples' Rights (June 1, 1981) OAU Doc. CAB/LEG/67/3 rev. 5, 21 I.L.M. 58 [hereinafter Banjul Charter].

57 Constitutive Act of the African Union, Lome, Togo, 11 July 2000 [hereinafter AU Constitution] (The preamble and art. 3(h) refer to the AU determination to "protect human and peoples' rights, consolidate democratic institutions and culture....").

58 *Id.* at arts. 3 (j), (k), (m), and (n).

59 *Human Rights Strategy for Africa*, Department of Political Affairs African Union Commission, https://au.int/sites/default/files/documents/30179-doc-hrsa-final-table_en3.pdf.

60 *See* Laurence R. Helfer, *Toward a Human Rights Framework for Intellectual Property*, 40 U.C. Davis L. Rev. 971 (2007); Peter K. Yu, *Ten Common Questions About Intellectual Property and Human Rights*, 23 Ga. State. Univ. L. Rev. 709 (2007); Audrey R. Chapman, *Approaching Intellectual Property as a Human Right: Obligations Related to ICESCR Article 15(1)(C)*, 35 UNESCO 4 (2001).

61 UDHR, *supra* note 55, at art. 25.

62 G.A. Res. 2200A (XXI), *International Covenant on Economic, Social and Cultural Rights*, at art. 12 (Dec. 16, 1966) [hereinafter ICESCR].

63 *Committee on Economic, Social and Cultural Rights, General Comment 14*, U.N. Doc. E/C.12/2000/4, at art. 16 (Aug. 11, 2000).

because adequate nutrition is a basic requirement for a healthy life.[64] The right to food is found in Article 11 of the ICESCR.[65] Articles 16 and 17 of the African Charter on Human and Peoples' Rights also guarantee the right to health and the right to education.[66] These human rights are relevant to the AU Goals of improving quality of life, health and education, as well as to several SDGs.

### *The Pan-African Intellectual Property Organization*

One of the initiatives of the AU was to adopt an instrument establishing the PAIPO to address IP throughout the African continent. Among other things, the PAIPO shall "harmonize intellectual property standards that reflect the needs of the AU," its member states, and regional organizations.[67] There are currently two regional African IP organizations: the African Regional Intellectual Property Organization and the Organisation Africaine de la Propriété Intellectuelle, which is the French equivalent. These institutions provide IP services and facilitate cooperation among member states.[68] They do not, however, set IP policy for the continent. In this regard, the PAIPO, once it receives the required ratifications, should play a significant role in developing Pan-African IP law and policy for the continent.

The statute creating the PAIPO was adopted by the AU on January 2016.[69] It will enter into force after it has been ratified by fifteen member states.[70] Only six of fifty-five member states have signed the agreement, but none have yet ratified

64 *Id.* at art. 3 ("The right to health is closely related to and dependent upon the realization of other human rights, as contained in the International Bill of Rights, including the rights to food, housing, work, education, human dignity, life, non-discrimination, equality, the prohibition against torture, privacy, access to information, and the freedoms of association, assembly and movement. These and other rights and freedoms address integral components of the right to health.").

65 *See Committee on Economic, Social and Cultural Rights, Twentieth Session, General Comment 12*, U.N. Doc. E/C.12/1999/5, at 3–4 (May 12, 1999) (The right to food includes both the availability of food and economic accessibility of food).

66 Banjul Charter, *supra* note 56.

67 African Union, *Statute of the Pan-African Intellectual Property Organisation*, art. 4 (adopted at Addis Ababa, Ethiopia, Jan. 31, 2016), https://au.int/sites/default/files/treaties/32549-treaty-0053_-_paipo_e.pdf [hereinafter PAIPO Statute]. Article 4 states: "The PAIPO shall harmonize intellectual property standards that reflect the needs of the AU, its member states, RECs; ARIPO and OAPI."

68 *See About ARIPO*, ARIPO, https://www.aripo.org (last visited June 11, 2020) ("The African Regional Intellectual Property Organization (ARIPO) is an inter-governmental organization (IGO) that facilitates cooperation among member states in intellectual property matters, with the objective of pooling financial and human resources, and seeking technological advancement for economic, social, technological, scientific and industrial development."); *See Member States*, AROPO, https://www.aripo.org/member-states/ (last visited June 11, 2020) (ARIPO has 19 Member states, mostly in eastern and southern Africa).

69 PAIPO Statute, *supra* note 67.

70 *Id.* at art. 24.

the PAIPO statute.[71] Interestingly, some African countries, such as Ghana, have signed the PAIPO statute, but other African economic powerhouses, such as Nigeria, South Africa, and Kenya, have not signed the agreement.[72] The most recent signatory was Tunisia on June 19, 2019.[73] Tunisia will host the PAIPO headquarters and Secretariat.[74]

The preamble to the PAIPO statute makes it clear that "development" is one of the priorities of the organization, stating that AU member states are "determined to promote a development-oriented intellectual property system in order to achieve the objectives of the African Union."[75] The preamble also references the WIPO Development Agenda and notes the importance of development and traditional and indigenous knowledge.[76] Article 1 of the PAIPO statute defines IP to include indigenous and traditional knowledge.[77] The PAIPO's stated mandate is to take responsibility for IP and emerging issues related to IP in Africa and to promote "effective use of the intellectual property system as a tool for economic, cultural, social, and technological development."[78] Finally, it is supposed to set standards that reflect the needs of the AU, its member states, and pertinent regional organizations.[79]

Despite its seemingly pro-development mandate, prior iterations of the PAIPO statute were criticized as reflecting the ideals of "true believers of IP-maximalist ideology" with an agenda of expanding IP protection and enforcement.[80] Commentators also observed that the language in the draft PAIPO statute referred to potential benefits of IP protection but made no reference to the need for balance between protection and access and was silent about protecting limitations and exceptions to IP protection.[81]

Some of the criticized provisions, such as Article 5 of the draft PAIPO statute, do not appear in the final version. Article 5 of the draft contained the

71 *See* Addis Ababa, *List of Countries Which Have Signed, Ratified/Acceded to the Statute of the Pan African Intellectual Property Organization (PAIPO)*, African Union, https://au.int/sites/default/files/treaties/32549-sl-STATUTE%20OF%20THE%20PAN%20AFRICAN%20INTELLECTUAL%20PROPERTY%20ORGANIZATION%20%28PAIPO%29%20%281%29.pdf (last visited June 13, 2020).

72 *Id.*

73 *Id.*

74 African Union, *Assembly of the Union, Twenty-Third Ordinary Session* (adopted at Malabo, Equatorial Guinea, 26–27 June, 2014), Assembly/AU, Dec. 522(XIII) *Decision on Pan-African Intellectual Property Organization*, Doc. Ex.CL/839/XXV, https://au.int/en/decisions/decisions-declarations-and-resolution-assembly-union-twenty-third-ordinary-session (last visited June 24, 2020).

75 PAIPO Statute, *supra* note 67, at pmbl.

76 *Id.*

77 *Id.* at art. 1.

78 *Id.* at art. 3.

79 *Id.*

80 Brook Baker, *Intellectual Property Incoherence at the African Union Threatens Access to Medicines*, InfoJustice (Sept. 28, 2012), http://infojustice.org/archives/27392.

81 *Id.*

objectives, which included: "the harmonization of intellectual property systems of its Member States, with particular regard to protection, exploitation, commercialization and enforcement of intellectual property rights ...."[82] It also referred to "activities that strengthen the human, financial and technical capacity of Member States to maximize the benefits of the intellectual property system to improve public health and eradicate the scourge of piracy and counterfeits on the continent ...."[83] This strong language – scourge of piracy – implies that the nonenforcement of IPR on the continent is highly damaging. Yet, the AU member states are not major producers of IP products, which leads one to ask whose interests did the draft PAIPO statute seek to protect?

It is evident from the draft statute that the drafters viewed high levels of IP protection as beneficial for the African continent, and as a tool for economic development.[84] Yet, this is contrary to the views held by many developing country advocates.[85] It is doubtful, for example, that increased IP enforcement to eradicate piracy and counterfeiting should be an African priority. This would be a relevant goal for IP owners, many of whom would be foreign-owned companies, but it is not clear how such language would align with African interests.[86] In light of all the criticism of the TRIPS standards as being inappropriate for developing countries, it is no surprise that the approach in the draft PAIPO statute was met with skepticism.

While the draft Article 5 did not find its way into the final version of the PAIPO statute, it was unfortunately not replaced with any development-oriented "objectives" or any objectives at all. The PAIPO statute does, however, have a "mandate" which, as discussed above, is to "promote the effective use of the intellectual property system as a tool for economic, cultural, social, and technological development."[87]

The absence of stated objectives in the PAIPO statute is a deficiency, particularly since, in the context of the TRIPS Agreement, the stated objectives and principles (found in Articles 7 and 8) have been central to the arguments

82 *Id.*

83 AU/STRC/522, African Union Scientific, Technical and Research Commission, Final Draft Statute of the PAIPO (2012). For a brief discussion of the history behind the draft statute, *see Final Text Agreed for the Creation of a Pan-African Intellectual Property Organization*, Inside Tech Media (Oct. 5, 2012) available at https://www.insidetechmedia.com/2012/10/05/final-text-agreed-for-the-creation-of-pan-african-intellectual-property-organization-paipo/.

84 *Id.* (The preamble states the "[d]etermin[ation] to promote the development of the continent through an effective intellectual property system in order to achieve objectives of the African Union; RECOGNIZING that Intellectual Property rights are tools for economic growth and dissemination of knowledge ....").

85 Baker, *supra* note 80; for a discussion of some of the criticisms of the TRIPS Agreement, *see* Yu, *supra* note 16.

86 Baker, *supra* note 80.

87 PAIPO Statute, *supra* note 67.

for IP policy flexibility for developing countries.[88] By comparison, the IP chapter of the Comprehensive and Progressive Agreement for Trans-Pacific Partnership (CPTPP)[89] reproduces Articles 7 and 8 of the TRIPS Agreement and expressly references the Doha Declaration on the TRIPS Agreement and Public Health.[90]

Article 7, the "objectives" of the TRIPS Agreement, makes clear the need for balance between protecting IPR and providing access, stating:

> The protection and enforcement of intellectual property rights should contribute to the promotion of technological innovation and to the transfer and dissemination of technology, to the mutual advantage of producers and users of technological knowledge and in a manner conducive to social and economic welfare, and to a balance of rights and obligations.

While Article 7 leaves no doubt that IP protection requires a balancing of interests with a view to the public welfare, Article 8(1) of the TRIPS Agreement creates policy space for the purpose of protecting public health and nutrition.[91] This moderating language can make a significant difference in the interpretation of IP obligations. Articles 7 and 8 of the TRIPS Agreement have been central to discussions about the appropriate IP balance for developing countries. For example, these core provisions have been cited repeatedly in academic articles about the effects of harmonized IP standards on access to medicines and education.[92] Many scholars have emphasized the policy space created by Articles 7 and 8 of the TRIPS Agreement, in addition to the exceptions and limitations to IP protection that are available for all forms of IP.[93]

88 *See* Matthew Flynn, *Corporate Power and State Resistance: Brazil's Use of TRIPS Flexibilities for Its National Aids Program, in* INTELLECTUAL PROPERTY, PHARMACEUTICAL AND PUBLIC HEALTH 149 (Kenneth C. Shadlen et al. eds., 2011).

89 *What is the CPTPP?*, INTERNATIONAL, https://www.international.gc.ca/trade-commerce/trade-agreements-accords-commerciaux/agr-acc/cptpp-ptpgp/index.aspx?lang=eng (last visited June 11, 2020) ("The Comprehensive and Progressive Agreement for Trans-Pacific Partnership (CPTPP) is a free trade agreement between Canada and 10 other countries in the Asia-Pacific region.").

90 CPTPP, arts. 18.2 and 18.3.

91 TRIPS Agreement, *supra* note 11, at art. 8 (1) ("Members may, in formulating or amending their laws and regulations, adopt measures necessary to protect public health and nutrition, and to promote the public interest in sectors of vital importance to their socio-economic and technological development, provided that such measures are consistent with the provisions of this Agreement.").

92 *See* Margaret Chon, *Intellectual Property from Below: Copyright and Capability for Education*, 40 U.C. DAVIS. L. REV. 803, 810 (2007) (discussing distributive justice as it relates to the global trading system).

93 *See* Sam Halabi, *International IP Shelters*, 90 TUL. L. REV. 903 (2016).

Similar language is notably absent from the PAIPO statute. Admittedly, the PAIPO statute includes some African innovations, such as defining IP to include indigenous and traditional knowledge systems, and folklore.[94] The PAIPO preamble also speaks to the need to strengthen national capacity and affirms the recommendations of the WIPO Development Agenda.[95] But there is little else in the PAIPO statute that indicates a desire to create IP laws and policies to address some of the concerns that have been expressed by developing countries, including African states, about harmonized IP standards under the TRIPS Agreement. Since the statute authorizes the PAIPO to lead negotiations on international IP issues for Africa and to ensure a common African position, it is troubling that the PAIPO statute says nothing about the need to appropriately calibrate the interests of users and producers of IP.

Regrettably, when it comes to health and IP, the PAIPO statute is also silent about the availability of measures to protect public health and nutrition, such as those found under Article 8 of the TRIPS Agreement.[96] Since it does not create any substantive IP provisions, one would not expect to find extensive details about IP standards in the statute. However, given that the statute characterizes IP policy and law as drivers of growth and an earlier draft described piracy on the continent as a "scourge," it would be appropriate, at a minimum, to reference the need for balance in IP law and policy.

Moreover, as discussed earlier, the PAIPO is supposed to harmonize IP standards with a view to the needs of its member states. The constitutive document is a disappointment in this regard. Fortunately, since there is not yet a Pan-African IP policy, it is still possible for the AU to improve upon what it has done thus far. The AU can advance the goals of African countries by ensuring a balanced system of IP protection that takes into account the human development needs of its member states.

As the Assessing Regional Integration in Africa Report IX notes, the AfCFTA will allow the AU "to advance a continental approach to a balanced IPR system that responds to the aspirations contained in Agenda 2063."[97]

94 PAIPO Statute, *supra* note 67, at pmbl.

95 *See The 45 Adopted Recommendations Under the WIPO Development Agenda*, World Intell. Prop. Org., https://www.wipo.int/ip-development/en/agenda/recommendations.html (last visited Sept. 6, 2020). The *WIPO Development Agenda*, which was created in 2007, contains 45 recommendations relating to IP and development.

96 TRIPS Agreement, *supra* note 11, art. 8 ("Members may, in formulating or amending their laws and regulations, adopt measures necessary to protect public health and nutrition, and to promote the public interest in sectors of vital importance to their socio-economic and technological development, provided that such measures are consistent with the provisions of this Agreement.").

97 U. N. Econ. Commission for Africa et al., *Assessing Regional Integration in Africa, ARIA IX: Next Steps for the Continental Free Trade Area*, at iv (2019), https://www.uneca.org/sites/default/files/PublicationFiles/aria9_report_en_4sept_fin.pdf.

## The African Continental Free Trade Area and IP

In 2012, the AU decided to establish a continental free trade area.[98] In line with that plan, the AU member states concluded the Agreement Establishing the African Continental Free Trade Area (AfCFTA) on March 21, 2018.[99] By May 2019, the AfCFTA had already secured the necessary signatures and ratifications for entry into force. The AfCFTA will cover, among other things, trade in goods, services, investments, and IP.[100]

The AfCFTA does not directly regulate IPR. However, according to Article 4 of the AfCFTA, the member states will cooperate on IP.[101] There is little substance to the provisions of the Agreement, but Article 6 clarifies that IP will be part of the AfCFTA through a Protocol on IP.[102] The Protocols will be an integral part of the Agreement and all members states of the AU will have to comply with the IP provisions of the AfCFTA.[103] This is similar to the requirement for all WTO member states to comply with the TRIPS Agreement.[104] The substantive IP provisions of the AfCFTA will be negotiated in "phase II" negotiations, which take place after the adoption of the agreement and which will be annexed as a Protocol to the AfCFTA.[105] The negotiations on the IP Protocol were anticipated to conclude by December 2020.[106]

Beyond the standards required by the TRIPS Agreement, one can only speculate about the IP obligations that will be created under the AfCFTA because,

98 AU Decision on Boosting Intra-African Trade and Fast Tracking The Continental Free Trade Area, Assembly/AU/Dec.394(XVIII), Doc. EX.CL/700(XX) https://au.int/en/decisions-21; *African Continental Free Trade Area (AfCFTA) Legal Texts and Policy Documents*, TRALAC, https://www.tralac.org/resources/our-resources/6730-continental-free-trade-area-cfta.html (last visited June 11, 2020) ("The 18th Ordinary Session of the Assembly of Heads of State and Government of the African Union, held in Addis Ababa, Ethiopia in January 2012, adopted a decision to establish a Continental Free Trade Area by an indicative date of 2017. This deadline was, however, not met. The Summit also endorsed the Action Plan on Boosting Intra-Africa Trade (BIAT) which identifies seven priority action clusters: trade policy, trade facilitation, productive capacity, trade related infrastructure, trade finance, trade information, and factor market integration.").

99 *African Continental Free Trade Area (AfCFTA) Legal Texts and Policy Documents*, TRALAC, https://www.tralac.org/resources/our-resources/6730-continental-free-trade-area-cfta.html (last visited June 11, 2020).

100 Agreement Establishing the African Continental Free Trade Area, Mar. 21, 2018 [hereinafter "AfCFTA"].

101 *Id.* at art. 4.

102 *Id.* at art. 6.

103 *Id.* at art. 8.

104 Marrakesh Agreement Establishing the World Trade Organization, Apr. 15, 1994, 1867 U.N.T.S. 154, art. II.2 [hereinafter Marrakesh Agreement].

105 AfCFTA, *supra* note 100, at art. 7.

106 Addis Ababa, *Assembly of the Union, Thirty-Third Ordinary Session*, AU Doc. Assembly/AU/Dec.749-795(XXXIII) (Feb. 2020), https://au.int/sites/default/files/decisions/38180-assembly_au_dec_749-795_xxxiii_e.pdf.

at the time of writing, there are no publicly available draft IP provisions. Even without having the IP Protocol in place, there are various AU documents that give some indication of what one might expect from the AfCFTA IP Protocol. The next section elaborates on how the IP Protocol might achieve development-oriented IP within the AfCFTA.

## *Possibilities for Pan-African IP in the AfCFTA*

The forthcoming IP Protocol creates new opportunities for discourse about IP that is tailored to the needs of African countries. The majority of WTO member states are developing countries, many of which are African nations.[107] It is logical for a Pan-African approach to IP to reflect African views on innovation, progress, and development. As this chapter has discussed, the AU policy, as reflected in its publicly available policy documents, emphasizes that development is an integral part of its innovation strategy. The inclusion of an IP Protocol in the AfCFTA could lead to human development-oriented IP that expressly mentions and reinforces respect for human rights.

National and regional approaches to IP obligations can influence the interpretation of international obligations. Article 31 of the Vienna Convention on the Law of Treaties[108] guides treaty interpretation at international law. It states that subsequent agreements and practice are relevant in interpreting international obligations.[109] It is essential, therefore, to have regional expressions of IP law that promote human development and human rights, and that recognize human development-oriented IP as consistent with the objectives of the TRIPS Agreement.[110]

The AfCFTA preamble references, among others, the aspirations of the AU Agenda 2063, the importance of human rights, and the flexibility for member states to "achieve legitimate policy objectives in areas including public health, safety, environment… and cultural diversity."[111] This matters because, under international law, preambular statements serve as important interpretive tools.[112] The terms of a treaty are to be interpreted in their context, of which the preamble is part, and in light of their object and purpose.[113]

107 *Who Are the Developing Countries in the WTO?*, World Trade Org., https://www.wto.org/english/tratop_e/devel_e/d1who_e.htm (last visited Feb. 2020).

108 Vienna Convention on the Law of Treaties, May 23, 1969, 1155 U.N.T.S. 33, art. 31.

109 *Id.*

110 International Law Commission, *Draft Conclusions on Subsequent Agreements and Subsequent Practice in Relation to the Interpretation of Treaties, with Commentaries*, GA Doc. A/73/10 (2018) https://legal.un.org/docs/?path=../ilc/texts/instruments/english/commentaries/1_11_2018.pdf&lang=EF.

111 AfCFTA, *supra* note 100, at pbml.

112 VCLT, arts. 31(1) and (2).

113 *Id.*

With this background and context, a Pan-African approach to IP may seek to emphasize African IP interests and priorities, such as those relating to cultural diversity, access to medicines, and traditional knowledge. In the IP Protocol, the AU could emphasize the importance of IP as it relates to agricultural production, medicines, and health. Of course, the AfCFTA must be consistent with existing international obligations, but there is some policy space to tailor the agreement to the needs of the AU member states. While the IP provisions must be drafted to comply with WTO obligations, they can and should also account for international and regional human rights instruments as well as the UN SDGs. This would reflect the AU's commitment to human rights and human development.[114]

There has been a great deal of discussion about exceptions to IP protection and the related flexibilities under the current international IP system. But rather than accepting a protectionist IP model, one could choose to expressly build human development and human flourishing objectives into the IP framework.[115] Further, to the extent that trade agreements express an understanding of IP's role in society, these regional agreements can contribute to norm-setting for international IP. For example, regional and domestic protections for traditional knowledge and folklore under national IP laws signal a commitment to protecting traditional cultural medicines within the context of an IP regime.[116] Similar to African approaches in other contexts, the AU could take leadership in this area.[117] The AU could also expressly include language within its Pan-African IP policy that signals that human development and human flourishing are explicit objectives of Pan-African IP policy.

The AfCFTA IP Protocol should have language that mirrors the language of the Doha Declaration on the TRIPS Agreement and Public Health (Doha Declaration) to ensure that IPR do not interfere with health-related objectives. The Doha Declaration reinforces policy space to protect public health. The IP Protocol could further emphasize the importance of this policy space. The Doha Declaration has been important in facilitating the ability of WTO members to resist IP enforcement that limits access to medicines. In the seizure of generic drugs in transit, for instance, India referenced the WTO

114 *See* section on Human Rights, *infra*.

115 *See* Osei-Tutu, *supra* note 40.

116 *See*, i.e. The Copyright Act 2005, § 4 (Ghana). (The Ghanaian Copyright Act recognizes a right to folklore, which vests in the President in trust for the people of Ghana. The folklore is protected indefinitely.)

117 For a discussion of Africa's leadership in developing regional standards that may have broader implications for international law, *see* Adulquwi A. Yusuf, ***The Public Law of Africa and International Law: Broadening the Scope of International Rules and Enriching Them for Intra-Africa Purposes***, ***in*** Shielding Humanity: Essays in International Law in Honour of Judge Abdul G. Koroma 513 (C. Jalloh & O. Elias eds., 2015).

Decision[118] to implement a waiver of the TRIPS domestic compulsory licensing provision. That decision arose as a result of the Doha Declaration.[119] India relied, in part, on that WTO decision and the Doha Declaration to buttress its argument that a patent owner cannot interfere with the transit of generic drugs legally manufactured in India.[120]

Additionally, the Comprehensive and Progressive Agreement for Trans-Pacific Partnership (CPTPP), which is a recently concluded agreement that involved both developing and developed countries, serves as an interesting comparison in this regard.[121] This agreement takes a relatively development-friendly approach to IP.[122] The IP chapter of the CPTPP not only reproduces Articles 7 and 8 of the TRIPS Agreement,[123] it also incorporates

118 *Implementation of Paragraph 6 of the Doha Declaration on the TRIPS Agreement and Public Health*, Doc. WT/L/540 and Corr.1 (July 29, 2005), https://docs.wto.org/dol2fe/Pages/FE_Search/FE_S_S009-DP.aspx?language=E&CatalogueIdList=51809,2548,53071,70701&CurrentCatalogueIdIndex=0&FullTextHash=&HasEnglishRecord=True&HasFrenchRecord=True&HasSpanishRecord=True.

119 European Union and a Member State – Seizure of Generic Drugs in Transit, WT/DS408/1/G/L/921/IP/D/28, 3 (May 19, 2010). "Article 28 read together with Article 2 of the TRIPS Agreement, Article 4bis of the Paris Convention, 1967 and the last sentence of paragraph 6(i) of the Decision of the General Council of August 30, 2003 on the Implementation of Paragraph 6 of the Doha Declaration on the TRIPS Agreement and Public Health (the 'August 30, 2003 Decision') because a cumulative reading of these provisions confirms, inter alia, that the rights conferred on the owner of a patent cannot be extended to interfere with the freedom of transit of generic drugs lawfully manufactured within, and exported from, India" *Id.*

120 *Id.* ("India considers further that the measures at issue also have a serious adverse impact on the ability of developing and least-developed country members of the World Trade Organization to protect public health and to provide access to medicines for all. Accordingly, the provisions of the TRIPS Agreement referred to above must be interpreted and implemented in light of the objectives and principles set forth in Articles 7 and 8 of the TRIPS Agreement, the Doha Ministerial Declaration on the TRIPS Agreement and Public Health adopted on 14 November 2001 and in the light of Article 12(1) of the International Covenant on Economic, Social and Cultural Rights, which recognizes the right of all persons to the enjoyment of the highest attainable standard of physical and mental health.").

121 *What is the CPTPP?*, *supra* note 89 ("On December 30, 2018 the CPTPP entered into force among the first six countries to ratify the agreement – Canada, Australia, Japan, Mexico, New Zealand, and Singapore. On January 14, 2019, the CPTPP entered into force for Vietnam.").

122 Heng Wang, *The Future of Deep Free Trade Agreements: The Convergence of TPP (and CPTPP) and CETA?*, 53 J. World Trade 317, 317–42 (2019) (comparing the CPTPP to the EU-Canada Comprehensive Economic Trade Agreement and "TPP entails a number of new and interesting formulations on protecting traditional knowledge, or the need to find an appropriate balance in IPs, which CETA does not address as a pact among industrialized countries.").

123 CPTPP, arts. 18.2 and 18.3.

the Doha Declaration.[124] The CPTPP clearly states that "the obligations of this Chapter do not and should not prevent a party from taking measures to prevent public health."[125] Further, Article 18.6(1)(b) explicitly references the parties' commitment to access to medicines, the Doha Declaration, and WTO decisions aimed at protecting the public health.[126] The CPTPP describes this as the "TRIPS/health solution."[127]

It would be helpful to include a similar provision in the AfCFTA IP Protocol. This kind of provision emphasizes the need for IP laws to promote public health and human development and underscores the importance of protecting public health. Such a provision does not automatically lead to reduced IP standards but focuses on the use of IP to improve human lives. Although much of the access to medicines discussion centers on the way patent rights can increase costs or limit access, it is also possible to recognize that patent rights may create incentives for health-related innovations that are relevant to the African continent. In addition, trademarks can be used as a tool to help promote authentic medicines in the marketplace.

Another pertinent area is traditional medicinal knowledge. Protection for traditional knowledge and cultural expressions have been important for African countries and can be an integral part of their development agendas. If the IP Protocol addresses traditional knowledge, it will not be the first multilateral agreement to do so. In Article 8(j), the Convention on Biological Diversity recognizes traditional knowledge by referencing the need to "preserve knowledge, innovations, and practices of indigenous and local communities" that embody traditional lifestyles and promote biological diversity.[128] The CPTPP IP chapter, though it creates no firm obligations in the area of traditional knowledge, recognizes its relevance to IP systems.[129] Given that African countries are among the demandeurs for traditional knowledge protection, the AfCFTA could reflect

124 *Id.* at art. 18.6.

125 *Id.* at art. 18.6(1)(a).

126 *Id.* at art. 18.6(1)(b) ("In recognition of the commitment to access to medicines that are supplied in accordance with the Decision of the WTO General Council of August 30, 2003 on the *Implementation of Paragraph Six of the Doha Declaration on the TRIPS Agreement and Public Health* (WT/L/540) and the WTO General Council Chairman's Statement Accompanying the Decision (JOB(03)/177, WT/GC/M/82), as well as the Decision of the WTO General Council of December 6, 2005 on the *Amendment of the TRIPS Agreement*, (WT/L/641) and the WTO General Council Chairperson's Statement Accompanying the Decision (JOB(05)/319 and Corr. 1, WT/GC/M/100) (collectively, the 'TRIPS/health solution'), this chapter does not and should not prevent the effective utilisation of the TRIPS/health solution.").

127 *Id.*

128 Convention on Biological Diversity, art. 8(j), UN (1992), https://www.cbd.int/doc/legal/cbd-en.pdf.

129 CPTPP, art. 18.16.

African interests by including provisions relating to the protection of traditional and indigenous knowledge.[130]

## Conclusion

As this chapter has outlined, there are reasons to expect that the AU will create an African-centered IP policy for Africa. An effective Pan-African IP policy will, in light of the AU Agenda 2063, recognize the need to protect public health and promote human development and human flourishing while encouraging innovation. Such goals should be an integral part of a Pan-African framework for IP that seeks to meet the needs of the ordinary citizen. While it is somewhat challenging to discern the direction the AU will take, this chapter has discussed the AU policies that suggest that human development, human flourishing, and human rights should influence the AU approach to IP.

Indeed, the language and history of the PAIPO statute might be an indication that the AU approach to IP could be inconsistent with its stated goals for the continent. If the AU chooses to adopt protectionist approaches to IP, which are more suitable to IP-producing industrialized countries, it may find that its IP policies conflict with its overarching commitments to human rights, development, and shared African values.

It will be critical, as a starting point, to recognize that IP laws and policies have implications for human rights and human development on the African continent, as in all nations. The AU decisions regarding its IP policies will influence the direction of IP for the African continent. In implementing its Agenda 2063 and developing the AfCFTA IP Protocol, the AU has a terrific opportunity to create human-centered IP policies for Africa.

130 Sri Ragavan, *Protection of Traditional Knowledge*, 2 Minn. Intell. Prop. L. Rev. 1, 10 (2001) ("Several incidents have occurred which developing countries describe as unauthorized appropriation of their knowledge. These countries find this appalling, especially since most of such indigenous people are living in conditions devoid of human rights, which the UN Charter regards as a condition for living with human dignity. These incidents are often viewed in the developing counties as instances where third parties steal information to expand their own industries and increase profit margins. That the developed nations are aware that if the holders were given even a portion of the profits, it would greatly improve their living conditions, only enhances the feelings of bitterness. This has led the indigenous people to organize themselves to protect their knowledge and resources by various means.").

# 7 US-Litigated Government-Funded Patents in Europe and Japan

## A First Look

*Teo Firpo and Michael S. Mireles**

## Introduction

The Bayh-Dole Act (Act), a landmark piece of legislation passed in the early 1980s[1] credited for invigorating the United States (US) economy during relative economic stagnation, may indeed have supported the development and growth of the biotechnology industry in the US, and for developing many health-related discoveries. The Act allows entities, including universities and nonprofits,[2] to own government-funded invention. Some opine that the Act has led to universities and other nonprofits significantly increasing their patenting and licensing activity.[3] In a thought-provoking paper, Professors Daniel Hemel and Lisa Ouellette propose a potential justification – although incomplete – for the Act, stating that patenting by recipients of government-funded inventions allows the US to internalize the benefits of such inventions.[4] They note, however, that a potential problem occurs when US government funding recipients choose not to patent in other countries. This essentially results in the US funding invention being free for use in other countries – meaning subsidized by the US. Presumably, in countries where they are not patented, these inventions will cost less. Professors Hemel and Ouellette also reviewed whether entities receiving government funding are patenting outside the US.[5]

In a prior paper, we explored the characteristics of litigated university and nonprofit patents covered in the Stanford Non-Practicing Entity Database (Stanford Database). The Stanford Database includes patents that have been

* This paper is partly based on our previously published paper, *see* Teo Firpo & Michael S. Mireles, ***Monitoring Behavior: Universities, Nonprofits, Patenting and Litigation***, 71 SMU Law Rev. 505 (2018).

1 University and Small Business Patent Procedures (Bayh-Dole) Act of 1980, Pub. L. No. 96-517, 94 Stat. 3015 (codified as amended at 35 U.S.C. §§ 200–11 (2000)).

2 Most universities are also nonprofits. For purposes of this chapter, the term "nonprofits" is used to describe nonuniversity and nonuniversity-related nonprofits.

3 *See* Firpo & Mireles, *supra* note *, at 530–31.

4 *See* Daniel J. Hemel & Lisa Larrimore Ouellette, *Bayh-Dole Beyond Borders*, 4 J. L. & Biosci. 282 (2017).

5 *See generally*, *Id.*

litigated – meaning where an actual patent litigation has been filed. This chapter extends the research by examining whether those litigated US patents are also covered by patents in the European Union (EU) and Japan. Examining the litigated patented inventions gives insight into the value of any contribution made to other countries. That the patents are litigated may indicate that they are relatively valuable. Moreover, this chapter examines whether the holders of these patents continue to pay maintenance fees to retain their patent rights, or allow their patent rights to essentially lapse.[6] The chapter also identifies the technical areas for litigated patents that are also part of a patent family extending to the EU and Japan. Notably, a significant number of litigated US patents which are part of patent families in the EU or Japan concern – or are related to – medical or pharmaceutical patents. Professor Hemel and Ouellette's paper suggests that patents in those technological fields are patented in the EU or Japan at a relatively higher rate than other US patents.

The first part of this chapter is the introduction. The second part provides an overview of the Act and its impact. The third part discusses Professor Hemel and Ouelette's theory and findings concerning patenting activity outside the US. The fourth part reviews the Stanford Database. The fifth part analyzes US patents litigated by universities and other nonprofits, and whether those patents are part of patent families in the EU and Japan. The last part offers a brief conclusion.

## Overview of the Bayh-Dole Act and Its Impact

The Act was principally designed to provide a solution to underuse of government-funded inventions.[7] Basically, many government-funded inventions were not commercialized prior to passage of the Act.[8] Some opined this was due to many different regulatory approaches for ownership of government-funded inventions.[9] Under the Act, which essentially harmonized the federal government's approach to ownership of government-funded inventions,[10] recipients of government-funded inventions are allowed to take title to – or ownership of – those inventions.[11] Thus, the government funds the invention and allows the recipient of the funding to obtain a patent, allowing it to charge a supra-competitive

6 The patents may also have been invalidated.

7 *See* Rebecca S. Eisenberg, *Public Research and Private Development: Patents and Technology Transfer in Government-Sponsored Research*, 82 Va. L. Rev. 1663, 1669–70 (1996).

8 *Id.*

9 *Id.*; Council on Governmental Relations, *University Technology Transfer: Questions and Answers* 1 (1996).

10 *See* Council on Governmental Relations, *supra* note 9.

11 *See* Michael S. Mireles, *States as Innovation System Laboratories: California, Patents and Stem Cell Technology*, 28 Cardozo L. Rev. 1133, 1141 (2006) [hereinafter Mireles, *States as Innovation Systems Laboratories*].

price to consumers.[12] The Act ensures that public interest is protected through various procedures. For example, the government retains a nonexclusive license to the invention[13] and march-in rights.[14] However, to date, march-in rights have not been exercised.[15] Also, most funding derived from the Act is supposed to be reinvested for research purposes.[16] Thus, it is supposed to create a virtuous circle of public investment of resources to invent and commercialize inventions, which should create funding for more research.

The Act further provides an incentive structure for recipients of public funding to create a system for the development and commercialization of government-funded inventions.[17] For example, allowance of ownership and the ability to secure funding from potential exploitation of the invention provide an incentive for grant recipients to create systems for disclosure of patentable inventions, administrative mechanisms to review potential patentable inventions, and to seek out commercialization partners.[18] Entitlement to royalties incentivizes researchers to participate in invention and commercialization activities necessary to bring inventions to market.[19] Potential licensees are incentivized to commercialize inventions by the possibility of receiving supra-competitive prices. The public is ultimately benefited by access to new inventions, as opposed to other publicly funded inventions which remain unused. Moreover, universities and other nonprofits receiving funding resulting from the Act are tasked with using those funds for additional research and development. The Act expressly provides its purposes:

> It is the policy and objective of Congress to use the patent system to promote the utilization of inventions arising from federally supported research or development; to encourage maximum participation of small business firms in federally supported research and development efforts; to promote collaboration between commercial concerns and nonprofit organizations, including universities; to ensure that inventions made by nonprofit organizations and small business firms are used in a manner to promote free competition and enterprise without unduly encumbering future research

12 Assuming there are no acceptable substitutes.

13 35 U.S.C. § 202(c)(4) (2000).

14 *Id.* § 203.

15 *See* Steven Seidenberg, *March-in Rights: A Lost Opportunity to Lower US Drug Prices*, Intell. Prop. Watch: Int'l IP Pol'y News (May 18, 2017), https://www.ip-watch.org/2017/05/18/march-rights-lost-opportunity-lower-us-drug-prices/.

16 *See* 35 U.S.C. § 202(c); 37 C.F.R. § 401.14(k) (2002).

17 *See* Theodore M. Hagelin, Technology Innovation Law and Practice: Cases and Materials 38–39 (2011).

18 *See* 35 U.S.C. § 202(c); 37 C.F.R. § 401.14(k); Mireles, *States as Innovation System Laboratories*, *supra* note 11, at 1144.

19 *See* Aline C. Flower, Intellectual Property Technology Transfer 28 (2006) (quoting 35 U.S.C. § 201(b) (2000)).

> and discovery; to promote the commercialization and public availability of inventions made in the U.S. by U.S. industry and labor; to ensure that the Government obtains sufficient rights in federally supported inventions to meet the needs of the Government and protect the public against nonuse or unreasonable use of inventions; and to minimize the costs of administering policies in this area.[20]

The Act stipulates that grant recipients must include a statement of government interest in the patent itself for government-funded patented inventions.[21] Unfortunately, many entities may have not complied with this requirement; thus, this data analysis may not fully capture the government-funded patenting of universities and other nonprofits.[22]

The Act has been lauded as providing a boost to the US economy. For example, the Association of University of Technology Transfer Managers recently described the Act as the silver lining in the Great Recession for the US. Essentially, the Great Recession would have been much worse without the economic activity generated from university spin-offs that benefit from the Act. Certainly, there has been an increase in patenting and licensing activity since the Act was passed.[23] Moreover, not all the patents concern Bayh-Dole inventions, but the Act certainly incentivized universities and other nonprofits to engage in patenting and licensing behavior – whether funded by the US government or not.

Another possible benefit could be the availability of US government–funded inventions to people worldwide. One argument is that the US government allowing the patenting of government-funded inventions led to commercialization of some inventions that would otherwise never have reached the public – even if patented worldwide. To that extent, the Act may have incentivized to bring unused government-funded inventions to the public. The Act principally incentivizes commercialization of inventions by allowing the grant recipient to take title to publicly funded inventions. This may result in global benefit, as important inventions – judged by willingness to invest to commercialize those inventions and their commercial success – reach the public. However, by restricting access, patents may also keep lifesaving and enhancing inventions from those without the ability to pay.

20 35 U.S.C. § 200.

21 35 U.S.C. § 202(c)(6); 37 C.F.R. § 401.14(f)(4) (2013).

22 *See* U.S. Gen. Accounting Office, GAO/RCED-99-242, Technology Transfer Reporting Requirements for Federally Sponsored Inventions Need Revisions 2–14 (1999).

23 *See* Nat'l Acad. of Sci., Managing University Intellectual Property in the Public Interest 19 (2011), https://www.nap.edu/read/13001/chapter/3#19.

There have been criticisms of the Act.[24] For example, some argue that it may shift research agendas from basic research to applied research[25] and simultaneously lead to patenting of basic research, which could impede the development and commercialization of inventions.[26]

Another impact of the Act is its adoption in other countries.[27] Many countries have attempted to garner the supposed success of the Act by enacting similar laws.[28] The supposed success of the Act in the US may have led to an increase in patenting of non-US government–funded inventions in other countries (and perhaps in the US) through similar Acts.[29]

## Professor Hemel and Ouellette's Internalization Theory and Study

In *Bayh-Dole Beyond Borders*, Professors Daniel J. Hemel and Lisa Larrimore Ouellette propose a new theory justifying the Act, at least partially. Basically, the theory is that patenting through the Act allows the US to internalize some of the benefits provided to citizens in other countries, benefits which grant recipients patent through foreign patenting. This may lead to additional research funding from public and private sources in the US. Additionally, the internalization theory applies to any country adopting legislation similar to the Act. Professors Hemel and Ouellette explain how the theory operates practically and the flow of benefits:

24 *See generally* Arti K. Rai & Rebecca S. Eisenberg, *The Public Domain: Bayh-Dole Reform and The Progress of Biomedicine*, 66 L. & CONTEMP. PROBS. 289, 295–301 (2003); Gary Pulsinelli, *Share and Share Alike: Increasing Access to Government-Funded Inventions Under the Bayh-Dole Act*, 7 MINN. J. L. SCI. & TECH. 393, 447–48 (2006).

25 *See* WILLIAM M. LANDES & RICHARD A. POSNER, THE ECONOMIC STRUCTURE OF INTELLECTUAL PROPERTY LAW 316 (2003) ("Being able to earn substantial income from patent licensing has, it appears, induced universities to substitute away from basic research, and the result may have been a net social loss."); Eisenberg, *supra* note 7, at 1714; *see also* Pierre Azoulay, Waverly Ding, & Toby Stuart, *The Impact of Academic Patenting on the Rate, Quality, and Direction of (Public) Research*, 57 J. IND. ECON. 637, 638 ("[S]urveys of academic scientists have found that patenting skews scientists' research agendas towards commercial priorities, causes delay in the public dissemination of research findings, and crowds out effort devoted to producing public research results.").

26 *See* Michael A. Heller & Rebecca S. Eisenberg, *Can Patents Deter Innovation? The Anticommons in Biomedical Research*, 280 SCIENCE 698 (1998).

27 *See* Michael S. Mireles, *Adoption of the Bayh-Dole Act in Developed Countries: Added Pressure for a Broad Research Exemption in the U.S.?*, 59 ME. L. REV. 259 (2007) [hereinafter Mireles, *Adoption of the Bayh-Dole Act in Developed Countries*]; Michael S. Mireles, *The Bayh-Dole Act and Incentives for the Commercialization of Government-Funded Invention in Developing Countries*, 76 UMKC L. REV. 525 (2007). For example, many countries in the EU have adopted the Act. *See* Mireles, *Adoption of the Bayh-Dole Act in Developed Countries*, *supra* note 27, at 265.

28 *Id.*

29 *Id.*

> Bayh-Dole patents allow the U.S. to internalize some of the benefits that its own direct public spending on innovation brings to consumers overseas. Foreign consumers benefit from the inventions generated by federally funded research at U.S. universities. And when foreign consumers pay supra competitive prices on these patented inventions, much of this patent 'shadow tax' flows back to the U.S. Some of this benefit goes to government labs and public universities; some goes to non-profit research universities and foundations that the federal government has chosen to support through tax exemptions; and some goes to U.S. manufacturers like Myriad Genetics (and thence to the U.S. government through taxation of these profits).[30]

Professors Hemel and Ouellette then examined the patenting practices of recipients of US government–funded inventions by analyzing data from the Economic and Statistics Division of the World Intellectual Property Organization (WIPO).[31] The WIPO data are "based on the PATSTAT database, which is compiled by the European Patent Office (EPO) and which combines data from over 100 national and regional patent offices."[32] The data include a representation of "patent families," a group of patents covering a single invention.[33] Those patents may be from different countries.[34] The data, from 2000 to 2011,[35] are divided by country income group: high-income economies, upper middle–income economies, lower middle–income economies, and lower income economies.[36] Of the 36,943 patent family filings in the US,[37] 13,175 (35.7 percent) were filed at the EPO. Hence, over 60 percent of the US university patent filings were not made in a major market – the EU. The numbers for other high-income economy countries are Canada (24.7 percent), Japan (22.6 percent), Australia (15.5 percent), Republic of Korea (10.9 percent), Israel (3.6 percent), and Singapore (0.6 percent).[38] In upper middle–income countries, the percentage is lower across several countries: China (15.4 percent), Mexico (4.8 percent), Brazil (3.1 percent), South Africa (0.6 percent), and Malaysia (0.3 percent).[39] Lower middle–income

30 Professors Hemel and Ouellette discuss three "caveats" to the theory: "(i) the results of government-funded invention cannot always be patented; (ii) investment in some kinds of research grants may not be suboptimal even without internalization of foreign benefits; and (iii) even if Bayh-Dole yields the internalization benefit … the costs associated with these patents may outweigh this benefit." Hemel & Ouellette, *supra* note 4, at 297.

31 *Id.* at 301.

32 *Id.*

33 *Id.*

34 *Id.* "Families are counted if any of the applicants are US universities as coded by WIPO; these data thus include filings made by US universities in conjunction with other entities such as for-profit firms." *Id.*

35 *Id.*

36 *Id.* at 303–05.

37 *Id.* at 303.

38 *Id.*

39 *Id.* at 304.

economies are also relatively low: India (6.7 percent), Philippines (0.6 percent), Ukraine (0.2 percent), and Vietnam (0.1 percent).[40] Lower income economies countries – including African Regional Intellectual Property Organization states (Botswana, Gambia, Kenya, Lesotho, Liberia, Malawi, Mozambique, Namibia, Rwanda, Sao Tome and Principe, Sierra Leone, Somalia, Sudan, Swaziland, Tanzania, Uganda, Zambia, and Zimbabwe) – are at 0.1 percent.[41]

Professors Hemel and Ouelette make three "observations" based on the data: (1) a significant number of inventions patented in the US are not patented in other countries by US universities; (2) US universities do seek patents in other countries – for each US patent filed in the US, on average, the university files "a family in two more jurisdictions"[42]; and (3) US universities tend to file more patents in higher income countries.[43]

## Stanford Database[44]

This ambitious project conducted at Stanford University Law School reviews nonpracticing entity litigation activity.[45] Among the most difficult issues concerning analysis of the impact of nonpracticing entity litigation is attempting to categorize those entities by behavior. Stanford researchers used the classification system developed by Professors Allison, Lemley, and Walker to categorize thousands of patent litigations filed in the US District Court from 2000 to 2014.[46] The 2017 database includes a "20% random sample of lawsuits filed in even years 2000 through 2014 and essentially every lawsuit filed in 2011, 2012 and 2013."[47]

The classification system consists of the following categories: (1) acquired patents; (2) university heritage or tie; (3) failed startup; (4) corporate heritage; (5) individual-inventor-started company; (6) university/government/nonprofit; (7) startup, pre-product; (8) product company; (9) individual; (10) undetermined;

40 *Id.*

41 *Id.* at 305. *See also* Shawn Miller et al., *Who's Suing Us? Decoding Patent Plaintiffs since 2000 with the Stanford NPE Litigation Dataset*, 21 Stan Tech. L. Rev. 235 (2018).

42 *Id.* at 302.

43 *Id.* at 305.

44 This section was first published in Firpo & Mireles, *supra* note *, at 527–28 (citing Shawn P. Miller et al., Introduction to the Stanford NPE Litigation Dataset 1 (Oct. 23, 2017 draft), https://law.stanford.edu/projects/stanford-npe-litigation-dataset/#slsnav-suggested-research-uses [https://perma.cc/D3JK-H7FA]). The cited draft was subsequently published in Shawn Miller et al., *Who's Suing Us? Decoding Patent Plaintiffs since 2000 with the Stanford NPE Litigation Dataset*, 21 Stan Tech. L. Rev. 235 (2018). The Stanford Database is available and described at the following website: *Stanford NPE Litigation Database*, https://law.stanford.edu/projects/stanford-npe-litigation-dataset/#slsnav-suggested-research-uses (Apr. 27, 2020).

45 *See generally* Firpo and Mireles, *supra* note *. A nonpracticing entity is generally an entity that did not develop or use the patented invention.

46 *Id.*

47 *Id.* at 528.

(11) industry consortium; (12) IP subsidiary of product company; and (13) corporate-inventor-started company.[48] In organizing the litigations, the researchers used Lex Machina's database concerning patent litigation and categorization information from other researchers. The researchers note that "only one type of patent asserter, Category 8 (product company)" is a practicing company that "makes products or offers services for sale."[49] Moreover, "entities ... [in] Category 1 (acquired patents), Category 4 (corporate heritage) or Category 5 (individual-inventor-started company) are typically known as 'patent trolls' by 'those who use the term.'"[50]

The most important categories in this chapter are (2) university heritage or tie and (6) university/government/nonprofit. According to the researchers, "Category 6 includes any patent asserter that is a university, government entity, or a not-for-profit institution."[51] Additionally, the researchers state,

> Category 2 entities are not themselves universities, but rather 'IP subsidiaries' of universities or separate licensing firms which primarily assert patent rights on behalf of universities. Examples include the Wisconsin Alumni Research Foundation, the University of Colorado Foundation, and Competitive Technologies Inc.[52]

The evidence used to categorize entities as Category 2 included: "[t]he pleadings, company website, news reports, or other filings indicate that the company has ties to a university and/or exists to license university intellectual property. There is no evidence suggesting the entity is actually the university itself or an alias for the university." [53] The evidence used for Category 6 included: "[t]he pleadings or website of the entity states that it is an institution for higher education, a government body, or a non-profit organization."[54]

## Results of Review of Patents

We used a mix of sources for analysis, starting from the dataset on litigated patents from the Stanford Database project. In our previous publications, we identified all the 585 legal cases in this dataset related to universities, nonprofits, or foundations, from which were derived the "university patents" dataset,

48 *Id.* at 244.
49 *Id.*
50 *Id.* at 237. The definition of a patent troll is somewhat controversial. *See generally* Firpo & Mireles, *supra* note *. Some may define a patent troll as an entity that did not use or develop the invention and solely exists to litigate the patent covering the invention. *Id.*
51 Miller et al., *supra* note 44, at 245.
52 *Id.*
53 *Id.* at 248.
54 *Id.* at 249.

containing 378 patents. We matched this dataset to the OECD Triadic Patent Families[55] (TPF) and OECD Patent Quality Indicators[56] databases to obtain data on patent families and the quality of characteristics of the patents, respectively.

Of the original 378 Stanford patents, 254 have corresponding records in the OECD TPF dataset, meaning they are part of a family that reaches other patent offices (primarily the EPO and Japan Patent Office [JPO]). Thus, over 60 percent of the litigated patents have corresponding patents filed in the EU, Japan, or both. Notably, this percentage of patents is significantly higher than noted in the Hemel and Ouellette study: 35.7 percent for the EU and 22.6 percent for Japan.[57] If a litigation has been filed in a particular case, we can assume that a determination was made that the patent was worth expending funding on litigation and covered a relatively valuable market. Indeed, when a party was infringing – or it was an Abbreviated New Drug Application (ANDA) case – a decision was made to file an ANDA in a valuable market. Moreover, these patents covered inventions that were probably studied carefully to determine whether patenting should occur or not – potentially starting with a grant funding proposal that was reviewed. Therefore, for US-litigated patents, there is much less patented invention essentially dedicated to other countries. Moreover, these may be some of the most valuable patents in the larger dataset of university and nonprofit patents.

For the patents in our sample with a record in the OECD TPF dataset, the technology fields break out as shown in Table 7.1. Predictably, most litigated patents fall under "pharmaceuticals," "biotechnology," or "organic fine chemistry" categories at well over 50 percent of the 254 patents associated with patent filings in the EU, Japan, or both. Most of the US litigation of these patents are likely to have involved ANDA litigation.

The OECD Triadic Families dataset shows the number of patents within a family for each patent, broken down by patent office. For most patents, the family to which they belong owns more patents in the US compared to the EPO and JPO (two patent offices for which there are data). We can further analyze these differences by considering the type of institution related to the patent (the dataset used in our previous publication allowed us to identify whether a patent was affiliated with a US-based institution, a foreign nongovernmental organization, or a foreign government. Tables 7.2 and 7.3 break down the average and median

55 OECD, Triadic Patent Families database (July 2019). This database is accessible by submitting an online form to the OECD. *See Intellectual Property Statistics and Analysis*, OECD, http://www.oecd.org/sti/inno/intellectual-property-statistics-and-analysis.htm.

56 OECD, Patent Quality Indicators database (July 2019). This database is accessible by submitting an online form to the OECD. *See Intellectual Property Statistics and Analysis*, OECD, http://www.oecd.org/sti/inno/intellectual-property-statistics-and-analysis.htm.

57 Hemel & Ouellette, *supra* note 4, at 303. The Hemel and Ouellette study primarily focuses on patenting activity of recipients of government funding. Some of the increase in percentage may be based on foreign entity patenting, which was not reviewed in Hemel and Ouellette.

*Table 7.1* Number of patents by technology field

| *Technology field* | *Number of patents* | *Percentage* |
|---|---|---|
| Electrical machinery, apparatus, energy | 8 | 3 |
| Audiovisual technology | 11 | 4 |
| Telecommunications | 2 | 1 |
| Digital communication | 2 | 1 |
| Computer technology | 14 | 6 |
| IT methods for management | 2 | 1 |
| Semiconductors | 13 | 5 |
| Measurement | 9 | 4 |
| Analysis of biological materials | 1 | 0 |
| Medical technology | 24 | 9 |
| Organic fine chemistry | 34 | 13 |
| Biotechnology | 53 | 21 |
| Pharmaceuticals | 64 | 25 |
| Macromolecular chemistry, polymers | 2 | 1 |
| Food chemistry | 8 | 3 |
| Surface technology, coating | 3 | 1 |
| Textile and paper machines | 1 | 0 |
| Transport | 3 | 1 |
| Total | 254 | 100 |

Source: OECD TFP OECD, Triadic Patent Families database, July 2019.

*Table 7.2* Average count by institution type

| *Institution type* | *USPTO count* | *EPO count* | *JPO count* |
|---|---|---|---|
| Foreign | 9.4 | 3 | 3.1 |
| Foreign gov't | 13 | 10 | 9 |
| US-based | 10.2 | 3.3 | 3.0 |
| Total | 10.1 | 3.3 | 3.1 |

*Table 7.3* Median count by institution type

| *Institution type* | *USPTO count* | *EPO count* | *JPO count* |
|---|---|---|---|
| Foreign | 11 | 1 | 2 |
| Foreign gov't | 13 | 10 | 9 |
| US-based | 7 | 2 | 2 |
| Total | 7 | 2 | 2 |

count, respectively, by type of institution (the median is a better measure in the presence of outliers). Both tables clearly indicate that even for patents related to foreign organizations or governments, patent families tend to have more patents registered at the US Patent and Trademark Office.

The OECD Patent Quality Indicators dataset has another advantage; its various measures of patent quality include the "simple count of years during which a granted patent has been kept alive, i.e. the latest year of renewal, or until it has lapsed, or has been withdrawn."

In our sample, the average patent has been kept alive for 12.3 years, slightly higher than 8.3 years in the OECD dataset. (A similar picture emerges when comparing medians.) This suggests that many patents filed in the EU and Japan are lapsing possibly by failure to pay maintenance fees or invalidation. Thus, even presumably valuable patents litigated in the US fall into the public domain in the EU or Japan well before the expiration of the complete patent term. This supports the theory – at least for patents where maintenance fees were not paid – that the US may be subsidizing some invention in the EU and Japan.[58]

## Conclusion

This chapter continues to explore the interesting question: what is the effect of the Act on access and development of inventions? Several possible effects include: the adoption of the Act in other countries; the availability of US-funded inventions in other countries covered by both US and other countries' patents; and the availability of US-funded inventions covered by US patents but not covered by patents in other countries. This chapter focuses on the last potential effect concerning the patenting behavior of patents which have been litigated in the US by universities, nonprofits, and their licensees. At least for the subset of patents litigated in the US, a high percentage are part of patent families in the EU, Japan, or both. Moreover, over half of those patents are in the medical and pharmaceutical field and are likely more valuable than other patents, given the decision to litigate them and seek patent protection in major jurisdictions – which is both expensive and time-consuming. Our future project will focus on patenting and litigation behavior concerning litigated patents in middle-income and lower income countries.

58 Importantly, that may be true with respect to government-funded invention. However, it is difficult to get an accurate count of government-funded patents in the United States because of an apparent failure by grant recipients to indicate that their patented invention is government funded in the patent. *See* Arti K. Rai & Bhaven N. Sampat, *Accountability in Patenting of Federally Funded Research*, 30 Nat. Biotechnol. 953 (Oct. 2012).

# Part II

# State Action and Access to Medicines Debate

## Second Generation

# 8 Brazil

## Patent Barriers and Access to Medicines Through the Public Health System*

*Gabriela Costa Chaves, Maria Auxiliadora Oliveira, and Jorge Antonio Zepeda Bermudez*

### Introduction

In 1996 and 2017, Brazil ranked sixth in the global pharmaceutical market in terms of sales output.[1] It was recently classified as a '*pharmerging*' country – a term used to describe developing countries with a fast expanding pharmaceutical market – and was therefore an important target in terms of growth and sales for transnational pharmaceutical companies.[2] The Brazilian pharmaceutical market was estimated to be worth BRL76 billion (around $23 billion) in 2017, of which 31 percent was from governmental spending and 69 percent from retail sales.[3]

Brazil's position in the global pharmaceutical market indicates why there has been such a pressure for the adoption of higher standards on intellectual property rights (IPR). Although the adoption of patent protection for pharmaceutical products and processes in the Industrial Property Law of 1996 (Law 9279/96) aimed at compliance with the Agreement on Trade-Related Aspects of Intellectual Property (TRIPS Agreement), such early adoption was also a result of continuous bilateral pressure from the United States (US).[4]

Efforts to implement public health IPR safeguards to increase access to medicines in the public system have since been a long-term battle, particularly against

* Disclaimer: This chapter brings a summary of some of the research results, experiences, and views developed by the authors in the past, at least, 20 years working on a public health approaches to intellectual property rights in Brazil, as well as research results from other researchers in this field. No new empirical data was produced specifically for the purpose of this chapter. The authors belong to the Department on Medicines Policy and Pharmaceutical Services (NAF), Sergio Arouca National School of Public Health (ENSP), Oswaldo Cruz Foundation (Fiocruz).

1 Alexis Jesus Velazquez Gonzalez, A indústria farmacêutica brasileira na década de 90: mudanças na pesquisa & desenvolvimento, na produção de fármacos e de medicamentos (1999) (Master's dissertation, Universidade Estadual de Campinas); *Guia 2018 – Interfarma, Dados do Setor*, Interfarma (2019), https://www.interfarma.org.br/guia/guia-2018/dados_do_setor/ [hereinafter *Guia 2018*].

2 Laura Lorenzetti, *Why Drug Companies are Betting Big on 'Pharmerging' Countries*, Fortune (Aug. 14, 2015), https://bit.ly/3lEddOd.

3 *Guia 2018*, *supra* note 1.

4 Maria Helena Tachinardi, A Guerra Das Patentes – Conflito Brasil X Eua Sobre Propriedade Intelectual (1993).

the backdrop of the right to health provided by the Federal Constitution of 1988.[5] A retrospective analysis of those efforts might provide important insights on present and future challenges faced.

This chapter provides a retrospective overview of the Brazilian government's adoption and use of public health TRIPS safeguards to increase access to medicines in the public health system. The analysis will assume that initiatives to address patent barriers and the local production[6] of medicines can have either a synergic or antagonistic effect on the reduction of the prices of monopoly medicines, depending on the approaches adopted.

Although governmental approaches to address patent barriers occurred within the context of several initiatives led by other stakeholders, especially civil society organizations (CSOs), we will not focus on the role they played at the time. We will also not focus on the Legislative's IP and medicines discussion regarding TRIPS flexibilities and TRIPS-plus proposed bills, or on the Judiciary's adjudication of emblematic cases on pharmaceutical patents. This is a limitation, as they add more context to the national environment and policy space for implementing public health TRIPS flexibilities, but would also go beyond the scope of this chapter.

Over the analyzed period, from 1996 to 2018, patent issues, as a barrier to access to medicines, varied in intensity in the governmental agenda. It became a growing priority between the end of 1990 and first years of the decade 2000 and weakened and became less of a priority after the issuance of Brazil's first compulsory license (CL) on pharmaceuticals in 2007, and the beginning of the implementation of the industrial policy involving local production and technology transfer.

## Background

Since the approval of the Federal Constitution of 1988, the Brazilian health system has been divided into the public and private subsystems in terms of funding. The public subsystem comprises the Unified Health System (*Sistema Unico de Saude* or SUS) and the one for civil servants (civil and military). All citizens are entitled to use the SUS free of charge. The private subsystem comprises voluntary health insurance often funded by individuals, families, and/or employers, and by out-of-pocket direct payment for health services. Although some individuals access health services and care through the private subsystem, they are also entitled to access the SUS.[7]

5 Brazil Const. of 1988, arts. 196–98 and 200.

6 We adopted the term 'local production' to refer to the production on the national territory of active pharmaceutical ingredients (APIs) and medicines, most often by private national companies or public manufacturers. In case the production in the national territory is made by multinational companies, it will be clarified in the text.

7 Maria Elizabeth Diniz Barros & Sérgio Francisco Piola, *O financiamento dos serviços de saúde no Brasil, in* Sistema de saúde no Brasil: organização e financiamento 101–38 (Rosa Maria Marques et al. eds., 2016).

The challenge to achieving universal access to medicines is reflected in the imbalance between private and public expenses in Brazil. Families' out-of-pocket expenses in 2010 and 2013 were equivalent to 1.6 percent and 1.5 percent, respectively, of Brazil's Gross Domestic Product, as opposed to 0.2 percent of governmental expenses for the same years.[8] This may suggest that public policies for promoting access to medicines have failed and may also indicate the challenges faced by the public sector in the provision of medicines. However, little is known about private expenses in terms of the types of technologies covered, and whether they strictly relate to public health needs or are influenced by pressure from pharmaceutical companies to increase demand.[9]

In any case, in 2013 or 2014, the SUS was exclusively responsible for providing health services to 71 percent of the population, which reflects its relevance in fulfilling the right to health and the unfinished agenda to become universal.[10] Some treatments are only publicly provided, such as those for tuberculosis and HIV/AIDS. Recent studies have also shown that treatments for highly prevalent diseases, such as diabetes and hypertension, have been mainly obtained from the SUS.[11]

At the SUS, medicines are funded by the federal, state, and municipal governments, although each level is responsible for a specific list of products. The Ministry of Health is generally responsible for the financing and, in some cases, (centralized) procurement of high-priced medicines. Following an international trend, its medicine expenses have been increasing more than the federal budget for health in the past years.[12]

8 IBGE – Instituto Brasileiro de Geografia e Estatística, *Conta-Satélite de Saúde Brasil* (2013).

9 Daniela Moulin Maciel de Vasconcelos et al., *Política Nacional de Medicamentos em retrospectiva: um balanço de (quase) 20 anos de implementação*, 22 Ciênc. Saúde Colet. 8, 2609–14 (2017).

10 *71% dos brasileiros têm os serviços públicos de saúde como referência*, Legado Brasil (June 2, 2015), http://legado.brasil.gov.br/noticias/saude/2015/06/71-dos-brasileiros-tem-os-servicos-publicos-de-saude-como-referencia (last visited Mar. 23, 2019).

11 *See, e.g.*, *National Research on Access, Utilization, and Promotion of Rational Use of Medicines in Brazil* (free translation), PNAUM, http://www.ufrgs.br/pnaum; Maria Auxiliadora Oliveira et al., *Access to Medicines for Chronic Diseases in Brazil: A Multidimensional Approach*, Rev. Saude Publica 50 (suppl. 2) (2016), http://www.scielo.br/scielo.php?script=sci_arttext&pid=S0034-89102016000300303&lng=en&tlng=en (last visited Oct. 9, 2019); Noemia Urruth Leão Tavares et al., *Free Access to Medicines for the Treatment of Chronic Diseases in Brazil*, Rev. Saude Publica 50 (suppl. 2) (2016), http://www.scielo.br/scielo.php?script=sci_arttext&pid=S0034-89102016000300313&lng=en&tlng=en (last visited Oct. 9, 2019).

12 Between 2008 and 2015, the expenses increased by 74 percent, from BRL8.5 billion to BRL14.8 billion, while the federal budget increased by 36.6 percent for the same period. *See* Grazielle David et al., *Direito a Medicamentos. Avaliação das Despesas com Medicamentos no Âmbito Federal do Sistema Único de Saúde entre 2008 e 2015*, Instituto de Estudos Socioeconômicos – INESC (2016). Another study showed that the Ministry of Health's medicines expenses increased by 53 percent between 2010 and 2016. *See* Fabíola Sulpino Vieira, *Evolução do gasto com medicamentos do sistema único de saúde no período de 2010 a 2016*, Instituto de Pesquisa Econômica Aplicada – IPEA (2018).

The patent system in Brazil plays a critical role in price increase resulting from the SUS' procurement of brand-name lifesaving medicines because it allows companies to charge high prices, thereby limiting government's strategies for price regulation. In addition to evergreening in the pharmaceutical field,[13] patents also affect the exclusivity situation of medicines in the country and the legal uncertainty resulting from the varying status of patent applications related to the same product.[14] 'Monopoly of law' – which results from a patent granted for the medicine – is distinguished from '*de facto* monopoly' – wherein there is no patent granted in the country for the product, but it is 'subject to patent protection' due to one or more applications that are still pending decision.[15]

After more than 20 years of the implementation of the TRIPS Agreement in Brazil, and considering the complex dynamics of the pharmaceutical market affecting public procurement of medicines, we believe that the government should systematically adopt public health TRIPS safeguards to challenge and overcome patent barriers and to regulate the price of monopoly medicines.

The next sections will describe how the Brazilian government approached patent problems related to some medicines procured by the SUS, highlighting oscillations across time in the orientation adopted.

## Changes in Industrial Property Legislation and the Adoption of Patented Medicines by the Unified Health System (1996–2002)

Law 9279/96 came into force during a very critical decade for the health sector, which saw the beginning of the SUS implementation, the HIV/AIDS epidemic crisis, and evidence of the efficacy of highly active antiretroviral (ARV) therapy to control HIV/AIDS.[16] The provision of ARVs by the public sector was initially concentrated in specific states and driven by lawsuits requesting for

13 Amy Kapczynski et al., *Polymorphs and Prodrugs and Salts (oh my!): An Empirical Analysis of "Secondary" Pharmaceutical Patents*, PLoS One 7, e49470 (2012); Dárcio Gomes Pereira & Eduardo P. S. Fiuza, *Os Direitos de propriedade intelectual nas estratégias de ciclo de vida para medicamentos de segunda geração: resultados parciais do inquérito brasileiro sobre a concorrência do setor farmacêutico*, Radar: Tecnol. Prod. Comér. Exter 29, 27–37 (2013); Roberto Silveira Reis, Panorama patentário dos medicamentos antirretrovirais no Brasil (2012) (Ph.D. thesis, Universidade Federal do Rio de Janeiro), http://www.ie.ufrj.br/images/pos-graducao/pped/defesas/05-Roberto_Reis.pdf (last visited Oct. 9, 2019).

14 Gabriela Costa Chaves et al., Contribution to the United Nations Secretary-General's High Level Panel on Access to Medicines (2016), http://www.unsgaccessmeds.org/inbox/2016/2/27/gabriel-chaves-english-translation?rq=gabriela (last visited Oct. 10, 2019).

15 Gabriela Costa Chaves et al., Medicines Under Exclusivity Situation Funded by the Ministry of Health: Analysis of the Patent Situation and Public Procurement 42 (1st ed. 2019), https://accessibsa.org/media/2019/08/Medicines-under-Exclusivity-Situation-funded-by-the-Ministry-of-Health.pdf (last visited Sept. 12, 2019).

16 Mario C. Scheffer, *Coquetel – A Incrível História dos Antirretrovirais e do Tratamento da Aids no Brasil* (1st ed. 2012).

medicines.[17] However, it was the enactment of Law 9313/96 on the free distribution of medicines to HIV/AIDS patients that established public funding to secure public sector pharmaceutical services for the control of HIV infections, and such services started to be nationally accessible.[18]

Although issued to comply with the TRIPS Agreement, Law 9279/96 was born TRIPS-plus – it included standards higher than those established by the TRIPS Agreement. Its early adoption (from May 1997) of patenting for pharmaceutical products and processes, which precluded Brazil from enjoying the transition period allowed by the TRIPS Agreement up to 2005, was followed by the inclusion of a pipeline mechanism[19] and was responsible for the patent protection of ARVs (*nelfinavir* in 1998; *efavirenz*, *abacavir*, and *amprenavir* in 1999; *lopinavir* in 2000), which were adopted by the SUS from 1998 as part of the free HIV/AIDS medicines program and the cancer medicine *imatinib*.[20]

Law 9279/96 also provided for an extension of the patent term when the decision to grant the patent is issued more than 10 years after its filing. As the backlog of the patent examination[21] may take more than 10 years, the patent monopoly is increased beyond the 20-year patent term. Competition is also inhibited because Article 44 of Law 9279/96 allows for the request of retrospective compensations for the exploitation by third parties during the pendency period in case the patent is granted.[22]

The first and only amendment to the Industrial Property Law was proposed in 1999, and later became Law 10196/2001. It included two public health

17 Mario C. Scheffer et al., *O remédio via Justiça – Um estudo sobre o acesso a novos medicamentos e exames em HIV/Aids no Brasil por meio de ações judiciais* (1st ed. 2005).

18 Maria Auxiliadora Oliveira & Angela Esher Moritz, *Acesso Universal ao Tratamento para as Pessoas Vivendo com HIV e aids no Brasil*, in JORGE ANTONIO ZEPEDA BERMUDEZ; MARIA AUXILIADORA OLIVEIRA; ÂNGELA ESHER. (ORG.). ACCESO A MEDICAMENTOS: DERECHO FUNDAMENTAL, PAPEL DEL ESTADO 233–50 (1st ed. 2004).

19 'The pipeline mechanism is a temporary provision whereby applications were accepted for existing patents in fields of technology that Brazil did not previously recognize, enabling patent protection for, among other things, food and pharmaceutical products. Pipeline patent applications would only be subject to a formal analysis and would follow the terms of the patent granted overseas, not being submitted to the Brazilian patent office, the National Industrial Property Institute (INPI), for a technical analysis of the patentability requirements – novelty, inventiveness, and industrial application. The pipeline mechanism was not required under the TRIPS Agreement'. (p. 172). Gabriela Costa Chaves, Marcela Fogaça Vieira & Renata Reis. *Access to Medicines and Intellectual Property in Brazil: Reflections and Strategies of Civil Society*, INT. J. HUM. RIGHTS. 8, 163–89 (2008).

20 Constance Meiners et al., *Modeling HIV/AIDS Drug Price Determinants in Brazil: Is Generic Competition a Myth?*, PLoS ONE 6, e23478 (2011).

21 Jussanã C de Abreu, Prospecção tecnológica aplicada na otimização da concessão de patentes no Brasil: estudo de caso em patentes de medicamentos imunossupressores (2017) (Ph.D. thesis, Universidade Federal do Rio de Janeiro).

22 CHAVES ET AL., *supra* note 15.

provisions – the prior consent[23] of the Brazilian Health Regulatory Agency (*Agência Nacional de Vigilância Sanitária* or Anvisa) to pharmaceutical patent applications (Article 229c) and the Bolar exemption (Article 43, VII).

When patented ARVs were incorporated in the SUS' medicines policy, their high prices raised concerns regarding the sustainability of the access policy and became a critical issue for the National AIDS Program agenda.[24] For this reason, health professionals from the National AIDS Program became the key government stakeholders at that time, influencing the Ministry of Health to defend and even propose better interpretation of public health TRIPS safeguards, such as Decree 3201/99,[25] which regulates Article 71 of Law 9279/96 on compulsory licensing for national emergency and public interest.[26]

To keep ARV prices low and increase access, the government focused on the procurement of medicines not protected by patents and locally produced by national private companies and public manufacturers. There were price negotiations between the Ministry of Health and pharmaceutical companies based on specific tools to increase government's bargaining power, such as the ability to establish a reference price from production cost estimates[27] developed by a public manufacturer (Farmanguinhos/Fiocruz) and threats of CL issuance.[28] The approval of Decree 3201/99 was in itself adopted as a threat to issue a CL in price negotiations with companies, resulting in significant reductions.[29] There was also no international market of generic ARVs yet, which strengthened the legitimacy of local production as part of the national response to the HIV/AIDS epidemic.[30]

23 This provision included the Brazilian Health Regulatory Agency (Anvisa) in the examination of patentability requirements of patent applications for pharmaceutical products and processes. The proposal was that Anvisa would give a consent on the granting (or not) of patents before (prior) the National Institute of Industrial Property (INPI – Brazilian Patent Office).

24 Alexandre Grangeiro et al., *Sustentabilidade da política de acesso a medicamentos antiretrovirais no Brasil*, 40 Rev. Saúde Pública 60–69 (2006).

25 This Decree was updated and improved in 2003 through Decree n.4.380 which incorporated the possibility of importation in case of issuing a compulsory license.

26 Gabriela Costa Chaves, Interfaces entre a produção local e o acesso a medicamentos no contexto do Acordo TRIPS da Organização Mundial do Comércio (2016) (Ph.D. thesis).

27 Those estimates were for the final products considering the importation of the APIs.

28 Matthew Brian Flynn, Pharmaceutical Governance in Brazil: Globalization, Institutions and AIDS (2010) (Ph.D. thesis, University of Texas), http://repositories.lib.utexas.edu/bitstream/handle/2152/ETD-UT-2010-12-2257/FLYNN-DISSERTATION.pdf?sequence=2 (last visited Sept. 12, 2019).

29 *Id.*; Marco Tulio de Barros e Castro, Licenciamento compulsório no Brasil: instituições e políticas (2013) (Ph.D. thesis, Universidade Federal do Rio de Janeiro), http://www.ie.ufrj.br/images/pos-graducao/pped/dissertacoes_e_teses/Marco_tulio_barros_e_castro.pdf (last visited Apr. 15, 2019).

30 Ellen t'Hoen, The Global Politics of Pharmaceutical Monopoly Power: Drug Patents, Access, Innovation and the Application of the WTO Doha Declaration on TRIPS and Public Health (2009).

The adoption of these price reduction strategies was part of a very specific context at the national level, with the establishment of several legal and institutional frameworks such as the National Medicines Policy in 1998 (Ministry of Health Ordinance Number 3916), the Generic Law in 1999 (Law Number 9787/99), and the creation of the Anvisa in 1999 (Law Number 9782/99).

At the end of the 1990s, approaches to address patent barriers to ARV medicines involved the inclusion of health issues in the foreign affairs agenda.[31] The Brazilian government started to engage in health diplomacy in 1998 by participating more actively in global arenas, such as in the World Health Organization (WHO) and World Trade Organization (WTO), in debates involving IPR and access to medicines. This created visibility over time, contributing to the expansion of policy space.

The National AIDS Program played an important role in 2000 during the XIII International AIDS Conference in South Africa by presenting the results of the Brazilian response to the epidemic in relation to access to medicines, based on local ARV production, and offering technological transfer to other developing countries.[32]

The involvement of the Ministry of Health in the negotiations at the 2001 WTO Ministerial Conference (that resulted in the approval of the Doha Declaration on the TRIPS Agreement and Public Health or the Doha Declaration) was also an effect of the government's mobilization of the National AIDS Program in relation to patent issues.[33] The Doha Declaration[34] marked the incorporation of public health-related issues into the WTO agenda. For the first time, the magnitude of the public health crisis was recognized, as paragraph 4 states that 'the TRIPS Agreement does not and should not prevent Members from taking measures to protect public health'. The Brazilian delegation, which included health professionals from the National AIDS Program, attended the conference primarily to highlight the problems caused by the TRIPS Agreement, especially on prices of patented medicines.

The inclusion of patent barriers as a concern in the Revised Drug Strategy resolutions approved by the WHO member states[35] was also critical in projecting Brazil as one of the developing country voices in the pro-public health interpretation of the TRIPS Agreement.[36]

31 Matthew Flynn, *Brazilian Pharmaceutical Diplomacy: Social Democratic Principles versus Soft Power Interests*, 43 Int. J. Health Serv. 67–89 (2013).

32 Alan Berkman et al., *A Critical Analysis of the Brazilian Response to HIV/AIDS: Lessons Learned for Controlling and Mitigating the Epidemic in Developing Countries*, 95 Am. J. Public Health 1162–72 (2005).

33 *Id.*

34 World Trade Organization, *Ministerial Declaration of 14 November 2001*, WTO Doc. WT/MIN(01)/DEC/2 (2001), https://www.wto.org/englilsh/thewto_e/minist_e/min01_e/mindecl_trips_e.htm.

35 Santiago Alcazar, *The Copernican Shift in Global Health* (Glob. Health Programme, Working Paper No. 3, 2008).

36 Flynn, *supra* note 31.

In 2002, the National AIDS Program also started to engage in international cooperation projects in which locally produced ARVs were donated to other developing countries in Latin America and Africa.

We can summarize this period as one in which patent problems related to access to medicines became part of the Ministry of Health's agenda after the incorporation of patented ARVs, reflected in changes to the legal framework to implement public health TRIPS flexibilities. Efforts to reduce the price of monopoly medicines were based on price negotiation in which the government's bargaining power was strengthened by showing local production capacity, the establishment of reference prices from production cost estimates, and the threat of CL issuance. It was also when the Brazilian government started to play an international role with regard to patents and access to medicines, including in the recognition of the problem in WHO resolutions and in negotiations around the approval of the Doha Declaration.

## Efforts to Implement Public Health TRIPS Flexibilities (2003–2007)

Brazil was one of the first developing countries to implement a universal, free, and comprehensive health-care program for people living with HIV/AIDS (PLHIV). Combining treatment and prevention, Brazil achieved excellent results in the fight against the HIV epidemic – a program which the World Bank advised against, as it instead advocated for a prevention only program.[37] Brazil thus became a reference for a successful health-care regime in the fight against the HIV epidemic in developing countries. It also spearheaded the adoption of such programs in most international forums.[38] Thus, the period between 2003 and 2007 saw several efforts by the Ministry of Health to increase the policy space and implement TRIPS flexibilities concerning HIV medicines in Brazil, including strengthening the role played by government in health diplomacy.

At that time, the global public health crisis was dramatic, especially because despite the existence of 17 ARVs, only 400,000 of the six million PLHIV who needed treatment received it.[39] Of these, 170,000 lived in Brazil, where access to ARV therapy has been universal and free since 1997.[40]

37 Jane Galvão, AIDS No Brasil – A agenda de Construção de uma Epidemia 256 (2000); World Bank, Confronting AIDS: Public Priorities in a Global Epidemic, A World Bank Research Report 353 (1997).

38 Maria Auxiliadora Oliveira & Elizabeth Moreira dos Santos, *Acesso universal ao tratamento para pessoas vivendo com o HIV e AIDS no Brasil*, *in* Políticas de controle do HIV/AIDS no Brasil e em Moçambique 139–68 (Nair Teles et al. eds., 2016).

39 World Health Organization & Joint United Nations Program on HIV/AIDS, *Treating 3 Million by 2005 Making It Happen The WHO Strategy* (2003), https://www.who.int/3by5/publications/documents/en/Treating3millionby2005.pdf (last visited Mar. 2, 2020).

40 Oliveira & Moreira dos Santos, supra note 38.

### *Efforts at the Regional and International Level*

The high prices of ARVs were affecting all of Latin America, bringing the common challenge around the same monopoly medicines. For that reason, countries from Latin America and the Caribbean, including Brazil, engaged in joint price negotiations with multinational pharmaceutical companies in 2003 and 2005. Although the success of these negotiations (in relation to the countries' ability to enforce the agreed price reductions) was uncertain, they at least contributed to bringing additional visibility to the problem of high medicine prices and the developing countries' challenge of providing universal access to treatment.[41]

IP issues related to access to medicines gained increasing relevance at the WHO arena, which is seen by developing countries as a multilateral space for bringing concerns such as health and the WTO-established IP system.[42] In the 167th session of the WHO Executive Board (EB) in January 2003, the Brazilian delegation proposed the inclusion the TRIPS Agreement and access to medicines in the agenda. They argued that the WTO had failed in finding a speedy solution to the problem of member countries with no pharmaceutical production capacity and their ability to issue CLs under paragraph 6 of the Doha Declaration.[43] The Brazilian delegation – with the support of other Latin American countries, the African Union, and some CSOs – requested the WHO Director-General to write to the WTO, showing concern for not complying with the mandate approved by WTO member states in November 2002. The proposal was considered radical and unsuitable by several EB members. After exhaustive negotiations, the EB members recognized the importance of broadening debates on the balance between innovation and access to health products. A draft resolution was approved by consensus, and later became Resolution WHA 56.27[44] at the 56th World Health Assembly (WHA) in May 2003.

The resolution addressed issues such as lack of innovation for neglected diseases, imbalance between the burden of diseases and the pharmaceutical market, as well as concerns for the current patent protection system, and reaffirmed the Doha Declaration. It also established a one-year deadline for the elaboration

41 Claudia G. S. Osorio-de-Castro et al., *Proposed Methodology for Monitoring Antiretroviral Drugs Price Negotiations in Latin America and the Caribbean*, 26 Rev. Panam. Salud Pública (2009), http://www.scielosp.org/scielo.php?script=sci_arttext&pid=S1020-49892009000800006&lng=en&nrm=iso&tlng=en (last visited Feb. 29, 2020).

42 Jordão Horácio da Silva Lima, *Saúde global e política externa brasileira: negociações referentes à inovação e propriedade intelectual*, 22 Ciênc. Saúde Colet. 2213–21 (2017); Alcazar, *supra* note 35.

43 Jorge Antonio Zepeda Bermudez, *Acesso a Medicamentos: Direito ou Utopia?* (1st ed. 2014).

44 *Global Strategy and Plan of Action on Public Health, Innovation and Intellectual Property*, Resolution WHA 61.21 (2008), http://www.wpro.who.int/health_research/wha61_21_global_strategy_poa_health_innovation_may2008.pdf [hereinafter Resolution WHA 61.21].

of terms of reference, and the setting up of a commission to collect data and proposals from different actors, and to produce an analysis of IPR, innovation, and public health.[45] The elaboration of the terms of reference and the establishment of the Commission for Intellectual Property Rights, Innovation and Public Health (CIPIH) took place in February 2004.

The CIPIH was tasked to investigate how to improve access to health products for diseases that mainly affect developing countries given IPR rules.[46] The process of collecting and analyzing data obtained through technical visits, meetings, workshops, and 32 studies took more than two years. The CIPIH's Final Report was published in April 2006 and approved during the 59th WHA in May 2006. It provided evidence-based analysis, concluding *inter alia* that the current patent protection system does not encourage the production of medicines for diseases prevalent in poorer populations of developing countries. It also made more than 50 recommendations to be implemented by different stakeholders.

There was no consensus among commissioners on how to fund research and development (R&D) to meet the needs of neglected diseases and populations. Given the broad scope of the Final Report's recommendations and the involvement of multiple interests in its implementation, Resolution WHA 59.24[47] – setting up an intergovernmental working group to develop a strategy and plan of action on public health, innovation, and intellectual property – was approved.

After considerable negotiations, the Global Strategy and Plan of Action on Public Health, Innovation, and Intellectual Property (GSPOA) was approved two years later as Resolution WHA 61.21[48] in May 2008. It provided a medium-term framework on needs-driven R&D for medicines of diseases that disproportionately affect developing countries. The Brazilian delegation was very active and purposeful throughout the drafting of this resolution. In fact, since delegates from Brazil raised the problem of the relationship between trade rules and access to medicines in 2003, the issue has been discussed at all WHAs. In these discussions, Brazil played a leading role, either by proposing resolutions or by supporting other countries that proposed resolutions on access to medicines.

### *Efforts at the National Level*

Many challenges emerged during the second decade of the SUS implementation (2000–2009). These included the sustainability of universal and free access to

45 Bermudez, *supra* note 43.

46 Carlos Correa, *Do Patents Work for Public Health?*, 84 Bull. World Health Organ. 349–51 (2006).

47 *Public Health, Innovation, Essential Health Research and Intellectual Property Rights: Towards a Global Strategy and Plan of Action*, Resolution WHA 59.24 (2006), http://apps.who.int/gb/ebwha/pdf_files/WHA59-REC1/e/WHA59_2006_REC1-en.pdf.

48 Resolution WHA 61.21, *supra* note 44.

newer patented medicines (especially those for HIV/AIDS treatment), which has been progressively incorporated into clinical protocols. Since the implementation of universal and free access to ARV therapy in 1997, the number of PLHIV being treated has increased from 35,800 to 231,146 in 2009.[49] During the same period, the cost of treatment decreased from $6526 per patient per year to $1609.[50] This was made possible by the local production of non-patented ARVs, by centralized purchasing of ARVs, and by the previously successful strategy of price negotiation of patented ARVs.

However, the Ministry of Health's spending on ARVs doubled from $209.9 million in 2004 to $496.9 million in 2005, and then to $407.6 million in 2006.[49,50] This alarming threat to the sustainability of access to HIV/AIDS medicines led to a series of cost containment measures.[51,52] At that time, patented ARVs accounted for 74.3 percent of the Ministry of Health's budget for universal access to HIV/AIDS medicines.[53]

To deal with this problem, negotiations with Abbott were commenced in 2005 to reduce the price of *lopinavir/ritonavir*. The Ministry of Health established a reference price based on estimates of production cost and declared the medicine of public interest, which was the first step in the issuance of a CL if the company refused to supply the medicine at the ceiling price established for negotiation.

The National Health Council, a body in the governance structure of the SUS allowing for society's participation, had previously issued Resolution 352/2005 approving the CL for *efavirenz*, *lopinavir*, and *tenofovir*.[54] A CL was not issued in this instance since Abbot agreed to reduce the price of *lopinavir/ritonavir* by 53 percent ($1.17–$0.63 per unit).[55] However, civil society groups led by the Working Group on Intellectual Property of the Brazilian Network for the Integration of Peoples (GTPI/REBRIP) and the Federal Prosecutor still filed a civil action against the Brazilian government, demanding the issuance of a CL for *lopinavir/ritonavir*.[56]

49 Rodrigo Silva Lopes dos Santos, A Sustentabilidade do Progama Nacional de DST/AIDS: Análise da capacidade de oferta e preços de medicamentos antiretrovirais (2010) (Master dissertation, Universidade federal do Rio de Janeiro).

50 Oliveira & Moreira dos Santos, *supra* note 38.

51 Grangeiro et al., *supra* note 24.

52 Amy S. Nunn et al., *Evolution of Antiretroviral Drug Costs in Brazil in the Context of Free and Universal Access to AIDS Treatment*, 4 PLoS Med. e305 (2007).

53 Dirceu B. Greco & Mariangela Simão, *Brazilian Policy of Universal Access to AIDS Treatment: Sustainability Challenges and Perspectives.* AIDS 21(suppl. 4), S37–45 (2007).

54 Carolinne Thays Scopel & Gabriela Costa Chaves, *Initiatives to Challenge Patent Barriers and Their Relationship with the Price of Medicines Procured by the Brazilian Unified National Health System*, Cad. Saúde Pública 32 (2016), http://www.scielo.br/scielo.php?script=sci_arttext&pid=S0102-311X2016001105001&lng=pt&tlng=pt (last visited Feb. 28, 2020).

55 Chaves, *supra* note 26.

56 Scopel & Chaves, *supra* note 54.

Another measure taken by the Ministry of Health to ensure the sustainability of universal access to ARV treatment was the issuance of a CL for the product *efavirenz* produced by Merck, Sharp, and Dohme. The license was issued in May 2007 after failed negotiations, even though the company offered a 30 percent discount on the price of the product. Brazilian authorities wanted to pay the same price paid by Thailand, about 136 percent lower.[57] In 2007, 40 percent of PLHIV on ARV therapy used *efavirenz* at a cost of $580 per patient per year. Savings from this CL were estimated at $107 million over the 2007 to 2011 period.

It is important to recognize that the results obtained in these price negotiations depended on various factors, including political will, support from international agencies, access to international drug price information, local production capacity, and availability of generic versions of *efavirenz*. Studies were published supporting this approach to access to medicines.[58] At the international level, there was the approval of the GSPOA and the CLs issued by the Thai government in 2006 and 2007 for several medicines.[59] At the national level, the National AIDS Program had accumulated years of knowledge on addressing patent barriers for ARVs and using price negotiations. As part of the Brazilian government negotiating team, they were thus able to leverage on this knowledge to build the case for the CL. Negotiations were also favored by the fact that the government was starting to implement an industrial policy targeting the pharmaceutical sector and local manufacturing, and the local production of *efavirenz* could showcase the potential effects of such policy.[60]

Thus, it can be argued that the convergence of these two interests within government – to reduce prices and to stimulate local production by national manufacturers – was critical in swinging the context in favor of CL issuance and in sustaining its implementation over subsequent years.[61]

The approach for the local production of *efavirenz* involved a consortium of private national API companies and the public manufacturer Farmanguinhos/Fiocruz. While the API companies first developed the API, the public

57 William C. V. Rodrigues & Orenzio Soler, *Licença compulsória do efavirenz no Brasil em 2007: contextualização*, 26 Rev. Panam. Salud Pública 553–59 (2009).

58 Carlos M. Correa, *Integrating Public Health Concerns into Patent Legislation in Developing Countries* (2000), http://www.who.int/medicinedocs/pdf/h2963e/h2963e.pdf (last visited Apr. 4, 2019); Ellen T'Hoen, *TRIPS, Pharmaceutical Patents, and Access to Essential Medicines: A Long Way from Seattle to Doha*, 3 Chic. J. Int. Law 1, 27–46 (2002); Jorge Antonio Zepeda Bermudez et al., *Acordo TRIPS da OMC e os desafios para a saúde pública*, *in* Acceso a Medicamentos: Derecho fundamental, papel del Estado 60–90 (Jorge Antonio Zepeda Bermudez et al. eds., 2004); Organización Panamericana de la Salud – OPS, *Aspectos de los Derechos de Propiedad Intelectual relacionados con el Comercio y Acceso a Medicamentos. Enfoque del Analisis en las Américas* (2004).

59 Nathan Ford et al., *Sustaining Access to Antiretroviral Therapy in Developing Countries: Lessons from Brazil and Thailand*, Aids 21 (suppl.), S21–29 (2007).

60 Chaves, supra note 26.

61 Chaves, supra note 26.

manufacturer developed the formulations for the final products.[62] Prior to the launch of the locally produced *efavirenz* in 2009, the government was importing Indian generic versions through the Pan-American Health Organization (PAHO) and the United Nations Children's Fund (UNICEF) to overcome regulatory barriers.[63]

Besides the threat and use of CL, other approaches adopted by the government to address patent barriers during this period included pre-grant oppositions, which allow third-party observations to patent applications. Farmanguinhos/Fiocruz presented pre-grant oppositions against *tenofovir* and *lopinavir/ritonavir* in 2005 and 2006, respectively.[64] In 2008, the Ministry of Health also requested the priority examination of *tenofovir disoproxil fumarate* (TDF) to speed up the decision on the patentability of the medicine.[65]

Although Brazil played an important role in advocating for the incorporation and use of TRIPS flexibilities, including the use of CLs, at the international level, it only issued one CL for one medicine. However, we consider that the use of a combination of measures to address patent barriers to different ARVs under monopoly during this period helps to explain why public expenditures for ARV from 2008 to 2015 were relatively stable (when comparing values adjusted to the inflation of 2015) despite the increase on the number of patients on treatment over the years.[66]

As newer and patented medicines are constantly incorporated, challenges to the sustainability of access policies remain and patent battles around specific medicines might take several years. However, we believe prices are likely to go down where patent barriers are being addressed by different stakeholders. Therefore, the knowledge culled from the experience in providing access to HIV medicines should be expanded to other diseases and expensive medicines in Brazil.

62 *Id.*

63 Rodrigues & Soler, *supra* note 57.

64 Wanise Borges Gouvea Barroso, *Processo de oposição (subsídio a exame) aplicado aos pedidos de patente na área farmacêutica: o caso do Tenofovir*, *in* Propriedade Intelectual e Politicas Publicas Para o Acesso a Antiretrovirais Nos Paises Do Sul 93–104 (Bernard Larouze & Cristina Possas eds., 2013).

65 While ARV expenditures amounted to BRL921,757,635.10 and the number of people on ARV treatment were 190,506 in 2008, these expenditures increased to BRL1,119,149,617.60 in 2015, when there were 454,615 people on ARV treatment. *See* Gabriela Costa Chaves et al., *Redução de preço de medicamento em situação de monopólio no Sistema Único de Saúde: o caso do Tenofovir*, 28 Physis: Rev. Saúde Colet. (2018), http://www.scielo.br/scielo.php?script=sci_arttext&pid=S0103-73312018000100400&lng=pt&tlng=pt (last visited Oct. 9, 2019).

66 Gabriela Costa Chaves et al., Mercosur-EU Free Trade Agreement: Impact Analysis of TRIPS-plus Measures Proposed by the EU on Public Purchases and Domestic Production of HIV and Hepatitis C Medicines in Brazil (2017), https://accessibsa.org/media/2018/01/Mercosur-EU-Free-Trade-Agreement-HIV-Hepatitis-C.pdf (last visited Sept. 12, 2019).

## New Approach to Stimulate Local Production and Price Reduction of Medicines at the SUS (2008–2015)

Since the first term of the Lula presidency (2003–2006), there have been several efforts to formulate and implement a policy to spur industrialization in key sectors and to strategically guide national industrial growth. Coordinated by the Ministry of Development, Industry, and Foreign Trade (MDIC) and formally launched in 2004, the Industrial, Technological, and Foreign Trade Policy (PITCE) represented the beginning of new approaches to stimulate national development based on the following orientation:

> The focus of industrial policy is to create conditions for increased systemic competitiveness, defined as increased economic efficiency and improved competition in international trade [...] by addressing what the functions of industrial policy would be, it unequivocally places the issue of innovation as a key element for increasing competitiveness. [translation by the authors][67]

To achieve the aims of the PITCE, the government divided the sectors into strategic options and future carriers. The pharmaceutical sector, covering industry for both APIs and medicines, was included under strategic options, while nanotechnology and biotechnology were selected as future carriers.[68]

Competitiveness Forums were created to encourage dialogue between representatives from the government, private sector, and civil society and to address bottlenecks related to the production chain of a specific sector.[69] The Competitiveness Forum of the Pharmaceutical Production Chain (FCCPF) was coordinated by the MDIC and Ministry of Health while activities were developed through Working Groups coordinated by different government agencies. The FCCPF's work between 2003 and 2006 was considered by several stakeholders as the starting point in formulating instruments to induce the national industry, which were adopted from 2003 and continued throughout the second term of the Lula presidency (2007–2010).[70]

67 Lia Hasenclever et al., *Uma análise das políticas industriais e tecnológicas entre 2003-2014 e suas implicações para o Complexo Industrial da Saúde*, *in* Desafios de Operação e Desenvolvimento do Complexo Industrial da Saúde 99–126, 138–39 (Lia Hasenclever et al. eds., 2016).

68 Jackson De Toni, *Novos arranjos institucionais na renovação da política industrial brasileira*, 28 Ensaios FEE 1, 127–58 (2007).

69 Ministry of Health and Ministry of Development, Industry and Foreign Trade, *Fórum de competitividade da cadeia produtiva farmacêutica 2003–2006: O desafio de prosseguir* (2007), http://bvsms.saude.gov.br/bvs/publicacoes/forum_competitividade_cadeia_farmac_2003a2006_1ed.pdf (last visited Aug. 24 2019).

70 Chaves, *supra* note 26.

At the end of 2007, the Ministry of Health launched the federal plan on health for 2008–2011 called 'More Health: Everyone's Right' (*Mais Saúde: Direito de Todos*).[71] The Health Industrial Complex (CIS) was included as one of the proposed interventions, indicating the Ministry of Health's role in coordinating industrial policy related to health and resource allocation for that purpose. CIS proposals were based on the Brazilian industry's lack of international competitiveness, especially in knowledge-based sectors. Other measures in the *Mais Saúde* also sought to stimulate local production by strengthening public manufacturers and the production of strategic API through technology transfer and regulation of the state's procurement power.

From 2008 onwards, several decrees and ordinances were issued – mostly by the Ministry of Health – to implement the industrial policy toward health.[72] The following highlights, which provide a brief context under which Productive Development Partnerships (PDPs) were implemented, are notable.

A PDP generally[73] involves a technology transfer to a public manufacturer of a list of selected medicines already procured by the SUS. The incentive for a company to engage in a PDP to transfer the technology is the exclusivity of the public market – through procurement by the Ministry of Health – during the transfer period.

Under this type of partnership, the API would also have to be locally produced. In fact, the model adopted in the local production of *efavirenz* issued under Brazil's first CL (which was based on an agreement between the public and national private manufacturers for both the API and the final product) was the basis for the PDP model.[74] The difference is that there was no technology transfer in the CL case.

According to some analysts,[75] the implementation of the PDP approach in subsequent years shifted the attention of health managers from dealing with high medicine prices (by addressing patent barriers) to local production, together with other strategies. Although some evidence indicates price

71 Ministry of Health, *Mais Saúde – Direito de Todos* (1st ed. 2008).

72 Chaves, *supra* note 26.

73 Although the first PDP was announced in 2009, its first regulation was formally published in 2012. *See* Ministry of Health, Ordinance 837 of 18 April 2012 – Define as diretrizes e os critérios para o estabelecimento das Parcerias para Desenvolvimento Produtivo (PDP) (2012), replaced by Ordinance No. 2,531 in 2014. There were some changes in its design and more detailed information about its four phases, but the essential idea of the approach described in this chapter remained the same. *See* Ministry of Health, Ordinance No. 2,531 of 12 April 2014 – Redefine as diretrizes e os critérios para a definição da lista de produtos estratégicos para o Sistema Único de Saúde (SUS) e o estabelecimento das Parcerias para o Desenvolvimento Produtivo (PDP) e disciplina os respectivos processos de submissão, instrução, decisão, transferência e absorção de tecnologia, aquisição de produtos estratégicos para o SUS no âmbito das PDP e o respectivo monitoramento e avaliação (2014).

74 Chaves, *supra* note 26.

75 *Id.*; Tulio de Barros e Castro, *supra* note 29.

reduction in the context of a PDP,[76] this was not the primary concern of the approach[77] as one of its premises is the inability of national industry to charge competitive international prices. This raised a number of concerns among different stakeholders as it potentially undermined previous experiences in dealing with high medicine prices. The incentive for local production in a PDP is based on a technology transfer that could last up to 10 years, on a temporary market exclusivity in public procurement with the agreed upon price reduction. In previous experiences, manufacturers themselves had to develop the existing technologies, allowing production cost estimates to support price negotiation. The incentive to strengthen local production thus 'displaced' national manufacturers from the role of developers of the medicines and contributors to production cost estimates, and relegating them to mere recipients of technology transfer.

The debate surrounding local medicine production in developing countries and strategies to link health and industrial policies is not a simple one. On one side, concerns regarding prices charged by national manufacturers are legitimate and must be considered; on the other side, the availability of alternative generic versions of patented medicines is more restricted in a post-2005 TRIPS era.

Brazil issued a CL for *efavirenz* because there was an alternative importable source before the availability of the nationally produced version. However, this option may no longer exist for certain newer medicines. Thus, approaches to local production that ignore patent barriers or create further market exclusivity without a guarantee of strengthening national manufacturers also create a risk to the public provision of medicines, as the incorporation of new technologies has accelerated over the years,[78] putting an increasing burden on public expenditures for medicines and the need to address high prices.

76 Gabriela Costa Chaves et al., *Strategies for Price Reduction of HIV Medicines Under a Monopoly Situation in Brazil*, 49 Rev. Saúde Pública (2015), http://www.scielo.br/scielo.php?script=sci_arttext&pid=S0034-89102015000100309&lng=en&tlng=en (last visited Oct. 9, 2019).

77 Considering the well-known lack of competitiveness in terms of price by the domestic sector, especially when compared to those charged by countries of similar level of development, the expectation of price reductions in the context of the PDP was unambitious, reaching 5 percent annually (Chaves, *supra* note 26). In Ordinance No. 837/2012, it is said to be one of the objectives of PDP 'IV – Negotiating significant and progressive price reductions as technology is transferred and developed, according to how strategic is considered for SUS' (Free translation by the authors). This Ordinance was replaced by Ordinance No. 2,531/2014 which brings detailed information as regards top price reductions expected in PDP proposals, also considering reference prices from countries at the same level as Brazil.

78 Jorge Antonio Zepeda Bermudez et al., *New Drugs: Who can Afford Them?*, 32 Cad. Saúde Pública (2016), http://www.scielo.br/scielo.php?script=sci_arttext&pid=S0102-311X2016001400301&lng=en&tlng=en (last visited Oct. 9, 2019).

A recent article by the Ministry of Health[79] identified the following strategies adopted between 2012 and 2015 to reduce medicine prices: centralized procurement; price agreement with manufacturers based on comparison of effectiveness and price of technologies already adopted by the SUS for the same therapeutic indication; application of the Price Adequacy Coefficient to define the Maximum Government Selling Price for almost all medicines from the Specialized Component of Pharmaceutical Services (which include high price medicines); request for tax exemption of medicines incorporated in the SUS to the National Council of Finance Policy of the Ministry of Finance; and efforts for local production, including technology transfer through PDPs. No measure for addressing patent barriers was mentioned.

Although a PDP might include a voluntary license (VL) to address patent barriers, it was not essentially designed to deal with patent protection. However, where a technology transfer was linked to a VL, concerns were raised regarding the lower price reductions achieved under the PDP compared to other experiences, such as the threat and use of CL.[80]

Case studies have been published analyzing the effect of PDPs on medicine price reduction. The *atazanavir* case includes a VL in the context of a PDP. The analysis by Chaves et al[81] indicated the *atazanavir* price charged by Bristol-Myers Squibb to the Brazilian government between 2005 and 2013 and estimated the prices for 2014–2016 in the context of a PDP. Although the prices observed after the PDP (2012 and 2013) were around the expected 5 percent reduction per year, reductions prior to the introduction of the PDP were 37.6 percent between 2009 and 2011 for the 200-mg capsule dosage form and 49 percent for the 300-mg capsule. The analysis of the PDP also indicated very restrictive clauses for public manufacturers. For instance, it limits any potential room for competition, which would have led to more significant price reduction. Other commentators[82] compared the CL for *efavirenz* and the PDP involving a VL for *atazanavir* based on an estimate of the Brazilian government's savings. For a period of five years (2007–2011), procuring the generic alternative (imported and locally produced) led to a 58 percent savings of the estimated expenditure in case the CL was not issued.[83] In relation to *atazanavir*, the authors estimated a savings of 6 percent between 2011 and 2016.

79 Rodrigo Fernandes Alexandre et al., *Acesso aos medicamentos incorporados no SUS: estratégias para garantia da sustentabilidade econômica*, 4 Rev Eletrônica Gest Saúde, 3338–53 (2015).

80 Marcela Cristina Fogaça Vieira et al., *A promoção do acesso a medicamentos por meio da produção local: estudo de caso da experiência brasileira sobre o uso da licença compulsória e licença voluntária do ponto de vista da sociedade civil*, *in* Políticas de produção local de medicamentos no Brasil: elementos para o debate 85–130 (Pedro Villardi et al. eds., 2017).

81 Chaves et al., *supra* note 76.

82 Vieira et al., *supra* note 80.

83 *Id.* Guimarães, Hallal, Viegas, 2012 *apud* Vieira et al., *supra* note 80.

In another example, Moraes et al.[84] analyzed the prices charged in federal procurements for *imatinib* 100 and 400 mg between 2004 and 2013. Price reductions were observed for both dosage forms during the period. From 2009 to 2010, the price difference observed was 30 percent (100 mg) and almost 50 percent (400 mg). In 2011, the Ministry of Health centralized the procurement of *imatinib* and reductions observed between 2010 and 2012 were 11.2 percent (100 mg) and 12.6 percent (400 mg). According to the authors, reductions were probably a result of the close expiration of the patent (2012) and the threat of CL issuance. The PDP for *imatinib* was signed in 2012 and supply to the Ministry of Health started in 2013. The price reductions observed prior to the PDP were higher than the expected target of 5 percent per year in the context of the technology transfer.

In another instance,[85] the price paid by the Ministry of Health for TDF from 2003 to 2013 was analyzed. Reductions were observed for the whole period, including after the establishment of the PDP (2011–2013). A 53.7 percent price reduction was observed from 2005 to 2006, which reflects the result of price negotiations. However, the patent application for TDF was rejected by the Patent Office (INPI) in 2009, and the Ministry of Health announced the local production of TDF through a PDP. As the Ministry of Health still bought TDF from the multinational company Gilead in 2010, a reduction of 40 percent on the unit price from 2009 to 2010 was observed, indicating the effect of a combined approach of addressing the patent barrier and announcing local production. Price reductions in the context of a PDP involving the supply of a locally produced version amounted to 6.2 percent (2010–2011), 5.5 percent (2011–2012), and 10.33 percent (2012–2013). According to the authors, the manufacturers involved in the PDP were also regulated by the price reduction charged by Gilead, as they had to apply the 2010 price as a reference to estimate the reductions under the PDP, which was lower than the price previously considered as reference.

Other commentators such as Costa et al[86] also analyzed the prices paid by the Minister of Health for Alzheimer medicines from 2008 to 2013, some of which were subject to a PDP (*donazepil* and *rivastigmine*). They found a price reduction for *donazepil* and an increase or stabilization of the price for *rivastigmine*.

84 Elaine Lazzaroni Moraes et al., *Compras federais de antineoplásicos no Brasil: análise do mesilato de imatinibe, trastuzumabe e L-asparaginase, 2004–2013*, 26 Physis: Rev. Saúde Colet. 1357–82 (2016).

85 Gabriela Costa Chaves et al., *Redução de preço de medicamento em situação de monopólio no Sistema Único de Saúde: o caso do Tenofovir*, 28 Physis: Rev. Saúde Colet. (2018), http://www.scielo.br/scielo.php?script=sci_arttext&pid=S0103-73312018000100400&lng=pt&tlng=pt (last visited Oct. 9, 2019).

86 Roberta Dorneles Ferreira da Costa et al., *Aquisição de medicamentos para a Doença de Alzheimer no Brasil: uma análise no sistema federal de compras, 2008 a 2013*, 20 Ciên. Saúde Colet. 3827–38 (2015).

The above cases provide different angles regarding the role of PDPs in price reductions of medicines procured by the SUS. On one hand, generic and biosimilar alternatives in the international market are limited as a consequence of manufacturing developing countries becoming TRIPS-compliant in the post-2005 period and the exclusion of Brazil as a beneficiary of VLs.[87] Therefore, an approach to strengthen local production might be crucial to address some vulnerabilities of access to medicines policies at the SUS, such as high prices of monopoly technologies and shortages of old and essential ones.[88]

On the other hand, there are concerns[89] regarding the ability of PDPs or technology transfer to address the SUS' vulnerabilities in relation to access to medicines. Other approaches could also be considered, as shown in previous experiences where public manufacturers and national API companies supported the Ministry of Health by estimating production cost, presenting pre-grant oppositions, or supplying generic versions upon issuance of a CL. To improve the development and launch of newer products, investments in human resources and R&D should also be considered as a complementary strategy to local production.

Other issues[90] regarding PDPs and the technology of transfer approach relate to the transferring partners (which up until 2016[91] were mostly national companies), selection of existing technologies already adopted by the SUS, conditions of public manufacturers as recipients of the technology, and their ability to absorb and accumulate technologies. Meanwhile, other authors argue that policies targeting the vulnerabilities of the Brazilian pharmaceutical industry must be linked with addressing the vulnerabilities of pharmaceutical policies, otherwise the sustainability of policies in achieving universal access might be at risk.

Another challenge for the SUS is the constant incorporation of technologies, mostly under high prices and monopoly. For example, between 2012 and 2014, 64 technologies were adopted by the SUS among 148 requested.[92] In 2015, the incorporation of the newer Direct Acting Antivirals (DAAs) for hepatitis C – sofosbuvir, daclatasvir, and simeprevir – affected the profile of procurement of medicines for the disease, with a 230 percent increase in expenditure compared

87 Medecins Sans Frontières Access Campaign for Essential Medicines, *Untangling the Web of Antiretroviral Price Reduction* (15th ed. 2012).

88 Gabriela Costa Chaves et al., *Acesso a medicamentos no Brasil e estratégias para a produção nacional: desafios para a sustentabilidade do Sistema Único de Saúde*, *in* Políticas de produção local de medicamentos no Brasil : elementos para o debate 31–84 (Pedro Villardi et al. eds., 2017).

89 *Id.*

90 *Id.*

91 Carolinne Thays Scopel, Análise da estratégia das Parcerias para Desenvolvimento Produtivo de medicamentos na perspectiva da saúde pública (2016) (Master dissertation, ENSP/Fiocruz).

92 Bermudez et al., *supra* note 78.

to that in 2014 (from BRL412.6 million to BRL945.5 million). Assuming the volume purchased as a proxy of use and based on the therapeutic regimen, Chaves et al estimated that the procurement covered around 30,000 treatments, far below the estimated population of 1.4 and 1.7 million hepatitis C virus patients in Brazil.[93] As a result, CSOs argue that this scenario does not fulfill the universal access principle of the SUS.[94]

## Challenges in the Context of Reducing Public Financing for Health (2016–2018)

We contend that the most recent period beginning after 2015 is the most complex. It saw the 'impeachment' of democratically elected President Dilma Rousseff in 2016,[95] and the announcement and implementation of different measures by the former Vice President Michel Temer, who became president after 2016. Profound regressive and more conservative changes were felt especially within the social areas, including health.

The most dramatic regressive change was related to the public financing of the SUS. The 'New Tax Regime' based on Constitutional Amendment 95/2016 established a ceiling for federal primary expenditures and the freezing of annual financing for 20 years over several areas, including health and education. Expenses were expected to be frozen in the amount of BRL1.3 trillion per year, from 2017 to 2036, and adjusted only for inflation.[96] A prospective analysis estimated that losses for the SUS during the same period could range from BRL168 billion to BRL738 billion.[97]

At the same time, new and more expensive (even unaffordable) medicines are being licensed and incorporated into the SUS, which does not bode well for the future of the Brazilian health-care system. Judicial demands have also grown regarding high priced medicines for rare diseases[98,99] and expensive

93 Gabriela Costa Chaves et al., *Public Procurement of Hepatitis C Medicines in Brazil from 2005 to 2015*, 22 Ciênc. Saúde Colet. 2527–38 (2017).

94 GTPI/Rebrip – Working Group on Intellectual Property from the Brazilian Network for the Integration of People, *Hepatite C – A cura fora do alcance*, ABIA (2015).

95 Petra Costa, *The Edge of Democracy* (Netflix 2019).

96 Isabela Soares Santos & Fabiola Sulpino Vieira, *Direito à saúde e austeridade fiscal: o caso brasileiro em perspectiva internacional*, 23 Ciênc. Saúde Colet. 2303–14 (2018).

97 Equivalent to BRL8.4 billion per year or BRL36.9 billion per year, respectively. *See* Fabiola Sulpino Vieira & Rodrigo Pucci De Sá E Benevides, *O Direito à Saúde no Brasil em Tempos de Crise Econômica, Ajuste Fiscal e Reforma Implícita do Estado*, 10 Revista de Estudos e Pesquisas sobre as Américas 10, 28 (2016).

98 In Brazil, rare diseases are those that affect less than 65 in every 100,000 persons.

99 Rosangela Wolf Moro, *Doenças raras: luta pelo acesso ao tratamento*, O Estado de São Paulo, https://saude.estadao.com.br/noticias/geral,doencas-raras-luta-pelo-acesso-ao-tratamento,70002738682 (last visited Oct. 14, 2019).

treatments.[100] As a result, the Ministry of Health issued a special ruling regarding rare diseases and access to diagnostics and treatment within the SUS.[101]

In addition to the constant incorporation of health technologies at high prices is the exclusivity situation from the supply side at the national level, involving multiple patent applications in varying status, which creates a legal uncertainty for generic competition. Chaves et al[102] identified medicines under this exclusivity situation that were financed by the Ministry of Health in 2016. From a total of 74 API (with all pharmaceutical presentations under exclusivity), 33 had pending patent applications, with the others rejected, dismissed, or expired. A total of 26 had at least one patent granted, with the other applications rejected, dismissed, or expired. This shows that the backlog in patent examination of secondary patent applications creates a *de facto* monopoly, as illustrated by the case of *sofosbuvir* below. This situation is even worse because if granted after 10 years of application in the country, the patent can enjoy an extension of the 20-year term, based on the TRIPS-plus provision under Brazilian law.

The worldwide launching in December 2013 of the so-called DAAs at unaffordable prices threatened developing countries as well as high-income economies and private health systems. The imminent incorporation of these technologies into the SUS triggered the development of a range of actions proposed and coordinated by the Oswaldo Cruz Foundation (Fiocruz) to increase the Ministry of Health's bargaining power in price negotiations, first by addressing patent barriers and stimulating local production. This included an international workshop and a public hearing at the Brazilian Parliament to bring the issue onto the political agenda.

The second step involved the definition by professionals from different public institutions of the patent landscape of DAAs in Brazil to distinguish primary applications (APIs and their synthetic process) from secondary ones (related to evergreening). All applications and patents related to one API were also analyzed in terms of their potential to block generic competition. For example, when analyzed in relation to their status, there were only pending applications and no patent granted at the time for *sofosbuvir*.

To address patent barriers, and based on the request from Fiocruz, the Ministry of Health requested the INPI in 2016 to conduct priority examination[103] of patent

100 Thaís Jeronimo Vidal et al., *The Lawsuits to Antineoplastic Drugs: The Tip of an Iceberg?*, 22 Ciênc. Saúde Colet. 2539–48 (2017).

101 Ministry of Health, Ordinance No. 199, 30 January 2014, Institui a Política Nacional de Atenção Integral às Pessoas com Doenças Raras, aprova as Diretrizes para Atenção Integral às Pessoas com Doenças Raras no âmbito do Sistema Único de Saúde (SUS) e institui incentivos financeiros de custeio (2014).

102 Gabriela Costa Chaves et al., *Medicines Under Exclusivity Situation Funded by the Ministry of Health: Analysis of the Patent Situation and Public Procurement* (1st ed. 2019), https://accessibsa.org/media/2019/08/Medicines-under-Exclusivity-Situation-funded-by-the-Ministry-of-Health.pdf (last visited Sept. 12, 2019).

103 Ministry of Health, Solicitação do exame prioritário do pedido de patente PI 0919404-5, Ofício No. 882/2016/SCTIE/MS (2016).

applications related to *sofosbuvir*, *daclatasvir*, *simeprevir*, and *ledipasvir* to bypass the backlog of patent analysis, which takes up to 13 years in Brazil.[104] This included a detailed description of each patent application to help in classifying the ones blocking generic competition. The Ministry of Health also requested priority examination for *adalimumab, atazanavir, pramipexole, sirolimus, formoterol fumarate dihydrate + budesonide, bevacizumab, glatiramer acetate, raltegravir, trastuzumab, clozapine, infliximab, everolimus,* and *imatinib* in 2017.[105]

Farmanguinhos/Fiocruz[106] also presented a pre-grant opposition in 2017 against one of the patent applications for *sofosbuvir*, following oppositions already presented in 2015 and 2016 by CSOs[107] and the national private company Blanver.

In relation to local production, a Technical Cooperation Agreement was signed in 2016 by Fiocruz and a consortium of national private companies for developing the API and the formulation of a generic version of *sofosbuvir*.[108] This was closely monitored by Anvisa, and the final product successfully obtained market approval in 2018.[109] The generic *sofosbuvir* was made available at a price lower than the originator product, and the Ministry of Health set up a tender to promote competition. Based on the lowest price, the national generic version was selected. However, Gilead was able to obtain a court injunction in December 2018 which blocked the supply of the generic medicine to the Ministry of Health.[110]

Post-2015 can also be seen as the period in which there were setbacks in addressing TRIPS-plus provisions under Brazilian law and the use of TRIPS flexibilities. Both TRIPS-plus provisions – the pipeline mechanism and the patent extension for delay in patent examination – are subject of Direct Actions

104 Mauro Sodré Maia, *Backlog de Patentes*, Revista Facto, 2018, at 20–21.

105 Ministry of Health, Exame prioritário dos pedidos de patente relacionados aos medicamentos adalimumabe, acetato de glatiramer, atazanavir, bevacizumabe, everolimus, fazaclo, glivec, infliximabe, kaletra, pramipexol, raltegravir, sevelamer, sirolimus, symbicort e trastuzumabe. tuzumabe. Ofício No. 1313/2017/SCTIE/MS (2017).

106 Alexandre Matos, *Contra preços abusivos, a favor da saúde pública*, Farmanguinhos (2017), https://www.far.fiocruz.br/2017/02/contra-precos-abusivos-a-favor-da-saude-publica/ (last visited May 24, 2019).

107 Working Group on Intellectual Property of the Brazilian Network for the Integration of People – GTPI/Rebrip, *Contestações de patentes*, http://deolhonaspatentes.org/contestacoes-de-patentes/ (last visited May 24, 2019).

108 *Fiocruz firma parceria para medicamento contra hepatite C*, Fiocruz (2016), https://portal.fiocruz.br/noticia/fiocruz-firma-parceria-para-medicamento-contra-hepatite-c (last visited Oct. 14, 2019).

109 *Anvisa aprova novo genérico para tratamento da hepatite C*, ANVISA (2018), http://portal.anvisa.gov.br/noticias/-/asset_publisher/FXrpx9qY7FbU/content/anvisa-aprova-novo-generico-para-tratamento-da-hepatite-c/219201/pop_up?inheritRedirect=false (last visited Oct. 14, 2019).

110 *Liminar barra entrega de genéricos contra hepatite C para 15 mil pacientes*, Folha de São Paulo (2018), http://agenciaaids.com.br/noticia/folha-de-s-paulo-liminar-barra-entrega-de-genericos-contra-hepatite-c-para-15-mil-pacientes/ (last visited Oct. 14, 2019).

of Unconstitutionality at the Federal Supreme Court. Although the 'pipeline case'[111] has been in court since 2009, it was only considered to be judged in September 2018. However, the judgment was unexpectedly cancelled the day before.[112]

The role of Anvisa in the examination of pharmaceutical patent applications (Anvisa's prior consent) has been subject to attacks since its incorporation in the law in 2001.[113] This was considered a crucial public health TRIPS flexibility in avoiding the grant of secondary patent applications. However, the new regulation approved by both Anvisa and the INPI in 2017 weakened Anvisa's prior consent by shifting its role in patent examination and approval. Anvisa was mandated to adhere to the role of providing third-party observations to the INPI's patent examination of applications related to medicines of interest to the SUS.[114]

Additionally, we need to consider that the expectation of patent grant (or not) also inhibits competition for several years and grants a *de facto* monopoly. For many patent holders, the delays in patent examination create an atmosphere of monopoly while causing legal constraints for generic companies who are unable to launch cheaper generic products, which would have expanded access to lower cost products within the health system. Recent initiatives proposed by the government to decrease and end the patent backlog may be considered as more problematic than straightforward. In 2017, a Parliamentary Commission Report aiming to decrease bureaucratic issues in Brazil included a reduction of the timing for the granting of patents. The proposal that was discussed, proposed, and eagerly adopted by government representatives was the automatic grant of all pending patents to expedite approval without merit examinations. Such proposal was severely criticized[115] as it would represent the approval of unnecessary patents that otherwise would not be granted. Although the proposal excluded pharmaceutical patent applications, there would be a clear risk that once the precedent of non-examination was put in place, it would end up being applied to all fields.

111 Lia Hasenclever et al., *O instituto de patentes Pipeline e o acesso a medicamentos: aspectos econômicos e jurídicos deletérios à economia da saúde*, 11 Rev. Direito Sanit. 2 (2010).

112 Marcela Fogaça Vieira, *Brazilian Supreme Court Refuses to Judge Its Biggest Case on IP and Access to Medicines, and Benefits Big Pharma with Undue Monopolies*, Intellectual Property Watch (2018), https://www.ip-watch.org/2018/09/13/brazilian-supreme-court-refuses-judge-biggest-case-ip-access-medicines-benefits-big-pharma-undue-monopolies/ (last visited Oct. 14, 2019).

113 Kenneth C. Shadlen, *The Political Contradictions of Incremental Innovation: Lessons from Pharmaceutical Patent Examination in Brazil*, 39 Polit. Soc. 143–74 (2011).

114 Brazil, Anvisa/INPI, Regulamenta os procedimentos para a aplicação do artigo 229-C da Lei no. 9.279, de 14 de maio de 1996, acrescido pela Lei no. 10.196, de 14 de fevereiro de 2001, e dá outras providências. Portaria Conjunta no. 1, de 12 de abril de 2017. Diário Oficial da União da 13/04/2017, Edição 72, Seção 1: 63 (2017).

115 Jorge Antonio Zepeda Bermudez et al., *Patentes por decreto: Brasil na contramão*, Fiocruz (2017), http://cee.fiocruz.br/?q=node/616 (last visited Oct. 14, 2019).

Other proposals include delegation to third parties and contractual arrangements with external parties to act as patent examiners. These proposals, we contend, pose a risk of being extremely liberal and do not align with the recommendations of the UN Secretary-General High-Level Panel on Access to Medicines that 'WTO Members should make full use of the policy space available in Article 27 of the TRIPS Agreement by adopting and applying rigorous definitions of invention and patentability that curtail the evergreening to ensure that patents are only awarded when genuine innovation has occurred'.[116]

## Final Considerations

This chapter aimed to provide an overview of the implementation of the TRIPS Agreement in Brazil by looking into the strategies adopted to implement and sustain medicine access policies in the public sector. Specific periods provided the context within which to analyze changes in strategies for obtaining price reduction for medicines in the SUS.

The first period indicated efforts to adopt and interpret the use of TRIPS flexibilities in the national legislation, the use of public production as a means of cost reduction, and the use of threats of CL issuance to support price negotiations.

The second period continued the trajectory developed in the first period in relation to strategies for price reduction of monopoly medicines. It also marked the issuance of a CL for *efavirenz* based on both importation and local production, and an expansion of the Brazilian government's participation at the international level on issues related to IPR and access to medicines.

The third period identified a shift in government strategies for local production based on the technology transfer approach (PDP), including for high-priced medicines already adopted by the SUS. Issues related to patent barriers and the need to use TRIPS flexibilities were not seen as a top priority by the Ministry of Health with regard to high prices of medicines until the adoption of the newer DAAs in 2015, which required the convergence of different governmental stakeholders in addressing patent barriers and pursuing generic local production to push for price reduction. However, this seemed to be an isolated case and was not a systematic approach in dealing with high medicine prices, especially considering the constant incorporation of high-priced medicines in the SUS.

In comparison to previous decades, there seem to be emerging changes at the international level as high prices of monopoly medicines are now being mentioned as affecting health systems in developed countries, and stakeholders are going public in discussions about the issuance of CLs – such as in the

116 UN Secretary-General's High-Level Panel on Access to Medicines, *Report of the United Nations Secretary-General's High-Level Panel on Access to Medicines – Promoting Innovation and Access to Health Technologies* 9 (2017).

Netherlands[117] and United Kingdom[118] – and the local production of generic medicines, which is being adopted by a group of hospitals in the US to address shortages and high prices.[119]

Although there is the prospect of the federal health budget being frozen for the next 20 years, with severe consequences to the fulfillment of the right to universal access, the Brazilian demand is still significant, especially as some technologies are only provided by the SUS. Therefore, we believe that the government's bargaining power in price reduction negotiations for monopoly medicines will only be strong if strategies to address patent barriers and stimulate local production are all in place to mitigate the vulnerabilities of the SUS' pharmaceutical services.

117 Ellen T'Hoen, *Medicines Excitement in the Netherlands – New Health Minister Announces Firm Action on 'Absurd' Medicines Pricing and Gets the European Medicines Agency*, Medicines Law and Policy (2017), https://medicineslawandpolicy.org/2017/11/medicines-excitement-in-the-netherlands-new-health-minister-announces-firm-action-on-absurd-medicines-pricing-and-gets-the-european-medicines-agency/ (last visited Oct. 15, 2019).

118 *Medicines for the Many: Public Health Before Private Profit*, UK Labor Party (2019), http://labour.org.uk/wp-content/uploads/2019/09/Medicines-For-The-Many.pdf (last visited Oct. 15, 2019).

119 Carolyn Y. Johnson, *Major US Hospitals Launch Not-for-profit Drug Company to Battle Pharmaceutical Corporations*, The Independent (2018), https://www.independent.co.uk/news/world/americas/us-healthcare-hospitals-drug-company-not-for-profit-pharmaceutical-corporations-civica-rx-a8525236.html. (last visited Oct. 15, 2019).

# 9 From Struggle to Surge

## China's TRIPS Experience and Its Lessons for Access to Medicines

*Peter K. Yu**

### Introduction

Entering into force on January 1, 1995, the Agreement on Trade-Related Aspects of Intellectual Property Rights (TRIPS Agreement) of the World Trade Organization (WTO) has imposed unprecedented burdens on countries in the developing world. In the public health arena, its high protection and enforcement standards have not only greatly jeopardized access to medicines – at both the domestic and international levels – but have also eroded the policy space and flexibilities developing countries need to devise solutions for public health challenges.[1]

The detrimental effects of the TRIPS Agreement were so overwhelming that the WTO members quickly adopted the Doha Declaration on the TRIPS Agreement and Public Health in November 2001, shortly after the expiration of the transition period for developing countries. For the world's poorest countries, known as "least developed countries," paragraph 7 of the Declaration delayed the mandatory protection of pharmaceutical patents and undisclosed test data until January 1, 2016. That deadline has since been extended to January 1, 2033. In December 2005, the WTO members further agreed to amend the TRIPS Agreement by introducing Article 31*bis*, which allows countries with insufficient or no manufacturing capacity to import generic versions of patented pharmaceuticals. Although it took more than a decade to ratify the amendment protocol, the new provision finally took effect on January 23, 2017.

While many developing and least developed countries continue to struggle with the high and arguably inappropriate TRIPS standards, large or populous emerging economies, such as Brazil, China, India, South Africa, and Thailand, have managed to adapt the TRIPS Agreement with some success.[2] Notable

 This chapter was adapted and expanded from Peter K. Yu, *China's Innovative Turn and the Changing Pharmaceutical Landscape*, 51 U. Pac. L. Rev. 593 (2020).

1 *See* Peter K. Yu, *The International Enclosure Movement*, 82 Ind. L.J. 827 (2007).

2 *See* Wu Handong, *One Hundred Years of Progress: The Development of the Intellectual Property System in China*, 1 WIPO J. 117, 118–19 (2009); Peter K. Yu, *TRIPS and Its Contents*, 60 IDEA 149, 207–15 (2020); Peter K. Yu, *When the Chinese Intellectual Property System Hits 35*, 8 Queen Mary J. Intell. Prop. 3, 12 (2018) [hereinafter Yu, *Chinese IP System*].

successes with significant public health implications include Brazil and Thailand's threats or issuance of compulsory licenses (CLs),[3] China's development of national intellectual property (IP) and patent development strategies (discussed in greater detail below), India's maximization of the transition period and introduction of Section 3(d) of the Indian Patents (Amendment) Act of 2005,[4] and South Africa's critical contributions to the global effort to combat the HIV/AIDS pandemic.[5]

As economic and technological conditions improved, these emerging economies began to secure even greater benefits from the TRIPS-based IP system, thereby initiating a self-reinforcing virtuous cycle. In recent years, some of these countries have also become more assertive, both as innovative powers and in the public health arena. As former WTO Director-General Roberto Azevêdo recalled,

> [I]n 1995, and earlier in the negotiations leading to the conclusion of TRIPS, the international IP system was largely seen as a trade interest of the developed economies. Today, the picture differs dramatically. Some middle-income countries are among the major users of the global IP system, and many other developing countries are increasingly engaged with it.[6]

Of all emerging economies, no country provides a better illustration for a complete transformation of its IP system and pharmaceutical landscape than China. This chapter therefore aims to document the country's journey from its struggle with the TRIPS Agreement to its recent surge in the global pharmaceutical arena. It begins by recounting China's initial reluctance to introduce high and externally driven IP standards, including the TRIPS standards that were introduced before and shortly after the country's accession to the WTO. The chapter then discusses China's innovative turn, which began in the mid-2000s

3 *See* Jonathan Burton-MacLeod, *Tipping Point: Thai Compulsory Licences Redefine Essential Medicines Debate*, *in* INCENTIVES FOR GLOBAL PUBLIC HEALTH: PATENT LAW AND ACCESS TO ESSENTIAL MEDICINES 406 (Thomas Pogge et al. eds., 2010); Yu, *supra* note 1, at 846–50; Peter K. Yu, *Virotech Patents, Viropiracy, and Viral Sovereignty*, 45 ARIZ. ST. L.J. 1563, 1578–81 (2013).

4 *See* Amy Kapczynski, *Harmonization and Its Discontents: A Case Study of TRIPS Implementation in India's Pharmaceutical Sector*, 97 CALIF. L. REV. 1571, 1588–616 (2009); Peter K. Yu, *Are Developing Countries Playing a Better TRIPS Game?*, 16 UCLA J. INT'L L. & FOREIGN AFFS. 311, 324–25 (2011).

5 *See* SUSAN K. SELL, PRIVATE POWER, PUBLIC LAW: THE GLOBALIZATION OF INTELLECTUAL PROPERTY RIGHTS 146–62 (2003); Debora Halbert, *Moralized Discourses: South Africa's Intellectual Property Fight for Access to AIDS Drugs*, 1 SEATTLE J. SOC. JUST. 257 (2002); Peter K. Yu, *Access to Medicines, BRICS Alliances, and Collective Action*, 34 AM. J.L. & MED. 345, 354–55 (2008).

6 Roberto Azevêdo, *Foreword* to THE MAKING OF THE TRIPS AGREEMENT: PERSONAL INSIGHTS FROM THE URUGUAY ROUND NEGOTIATIONS xiii, xiii (Jayashree Watal & Antony Taubman eds., 2015).

when its leaders made a major policy push toward the development of independent innovation. The chapter further examines the recently proposed amendments to Chinese patent law and pharmaceutical regulations. It concludes with five distinct lessons that China's TRIPS experience has provided for the debate on the TRIPS Agreement and access to medicines.

## Pre-TRIPS and TRIPS Struggle

Although the history of Chinese medical innovations dates back to more than two millennia[7] and China adopted patent laws in 1912 and 1944,[8] the country did not establish a modern patent system until its economy reopened to the outside world in the late 1970s. In 1984, China established the Patent Law, reviving the protection that inventions had once enjoyed. Except for a brief period from 1950 to 1954, during which patents were granted in the then newly founded People's Republic of China, inventors obtained protection through inventors' certificates (*faming zhengshu*) and other types of awards or remuneration.[9] A few months after the adoption of the 1984 Patent Law, China acceded to the Paris Convention for the Protection of Industrial Property, which took effect on March 19, 1985.

Even though the 1984 statute ushered in a new innovation system, its effectiveness "was greatly limited by a lack of experience with patent protection, the uneasiness about introducing private rights in a socialist environment and a myriad of compromises struck in the drafting process."[10] Notably, Article 25 excluded "pharmaceutical products, and substances obtained by means of a chemical process," similar to the exclusions found in the patent laws of India and other developing countries.[11] Such limited protection in the patent area, as well as in other areas of IP law such as copyright,[12] eventually led to increased external pressure from the United States (US) and other developed countries.[13]

7 *See* Teresa Schroeder, Comment, *Chinese Regulation of Traditional Chinese Medicine in the Modern World: Can the Chinese Effectively Profit from One of Their Most Valuable Cultural Resources*, 11 Pac. Rim L. & Pol'y J. 687, 689 (2002).

8 *See* Peter K. Yu, *Building the Ladder: Three Decades of Development of the Chinese Patent System*, 5 WIPO J. 1, 4 (2013).

9 *See* Zheng Chengsi with Michael D. Pendleton, Chinese Intellectual Property and Technology Transfer Law 52 (1987); Yu, *supra* note 8, at 5.

10 Yu, *supra* note 8, at 7. On the drafting of the 1984 Patent Law, see William P. Alford, To Steal a Book Is an Elegant Offense: Intellectual Property Law in Chinese Civilization 66, 70 (1995); Andrew C. Mertha, The Politics of Piracy: Intellectual Property in Contemporary China 82–87 (2005).

11 Yu, *supra* note 3, at 1632–33.

12 *See* Yu, *supra* note 8, at 8.

13 *See* Warren H. Maruyama, *U.S.-China IPR Negotiations: Trade, Intellectual Property, and the Rule of Law in a Global Economy*, *in* Chinese Intellectual Property Law and Practice 165, 186 (Mark A. Cohen et al. eds., 1999); Peter K. Yu, *From Pirates to Partners: Protecting Intellectual Property in China in the Twenty-first Century*, 50 Am. U. L. Rev. 131, 140–51 (2000).

In January 1992, China signed the Memorandum of Understanding on the Protection of Intellectual Property with the United States, in large part to avert an impending trade war. Included in this instrument were strengthened protection for pharmaceuticals and commitments in other areas of IP law. Article 1(a) stated explicitly: "Patents shall be available for all chemical inventions, including pharmaceuticals and agricultural chemicals, whether products or processes." Article 2 further memorialized China's "agree[ment] to provide administrative protection to U.S. pharmaceutical and agricultural chemical product inventions."

Pursuant to this memorandum of understanding, China amended its patent law in September 1992, expanding the scope of protection in Article 25 to cover foods, beverages, condiments, pharmaceutical products, and "substances obtained by means of a chemical process." In addition, the amended law added the right to import, extended patent protection to both products and processes, and lengthened the duration of protection from 15 to 20 years. The law also severely curtailed the scope of CLs, which were of great concern to the US pharmaceutical industry. Taken together, these amended provisions gave China the high patent standards then under negotiation at the Uruguay Round of Multilateral Trade Negotiations and that would soon find their way to the final text of the TRIPS Agreement. A year after the adoption of the 1992 Patent Law, China joined the Patent Cooperation Treaty (PCT).

In the next few years, China prepared to join the WTO and worked hard to conform its IP laws to the TRIPS requirements.[14] In August 2000, China amended its patent law for the second time. Consistent with the TRIPS Agreement, the law prohibited "offers for sale" of infringing products, tightened the standards for obtaining CLs, and allowed for the judicial review of patent invalidations. To strengthen protections for both local and foreign rights holders, the law required innocent infringers to prove the legitimate source of the patented product. When it was difficult to determine damages, the amended law allowed for compensation based on appropriate royalties. In December 2001, China finally became the 143rd member of the WTO.[15]

Immediately after joining the WTO, China did not receive as much international pressure as it did before the accession. From 2002 to 2004, the Office of the US Trade Representative (USTR) removed China from the Section 301 Watch List or Priority Watch List, thereby allowing it to enjoy a rarely available honeymoon period.[16] Nevertheless, countries and their supportive IP rights holders – including those in the pharmaceutical industry – remained highly concerned about inadequate enforcement. As the *2005 National Trade Estimate*

14 *See* Yu, *supra* note 8, at 10.

15 On China's performance in the intellectual property area in its first decade in the WTO, see Peter K. Yu, *The First Decade of TRIPS in China*, *in* CHINA AND GLOBAL TRADE GOVERNANCE: CHINA'S FIRST DECADE IN THE WORLD TRADE ORGANIZATION 126 (Zeng Ka & Liang Wei eds., 2013).

16 *See* Peter K. Yu, *The Rise and Decline of the Intellectual Property Powers*, 34 CAMPBELL L. REV. 525, 526 n.2 (2012).

*Report on Foreign Trade Barriers* stated, "while China has made significant progress in its efforts to make its framework of laws, regulations and implementing rules WTO-consistent, serious problems remain, particularly with China's enforcement of intellectual property rights."[17] In April 2005, the USTR added China back to the Priority Watch List, on which the country has remained ever since.[18] Two years later, the US filed its first TRIPS complaint against China, focusing on its noncompliance with WTO rules in the areas of criminal enforcement, border control, and censorship.[19]

## China's Innovative Turn

Although the Chinese patent system experienced considerable changes in its first two decades of existence, its repeated reforms were tailored more to external demands than to changing internal conditions.[20] Indeed, the system was built mostly upon legal transplants from abroad.[21] It was not until the adoption of the third amendment to the Patent Law in December 2008 that China was able to make major adjustments to the patent system based on its own needs, interests, conditions, and priorities. As Guo He recounted, "The impetus for the early amendments came from outside, whilst the need for the third amendment originated from within China, that is to say, the majority of the third amendment was to meet the needs of the development of the domestic economy and technology originating in China."[22]

Reflecting "the country's growing emphasis on using patents to help develop a knowledge-based economy,"[23] the 2008 Patent Law increased the amount of damages and fines, including statutory damages. The law also allowed for parallel importation while introducing the Chinese equivalent of a Bolar exception,

17 Office of the U.S. Trade Representative, 2005 National Trade Estimate Report on Foreign Trade Barriers 95 (2005).

18 *See* Peter K. Yu, *From Pirates to Partners (Episode II): Protecting Intellectual Property in Post-WTO China*, 55 Am. U. L. Rev. 901, 925 (2006).

19 On this complaint, see Peter K. Yu, *The TRIPS Enforcement Dispute*, 89 Neb. L. Rev. 1046 (2011); Peter K. Yu, *TRIPS Enforcement and Developing Countries*, 26 Am. U. Int'l L. Rev. 727 (2011).

20 In addition to conforming Chinese patent law to TRIPS standards, the Second Amendment addressed the rapidly changing local conditions, such as "the Chinese leaders' changing attitude towards the rule of law, the emergence of private property rights and local stakeholders, the increasing concerns about ambiguities over relationships in state-owned enterprises, and the government's active push for modernization." Yu, *supra* note 18, at 908, 914–22.

21 *See* Peter K. Yu, *The Transplant and Transformation of Intellectual Property Laws in China*, *in* Governance of Intellectual Property Rights in China and Europe 20 (Nari Lee et al. eds., 2016).

22 Guo He, *Patents*, *in* Chinese Intellectual Property and Technology Laws 25, 28 (Rohan Kariyawasam ed., 2011).

23 Yu, *supra* note 8, at 10.

which enables generic pharmaceutical producers to import, manufacture, or test a patented product prior to the expiry of the patent "for the purpose of scientific research and experimentation" or "providing information required for administrative examination and approval."

A few months before adopting this third amendment, the State Council instituted a new National Intellectual Property Strategy, which "provided a comprehensive plan to improve the creation, utilization, protection, and administration of intellectual property rights."[24] Paragraph 7 specifically emphasized the need for active development of independent or self-controlled IP (*zizhu zhishi chanquan*). Building on this strategy and taking advantage of the new patent law amendment, the State Intellectual Property Office (SIPO), now the National Intellectual Property Administration of China (CNIPA), adopted a National Patent Development Strategy in November 2010.[25] Although the SIPO strategy set a highly ambitious target of two million patents per year by 2015, China surpassed that target three years before.[26]

Today, China no longer hesitates to offer protection to patents and pharmaceutical products – a significant contrast from three decades ago. Instead, the country has slowly emerged as a major player in the international patent system. In 2019, China became the world's leader in PCT applications, overtaking the US for the first time.[27] Based on statistics provided by the World Intellectual Property Organization (WIPO), Huawei Technologies, Guangdong Oppo Mobile Telecommunications, the BOE Technology Group, and Ping An Technology – all Chinese companies – ranked among the world's top eight corporate PCT applicants.[28]

At the domestic level, the total number of patent applications has been equally impressive. Based on CNIPA statistics, China processed over 4.3 million patent applications in 2019, with over 4.1 million originating from domestic applicants.[29] While these figures included three types of patents – inventions, designs, and utility models – the number of invention patents issued in China in 2019

24 Peter K. Yu, *A Half-Century of Scholarship on the Chinese Intellectual Property System*, 67 Am. U. L. Rev. 1045, 1079–85 (2018).

25 *See* Peter K. Yu, *Five Oft-Repeated Questions About China's Recent Rise as a Patent Power*, 2013 Cardozo L. Rev. De Novo 78, 80–82.

26 *See* Yu, *Chinese IP System*, *supra* note 2, at 5.

27 Press Release, World Intellectual Property Organization, China Becomes Top Filer of International Patents in 2019 amid Robust Growth for WIPO's IP Services, Treaties and Finances (Apr. 7, 2020), https://www.wipo.int/pressroom/en/articles/2020/article_0005.html.

28 *Annex 2: Top PCT Applicants*, World Intell. Prop. Org. (Apr. 7, 2020), https://www.wipo.int/export/sites/www/pressroom/en/documents/pr_2020_848_annexes.pdf#annex2.

29 National Intellectual Property Administration of China, *Table 1 Statistics on Applications for Inventions from Home and Abroad*, http://english.cnipa.gov.cn/statistics/2019/201912/1146705.htm (last visited June 28, 2020).

(452,804) compared favorably with that of utility patents issued in the US in the same year (336,855).[30]

To be sure, questions have arisen over the quality of patents that the CNIPA and its predecessor, SIPO, have issued.[31] Nevertheless, Chinese firms have been actively applying for and obtaining patents at both the European Patent Office and the US Patent and Trademark Office. Based on the 2017 statistics concerning patent applications filed in the US, residents of mainland China (32,127) were behind only those from Japan (89,364), South Korea (38,026), and Germany (32,771).[32] According to the European Patent Office, about 16 percent of its patent filings in that same year originated in China, which trailed behind only the US and Japan.[33]

If these statistics are not impressive enough, China ranked 14th in both the 2020 and 2019 Global Innovation Index, moving up from 17th in 2018, 22nd in 2017, and 25th in 2016.[34] As the 2019 report stated, "China continues its upward rise … and firmly establishes itself as one of the innovation leaders."[35] The country "was [also] responsible for 24% of the world's [research-and-development] expenditures in 2017, up from only 2.6% in 1996."[36] In sum, China's innovative turn has significant ramifications, not only at the domestic level but also at the international level.

30 *Compare* National Intellectual Property Administration of China, *Table 3 Distribution of Grants for Inventions Received from Home and Abroad*, http://english.cnipa.gov.cn/statistics/2019/201912/1146707.htm (last visited June 28, 2020), *with* U.S. Patent & Trademark Office, FY 2019 Performance and Accountability Report 166 (2019).

31 *See* Dan Prud'homme, Dulling the Cutting-Edge: How Patent-Related Policies and Practices Hamper Innovation in China 1 (2012); Zhuang Wei, *Evolution of the Patent System in China*, *in* Emerging Markets and the World Patent Order 155, 156–58 (Frederick M. Abbott et al. eds., 2013); Mark Liang, *Chinese Patent Quality: Running the Numbers and Possible Remedies*, 11 J. Marshall Rev. Intell. Prop. L. 478 (2012).

32 U.S. Patent & Trademark Office, *supra* note 30, at 184–85.

33 European Patent Office, *European Patent Filings per Country of Origin*, https://www.epo.org/about-us/annual-reports-statistics/annual-report/2017/statistics/patent-filings.html#tab3 (last visited June 28, 2020).

34 *Rankings*, *in* Global Innovation Index 2020: Who Will Finance Innovation? xxxii, xxxii (Soumitra Dutta et al. eds., 2020); *Rankings*, *in* Global Innovation Index 2019: Creating Healthy Lives – The Future of Medical Innovation xxxiv, xxxiv (Soumitra Dutta et al. eds., 2019) [hereinafter Global Innovation Index 2019]; *Rankings*, *in* Global Innovation Index 2018: Energizing the World with Innovation xx, xx (Soumitra Dutta et al. eds., 2018); *Rankings*, *in* Global Innovation Index 2017: Innovation Feeding the World xviii, xviii (Soumitra Dutta et al. eds., 2017); *Rankings*, *in* Global Innovation Index 2016: Winning with Global Innovation xviii, xviii (Soumitra Dutta et al. eds., 2016).

35 Soumitra Dutta et al., *The Global Innovation Index 2019*, *in* Global Innovation Index 2019, *supra* note 34, at 1, 9.

36 *Id.* at 3.

## Changing Pharmaceutical Landscape

Thus far, the key driving force behind China's innovative turn is the developments in the electronics and telecommunications industries. Huawei, Oppo, BOE, and Ping An – the four leading corporate PCT applicants worldwide in 2019 – all belong to these industries. Nevertheless, recent years have seen Chinese leaders making a major policy push to actively strengthen the indigenous pharmaceutical industry, including the development of national champions.

In February 2006, the State Council released the *National Medium- and Long-Term Plan for Science and Technology Development* (2006–2020), which listed biotechnology as one of the eight frontier technologies. A decade later, the State Council issued a notice for the *Made in China 2025* strategic plan, which also identified biomedicine and high-performance medical devices as one of the ten priority sectors.[37] Among the medical products and technologies that China intends to develop are "biologic-based therapeutics, such as antibody drugs, antibody-drug conjugates, new structural proteins, polypeptide drugs, and new vaccines; technologies to support individualized drug treatments (i.e., precision medicine); and breakthrough technologies, such as induced pluripotent stem cells."[38]

For more than a decade, China has been the world's leading supplier of active pharmaceutical ingredients (APIs).[39] Today, it has the world's second largest pharmaceutical market, behind only the US.[40] With a market "worth more than $120 billion,"[41] China "account[s] for 20% of total global API output" and "produces over 2000 API drug products, with annual production capacity exceeding 2 million tons."[42] In addition, the country produces about 4 percent of the world's new pharmaceutical products.[43] It also has a strong and vibrant market in traditional medicine,[44] which in 2015 "account[ed] for 28.55% of the total [output value] generated by the country's pharmaceutical industry."[45]

37 *See* U.S. Chamber of Commerce, Made in China 2025: Global Ambitions Built on Local Protections 10 (2017).

38 Gryphon Scientific, LLC & Rhodium Group, LLC, China's Biotechnology Development: The Role of US and Other Foreign Engagement: A Report Prepared for the U.S.-China Economic and Security Review Commission 38 (2019).

39 *See* World Health Organization, China Policies to Promote Local Production of Pharmaceutical Products and Protect Public Health 17–18 (2017) (prepared by Frederick Abbott); Yu, *supra* note 5, at 363.

40 *See* Issaku Harada, *China Extends Drug Patents to 25 Years*, Nikkei Asian Rev. (May 16, 2018), https://asia.nikkei.com/Politics/China-extends-drug-patents-to-25-years.

41 *Id.*

42 World Health Organization, *supra* note 39, at 17.

43 *See* China Pharmaceutical Enterprises Association et al., Fostering a Sustainable Ecosystem for Drug Innovation in China 3 (2016); Ma Huateng, Tencent, *Application of Artificial Intelligence and Big Data in China's Healthcare Services*, *in* Global Innovation Index 2019, *supra* note 34, at 103, 108.

44 *See* World Health Organization, *supra* note 39, at 21–22.

45 World Health Organization, WHO Global Report on Traditional and Complementary Medicine 2019, at 164 (2019).

Finally, China has played important roles in pushing for the greater use and development of artificial intelligence (AI) and machine learning in the health area.[46] As Tencent CEO Ma Huateng observed in the *Global Innovation Index 2019* report:

> Th[e] growth in national health expenditures is creating opportunities for medical AI in China. According to Tractica's forecast, China's AI medical market is developing rapidly, with the market size soaring from 9.661 billion yuan in 2016, and 13.65 billion yuan in 2017, to 20.4 billion yuan in 2018, maintaining a compound annual growth rate of more than 40%. At the same time, Chinese medical institutions and businesses are taking a proactive attitude towards AI. Nearly 80% of hospitals and medical companies are planning to, or already have, carried out medical AI applications and more than 75% of hospitals believe that such applications will become popular in the future.[47]

In terms of health patent publications, the *Global Innovation Index 2019* placed China among the top three in the world in the areas of biotechnology, pharmaceuticals, and medical technology, based on publications from 2010 to 2017.[48] From 1985 to 2017, "China ranked fourth in the total number of healthcare AI patent applications filed, contributing to 12% of the total."[49] In 2016, China already "surpassed Japan and the European Union to become the world's second largest healthcare AI applicant ..., which reflects the strong momentum of medical technology innovation in China."[50]

When all these developments are taken together, China's pharmaceutical landscape has significantly transformed from the time it struggled painfully through the transplant and reception of foreign and, later, TRIPS-based IP standards. Today, Chinese leaders are determined to introduce laws and policies that would actively strengthen the indigenous pharmaceutical industry. The *Global Innovation Index 2019* statistics on health patent publications and AI patent applications have also revealed many forward-looking developments in the Chinese pharmaceutical sector. It can therefore be reasonably predicted that China will play an even bigger role in the global pharmaceutical arena in the near future.

## Legal and Regulatory Changes

In April 2018, the National Medical Products Administration of China, formerly the Food and Drug Administration of China, released the draft Provisional

46 On AI developments in China, see LEE KAI-FU, AI SUPERPOWERS: CHINA, SILICON VALLEY, AND THE NEW WORLD ORDER (2018).

47 Ma, *supra* note 43, at 103.

48 Dutta et al., *supra* note 35, at 48.

49 Ma, *supra* note 43, at 104.

50 *Id.*

Measures for the Implementation of Test Data Protection for Pharmaceutical Products. Article 5 of these measures not only provides six years of protection to data submitted for the regulatory approval of innovative drugs (*chuangxin yao*), but also 12 years of protection to undisclosed test or other data for innovative therapeutic biological products (*chuangxin zhiliao yong shengwu zhipin*). While the WTO accession protocol required China to offer at least six years of protection to undisclosed test or other data for pharmaceutical products[51] – a duration that Article 39.3 of the TRIPS Agreement does not require[52] – the accession protocol did not include any provision on biological products.[53] In fact, the protections for these products have been the subject of major controversies in the negotiations for TRIPS-plus bilateral, regional, and plurilateral agreements, including most notably the Trans-Pacific Partnership (TPP) Agreement.[54]

More recently, China amended its Patent Law. Article 42 grants a limited extension of the patent term for up to five years to compensate for the time lost when a pharmaceutical product is undergoing regulatory review. Should the duration of patent protection be extended under this provision, the maximum protection will last for 14 years. This new provision parallels the Hatch-Waxman Act of 1984 in the US and similar provisions on patent term extension in TRIPS-plus bilateral, regional, and plurilateral agreements.[55]

Taken together, these two sets of regulatory changes are important at both the national and international levels. Domestically, China continues to face serious problems in the public health arena, as illustrated by its past problems with SARS, bird flu, and swine flu, and its ongoing struggle with COVID-19. With a gross national income per capita of $9470 in 2018, China now ranks in the

51 World Trade Organization, *Report of the Working Party on the Accession of China* ¶ 284, WTO Doc. WT/ACC/CHN/49 (Oct. 1, 2001).

52 *See* Peter K. Yu, *Data Exclusivities and the Limits to TRIPS Harmonization*, 46 Fla. St. U. L. Rev. 641, 651–52 (2019).

53 *See* Srividhya Ragavan, *The (Re)Newed Barrier to Access to Medication: Data Exclusivity*, 51 Akron L. Rev. 1163, 1185 (2017); Yu, *supra* note 52, at 689–90.

54 *See* Frederick M. Abbott, *The Evolution of Public Health Provisions in Preferential Trade and Investment Agreements of the United States*, *in* Current Alliances in International Intellectual Property Lawmaking: The Emergence and Impact of Mega-Regionals 45, 55 (Pedro Roffe & Xavier Seuba eds., 2017); Burcu Kilic & Courtney Pine, *Decision Time on Biologics Exclusivity: Eight Years Is No Compromise*, Intell. Prop. Watch (July 27, 2015), https://www.ip-watch.org/2015/07/27/decision-time-on-biologics-exclusivity-eight-years-is-no-compromise/.

55 *See* Dominican Republic–Central America Free Trade Agreement, art. 15.9.6, Aug. 5, 2004, https://ustr.gov/trade-agreements/free-trade-agreements/cafta-dr-dominican-republic-central-america-fta/final-text; United States–Australia Free Trade Agreement, Austl.-U.S., art. 17.9.8, May 18, 2004, https://ustr.gov/trade-agreements/free-trade-agreements/australian-fta/final-text; United States–Singapore Free Trade Agreement, Sing.-U.S., art. 16.7.8, May 6, 2003, https://ustr.gov/trade-agreements/free-trade-agreements/singapore-fta/final-text.

middle among the upper middle-income economies.[56] In light of these conditions and China's continued eagerness to assume leadership in the developing world, the recent legal and policy changes in the pharmaceutical arena are indeed surprising, as they will move China's policy position closer to those of developed countries.[57] Such a policy shift is particularly troubling considering the aging Chinese population, which will require higher levels of health care while imposing a greater internal demand for pharmaceutical and biological products.[58]

Globally, having 12 years of protection for undisclosed test or other data for biological products in China is equally significant, because this duration is not only the current US standard[59] but is also longer than what existing TRIPS-plus bilateral, regional, and plurilateral agreements require. Although US negotiators had pushed aggressively for this particular standard in TPP negotiations, the TPP negotiating parties settled on protection, in Article 18.51, for "at least eight years from the date of first marketing approval," with only five years of such protection guaranteed through market exclusivity.[60] Worse still, this provision was suspended in its entirety when the Comprehensive and Progressive Agreement for Trans-Pacific Partnership was established to replace the TPP Agreement, following the withdrawal of the US from the regional pact.[61] Likewise, in fall 2018, the US sought to resuscitate the now-suspended TPP standard through the negotiation of the United States–Mexico–Canada Agreement, which aimed to replace the North American Free Trade Agreement.[62] Although Article 20.49 of the initial agreement text offered protection to undisclosed test or other data for biological products "for a period of at least ten years from the date of first marketing approval of that product,"[63] this provision was removed in December 2019 when the agreement was amended.

In sum, the proposed 12 years of protection for undisclosed test or other data for biological products in China is the world's highest watermark. This standard is not only in parity with US law, but also higher than those laid down

56 *GNI per Capita, Atlas Method (Current US$)*, World Bank, https://data.worldbank.org/indicator/NY.GNP.PCAP.CD (last visited June 28, 2020). As the World Bank stated, "[f]or the current 2020 fiscal year, ... upper middle-income economies are those with a [gross national income] per capita between $3,996 and $12,375." *World Bank Country and Lending Groups*, World Bank, https://datahelpdesk.worldbank.org/knowledgebase/articles/906519-world-bank-country-and-lending-groups (last visited June 28, 2020).

57 *See* Yu, *supra* note 25, at 113; Peter K. Yu, *The RCEP and Trans-Pacific Intellectual Property Norms*, 50 Vand. J. Transnat'l L. 673, 722 (2017).

58 *See* World Health Organization, *supra* note 39, at 1; Ren Shuli, *Selling Drugs Is No Longer a Free Lunch in China*, Bloomberg (Jan. 2, 2019), https://www.bloomberg.com/opinion/articles/2019-01-02/china-s-drug-market-is-no-longer-a-free-lunch.

59 42 U.S.C. § 262(k)(7)(A) (2018).

60 *See* Kilic & Pine, *supra* note 54; Yu, *supra* note 52, at 674–78.

61 *See* Peter K. Yu, *Thinking About the Trans-Pacific Partnership (and a Mega-Regional Agreement on Life Support)*, 20 SMU Sci. & Tech. L. Rev. 97, 105 (2017).

62 *See* Yu, *supra* note 52, at 680–83.

63 *See id.* at 682–83.

in TRIPS-plus bilateral, regional, and plurilateral agreements. While offering stronger data exclusivity will certainly attract foreign providers of biological products to undertake research and development in China,[64] such protection also reveals China's eagerness to become more assertive in the global pharmaceutical arena.[65] Just as Huawei, ZTE, BOE, and other Chinese companies have built up their portfolios of PCT applications in the past few years, China is now actively undertaking legal, regulatory, policy, and institutional reforms to create national champions in the pharmaceutical sector.

## Lessons for the TRIPS Agreement and Access to Medicines

In view of China's growing assertiveness in the pharmaceutical arena and the ongoing changes to its patent laws and pharmaceutical regulations, one naturally wonders what ramifications these developments will have in the fields of IP and public health. This section identifies five distinct lessons these developments have provided for the debate on the TRIPS Agreement and access to medicines.

First, China's struggle-to-surge experience will change the perception of the strengths and weaknesses of the TRIPS Agreement and its international harmonization efforts. Although commentators have widely condemned the Agreement's deleterious effects on developing countries, especially in the public health arena, the recent developments in Brazil, China, India, South Africa, Thailand, and other large or populous emerging economies show that countries can deploy selective adaptation strategies to maximize benefits from the TRIPS-based IP regime. Learning more deeply about China's TRIPS experience – including the country's use of selective adaptation strategies and its changing pharmaceutical landscape – will enable the development of more complex and nuanced assessments of the benefits and drawbacks of the TRIPS Agreement.[66] As I noted in an earlier article, this Agreement "has been a 'mixed bag' because it can help and simultaneously hurt developing countries."[67]

Second, the ongoing developments in the Chinese pharmaceutical landscape will undoubtedly widen the domestic gap between those with access to medicines and those without. Although policy makers and commentators have widely criticized the TRIPS Agreement for fostering global inequality, the

64 *See id.* at 696; Mark Cohen, *Draft of Data Exclusivity Rules Released by CFDA*, China IPR (Apr. 26, 2018), https://chinaipr.com/2018/04/26/draft-of-data-exclusivity-rules-released-by-cfda/.

65 *See* Gryphon Scientific, LLC & Rhodium Group, LLC, *supra* note 38, at 3; World Health Organization, *supra* note 39, at 17, 29; Yu, *supra* note 52, at 694.

66 *See* Yu, *supra* note 52, at 702.

67 Yu, *supra* note 24, at 1124.

Agreement has also fostered national and sub-national inequalities.[68] China, for example, has some of the world's widest regional disparities in innovative capacities, with 200,000 annual patent applications for its leading province and fewer than 4000 applications for its weakest provinces.[69] In addition, the overall gains from the development of national champions in the pharmaceutical sector are unlikely to diffuse to those who have to pay higher drug prices or suffer from more limited access to medicines and health care.[70] At the time of writing, China has prioritized the provision of universal health care as a counterbalancing measure,[71] while also introducing centralized drug procurement,[72] exceptions and limitations to patent rights, and the more active use of competition or anti-monopoly law. Nevertheless, ample evidence exists in both the developed and developing worlds to show that an out-of-balance patent system will greatly reduce the health-care quality for those who cannot afford high-priced drugs and medical treatments. It is therefore no surprise that a substantial part of the

68 *See* Peter K. Yu, *Intellectual Property, Global Inequality and Subnational Policy Variations*, *in* INTELLECTUAL PROPERTY, INNOVATION AND GLOBAL INEQUALITY (Daniel Benoliel et al. eds., forthcoming 2021); Peter K. Yu, *A Spatial Critique of Intellectual Property Law and Policy*, 74 WASH. & LEE L. REV. 2045, 2091–100 (2017).

69 As I noted in an earlier article: "Based on CNIPA statistics, in 2018 Guangdong, Jiangsu, and Zhejiang – the provinces with the three largest volumes of applications – had 216,469, 198,801, and 143,081 applications, respectively. Meanwhile, Jilin, Yunnan, and Shanxi (those provinces that ranked eighteenth to twentieth) had only 10,530, 9,606, and 9,395 applications, respectively. In the same year, the total numbers of patent grants for Guangdong, Jiangsu, and Zhejiang were 53,259, 42,019, and 32,550, respectively. By contrast, the total numbers for Jilin, Yunnan, and Shanxi were 2,868, 2,297, and 2,284, respectively. For either patent applications or grants, the figures for the less developed provinces were less than one-tenth of the figures for their more developed counterparts. If we include in the second group those provinces and autonomous regions that have fewer than 4,000 patent applications and 1,000 patent grants, such as Inner Mongolia, Xinjiang, Ningxia, Hainan, Qinghai, and Tibet, the statistical contrasts between these two groups will become even starker." Peter K. Yu, *China's Innovative Turn and the Changing Pharmaceutical Landscape*, 51 U. PAC. L. REV. 593, 612 (2020).

70 As Frederick Abbott rightly reminded us: "[I]n order for the health sector not to be adversely affected, there must be some type of transfer payment, whether in the form of increased public health expenditures on pharmaceuticals, by providing health insurance benefits, or other affirmative acts. In a world of economic scarcity, the prospect that governments will act to offset increases in medicines prices with increased public health expenditures is uncertain." Frederick M. Abbott, *The Cycle of Action and Reaction: Developments and Trends in Intellectual Property and Health*, *in* NEGOTIATING HEALTH: INTELLECTUAL PROPERTY AND ACCESS TO MEDICINES 27, 33 (Pedro Roffe et al. eds., 2006).

71 *See* WORLD HEALTH ORGANIZATION, *supra* note 39, at 1, 6–7.

72 *See* Eric Ng, *China Pharma Must Swallow That Jagged Little Pill Called R&D as Government Slashes Profit Margins of Generic Drugs*, S. CHINA MORNING POST (Jan. 19, 2019), https://www.scmp.com/business/companies/article/2182740/china-pharma-must-swallow-jagged-little-pill-called-rd-government. Included in the reported centralized medicine procurement scheme were Beijing, Chengdu, Chongqing, Dalian, Guangzhou, Shanghai, Shenyang, Shenzhen, Tianjin, Xi'an, and Xiamen.

Chinese populace has concerns over inadequate or unaffordable health care.[73] Worse still, as we have seen with SARS, bird flu, swine flu, and most recently COVID-19, the public health problems in China often have serious global ramifications.[74] Indeed, "[b]ecause of the climate, crowdedness, and huge population, China and countries in Southeast Asia have … been the breeding places for outbreaks of influenza and other infectious diseases."[75]

Third, the policy position China now takes in the pharmaceutical arena will likely differ significantly from those taken by other developing countries, including the large or populous emerging economies discussed in this chapter. Since China entered the WTO in December 2001, it has joined Brazil and India in pushing for stronger accommodation of developing countries' interests in the international trading and IP systems.[76] Together with Russia and South Africa, these three countries have also worked hard to facilitate greater cooperation in the BRICS context.[77] Nevertheless, China's recent policy shift in the pharmaceutical arena has created tensions, if not conflicts, with India (and probably other developing countries).[78] While India remains the "pharmacy of the world"[79] and is eager to provide strong support for generic drugs at the international level[80] – notwithstanding the changing dynamics in its pharmaceutical industry[81] – China's

73 Such concern may explain why the film *Dying to Survive* (*Wo bu shi yaoshen*) resonated with tens of millions in China and became a local blockbuster. Based on a real-life story, this film told the story of a Chinese aphrodisiac store owner who smuggled cheap generic medicine from India for sale at affordable prices to leukemia patients in China.

74 *See* Nina Hachigian & Mona Sutphen, The Next American Century: How the U.S. Can Thrive as Other Powers Rise 41 (2010); Yu, *supra* note 3, at 1652.

75 Yu, *supra* note 3, at 1652.

76 *See* Peter K. Yu, *Intellectual Property Negotiations, the BRICS Factor and the Changing North-South Debate*, *in* The BRICS-Lawyers' Guide to Global Cooperation 148, 149 (Rostam J. Neuwirth et al. eds., 2017); Yu, *supra* note 5, at 358–62; Yu, *supra* note 3, at 1645.

77 "BRICS" refers to Brazil, Russia, India, China, and South Africa. *See* Yu, *supra* note 76; Yu, *supra* note 24, at 1116.

78 *See* World Health Organization, *supra* note 39, at 17; World Health Organization, Indian Policies to Promote Local Production of Pharmaceutical Products and Protect Public Health 33 (2017) (prepared by Frederick Abbott).

79 Shamnad Basheer & Pankhuri Agarwal, *India's New IP Policy: A Bare Act?*, 13 Indian J.L. & Tech. 1, 22 (2017).

80 *See* Kenneth C. Shadlen, *Is AIDS Treatment Sustainable?*, *in* The Global Governance of HIV/AIDS: Intellectual Property and Access to Essential Medicines 29, 36 (Obijiofor Aginam, John Harrington & Peter K. Yu eds., 2013); Colleen V. Chien, *HIV/AIDS Drugs for Sub-Saharan Africa: How Do Brand and Generic Supply Compare?*, 2 PLoS One e278, 2 (2007); Srividhya Ragavan, *Data Exclusivity: A Tool to Sustain Market Monopoly*, 8 Jindal Global L. Rev. 241, 260 (2017).

81 *See* Sudip Chaudhuri, *Is Product Patent Protection Necessary to Spur Innovation in Developing Countries?: R&D by Indian Pharmaceutical Companies After TRIPS*, *in* The Development Agenda: Global Intellectual Property and Developing Countries 265, 285–86 (Neil Weinstock Netanel ed., 2009); Dwijen Rangnekar, *Context and Ambiguity in the Making of Law: A Comment on Amending India's Patent Act*, 10 J. World Intell. Prop. 365, 379–80 (2007); Yu, *supra* note 5, at 390–91.

position is now closer to those of the European Union (EU), Japan, Switzerland, the US, and other developed countries. This position shift has therefore raised questions about the ongoing negotiations at the WTO, WIPO, and regional level, such as the development of the Regional Comprehensive Economic Partnership (RCEP).[82] Will both China and India continue to team up to push for international or regional standards that align with the positions of developing countries? Or will the changing global pharmaceutical landscape cause these two developing world leaders to slowly drift apart? If so, how can other developing countries maintain an effective coalition to push for positions more in line with their needs, interests, conditions, and priorities?

Fourth, as China continues to become more assertive in the pharmaceutical arena, its poorer or smaller neighbors and trading partners may begin to wonder – if they have not already – whether China will become a new bully in this arena, with its posture moving from struggle to surge and finally to strike.[83] Policy makers and commentators have already registered neocolonialist concerns in China's engagement with Africa, South America, Southeast Asia, and other parts of the developing world.[84] In the last two decades, China has actively utilized development aid, preferential trade, loan support, and other measures (such as the donation of masks and other personal protective equipment amid the COVID pandemic) to generate soft power – or to mount what Joshua Kurlantzick has described as the "charm offensive."[85] Nevertheless, the growing suspicion among China's neighbors and trading partners has raised questions about the intentions behind its ongoing international and regional engagements, including the development of the massive Belt and Road Initiative. While this initiative has thus far focused on interconnectivity and infrastructure

82 *See* Peter K. Yu, *The RCEP Negotiations and Asian Intellectual Property Norm Setters*, *in* The Future of Asian Trade Deals and IP 85 (Liu Kung-Chung & Julien Chaisse eds., 2019); Anupam Chander & Madhavi Sunder, *The Battle to Define Asia's Intellectual Property Law: From TPP to RCEP*, 8 U.C. Irvine L. Rev. 331 (2018). The RCEP negotiations have involved Australia, China, India, Japan, New Zealand, South Korea, and the Association of Southeast Asian Nations (ASEAN). Although both China and India have played important roles in the negotiations, India withdrew in November 2019 and did not rejoin when the RCEP Agreement was signed a year later.

83 *See* Peter K. Yu, *The Middle Intellectual Property Powers*, *in* Law and Development of Middle-Income Countries: Avoiding the Middle-Income Trap 84, 103 (Randall Peerenboom & Tom Ginsburg eds., 2014).

84 *See* Fantu Cheru & Cyril Obi, *Introduction – Africa in the Twenty-First Century: Strategic and Development Challenges*, *in* The Rise of China and India in Africa: Challenges, Opportunities and Critical Interventions 1, 6 (Fantu Cheru & Cyril Obi eds., 2010); R. Evan Ellis, China in Latin America: The Whats and Wherefores 1 (2009); Dot Keet, *The Role and Impact of Chinese Economic Operations in Africa*, *in* China's New Role in Africa and the South: A Search for a New Perspective 78, 81 (Dorothy-Grace Guerrero & Firoze Manji eds., 2008); Tom Miller, China's Asian Dream 80 (2017); Ian Taylor, China's New Role in Africa 2 (2009).

85 Joshua Kurlantzick, Charm Offensive: How China's Soft Power Is Transforming the World (2007).

developments, it has serious implications in the fields of IP and public health.[86] It is therefore understandable why policy makers and commentators have started exploring what greater Chinese leadership in the global pharmaceutical arena would mean for the rest of the world.

Finally, although the closer alignment of China's policy position in the pharmaceutical arena with those of the EU, Japan, Switzerland, the US, and other developed countries could help consolidate international and regional norm-setting efforts, such alignment could also lead to greater rivalries between China and these countries. As China becomes stronger economically and technologically, the distrust other countries and their peoples have over China will also grow, not to mention additional and often heightened competition.[87] In the US, for example, the growing distrust and animosities were a key driver behind the ongoing US-China trade war and the rising concerns among the American public about their country's heavy dependence on pharmaceutical products and ingredients from China.[88] At the moment, China is not yet well positioned to rival the EU, Japan, the US, or other major players in the pharmaceutical arena. China only produces about 4 percent of the world's new pharmaceutical products,[89] and its pharmaceutical companies do not compare favorably with other internationally recognized brands, such as Johnson & Johnson, Merck, Novartis, Pfizer, Roche, and Sanofi.[90] Nevertheless, it is only a matter of time before Chinese companies catch up with those major players, especially with the country's ongoing developments and policy pushes in the area of biological

86 Launched in fall 2013, this initiative covers over 60 countries, more than 60 percent of the world's population, and about a third of global gross domestic product. As David Shambaugh described, the Belt and Road Initiative sought "to build infrastructure and facilitate commercial 'connectivity' from northwestern China across Eurasia and from southeast China to Africa and the eastern Mediterranean. Through [this and other] initiatives, China is meticulously constructing an alternative and parallel global institutional architecture to the postwar western order." David Shambaugh, China's Future 162–63 (2016). On the intellectual property issues relating to this initiative, see Lee Jyh-an, *The New Silk Road to Global IP Landscape*, *in* Legal Dimensions of China's Belt and Road Initiative 417 (Lutz-Christian Wolff & Xi Chao eds., 2016); Peter K. Yu, ***Building Intellectual Property Infrastructure Along China's Belt and Road***, 14 U. Pa. Asian L. Rev. 281 (2019); Peter K. Yu, ***China, "Belt and Road" and Intellectual Property Cooperation***, 14 Global Trade & Customs J. 244 (2019).

87 *See* Yu, *supra* note 16, at 549–54.

88 *See* Rosemary Gibson & Janardan Prasad Singh, China Rx: Exposing the Risks of America's Dependence on China for Medicine (2018); Ana Swanson, *Coronavirus Spurs U.S. Efforts to End China's Chokehold on Drugs*, N.Y. Times (Mar. 11, 2020), https://www.nytimes.com/2020/03/11/business/economy/coronavirus-china-trump-drugs.html; Guy Taylor, *"Wake-Up Call": Chinese Control of U.S. Pharmaceutical Supplies Sparks Growing Concern*, Wash. Times (Mar. 17, 2020), https://www.washingtontimes.com/news/2020/mar/17/china-threatens-restrict-critical-drug-exports-us/.

89 *See* China Pharmaceutical Enterprises Association et al., *supra* note 43, at 3; Ma, *supra* note 43, at 108.

90 *See* Yu, *supra* note 69, at 594.

products and personalized medicines[91] and in the use of AI in drug research and development.[92]

## Conclusion

In the last three decades, China has been slowly but actively building its patent system while increasing its assertiveness in the global pharmaceutical arena. Having undergone multiple developmental phases – from imitation to standardization to integration to indigenization[93] – the Chinese patent system has arguably advanced much faster than any system ever built.[94] More importantly for this volume, the Chinese experience has shown how the TRIPS Agreement can be selectively adapted to a country's benefit. Although China's size, population, geopolitical influence, and other unique conditions have raised questions about the replicability of this experience, its recent surge in the pharmaceutical arena has called for a more cautious analysis of the struggles and successes brought about by the TRIPS Agreement. The country's continuous improvements in the pharmaceutical sector and the accompanying changes in laws, regulations, policies, and institutions also suggest an increasingly complex debate on access to medicines – at both the domestic and international levels.

91 *See* World Health Organization, *supra* note 39, at 19–21.

92 *See* Ma, *supra* note 43.

93 *See* Yu, *supra* note 24, at 1058–87.

94 *See* Yu, *supra* note 8, at 2; Peter K. Yu, *Trade Secret Hacking, Online Data Breaches, and China's Cyberthreats*, 2015 Cardozo L. Rev. De Novo 130, 139.

# 10 Canada

## Access to Medicines in High-income Countries

*Gaëlle Groux and Jeremy de Beer*

### Introduction

The Agreement on Trade-Related Aspects of Intellectual Property Rights (TRIPS Agreement) catalyzed a global debate about trade, intellectual property (IP), and access to medicines. Much of the debate has centered on impacts of IP and trade law on access to medicines in low- and middle-income countries. Access to patented medicines became an especially high-profile issue around the turn of the 21st century in the context of the global HIV/AIDS crisis. This contributed to action at the World Trade Organization, including the Doha Declaration on the TRIPS Agreement and Public Health (Doha Declaration).

Yet minimum IP standards continue to rise as some countries push for longer and stronger IP rights (IPR) in bilateral, regional, mega-regional, or other preferential trade agreements. High-income countries are not always the ones pushing for more IP protection. Canada, for example, has signed three recent trade deals, including IP obligations it accepted but did not ask for – the Canada-European Union Comprehensive Economic and Trade Agreement (CETA), the Comprehensive and Progressive Agreement for Trans-Pacific Partnership (CPTPP), and the Canada-United States-Mexico Agreement (CUSMA).[1] These agreements require Canada to provide more protection for patents and undisclosed data.

According to a blue-ribbon advisory council on the implementation of national pharmacare in Canada, "almost one million Canadians had cut their household spending on food and heat to pay for medication [and] one in five households reported a family member who, in the past year, had not taken a prescribed

1 Canada-European Union Comprehensive Economic and Trade Agreement, Can.-E.U., Oct. 30, 2016, O.J. (L 11) 23 (entered into force Sept. 21, 2017) [hereinafter CETA]; Comprehensive and Progressive Agreement for Trans-Pacific Partnership, Mar. 8, 2018, Can TS 2018 (entered into force Dec. 30, 2018, for all countries except Vietnam), https://www.international.gc.ca/trade-commerce/trade-agreements-accords-commerciaux/agr-acc/cptpp-ptpgp/index.aspx?lang=eng [hereinafter CPTPP]; Canada-United States-Mexico Agreement, Can.-U.S.-Mex., Nov. 30, 2018 (not in force), https://www.international.gc.ca/trade-commerce/trade-agreements-accords-commerciaux/agr-acc/cusma-aceum/index.aspx?lang=eng [hereinafter CUSMA].

medicine due to its cost."[2] Canadians' access to medicines will be affected by the recent trade deals that ratchet up IP protection.

This chapter explains how IP provisions in recent trade agreements may impact access to medicines in Canada. It shows that as minimum IP standards have increased through trade law, access to medicines is affected not just in low- and middle-income countries but also in high-income countries. This chapter also shows how IP provisions in trade deals impact subregions and subpopulations differently within a high-income country like Canada. For example, IP affects access to medicines for Indigenous peoples and recent immigrants differently, and its impact is gendered. The chapter concludes with lessons from Canada's challenges and solutions to ensure that IP is not a barrier to accessing medicines.

## The Issue of IP and Access to Medicines

In 1998, pharmaceutical companies challenged a South African law that allowed importing generic medicines from elsewhere. Drug companies argued that the law breached the TRIPS Agreement and violated South Africa's Constitution.[3] Around that time, South Africa was facing a growing HIV/AIDS crisis: 1.8 million South Africans had HIV, causing about 79,000 deaths per year.[4] The event brought to the forefront international debates on the appropriate balance between IPR and access to medicines.

Two types of IPR are especially relevant to the development of and access to innovative medicines: patents and data exclusivity.[5] By providing a limited window of time during which only the patent owner may make, use, or sell an invention, patents and data exclusivity lead to higher prices and thereby reward or encourage further invention. In the context of medicines, inventions might include new, useful, and nonobvious chemical compounds or combinations of compounds, i.e., drugs, or methods of manufacturing, delivering, or administering those compounds.[6] Inventions can also be biologics, which are medicines derived from living organisms.[7]

2 Gov't Can., A Prescription for Canada: Achieving Pharmacare for All: Final Report of the Advisory Council on the Implementation of National Pharmacare 2 (2019) [hereinafter A Prescription for Canada].

3 *See Pharmaceutical Manufacturers Association of South Africa and Another: In Re Ex Parte President of the Republic of South Africa and Others 2000* (2) SA 674 (CC) (S. Afr.).

4 AIDSinfo | UNAIDS, *People Living with HIV Receiving Art – As of June 30, 2019*, https://aidsinfo.unaids.org/ (last visited June 8, 2020).

5 Md. Deen Islam et al., *Impacts of Intellectual Property Provisions in Trade Treaties on Access to Medicine in Low and Middle Income Countries: A Systematic Review*, 15 Global Health 88 (2019).

6 Patent Act, R.S.C. 1985, c. P-4, art. 2; Patent Act 57 of 1978 § 25 (S. Afr.).

7 Gov't Can., *Biologics and Genetic Therapies Directorate* (2007), https://www.canada.ca/en/health-canada/corporate/about-health-canada/branches-agencies/health-products-food-branch/biologics-genetic-therapies-directorate.html (last modified Jan. 4, 2019).

Data exclusivity laws also impact both the invention of and access to medicines. Before a medicine can be marketed, it must be proven safe and effective. That usually requires expensive clinical trials, the data from which must be submitted to obtain regulatory approval for the drug.[8] When a patent expires, generic drug makers who wish to market a competing version also require approval. Rather than redoing clinical trials, which is inefficient and often unethical, makers of generic equivalent drugs can cite the data already submitted by brand-name drug companies. Data exclusivity limits the ability of competitors to rely on the previously submitted data for regulatory approval.[9] The longer and stronger the data exclusivity, the more expensive drugs remain.

There are two side of the debate regarding IP and access to medicines. One view emphasizes that higher IP protections resulting in unjustifiably high monopoly prices affect access to medicines.[10] The other emphasizes that strong IP protection promotes innovation.[11] There is truth in both positions. Much evidence shows that drug prices fall significantly after a patent expires.[12] For example, one United States (US) study showed that generics that entered the US market between 2002 and 2014 reduced the price of medicines by 51 percent in the first year and 57 percent in the second year following loss

8 Linda Martin et al., *How Much Do Clinical Trials Cost?* 16 Nat. Rev. Drug Discov. Lond. 381–82 (2017); Gov't Can., *Clinical Trials and Drug Safety* (2013), https://www.canada.ca/en/health-canada/services/healthy-living/your-health/medical-information/clinical-trials-drug-safety.html.

9 Charles Clift, *Data Protection and Data Exclusivity in Pharmaceuticals and Agrochemicals*, *in* Intellectual Property Management Health and Agricultural Innovation: A Handbook of Best Practices (Anatole Krattiger et al. eds., 2007).

10 *Patents and Intellectual Property: An Overview*, MSF Access Campaign, https://www.msfaccess.org/patents-and-intellectual-property; Ellen F. M. 't Hoen, Private Patents and Public Health: Changing Intellectual Property Rules for Access to Medicines 1–6, 134–37 (2016); Commission on Intellectual Property Rights, Innovation and Public Health & World Health Organization, Public Health, Innovation and Intellectual Property Rights IX, 116–20 (2006).

11 *R&D, Innovation and Patents*, World Intell. Prop. Org., https://www.wipo.int/patent-law/en/developments/research.html (last visited June 8, 2020); Dan Andrews & Chiara Criscuolo, *Knowledge Based Capital, Innovation and Resource Allocation Economics Department* 1–7 (OECD Econ. Dep't, Working Paper No. 1046, 2013).

12 FDA – Center for Drug Evaluation and Research, Generic Competition and Drug Prices (2019); IMS Institute for Healthcare Informatics, *Price Declines After Branded Medicines Lose Exclusivity in the U.S.* 2 (2016); Omotayo Fatokun et al., *Generic Competition and Drug Prices in the Malaysian Off-Patent Pharmaceutical Market*, 9 J. Appl. Pharm. Sci. 5 (2011); Association for Accessible Medicines, Generic Drug Access and Savings in the US 8, 18 (2018); Council of Economic Advisers, Executive Office of the President of the United States, *The Administration's FDA Reforms and Reduced Biopharmaceutical Drug Prices* (2018); Congressional Budget Office, Congress of the United States, *How Increased Competition from Generic Drugs has Affected Prices and Returns in the Pharmaceutical Industry* (1998); The Pew Charitable Trusts, *FDA Approves More Generic Drugs, But Competition Still Lags: FY 2012–17 Program Achieves Mixed Results* (2019).

of exclusivity.[13] However, post-patented drug prices will vary between countries because they are also dependent on national drug price control laws.[14] Studies done in Canada also show a reduction in overall drug prices in the market when generics enter the market, and the overall price decreases with every new generic entrant.[15] IP is merely one of the factors affecting drug pricing. Yet, overall, it is widely accepted that stronger IP protection leads to higher drug prices. The ability to charge higher prices is the primary goal of IP law; the debate is about the appropriate balance between incentives and access.

Clearly, IP incentivizes research and development (R&D) in the pharmaceutical and biomedical sector. Numerous surveys show that companies in the pharmaceutical sector list patents as a top incentive for innovation, to a far greater degree than other innovative sectors.[16] While many studies on the effect of patents on overall innovation – usually measured by number of patents filed – show minimal impact, most studies that disaggregate by sector find that patents are important in the pharmaceutical, medical technology, and/or biomedical fields.[17] Nevertheless, the costs of R&D for developing one drug remain contested, with estimates ranging from $40 million to $2.5 billion.[18]

Not all pharmaceutical research, of course, comes from the private sector. One global estimate shows that governments' public funding accounts for about

13 IMS Institute for Healthcare Informatics, *supra* note 12.

14 Laura Magazzini et al., *Dynamic Competition in Pharmaceuticals: Patent Expiry, Generic Penetration, and Industry Structure,* 5 EUR. J. HEALTH ECON. 180–81 (2004).

15 Joel Lexchin, *Effect of Generic Drug Competition on the Price of Prescription Drugs in Ontario*, 148 CMAJ CAN. MED. ASSOC. J. 35–38 (1993); Joel Lexchin, *The Effect of Generic Competition on the Price of Brand-Name Drugs*, 68 HEALTH POLICY 47–54 (2004); J. C. H. Jones et al., *Patents, Brand-Generic Competition and the Pricing of Ethical Drugs in Canada: Some Empirical Evidence from British Columbia, 1981–1994*, 33 APPL. ECON. 947–56, 20 (2001).

16 Bhaven N. Sampat, *A Survey of Empirical Evidence on Patents and Innovation* (Nat'l Bureau Econ. Rsch., Working Paper No. 25383, 2018); C. T. TAYLOR, THE ECONOMIC IMPACT OF THE PATENT SYSTEM; A STUDY OF THE BRITISH EXPERIENCE (1973); Richard C. Levin et al., *Appropriating the Returns from Industrial Research and Development*, 18 SPECIAL ISSUE MICROECONOMICS 783 (1987); Edwin Mansfield, *Patents and Innovation: An Empirical Study*, 32 MANAG. SCI. 173 (1986); Josh Lerner, *The Empirical Impact of Intellectual Property Rights on Innovation: Puzzles and Clues*, 99 AM. ECON. REV. 343 (2009); ANTHONY ARUNDEL ET AL., INNOVATION STRATEGIES OF EUROPE'S LARGEST INDUSTRIAL FIRMS: RESULTS OF THE PACE SURVEY FOR INFORMATION SOURCES, PUBLIC RESEARCH, PROTECTION OF INNOVATIONS AND GOVERNMENT PROGRAMMES; FINAL REPORT (1995); Wesley M. Cohen et al., *R&D Spillovers, Patents and the Incentives to Innovate in Japan and the United States*, 31 RES. POL'Y 1349 (2002); Stuart J. H. Graham et al., *High Technology Entrepreneurs and the Patent System: Results of the 2008 Berkeley Patent Survey*, 24 BERKELEY TECH. L. J. 255 (2009).

17 *Id.*

18 ELLEN F. M. 'T HOEN, *supra* note 10, at 129.

30 percent of global investments in health R&D.[19] The largest public funder of R&D in the world is the US National Institutes of Health (NIH) at $26.1 billion. Its funding contributed to all of the 210 new drug molecules approved by the Food and Drug Administration from 2010 to 2016.[20]

This debate over IP and access to medicines has not abated since the 1990s. However, much of the discussion has been in or about access to medicines in low- and middle-income countries. Articles discussing access to medicines rarely addressed high-income countries during this time, except to mention their role in imposing IP rules.[21] Early papers on the TRIPS Agreement argued that high-income countries benefitted more from it because their IP laws were already in line with the TRIPS Agreement, and they housed significantly more innovative industries.[22] However, high-income countries also face rising drug prices, stagnating wages, and greater inequality.[23] IP chapters of trade agreements have therefore brought the access to medicine debates to countries like Canada.

19 John-Arne Røttingen et al., *Mapping of Available Health Research and Development Data: What's There, What's Missing, and What Role is There for a Global Observatory?*, 382 Lancet 1286 (2013).

20 Margaret E. Blume-Kohout, *Does Targeted, Disease-specific Public Research Funding Influence Pharmaceutical Innovation?*, 31 J. Policy Anal. Manag. 641 (2012).

21 Ellen F. M.'t Hoen, *TRIPS, Pharmaceutical Patents, and Access to Essential Medicines: A Long Way from Seattle to Doha*, 3 Chic. J. Int. Law 27, 42–45 (2002); Susan K. Sell, *TRIPS and the Access to Medicines Campaign*, 20 Wis. Int. Law J. 481 (2001); Carlos María Correa, *Implications of Bilateral Free Trade Agreements on Access to Medicines*, 84 Bull. World Health Org. 399 (2006); Valbona Muzaka, The Politics of Intellectual Property Rights and Access to Medicines Palgrave Macmillan; Mandisa Mbali, South African AIDS Activism and Global Health Politics 136–46 (2013).

22 F. M. Scherer & Jayashree Watal, *Post-TRIPS Options for Access to Patented Medicines in Developing Nations*, 5 J. Int. Econ. Law 913 (2002); John Hudson & Alexandru Minea, *Innovation, Intellectual Property Rights, and Economic Development: A Unified Empirical Investigation*, 46 World Dev. 66 (2013); Constantine Vaitsos, *Patents Revisited: Their Function in Developing Countries*, 9 J. Dev. Stud. 71 (1972).

23 *New Poll Reveals Overwhelming Support for Pharmacare*, Can. Federation of Nurses Union (Sept. 24, 2019), https://nursesunions.ca/new-poll-reveals-overwhelming-support-for-pharmacare/ [hereinafter New Poll]; Steven G. Morgan et al., Pharmacare 2020: The Future of Drug Coverage in Canada (2015); Matthew Brzozowski et al., *Consumption, Income, and Wealth Inequality in Canada*, 13 J. Econ. Lit. 52 (2010); Thomas Piketty, Capital in the Twenty-First Century (2017); John Cassidy, *Piketty's Inequality Story In Six Charts*, New Yorker (Mar. 26, 2014), https://www.newyorker.com/news/john-cassidy/pikettys-inequality-story-in-six-charts; Nicole Fortin et al., *Canadian Inequality: Recent Developments and Policy Options*, 38 Can. Public Policy 121 (2012); Patented Medicines Price Review Board, *Annual Report 2017* (2018), http://www.pmprb-cepmb.gc.ca/view.asp?ccid=1380&lang=en [hereinafter PMPRB]; Gov't Can., *Patented Medicines Price Review Board, Generics360 – Generic Drugs In Canada*, 2018 (2019), http://www.pmprb-cepmb.gc.ca/view.asp?ccid=1469&lang=en; Andrew Sharpe et al., *Why Have Real Wages Lagged Labour Productivity Growth in Canada?*, 17 Int'l Productivity Monitor 16 (2008); Lancet Global Health, *Access to Medicines—Business as Usual?*, 7 Lancet Global Health 385 (2019).

## The Historical and Current Context for Canadian Pharmacare

While Canada has also been impacted by the TRIPS Agreement and subsequent trade deals, access to medicine debates are different in Canada than elsewhere. Drug prices have only recently begun to gain regular national attention, as Canadians are increasingly vulnerable to high medicine prices.[24] To understand the issue in Canada, it is important to understand the context of medicare, pharmacare, and IP in the country.

A government-paid health-care system, colloquially known as medicare, was first implemented in the province of Saskatchewan by Premier Tommy Douglas in 1947 and implemented in the rest of Canada in the 1960s.[25] All provinces now provide medical care that is funded through taxpayer contributions, not user fees, although there are significant differences across provinces.[26] In hospitals, patients do not pay for the medicines used to treat them. However, medicare does not cover patients' costs for medicines purchased outside of hospitals.[27]

After the system was implemented in the 1960s, calls for medicare to include medicines came swiftly. The first report to recommend a national pharmacare system was the 1964 Royal Commission on Health Services, which famously called it the "unfinished business of medicare."[28] Pharmacare was subsequently recommended by numerous government reports, including the National Forum on Health in 1997,[29] a second Royal Commission on the Future of Health Care in Canada,[30] the Parliamentary Standing Committee on Health in 2018,[31] and the Advisory Council on the Implementation of National Pharmacare in 2019.[32]

Despite these repeated calls, Canada remains the only member of the Organization for Economic Cooperation and Development to have a single payer health system without pharmacare.[33] Supporters of an expanded health coverage in the country frequently refer to pharmacare as the "lost business" of

24 Morgan et al., *supra* note 23.

25 Health Canada, CANADA'S HEALTH CARE SYSTEM, (May 26, 2011), https://www.canada.ca/en/health-canada/services/health-care-system/reports-publications/health-care-system/canada.html.

26 Colleen M. Flood et al., UNIVERSAL PHARMACARE AND FEDERALISM: POLICY OPTIONS FOR CANADA (2018).

27 Morgan et al., *supra* note 23.

28 Emmett M. Hall, *Royal Commission on Health Services, 1961–64* (1964).

29 NATIONAL FORUM ON HEALTH, CANADA HEALTH ACTION: BUILDING ON THE LEGACY – VOLUME I – THE FINAL REPORT (2004), https://www.canada.ca/en/health-canada/services/health-care-system/reports-publications/health-care-renewal/canada-health-action-building-legacy-volume1.html.

30 ROY J. ROMANOW, BUILDING ON VALUES: THE FUTURE OF HEALTH CARE IN CANADA : FINAL REPORT (2002).

31 BILL CASEY, PHARMACARE NOW: PRESCRIPTION MEDICINE COVERAGE FOR ALL CANADIANS REPORT OF THE STANDING COMMITTEE ON HEALTH (2018).

32 A PRESCRIPTION FOR CANADA, *supra* note 2, at 2.

33 Flood et al., *supra* note 26, at 4.

medicare.[34] As a result, each province offers its own patchwork of pharmaceutical coverage programs, and the private pharmaceutical insurance industry has flourished.

Meanwhile, medicine prices in Canada continue to rise. Canadians pay $832 per person per year for medicines, the fourth highest in the world, behind only the US, Switzerland, and Japan.[35] Patented medicines tend to be the most expensive, as patented drugs accounted for 26 percent of sales by volume, but 60 percent of sale values (in C$) in Canada in 2016.[36] A 2017 report by Canada's Patented Medicines Prices Review Board (PMPRB) showed that higher cost medications are the norm for new launches of pharmaceutical medicines.[37] For example, over a quarter of new medicines in 2016 and 2017 were developed for cancer treatment, which average a price of $13,700 for 28 days.[38] In addition, Canadians are not necessarily getting the benefit of innovation with these new high-priced medicine launches: of eight newly launched medicines assessed by the PMPRB in 2016, only one demonstrated more than a slight therapeutic improvement upon previously available medication.[39]

Researchers have shown that high drug prices have affected drug spending and access to medicines. Drug spending outside of hospitals, where drugs are covered by medicare, has grown from C$2.6 billion in 1985 to C$33.7 billion in 2018.[40] Yet in Statistics Canada's 2016 Canadian Community Health Survey, 19 percent (about 7.5 million people) reported they did not have insurance that covered part or all of the cost of their prescription drugs.[41] As a result, about 17 percent of drug spending is paid out of pocket (C$4.7 billion).[42]

Several studies have also shown that medicine prices are having a deleterious impact on well-being. According to a 2019 study, one in four Canadians did not take medication as prescribed or did not renew a prescription, due to cost. One in four reported that their health-care benefits have caused them to hesitate in quitting or changing jobs.[43] Finally, 35 percent of households have experienced budgetary stress due to medicine costs.[44] This is a significant increase from a survey in 2015, which showed that one in ten Canadians were not taking their medicine as prescribed due to cost.[45]

34 A Prescription for Canada, *supra* note 2.
35 *Health Resources – Pharmaceutical Spending – OECD Data*, OECD, http://data.oecd.org/healthres/pharmaceutical-spending.htm.
36 PMPRB, *supra* note 23.
37 *Id.*
38 *Id.*
39 *Id.*
40 Parliamentary Budget Officer, House of Commons Canada, *Federal Cost of a National Pharmacare Program* (2017).
41 *Id.* at 41.
42 *Id.* at 5.
43 New Poll, *supra* note 23; PMPRB, *supra* note 23.
44 *Id.*
45 Morgan et al., *supra* note 23.

## The Evolution of Canadian IP Law

### *Canadian Law Before Free Trade*

Prior to signing the Canada-US Free Trade Agreement (CUSFTA)[46] in the late 1980s, and the North American Free Trade Agreement (NAFTA)[47] and TRIPS Agreement in the 1990s,[48] Canada had more flexible IP laws.[49] Canadian law granted only a 17-year term of patent protection, and undisclosed clinical trial and other test data were not protected. Canada also attempted to develop its domestic generic pharmaceutical industry and kept drug prices low through a compulsory licensing policy from 1923 to 1988.[50]

Initially, the compulsory licensing regime required generic drugs to be locally manufactured. The law was amended in 1969 in response to provincial government pharmaceutical insurance programs in the 1960s.[51] The new law allowed industries to import generic drugs with a compulsory license (CL) and required the Commissioner of Patents to grant the CL unless there were "good reasons" to deny it.

The evolving compulsory licensing regime was eventually successful in building Canada's generic industry and fostering access to generic medicines in the country. By 1970, there were already 52 new generic drugs available in Canada.[52] During the period when compulsory licensing was popular in Canada, 1030 applications were filed and 613 licenses were granted (compared to an earlier total from 1923 to 1969 of 22 CL grants out of 49 applications).[53]

However, Canada's approach to pharmaceutical patent licensing caused political and economic tension with its neighbor to the south. The US continually pushed Canada to abandon its compulsory licensing regime, putting it on the Special 301 watch list and threatening trade sanctions. As a result, Canada changed its patent laws.

46 Free Trade Agreement, Can.-U.S., Jan. 2, 1988, Can TS 1989 No 3 (entered into force Jan. 1, 1989; suspended Jan. 1, 1994) [hereinafter CUSFTA].

47 North American Free Trade Agreement, Can.-Mex.-U.S., Dec. 17, 1992, 32 I.L.M 289 [hereinafter NAFTA].

48 TRIPS: Agreement on Trade-Related Aspects of Intellectual Property Rights, Apr. 15, 1994, Marrakesh Agreement Establishing the World Trade Organization, Annex 1C, 1869 U.N.T.S. 299, 33 I.L.M. 1197 (1994) [hereinafter TRIPS Agreement].

49 Joel Lexchin, Private Profits versus Public Policy: The Pharmaceutical Industry and the Canadian State 135–56 (2016).

50 Joel Lexchin, *After Compulsory Licensing: Coming Issues in Canadian Pharmaceutical Policy and Politics*, 40 Health Pol'y 69 (1997).

51 *Id.* Mélanie Bourassa Forcier & Jean-Frédéric Morin, *Canadian Pharmaceutical Patent Policy: International Constraints and Domestic Priorities*, in An Emerging Intellectual Property Paradigm 85 (Ysolde Gendreau ed., 2008).

52 A. H. Anis et al., *A Dog's Breakfast: Prescription Drug Coverage Varies Widely Across Canada*, 39 Med. Care 315 (2001); Lexchin, *supra* note 50, at 79.

53 Forcier & Morin, *supra* note 51, at 84–85.

### *Canada After the CUSFTA, NAFTA, and TRIPS Agreement*

The CUSFTA, NAFTA, and TRIPS Agreement required numerous changes in Canadian patent law.[54] Canada extended the term of patent protection from 17 years to 20 years, adopted five years of data exclusivity for pharmaceuticals, created a more restrictive framework for importing generic drugs, and limited circumstances where compulsory licensing can be used.[55] Consequently, rates of CLs fell significantly.

Then-Prime Minister Brian Mulroney attempted to mitigate the impacts of trade deals by entering into an agreement with innovative pharmaceutical companies – increased IP protection in return for increased investment in innovation. Although investments in R&D grew for a few years after the agreement, it has since fallen to levels below those prior to the trade agreements.[56]

Canada also created the PMPRB to regulate medicine prices. The PMPRB reviews the reasonableness of prices of patented medicines that have recently entered the market. Changes to the PMPRB's practices, which are expected to enter into force in July 2021, will make it even more effective.[57] To determine reasonable pricing, Canada will stop comparing itself to the US and Switzerland, instead focusing on comparisons with markets where medicines are more affordable.[58]

## A New Generation of Trade Agreements

### *Background*

New trade agreements have inflamed the Canadian debate on IP and access to medicines. Three recently signed trade deals contain IP obligations more stringent than Canada's IP laws prior to 2016. The CETA was signed in 2016, the CPTPP with 10 countries across the Asia-Pacific region was signed in 2018, and the CUSMA that updates the NAFTA was signed in 2018.[59] Legislation implementing

54 NAFTA, *supra* note 47; CUSFTA, *supra* note 46; TRIPS Agreement, *supra* note 48.

55 Lexchin, *supra* note 49.

56 *Id.* at 190.

57 Patented Medicine Prices Review Board Canada, *PMPRB Draft Guidelines Consultation* (Dec. 2, 2019), https://www.canada.ca/en/patented-medicine-prices-review/services/consultations/draft-guidelines.html.

58 *Regulations Amending the Patented Medicines Regulations (Additional Factors and Information Reporting Requirements)*, Canada Gazette, Part II, (Aug. 21, 2019).

59 Global Affairs Canada, *Statement by Minister Champagne on Signing of Comprehensive and Progressive Agreement for Trans-Pacific Partnership* (Mar. 8, 2018), https://www.canada.ca/en/global-affairs/news/2018/03/statement-by-minister-champagne-on-signing-of-comprehensive-and-progressive-agreement-for-trans-pacific-partnership.html; Gov't Can., *Comprehensive and Progressive Agreement for Trans-Pacific Partnership (CPTPP)* (2018), https://international.gc.ca/trade-commerce/trade-agreements-accords-commerciaux/agr-acc/cptpp-ptpgp/index.aspx?lang=eng; CETA, *supra* note 1; Global Affairs Canada-Affaires Mondiales Canada, *A New Canada-United States-Mexico Agreement* (Feb. 20, 2020), https://www.international.gc.ca/trade-commerce/trade-agreements-accords-commerciaux/agr-acc/cusma-aceum/index.aspx?lang=eng.

*Table 10.1* Summary of changes to Canadian patent and data exclusivity laws[a]

| | *Patent term restoration* | *Data and marketing exclusivity* | *Protection for biologics* |
|---|---|---|---|
| CETA | Up to two–five years | Eight years for pharmaceuticals | None |
| CPTPP | None | None; three and five years for pharmaceuticals until the US withdrew | None; five and eight years until US withdrew and provisions suspended |
| CUSMA | Up to two years | Five years for pharmaceuticals | None; 10 years until deleted by the Protocol of Amendment |

a Canada-European Union Comprehensive Economic and Trade Agreement Between the Government of Canada and the States of the European Union, 30 October 2016, Can TS 2017 (entered into force 21 September 2017) [CETA], online https://www.international.gc.ca/gac-amc/campaign-campagne/ceta-aecg/index.aspx?lang=eng; Comprehensive and Progressive Agreement for Trans-Pacific Partnership, 8 March 2018, Can TS 2018 (entered into force 30 December 2018, for all countries except) [CPTPP], online https://www.international.gc.ca/trade-commerce/trade-agreements-accords-commerciaux/agr-acc/cptpp-ptpgp/index.aspx?lang=eng; Canada-United States-Mexico Agreement between the Government of Canada, the Government of the United States and the Government of Mexico, 30 November 2018 (not in force) [CUSMA], online https://www.international.gc.ca/trade-commerce/trade-agreements-accords-commerciaux/agr-acc/cusma-aceum/index.aspx?lang=eng; Patent Act, RSC, 1985, c P-4.

the CETA and CPTPP has already been enacted.[60] Implementation of the CUSMA occurred in 2020, although some changes come into force over several years.[61] Nevertheless, these three trade deals change Canadian patent and data exclusivity laws in key respects (Table 10.1).[62]

## *Legislative and Regulatory Changes*

### *Patent Term Extensions*

Patent term extensions compensate for delays in the administrative process of examining a patent application or in the marketing approval of a drug. The CETA is the first agreement to mandate the addition of two years of patent protection where there are delays in the regulatory approval of drugs.[63] It also

60 CUSMA, *supra* note 1; CETA, *supra* note 1.

61 Canada–United States–Mexico Agreement Implementation Act (SC 2020, c 1).

62 Lexchin, *supra* note 49.

63 Joel Lexchin & Marc-André Gagnon, *CETA and Pharmaceuticals: Impact of the Trade Agreement Between Europe and Canada on the Costs of Prescription Drugs*, 10 Global Health 30 (2014); Joel Lexchin & Marc-André Gagnon, CETA and Intellectual Property: The Debate over Pharmaceutical Patents (2013); Jeremy De Beer, *Implementing International Trade Agreements in Federal Systems: A Look at the Canada-EU CETA's Intellectual Property Issues*, 39 Lege. Issues Econ. Integr. (2012).

encourages additional protection to incentivize or reward research in certain target populations.[64] The CUSMA also mandates term extensions for up to two years to compensate for unreasonable delays in patent examination and market approval.[65]

### *Market and Data Exclusivity*

Other common ways of extending a drug makers' monopoly on the market beyond the patent term are market and data exclusivity clauses. Data exclusivity laws prevent generic companies from relying on data generated by brand-name manufacturers in their own applications for market approval for a minimum number of years.[66] Market exclusivity laws grant a company exclusive marketing rights over a drug upon its approval for sale in the country.

The CETA, CPTPP, and CUSMA all have data and/or market exclusivity provisions. The periods of data and market exclusivity have increased in each subsequent agreement. For example, the CETA mandates data exclusivity periods of six years for new pharmaceutical products, and generic companies cannot seek marketing approval for eight years after the submission of the originator drug's clinical trial data to approval agency.[67] The CETA also encourages, but does not require, compensation for companies that decide to publish or share their own clinical trial data.[68] Meanwhile, the CUSMA goes further by requiring five years of data exclusivity on new chemical entity drugs, and three years for chemicals that have already been submitted for approval.[69] The CPTPP and CUSMA both do not permit exceptions to data exclusivity unless used in conjunction with the Doha Declaration.[70]

### *The Next Generation of Medicines: Biologics*

Biologics are a relatively new type of therapeutic which manufactures antibodies – a type of molecule used in mammalian immune responses to target foreign objects in the body – in order to administer them as medicines.[71] These drugs

64 CETA, *supra* note 1, at art. 20.27.5.
65 CUSMA, *supra* note 1, at arts. 20.44 and 20.46.
66 Clift, *supra* note 9.
67 CETA, *supra* note 1, at art. 20.29.
68 *Id.* at art. 20.30.7.
69 CUSMA, *supra* note 1, at art. 20.48.
70 CPTPP, *supra* note 1, at art. 18.48; CUSMA, *supra* note 1, at art. 20.48.
71 Health Canada, *Biosimilar Biologic Drugs in Canada: Fact Sheet* (Dec. 7, 2016), https://www.canada.ca/en/health-canada/services/drugs-health-products/biologics-radiopharmaceuticals-genetic-therapies/applications-submissions/guidance-documents/fact-sheet-biosimilars.html#a1; Center for Biologics Evaluation and Research, *What are "Biologics" Questions and Answer* (2018), http://www.fda.gov/about-fda/center-biologics-evaluation-and-research-cber/what-are-biologics-questions-and-answers>.

show much therapeutic promise but are more expensive to research and manufacture than chemical medications.[72]

The CUSMA IP chapter was supposed to contain sections that increase IP protection solely for biologics, but such provisions were removed post-signing by a Protocol of Amendment at the insistence of Democratic Party lawmakers.[73] The CUSMA would have mandated a data exclusivity period of 10 years from the date of the first marketing approval for the biologic.[74] It also would have created a very broad definition of biologics: "a product that is produced using biotechnology processes and that is, or, alternatively, contains, a virus, therapeutic serum, toxin, antitoxin, vaccine, blood, blood component or derivative, allergenic product, protein, or analogous product, for use in human beings for the prevention, treatment, or cure of a disease or condition."[75] The expectation of many analysts was that future US trade agreements would contain sections on biologics, with increasingly strong market and data exclusivity protections, although developments in the CUSMA call that into question.[76]

## Summary

### *Interpretation and Enforcement*

Increasing statutory protection for patents and test data is one thing. Interpreting legislation and enforcing IPR is another. Canada has experienced several recent controversies around the interpretation and enforcement of IP that affect access to medicines. The most notable controversies involved a legal rule called the promise doctrine.

72 Oliver Sachgau, *The Price of Being Pain Free: Why are Life-Changing Biologics Out of Reach for So Many?*, The Globe and Mail (Sept. 13, 2013), https://www.theglobeandmail.com/life/health-and-fitness/health/the-price-of-being-pain-free-why-are-biologics-out-of-reach-for-so-many/article26332629/; Thomas Morrow & Linda Hull Felcone, *Defining the Difference: What Makes Biologics Unique*, 1 Biotechnology Healthcare (2004).

73 John E. Osborn, *Biologics Lose Protection as Trade Agreement Moves Forward*, Stat (Dec. 20 2019), https://www.statnews.com/2019/12/20/biologics-lose-protection-us-canada-mexico-trade-agreement/; Kevin Freking et al., *North America Trade Pact Deals Rare Setback to Big Pharma*, AP NEWS (Dec. 19, 2019), https://apnews.com/fb54abbce60e1fe44926becb84e86edf; Eric Martin & Jenny Leonard, *Mexico Weighs U.S. Plan to Strip Drugs Provision From USMCA*, Bloomberg (Dec. 3, 2019), https://www.bloomberg.com/news/articles/2019-12-03/mexico-weighs-u-s-plan-to-strip-biologic-drugs-from-trade-pact.

74 CUSMA, *supra* note 1, art. 20.48.

75 *Id.* at art. 20.49.

76 Maria Fabiana Jorge, *Biologics and Trade Agreements: Defining the New Frontier*, 10 J. Generic Med. 105 (2013); Lexchin & Gagnon, *supra* note 63; David A. Gantz, *The TPP and RCEP: Mega-Trade Agreements for the Pacific Rim*, 33 Ariz. J. Int. Comp. Law 57 (2016); Jeremy de Beer, *International Intellectual Property After the New NAFTA*, Centre for Internat'l Governance Innovation (Jan. 6, 2020), https://www.cigionline.org/publications/international-intellectual-property-after-new-nafta.

The promise doctrine was articulated in a series of judicial decisions considering the utility requirement in patent law – that to be a patentable invention, the claimed subject matter must be "useful," a requirement synonymous with "capable of industrial application" in the language of the NAFTA and TRIPS Agreement.[77]

Under earlier Supreme Court of Canada case law, a "sound prediction" that the drug would work was sufficient to fulfill the utility requirement.[78] The sound prediction doctrine was used by the Supreme Court to uphold a patent for a new use – the prevention and treatment of HIV/AIDS – of an old drug called *azidothymidine* (AZT).

Pharmaceutical companies sometimes filed patent applications for chemical compounds that were not, at the time of the application, known for certain to be useful. Instead, the applicants made promises about a drug's potential, leaving the generic drug companies to challenge the validity of those patents on the basis that, while the drugs did *something*, the drugs did not do *exactly* or *everything* the patent applicants had promised.[79]

Before the Supreme Court of Canada struck down the promise doctrine as "bad law" in its 2017 decision in *AstraZeneca Canada Inc. v. Apotex Inc.*,[80] several valuable patents had been invalidated or undermined. For example, Canadian generic company Apotex was allowed to make a generic version of *Latanoprost*, a drug to treat glaucoma, because Pfizer's prediction fell short of the requirements for patentability.[81] Two blockbuster drugs from US pharmaceutical company Eli Lilly (Lilly) suffered a similar fate – *Strattera* (*atomoxetine*, used to treat attention deficit hyperactivity disorder or ADHD)[82] and *Zyprexa* (*olanzapine*, an antipsychotic to treat schizophrenia and bipolar disorder).[83] French pharmaceutical company Sanofi saw its patent for *clopidogrel*, a blood thinner sold under the brand name *Plavix*, invalidated around the same time.[84]

While the Canadian courts' decisions affected numerous brand-name drug companies, Lilly took the most aggressive legal action. It brought an action under the investor-state dispute settlement rules of the NAFTA to arbitrate the alleged expropriation of its IP and Canada's failure to comply with international obligations.[85]

77 TRIPS Agreement, *supra* note 48, at art. 47; NAFTA, *supra* note 47, at art. 1709(1).

78 *Apotex Inc. v. Wellcome Foundation Ltd.*, (2002) 4 S.C.R. 153 (Can.).

79 Norman Siebrasse, *The False Doctrine of False Promise*, 29 Can. Intellect. Prop. Rev. 56 (2013); E. Richard Gold & Michael Shortt, *The Promise of the Patent in Canada and Around the World*, 30 Can. Intellect. Prop. Rev. 35, 201 (2014).

80 *AstraZeneca Canada Inc v. Apotex Inc.*, (2017) 1 S.C.R. 943 (Can.).

81 *Apotex Inc. v. Pfizer Canada Inc.*, (2011) FCA 236 (Can.).

82 *Eli Lilly & Co. v. Teva Canada Ltd.*, (2011) FCA 220 (Can.).

83 *Eli Lilly Canada Inc. v. Novopharm Ltd.*, (2012) FCA 232 (Can.).

84 *Apotex Inc. v. Sanofi-Aventis*, (2013) FCA 186 (Can.).

85 *Eli Lilly and Company v. The Government of Canada*, ICSID Case No. UNCT/14/2, Notice of Intent to Submit a Claim to Arbitration under NAFTA Chapter Eleven (Nov. 7, 2012).

Lilly alleged that Canada's promise doctrine contradicted international trade law. It also alleged that Canadian judicial decisions could be considered and reviewed by trade lawyers arbitrating a dispute under the NAFTA. In effect, that would take the final say about how patent law impacts access to medicines out of the hands of the domestic courts of a sovereign nation and give that decision-making power to a panel of arbitrators interpreting trade law.

Lilly's lawsuit against the Government of Canada sought damages of C$500 million.[86] Canada was ultimately successful when the arbitrators ruled that courts in a common law system are allowed to develop law incrementally from case to case and that the promise doctrine did have roots in earlier precedent.[87] In a curious chronology, the arbitrators' decision under international trade law was released before the Supreme Court's decision on domestic law. While the arbitrators said the promise doctrine was justified, it was the Supreme Court that held that the promise doctrine should be abolished.

This dramatic saga worked out in the end. Canada won the case and even recovered some of its legal fees. The lesson, however, is a harsh one for developed and developing countries alike. If a well-resourced country like Canada is not immune to threats by foreign pharmaceutical companies over allegedly weak IP laws, how does that bode for developing countries? The message Lilly sent was loud and clear: do not mess with patent law, or you too could be sued for violating international trade law. In this way, what happened to Canada was not much different than what happened to South Africa nearly two decades earlier.

### *The Cost of More IP*

In combination, the changes to Canada's IP laws in these three recent trade agreements will likely affect the overall prices of medicines. One study predicts that the price of brand-name pharmaceuticals will increase by 6.2 percent in the long run as a result of the CETA.[88] This would be an estimated cost of C$850 million per year to Canadians.[89] Estimates calculated by Canada's Parliamentary Budget Office (PBO) also show increased costs as a result of both the CETA and CUSMA. The PBO estimates that the annual cost of the patent restoration clauses in the CETA would reach C$392 million (in 2015 values)

86 *Id.*

87 *Eli Lilly and Company v. The Government of Canada*, ICSID Case No. UNCT/14/2, Final Award, (Mar. 16, 2017) (International Centre for Settlement of Investment Disputes) (Arbitrators: Professor Albert Jan Van Den Berg (President), Sir Daniel Bethlehem QC and Mr. Gary Born).

88 Lexchin & Gagnon, *supra* note 63.

89 *Id.*

had they been in place in 2015.[90] This would have amounted to a cost of C$214 million for provincial public programs.[91]

Studies estimating the impact of the CUSMA also predict an increase in costs. The PBO predicts a cost of C$23.8 million per year between 2015 and 2023, had the CUSMA's provisions been in force starting in 2015.[92] However, considering future drug consumption and the increasing share of biologics in the market, the PBO estimates that the increase in combined cost for consumers and drug plans would be at least C$169 million in 2029 and would increase every year thereafter.[93]

Another study, by Lexchin, focuses only on the impact of the CUSMA on the cost of biologics, noting that "depending on how much of the market is captured by biologic competitors and how strong the patents are, lost savings from data protection extension could range from $0 to $305.8 million."[94]

Finally, the latest research indicates that the combined impact of the CETA and CUSMA will be the increase in the length of patent protection by 11 percent, on average, which will likely cost about C$410 million annually.[95]

Despite the increasing prices, significant innovation is unlikely to be stimulated within Canada. Rather, one study shows that these changes may stymie innovation rather than encourage it. Innovative industries are likely to face increased competition from much larger multinational industries in the US, Japan, Chile, and many European countries following the signing of all three trade deals.[96] Thus, predictive studies to date indicate broadly negative impacts

90 Office of The Parliamentary Budget Officer, Patent Restoration and the Cost of Pharmaceuticals 2 (2018).

91 *Id.* at 23. This figure is significantly different from Gagnon and Lexchin's estimates in their earlier study, and the PBO addresses this discrepancy. Gagnon and Lexchin's study estimates are based on a pool of drugs about five times larger than the PBO, as implementing legislation was not yet published at the time of their study. The implementing legislation limited the application of patent restoration clauses more than expected, according to the PBO. In addition, the Gagnon and Lexchin study incorporates the potential impacts of changes to the regulatory approval process, while the PBO only estimates the impact of patent restoration clauses.

92 *Id.*

93 Office of The Parliamentary Budget Officer, The Impact of the Canada – United States – Mexico Agreement on Prescription Drug Expenditures in Canada 2 (2019).

94 Joel Lexchin, *Increase in Drug Spending in Canada Due to Extension of Data Protection for Biologics: A Descriptive Study*, 14 Health Pol'y 10–18 (2019).

95 Reed F. Beall et al., *How Will Recent Trade Agreements That Extend Market Protections for Brand-Name Prescription Pharmaceuticals Impact Expenditures and Generic Access in Canada?*, 123 Health Policy 1251–58 (2019).

96 Olena Ivus, *The TPP and the New Intellectual Property Regime*, Centre Int'l Governance Innovation (2016), https://www.cigionline.org/publications/tpp-and-new-intellectual-property-regime; Olena Ivus & Marta Paczos, *Does Canada's Foreign Trade Policy Give Innovating Canadian Firms a Competitive Edge Internationally?*, Centre Int'l Governance Innovation (2019), https://www.cigionline.org/publications/does-canadas-foreign-trade-policy-give-innovating-canadian-firms-competitive-edge.

of these IP chapters on Canadians' access to medicines. The overall costs of the agreements' IP chapters may outweigh their benefits. Retrospective research on the impacts will be needed once they are all implemented.

## Impacts on Canadian Subpopulations

### *Background*

While the effects of IP on access to medicines are different in high-income countries compared to low- and middle-income countries, they are nonetheless real. The remainder of this chapter exposes a related issue: the unequal impacts of IP in trade agreements for different subpopulations of Canadians.

Overall, Canada has a confusing mix of policies. An individual may pay full price for a drug in one province, but nothing in other provinces. As a result, different populations with different types of health coverage are affected by rising prices differently. The effects will be felt differently in each province, given that pharmacare coverage, when provided, is paid for by provincial governments, not the federal government. The effects will also be felt differently by various groups who have different pharmacare coverage, such as Indigenous peoples, refugees, and people without private or employer-provided insurance.

Canada does not currently have a national pharmacare program. Instead, Canadians are covered by a patchwork of provincial insurance plans, federal drug coverage, and private insurance plans, if they are covered at all. "About 46 percent of the total drug expenditure ($13.1 billion) was covered primarily by public sources; 37 percent ($10.7 billion) was covered primarily by private insurance; the remaining 17 percent ($4.7 billion) was primarily paid for out-of-pocket."[97] Many Canadians pay for their drug coverage. Estimates show that five percent of Canadians have no insurance whatsoever, private or public. About 20 percent are either not insured or underinsured, such that their insurance does not cover part or all of their prescription costs.[98] At the moment, private insurance is the most common source of drug coverage in Canada. Indeed, almost 60 percent of the population is at least partially covered through private insurance.[99] Nevertheless, private insurance plans are only responsible for about 36 percent of Canada's total prescription drug spending, and about one-third of Canadians do not have employer-funded prescription drug coverage.[100]

These private plans tend to exacerbate inequalities.[101] Canadians in precarious jobs are unlikely to have private health insurance, and women and young workers

97 *Federal Cost of a National Pharmacare Program*, *supra* note 40, at 5.
98 *Id.* at 41.
99 A Prescription for Canada, *supra* note 2, at 18.
100 *Id.*
101 *Id.* at 44.

are less likely to have health-care benefits from an employer.[102] On the other hand, those with incomes over C$55,000 often rely entirely on private drug coverage or out-of-pocket payments.[103]

The federal government also pays for private insurance costs. It employs about 450,000 individuals (including reservists), although this varies every year, and all those employees benefit from health insurance.[104] The federal government spends about C$658 million on private drug insurance plans.[105] Therefore, the federal government is an important provider of drug coverage through its contractual employer relationship alone. It also attempts to offset medicine costs with the Medical Expense Tax Credit, which gives Canadians with significant medical expenses – meaning three percent of their net income – a 15 percent nonrefundable tax credit.

### *Different Impacts Across Provinces*

There are over 100 different provincial government drug insurance programs. These are often tailored for specific groups, such as children, seniors, individuals with low incomes, or individuals with specific illnesses. The plans vary widely in their co-pays, deductibles, and premiums. Individuals receiving social assistance do not pay medicines out of pocket in six provinces: British Columbia, Alberta, Manitoba, Quebec, Prince Edward Island, and Newfoundland and Labrador. There is only partial coverage of medications for low-income people in other provinces.[106] Nevertheless, all provinces have at least some drug coverage for those over 65. Quebec is the only province where pharmaceutical insurance is mandatory, and much of it is covered by the government.[107]

In addition, medicines administered to patients while they are in the hospital are covered by the hospital in all provinces. Thus, hospitals spend about C$2 billion on medicines per year.[108] That impact is inevitably felt differently depending on each province's fiscal situation. As regional economies cycle through ups and downs, in-hospital pharmacare costs will consume lower and higher proportions of provincial budgets. Adding to the patchwork of drug coverage, each hospital determines the formulary of drugs that are distributed.[109]

102 A Prescription for Canada, *supra* note 2, at 18.

103 David J. T. Campbell et al., *Comparison of Canadian Public Medication Insurance Plans and the Impact on Out-of-Pocket Costs*, 5 CMAJ Open E808–13 (2017).

104 Gov't Can., Statistics Canada (Jan. 17, 2018), https://www150.statcan.gc.ca/n1/pub/11-402-x/2011000/chap/gov-gouv/gov-gouv-eng.htm.

105 *Federal Cost of a National Pharmacare Program*, *supra* note 40.

106 Jamie R. Daw & Steven G. Morgan, *Stitching the Gaps in the Canadian Public Drug Coverage Patchwork? A Review of Provincial Pharmacare Policy Changes from 2000 to 2010*, 104 Health Pol'y 19–26 (2012); Campbell et al., *supra* note 104.

107 Daw & Morgan, *supra* note 107; Campbell et al., *supra* note 104.

108 *Federal Cost of a National Pharmacare Program*, *supra* note 40.

109 *Id.* at 16.

Provinces also vary in the drugs that are covered in their formulary. Various studies have found that 30–50 percent of drugs are covered by all nine provinces.[110] Still, the Common Drug Review (CDR) was created in 2002 to help align provincial drug formularies. It is managed by the Canadian Agency for Drugs and Technologies in Health, and all provinces except Quebec participate in the CDR process. There is a disagreement on whether it has helped to align drug formularies.[111] Nevertheless, the most recent studies on drug formularies indicate that there is substantial agreement between provincial formularies.[112] Thus, there may be less variance throughout the country at present, and this trend may continue as there are many calls for a national drug formulary to entirely replace provincial drug formularies.[113]

Finally, another challenge of the public insurance system is uptake. One study found that 4.1 million eligible Canadians do not enroll for public insurance, possibly because they know their drug costs will not be high enough to meet plan deductibles or they do not know about the plans.[114] The patchwork of drug coverage policies is also confusing to navigate, even for expert policy makers. Academic journal articles are needed to describe the wide range of pharmaceutical coverage programs across Canada.[115] Thus, while provincial drug insurance plans are certainly important, the patchwork of policies leads to inequality between provinces and to many Canadians being underinsured.

Only the following groups are covered by a federal government program: Indigenous peoples, newly arrived refugees, federal prison inmates, and Canadian military veterans. The federal government programs only add to the confusing patchwork of eligibility for drug coverage.

110 Steve Morgan et al., *Breadth, Depth and Agreement Among Provincial Formularies in Canada*, 4 Health Pol'y E162 (2009); Kara MacDonald & Ken Potvin, *Interprovincial Variation in Access to Publicly Funded Pharmaceuticals: A Review Based on the WHO Anatomical Therapeutic Chemical Classification System*, 137 Can. Pharm. J. 29–34 (2004); J. P. Grégoire et al., *Inter-provincial Variation in Government Drug Formularies*, 92 Can. J. Public Health 307–12 (2001); Anis et al., *supra* note 52.

111 John-Michael Gamble et al., *Analysis of Drug Coverage Before and After the Implementation of Canada's Common Drug Review*, 183 CMAJ Open E1259 (2011); Amir Attaran & Andree Taylor, *The Effectiveness of the Common Drug Review in Canada's National Drug Strategy*, Atlantic Inst. AIMS, Dec. 2011, at 1, 10; Morgan et al., *supra* note 111.

112 Nicola Allen et al., *Evaluating Alignment Between Canadian Common Drug Review Reimbursement Recommendations and Provincial Drug Plan Listing Decisions: An Exploratory Study*, 4 CMAJ Open E674 (2016); Patented Medicine Prices Review Board, Alignment Among Public Formularies in Canada, Part 1, 1, 10 (2017).

113 A Prescription for Canada, *supra* note 2; Aidan Hollis & Stephen Law, *A National Formulary for Canada*, 30 Univ. Toronto Press 445 (2004).

114 Greg Sutherland & Thy Dinh, *Understanding the Gap: A Pan-Canadian Analysis of Prescription Drug Insurance Coverage*, Conference Board Of Can. 114 (2017).

115 Daw & Morgan, *supra* note 107; Campbell et al., *supra* note 104.

### *Different Impacts Across Groups*

#### *The Plight of Canada's Indigenous Peoples*

Medicines are covered by the federal government through the Non-Insured Health Benefits (NIHB) program because Indigenous services constitutionally fall under federal jurisdiction.[116] In addition, some treaties between the government and Indigenous groups bind the government to provide health care to that group. Drugs covered by the NIHB are listed in the drugs benefit list (DBL).[117] The NIHB does not require individuals to pay any money up-front or paying any premiums, co-pays, or deductibles.[118] As a result, some Indigenous people have adequate coverage compared to other segments of the population.

Nevertheless, there are some shortcomings of the program. First, many Aboriginal Canadians are not covered by the NIHB. There are three broad groupings for Indigenous peoples in Canada: Inuit, Métis, and First Nations.[119] Only First Nations individuals who have the "Indian" status as defined by the *Indian Act*, and recognized Inuit people, have access to this health coverage.[120] Métis and non-Indian First Nations individuals, representing 32 percent and 14 percent of aboriginal peoples, respectively, are not covered by the NIHB.[121] Second, some medicines are not covered under the DBL, although requests for coverage can be made under an exception process.[122] Third, changes may be made to the DBL without notifying NIHB recipients.[123] Fourth, the government sees this as a program of last resort, as it only covers "a range of medically necessary health benefits when these benefits are not otherwise covered through

116 Constitution Act, 1982, § 35(2), being Schedule B to the Canada Act 1982 (U.K.) (1982), c. 11.

117 *Guide for Pharmacy Benefits: Non-Insured Health Benefits*, HEALTH CAN. (Feb. 6, 2017), https://www.canada.ca/en/indigenous-services-canada/services/first-nations-inuit-health/reports-publications/non-insured-health-benefits/guide-pharmacy-benefits-non-insured-benefits.html#chp2_1 [hereinafter *Guide for Pharmacy Benefits*].

118 *Drugs and Pharmacy Benefits*, HEALTH CAN. (Apr. 12, 2016), https://www.canada.ca/en/indigenous-services-canada/services/non-insured-health-benefits-first-nations-inuit/benefits-services-under-non-insured-health-benefits-program/drugs-pharmacy-benefits.html.

119 Constitution Act, 1982, *supra* note 117; D. N. COLLINS, ABORIGINAL PEOPLE AND OTHER CANADIANS: SHAPING NEW RELATIONSHIPS (2001).

120 *Guide for Pharmacy Benefits, supra* note 118.

121 NATIONAL HOUSEHOLD SURVEY, ABORIGINAL PEOPLES IN CANADA: FIRST NATIONS PEOPLE, MÉTIS AND INUIT, ANALYTICA REPORTS 2011 (2018); *Guide for Pharmacy Benefits, supra* note 118.

122 Zeeshan Rana et al., *Access to Essential Medicines and the Canadian Aboriginal Population: Core Features of the Drug Program and Policy Issues* 24 (Compar. Program on Health and Soc'y, Working Paper Series 2003/2004, 2004).

123 Jessie Loyer & Marija Small Legs, *Non-Insured Health Benefits for First Nations and Inuit People: An Overview for Information Providers*, 35 J. CAN. HEALTH LIBR. ASSOC, 24 (2014); Jeff Morrison, *The Time has Come to Fix the Non-Insured Health Benefits (NIHB) Program*, 148 CAN. PHARM J. 217 (2015).

private or provincial/territorial health insurance plans or social programs."[124] As a result, Indigenous peoples and their pharmacists are required to submit their claims to other plans before submitting them to the NIHB.[125]

In addition, Indigenous peoples' medical needs are on average greater than the rest of the Canadian population. They have higher rates of injuries, mental illness, suicide, most chronic diseases, diabetes, asthma, cardiovascular disease, tuberculosis, hepatitis, syphilis, HIV/AIDS, and pulmonary illnesses.[126] Some particularly striking statistics are as follows: rates of diabetes are three to five times higher than the national average, the rate of tuberculosis in on-reserve First Nations is 40 times higher than the national average and over 300 times higher among the Inuit, and suicide is one of the leading causes of death among children and youth in many First Nations communities and Inuit Nunangat.[127] They also have lower incomes on average, while accessing safe water and adequate housing is also a challenge in many Indigenous communities.[128] As a result, they face barriers to accessing medication, such as securing financial support for paid time off work when a treatment or medication is required.[129] While Indigenous peoples may be shielded from most of the costs of the increased prices, they would struggle far more to access any medicine not covered on the DBL.

124 *Guide for Pharmacy Benefits*, *supra* note 118.

125 *Id.*; Loyer & Legs, *supra* note 124.

126 Sandra J. Romain, *Pharmaceutical Health Care and Inuit Language Communications in Nunavut, Canada*, 72 Int. J. Circumpolar Health 21409 (2013).

127 Mohan B. Kumar & Michael Tjepkema, *Suicide Among First Nations People, Métis and Inuit (2011–2016): Findings from the Canadian Census Health and Environment Cohort (CanCHEC)*, National Household Survey: Aboriginal Peoples 23 (2019); Health Canada, *Map – Tuberculosis in Inuit Nunangat* (Mar. 23 2018), https://www.canada.ca/en/indigenous-services-canada/services/first-nations-inuit-health/diseases-health-conditions/tuberculosis/tuberculosis-resources-first-nations-inuit-aboriginal-health-health-canada/map-tuberculosis-inuit-nunangat.html; *Indigenous Services Canada, Tuberculosis in First Nations in Canada*, Gov't Can. (Mar. 22 2019), https://www.canada.ca/en/indigenous-services-canada/services/first-nations-inuit-health/diseases-health-conditions/tuberculosis/tuberculosis-resources-first-nations-inuit-aboriginal-health-health-canada/tuberculosis-first-nations-canada.html; Chantelle A. M. Richmond & Catherine Cook, *Creating Conditions for Canadian Aboriginal Health Equity: The Promise of Healthy Public Policy*, 37 Public Health Rev. 2 (2016).

128 Richmond & Cook, *supra* note 128; Naomi Adelson, *The Embodiment of Inequity: Health Disparities in Aboriginal Canada*, 96 Can. J. Public Health S45 (2005); Maya Basdeo & Lalita Bharadwaj, *Beyond Physical: Social Dimensions of the Water Crisis on Canadas First Nations and Considerations for Governance,* 23 Indig Pol'y J. (2013); Heather Castleden & Emily Skinner, *Whitewashing Indigenous Water Rights in Canada: How Can We Indigenize Climate Change Adaptation If We Ignore the Fundamentals?, in* Adaptation to Climate Change through Water Resources Management: Capacity, Equity and Sustainability 221 (Dominic Stucker & Elena Lopez-Gunn, eds., 1st ed. 2014).

129 Tara C. Horrill et al., *Access to Cancer Care Among Indigenous Peoples in Canada: A Scoping Review*, 238 Soc. Sci. Med. 112495 (2019).

*Poor Coverage for Newcomers*

Refugees are the only immigrant group that has dedicated federal funding as they are covered by the interim federal health program.[130] Thus, refugees that come to Canada through a formal refugee resettlement program have medicare for six months that is comparable to citizens' coverage.

Most immigrants do not have coverage for medicines like refugees. They are dependent on provincial health-care policies that vary widely between provinces.[131] In addition, immigrants' precarity often makes access to medicines particularly challenging. For instance, individuals with temporary status often have no, or very limited, health coverage. International students with visas have no access to health care in three provinces, have conditional access to health care in others, and must wait 12 months to access health care in others.[132] Even after obtaining a status that provides access, immigrants must often wait several months before they can access health-care services in four provinces. However, some doctors estimate that the delay takes closer to two years.[133] Many immigrants start their time in Canada on a temporary visa and gradually obtain permanent status.[134] They are mandated to buy health insurance in several provinces in the meantime, which can have high premiums. As a result, migrants may reside in Canada for years without health care or have to pay high prices for health care.

Immigrants also have different sets of health needs and challenges than the rest of the population. Although about 90 percent of migrants arrive in Canada with excellent health (the "healthy migrant effect") due to health screening and selection effects of the immigration system, their health relative to the general population tends to decline with time spent in Canada.[135] They are twice as likely to have difficulties in accessing immediate care as those born in Canada.[136] There are also significant language and cultural barriers to accessing

130 *Refugees and Citizenship Canada Immigration, Interim Federal Health Program: Summary of coverage*, Gov't Can. (Dec. 2, 2019), https://www.canada.ca/en/immigration-refugees-citizenship/services/refugees/help-within-canada/health-care/interim-federal-health-program/coverage-summary.html.

131 Y. Y. Brandon Chen, *Extending Health Care Entitlement to Lawful Non-Transient International Migrants: Untapped Potential of the Universality Principle in the Canada Health Act*, 48 Univ. B.C. L.R. 81 (2015).

132 *Id.*

133 P. Caulford, *Providing Health Care to Medically Uninsured Immigrants and Refugees*, 179 Can. Med. Assoc J. 1253 (2006); Ritika Goel et al., *Waiting for Care: Effects of Ontario's 3-Month Waiting Period for OHIP on Landed Immigrants*, 59 Can. Fam. Physician Med. E269 (2013).

134 Chen, *supra* note 132.

135 Statistics Canada, Zotero (Government of Canada), *Health Reports: Healthy Immigrant Effect by Immigrant Category in Canada.*

136 B. D. Gushulak et al., *Migration and Health in Canada: Health in the Global Village*, 183 Can. Med. Assoc. J. E952 (2011).

health care.[137] Difficulties in language and in social support in their new country will also affect access.[138]

### *Different Impacts Based on Gender*

IP also affects access to medicines differently depending on gender. Gender identity is defined broadly by the Ontario Human Rights Code as "each person's internal and individual experience of gender… anywhere along the gender spectrum." They may be a man, woman, both, neither, or anywhere along the spectrum, and "a person's gender identity may be the same as or different from their birth-assigned sex."[139]

The medical field has a long history of gender bias, and this is also evident in medicine access. Women in Canada were not afforded medical education until the 1890s.[140] Clinical trial studies were usually done with exclusively or primarily cisgender white male participants prior to the 1970s.[141] In addition, the symptoms of men are investigated and treated more extensively for a number of diseases.[142]

Women are more likely to require medication but are less likely to have employer-funded health care and have lower income on average than men.[143] They are also more likely to be buying medication for children, yet female single parents had the lowest median income in 2016 of any family type.[144] Women account for 54 percent of spending on medication and 57 percent of prescriptions in

137 Salim Ahmed et al., *Barriers to Access of Primary Healthcare by Immigrant Populations in Canada: A Literature Review*, 18 J. Immigr. Minor Health 1522 (2016).

138 *Id.*

139 *Policy on Preventing Discrimination Because of Gender Identity and Gender Expression*, Ontario Hum Rights Comm. (2014), http://www.ohrc.on.ca/en/policy-preventing-discrimination-because-gender-identity-and-gender-expression.

140 Charles G. Roland, *History of Medicine to 1950*, Can. Encyclopedia, https://thecanadianencyclopedia.ca/en/article/history-of-medicine (Sept. 6, 2020).

141 Katarina Hamberg, *Gender Bias in Medicine*, 4 Womens Health 237 (2008).

142 Caroline Daly et al., *Gender Differences in the Management and Clinical Outcome of Stable Angina*, 113 Circulation 490 (2006); G. M. Hariz & G. M. Hariz, *Gender Distribution in Surgery for Parkinson's Disease*, 6 Parkinsonism & Relat. Disord. 155 (2000); Fazlul Karim et al., *Gender Differences in Delays in Diagnosis and Treatment of Tuberculosis*, 22 Health Pol'y Plan 329 (2007); Anna Marie Chang et al., *Gender Bias in Cardiovascular Testing Persists After Adjustment for Presenting Characteristics and Cardiac Risk*, 14 Acad. Emergency Med. 599 (2007); Rita F. Redberg, *Gender, Race, and Cardiac Care: Why the Differences?*, 46 J. AM. Coll. Cardiol. 1852 (2005); Katarina Hamberg et al., *Male and Female Physicians Show Different Patterns of Gender Bias: A Paper-Case Study of Management of Irritable Bowel Syndrome*, 32 Scand J. Public Health 144 (2004); Katarina Hamberg et al., *Gender Bias in Physicians' Management of Neck Pain: A Study of the Answers in a Swedish National Examination*, 11 J. Womens Health Gend. Based Med. 653 (2002); J. N. Katz et al., *Differences Between Men and Women Undergoing Major Orthopedic Surgery for Degenerative Arthritis*, 37 Arthritis Rheum. 687 (1994).

143 A Prescription for Canada, *supra* note 2.

144 Statistics Canada Government of Canada, Lone-Parent Families (June 24, 2015), https://www150.statcan.gc.ca/n1/pub/75-006-x/2015001/article/14202/parent-eng.htm.

Canada.[145] Most Canadian women of reproductive age must also regularly use contraception, yet not all contraceptive options are covered in numerous insurance plans.[146] Women also experience a greater need for antidepressants, hormone replacement therapy, and drugs for multiple sclerosis, and antibiotics.[147] As a result, drug spending for women between the ages of 19 and 39 are 60 percent higher than men of the same age.[148] However, drug spending is on an average higher for men before 18 years and after 65 years of age due to antipsychotics, ADHD, and asthma drugs for boys and cholesterol, hyperplasia, and erectile dysfunction drugs for elderly men.[149] Better data on the impact of these clauses on medicine prices, with data disaggregated by gender, would give a more detailed portrait of the gendered impacts of trade agreements on access to medicines.

Gender nonconforming and/or transindividuals have been marginalized even more than women by the medical literature.[150] Their particular challenges affect accessing and affording medicines. They experience higher levels of violence, poverty, unemployment, and homelessness.[151] This poses challenges for accessing health care because trans- and/or gender nonconforming individuals may not have the time or resources to prioritize their medical concerns or to see their doctor.[152] They are also more likely to experience challenges affording medication and less likely to be covered by insurance policies.[153]

145 Steve Morgan et al., *The Canadian Rx atlas, 3rd edition*, UBC CENTRE HEALTH SERVS. & POL'Y RESEARCH (2013), https://open.library.ubc.ca/cIRcle/collections/facultyresearchandpublications/52383/items/1.0048514.

146 Amanda Black et al., *Contraceptive Use Among Canadian Women of Reproductive Age: Results of a National Survey*, 31 J. OBSTET. GYNAECOL. CAN. 627 (2009).

147 Morgan et al., *supra* note 146.

148 *Id.*

149 *Id.*

150 For definitions of gender identity, *see Terminologies of Oppression: Comprehensive List of Working Definitions,* ANTI-OPPRESSION NETWORK (Mar. 10, 2014), https://theantioppressionnetwork.com/resources/terminologies-of-oppression/.

151 Greta Bauer & Ayden I. Scheim, *Transgender People in Ontario, Canada: Statistics from the Trans PULSE Project to Inform Human Rights Policy*, TRANS PLUS PROJECT (2015), https://transpulseproject.ca/wp-content/uploads/2015/06/Trans-PULSE-Statistics-Relevant-for-Human-Rights-Policy-June-2015.pdf; Tiffany K. Roberts & Corinne R. Fantz, *Barriers to Quality Health Care for the Transgender Population*, 47 CLIN. BIOCHEM. 983 (2014). In one survey, 34 percent of trans respondents were living in poverty, compared to 13.5 percent of the Canadian general population, and 21 percent had experienced physical or sexual violence due to being trans. In the United States, transgender individuals experience twice the rate of unemployment and nearly seven times the rate of homelessness compared to the United States general population.

152 Jae M. Sevelius et al., *Barriers and Facilitators to Engagement and Retention in Care Among Transgender Women Living with Human Immunodeficiency Virus*, 47 ANNALS BEHAVIOR MED. 5 (2014); Robert H. Remien et al., *Barriers and Facilitators to Engagement of Vulnerable Populations in HIV Primary Care in New York City*, 69 J. ACQUIRE IMMUNE DEFICIENCY SYNDROME S16 (2015).

153 Roberts & Fantz, *supra* note 152; Daphna Stroumsa, *The State of Transgender Health Care: Policy, Law, and Medical Frameworks,* 104 AM. J. PUBLIC HEALTH E31 (2014).

In addition, they report facing discrimination by health-care providers.[154] For instance, a diagnosis of gender dysphoria listed in the Diagnostic and Statistical Manual of Mental Disorders is still necessary to access publicly funded gender-affirming surgeries in many cases. Some researchers argue that this serves to further stigmatize trans- and gender nonconforming individuals in the medical field.[155] Transindividuals may avoid health care as a result. One survey in Ontario showed that 25 percent of transgender people avoided emergency services when needed due to discrimination against transgender people.[156]

Finally, this community has unique health needs compared to the general population, as they may require access to gender-affirming treatments, hormone therapy, and others.[157] They also face higher rates of mental illness, HIV/AIDS, and depression.[158,159]

In sum, the impact of IP chapters in trade deals will vary for different populations, and the government must understand and measure how the agreements will impact access to medicines in different countries.

## Conclusions

As IP has increasingly strong protections in each new trade agreement, and as the prices of medicines continue to increase, high-income countries like Canada are feeling the effects. This chapter has shown that three recent trade deals will significantly increase IP protections in Canada and has summarized research showing this will likely increase drug prices but not innovation. Contrasting this with Canada's pharmaceutical policy landscape, these overall increases in prices will have significantly different impacts on different Canadians across the country. Indeed, those already without coverage, or with increased health needs, will likely be affected by these changes in IP laws more than others.

154 Greta R. Bauer et al., *Factors Impacting Transgender Patients' Discomfort with Their Family Physicians: A Respondent-Driven Sampling Survey*, 10 PLoS One (2015); Greta R. Bauer et al., *Reported Emergency Department Avoidance, Use, and Experiences of Transgender Persons in Ontario, Canada: Results from a Respondent-Driven Sampling Survey*, 63 Annals Emergency Med. 713 (2014); Sevelius et al., *supra* note 153; Stroumsa, *supra* note 154; Ella Vermeir et al., *Barriers to Primary and Emergency Healthcare for Trans Adults*, 20 Cult Health Sex 232 (2018); Edward McCann & Danika Sharek, *Mental Health Needs of People Who Identify as Transgender: A Review of the Literature*, 30 Arch. Psychiatric Nurse 280 (2016).

155 Stroumsa, *supra* note 154; Roberts & Fantz, *supra* note 152; Vermeir et al., *supra* note 155.

156 Bauer et al., *supra* note 155.

157 Stroumsa, *supra* note 154.

158 Remien et al., *supra* note 153; Stroumsa, *supra* note 154; Bauer & Scheim, *supra* note 152; Jaime M Grant et al., National Transgender Discrimination Survey: Full Report (2015), https://www.transequality.org/sites/default/files/docs/resources/NTDS_Report.pdf.

159 Bauer & Scheim, *supra* note 152.

# 11 India

## Pharmaceutical Patents and Evergreen Battle for Access to Medicines

*Anand Grover*

### Introduction

In April 2013, the Supreme Court of India upheld the strict application of a pivotal provision in the Indian patent law, i.e. section 3(d) of the Patents Act, which restricts the evergreening of pharmaceutical patents. The "Novartis case," as it has come to be known, captured the imagination of the global health community through the eight years of ill-advised litigation launched by Swiss pharmaceutical major, Novartis, against those who opposed its patent application for the drug *Glivec*. But the history of the Novartis case lay much more in the events that preceded it by several decades.

### TRIPS Agreement and Health

In many ways, the Novartis story starts in the 1980s, when Western Multinational Corporations (MNCs), notably the pharmaceutical and music industries in the United States (US), pushed for the global dissemination of the US intellectual property (IP) regime – a vision they pursued through their governments in the negotiations to establish the World Trade Organization (WTO). India and other developing countries initially resisted, but their alliances were eventually broken by US pressure and threats to use unilateral sanctions under the US Special 301 law, i.e. to increase US tariffs on imports from those countries. Eventually, developing countries stopped resisting the global dissemination of the US IP regime. A compromise was ultimately arrived at – the Agreement on Trade-Related Aspects of Intellectual Property Rights (TRIPS Agreement). Why did the developing countries agree? While the TRIPS Agreement did set out mandatory minimum standards of IP rights protection and enforcement measures for WTO members, developing countries were able to extract certain flexibilities, including what would be the criteria for patent products and processes. However, they failed to realize that the agenda of a unitary international IP regime would continue to be pursued through other means.[1]

The impact of the TRIPS Agreement on public health and access to medicines was most notable in the context of the HIV epidemic. In the first decade and a half after the discovery of HIV, neither cure nor treatment was available. This inevitably meant that once a person was HIV positive, death due to AIDS was a certainty. However, with the advent of triple-drug combination antiretroviral (ARV) therapy in the mid-1990s, HIV became a treatable disease for the vast majority of People Living with HIV (PLHIV). With ARV therapy (ART), PLHIV could, for all practical purposes, have lives that are primarily normal and fulfilling. Those diagnosed with HIV need ART throughout their lives. However, the costs of these drugs and various monitoring tests made the treatment unaffordable for most PLHIV, especially those living in developing countries and least developed countries (LDCs). In the West, the cost of ART was borne either by the state or insurance companies. As a result, there was a marked decrease in the number of HIV-related deaths in the last seven years of the last millennium in the developed world. In contrast, HIV was wreaking havoc in the developing countries. PLHIV were dying by the thousands in sub-Saharan Africa. As HIV was largely affecting the young and productive populations, economies in some countries were literally being devastated by the HIV pandemic.

In 1996, the Brazilian government took a political decision, based on the principle that no Brazilian should die on account of HIV if they could be treated with ART. The Brazilian government introduced and implemented, with the help of nongovernmental organizations, the policy of universal access to ART. At the time, ARVs in Brazil were manufactured by companies controlled by the government. ARV prices were thus considerably lower. As part of this program, approximately 95,000 patients received free ART through the public health system in September 2000. Within three years, AIDS-related mortality nearly halved and opportunistic infections were reduced by 60–80 percent.[2] By 2005, 160,000 PLHIV received free ART from the public health system, including 17 ARVs, eight of which were domestically produced generic drugs. While ART costs reached $400 million in 2005, government estimates showed that the provision of treatment early in the epidemic resulted in savings of over $2 billion in health-care costs.[3]

1 The unfinished agenda is now being pursued through free trade or bilateral agreements; *see, e.g.*, TRIPS: Agreement on Trade-Related Aspects of Intellectual Property Rights, Apr. 15, 1994, Marrakesh Agreement Establishing the World Trade Organization, Annex 1C, 1869 U.N.T.S. 299, 33 I.L.M. 1197 (1994) [hereinafter TRIPS Agreement].

2 United Nations, Report on the Global HIV/AIDS Epidemic, UNAIDS/00.13E (2000), http://data.unaids.org/pub/report/2000/2000_gr_en.pdf.

3 World Health Organization, *Developing Countries & Free Access Fact Sheet* (2005), https://www.who.int/hiv/countries_freeaccess.pdf.

In other countries, TRIPS-compliant regimes had already been put in place. However, despite the fact that their patent laws were compliant with the TRIPS Agreement, governments were bullied by pharmaceutical MNCs into not using any flexibilites allowed by the TRIPS Agreement to access generic medicines. South Africa was a classic case in point.

In Southern Africa and other parts of the developing world, thousands were dying of HIV every day. A movement against this inequality in access to drugs in the international system was led by South African activists. During the 2000 International AIDS Conference in Durban, Justice Edwin Cameron, an openly gay and HIV-positive judge of the South African High Court and ultimately the judge of the Constitutional Court of South Africa, put it thus:

> In this I exist as a living embodiment of the iniquity of drug availability and access in Africa. My presence here embodies the injustices of AIDS in Africa because, on a continent in which 290 million Africans survive on less than one US dollar a day, I can afford monthly medication costs of about US$400 per month. Amidst the poverty of Africa, I stand before you because I am able to purchase health and vigor. I am here because I can afford to pay for life itself.[4]

The indignation at this inequality and injustice in matters concerning life and death reverberated globally. The call was for all persons, from the rich or poor countries, black or white, irrespective of gender or sexual orientation, to have their right to life respected unequivocally through the provision of ART. South Africa's attempt to include provisions in its medicines law that would have allowed it to access generic ART led to retaliation by way a lawsuit by 39 pharmaceutical MNCs to prevent the government from going ahead with its plans to expand ART coverage with generic company support.[5] The outrage against the case spread globally. By early 2001, the critical importance of generic competition was clear through Brazil's experience and with Indian generic companies launching first-line ART at $350 per patient per annum.[6] The new prices made it possible to launch a huge global effort of providing ARVs across the world to the people who needed them, saving millions of lives. These events prompted the Ministerial Declaration on the TRIPS Agreement and Public Health in November 2001 (Doha Declaration).[7]

4 Edwin Cameron, *The Deafening Silence of AIDS*, Health and Human Rights (2000), https://cdn2.sph.harvard.edu/wp-content/uploads/sites/13/2014/04/3-Cameron.pdf.

5 Rachel L. Swarns, *Drug Makers Drop South Africa Suit over Aids Medicine*, N.Y. Times (Apr. 10, 2001), https://www.nytimes.com/2001/04/20/world/drug-makers-drop-south-africa-suit-over-aids-medicine.html.

6 Donald G. McNeil Jr., *Indian Company Offers to Supply AIDS Drugs at Low Cost in Africa*, N.Y. Times (Feb. 7, 2001), https://www.nytimes.com/2001/02/07/world/indian-company-offers-to-supply-aids-drugs-at-low-cost-in-africa.html.

7 World Trade Organization, *Ministerial Declaration of 14 November 2001, WTO Doc. WT/MIN(01)/DEC/W/2*, 41 ILM 746 (2002), https://www.who.int/medicines/areas/policy/tripshealth.pdf?ua=1.

The Doha Declaration recognized the concerns of developing countries and LDCs regarding the implications of the TRIPS Agreement on public health, especially in the context of diseases like HIV/AIDS, malaria, and tuberculosis (TB). Paragraph 4 of the Doha Declaration affirms that the TRIPS Agreement should be interpreted and implemented so as to protect public health and promote access to medicines for all. The Doha Declaration explicitly recognized the right of WTO members to grant compulsory licenses (CLs), to determine the grounds for granting them, and to determine what constitutes national emergency or other circumstances of extreme urgency. It further clarifies that members are free to establish their own regime as regards the principle of exhaustion without challenge, thus leaving countries free to determine the rules for parallel importing. While these TRIPS flexibilities found specific mention in the Doha Declaration, there are several other public health TRIPS flexibilities that can ensure access to affordable generic medicines. However, it must be noted that to make use of TRIPS flexibilities, it is essential that national laws contain provisions reflecting them.

## India's Patent Law

India's experience with pharmaceutical patents predates the TRIPS Agreement, and thus the history of the Novartis case stretches even further into the past. Before the 1970s, Indian patent law followed along the lines of British law, allowing foreign companies to make huge profits.[8] At the time of independence, India was one of the countries with the highest medicine prices in the world. In the 1970s, after detailed reports at the instance of the then Prime Minister, Indira Gandhi, by Justice Bakshi Tek Chand[9] and Justice N. Rajagopala Ayyangar[10] recommending the reform of the Indian patent law in the interest of citizens, Indian patent law was amended to protect only process patents, not product patents on medicines and food.[11] The period for protection was limited to seven years. Product patents give an absolute monopoly to owners, enabling them to charge monopolist exorbitant prices for medicines. Process patents, on the other hand, allow relative competition, as better processes are developed to make a product and compete with others, resulting in lower prices. Several Indian generic companies thus came up with effective processes and began to compete with foreign companies. From a relatively low presence, the Indian generic drugs industry became a dominant player domestically, and by the turn of the millennium, in the developing world. By 1988, the industry had turned into a net earner of

8 Indian Patents and Designs Act, 1911.

9 Bakshi Tek Chand, Patents Enquiry Committee 1948 – Report, Ministry of Industry and Supply, New Delhi, (1950).

10 Shri Justice N. Rajagopala Ayyangar, Report on the Revision of the Patents Law (1959).

11 The Patents Act, 1970 (India).

foreign exchange[12] and by the 2000s, it had become the largest supplier of safe and effective ARVs in the developing world.[13] Indian generic pharmaceutical companies were "making in India" not only for Indians but also for the rest of the world.

It was in this backdrop that the TRIPS Agreement came into force on 1 January 1995; India had to fully comply with its obligations under the TRIPS Agreement by 1 January 2005. The Indian Parliament amended the patent law in 1999 to introduce the interim Exclusive Marketing Rights regime required under the Agreement,[14] and later amended the Patents Act in 2002 for India's full compliance to the Agreement in 2005. When the final amendments to the Patents Act had to be carried out by the beginning of 2005, Parliament was not only mindful of its obligation under the TRIPS Agreement, but also of its obligation to protect the right to health of its citizens and the developing world.[15] Given that drug patents are mostly internationally owned by Western and Japanese MNCs who were likely to patent most of the new generation medicines, including ARVs, Indian pharmaceutical companies faced the very real prospect of not being able to use the generic route to manufacture medicines at lower prices. The world had already seen the crisis in access to medicines over the AIDS epidemic, when drugs were being sold at $10,000 per patient per annum, leaving huge populations to die.

There was an additional problem. In the US, Europe, and Japan, patents were being granted not only for new molecular (or chemical) entities (NMEs or NCEs), but also for new forms of the same. For instance, if a base of a compound is the NCE or NME and had been granted a patent, then even the new form of the same compound, a salt or crystalline form, was also being granted patents even though it may not have any additional therapeutic benefit, provided that it satisfied the criteria of novelty, inventive step, and industrial applicability. In fact, nearly 76 percent of patented drugs were such forms of known substances.[16]

12 Biswajit Dhar & C. Niranjan Rao, *Transfer of Technology for Successful Integration into the Global Economy, A Case Study of the Pharmaceutical Industry in India* (2002), https://unctad.org/en/Docs/iteipcmisc22_en.pdf.

13 Brenda Waning et al., *A Lifeline to Treatment: The Role of Indian Generic Manufacturers in Supplying Antiretroviral Medicines to Developing Countries*, 13:35 J. Int. AIDS Soc. (2010).

14 Earlier Parliament had refused to introduce the EMR regime, as a result of which India was taken to the WTO's Dispute Settlement Body where India lost both before the Panel and the Appellate Body. Parliament had no choice but to introduce the interim regime of EMR to avoid trade sanctions. *See* World Trade Organization, *India – Patent Protection for Pharmaceuticals* (1999), https://www.wto.org/english/tratop_e/dispu_e/cases_e/ds50_e.htm.

15 Sanya Reid Smit et al., *Our Health, Our Right: The Role and Experiences of PLHIV Networks in Securing Access to Generic ARV Medicines in Asia, Asia Pacific Network of People Living with HIV/AIDS* 32 (2008), https://hivlawcommission.org/wp-content/uploads/2017/06/Our-Health-Our-Right-Securing-access-to-generic-ARV-medicines-in-Asia.pdf.

16 National Institute for Health Care Management Research and Educational Foundation, *Changing Patterns of Pharmaceutical Innovation* (2002).

This allowed what is known as "evergreening," effectively extending the patents on medicines and preventing the manufacture of generic versions even after the 20-year patent term on the NME or NCE ran out. Evergreening extend monopolies tends to eliminate competition, making drugs unaffordable and inaccessible, and adversely impacting the right to health.

The challenge for the Indian Parliament, therefore, was to strike a balance between complying with the TRIPS obligations by providing patent protection for both products and processes for 20 years, and substantially limiting evergreening and promoting generic competition, thereby protecting the right to health. It was guided in its deliberations by the Doha Declaration[17] and by several representatives from around the world, including from the World Health Organization (WHO) and the Joint United Nations Program on HIV/AIDS.[18] Importantly, several Members of Parliament cut across party lines voiced their concerns and hopes for protecting access to medicines.

These efforts crystallized into a provision engrafting section 3(d) onto the Patents Act, among other provisions. Section 3(d) provides that a new form of a known substance would not be patented unless it had enhanced efficacy over the known substance, while new uses could not be patented at all. The provision is compliant with the TRIPS Agreement when one considers the flexibilities available to member states. Although Article 27.1 of the TRIPS Agreement mandates that member countries have to provide patent protection for a period of 20 years for products and processes that are novel, not obvious, and industrially applicable, it does not stipulate what is "new" or what is an "inventive step." This is a key flexibility that developing countries secured in the TRIPS Agreement which allowed them to define these terms narrowly or broadly depending on their own socioeconomic needs and concerns. This is what India used.

It is section 3(d) that Novartis challenged and relentlessly campaigned against.[19] Interestingly, during the debate in Parliament, the one medicine that exemplified this concern was *imatinib mesylate*, sold by Novartis as *Glivec*. Members of Parliament cited Novartis' high costs (₹120,000 per person per month) against the generic versions (₹8000 to ₹10,000 per person per month). It seems fitting then that it is the legal battle on this very medicine that finally affirmed this public health safeguard and the requirement for its "strict and narrow interpretation."

17 *See* McNeil, *supra* note 6.

18 Interestingly, the letter from the WHO was signed by the erstwhile president of the World Bank Jim Young Kim. *See* http://www.cptech.org/ip/health/c/india/unaids02232005.html, and http://www.cptech.org/ip/health/c/india/who12172004.html.

19 Thus, in India, the MNCs have, with the local industry formed the US-India Business Coalition, which has issued documents about the need to delete section 3(d) from the Patents Act; *see* Indian Patent and Designs Act, 1911, section 3(d) (India).

## The Novartis Case

### *In General*

In 1997, Novartis filed a patent application for its claimed invention, the drug *Glivec* – the β-crystalline form of the salt *imatinib mesylate* – before the Chennai Patent Controller. The application was kept in the mailbox. After 1 January 2005, the mailbox facility was opened. Five pre-grant patent oppositions were filed against Novartis' application, one by the Cancer Patients Aid Association (CPAA), and the other four by Indian generic companies.[20]

Novartis contended that the claimed invention was novel, inventive, and industrially applicable. The oppositionists contended otherwise and argued that the claimed invention was hit by section 3(d) of the Patents Act. In this respect, Novartis filed additional affidavits to ostensibly to show that on account of the alleged increased bioavailability, higher hygroscopicity, and free flow of the β-crystalline form of *imatinib mesylate*, there was a significant increase in the efficacy in the claimed invention.[21] While there was no dispute as to the claimed invention's industrial applicability, the Patent Controller concluded that it was neither novel nor inventive and was also hit by section 3(d), thus rejecting the application for its patent.

Novartis filed appeals against this order before the Madras High Court. These were later transferred to the Intellectual Property Appellate Board (IPAB) on account of the change of procedure. Both Novartis AG and Novartis India also challenged the constitutional validity of section 3(d) in the Madras High Court, purportedly for noncompliance with the TRIPS Agreement, and on the ground that the term "efficacy" was vague and therefore in violation of the Indian Constitution. The Madras High Court dismissed both the Writ Petitions and held that section 3(d) had been enacted, among other reasons, to protect public health, observing: "[W]e have borne in mind the object which the amending Act wanted to achieve namely, to prevent evergreening; to provide easy access to the citizens of the country to life saving drugs and to discharge their constitutional obligation of providing good health care to its citizens."[22] Importantly, Novartis did not challenge this order of the Madras High Court.

On the other hand, the IPAB, in appeal, partially reversed the Patent Controller's order and held that the claimed invention was novel and inventive. It also granted

20 Under the Indian Patents Act, any person can file a pre-grant opposition on the grounds indicated in section 25(1). Post-grant opposition can be filed only by a person "interested"; *see* Indian Patent and Designs Act, 1911, section 25(1) (India).

21 The study was conducted on rats, but the comparison was with the base form of imatinib and not with the mesylate form of *imatinib*, which was also known at that time. *See M/s Novartis AG, Switzerland v. M/s Cancer Patients Aid Association*, *India*, Decision of the Patent Office (Jan. 25, 2006).

22 Madras High Court Writ Petition No. 24759 and 24760 of 2006, ¶ 19.

the process patent to Novartis. However, it agreed with the Patent Controller that the claimed invention was hit by section 3(d) and rejected the patent application. It was against this order that Novartis filed a Special Leave Petition directly to the Supreme Court, though by law, it should have filed a petition in the Madras High Court.

In the Supreme Court, the question of the maintainability of Novartis' petition was dropped and the case was heard on merits. At this stage, Novartis did not challenge section 3(d) and instead sought to weaken its interpretation.

### *On Merits*

The CPAA and the generic companies that opposed Novartis' patent application argued that the alleged "invention" lacked novelty, was obvious to a person skilled in the art, and that it was merely a "new form" of a "known substance" that did not enhance the known substance's efficacy, and was thus not patentable under section 3(d). These arguments were based on the fact that Novartis had already been granted a patent in 1993 in the US and other jurisdictions for the active molecule, *imatinib*, and that the application in India only concerned a specific β-crystalline form of the salt form of that compound, *imatinib mesylate*. The CPAA and the generic companies contended that the 1993 patent (also known as the Zimmerman patent) effectively disclosed both the free base *imatinib* and the acid addition salt *imatinib mesylate*. They also argued that different crystalline forms of *imatinib mesylate* did not differ in properties with respect to efficacy, and thus the various forms of *imatinib mesylate* must be considered the "same substance" under section 3(d).

*Imatinib* was exemplified in Example 21 of the Zimmerman patent. Novartis argued that the claimed invention in its 1997 application involved a twofold step over the Zimmerman patent, firstly from *imatinib* to *imatinib mesylate*, the salt form and, secondly, from the *mesylate* form to the β-crystalline form of *imatinib mesylate*.

It is a little-known fact that for the first week of arguments in the Supreme Court, Novartis flew down Dr. Jurg Zimmerman, the inventor named in the 1993 patent, to sit through the proceedings.

### *On Novelty*

Novartis contended that the Zimmerman patent did not teach the *mesylate* salt. However, the Supreme Court noted that the salt forms of *imatinib* were actually described and claimed in the Zimmerman patent. Moreover, the acid addition salt forms could be made in a customary manner or the manner known *per se*. That apart, Novartis itself had submitted a patent-term extension application in the US for the Zimmerman patent in respect of the *mesylate* form, which was granted for a period of 586 days on the basis that the Zimmerman patent covered the *mesylate* form. Much later, Novartis also submitted an application in the US for the β-crystalline form of *imatinib mesylate* which was rejected by the examiner. Novartis appealed the rejection, and the Board of Appeals held that the Zimmerman patent did not go beyond *imatinib mesylate* and did not extend to the β-crystalline form of *imatinib mesylate*. It also came to light in the Supreme Court hearings that Novartis had issued a notice in the United Kingdom for possible infringement against Natco Pharma Ltd., one of the generic company oppositionists, from marketing the *mesylate* form. This notice stated that the Zimmerman patent claimed the *mesylate* form. Therefore, it was Novartis's own case that the Zimmerman patent covered the *imatinib mesylate*. The Court thus found that *imatinib mesylate*, marketed as *Glivec*, was covered by the Zimmerman patent.

The Court also observed that the properties of *imatinib*, namely, the inhibition of tyrosine kinase activity, were also found in all the pharmaceutically acceptable salt forms, particularly noting that the authors of two articles in *Cancer Research* had concluded that in respect of properties, "no significant difference in results could be seen between the two forms of CGP 57148."[23] Similar findings were recorded in an article in the journal *Nature Medicines*. The Court therefore concluded that it was "unable to see how Imatinib Mesylate can be said to be a new product" and was in fact covered by the Zimmerman patent.

To overcome this hurdle, Novartis submitted that though *imatinib mesylate* may have been claimed and therefore covered under the Zimmerman patent, it was not disclosed, as there was no enabling disclosure in the Zimmerman patent. Novartis relied on the decision of the US Court of Customs and Patent Appeals in *In re Hogan*,[24] among other decisions. The argument was that coverage was larger than the disclosure, which in any case was not enabling. While rejecting this argument, the Supreme Court held that "to say coverage in a patent may go much beyond the disclosure thus seem to negate the fundamental rule underlying the grant of patents." The Supreme Court found that *Hogan* was rendered in very specific circumstances and later decisions of US courts had narrowed down *Hogan*'s impact. In addition, Novartis' own showing that the *mesylate* form was known in the Zimmerman patent made *Hogan* not applicable. The Court did not want Indian law to develop on the lines as in the US, "where there was big gap between coverage and disclosure under the patent; where the scope of patent is determined not on the intrinsic worth of the invention but on the artful drafting of claims by skillful lawyers...." Thus, the argument that *imatinib mesylate* was a new product over and above the Zimmerman patent was rejected.

## *On Interpreting Section 3(d)*

Once the Supreme Court determined that *imatinib mesylate* was known, it turned its attention to the β crystal form of *imatinib mesylate*, accepting "for the purposes of argument" that it was new. The Court also observed that whether it involved an inventive step or not was another unrelated matter. What was evident was that as a pharmaceutical substance and a polymorph of *imatinib*

23 *Novartis AG v. Union of India (UOI) and Ors.; Natco Pharma Ltd. v. UOI & Ors.; M/s Cancer Patients Aid Association v. UOI & Ors. (2013)*, referring to the *imatinib* base and the mesylate salt form of *imatinib*.

24 *In re Hogan*, 559 F.2d 595 (C.C.P.A. 1977).

*mesylate*, "it directly runs into section 3(d) of the Act with the explanation appended to the provision." The crucial question before the Court was whether, in view of section 3(d) as amended, Novartis could be granted a patent on the claimed invention of the β-crystalline form of *imatinib mesylate.*

As Novartis's legal team posited multiple arguments to diminish the importance of section 3(d), the Court went into the legislative history of the provision and of India's patent law, noting that this was necessary to "correctly understand the present law." Novartis argued that evergreening simply referred to trifling changes and that section 3(d) was included only as a matter of abundant caution. It further argued that the patenting of trifling changes would be prevented by the definition of invention in the law and that any public health concerns would be addressed by the provisions on patent oppositions, revocation, and compulsory licensing.

Rejecting this argument, the Court noted that Novartis' submission completely missed the vital distinction between patentability and invention, a distinction that lies at the heart of India's patent law. Stating that the amendment made to section 3(d) could not be underestimated, the Court observed that:

> In the course of the Parliamentary debates, the amendment in section 3(d) was the only provision cited by the Government to allay the fears of the Opposition members concerning the abuses to which a product patent in medicines may be vulnerable. We have, therefore, no doubt that the amendment or addition made in section 3(d) is meant specially to deal with chemical substances, and more particularly pharmaceutical products. The amended portion of section 3(d) clearly sets up a second tier of qualifying standards for chemical substances/pharmaceutical products in order to leave the door open for true and genuine inventions but, at the same time, to check any attempt at repetitive patenting or extension of the patent term on spurious grounds.

Even if taken as an extension of the definition of invention by ignoring the legislative history or the other provisions of section 3, the Court stated that reading together the provisions related to invention and section 3(d), "it would appear that the Act sets different standards for qualifying as 'inventions' things belonging to different classes, and for medicines and drugs and other chemical substances, the Act sets the invention threshold further higher, by virtue of the amendments made in section 3(d) in the year 2005."

Essentially, the Court was telling Novartis that one way or the other, its alleged invention would have to meet the standards of section 3(d) before it could be patented.

### *On the β-crystalline Form*

Even as the Supreme Court found that section 3(d) would apply as the β-crystalline form was a new form of *imatinib mesylate*, Novartis took to arguing on the specific terms and phrases in section 3(d). It contended that neither *imatinib* nor *imatinib mesylate* were "known substances" or had "known efficacy," thus no comparison could be made of the β-crystalline form of *imatinib mesylate* with a "known substance" with "known efficacy" as required under section 3(d). This was rejected by the Court on the grounds that it is well established by the Court itself, as interpreted in *Monsanto Co. v. Coramandal Indag Products (P) Ltd.*,[25] that the expression "publicly known" used in section 64 of the Indian Patents Act does not mean that it was widely used to the knowledge of the consumer public, but that it is "known to the persons who are engaged in the pursuit of knowledge of the patented product or process either as men of science or men of commerce or consumers." Moreover, given the extension application in the US, it was evident that *imatinib mesylate* had undergone extensive studies, including efficacy studies, and the Court found that the efficacy of *imatinib* and *imatinib mesylate* was well known. Therefore, as *imatinib mesylate* was the known substance, and β-crystalline form the new form of the known substance, section 3(d) was squarely applicable.

Further, in examining the efficacy of the different forms of *imatinib* (that is *imatinib* free base, non-crystalline form of *imatinib mesylate*, and the β-crystalline form of *imatinib mesylate*), the Court noted that it was Novartis' own case that all the properties possessed by the *imatinib* free base were possessed by the β-crystalline form of *imatinib mesylate.* Under the circumstances, the Court legitimately queried how there could be any enhanced efficacy in the β-crystalline form of *imatinib mesylate.*

### *On Efficacy*

In this respect, Novartis filed two affidavits to satisfy the requirements of section 3(d) for consideration. One of these stated that upon conducting experiments, it was found that there was a 30 percent increase in bioavailability in the β-crystalline form of *imatinib mesylate*, it was more soluble, had better flow properties, was thermodynamically more stable, and had lower hygroscopicity as compared to the *imatinib* free base. The Court noted Novartis was bound to show the enhanced efficacy of β-crystalline *imatinib mesylate* over the non-crystalline *imatinib mesylate*, but that there was no material on efficacy produced by Novartis.

Section 3(d) prohibits patents on new forms of known medicines unless there is a significant increase in efficacy. Novartis tried to argue that the physiochemical properties of the new form of the *imatinib* molecule (β-crystalline *imatinib mesylate*) had better flow properties, better thermodynamic stability, and lower hygroscopicity, resulting in improved efficacy. The Supreme Court firmly rejected this contention, holding that in the case of medicines, efficacy means "therapeutic efficacy" and these properties, while they may be beneficial to some patients, do not meet this standard. The Court also held that patent applicants must prove the increase in therapeutic efficacy based on research data *in vivo* in animals.

The Court held that the term "efficacy" in section 3(d) has to be understood as the ability to produce the desired or intended effect. This would differ in the context of the product, its function, utility, or purpose under consideration.

25 *Monsanto Co. v. Coramandal Indag Products (P) Ltd.*, (1986) 1 S.C.C. 642 (India).

In the context of medicines that claim to cure a disease, it has to be therapeutic efficacy. Thus, the Court held, "with regard to the genesis of section 3(d), and more particularly the circumstances in which section 3(d) was amended to make it even more constrictive than before, we have no doubt that the 'therapeutic efficacy' of a medicine must be judged strictly and narrowly."

Accordingly, "not all advantageous or beneficial properties are relevant, but only such properties that directly relate to efficacy, which in case of medicine…is its therapeutic efficacy." Thus, holding that the physiochemical properties of the β-crystalline form of *imatinib mesylate* contended by Novartis to be properties "with regard to efficacy" – namely, more beneficial flow properties, better thermodynamic stability, and lower hygroscopicity – may be helpful but cannot be considered for the purpose of the test of section 3(d) as they have nothing to do with therapeutic efficacy.

That left bioavailability and its role in efficacy. There were two rival contentions here. The CPAA, through the present author, argued that in the pharmaceutical field, drug action is explained by "pharmacokinetics" (effect of the body on the drug) and "pharmacodynamics" (effect of the drug on the body). Efficacy is the capacity of a drug to produce an effect, an aspect of pharmacodynamics. The generation of response from the drug-receptor complex is governed by efficacy. Bioavailability, on the other hand, is a pharmacokinetic property. It is the term used to indicate the extent to which a dose of drug reaches its site of action or a biological fluid from which the drug has access to its site of action. On the other hand, intervenor-cum-*amicus* Shamnad Basheer argued that safety or significantly reduced toxicity should also be taken into consideration to judge the enhanced therapeutic efficacy of a pharmaceutical product in terms of section 3(d).

While the Court left these submissions untouched, it held that bioavailability by itself may or may not result in efficacy being affected; and certainly, a bold assertion of increased bioavailability would not suffice. In terms of section 3(d), it must be claimed and established by the claimed inventor through research data with *in vivo* animal models, which Novartis had not done. Therefore, the claimed invention (β-crystalline form of *imatinib mesylate*) failed the test of section 3(d). Novartis's appeal was dismissed and those of the CPAA and the generic companies were allowed.

In concluding its judgment, the Supreme Court clarified that the finding in this case did not preclude other incremental innovations from being patented under the Indian patent law should they meet the standards of section 3(d):

> 191. We have held that the subject product, the beta crystalline form of Imatinib Mesylate, does not qualify the test of section 3(d) of the Act but that is not to say that section 3(d) bars patent protection for all incremental inventions of chemical and pharmaceutical substances. It will be a grave mistake to read this judgment to mean that section 3(d) was amended with the intent to undo the fundamental change brought in the patent regime by deletion of section 5 from the Parent Act. That is not said in this judgment…
>
> 192. section 2(1)(j) defines "invention" to mean, "a new product or …", but the new product in chemicals and especially pharmaceuticals may not

> necessarily mean something altogether new or completely unfamiliar or strange or not existing before. It may mean something "different from a recent previous" or "one regarded as better than what went before" or "in addition to another or others of the same kind" [53]. However, in case of chemicals and especially pharmaceuticals if the product for which patent protection is claimed is a new form of a known substance with known efficacy, then the subject product must pass, in addition to clauses (j) and (ja) of section 2(1), the test of enhanced efficacy as provided in section 3(d) read with its explanations.

## Aftermath of the Judgment

While patients' groups around the world expressed joy over the Novartis decision, Western MNCs and their governments expressed extreme displeasure about it. Throughout the case, there was an orchestrated chorus on the part of the pro-foreign MNC section of the industry to remove section 3(d). The US-India Business Council, actively supported by the US Trade Representative, was quite vociferous in its antipathy toward the provision. The opponents of section 3(d) left no stone unturned. Before the judgment, Novartis threatened that it would not register any new drugs and invest "in innovation in India" if it lost the case. The US pharmaceutical industry, through its fellow travelers in academia, also actively tried to influence academics and judges in India to show them how Indian law should be reframed, section 3(d) being the prime culprit. One of the two judges of the Supreme Court which recused himself from the Novartis case did so after it came to light that he had attended conferences in the US promoted by such interests with an aim, among other things, to water down section 3(d). After the judgment, some in the US urged their administration to take India to the Dispute Panel under the WTO, as according to them, Indian patent law is not compliant with the TRIPS Agreement. They even found supporters in the business community in India. Unfortunately, these kinds of criticism reflect either ignorance at worst or poor understanding of the debate at best. Worse still, the criticism appears to be motivated.

Eventually, no WTO dispute was raised. This does not mean that the attempts to remove or make section 3(d) ineffective have stopped. The European Union and the US have been putting significant pressure on India through their Trade Representatives to change Indian patent law to allow easier patenting, including provisions through the free trade agreements.

Some of this pressure may have worked.

## Emerging Challenges

### *In General*

The Supreme Court in the Novartis case not only saw the significance of section 3(d), but also gave it a fuller meaning. Had it not been for section 3(d), *imatinib mesylate* and a large number of other new forms of existing medicines would be granted patents as illustrated in Table 11.1.

*Table 11.1* List of selected patent oppositions in which the Lawyers Collective has provided legal representation

| *Medicine: international nonproprietary name* | *Patent applicant* | *Patent opponent* | *Year of opposition* | *Status* |
|---|---|---|---|---|
| Imatinib mesylate (β-crystalline form) | Novartis AG | Cancer Patients Aid Association | 2005 | Patent Application REJECTED |
| Zidovudine + lamivudine | Glaxo Group | Manipur Network of Positive People | 2006 | Patent Application WITHDRAWN |
| Amprenavir agenerase | Glaxo Group | Uttar Pradesh Network of Positive People and Indian Network for People Living with HIV/AIDS | 2006 | Patent Application ABANDONED |
| Atazanavir | Novartis AG | Indian Network for People Living with HIV/AIDS and Karnataka Network of People Living with HIV/AIDS | 2006 | Patent Application ABANDONED |
| Tenofovir disoproxil fumarate | Gilead Sciences | Indian Network for People Living with HIV/AIDS and Delhi Network of Positive People | 2006 | Patent Application REJECTED |
| Nevirapine hemihydrate | Boehringer Ingelheim | Indian Network of People Living with HIV/AIDS and Positive Women's Network | 2006 | Patent Application REJECTED |
| Abacavir sulfate | Glaxo Group | Indian Network for People Living with HIV/AIDS | 2006 | Patent Application WITHDRAWN |
| Lopinavir (crystalline) | Abbott Laboratories | Indian Network for People Living with HIV/AIDS, Delhi Network of Positive People, and Network of Maharashtra by People Living with HIV/AIDS | 2006 | Patent Application REJECTED |

(*Continued*)

*Table 11.1* List of selected patent oppositions in which the Lawyers Collective has provided legal representation (*Continued*)

| *Medicine: international nonproprietary name* | *Patent applicant* | *Patent opponent* | *Year of opposition* | *Status* |
|---|---|---|---|---|
| Ritonavir | Abbott Laboratories | Indian Network for People Living with HIV/AIDS and Delhi Network of Positive People v. | 2006 | Patent Application ABANDONED |
| Tenofovir disoproxil | Gilead Sciences | Sahara Centre for Residential Care and Rehabilitation and Associação Brasileira Interdisciplinar de AIDS | 2008 | Patent Application REJECTED |
| Tenofovir disoproxil fumarate | Gilead Sciences | Delhi Network of Positive People | 2012 | Patent Application REJECTED |
| Elvitegravir | Gilead Sciences | Nai Umang | 2014 | Pending |
| Sofosbuvir | Gilead Sciences | Sankalp Rehabilitation Trust, HepCon & APN+ | 2014 | Pending |
| Sofosbuvir base | Gilead Sciences | Sankalp Rehabilitation Trust | 2014 | Appeal pending against patent grant |
| Daclatasvir | Bristol Myers Squibb | Sankalp Rehabilitation Trust, HepCon & APN+ | 2015 | Pending |
| Dolutegravir | ViiV Healthcare Company, Shionogi & Co. Ltd. | Bengal Network of People living with HIV/AIDS & Feroz Khan | 2015 | Pending |
| Tenofovir alafenamide fumarate (TAF) – prodrug | Gilead Sciences | Gujarat State Network of People living with HIV/AIDS | 2015 | Patent Application ABANDONED |
| Velpatasvir Polymorph | Gilead Sciences, Pharmasset LLC | Delhi Network of Positive People | 2016 | Pending |
| Velpatasvir + Sofosbuvir combination | Gilead Sciences, Pharmasset LLC | Delhi Network of Positive People | 2016 | Pending |
| Bedaquiline fumarate salt | Janssen Pharmaceuticals | Nandita Venkatesh & Phumeza Tisile | 2019 | Pending |
| Cabotegravir long-acting parenteral | ViiV Healthcare Company | Henminlun | 2019 | Pending |

A recent set of studies has demonstrated both the power and, unfortunately, the weakness of India's strict patentability criteria, including section 3(d). A study of pharmaceutical patent applications rejected by the Indian Patent Office between 2009 and 2016 found that 1723 applications were rejected, and section 3(d) was cited in 771 of the rejections. The study found a much greater application of section 3(d) in the two years after the Novartis judgment, likely due to the legal certainty of the provision.[26] Unfortunately, a concomitant study of granted pharmaceutical patents showed that the application of section 3(d) was nowhere near what it should have been. The second study found that 72 percent of the 2293 pharmaceutical patents granted by the Indian Patent Office were secondary patents that were granted for marginal improvements over previously known drugs that had been patented; this included formulations, physical variants, salts, esters, ethers, prodrugs, new uses, and isomers,. These are precisely the sort of patent applications that section 3(d) is meant to address.[27] This is of serious concern.

## *Injunctions*

Additionally, there have been growing concerns about the dilution of other public interests based on jurisprudence related to the implementation of the patent law in India. This includes the increasing ease with which injunctions are being granted to patent holders in the pharmaceutical field. Under India's patent law, there is no presumption of the validity of a patent.[28] The granting of an interim injunction is discretionary and governed by equitable considerations. In cases of interlocutory injunctions, including any patent action, the principles are normally the same, namely,[29] (1) the plaintiff or patentee must show a *prima facie* case that it has a valid patent and it is infringed or likely to be infringed, (2) the balance of convenience is in favor of the plaintiff or patentee, (3) irreparable loss would be caused to the plaintiff or patentee if the injunction is not granted, and (4) the plaintiff cannot be compensated in terms of money.

Most courts usually followed the so-called six-year rule based on the judgment in *V. Manicka Thevar v. M/s Star Plough Works*,[30] where the Madras High Court held that if from the objections raised by the defendant, it is clear that a serious controversy exists as to whether or not the invention involves any new inventive skill, having regard to what was known or used prior to the date of the

26 Dr. Feroz Ali et al., *Rejected in India: What the Indian Patent Office Got Right on Pharmaceuticals Patent Applications (2009–2016)*, ACCESSIBSA (2017), https://accessibsa.org/media/2017/12/Rejected-in-India.pdf.

27 Dr. Feroz Ali et al., *Pharmaceuticals Patent Grant in India: How Our Safeguards Against Evergreening Have Failed and Why the System must be Reformed*, ACCESSIBSA (2018), https://accessibsa.org/media/2018/04/Pharmaceutical-Patent-Grants-in-India.pdf.

28 The Patents Act, 1970, India Code, Section 13(4) (India).

29 *Wander Ltd. & Anr. v. Antox India P. Ltd.*, (1990) Supp (1) S.C.C. 727 (India).

30 *V. Manicka Thevar v. M/s Star Plough Works*, A.I.R. 1965 Madras 327 (India).

patent, and if the patent was a recent one (less than six years old), courts would not grant an injunction restraining the defendant from pursuing his normal business activity.

In 2009, attempts by Roche to stop the launch by Cipla of the generic version of the cancer drug *erlotinib* led to a set of significant decisions from the Delhi High Court that reinforced the notion that public interest was critical in the interpretation and application of India's patent law. The Delhi High Court held in *F.Hoffman-La Roche Ltd. v. Cipla Ltd.*[31] that "without indulging in an exercise in semantics, the court when faced with a prayer for grant of injunction and a corresponding plea of the defendant challenging the validity of the patent itself, must enquire whether the defendant has raised a credible challenge."[32] Also, while requiring patent holders to reveal several details such as specifications and pending applications,[33] the court held that public interest would be an important factor, stating that "where question of general public access to life saving drugs assumes great significance, the adverse impact on such access which the grant of injunction in a case like the instant one is likely to have, would have to be accounted for."

In practice, however, it appears that these strict notions of public interest and the multiple factors in granting injunctions are rarely applied. A study of pharmaceutical patent–related injunctions that have been granted found that most pharmaceutical patentees obtain injunctions quickly and have been successful in preventing the launch of generic versions; most are granted *ex parte* (without granting a full hearing to the defendant) or without any injury to the plaintiff.[34] Moreover, the principles related to injunctions are being applied unevenly. A key principle that emerged in the context of MNC patent holders provided

31 *F. Hoffmann-La Roche Ltd. & Anr. v. Cipla Ltd.*, 2009 (40) P.T.C. 125 Delhi (India).

32 *Id.* at para. 55, the Court further held, "At this stage of course the court is not expected to examine the challenge in any great detail and arrive at a definite finding on the question of validity. That will have to await the trial. At the present stage of considering the grant of an interim injunction, the defendant has to show that the patent that has been granted is vulnerable to challenge."

33 *Id.* at para. 40 the Court held that, "in an application seeking ad interim injunction in a suit for infringement of patent, it would be incumbent on the plaintiffs to make a full disclosure of the complete specification of the product whose patent is claimed to have been infringed. The plaintiffs will also have to disclose to Court the x-ray diffraction data of the product, particularly if it is a pharmaceutical drug. The plaintiffs have to make an unequivocal disclosure that the patent they hold covers the drug in question; whether there are any other pending applications seeking the grant of patent in respect of any derivatives or forms of the product for which they already hold a patent and the effect of such applications on the suit patent. Short of the above details, the Court being approached for the grant of an ad interim relief will be unable to form a view on whether the plaintiff has made out a prima facie case. Otherwise it would be a case of suppression of material facts that would have a bearing on the question."

34 Sandeep Rathod, *Injunctions in Indian Pharmaceutical Patent Infringement Actions: Some Observations*, SSRN (2016), https://papers.ssrn.com/sol3/papers.cfm?abstract_id=2758327.

that interim injunctions would not be granted where the patent holder had not worked the patent in India by bringing the product in the market.[35] While this important principle was applied in the case of *Bayer Intellectual Property Gmbh v. Ajanta Pharma Ltd.*,[36] it was not followed in *Eisai Co. Ltd. & Anr. v. Satish Reddy & Anr.*[37] despite the fact that in both cases, the patent had not been worked in India; nor was it applied in *Bayer Intellectual Property Gmbh v. BDR Pharmaceuticals International*,[38] also a case of exports.

### *Buyouts*

Access to medicines has been determined by the local manufacturing capacity in the state concerned. Local production must be encouraged as a long-term investment in the security of access to medicines. This involves states considering statutory and policy measures that create an enabling environment for local producers to promote the growth of the pharmaceutical industry. India has done this quite well in the past, leading to the creation of a vibrant generic industry.

But today, apart from concern about the weakening of the public interest underpinnings of Indian patent law, there is also the question of how long Indian pharmaceutical companies will remain "Indian" and generic. Some have already been bought out by international MNCs, both originating and generic.[39] This has already reduced the incentive for them to challenge patent applications or file for compulsory licenses (CLs) instead of entering into restrictive voluntary licenses (VLs) bilaterally or through the Medicines Patent Pool. For example, generic companies in India withdrew their patent oppositions to the hepatitis-C drug *Sofosbuvir* and did not even demand a CL because of the VLs offered to them, despite the exclusion of many developing countries from the licenses. Unless we have independent Indian companies to produce generic drugs, our efforts are not going to be very successful in the long run.

The threat of Indian generic companies' inability to deliver affordable medicines in the coming decades is thus quite real. For many middle-income countries, this is already a reality with the restrictive VLs they have signed. Although there are counterstrategies, some of which we in the communities are pursuing effectively, the outcome is anybody's guess.

35 *Franz Xavier Heumer v. New Yash Engineers*, A.I.R. 1997 Delhi 79 (India).

36 *Bayer Intellectual Property Gmbh v. Ajanta Pharma Ltd. & Ords.*, CS(COMM) 1648/2016 (India).

37 *Eisai Co. Ltd. & Anr. v. Satish Reddy & Anr.*, CS(COMM) 1169/2018 & I.As. 13934/2018, 15885/2018, (India).

38 *Bayer Intellectual Property Gmbh v. BDR Pharmaceuticals*, CS(COMM)107/2017 (India).

39 Beena Saraswathy, *An Analysis of Foreign Acquisitions in India's Manufacturing Sector*, ISID (2016), http://isid.org.in/pdf/WP193.pdf.

### *Compulsory Licenses or Voluntary Licenses*

There has been vigorous debate about pharmaceutical MNCs' use of VLs to make drugs available when the state has the power to issue a CL under patent laws in all countries.

Article 31 of the TRIPS Agreement deals with other use of patented products without authorization of the patent holder, commonly known as a CL. A CL can only be issued only if, apart from other things, the proposed user has made efforts to obtain authorization from the patentee on reasonable commercial terms and conditions and has been unsuccessful within a reasonable period of time. If the proposed user gets the authorization, a VL will issue, though the TRIPS Agreement talks of the proposed user initiating the action that need not be the case. A VL can also be offered by the patentee. In case the patentee does not agree, the proposed user can then move for a CL.

In India, such an action lies before the Patent Controller. This is what happened in respect of the drug *sorafinib tosylate*, sold as *Nexavar* by the patent holder Bayer. The drug, which is used to treat liver and kidney cancer, was being sold for approximately $5000 a month even as imported quantities remained low. The Indian generic company Natco successfully received a CL to manufacture and sell *sorafanib tosylate* in India at the price of $170 a month.[40] This is in the case of nonemergency situations. The applications is these kind of situations is made by the generic to the Patent Controller under Section 84 of the Indian Patents Act.

In case of national emergency or other circumstances of extreme urgency, or in cases of public noncommercial use, the TRIPS Agreement allows for the issuance of a license without the authorization of the patentee. Section 92 of the Indian Patents Act deals with these situations. The Government can also issue an order for "government authorization" under Section 100 of the Indian Patents Act.

Over the past decade, some pharmaceutical MNCs have been strategically offering VLs to generic companies. Although there has been considerable debate about the utility of such VLs, the scope of this chapter does not allow discussion in detail here. Suffice it to say that the opponents of VLs have pointed out that VLs have a negative impact on the use of other TRIPS-compliant flexibilities, including IP reform and oppositions; are used as a strategy to divide the market and control competition or dissuade governments from issuing CLs; are timed to scuttle the issuance of CLs or portray the patentees offering the VL in a favorable light; and give the false impression that access is being granted to all. They also argue that conditionalities imposed on VLs are not sufficient, especially coverage and sourcing of active pharmaceutical ingredients, to ensure access to all; and that most of the resources are being used to pursue VLs notwithstanding allocation and use of some funds for pursuing oppositions and obtaining CLs.

40 Lawyers Collective, *Supreme Court Says No to Bayer, Upholds Compulsory License on Nexavar* (Dec. 13, 2014), https://lawyerscollective.org/2014/12/13/supreme-court-says-no-to-bayer-upholds-compulsory-license-on-nexavar/.

Proponents of VLs argue that both VLs and CLs are complementary strategies; access to medicines has always been incremental; sufficient coverage has been ensured; VLs have made medicines more accessible to nearly 90 percent of those who need them, and the remaining 10 percent can be covered by pursuing the CL strategy in individual countries; and that as opposed to following the VL strategy, which covers vast numbers in one go, the CL country-by-country strategy would be too cumbersome.

### *Only Time Will Tell What Is a Better Strategy*

However, it is important to note that Indian generic companies have previously supplied over 80 percent of the generic ARV requirement to the whole of the developing world. Under VLs, they cannot supply to middle-income countries in South America, the Middle East, North Africa, or Eastern Europe. Without Indian generic companies agreeing to VLs, that strategy will not work. MNCs have therefore wooed Indian generic companies to opt for VLs, and they have fallen for the bait. This will be easier for generics who are no longer Indian. In any event, for generic companies, the rationale is very simple: VLs are cost-effective and allow them to stay in business. Thus, for any CL strategy to succeed, the core Indian generic companies must be on board. That is a challenging task.

It should be noted that although some CLs and VLs were granted for hepatitis C, the vast majority were for HIV ARVs. The ailment that is most widespread and has affected the largest number of persons, TB, does not have any CL and has extremely restricted and fragmented VLs for new drugs which are effective, *Bedaqualine* and *Delaminid*. This shows that the VL strategy is not working in this sector. Pursuing a VL strategy takes away the powers of the state and transfers it to the MNC, where it does not belong; it passes the ability to control the accessibility and affordability of medicines to MNCs. This challenge has to be met internationally; unfortunately, civil society organizations that were united at the turn of the century are now divided over VLs, not only internationally but also domestically in India. Diverse groups in India are no longer working in unison.

Both strategies are up for trial in the COVID-19 pandemic. Interestingly, some governments have amended their laws to issue CLs for drugs that may be effective, such as Germany, Israel, and Canada. However, VL proponents are working to get a pool setup. Civil society would be left to pursue both opposition and CL strategies, which generic companies can take advantage of if they do succeed. But knowing their past practice, they will go for VLs if so offered.

## Hope for the Future

Access to essential medicines is integral to the right to health and has been specifically enunciated under a number of international instruments, including the International Covenant on Economic, Social and Cultural Rights (ICESCR). Article 12 of the ICESCR provides for the right of everyone to the highest attainable standard of physical and mental health. States are obliged to respect (not to interfere with the right itself), protect (prevent interference by others), and fulfill (take all administrative measures) the right to health. This is elaborated by the Committee on Economic, Social, and Cultural Rights in General Comment Number 14 (2000), which provides that all health services, goods, and facilities, including medicines, are to be made available, accessible, acceptable, and of good quality. Furthermore, the provision of essential medicines to all persons in a non-discriminatory manner is a core non-derogable obligation of the state and also includes ensuring availability and access to quality affordable medicines.

The framework of the right to health makes it clear that medicines must be available, accessible, acceptable, and of good quality, and reach ailing populations all over the world without discrimination. Affordable access to medicines cannot be sustainably achieved without sufficient market competition. The need of the hour is for developing countries to utilize and preserve the flexibilities embodied in the TRIPS Agreement in their national laws, and prioritize the right to health above all. For this, civil society needs to be reunited domestically and across continents to challenge the agenda of pharmaceutical MNCs and even generic companies so that the state can be back in the driver's seat to make medicine accessible and affordable to its own people.

As the COVID-19 pandemic grips the world, the imperative for equitable and affordable access to diagnostics, treatment, and vaccines for all people in all countries has never been greater. This past year has painfully demonstrated the extent to which intellectual property barriers can hamper access to health technologies. It has resulted in nearly two-thirds of the WTO membership demanding a waiver of their obligations under the TRIPS Agreement to be able to properly address the challenges of the pandemic. The proposal first put forward by India and South Africa in October 2020[41] has gathered considerable support as well as opposition by developed countries.[42] While the waiver, if it materializes will be limited to the Covid pandemic, for non-Covid diseases and other epidemics, the full use of TRIPS flexibilities by all governments will be even more crucial in the coming years. And restricting pharmaceutical patents to genuine inventions will be key among these flexibilities.

Despite the many developments in the years since the Novartis case that have cast a shadow over India's strict patent law, the potential of section 3(d) and the Supreme Court's decision to ensure access, availability, and affordability of medicines remains. With section 3(d) and the Supreme Court firmly behind the intent of this provision, India's patent law provides the right check and balance

41 Council for Trade Related Aspects of Intellectual Property Rights, *Waiver from Certain Provisions of The TRIPS Agreement for the Prevention, Containment and Treatment of Covid-19: Communication From India And South Africa*, IP/C/W/669. (2 October 2020), https://docs.wto.org/dol2fe/Pages/SS/directdoc.aspx?Filename=q:/IP/C/W669.pdf &Open=True.

42 Third World Network, *Opponents of TRIPS Waiver Asked to Respond to Questions by Proponents* (15 January 2021), https://www.twn.my/title2/wto.info/2021/ti210104.htm.

to the runaway patent systems of the West. In the words of the Supreme Court, section 3(d) leaves "the door open for true and genuine inventions but, at the same time, to check any attempt at repetitive patenting or extension of the patent term on spurious grounds." The Supreme Court decision has encouraged other developing countries to follow suit, as the Philippines, Argentina, and Zanzibar have already done. This is now a key recommendation for patent law reform across the developing world.

If fundamental changes to the runaway patent system of the West can be affected in the way India has tried to do, we may truly have an IP system that works not just for firms but for everyone. Novartis' assertions that the ruling will affect investment or future innovations have been belied time and again, including at the WHO, which has found that IP does not result in the kind of innovation in medicines required by India as a developing country.

Novartis' threat that it would not introduce new medicines in India after the verdict was also hollow. It knew fully well that Indian companies will step into its shoes and be able to produce medicines at one tenth of the cost. But it further adds strength to the assertion of health groups that India must jealously guard its generic manufacturing capacity in the face of such threats from multinationals if they do not have their way. It is also a strong lesson for other developing countries to invest in local independent production of medicines.

The Supreme Court's decision is a tribute to the hard-fought battles of people living with cancer, HIV, and many other ailments who have tirelessly campaigned for the right to health to be placed before the profits of pharmaceutical companies. As we mark 15 years of section 3(d) and the pressure from MNCs intensifies for India to change its IP laws, there is enough reason to protect and celebrate section 3(d) and not allow it to be dismantled – not just to keep medicines affordable for people in India and overseas, but also to ensure that only true innovations are rewarded with patent protection.

# 12 South Africa's Three Decades of Access to Medicine Discourse

## Blight or Benefit

*Caroline B. Ncube*[1]

## Introduction

Access to medicines is imperative in South Africa where essential medicines remain beyond the reach of the majority of its citizenry and the poor.[2] The national discourse regarding access to medicines is as old as democratic South Africa, and many stakeholders have been engaged in it in various ways, including through participation in policy formulation, litigation, advocacy campaigns, complaints to the competition authorities, and the threat of trade sanctions. The dawn of a democratic South Africa in April 1994 and the entry into force of the Constitution (Act 108 of 1996) coincided with her membership into the World Trade Organization (WTO) and the twinned adoption of the Agreement on Trade-Related Aspects of Intellectual Property Rights (TRIPS Agreement), which both came into effect on 1 January 1995.[3]

The state's goal of achieving access to medicines for its populace is mandated by national policies[4] and the constitutional protection of the right of access to

1 Thanks to Simamkele Gosa and Omowamiwa Kolawole for their research and editorial assistance, respectively. This work is based on the research supported in part by the National Research Foundation (NRF) of South Africa (Grant Numbers: 115716). Any opinion, finding, and conclusion or recommendation expressed in this material is that of the author and the NRF does not accept any liability in this regard.

2 C. Tomlinson et al., *How Patent Law Reform Can Improve Affordability and Accessibility of Medicines in South Africa: Four Medicine Case Studies*, 109 S. Afr. Med. J. 387, 387–91 (2019).

3 Heinz Klug, *Access to Medicines and the Transformation of the South African State: Exploring the Interactions of Legal and Policy Changes in Health, Intellectual Property, Trade, and Competition Law in the Context of South Africa's HIV/AIDS Pandemic*, 37 L. & Soc. Inquiry 297, 302 (2019).

4 *See, e.g.*, *National Policy for the Establishment and Functioning of Pharmaceutical and Therapeutics Committees in South Africa,* Republic of S. Afr., Dep't of Health (Jan. 19, 2015).

health-care services.[5] The state has sought to fulfill this mandate through the creation of an enabling regulatory framework coupled with implementing institutions.

The most recent significant development in relation to access to medicines and patents in South Africa was the passage of the National Intellectual Property Policy – Phase 1 in 2018 (IP Policy 2018).[6] The IP Policy 2018 was the culmination of decades' worth of work by the state and other national and international stakeholders. This chapter analyzes the state action that led to this point and the related discourse. Of the state's three arms, this chapter will focus on the legislature and the executive, and specifically on the two lead departments, the Department of Health and the then Department of Trade and Industry (DTI), which has been renamed to the Department of Trade, Industry and Competition. This chapter will consider how the national discourse has both harmed and benefitted the efforts of parliament and these two departments to fulfill the constitutional mandate of access to health-care services, of which access to medicines is a fundamental part.

The chapter will proceed in four sections, including this introduction. The second section will be an overview of the regulatory framework pertaining to patents, competition, and medicines control. It will highlight the campaigns for, and contestations against, legislative reforms intended to secure access to medicines. It will also reflect on the use of competition law and institutions by advocacy groups. The third section will focus on the IP Policy 2018, summarizing the reforms put forward in the policy. The last section will conclude the chapter by commenting on the learnings that can be drawn from policy and legislative reform discourse and developments in South Africa over the last 25 years.

## The Regulatory Framework

The regulatory framework that governs the right to access to medicines consists of patent law, competition law, and medicines control regulation together with their institutional arrangements. Each of these is briefly outlined in the following sections.

5 For a full discussion, *see* Lonias Ndlovu, *The WTO TRIPS Agreement and Access to Medicines in South Africa Twenty Years into Democracy*, 28 Speculum Juris 2, 70–98 (2014). For a discussion of the relevant sections of the Constitution, *see* Cipla Medpro, Ltd. v. Aventis Pharma SA, Aventis Pharma SA v Cipla Life Sciences (139/2012, 138/2012) (2012) ZASCA 108; 2013 (4) SA 579 (SCA) (26 July 2012) (providing the relevant sections as follows: "S 27(1)(a) Everyone has the right to have access to health care services, including reproductive health care"; "S 27(2) The state must take reasonable legislative and other measures, within its available resources, to achieve the progressive realisation of each of these rights"; "28(1)(c) Every child has the right to basic nutrition, shelter, basic health care services and social services"). *See also* Minister of Health v. Treatment Action Campaign (No. 2) 2002 (5) SA 721 (CC), Minister of Health v. New Clicks South Africa, Ltd. (2006) (2) SA 311 (CC).

6 Intellectual Property Policy of the Republic of South Africa Phase I, GN 518 of GG 41870 (Aug. 31, 2018).

### *Patent Law*

Patents are regulated by the Patents Act 57 of 1978, which requires an invention to meet the following patentability criteria to secure protection: novelty, inventive step, and industrial application.[7] Further, the patent application must adequately disclose the invention. South Africa grants pharmaceutical patents, but methods of treatment of the human or animal body by surgery or therapy or of diagnosis practices on the human or animal body are not patentable.[8]

The Patents Act was amended in 1997 to provide that the duration of a patent, in accordance with the TRIPS Agreement, is 20 years.[9] Section 45(1) was also amended to provide the following scope of patent protection:

> The effect of a patent shall be to grant to the patentee in the Republic, subject to the provisions of this Act, for the duration of the patent, the right to exclude other persons from making, using, exercising, disposing or offering to dispose of, or importing the invention, so that he or she shall have and enjoy the whole profit and advantage accruing by reason of the invention.[10]

Applications for patents may be made nationally through the Companies and Intellectual Property Commission (CIPC) or through the Patent Cooperation Treaty (PCT) system. If an application is made through the PCT system, an international search is conducted to establish patentability. On the other hand, the CIPC is a registration patent office that does not undertake substantive patent examination to establish whether an invention meets the patentability criteria. This has been highlighted as a weakness of South Africa's patent system and several commentators have argued for the introduction of substantive examination,[11] an improvement that has been taken up in the IP Policy 2018, as discussed below. The introduction of a pre-grant opposition process would also strengthen the application process by enabling interested parties to participate in the patent grant process.[12]

South Africa is not a member of the African Regional Intellectual Property Organization (ARIPO) so there is no avenue for a regional patent application.[13]

7 Patents Act 57 of 1978 § 25(1) (S. Afr.).
8 Patents Act 57 of 1978 § 25(2) (11) (S. Afr.).
9 Intellectual Property Laws Amendment Act 38 of 1997 § 41 (S. Afr.), amending Patents Act 57 of 1978 § 46 (S. Afr.).
10 *Id.*
11 Jonathan Berger & Andrew Rens, *Innovation and Intellectual Property in South Africa: The Case for Reform*, Univ. of Cape Town (Apr. 2018), https://www.accessibsa.org/media/2018/05/Innovation-IP-in-SA.pdf; *see also* Caroline B. Ncube, *The Draft National Intellectual Property Policy Proposals for Improving South Africa's Patent Registration System: A Review*, 9 J. Intell. Prop. L. & Prac. 10, 822–9 (Sept. 12, 2014).
12 *Id.*
13 However, the country has observer status at ARIPO.

The Patents Act contains the following flexibilities that may be used to advance access to medicines. Section 55 provides for compulsory licenses (CLs) on dependent patents[14] and as of November 2018, there had been only one reported case founded on this section.[15] Section 56(1) provides for CLs for abuse of patent rights. Section 56(2)(a) then states that the rights in a patent shall be deemed to be abused if:

> [T]he patented invention is not being worked in the Republic on a commercial scale or to an adequate extent, after the expiry of a period of four years subsequent to the date of the application for the patent or three years subsequent to the date of the application for the patent or three years subsequent to the date on which that patent was sealed, whichever period last expires, and there is in the opinion of the commissioner no satisfactory reason for such non-working'2. s56(2)(c): 'the demand for the patented article in the Republic is not being met to an adequate extent and on reasonable terms'3. s56(2) (d); 'by reason of the refusal of the patentee to grant a license or licenses upon reasonable terms, the trade or industry or agriculture of the Republic or the trade of any person or class of persons trading in the Republic, or the establishment of any new trade or industry in the Republic[16]

CLs are issued upon successful application to the Commissioner of Patents, who is a Judge of the High Court.[17] The application may be opposed by the patent holder,[18] and the Commissioner may impose conditions on the CL upon grant.[19] CLs have not yet been granted for pharmaceuticals in South Africa under

14 Patents Act 57 of 1978 § 55 (S. Afr.) (providing that "Compulsory licences in respect of dependent patents.—Where the working of a patent (hereinafter referred to as a dependent patent) without infringement of a prior patent is dependent upon the obtaining of a licence under that prior patent, the proprietor of the dependent patent may, if agreement cannot be reached as to such licence with the proprietor of the prior patent, apply to the commissioner for a licence under the prior patent, and the commissioner may grant such a licence on such conditions as he may impose, but including a condition that such licence shall be used only for the purpose of permitting the dependent patent to be worked and for no other purpose: Provided that the commissioner shall not grant such a licence unless—
(a) the invention claimed in the dependent patent involves an important technical advance of considerable economic significance in relation to the invention claimed in the prior patent;
(b) the proprietor of the dependent patent granted the proprietor of the prior patent on reasonable terms a cross-licence to use the invention claimed in the dependent patent; and
(c) the use authorised in respect of the prior patent is not assignable except with the assignment of the dependent patent."

15 Atomic Energy Corporation of South Africa v. The Du Pont Merck (1997) BIP 90 (CP).

16 Patents Act 57 of 1978 §§ 8 & 56 (S. Afr.).

17 Patents Act 57 of 1978 § 8 (S. Afr.) (detailing terms of assignment by the Judge President).

18 *Id.* at § 56(3).

19 *Id.* at § 56(4)(a).

these provisions.[20] However, there have been several cases that have dealt with the interpretation of these provisions in the Patents Act.[21] The Commissioner of Patents' denial of CL applications is attributable to the applicant's failure to satisfy the evidentiary burden.[22]

CL applications are not filed frequently because of the prohibitive costs of the requisite litigation, which would deter pharmaceutical firms with limited resources, the limited grounds upon which an application may be founded, and the precedent of "an overly formal approach to judicial interpretation and adjudication" which has so far not led to the grant of CL.[23] An administrative CL application, rather than a judicial process, will probably be more appropriate because it will exclude the delays and costs associated with litigation.

The Patents Act also contains Section 69A "Bolar" provisions that allow the use of patented pharmaceutical products without license to obtain regulatory approval for generic versions.[24] This is essential to enable the introduction of generics to the market soon after the expiry of the relevant patent. Without this provision, the regulatory approval process may take up to two years after the patent expires.[25]

TRIPS flexibilities are an important mechanism in enabling and enhancing access to medicines, and in November 2001, WTO members signed the Doha Declaration on the TRIPS Agreement and Public Health (Doha Declaration) reaffirming countries' rights to utilize safeguards in the TRIPS Agreement to

20 *The TRIPS Flexibilities Database*, MEDICINES LAW & POLICY, http://tripsflexibilities.medicineslawandpolicy.org/ (last visited Jan. 31, 2020).

21 *See Sanachem (Pty) Ltd v. British Technology Group PLC* (1992) BP 276 (CP) (agrochemical substance); *Delta G Scientific (Pty) Ltd v. Janssen Pharmaceutical NV and Another* (1996) BP 455 (CP) (agricultural fungicides); *Afitra (Pty) Ltd and Another v. Carlton Paper of SA (Pty) Ltd* (1992) BP 331 (CP) (device for a baby diaper). For a discussion of the case law, *see* Yousuff A. Vadwa, *Compulsory Licensing Jurisprudence in South Africa: Do We Have Our Priorities Right?* Research Paper, 90, SOUTH CENTRE (Dec. 2018), https://www.southcentre.int/wp-content/uploads/2018/12/RP90_Compulsory-Licensing-Jurisprudence-in-South-Africa-Do-We-Have-Our-Priorities-Right_EN-1.pdf.

22 Vadwa, *supra* note 21, at 19; Vuyisile Hobololo, *Strategic Patenting of Pharmaceutical Inventions and the Public's Right to Access Medicines: The South African Context* 16, AFR. J. INFORM. COMMUN. (AJIC) 1, 80 (2015).

23 Vadwa, *supra* note 21, at 19.

24 Patents Act 57 of 1978 § 69A (S. Afr.) (last amended by Act No. 58 of 2002) ("Acts of non-infringement.—(1) It shall not be an act of infringement of a patent to make, use, exercise, offer to dispose of, dispose of or import the patented invention on a non-commercial scale and solely for the "purposes reasonably related to the obtaining, development and submission of information required under any law that regulates the manufacture, production, distribution, use or sale of any product. (2) It shall not be permitted to possess the patented invention made, used, imported or acquired in terms of subsection (1) for any purpose other than for the obtaining, development or submission of information as contemplated in that subsection.").

25 JONATHAN BERGER, HEALTH & DEMOCRACY: A GUIDE TO HUMAN RIGHTS, HEALTH LAW AND POLICY IN POST-APARTHEID SOUTH AFRICA 449 (Mark Heywood et al. eds., 2007).

protect health. Another significant development is the 2005 WTO Decision that culminated in the TRIPS Amendment, which came into force in 2017. South Africa accepted the Protocol amending the TRIPS Agreement in 2016.[26] Other notable state declarations of the intent to fully utilize TRIPS flexibilities include the 2011 Beijing Declaration signed by the health ministers of BRICS countries (Brazil, Russia, India, China, and South Africa), which reiterated their intent to use TRIPS flexibilities in the interest of public health to maximum benefit.[27] There are several other examples, but a full reprise of these falls beyond the scope of this chapter.

### *Competition Law*

Resort can also be had to competition law to enable or to enhance access to medicines.[28] The Competition Act 89 of 1998 seeks to eliminate or reduce anticompetitive behavior. Section 8's prohibition of abuse of dominance is of specific relevance to access to medicines. This section previously provided as follows:

> 8. Abuse of dominance prohibited—It is prohibited for a dominant firm to—
>
> a charge an excessive price to the detriment of consumers;
> b refuse to give a competitor access to an essential facility when it is economically feasible to do so;
> c engage in an exclusionary act, other than an act listed in paragraph (d), if the anti-competitive effect of that act outweighs its technological, efficiency or other pro-competitive, gain; or
> d engage in any of the following exclusionary acts, unless the firm concerned can show technological, efficiency or other pro-competitive, gains which outweigh the anti-competitive effect of its act:
> i requiring or inducing a supplier or customer to not deal with a competitor;
> ii refusing to supply scarce goods to a competitor when supplying those goods is economically feasible;

26 *South Africa Accepts Protocol Amending the TRIPS Agreement*, World Trade Org. (Feb. 23, 2016), https://www.wto.org/english/news_e/news16_e/trip_23feb16_e.htm; *see also* Xolelwa Mlumbi-Peter, *South Africa's Acceptance of Amending the TRIPS Agreement*, Dep't Trade & Indus.: Repub. S. Afr. (Nov. 24, 2015), http://www.dti.gov.za/parliament/2015/Protocol_Amending_TRIPS_Agreement.pdf.

27 *First Meeting of BRICS Health Ministers Brings New Leadership to Global Health*, UNAIDS (July 11, 2011), https://www.unaids.org/en/resources/presscentre/featurestories/2011/july/20110711bchinabrics.

28 *Using Law to Accelerate Treatment Access in South Africa*, United Nations Dev. Programme (Dec. 7, 2015), https://www.undp.org/content/undp/en/home/librarypage/hiv-aids/using-law-to-accelerate-treatment-access-in-south-africa.html.

iii selling goods or services on condition that the buyer purchases separate goods or services unrelated to the object of a contract, or forcing a buyer to accept a condition unrelated to the object of a contract;
iv selling goods or services below their marginal or average variable cost; or
v buying-up a scarce supply of intermediate goods or resources required by a competitor.

This section may be applicable to pharmaceutical companies in a number of different scenarios. For instance, a refusal to license a patent could arguably be the denial of an essential facility in contravention of Section 8(a).[29] Companies may only escape liability if they have secured an exemption under Section 10(4) of the Competition Act.

Neither the Competition Tribunal nor the Competition Appeal Court has made a ruling on anticompetitive practices by pharmaceutical companies. However, a complaint was filed with the Competition Commission in 2002 by Hazel Tau, the Treatment Action Campaign (TAC), and others against GlaxoSmithKline (GSK) and Boehringer Ingelheim, accusing them of excessive pricing of antiretroviral drugs to the detriment of consumers, which is prohibited by Section 8(a) of the Competition Act.[30] The Competition Commission found against the pharmaceutical companies and held that there were grounds for a referral of the matter to the Competition Tribunal.[31] Specifically, it found that the companies had contravened Sections 8(a) (excessive pricing), 8(b) (refusing a competitor access to an essential facility), and 8(c) (an exclusionary act).[32] However, the matter was ultimately settled, and seven voluntary licenses (VLs) were issued.[33] The complainants entered into a settlement with the pharmaceutical companies because, in their view, this would facilitate the provision of cheaper medicines

29 Pieter Francois Van Aswegen, *The Right to Exclude Others From Using Claimed Intellectual Property: A Perspective From Competition Law*, 14 STELLENBOSCH L. REV. 1, 115, 120 (2003); Tim Ball, *Patented Inventions as Essential Facilities Under the Competition Act 69 of 1998: Analyses*, 18 SA MERCANTILE L. J. 2, 1, 186–95 (2006); James Brand, *Intellectual Property and the Abuse of Dominant Position in South African Competition Law,* 122 S. AFR. L. J. 4, 1, 907–28 (2005).

30 Hazel Tau et al., *Statement of Complaint in Terms of Section 49b(2)(B) of the Competition Act 89 of 1998*, http://www.section27.org.za/wp-content/uploads/2010/10/TauvGSKevidenceAndLegalSubmissions.pdf (last visited Jan. 31, 2020).

31 EDWIN CAMERON, WITNESS TO AIDS, 179–82 (Kate Sherratt ed., 1st ed. 2005); Brook K. Baker, *Threat of Compulsory Licenses at the South African Competition Commission Results in Generic Licenses for AIDS Medicines*, briefing paper, Health Global Access Project ("GAP") (Dec. 10, 2003).

32 Newsletter of the Competition Commission of South Africa, *GSK and BI Issue Antiretroviral Licenses,* (15th ed. Mar. 2004).

33 The Competition Commission of South Africa, *2003–2004 Annual Report*, 8.

compared to fully litigating the matter before the Competition Tribunal.[34] The licenses were for *AZT* (branded as *Retrovir*), *Lamivudine* (branded as *3TC*), *AZT/lamivudine AZT/3TC* (branded as *Combivir*), and *Nevirapine NVP* (branded as *Viramune*).

Other complaints filed over the years include the complaint filed in November 2007 by the TAC against MSD (Pty) Ltd., Merck & Co. Inc., and related companies for abuse of dominance through the refusal to grant licenses permitting generic production of and affordable access to generic *Efavirenz*.[35] The Competition Commission did not refer the matter to the Competition Tribunal because the companies issued VLs in June 2008.[36] In 2009, the TAC filed a submission to the Competition Commission during its consideration of the merger between GSK's South African operations and Aspen Pharmacare Holdings Ltd. (Aspen), a local generic pharmaceutical manufacturer.[37] The Competition Commission approved the merger on condition that GSK "grant licences, on a non-exclusive basis, to Adcock Ingram, Cipla Medpro, Ranbaxy, Biotech Laboratories and Feza Pharmaceutical and any other interested generic manufacturer for the manufacture and/or import of Abacavir, on terms and conditions no less favourable than those granted to Aspen."[38]

In June 2017, the Competition Commission commenced an investigation for suspected abuse of dominance and excessive pricing in the provision of specific cancer medicines in South Africa by Roche Holding AG, Genentech Inc., Pfizer Inc., Equity (Pty) Ltd. (Equity), and Aspen.[39] The investigation against Aspen and Equity were withdrawn shortly thereafter.[40] The outcome of this investigation is not publicly available.

The other examples given above that resulted in the issuance of VLs show that competition law can successfully be used to improve access to medicines. However, these arrangements remain voluntary and, in the above cases, have to be forced by resort to competition institutions. Therefore, it is clear that other avenues are necessary to enhance access to medicines.

34 *Id.*; *see also* The TRIPS Flexibilities Database, Medicines Law & Policy, http://tripsflexibilities.medicineslawandpolicy.org/ (last visited Jan. 31, 2020).

35 TAC v. MSD (Pty) Ltd., Merck & Co. Inc. and related companies, https://section27.org.za/wp-content/uploads/2010/10/TACvMSDlegalsubmissions.pdf (last visited Jan. 31, 2020).

36 TAC Statement, *Access to Generic Efavirenz in South Africa: MSD Agrees to Grant Licenses on Reasonable Terms*, I-BASE.INFO (Aug. 30, 2008), http://i-base.info/htb/560.

37 TAC v. MSD (Pty) Ltd., *supra* note 35.

38 Press Release, *Competition Commission, Competition Commission Approves Pharma Merger on Condition that Abacavir is Out-licensed to Generic Manufacturers* (Sept. 2, 2009), http://www.compcom.co.za/wp-content/uploads/2014/09/02-Sept-09-Competition-Commission-approves-pharma-merger-on-condition-that-Abacavir-is.pdf.

39 *Competition Commission Media Statement: Update: Pharmaceutical Investigations* (Oct. 4, 2019), http://www.compcom.co.za/wp-content/uploads/2017/01/Update-Pharmaceutical-Investigations.pdf.

40 *Id.*

### *Amendments to the Competition Act*

Section 8 of the Competition Act has been amended by Section 5 of the Competition Amendment Act Number 18 of 2018.[41] The new expanded section broadly notes under Section 8 that a statutorily prohibited abuse of dominance occurs when a dominant firm (a) charges an excessive price to the detriment of consumers or customers; (b) refuses to give a competitor reasonable access to an essential facility; (c) engages in an (unpermitted) exclusionary act; (d) if the anticompetitive effect of a dominant firm's action outweighs its technological, efficiency, or other pro-competitive gains except where there are overwhelming pro-competitive gains. Under the section, if there is a prima facie case of abuse of dominance because of excessive pricing, the dominant firm has the burden to prove that the price was reasonable taking into account listed statutory factors. A firm designated as dominant by the Minister has an obligation to engage in fair trade practices in pricing, trading, and dealing in a fair manner, as required under regulations under Section 78 of the statute, with historically disadvantaged persons.[42]

### *Medicines Regulation*

The bedrock of medicines regulation is the National Drug Policy of 1996 and one of the key elements of the medicines regulatory framework is the Medicines and Related Substances Act 101 of 1965 and its regulations. It was amended in 1997 by the Medicines and Related Substances Amendment Act 90 of 1997 to provide for parallel importation in Section 15C,[43] generic substitution in Section 22F, and the establishment of a Pricing Committee in Section 22G. In 2002,

41 Government Gazette 42231, GN 644, Feb. 14, 2019, Section 8(1)–(3) with effect from July 19, 2019 (proclaimed by Government Gazette 42578, July 12, 2019).

42 *Id.* Section 8(4) with effect Feb. 13, 2020 (proclaimed by Government Gazette 43018, Feb. 13, 2020).

43 Medicines and Related Substances Control Amendment Act, No. 101 (1997) (S. Afr.) § 15(C). The entirety of section 15C reads as follows:
Measures to ensure supply of more affordable medicines. The Minister may prescribe conditions for the supply of more affordable medicines in certain circumstances so as to protect the health of the public, and in particular may:
(a) notwithstanding anything to the contrary contained in the Patents Act, 1978 (Act No. 57 of 1978), determine that the rights with regard to any medicine under a patent granted in the Republic shall not extend to acts in respect of such medicine which has been put onto the market by the owner of the medicine, or with his or her consent;
(b) prescribe the conditions on which any medicine which is identical in composition, meets the same quality standard and is intended to have the same proprietary name as that of another medicine already registered in the Republic, but which is imported by a person other than the person who is the holder of the registration certificate of the medicine already registered and which originates from any site of manufacture of the original manufacturer as approved by the Authority in the prescribed manner, may be imported;
(c) prescribe the registration procedure for, as well as the use of, the medicine referred to in paragraph (b).

both Sections 22F and 22G were amended.[44] Section 22G provides for a single exit price (SEP) "at which manufacturers shall sell medicines and Scheduled substances to any person other than the State," which would be prescribed under Regulations. The Amendment Act entered into force in 2003 after the promulgation of pricing regulations.[45]

The passing of the amendment spurred some litigation which was ultimately withdrawn.[46] A High Court Application was brought in 1998 by the Pharmaceutical Manufacturers Association and international pharmaceutical companies to stop the implementation of part of the Medicines and Related Substances Control Amendment Act.[47] The companies initially had support from the United States (US) government expressed through the inclusion of South Africa in the Special 301 List of the Office of the US Trade Representative (USTR).[48] There was a public outcry against these developments that included demonstrations and culminated with the joinder of the TAC to the litigation as *amicus curiae*.[49] However, as stated above, the matter was withdrawn before hearing after a settlement was reached.

An agreement was also reached between the South African and US governments that led to the removal of South Africa from the USTR 301 list. An executive order was passed by the US government in May 2000, in terms of which the US:

> shall not seek, through negotiation or otherwise, the revocation or revision of any intellectual property law or policy of a beneficiary sub-Saharan

44 Medicines and Related Substances Control Amendment Act, No. 59 (2002) (S. Afr.).

45 Government Gazette 24727, GN R510, Apr. 10, 2003.

46 *See* Caroline B. Ncube, *Enforcing Patent Rights Against Goods in Transit: A New Threat to Transborder Trade in Generic Medicines*, 21 S. Afr. Mercantile L. J. 680, 691 (2009).

47 Pharm. Mfrs.' Ass'n of S. Afr. v. President of the Republic of S. Afr., Case No. 4183/98, High Court of South Africa (Transvaal Provincial Division).

48 Office of the U.S. Trade Representative, *199 Special 301 Report* (1999).

49 Ellen F.M. 't Hoen, *Practical Applications of the Flexibilities of the Agreement on Trade-Related Aspects of Intellectual Property Rights: Lessons Beyond HIV for Access to New Essential Medicines,* 33–6 (2018) (Ph.D. dissertation, University of Groningen-Netherlands); Caroline B. Ncube, *The Politics of National Intellectual Property Policy Design and the Provision of Health Services in South Africa*, 3 S. Afr. Intell. Prop. L. J. 15, 15–39 (2015); Mark Heywood, *Debunking "Conglomo-talk": A Case Study of the Amicus Curiae as an Instrument for Advocacy, Investigation and Mobilisation*, 5 Law, Democracy & Dev. 2, 133, 139–44 (2001); William W. Fisher III & Cyrill P. Rigamonti, *The South Africa AIDS Controversy: A Case Study in Patent Law and Policy*, Law & Bus. Patents, (Feb. 10, 2005), http://cyber.law.harvard.edu/people/tfisher/South%20Africa.pdf; Susan Cleary & Don Ross, *The 1998–2001 Legal Struggle Between the South African Government and the International Pharmaceutical Industry: A Game-Theoretic Analysis*, 27 J. Soc. Pol. Econ. Stud. 445 (2002); Solomon Frank Sacco, *A Comparative Study of the Implementation in Zimbabwe and South Africa of the International Law Rules That Allow Compulsory Licensing and Parallel Importation for HIV/AIDS Drugs*, 5 African Human Rights L.J. 105 (2005).

> African country, as determined by the President, that regulates HIV/AIDS pharmaceuticals or medical technologies if the law or policy of the country: (1) promotes access to HIV/AIDS pharmaceuticals or medical technologies for affected populations in that country; and (2) provides adequate and effective intellectual property protection consistent with the TRIPS Agreement.[50]

Soon thereafter, the Doha Declaration was signed in November 2001 by WTO members.

Following the withdrawal of the litigation and the agreement between South Africa and the US, South Africa was able to proceed with the implementation of the SEP. The SEP was first prescribed by the pricing regulations in 2004 and comprises the manufacturer's price and a logistics fee plus value-added tax.[51] It has been noted that the establishment of the logistics fee is not transparent.[52] Therefore, price controls have somewhat, but have not completely, eradicated the price-related challenges that may hinder access to medicines.

## The IP Policy 2018

The most notable development in relation to access to medicines and patents in South Africa has been the passing of the IP Policy 2018, a process led by the then DTI. The formulation of this policy has spanned almost a decade[53] and involved a shift from the original lead division, the Consumer Corporate Division, to the current lead and custodian division, the International Trade and Economic Development.[54] The policy also included various consultative phases, with the first draft being circulated for comment in 2013[55] and the last call for comments being made in August 2017.[56] Soon after the publication

50 Exec. Order No. 13155, Fed. Reg. 30, 521–3, May 12, 2000.

51 V. Bangalee & F. Suleman, *Is There Transparency in the Pricing of Medicines in the South African Private Sector?*, 108 S. Afr. Med. J. 2, 82–3 (2018); Price control Minister of Health v. New Clicks South Africa (Pty) Ltd. (2005) ZACC 14.

52 *Id.*

53 Linda Daniels, *South Africa Approves New IP Policy, with Guidance from UN Agencies*, IPWatch (May 27, 2018), https://www.ip-watch.org/2018/05/27/south-africa-approves-new-ip-policy-guidance-un-agencies/.

54 South African Institute of Intellectual Property Law Council Meeting (2016), Minutes of Meeting dated Aug. 18, 2018.

55 Draft National Policy on Intellectual Property 918, GenN 36816 in GG 36816 of Sept. 4, 2013.

56 Draft Intellectual Property Policy of the Republic of South Africa Phase 1 (2017): For Broader Public Comments GenN 636 of 2017, Government Gazette 626, GN 41064, Aug. 25, 2017.

of the draft policy for comment in 2013, a document detailing a counter-strategy entitled "A Proposal Prepared for PhRMA and IPASA: Campaign to Prevent Damage to Innovation from the Proposed Draft National IP Policy in SA"[57] was leaked, leading to a spirited response from the Minister of Health, civil society protests, and academic commentary.[58] This episode was popularly known as PharmaGate. A full discussion of this is beyond the scope of this chapter, but suffice it to say that the strategy was disavowed by the Innovative Pharmaceutical Association of South Africa and the policy formulation process unfolded to its culmination.

Many stakeholders provided comments on the IP Policy drafts to parliament, some of which are publicly available.[59] In addition, scholarly analyses were

57 Public Affairs Engagement (PAE), *A Proposal Prepared for PhRMA and IPASA: Campaign to Prevent Damage to Innovation from the Proposed Draft National IP Policy in South Africa: Stage 1: Jan–Feb 2014*, http://cdn.mg.co.za/content/documents/2014/01/16/skmbt36314011511040.pdf (last visited Jan. 31, 2020).

58 For a discussion, *see* Caroline B. Ncube, *The Politics of National Intellectual Property Policy Design and the Provision of Health Services in South Africa*, 3 S. Afr. Intell. Prop. L.J. 15–39 (2015).

59 For example, Mail & Guardian published submissions on sourcenet. *See* sourceAFRICA, https://dc.sourceafrica.net/public/search/Draft%20IP%20policy (last visited June 23, 2020). Persons who had submitted comments also published them on various websites. *See, e.g.*, Innovative Pharm. Ass'n S. Afr. (IPASA), *Extracts from Submission: Focus on Matters of IP and Public Health* (2013), http://ipasa.co.za/wp-content/uploads/2016/03/IPASA-Extracts-from-Submission-made-on-the-DRAFT-NATIONAL-POLICY-ON-IP....pdf; LTC Harms Comment, *Draft National Policy on Intellectual Property 2013*, http://blogs.sun.ac.za/iplaw/files/2013/09/HARMS-Comment-IP-POLICY.pdf (last visited Jan. 31, 2020); Tobias Schonwetter et al., *Draft National Policy on Intellectual Property (IP) of South Africa, 2013* (Oct. 17, 2013), http://ip-unit.org/wp-content/uploads/2013/10/IP-Policy-Academics-Submission_final171013.pdf; [AmaBele Belles' Project FlamingoBreast Course 4 Nurses, Breast Health Foundation (BHF), Cancer Association of South Africa (CANSA), Can-Sir, CanSurvive Cancer Support, Cape Mental Health (CMH), Childhood Cancer Foundation of South Africa (CHOC), DiabetesSA, Doctors without Borders (MSF), EpilepsySA, Hospice Palliative Care Association (HPCA), Igazi Foundation, Lymphoedema Association of South Africa (LAOSA), Look Good Feel Better, Marie Stopes South Africa, Men's Foundation, National Council Against Smoking, Oncology Nursing Association of SA, Pancreatic Cancer Network of SA, People Living With Cancer (PLWC), Pink Trees for Pauline, Pocket Cancer Support, Rainbows and Smiles, Reach for Recovery, Schizophrenia and Bipolar Disorders Alliance (SABDA), SECTION27, South African Depression and Anxiety Group (SADAG), South African Federation of Mental Health (SAFMH), South African Non-Communicable Diseases Alliance (SANCD Alliance), Stop Stock Outs Project (SSP), The Pink Parasol Project, The Sunflower Fund, Treatment Action Campaign (TAC), Vrede Foundation, and Wings of Hope.], *Fix the Patent Laws Submission on the Draft Intellectual Property Policy of the Republic of South Africa, Phase I, 2017* (Nov. 17, 2017), http://section27.org.za/wp-content/uploads/2018/06/FTPL-Submission-and-Appendices-Nov-17.pdf.

published by legal scholars and practitioners.[60] In summary, the feedback to the 2013 draft IP Policy was mostly negative but it had become largely positive by 2017 due to the revisions that had been made to the policy, coupled with a very inclusive consultative process.[61]

A key part of the consultation process was that it was anchored in the Inter-Ministerial Committee on Intellectual Property, which is a consultative forum with some oversight of the policy formulation process.[62] It currently comprises representatives from the departments of Trade, Industry and Competition, Health; Economic Development; International Relations and Cooperation; Science and Technology; Communications; Telecommunications and Postal Services; Higher Education and Training; Agriculture Forestry and Fisheries; Arts and Culture, Energy; and Environmental Affairs.[63] The policy formulation process, inclusive of stakeholder consultation, has been commented upon by other scholars and civil society,[64] therefore this chapter will focus on the actual content of the policy.

In its own words, the IP Policy 2018:

> covers IP and public health, coordination in international forums, and the implementation of commitments undertaken in international agreements … [and its] priorities have been identified on the basis of South Africa's development objectives, supplemented by research, analysis, and experience, as well as assessments of existing capacity to implement the [proposed] measures.

The IP and public health–related reforms taken up by the IP Policy 2018 which had been initially and partially identified as requiring immediate review in the Consultative Framework[65] are given in Table 12.1.[66]

60 *See, e.g.*, Madelein Kleyn, *Public Health Sector and the South African National Policy on Intellectual Property*, ANSTON MOSTERT CHAIR OF INTELL. PROP. (Jan. 24, 2014), https://blogs.sun.ac.za/iplaw/2014/01/24/public-health-sector-and-the-south-african-national-policy-on-intellectual-property/; Yousuf A. Vawda, *After the Novartis judgment – 'Evergreening' Will Never Be the Same Again!*, 18 L., DEMOCRACY & DEV. 305 (2014); Caroline B Ncube, *The Draft National Intellectual Property Policy Proposals for Improving South Africa's Patent Registration System: A Review*, 9 J. INTELL. PROP. L. & PRAC. 822 (2014).

61 *Intellectual Property Consultative Framework*, DEP'T TRADE & INDUS.: REPUB. S. AFR. (July 6, 2016), https://www.thedti.gov.za/news2016/IPConsultativeFramework.pdf [hereinafter *IP Consultative Framework*].

62 *Id.* at 4; *Intellectual Property Policy of the Republic of South Africa, Phase I*, REPUBLIC OF S. AFR., INT'L TRADE & ECONOMIC DEV. TRADE & INDUSTRY DEP'T 184 § 6 (2018), https://www.gov.za/sites/default/files/gcis_document/201808/ippolicy2018-phasei.pdf [hereinafter *IP Policy of South Africa*].

63 *IP Policy of South Africa*, *supra* note 62, at 184.

64 *A Timeline of Intellectual Property Reform in South Africa 1994–2015*, FIX THE PATENT LAWS (Oct. 29, 2015), https://www.fixthepatentlaws.org/a-timeline-of-intellectual-property-reform-in-south-africa-1994-2015/.

65 *IP Consultative Framework*, *supra* note 61, at 5.

66 *IP Policy of South Africa*, *supra* note 62, at 185.

*Table 12.1* IP and public health–related reforms in the 2018 IP Policy

| *Aspect* | *Suggested reforms* |
|---|---|
| 1. Local manufacture and export in line with industrial policy | The reforms below are all intended to create an enabling environment for the growth of this industry for local production and export.[a] |
| 2. Patents – substantive search and examination (SSE) | SSE to be introduced after the development of SSE Guidelines to selected fields to be determined in consultation with stakeholders, including, the IMCIP, industry, and civil society.[b] |
| 3. Patent opposition | • A third-party observation for interested parties to make written submissions to oppose patent grant.[c]<br>• Regulations for a post-grant opposition mechanism by administrative review under the Promotion of Administrative Justice Act 3 of 2000 (pending the creation of post-grant opposition system).[d]<br>• Legislative provisions for pre-grant opposition proceedings once there is sufficient capacity within the substantive examination system to make appropriate use of such proceedings.[e] |
| 4. Patentability criteria | Legislative reforms to be introduced to "raise the bar" and ensure that only deserving patents are granted.[f] |
| 5. Disclosure requirements | Suggested the introduction of legislative provisions requiring patent applicants to provide information regarding the status of similar and related applications filed in other international jurisdictions.[g] |
| 6. Parallel importation | Recommends that the Patents Act should be amended to clarify that parallel importation of medicines under s15C of the Medicines Act does not constitute an infringement of a patent.[h] |
| 7. Exceptions | Recommends legislative reforms for a carefully crafted set of exceptions for research and experimental activities.[i] |
| 8. Voluntary licenses | No recommended legislative reform. The policy encourages the use of voluntary licenses.[j] |
| 9. Compulsory licenses | Recommends the development of guidelines that ought to include government use and export, together with the replacement of the court application process with a less cumbersome process.[k] |
| 10. IP and competition law | Recommends jointly developed guidelines on the interface between IP and competition law, by the competition authorities, and other relevant authorities.[l] |
| 11. Rule of law and legal certainty | No reforms suggested. This section is a confirmation that, as required by law, the proposed reforms will be "implemented in a lawful, transparent, fair, and open process. Furthermore, the proposed changes increase legal certainty with respect to patents and other forms of intellectual property in South Africa, in comparison to the status quo. Finally, the patent system as envisaged is designed to increase and diversify investment in the country."[m] |

a *Id.* at 186.
b *Id.* at 188.
c *Id.* at 190.
d *Id.*
e *Id.*
f *Id.* at 192–3.
g *Id.* at 193.
h *Id.* at 194–6.
i *Id.* at 196–7.
j *Id.* at 198.
k *Id.* at 198–9.
l *Id.* at 200–1.
m *Id.* at 202.

VLs and the rule of law and legal certainty were not included in the Consultative Framework's priority aspects list. The abovementioned listed reforms have been debated at length by scholarly commentators and advocacy groups, as cited in preceding sections of this chapter. It is yet to be seen exactly how the recommended legislative provisions would be phrased but the policy has given clear guidelines as to the import of its suggested legislative reforms. It is clear that there will be an extensive legislative reform process flowing from these suggestions.

The policy-making process presented another opportunity for the development of the tripartite relationship between the state, private sector, and civil society. Civil society was instrumental in the instigation of the policy reform process, through concerted campaigns that highlighted access to medicines challenges. This "bottom-up" approach is distinguishable from a "top-down" approach in which the state or international regulators initiate the reform process.[67] The beginning of the process, around 2013, showed tension between the parties due to the dissatisfaction with the first iteration of the policy and at that stage, the parties – at times – were antagonistic toward each other. However, as the consultative process unfurled and the policy was refined, the relationship became increasingly collaborative.

## Commentary and Conclusion

The previous section on the regulatory framework governing the right to access to medicines has given a summary of the legislative reforms that have been enacted to date as given in Table 12.2.

*Table 12.2* Legislative reforms enacted up to date (2019)

| *Legislation* | *Nature of reform* | *Year* |
|---|---|---|
| Patents Act | Extension of patent duration from to 20 years s. 46 | 1997 |
| Patents Act | Effect of a patent s. 45(1) | |
| Medicines and Related Substances Act | S15C parallel importation<br>S22F generic substitution<br>S22G price control | 1997 |
| Medicines and Related Substances Act | S22F generic substitution<br>S22G price control | 2002 |
| Competition Act | S8 abuse of dominance | 2019 |

67 Saeed Ahmadiani & Shekoufeh Nikfa, *Challenges of Access to Medicine and the Responsibility of Pharmaceutical Companies: A Legal Perspective*, 24 DARU J. PHARM. SCI. 13, 17 (2016), https://doi.org/10.1186/s40199-016-0151-z.

The abovementioned tabular summary and the previous account regarding South Africa's regulatory framework show that the government has been pursuing legislative reforms related to access to medicines since 1997, with the amendments to the Patents Act and the Medicines and Related Substances Control Act. Further, from the outset, there has been advocacy in support of, and against, these reforms.

While the reforms are generally welcomed, it can reasonably be said that they do not go far enough. Indeed, the South African government has admitted as much in the Consultative Framework.[68] For instance, the CL provisions in the Patents Act have not resulted in the issuance of a CL. However, resort to the competition authorities by the filing of several complaints has resulted in the issuance of VLs. Reliance on the negotiation of VLs is inadequate because it does not "provide the requisite level of access in other disease areas. Hence, government requires a mix of policy options for instances where voluntary mechanisms prove inadequate."[69]

These developments in South Africa have had an effect on regional and global discourse regarding IP and access to medicines, as evidenced by the reliance on South Africa as an example of the contestation of positions which led to a favorable outcome for access to medicines in scholarly writing,[70] and the adoption of similar human rights and developmental arguments or positions in other national contexts in Africa.[71] A third, and perhaps the most significant, indicator of impact is the citation of the country's civil society's initiatives as a good model to follow in the Report of the United Nations Secretary-General's High-Level Panel (HLP) on Access to Medicines.[72] The HLP's Global Hearing and Dialogue held in Johannesburg in March 2016 provided a further opportunity for South African stakeholders to engage and work with their counterparts from across the African continent[73] and for the dynamics of South African national discourse to be witnessed by all in attendance. The symbiosis of national discourse and the impact of civil society's stance in the tripartite negotiation over

68 *IP Consultative Framework*, *supra* note 61, at 5, para. 3 ("the South African government has to date not made full use of the flexibility within international law through the pursuit of appropriate policy and legislation.").

69 *Id.* at 9–10.

70 For example, Ahmadiani & Nikfa, *supra* note 67.

71 Abigail A. Ekeigwe. *Drug Manufacturing and Access to Medicines: The West African Story. A Literature Review of Challenges and Proposed Remediation*, 5 AAPS Open 3 (2019), https://doi.org/10.1186/s41120-019-0032-x.

72 Report of the United Nations Secretary-General's High-Level Panel on Access to Medicines. Promoting innovation and access to health technologies 63 (Sept. 2016).

73 For example, *see* Gerard Best, *A Joint Position Statement from Africa Continent Civil Society and Community Groups is Issued Ahead of the of UN High Level Meeting on Ending AIDS 2016, Following a Consultation Convened on 1 April in Nairobi* (Apr. 6, 2016), http://itpcglobal.org/african-civil-society-statement-to-un-general-assembly-high-level-meeting-to-end-aids/.

intellectual property and access to medicines are most aptly captured by Shiba Phurailatpam, as follows:

> A band of determined patients and activists stand in the way of this tightening grip of corporate power over medicines...The legal work pursued by these groups have played a critical role in the shaping, implementation and evolution of TRIPS flexibilities as we understand them today; whether it was the competition case brought by the Treatment Action Campaign in South Africa, the DDI case in Thailand that established the standing of public interest groups in patent challenges, the patent opposition work in India, Brazil, Argentina, China, Thailand etc...The list is far longer and support for the legal work of public interest groups is critical for the successful use of TRIPS flexibilities.[74]

In closing, it is important to contextualize the above quotation by acknowledging that, as is to be expected, the HLP's Report and its aftermath have become another site of contestation through scholarly debate[75] and continued activism.[76] The discussion regarding the IP Policy 2018 has outlined the upcoming legislative reforms based on the policy. From that, it is clear that extensive legislative reform is to be anticipated. Based on the past engagement by stakeholders in access to medicines–related patent reform, another robust wave of discourse can be expected. If past patterns are anything to go by, it can also reasonably be expected that the progress of the future reform process will be lengthy as the various stakeholders each have their say and employ their full arsenal of campaign and advocacy tactics.

74 *Id.*

75 For example, *see* Eric M. Solovy and Pavan S. Krishnamurthy, *TRIPS Agreement Flexibilities and Their Limitations: A Response to the UN Secretary-Generals's High-Level Panel Report on Access to Medicines*, 50 Geo. Wash. Int'l L. Rev. 69 (2017–2018); Jorge Bermudez, *Contemporary Challenges on Access to Medicines: Beyond the UNSG High-Level Panel Debate*, 22 Ciên. Saúde Colet. 8 (Aug. 2017), https://doi.org/10.1590/1413-81232017228.29362016; Frederick M. Abbott, *Reflections on the Report of the UN Secretary General's High-Level Panel on Access to Medicines*, 22 Ciên. Saúde Colet. 8, 2440–2 (2017), https://dx.doi.org/10.1590/1413-81232017228.16262017; Jacob Robin, *Comment on the UN High-level Panel Report on Access to Medicines*, 16 Bio-Science Law Review 2, 56–90 (2017).

76 Resulting in, for instance, the *Political Declaration on the Fight against Tuberculosis Co-Facilitators' Final Text 1 United to End Tuberculosis: An Urgent Global Response to a Global Epidemic* (2018), https://www.un.org/pga/72/wp-content/uploads/sites/51/2018/07/TB.pdf.

# 13 Thailand

## Shooting Star for Access to Medicines Through Compulsory Licensing

*Van Anh Le*

### Introduction

Compulsory licensing is often used in contemporary debates as an umbrella term for many types of nonvoluntary authorization by the State – or by some part of the State's machinery – to exercise patent holders' rights without their authorization. Examples include ex officio licenses, government use, licenses to remedy anticompetitive practices, mandatory licenses, and statutory licenses.[1] This legal measure is a highly controversial topic[2] because it directly touches on the core value of a patent – the exclusivity by which a patent holder can prohibit others from using his invention – and enables the patentee to be its only beneficiary. Article 31 of the Agreement on Trade-Related Aspects of Intellectual Property Rights (TRIPS Agreement) provides the legal basis for compulsory licensing at the international level.[3] A compulsory license (CL) can be given for any kind of intellectual property rights (IPRs). In no other field, however, has it been

1 Coenraad Visser, *Patent Exceptions and Limitations in the Health Context*, SCP/15/3, Annex V, Experts' Study on Exclusions from Patentable Subject Matter and Exceptions and Limitations to the Rights (2010), https://www.wipo.int/edocs/mdocs/scp/en/scp_15/scp_15_3-annex5.pdf (last visited Nov. 5, 2019).

2 Jamie Feldman, *Compulsory Licenses: The Dangers Behind the Current Practice*, 8 J. Int'l Bus. & L., 137 (2009), https://scholarlycommons.law.hofstra.edu/cgi/viewcontent.cgi?article=1107&context=jibl (last visited Nov. 5, 2019); Jerome H. Reichman, *Comment: Compulsory Licensing of Patented Pharmaceutical Inventions: Evaluating the Options*, 37 J. L. Med. & Ethics 2, 247–63 (2009); Daniel Gervais, The TRIPS Agreement: Drafting History and Analysis (4th ed. 2012); Kristina M. Lybecker & Elisabeth Fowler, *Compulsory Licensing in Canada and Thailand: Comparing Regimes to Ensure Legitimate Use of the WTO Rules*, 37 J. L. Med. & Ethics 2, 222–39 (2009).

3 TRIPS: Agreement on Trade-Related Aspects of Intellectual Property Rights, Apr. 15, 1994, Marrakesh Agreement Establishing the World Trade Organization, Annex 1C, 1869 U.N.T.S. 299, 33 I.L.M. 1197 (1994), https://www.wto.org/english/docs_e/legal_e/31bis_trips_e.pdf (last visited Nov. 5, 2019) [hereinafter TRIPS Agreement], art. 31.

more debated, contextualized, and disputed than in the case of pharmaceutical patents.[4]

Within two relatively short periods – from November 2006 to January 2007 and in January 2008 – the government of Thailand, which has been a World Trade Organization (WTO) member since 1995, issued seven CLs, citing public health as a ground to justify its actions.[5] The Thai example is critical in understanding the impacts of the TRIPS Agreement on access to medicines and it is a "collection" of many first-time-ever events. That is, in addition to issuing CLs against patents over HIV drugs, Thailand is the *first* nation to use such licenses for medicines to treat chronic diseases as earlier CLs were limited to medicines for treating communicable illnesses, or epidemics such as HIV/AIDS.[6] Adding another layer of complexity to this case study is the *extraordinary* involvement of politics, since the government that granted the licenses was a postcoup cabinet.[7] Due to significant quantities of the CLs issued and their broad range, the Thai government, for the *first* time, felt obliged to justify its policy in two so-called

4 Padmanabha Ramanujam & Yugank Goyal, *One View of Compulsory Licensing: Comparative Perspectives from India and Canada*, 18 Marq. Intell. Prop. L. Rev., 375, 378 (2014); Chang-fa Lo, *Compulsory Licensing: Threats, Use and Recent Trends*, *in* Contemporary Issues in Pharmaceutical Patent Law: Setting the Framework and Exploring Policy Options, 147 (Bryan Mercurio & Daria Kim eds., 1st ed. 2018).

5 The notifications of these compulsory licenses are reprinted in the documents (a) The Ministry of Public Health and the National Health Security Office, Thailand, *Facts and Evidences on the 10 Burning Issues Related to the Government Use of Patents on Three Patented Essential Drugs in Thailand* (2007), https://apps.who.int/medicinedocs/documents/s18718en/s18718en.pdf (last visited Nov. 5, 2019) [hereinafter White Paper 2007]; (b) The Ministry of Public Health and the National Health Security Office, *The 10 Burning Questions on the Government Use of Patents on the Four Anti-cancer Drugs in Thailand* (2008), https://www.publiceye.ch/fileadmin/doc/_migration/Gesundheit/White_paper_CL_II_FEB_08-ENG.pdf (last visited Nov. 5, 2019) [hereinafter White Paper 2008]. There is no official definition of a so-called White Paper within the Thai legal system. In fact, these two White Papers can be considered as official reports which compile letters and communications, in addition to compulsory licensing notifications, from various parties involved in the situation, for example, letters from the Thai government, pharmaceutical companies, the United States, nongovernmental organizations (NGOs), and others. The reports also detail the rationale, legal issues, and decision-making process of Thai compulsory licensing. These two White Papers are the Thai government's effort to inform the public and garner support.

6 Read Beall & Randall Kuhn, *Trends in Compulsory Licensing of Pharmaceuticals Since the Doha Declaration: A Database Analysis*, 1 PLoS Med. 9 (Jan. 10, 2012), https://journals.plos.org/plosmedicine/article?id=10.1371/journal.pmed.1001154 (last visited Nov. 5, 2019).

7 Until 2006, Thailand was represented by Prime Minister Thaksin Shinawatra. On Sept. 19, 2006, taking advantage of the absence of Thaksin at the United Nations General Assembly, the Thai military seized power, appointing a new cabinet and a new National Assembly. *See Thailand Profile-Timeline*, BBC, https://www.bbc.com/news/world-asia-15641745 (last visited May 22, 2019).

White Papers, published in February 2007 and February 2008.[8] In addition, Thailand is also the *first* country to assess the economic impacts of all seven CLs *after* they were issued.[9]

Thailand's bold moves provoked retaliation by Abbott Laboratories Limited (Abbott). The company, which held a patent of *Kaletra* – one of the medicines issued under Thai compulsory licensing – withdrew seven new medicines from the Thai market in reprisal.[10] This was believed to be the *first* tit-for-tat action of a rights owner since the history of TRIPS compulsory licensing. Such withdrawal raises the question of whether the balance of interest is achieved, if enhancing accessibility to one set of medication to a class of patients leads to denying access to other medications to the entire market, because of a patent holder's retaliation.

## Thai Government Uses Licensing

Thailand's compulsory licensing was first issued in 2006, although the first attempt to issue such a license was made in 1999, when the Government Pharmaceutical Organization (GPO) requested for a CL to manufacture *Didanosine*, an HIV drug.[11] The request was rejected when it was lodged before the WTO Ministerial Meeting in Seattle, as the Thai government wanted to avoid any potential trade dispute with the United States (US).[12] To circumvent patent infringement of *Didanosine*, the GPO had to develop a new formulation – in powder form – of the medicine.[13] However, the new drug caused digestive and other undesirable side effects.[14] Clearly, there was a substantial market demand for generic versions of HIV medications in Thailand at that time.

In order to analyze the Thai government's compulsory licensing, the author will group these licenses into two time periods linked to the White Papers: 2006–2007 and 2008.[15]

8 White Paper 2007, *supra* note 5.

9 Inthira Yamabha et al., *Assessing the Implications of Thailand's Government Use Licenses, Issued in 2006–2008 A Draft for Consultation of the Health Intervention and Technology Assessment Program, Ministry of Public Health* (May 2009), http://www.hitap.net/wp-content/uploads/2014/09/completed_compulsoly_licensingeng.pdf (last visited Apr. 28, 2020).

10 Cynthia M. Ho, Access to Medicine in the Global Economy: International Agreements on Patents and Related Rights, 169 ( 2011).

11 Suwit Wibulpolprasert et al., *Government Use Licenses in Thailand: The Power of Evidence, Civil Movement and Political Leadership*, 7 Glob. Health 1, 3 (2011).

12 *Id.*

13 *Id.*

14 *Id.*

15 White Paper 2007, *supra* note 5.

### *The First Period: From Late 2006 Until Early 2007*

The government is mainly responsible for health-care expenditure in Thailand. In 2002, Thailand adopted the National Health Security Act,[16] which covered most Thai citizens under a national insurance scheme.[17] The beneficiaries were entitled to full access to medicines on an essential drug list with almost 900 items.[18] In 2003, Thailand started providing free antiretroviral drugs (ARVs) for HIV/AIDS patients.[19] To achieve these national goals, Thailand raised the health-care budget from around 4 percent of the overall national budget in the 1980s to almost 10 percent in 2007. The ARV expenditure increased more than tenfold from 2001 to 2007 due to high drug prices.[20] The financial difficulties were further aggravated by the growing number of patients: from 20,000 in 2003 to approximately 120,000 in 2007.[21] The budget deficit, together with high prices, hindered the government from accomplishing these national goals.

Left with limited alternatives, Thailand decided to issue CLs.[22] On November 29, 2006, citing public health reasons, the Thai Minister of Health announced the government use of *Efavirenz* for noncommercial purposes, as regulated by Section 51 of the Thai Patent Act.[23] This section outlines CLs in public interest by allowing any ministry, bureau, or department of the government, either by themselves or through a third party, to issue such a license.[24] Two months after the first announcement, on January 25, 2007, Thailand announced the compulsory licensing of the *Lopinavir* and *Ritonavir* (*Kaletra*)[25]

Even though these licenses were controversial, they did not make headlines. On January 26, 2007, after the decision involving *Kaletra*, Thailand issued a CL for *Clopidogrel* (*Plavix*), a blood thinner used to treat heart diseases.[26] This was a further blow to the global pharmaceutical industry, because a CL covered a chronic disease for the first time.

In February 2007, the Ministry of Public Health and the National Health Security Office issued the first White Paper entitled "Facts and Evidence on the

16 National Health Security Act, B.E. 2545 (2002) (Thai).

17 White Paper 2007, *supra* note 5, at Issue No. 1.

18 *Id.*

19 *Id.*

20 *Id.*

21 Beatrice Stirner, *Learning From Practice: Compulsory Licensing Cases and Access to Medicines*, 1 PHARM. PAT. ANALYST 5, 555, 562 (Nov. 21, 2012).

22 White Paper 2007, *supra* note 5.

23 Compulsory license for Efavirenz (Nov. 29, 2006) [hereinafter Compulsory License for Efavirenz]. The notification was reprinted in the White Paper 2007, *supra* note 5.

24 Patent Act § 51, B.E. 2542 (1999) (Thai).

25 Compulsory license for Kaletra (Jan. 24, 2007) [hereinafter Compulsory License for Kaletra]. The notification was reprinted in the White Paper 2007, *supra* note 5.

26 Compulsory license for Plavix (Jan. 25, 2007) [hereinafter Compulsory License for Plavix]. The notification was reprinted in the White Paper 2007, *supra* note 5.

Ten Burning Issues Relating to the Government Use of Patents in Thailand" to allay the apprehensions of the pharmaceutical industry, stating:

> does not only aim at answering all the questions [raised by the public and the concerned partners], but more importantly as a tool to inform and educate the Thai and Global Society as a whole, on the issue of pharmaceutical patent and the public health. This is to ensure the success of the future movements to improve the intellectual property systems so that it is more conducive to social development.[27]

This White Paper listed the selection of drugs and disclosed Thailand's intention to compulsorily license up to 15 percent of all patented drugs.[28] Meanwhile, there was political crisis as a result of a coup in 2006. Until 2006, the Prime Minister was Thaksin Shinawatra, who was responsible for the initiation of Thai-US free trade agreement (FTA) negotiations in June 2004. Through this FTA, the US sought to restrict the compulsory licensing mechanism.[29] However, due to the political turmoil within Thailand, the FTA was put on hold.

### *The Second Period: Early 2008*

In June 2007, in fulfillment of its stated intention to issue additional licenses, the Thai government established two exploratory committees to consider compulsory licensing of cancer medications. However, 12 rounds of negotiations from October to December 2007 yielded no significant results.[30]

A general election was also held in Thailand in December 2007, the first legislative election since the 2006 coup. A new government was established, and on January 4, 2008, less than a month before demitting office, the Minister of Health announced the government use of four anticancer medicines under Section 51 of the Thai Patent Act.[31] However, unlike previous licenses that had

27 White Paper 2007, *supra* note 5, at preface.
28 *Id.* at Issue No. 4.
29 *Thailand Free Trade Agreement*, Office of US Trade Representative, https://ustr.gov/archive/Trade_Agreements/Bilateral/Thail_FTA/Section_Index.html (last visited May 22, 2019).
30 White Paper 2008, *supra* note 5.
31 Ministry of Public Health, Compulsory License for Patented Medicines and Medical Devices: Letrozole, B.E. 2551 (Jan. 4, 2008) [hereinafter Compulsory License for Letrozole]; Ministry of Public Health, Compulsory License for Patented Medicines and Medical Devices: Docetaxel, B. E. 2551 (Jan. 4, 2008) [hereinafter Compulsory License for Docetaxel]; Ministry of Public Health, Compulsory License for Patented Medicines and Medical Devices: Erlotinib, B.E. 2551 (Jan. 4, 2008) [hereinafter Compulsory License for Erlotinib]; Ministry of Public Health, Compulsory License for Patented Medicines and Medical Devices: Imitinab, B. E. 2551 (Jan. 4, 2008) [hereinafter Compulsory License for Imitinab]. All these compulsory licensing notifications were reprinted in the White Paper 2008, *supra* note 5.

been implemented immediately, the Thai government chose to hold further negotiations with the patent owners, leading to an acceptable result; Novartis agreed to supply the medicine free to hundreds of Thai patients meeting certain requirements.[32] The government therefore revoked the decision to issue a CL for Novartis-owned *Glivec*. For the remaining three medicines, no agreement could be reached, so Thailand continued to issue CLs.

On February 7, 2008 – the day the new Minister of Health took office – he announced that he would reevaluate his predecessor's decisions and their impact on the relationship with the US.[33] Meanwhile, the US placed Thailand on the Priority Watch List under Section 301 of the US Trade Act of 1974,[34] which the Thai minister mentioned as the main reason for the review. Ultimately, no CLs were revoked.

In 2008, Thailand published its second White Paper defending the additional licenses issued. Like the first White Paper of 2007, this one also provided supporting evidence for Thai government use.[35] The evidence included the exorbitant cost of patented cancer drugs versus the reduced prices of their generic versions, the genuine implementation of Thai compulsory licensing for public health purposes, the transparency of the decision-making process, the potential impacts of those licenses on Thai exports to the US, and the high quality of Thailand's generic drugs.[36]

## Reactions to Thai Compulsory Licenses

Thailand's government use licenses, like other compulsory licensing activities, created a dichotomy between supporters and objectors. Internationally, public health activists praised and congratulated Thailand for advancing access to medicines, while patent advocates fiercely criticized the Thai policy for expropriating private property. For example, the Joint United Nations Programme on

32 Letter from Novartis Asia Pacific Pharmaceuticals Pte Ltd., to Minister of Public Health (Jan. 23, 2008) and to Compulsory License for Imatinib (Jan. 25, 2008). This document was reprinted in the White Paper 2008, *supra* note 5.

33 Ho, *supra* note 10, at 170.

34 Trade Act of 1974 (Omnibus Trade and Competitveness Act), Pub. L. No. 93-618, tit. III, ch. 1, § 301, 88 Stat. 1978, 2041 (codified as amended by the Trade Act of 1988, at 19 U.S.C. §§ 2411–20 (1988)). Section 301 is a key enforcement tool that allows the United States Trade Representative (USTR) to initiate trade sanctions, including tariffs and import duties against nations failing to protect United States IPRs. Under Section 301, US trading partners with IPR deficiencies were listed under the following classifications: watch lists, priority watch lists, and priority foreign countries. The last is the worst classification, and countries on it are likely to face trade retaliation by the United States. *See* Office of the U.S. Trade Rep., 2007 Special 301 Report, 27 (Apr. 2007), https://ustr.gov/sites/default/files/2007%20Special%20301%20Report.pdf (last visited Nov. 5, 2019) [hereinafter 2007 Special 301 Report].

35 White Paper 2008, *supra* note 5.

36 White Paper 2008, *supra* note 5.

HIV/AIDS (UNAIDS) described Thai actions as "strong and steadfast efforts" for HIV patients.[37] Similarly, the Médecins Sans Frontières (MSF) welcomed the Thai licenses[38] and wrote to the US Trade Representative Ambassador Schwab, asking the US and the Office of the US Trade Representative (USTR) not to interfere with the Thai decisions.[39] According to the MSF, Thailand's CLs "will create a larger global market for generic drugs, stimulate competition and lower prices everywhere for the newer products."[40] The Third World Network (TWN)[41] asserted these licenses were consistent with the TRIPS Agreement and encouraged the country to make further use of TRIPS flexibilities.[42] The Consumer Project on Technology (currently known as Knowledge Ecology International [KEI])[43] supported Thailand through a series of blogs[44] and requested the US not to put pressure on the country.[45] Expressing similar support, the Clinton Foundation opined that these licenses "ensure more affordable access to high quality ARV drugs."[46] Obviously, the general public welcomed this move promoting medicines' accessibility.

But the Thai series of CLs also provoked many controversies. The BBC portrayed Thailand as the "violator of IPRs."[47] The Wall Street Journal characterized the CLs as "theft,"[48] a "seizure of foreign drug patents," and a "frontal

37 Letter from UNAIDS, to the Thai Minister of Health (Dec. 26, 2006). This was reprinted in the White Paper 2007, *supra* note 5.

38 Médecins Sans Frontières (MSF) is an international, independent, medical humanitarian organization, providing medical assistance to people affected by conflict, epidemics, disasters, or exclusion from healthcare. *See* Médecins Sans Frontières Int'l, https://www.msf.org/ (last visited May 22, 2019).

39 Letter from MSF to US Trade Representative Susan Schwab (Dec. 29, 2006). This was reprinted in the White Paper 2007, *supra* note 5.

40 *Id.*

41 TWN, headquartered in Malaysia, is an NGO providing international research and advocacy in issues relating to development, developing countries and North-South affairs. *See Introduction,* Third World Network, https://www.twn.my/twnintro.htm (last visited May 30, 2019).

42 Letter from TWN, to the Thai Minister of Health (Feb. 23, 2007). This was reprinted in the White Paper 2007, *supra* note 5.

43 KEI, an NGO, was created in 2006 to continue work undertaken earlier by the Consumer Project on Technology. This think tank and advocacy organization has been extensively working on access to medicines, including tremendous efforts on compulsory licensing of patents. *See KEI's Mission*, Knowledge Ecology International, https://www.keionline.org/about/mission (last visited May 30, 2019).

44 *Thailand's Compulsory Licensing Controversy*, Knowledge Ecology Int'l, https://www.keionline.org/25989 (last visited May 30, 2019).

45 Letter from Consumer Project on Technology, to the Thai Minister of Health (Dec. 11, 2006). This was reprinted in the White Paper 2007, *supra* note 5.

46 Letter from Clinton Foundation to the Thai Minister of Public Health (Feb. 16, 2007). This was reprinted in the White Paper 2007, *supra* note 5.

47 Jonathan Head, *Thailand Takes on Drugs Giants*, BBC (Apr. 26, 2007, 21:09 GMT), http://news.bbc.co.uk/1/hi/world/asia-pacific/6587379.stm (last visited Nov. 5, 2019).

48 Editorial, *Theft in Thailand*, Wall St. J. (Feb. 10, 2007, 12:01 AM), https://www.wsj.com/articles/SB117097198633602800.

attack on property rights" in its editorials and described Thailand's supporters as "anti-patent hooligans."[49] Other journals hinted that Thailand was violating international law.[50]

Counteractions also came from Western governments. In March 2007, US Senators urged USTR to respond strongly to Thailand, expressing worry that such a practice might initiate new policies to expropriate patents without any significant public health grounds.[51] In April 2007, USTR's condemnation stated that Thailand's CLs represented "a serious concern" and placed it on its Special 301 Priority Watch List.[52] In July 2007, USTR removed some Thai products from the Generalized System of Preferences (GSP) program.[53] Meanwhile, Ralph Boyce, the US Ambassador at that time, wrote to Thailand's Prime Minister, criticizing Thai decisions.[54] Though the ambassador agreed that WTO members could make appropriate use of flexibilities for urgent situations, he asserted that "these decisions should not be made lightly and only as a last resort."[55] He also requested the Ministry of Public Health to involve the pharmaceutical companies in the decision-making process in an open and transparent manner,[56] although such a request is not mandatory under Article 31 of the TRIPS Agreement.

Although the Thai government's CLs were issued by the Ministry of Public Health, the Ministry of Commerce was unavoidably involved. In July 2007, the European Union (EU) Trade Commissioner, Peter Mandelson, wrote to

49 Editorial, *Bangkok's Drug War Goes Global*, THE WALL ST. J. (Mar. 7, 2007, 12:01 AM), https://www.wsj.com/articles/SB117322181443628799.

50 David Batty, *Clinton Backs Violation of Aids Drug Patents*, THE GUARDIAN (May 9, 2007), https://www.theguardian.com/world/2007/may/09/aids.davidbatty (last visited Nov. 5, 2019); Amy Kazmin & Andrew Jack, *Thai Government to Break Drug Patents*, FIN. TIMES (Nov. 3, 2007), https://www.ft.com/content/6889bbbc-ac98-11db-9318-0000779e2340?mhq5j=e2.

51 Letter from US Senators J. I. Lieberman, T. R. Carper, R. Menendez, D. Feinstein, & F. Lautenberg to US Trade Representative Susan Schwab (Mar. 20, 2007), http://www.keionline.org/misc-docs/liebermanplus4.pdf (last visited Nov. 5, 2019).

52 2007 SPECIAL 301 REPORT, *supra* note 34.

53 Wibulpolprasert et al., *supra* note 11, at 5. The Generalized System of Preferences (GSP), a United States trade program established by the Trade Act of 1974, provides preferential duty-free entry to the United States market for certain products originating from designated beneficiary developing countries. To qualify for GSP, a beneficial country must meet certain requirements, including providing adequate and effective IPRs protection for United States companies. For more detailed information on GSP, see *Generalized System of Preferences*, USTR, https://ustr.gov/issue-areas/trade-development/preference-programs/generalized-system-preference-gsp (last visited May 22, 2019).

54 Letter from Ralph Boyce, US Ambassador, to Surayud Chulanont, Thailand's Prime Minister (July 20, 2007), cited in *Timeline for US-Thailand Compulsory License Dispute*, INFOJUSTICE (Apr. 3, 2009) http://infojustice.org/wp-content/uploads/2012/11/pijip-thailand-timeline.pdf (last visited Nov. 5, 2019).

55 *Id.*

56 *Id.*

Thailand's Minister of Commerce, complaining about the Thai approach.[57] While recognizing the right to grant compulsory licensing, the letter indicated that this legal measure should be used as a last resort.[58] He requested the Minister of Commerce to review the policy in liaison with the Ministers of Foreign Affairs and Public Health, and to enter into negotiations with patent holders.[59] This is a classic example of how trade pressure can potentially modify the IPRs policies of a developing country. The close interconnection between trade and IPRs is getting clearer, particularly in the modern economy, where countries are becoming economically interdependent and also want to ensure cooperation in different areas, including IPRs.

At the same time, Switzerland – home to Novartis and Roche, two pharmaceutical companies that were targets of Thai CLs – sent an aide-memoire to the Thai government.[60] The aide memoire, which is an informal diplomatic message, expressed the Swiss government's concern over Thai actions.[61] It stated that if compulsory licensing was "used not only in emergencies and other exceptional cases, but systematically for all kinds of pharmaceuticals," patent research would be detrimentally affected. Switzerland recommended negotiations as a cooperative and constructive solution.[62] Similarly, other patent owners such as Sanofi-Aventis, patent owners of *Plavix*, threatened legal action against Cadila, an Indian company that was about to supply its generic version to Thailand.[63] Owing to prospective litigation, Cadila postponed the delivery to the GPO until June 2008, though its CL had been issued in January 2007.[64]

Meanwhile, Novartis, another patent owner, warned the Thai government that its decision might have an adverse effect on 900 leukemia patients receiving treatment through the company's philanthropic program.[65] This warning seemed more effective, as the assistance centers and physicians working in

57 Letter from Peter Mandelson, European Union Trade Commissioner, to Thailand's Minister of Commerce (July 10, 2007), https://www.keionline.org/wp-content/uploads/mandelson07102007.pdf (last visited Nov. 5, 2019).

58 *Id.*

59 *Id.*

60 Aide Memorie, *Compulsory Licenses in Thailand on Pharmaceuticals Under Patent Protection*, KEIONLINE (Feb. 25, 2008), http://www.keionline.org/misc-docs/1/swiss2thailand_cl.pdf (last visited Apr. 28, 2020).

61 *Id.*

62 *Id.*

63 Rupali Mukherjee, *Pharma Firms Under US Pressure to Stop Generic Sale*, TIMES OF INDIA (Feb. 3, 2008), https://timesofindia.indiatimes.com/business/india-business/Pharma-firms-under-US-pressure-to-stop-generic-sale/articleshow/2777692.cms (last visited Apr. 28, 2020).

64 *Id.*

65 Gaëlle Krikorian, *The Politics of Patents: Conditions of Implementation of Public Health Policy in Thailand*, *in* POLITICS OF INTELLECTUAL PROPERTY CONTESTATION OVER THE OWNERSHIP, USE, AND CONTROL OF KNOWLEDGE AND INFORMATION, 34 (Sebastian Haunss & Kenneth C. Shadlen eds., 2009).

this program in Thailand also expressed concern about the Thai government's decision.[66]

In its first retaliatory reaction to the Thai government's grant of a CL, Abbott, the patent-holding company of *Kaletra* – one of the medicines subject to Thailand's compulsory licensing[67] – took the most antagonistic approach of withdrawing all seven new patent registrations of medicines from the Thai market, including the newest version of *Kaletra* (*Aluvia*), the HIV/AIDS drug carefully formulated to work effectively in tropical climates like Thailand's.[68] Abbot also sued Act Up-Paris, a group of HIV/AIDS patients, for attempting to overload the company's website by multiplying simultaneous connections.[69] This was the first time that a pharmaceutical company sued a nongovernmental organization (NGO). This action not only expressed the hostile attitude of Abbott but also demonstrated that the battle of compulsory licensing had gone far beyond the conventional boundaries of legal issues. Abbott's withdrawal of new medicines generated a public outcry and sparked protests in Thailand, and led to consumer boycotts of Abbott products globally.[70] Some NGOs participated in Abbott's annual shareholders' meeting to confront the company's actions.[71] The MSF described Abbott's decision as an "immoral act"[72] while other NGOs filed a complaint to the Thai Trade Competition Commission, alleging that Abbott's withdrawal of new medicine registrations violated the Trade Competition Act.[73] However, the company was held not to be in breach of the Act.[74] Eventually, Abbott allowed *Aluvia* to be sold in Thailand, but only if no CL were imposed on *Aluvia*.[75] Abbott withheld six other new drugs from entry into the Thai market.[76]

66 *Id.*

67 Compulsory License for Kaletra, *supra* note 25.

68 Stephanie Skees, *Thai-ing Up the TRIPS Agreement: Are Compulsory Licenses the Answer to Thailand's AIDS Epidemic?* 19 Pace Int'l L. Rev. 233, 242 (2007).

69 Krikorian, *supra* note 65, at 46.

70 Thomas Fuller, *Thailand Takes on Drug Industry, and May be Winning,* N.Y. Times (Apr. 11, 2007), http://www.nytimes.com/2007/04/11/world/asia/11iht-pharma.4.5240049.html?pagewanted=alland_r=0 (last visited Apr. 28, 2020).

71 Jiraporn Limpananont & Kannika Kijtiwatchakul, *TRIPS Flexibilities in Thailand: Between Law and Politics, in* Access to Knowledge in the Age of Intellectual Property, 447 (Gaëlle Krikorian & Amy Kapczynski eds., 2010).

72 Darren Schuettler, *Angered U.S. Firm Excludes Thailand from New Drugs*, Reuters (Mar. 14, 2007), https://www.reuters.com/article/us-thailand-drugs-abbott/angered-u-s-firm-excludes-thailand-from-new-drugs-idUSBKK27714620070314 (last visited Apr. 28, 2020).

73 R. Ian McEwin & Sakda Thanitcul, *Thailand: Medicines, Competition Law and Compulsory Licensing*, *in* Intellectual Property, Competition Law and Economics in Asia, 296, ch. 12 (R. Ian McEwin ed., 2011).

74 *Id.*

75 Skees, *supra* note 68, at 242.

76 *Id.*

Thailand's compulsory licensing also sparked criticism from several quarters. NGO group USA for Innovation condemned the postcoup government for turning Thailand into a dictatorship like Burma by issuing CLs.[77] However, other health-related NGOs revealed that this group was the partner of a public relations company, with their most important clients being Abbott and the ousted Prime Minister Thaksin.[78] Whatever the truth of the accusation, both sides pushed the limits to the extreme. Similarly, academics such as Bate condemned Thailand's lack of dialogue with pharmaceutical companies and described the CLs as "attacks" on the industry and the worldwide patent system.[79] Most interestingly, in 2011, well-known Thai IP expert Kuanpoth warned against compulsory licensing and suggested that developing countries should consider this option carefully before adopting it.[80] However, he contradicted himself in 2014 by praising these licenses and strongly recommending other developing countries to follow suit.[81] Lybecker and Fowler opined that, in Thailand's case, compulsory licensing was invoked to serve industrial policy (the GPO) rather than public health policy.[82] Adelman expressly described the Thai actions as "theft."[83]

## An Evaluation of Thailand's Policy from a Legal Perspective

Thailand's government use licenses were subject to strong criticism for many reasons. This section evaluates Thai policy, taking each criticism in turn.

### *Justification for the Thai Government's Policies*

The Thai CLs were issued under Section 51 of the Thai Patent Act for a public health noncommercial purpose.[84] However, patent advocates felt that this justification was open to serious doubts.[85] That the government could use licensing as a solution to a lack of finances failed to convince critics. Many believed that

77 Limpananont & Kijtiwatchakul, *supra* note 71, at 444.

78 *Id.*

79 Roger Bate, Thailand and the Drug Patent Wars, American Enterprise Institute (Apr. 4, 2007), https://www.aei.org/wp-content/uploads/2011/10/20070404_HPO.pdf (last visited Apr. 28, 2020).

80 Jakkrit Kuanpoth, *Proceed with Caution on Compulsory Licensing*, Tilleke and Gibbins (Feb. 28, 2011), https://www.tilleke.com/sites/default/files/informed_counsel_vol2_no1_p3.pdf (last visited Apr. 28, 2020).

81 Jakkrit Kuanpoth, *Compulsory Licenses: Law and Practice in Thailand*, *in* Compulsory Licensing: Practical Experiences and Ways Forward, 75 (Reto M. Hilty & Kung-Chung Liu eds., 2015).

82 Lybecker & Fowler, *supra* note 2, at 229.

83 10 Hugh C. Hansen, Intellectual Property Law and Policy 961 (2008).

84 Patent Act, *supra* note 24.

85 Skees, *supra* note 68, at 244; Bate, *supra* note 79.

Thailand, having a middle-income status, could have afforded the medicines without resorting to compulsory licensing.[86]

However, nowhere among the dozen clauses of Article 31 of the TRIPS Agreement,[87] which is directly implicated in this case, stated that middle-income countries are excluded from granting CLs. Therefore, alleging that Thailand's wealth precluded its right to use CLs is an invalid argument since even developed nations have used this legal solution.[88]

The opponents also stated that while the public health-care budget was reduced by $12 million per annum,[89] the military budget increased by almost 50 percent from 2006.[90] Yet this counterargument has merit, considering the political climate when those licenses were implemented. In fact, due to frequent military coups, Thailand often increased the defense budget at the expense of other priorities.[91] But defense spending, a matter of sovereign priority, is not meant for scrutiny by other countries.

Moreover, Thailand levying a 10 percent tariff on almost all imported medicines (excluding vaccines and therapies for HIV, malaria, and thalassemia) and a 7 percent Value Added Tax on all medicines also caused price increases.[92] A World Health Organization (WHO) study in 2006 identified that taxes and duties levied on medicines, as well as markups, frequently contribute more to the final price than the actual manufacturers' price.[93] Pipes voiced the criticism that Thailand did not want to pay more for patented medicines, and described its actions of

86 *Id.* At that time (2006), the country's Gross Domestic Product (GDP) ranked 33rd among 183 nations.

87 TRIPS Agreement, *supra* note 3.

88 For examples of compulsory licensing issued in Europe on the grounds of competition law, see Case T-201/04 *Microsoft Corp. v. Comm'n*, 2007 E.C.R. II-03601; Case C-418/01 *IMS Health GmbH & Co. OHG v. NDC Health GmbH & Co. KG*, 2004 E.C.R. I-05039; Joined cases C-241/91 P & C-242/91 *P Radio Telefis Eireann ("RTE") & Indep. Television Publ'ns Ltd. ("ITP") v. Comm'n*, 1995 E.C.R. I-00743; *see also* Jerome H. Reichman & Catherine Hasenzahl, *Non-Voluntary Licensing of Patented Inventions: Historical Perspective, Legal Framework Under TRIPS, and an Overview of the Practice in Canada and the USA*, Intell. Prop. Rts. & Sustainable Dev. (2003), https://www.ictsd.org/sites/default/files/downloads/2008/06/cs_reichman_hasenzahl.pdf (last visited Apr. 28, 2020); *Recent European Union Compulsory Licenses*, Knowledge Ecology Int'l (Mar. 1, 2014), https://www.keionline.org/wp-content/uploads/Annex_B_European_Union_Compulsory_Licenses_1Mar2014_8_5x11_0.pdf (last visited Apr. 28, 2020).

89 Lybecker & Fowler, *supra* note 2, at 233.

90 Skees, *supra* note 68, at 244–45.

91 Edward Kelly, *Thailand: Compulsory Licenses. Finding a Middle Ground*, Managing IP (2011), https://www.managingip.com/article/b1kc12y5xlwl9s/finding-a-middle-ground (last visited Apr. 28, 2020).

92 Lybecker & Fowler, *supra* note 2, at 233.

93 Susanne Gelders et al., *Price, Availability and Affordability an International Comparison of Chronic Disease Medicines*, World Health Org. (2006), http://archives.who.int/medprices/CHRONICANN.pdf (last visited Apr. 28, 2020).

breaching patents as those of a "21st Century Robin Hood."[94] Some authors also arrived at the same conclusion that Thailand's CLs have very little to do with public health emergencies and much more to do with economic and political priorities.[95] Indeed, political exigencies in Thailand necessitated increasing defense spending, leading to cuts in other areas, including public health.

### *Public Noncommercial Use*

Some contend that Thailand's government use licenses did not qualify as public noncommercial licenses.[96] The source of this distrust was the GPO, the only organization which manufactured or imported the generics under CLs. It is claimed that the GPO, being a profit-making enterprise, does not qualify as "noncommercial."[97] Moreover, some authors have questioned the quality of the medicines manufactured by the GPO.[98] A 2005 study by Thailand's Mahidol University, for instance, found that resistance to GPO-VIR – a copy HIV treatment GPO made – grew significantly in the previous few years.[99] Even after four years of pretesting, the WHO refused to list GPO-VIR in its prequalification program.[100] Since 2002, the WHO has recommended that this medicine should not be sold outside of Thailand, because the country had failed to prove its bioequivalence.[101]

From a health-care perspective, drug resistance will lead to higher treatment costs, thus undermining the justification for Thai compulsory licensing.[102] The WHO explains that when such a deleterious effect reduces the efficacy of current first-line treatments of ARVs in some patients, they need to be switched to more expensive second-line – or even third-line – regimes.[103] Higher levels of drug

94 Sally C. Pipes, *Thailand's Misuse of 'Compulsory Licensing' Allowed Corrupt Officials to Steal Millions*, Pac. Research Inst. (Mar. 31, 2008), https://www.pacificresearch.org/thailands-misuse-of-compulsory-licensing-allowed-corrupt-officials-to-steal-millions/ (last visited Apr. 28, 2020).

95 *See Id.*; Lybecker & Fowler, *supra* note 2, at 229.

96 Lybecker & Fowler, *supra* note 2, at 233; Skees, *supra* note 68; Bate, *supra* note 79.

97 Lybecker & Fowler, *supra* note 2, at 232.

98 *Safe at Any Cost?*, Asia Sentinel (Jan. 4, 2007), https://www.asiasentinel.com/society/safe-at-any-cost/ (last visited Apr. 28, 2020).

99 Ruengpung Sutthent et al., *HIV-1 Drug Resistance in Thailand: Before and After National Access to Antiretroviral Program*, 34 J. Clin. Virol. 4, 272–76 (2006).

100 *Safe at Any Cost*, *supra* note 98.

101 *Id.*

102 At Thailand's 10th National Seminar on AIDS in Bangkok in 2005, it was reported that the resistance rate of locally made GPO-VIR antiretroviral drug treatment had grown dramatically over the past couple of years and was expected to get worse. *See U.S. Centers for Disease Control & Prevention, Thailand: HIV Drugs Losing Their Power*, BodyPro (July 19, 2005), https://www.thebodypro.com/article/thailand-hiv-drugs-losing-power (last visited Apr. 28, 2020).

103 *Development of the Global Action Plan on HIV Drug Resistance, 2017–2021*, World Health Org., https://www.who.int/hiv/drugresistance/hivdr-action-plan-2017-2021/en/ (last visited Apr. 28, 2020).

resistance need more resources to treat the same number of patients, or fewer patients could be treated with the same resources.[104]

Further, the historical corruption within the GPO also raised doubt on whether Thai compulsory licensing was granted for the public purpose. In 2002, the GPO was found to have misappropriated approximately $13 million from the government over the previous four years.[105] It was criticized for selling about 60 percent of its medical products to government agencies at inflated prices.[106] Some products were marked up by 1000 percent.[107] Consequently, the government's motivation and its claim to be promoting public health were questionable.

Neither the TRIPS Agreement nor the Doha Declaration[108] defines "public non-commercial use," hence national laws have complete freedom in its interpretation. Even when a CL is issued to a private entity, it is largely meant as an intrusion into private rights *for public benefit*. Thai licenses were also issued by the government to render a benefit to the nation. But they were extraordinary in that such licenses only applied to those covered by public health insurance, as stated in the grants. Those who could afford out-of-pocket payment were excluded. Although many attacked the profit-making nature of the GPO, it is important to draw a clear distinction between the character of the entity which undertakes the CLs and the nature of those licenses. As long as a CL aims to serve society, it is regarded as not-for-profit, though the entity exploiting the license is a commercial entity. That was the case of the GPO. It is submitted that the GPO's questionable role could have been dispelled had the government's policy enabled more competition among license holders and/or patent owners while ensuring medicine quality. The GPO's monopoly position became controversial and there was a lack of transparency in implementing the compulsory licensing.

### *The Legitimacy of the Thai Postcoup Government*

Another factor causing great controversy over Thailand's government use is the presence of the military junta. The postcoup government, condemned for ignoring IPRs, was accused of using populist rhetoric and policies to enhance

104 *Id.*
105 Skees, *supra* note 68, at 246.
106 *Id.*
107 Bate, *supra* note 79.
108 World Trade Organization, Declaration on the TRIPS Agreement and Public Health, WTO Doc. WT/MIN(01)/DEC/2 (2001), https://www.wto.org/english/thewto_e/minist_e/min01_e/mindecl_trips_e.htm, (last visited Nov. 6, 2019) [hereinafter Doha Declaration]. The Doha Declaration recognized the gravity of the public health problems afflicting many least-developed and developing countries and hence reaffirmed flexibility of TRIPS member states in circumventing patent rights for better access to essential medicines.

its popularity.[109] Also, owing to the coup d'état, with *carte blanche* in decision-making, the Thai Minister of Health did not consult other ministries.[110] The interim government was accused of irresponsibility while granting several CLs, as it was not accountable to anyone.[111] Such criticism is valid, as the country's policy changed right after a democratic government was elected in 2007. After the election, the newly appointed Minister of Health announced he would reconsider the CLs – but did not revoke any. He was also alleged to have removed the Chairman of the GPO, a key supporter of the compulsory licensing.[112]

One could argue that the military government was not recognized by law. Yet the uniqueness of Thai politics – the high frequency of coups – might invite a rethinking of the issue. With a long history of military regimes and military interventions, coups d'état have been intrinsic in Thai politics. Political uncertainty raises questions on the purpose behind Thai licensing, yet military coups regularly occur in the country's politics.[113]

### *Scope of Thai Licenses*

The scope of the Thai government's use licensing was considered wider than the TRIPS Agreement because it covered chronic diseases.[114] The CL for *Plavix* treating cardiovascular diseases was considered a breach of patent, since it is assumed that compulsory licensing is permitted only for epidemics and infectious diseases. Heart diseases – being chronic conditions – were considered ineligible, hence the CL for *Plavix* was regarded to be inappropriate, as it signified a new era where CLs would be authorized even to treat illnesses other than infectious diseases.[115]

Bate argued that as less than 1 percent (approximately 300,000) of the Thai population suffered from heart diseases, it could not be considered as a public health emergency in Thailand.[116] Similarly, Skees asserts that the CL constituted

109 James Hookway & Nicholas Zamiska, *Thai Showdown Spotlights Threat to Drug Patents*, WALL STREET J. (Apr. 24, 2007), http://www.wsj.com/articles/SB117735181629579246 (last visited June 20, 2019).

110 This situation contrasts with that of Brazil, where there was discussion between ministries. In 2005, Brazil's intention of issuing a compulsory license of Kaletra did not materialize partly due to the internal conflict between two of Brazil's Ministries. JENNIFER CHAN, POLITICS IN THE CORRIDOR OF DYING: AIDS ACTIVISM AND GLOBAL HEALTH GOVERNANCE, 99 (2015).

111 Skees, *supra* note 68, at 240.

112 *Thai Govt Purge Indicates CL Shift*, THE PHARMA LETTER (March 3, 2008), https://www.thepharmaletter.com/article/update-thai-govt-purge-indicates-cl-shift (last visited May 22, 2019).

113 Between 1932 and 2014, 19 military coups and attempted coups occurred in Thailand. Nicholas Farrelly, *Thailand's Elite Coup Culture*, AUSTRALIAN INST. OF INT'L AFFAIRS (MAR. 28, 2014), http://www.internationalaffairs.org.au/australianoutlook/thailands-elite-coup-culture (last visited Apr. 28, 2020).

114 Fieldman, *supra* note 2, at 151–54; Skees, *supra* note 68, at 243.

115 Fieldman, *supra* note 2, at 151.

116 BATE, *supra* note 79.

"a contempt for patents rather than a genuine effort to relieve a public health crisis."[117] McGill characterized the Thai action as an example of failure in the widespread use of compulsory licensing.[118]

This view is factually improper, both from the health-care and legal perspectives; limiting a CL to a number of specific diseases goes against the current understanding of the shifting global burden of diseases, from common communicable to chronic diseases. According to the WHO, ischemic heart disease was the world's most common cause of death in 2015.[119] Upper middle–income countries, including Thailand, displayed the same tendency belying popular belief that infectious diseases are the main cause of fatality there.[120] A similar shift is seen in low-income countries, albeit to a lesser extent.[121]

Pharmaceutical companies need to change their products and opinions, balancing profits with social responsibility, in line with demographic changes in diseases occurring in developing nations. The variation in each country's epidemiological profile requires individual analysis. Developing countries are far from being homogeneous, and such an understanding should also be applied in the health context. For example, HIV/AIDS is still a health emergency in sub-Saharan countries, but not in Brazil or Thailand.

From the legal perspective, the arguments for a limited scope of diseases subject to a CL are flawed. It is reiterated that all Thai CLs were issued in accordance with Section 51 of the Thai Patent Act,[122] under the rubric of "public non-commercial use" and not national emergency. Therefore, the argument that heart disease does not constitute an emergency is invalid. But in this debate, the term "public non-commercial use" drew less attention, while "national emergency" drew greater emphasis.[123]

One document, commonly (but falsely) mentioned to justify exclusion of chronic diseases from using such licenses, is the Doha Declaration.[124] Some authors insisted that only HIV/AIDS, tuberculosis, malaria, and other epidemics are sufficient grounds.[125] However, it is reasserted that the Doha

117 Skees, *supra* note 68, at 243.

118 Aileen M. McGill, *Compulsory Licensing of Patented Pharmaceuticals: Why a WTO Administrative Body Should Determine What Constitutes a Public Health Crisis Under The Doha Declaration*, 10 Wake Forest Intell. Prop. L. J., 89 (2010).

119 *The Top 10 Causes of Death*, World Health Org. (May 24, 2018), https://www.who.int/news-room/fact-sheets/detail/the-top-10-causes-of-death (last visited Apr. 28, 2020).

120 *Id.*

121 *Id.*

122 Patent Act, *supra* note 24.

123 Kelly, *supra* note 91, at 67.

124 Doha Declaration, *supra* note 108.

125 Ronald A. Cass, *Compulsory Licensing of Intellectual Property: The Exception That Ate the Rule?*, Wash. Legal Found. (Sept. 7, 2007), https://www.wlf.org/2007/09/07/publishing/compulsory-licensing-of-intellectual-property-the-exception-that-ate-the-rule (last visited Apr. 28, 2020); McGill, *supra* note 118, at 84.

Declaration does not intend to limit the diseases subject to a CL.[126] Paragraph 5 of the Doha Declaration clearly mentions: "HIV/AIDS, tuberculosis, malaria"[127] are mere examples of public health crises. Since this list is not exhaustive, the claim that chronic diseases cannot justify the use of CLs is an untenable distortion of the Doha Declaration.[128] Nor does the TRIPS Agreement restrict the type of disease eligible for compulsory licensing.

Considering the above analysis, the author asserts that by law, Thai compulsory licensing of *Plavix* was entirely consistent with the TRIPS Agreement. Nevertheless, any government planning to issue a CL should carefully assess whether a victory in the patent battle might be overshadowed by the negative or deleterious effects associated with compulsory licensing. Such effects could include patent holders' retaliation and/or trade sanctions of the US.

### *Prior Negotiation*

Article 31(b) of the TRIPS Agreement mandates that the prospective licensee should consult first with the patentee for acquiring a voluntary license (VL) "on reasonable commercial terms and conditions." When such an effort made "within a reasonable period" is fruitless, the licensee can proceed to the CL. However, the law does not define what constitutes "reasonableness."[129] It should be noted that in the case of "national emergency," "other circumstances of extreme urgency," or "public non-commercial uses," the requirement of prior negotiation can be waived, meaning that the government can proceed with compulsory licensing without holding talks with the patent holder.[130] All the Thai CLs were issued under the "public non-commercial use" criterion, by which prior negotiation may be waived and compulsory licensing activated immediately.[131] Therefore, the patentees and other concerned parties directly contravened Article 31 of the TRIPS Agreement *ex post facto* by stating that prior negotiation should have been conducted.

Further, though consultation is not mandatory, Thailand's government claimed it had been in discussion with the pharmaceutical companies since 2004.

126 Doha Declaration, *supra* note 108, ¶ 5(b) (stating that "Each Member has the right to grant compulsory licenses and the freedom to determine the grounds upon which such licenses are granted.").

127 *Id.* ¶ 5(c) (stating that "Each Member has the right to determine what constitutes a national emergency or other circumstances of extreme urgency, it being understood that public health crises, including those relating to HIV/AIDS, tuberculosis, malaria and other epidemics, can represent a national emergency or other circumstances of extreme urgency").

128 *Id.*

129 TRIPS Agreement, *supra* note 3, at art. 31(b).

130 *Id.*

131 Compulsory License for Efavirenz, *supra* note 23; Compulsory License for Kaletra, *supra* note 25; Compulsory License for Plavix, *supra note 26*; Compulsory License for Letrozole, *supra* note *31*.

Regarding cancer drugs, it argued that although the Minister of Health could have exercised his authorization immediately, he still had consultations with the right owners before final actions were taken. Although the Thai government's prior negotiation with the patent holders is legally waived under the TRIPS Agreement and the Thai Patent Act,[132] patent-holding companies were unhappy that the government did not attempt to negotiate a reasonable price. Steinbrook criticized the Thai government's unilateral action for rejecting dialogues with the right owners, asserting it could have resulted in discounted prices or VLs.[133] A representative of the Pharmaceutical Research and Manufacturers of America opined that there were many alternative ways to increase access to medicines, but Thailand chose only compulsory licensing.[134] The representative contended that the negotiating process with Thailand was a mere formality, because either the patent owners did not have any voice or the government was not in a genuine dialogue with them.[135] Merck, patent owner of *Efavirenz*, stated that the company came to know about the decision only 2 days in advance, whereas the normal consultation period is 90 days.[136] Clearly, the averment of "lack of prior negotiation" is another common but false charge against Thailand.

### *Adequate Remuneration*

Under Article 31(h) of the TRIPS Agreement, the patent owner is entitled to "adequate remuneration" that takes into account the "economic value of the authorization."[137] However, the TRIPS Agreement fails to provide any criteria for determining such remuneration.[138] The 0.5 percent royalty that Thailand offered was considered too low.[139] Calling it an embarrassment, Adelman stated the Thai government should not have made this kind of offer.[140] James Love, a health activist who supported Thailand's licensing, also suggested that the royalty was inadequate.[141] The patent owners, nevertheless, made no counteroffers.[142] This prompts a question: why did the pharmaceutical companies not negotiate or appeal to the Board of Patents when they were entitled to do so?[143] The patent holders, in all probability, tried to avoid establishing a precedent of royalty standard that others were likely to use in future. By compromising on a government-stipulated

132 TRIPS Agreement, *supra* note 3; Patent Act, *supra* note 24.
133 Robert Steinbrook, *Thailand and the Compulsory Licensing of Efavirenz*, 6 New Eng. J. Med. 356, 544–46 (Feb. 8, 2007).
134 Hansen, *supra* note 83, at 955.
135 *Id.* at 954, 958.
136 Kazmin & Jack, *supra* note 50.
137 TRIPS Agreement, *supra* note 3, at art. 31(h).
138 *Id.*
139 Skees, *supra* note 68, at 254.
140 Hansen, *supra* note 83, at 958.
141 *Id.*
142 *Id.*
143 Patent Act, *supra* note 24.

remuneration, pharmaceutical companies would effectively be facilitating more such licenses. For patent advocates, the optimal solution is to preclude compulsory licensing, rather than to negotiate terms and conditions. In the patent holders' view, compulsory licensing is nonnegotiable; it is a dead-end and cancellation of the license is the only solution. Accordingly, pharmaceutical companies did not propose an alternative remuneration, but focused on eliminating CLs.

In fact, the author opines that there was no bargaining process in the context of Thailand because the government and the patent holders held completely different expectations about the final result. While the government shaped the negotiation around the central idea of how to use compulsory licensing to obtain price cuts, the patent holders wanted absolute rejection.

The topic of adequate remuneration is conspicuously missing in scholarly literature about CLs. When a CL is granted, it is solely the ground for the grant that is in focus; neither the remuneration nor the terms and conditions are worthy of discussion. This is mainly because the existing global framework has given inadequate attention to royalty payments. For example, the Paris Convention,[144] the first international treaty regulating IP law – including compulsory licensing – does not even mandate the requirement of remuneration.[145] Additionally, the concept of "adequate amount" is not defined under the TRIPS Agreement. International guidelines on this matter do not attract public attention. How much a granting country pays to the patentee in order to achieve "adequacy" is left to the parties. When developing countries' governments have tried to issue compulsory licensing for a public health purpose, patent holders have avoided negotiating royalty rates, while international law fails to outline a comprehensive process or a set of detailed conditions, leaving the matter to the discretion of national governments.[146] Hence opposing views on defining "adequate remuneration" are inevitable.

144 Paris Convention for the Protection of Industrial Property, March 20, 1888, as revised at the Stockholm Revision Conference, July 14, 1967, 21 U.S.T. 1538, T.I.A.S. No. 6903, 828 U.N.T.S. 305 [hereinafter Paris Convention].

145 *Id.* at art. 5A.

146 Ho, *supra* note 10, at 138 (discussing the difficulties of setting out an adequate remuneration for TRIPS compulsory licensing). Some international organizations have proposed different methods to calculate the remuneration. UNCTAD suggested the adequate amount can be based on the ordinary course of trade, on the patent owners' justification for their request, on the benchmark established by an independent international organization, or on a percentage of its income from sales of the licensed product. *See* UNCTAD-ICTSD, Resource Book on TRIPS and development, 476 (2004), https://unctad.org/en/PublicationsLibrary/ictsd2005d1_en.pdf (last visited Apr. 28, 2020). UNDP recommended that the normal rates could be set at 4 percent and adjusted within the range of 2 percent, i.e. from 2 to 6 percent. The 1998 Japan Patent Office Guidelines (for government-owned drug patents) specify royalties between 2 and 4 percent of the generic product price, vary by up to 2 percent, in a range of 0–6 percent. *See also* James Love, *Remuneration Guidelines for Non-voluntary Use of a Patent on Medical Technologies*, World Health Org. (2005), https://www.who.int/hiv/amds/WHOTCM2005.1_OMS.pdf (last visited Apr. 28, 2020).

## An Evaluation of Thailand's Policy from an Economic Perspective

In 2009, Thailand conducted a study to assess the economic impacts of its compulsory licensing policies.[147] However, its scope was limited because the generic versions of three anticancer drugs – *Letrozole*, *Docetaxel*, and *Erlotinib* – were not yet imported into the country. Accordingly, the 2009 study could only make a projection,[148] which resulted in the inaccuracy of the overall assessment. Despite these shortcomings, Thailand is arguably the only country that has attempted to ensure transparency after compulsory licensing was implemented. This could be an effort to compensate for its nontransparency during its implementation of the issued licenses between 2006 and 2008.

Following the 2009 study, similar research was carried out in 2011–2012 when some CLs expired, allowing a more comprehensive and accurate assessment.[149] From 2007 to 2012, it was estimated that Thailand's policy saved the country $370 million.[150] However, there were wide discrepancies among the medicines' economic impact. For example, *Efavirenz* received the lowest discount but was used by the greatest number of patients. It thus had the greatest economic effect.[151] The cost saving of *Efavirenz* was between $116.45 and $118.84 million.[152] But *Erlotinib*, a cancer drug, and *Clopidogrel*, a heart disease medicine, had minimal impact due to fewer recipients.[153] *Clopidogrel* saved the government around $22 million, while the savings on *Erlotinib* was the smallest: between $6.33 million and $7.57 million.[154] If the Thai government could have estimated the significant differences in economic savings between medicines, it might have chosen better alternatives for medicines with smaller impacts. These figures lead to an important conclusion: selection of drugs plays a key role in optimizing the benefit of CLs.

The data revealed that the manufacturing of generics in Thailand encountered substantial delay.[155] It took the generic equivalent of *Kaletra* one year and *Clopidogrel* 20 months to be delivered.[156] Such delays occurred because some patent-holding companies threatened legal action against the generic companies

147 Yamabha et al., *supra* note 9.

148 *Id.* at 14, 30–32.

149 Adun Mohara et al., *Impact of the Introduction of Government Use Licenses on the Drug Expenditure on Seven Medicines in Thailand*, 15 Value in Health S95 (2012); Inthira Yamabhai et al., *Government Use Licenses in Thailand: An Assessment of the Health and Economic Impacts*, 28 Glob. Health 7, 1 (2011); Wibulpolprasert et al., *supra* note 11.

150 Mohara et al., *supra* note 149.

151 *Id.* at S98.

152 *Id.*

153 *Id.*

154 *Id.*

155 Inthira Yamabhai et al., *Government Use Licenses in Thailand: An Assessment of the Health and Economic Impacts*, 28 Glob. Health 7, 3 (2011).

156 *Id.*

that were about to supply the low-cost medicines to Thailand. *Efavirenz* had the shortest delay, as the generic from India was imported within one month after the grant.[157] In essence, the successful grant of a CL might merely remain a moral victory if practical challenges cannot be defeated.

## Conclusions

Thailand has provided a very fine example of how law and politics are strongly and inevitably intertwined in government use licensing. The distinctive presence of politics shaped this into a very exceptional case when compared with other country case studies. Thailand's compulsory licensing granted by a postcoup government was seen as a solution for bridging financial shortage resulting from its political turmoil, rather than an appropriate means to reduce public health costs. The backlash caused by the government's action had less to do with legal issues than with the rationale behind its decisions. Although Thai compulsory licensing complied with the TRIPS Agreement, the ulterior motives of the government, nevertheless, remain questionable.

Yet Thailand also serves as a classic example of how the use of CLs can create a melding of different versions of truth and fallacy. All the details are unclear and ambiguous, so it is no easy task to extract facts from biased opinions presented by both sides. Also, it dramatically demonstrates how patents and CLs pertaining to access to medicines cause heated confrontations on many fronts: political, economic, and media.

By publishing two White Papers in 2007 and 2008, Thailand made great efforts to explain the validity of its decisions in great detail. Consequently, its actions were hailed "as a model of gentleness and transparency" and "generosity and courage," since Thailand was not obliged to explain its actions.[158] However, it is equally true that these papers were published *ex post facto*, i.e. *after* the grant of compulsory licensing in order to allay the right owners' mounting concerns, and also to present Thailand's version to the world, possibly to garner public support. One can only speculate that the Thai government possibly did not fully anticipate the negative reactions arising from its decisions. Otherwise, the two White Papers could have been published before the licenses were announced.

Thailand's example also demonstrates that CLs prompt furious retaliation from patent owners. To mitigate and circumvent such situations, prior negotiation with patentees is therefore always advisable, even when not required by the TRIPS Agreement. This will convey the government's willingness to consult and also legitimize the patents' further use. Moreover, prior negotiation should be buttressed by explicitly stating that a CL could be imposed if the talks fail to reach a consensus or cause substantial delays.

157 *Id.*
158 *Q&A Session on Thai White Paper*, KNOWLEDGE ECOLOGY INT'L (Mar. 8, 2007), https://www.keionline.org/25973 (last visited Apr. 28, 2020).

Remarkably, by extending CLs to chronic disease medications – albeit provoking controversy – Thailand has indicated the possibility of similar CLs in the near future. Chronic diseases have an even greater economic impact on developing countries than HIV/AIDS. If pharmaceutical companies and developed nations want to avoid compulsory licensing, they should anticipate those needs and give the poor greater access to medicines. The truth regarding the decision to grant CLs remains unclear in the Thai case, but the underlying public health pressures driving similar decisions in other countries may lead all the players to take unambiguous stances and formulate a mutually acceptable *modus operandi*.

A final observation: patent advocates expound the very restrictive view on compulsory licensing – that financial constraints can be removed by means other than granting CLs (including by eliminating all taxes or allocating more funds), but not by "taking away" the patentees' private rights. Patent-holding companies have put up strong resistance whenever the legal mechanism of compulsory licensing was employed, thus repulsing any further discussion. That leads to a question: *can* a country issue a CL if its people cannot afford the patented medicines? Prima facie, this question seems too easy to answer. Under global law, yes, it can. If one looks a little deeper, however, this practice is more complex, dubious, and cumbersome than in legal theory. This chapter on Thailand has further emphasized that impediments – such as retaliation from patent-holding companies and economic coercion of countries supporting those companies – are magnified when the market is much smaller and the licensee country is less significant.

# 14 United States

## Unilateral Norm Setting Using Special 301

*Michael Palmedo**

### Introduction

Every year since 1989, the Office of the United States Trade Representative (USTR) has released the Special 301 Report, which identifies countries that "deny adequate and effective protection of intellectual property (IP) rights or deny fair and equitable market access to U.S. persons who rely on IP protection."[1] USTR is obligated to publish the report annually under the Trade Act.[2] The report classifies countries according to the seriousness of their alleged shortcomings. USTR designates countries it finds to "have the most onerous or egregious acts, policies, or practices and whose acts, policies, or practices have the greatest adverse impact (actual or potential) on the relevant U.S. products" as Priority Foreign Countries (PFCs).[3] Designation of a country as a PFC triggers a Trade Act investigation, which, in turn, can lead to sanctions.[4] A country may also be placed on a "Priority Watch List" (PWL) or "Watch List" (WL), which indicates that the United States will further engage with it regarding the policy or policies at issue. Countries on the PWL or WL are usually the subject of further diplomatic and trade pressures to change their domestic policies.[5] Some countries, even if removed from these lists, may feature in the reports for being monitored under Section 306, and some receive Out-Of-Cycle Reviews, which are more detailed reviews of the IP or market access policies.

The Omnibus Trade and Competitiveness Act of 1988 created the Special 301 Review. At the time, the Guaranteed Agreement on Tariffs and Trade (GATT)

* The author wishes to thank Sri Ragavan (Texas A&M University Law School) and Jonathan Kimball (Association for Affordable Medicines) for their comments.

1 Office of the United States Trade Representative, *Request for Comments and Notice of a Public Hearing Regarding the 2020 Special 301 Review*, FEDERAL REGISTER (Dec. 23, 2019), https://www.federalregister.gov/documents/2019/12/23/2019-27572/request-for-comments-and-notice-of-a-public-hearing-regarding-the-2020-special-301-review.

2 *See* 19 U.S.C. § 2242.

3 OFFICE OF THE U.S. TRADE REP., 2020 SPECIAL 301 REPORT, 88 (2020), https://ustr.gov/ [hereinafter 2020 Special 301 Report].

4 19 U.S.C. § 2411. *See also* Congressional Research Service, *Section 301 of the Trade Act of 1974* (Apr. 20, 2020).

5 2020 SPECIAL 301 REPORT, *supra* note 3.

loosely governed global trade, but it lacked IP rules and had only weak enforcement provisions. The Uruguay Round of trade negotiations was underway, and the United States wanted to include an agreement on IP that would be subject to stronger enforcement measures, but many countries in the Global South opposed this. Special 301 served two purposes – it threatened countries the United States accused of lacking adequate IP protections with trade sanctions, and it made a multilateral IP framework seem more appealing than facing unilateral pressure from the United States.[6] However, the establishment of the WTO did not end unilateral pressure through Special 301. The US legislation passed to join the WTO in 1994 added text to the Special 301 provision clarifying that "a country may be determined to deny adequate and effective protection of intellectual property rights, notwithstanding the fact that the foreign country may be in compliance with the specific obligations" of the WTO's Agreement on Trade-Related Aspects of Intellectual Property Rights (TRIPS Agreement).[7] The Special 301 Report has since become a tool used to coerce countries to strengthen IP rights beyond the level required by TRIPS.

To conduct its annual review, USTR leads a Special 301 Subcommittee of an interagency team called the Trade Policy Staff Committee. This group solicits comments from interested parties. Most of the comments are submitted by IP-owning firms and industry groups that ask to have certain countries included for various alleged IP deficiencies. Since 2010, it has hosted a public hearing to gather additional information to inform the report. Although the process by which the Committee receives input is clear, there is a lack of concrete criteria to determine (a) which countries are identified in the report, and (b) which countries are placed on the PWL rather than the WL.[8] However, it is clear that industry input drives much of the process. The Pharmaceutical Research and Manufacturers Association (PhRMA) submits detailed comments each year. Many of the countries PhRMA asks to have included in the report on an annual basis are regularly included in it.

This chapter reviews USTR's Special 301 Reports from 2009 to 2020, with a focus on countries identified by PhRMA in its Special 301 comments. It examines (a) trends in the identification and listing of countries; (b) the qualities of the countries included; and (c) the particular reasons for inclusion in the Special 301 Reports. Thus, this chapter focuses on the Special 301 listings that apply to IP and health care to examine how USTR's actions threaten countries that use TRIPS flexibilities to increase access to medicines, how USTR's actions threaten countries that refuse to implement TRIPS-plus IP protections, and how USTR uses Special 301 to promote trade interests outside the realm of IP.

6 Jagdish Bhagwati. In Defense of Globalization 183 (2004).
7 *See* Pub. L. 103–465, § 313(2)(B).
8 After the creation of the WTO, few countries have received a Priority Foreign Country designation, where the investigations can lead to unilateral sanctions, despite industry requests.

I reviewed the Special 301 Reports and PhRMA Special 301 Comments (as opposed to testimonies) from 2009 through 2020 and recorded the specific complaints against each country in each year that were *related to access to health care*. I did not record complaints against countries in Special 301 Reports that were unrelated to patents, data exclusivity, or medicines. This focus on IP and healthcare is not meant to downplay the significance of USTR blacklisting countries that use TRIPS flexibilities to expand access to information (which is clearly important for development).[9]

The review produced a dataset demonstrating how the prevalence of different country listings and particular policy complaints have changed over time. The dataset records USTR's specific allegations for each country and PhRMA's listing recommendations for each year, and allows one to see the changing landscape of the USTR Special 301 Report and its responsiveness to PhRMA's input. Reasons cited for including a country on a Special 301 List typically fit into one of three categories: (a) use of TRIPS flexibilities (b) poor enforcement of IP rights; and (c) inadequate market access for firms that rely on IP. The following section will explain the reasons for listing in these categories.

## Typology of Complaints Against Countries in the Special 301 Report

### *Use of TRIPS Flexibilities*

The TRIPS Agreement sets minimum global standards for IP protection, but it leaves policy space (referred to as "flexibilities") for countries to implement these standards as they see fit. USTR routinely lists countries for exercising TRIPS flexibilities to allow generic medicines. This section identifies specific health-related TRIPS flexibilities that USTR has criticized countries for using in its Special 301 Reports.

#### *Test Data Protection*

Pharmaceutical manufacturers need to obtain marketing approval from health regulators in order to sell their products in most markets. Brand name manufacturers submit clinical test data to regulators to prove the safety and effectiveness of the drug. Much of the cost of drug development is the cost of conducting clinical trials to generate this data. Generic firms typically obtain marketing approval based on the originator's clinical trial data (and their own bioequivalence data), allowing them to bring their products to the market at a lower price.

Article 39.3 of the TRIPS Agreement requires companies to protect test data against "unfair commercial use." In the U.S. and most other developed

9 Ruth Okediji, *The Limits of International Copyright Exceptions for Developing Countries*, 21 Van. J. Environ. Technol. L. 3, 689, 725 (2019).

countries, this protection takes the form of data exclusivity – a period of time during which generic firms may not apply for marketing approval based on the originator's test data. Data exclusivity is a second IP barrier to the entry of generic products to the market. It has the potential to block generic entry in situations where a patent has expired or was never in force.

The United States promotes data exclusivity as the proper way for countries to implement TRIPS Article 39.3 Hence, data exclusivity requirements are included in all the bilateral and regional trade agreements the United States has negotiated since the creation of the WTO. Countries that do not provide data exclusivity for a wide range of pharmaceutical products are often cited in the Special 301 Report for failing to adequately protect test data.

However, there is no WTO rule mandating data exclusivity. Under the TRIPS Agreement, countries are free to implement Article 39.3 in other ways, including through restrictive definitions of "unfair commercial use" and through limiting the scope of new products eligible for data protection.[10]

### *Patent Linkage*

Patent linkage refers to a mechanism for ensuring that health regulatory authorities do not approve a generic product for sale while an unexpired patent protects the drug, or a mechanism to ensure that patent owners are notified when a generic manufacture applies for regulatory approval to sell a follow-on product. In practice, patent linkage has led to problems with follow-on patents (and with patents of poor quality) delaying the entry of generics, sometimes even after the expiration of the relevant patent. Patent linkage is not required under the TRIPS Agreement but has been included in most bilateral and regional free trade agreements (FTAs) with the United States after the TRIPS Agreement took effect.

### *Scope of Patentability*

The TRIPS Agreement requires patents to be made available for inventions that are "new, involve an inventive step and are capable of industrial application."[11] However, countries are free to define what is new and what is useful according to their own laws. The ability to define patentable subject matter is one of the most important flexibilities in the TRIPS Agreement.[12]

10 Pedro Roffe & Christoph Spennemann, Resource Book on TRIPS and Development 530–531 (1995).

11 TRIPS: Agreement on Trade-Related Aspects of Intellectual Property Rights, Apr. 15, 1994, Marrakesh Agreement Establishing the World Trade Organization, Annex 1C, 1869 U.N.T.S. 299, 33 I.L.M. 1197 (1995), https://www.wto.org/english/docs_e/legal_e/27-trips_04c_e.htm#5 [hereinafter TRIPS Agreement], art. 27.

12 Carlos Correa, *Guidelines for Pharmaceutical Patent Examination: Examining Pharmaceutical Patents from a Public Health Perspective*, UNDP (2016), https://www.researchgate.net/publication/304396604_.

The scope of patentability varies between countries Many have implemented strict standards of patentability to avoid granting patents on innovations that are not completely new, like second uses of existing medical products or common derivatives of known substances (such as polymorphs and isomers).[13] Some countries have different rules for biologic inventions, which may be simulations of substances created in nature. Other countries have relatively loose standards of patentability, making it easier for firms to patent variations of existing products. The United States advocates broad standards of patentability to allow protection for a wide range of products. USTR lists countries in the Special 301 Report for alleged inadequacies regarding what a firm can patent.

### *Compulsory Licensing*

A compulsory license (CL) authorizes a third party to produce and/or sell a patented invention without the permission of the patent holder, subject to conditions listed under Article 31 of the TRIPS Agreement. CLs have been part of the international patent law landscape since at least the Paris Convention of 1883. Most countries' domestic laws have provisions for CLs, including the United States. Domestic laws typically allow CLs for a variety of public interest purposes, including (but not limited to) meeting public health needs. They often establish conditions that must be met for the issuance of a license, such as payment of royalties to the patent holder. The specific details of compulsory licensing policies vary from one country to the next.

Countries at all levels of development have issued CLs to meet health needs. Since the 1990s, many CLs have been issued for medicines needed to treat HIV/AIDS.[14] The US government has a history of opposing the issuance of CLs for medicines, through listing in the Special 301 Report as well as other means.

### *Other IP Policies Drawing Criticism in Special 301 Reports*

Special 301 Reports also include IP complaints unrelated to the use of TRIPS flexibilities. For instance, many patent offices have large backlogs; there may be few examiners, or a patent office may face other resource constraints that delay patent prosecution. Other alleged problems with patent application processes

13 A polymorph has minor modifications of the structure or chemical makeup of a molecule and is different from crystalline form. An isomer has the same molecular formula but with a different atomic arrangement. *See* Amy Kapczynksi et al., *Polymorphs and Prodrugs and Salts (Oh My!): An Empirical Analysis of "Secondary" Pharmaceutical Patents*, 7 PLoS ONE 12, e49470 (2012), https://doi.org/10.1371/journal.pone.0049470.

14 *See* TRIPS Flexibilities Database, HEALTH LAW & POLICY, http://tripsflexibilities.medicineslawandpolicy.org. *See also* Ellen t' Hoen et al., *Medicine Procurement and the Use of Flexibilities in the Agreement on Trade-Related Aspects of Intellectual Property Rights, 2001–2016*, 96 BULL. WORLD HEALTH ORGAN. 185–193 (2018), http://dx.doi.org/10.2471/BLT.17.199364.

include a lack of transparency, overly meticulous patent examination, and prosecution processes allegedly discriminating against foreign patent applicants.

Special 301 Reports also include complaints about trade secret protection and trademark squatting, which are outside the scope of this chapter.

### *Intellectual Property Enforcement*

Many of the complaints against countries in the Special 301 Report focus on the enforcement of IP, rather than IP provisions themselves. Under the WTO Dispute Settlement Understanding, countries should settle disputes related to TRIPS enforcement through the WTO's system, yet USTR alleges TRIPS noncompliance regarding enforcement for most of the countries listed. The following enforcement-related complaints are often found in Special 301 Reports and in PhRMA's comments:

- The presence of excessive counterfeit goods in the market
- Underfunded or under-resourced enforcement agencies (including police, courts, and border authorities)
- Enforcement officials (including police and border authorities) lacking *ex officio* authority to take action on their own, without the request of a right holder, for suspected IP infringement
- Penalties for IP infringement deemed insufficiently severe to have a deterrent effect
- Problems with judicial systems, including administrative delays and nontransparent proceedings
- Border enforcement deficiencies resulting in inflow of infringing goods or export of counterfeit goods

### *Market Access Issues Other Than Intellectual Property Protection*

Other complaints allege that countries "deny fair and equitable market access to U.S. persons who rely on IP protection." These types of complaints include:

- Import substitution, used to block imports of drugs if a local (generic) manufacturer is producing it. This is rare, and when described in PhRMA complaints it has been used for high-value medications.
- Tariffs and high taxes on medicines. In some cases, PhRMA has alleged discriminatory taxes if they are applied differently to multinational companies than domestic ones.
- Licensing or permitting policies that discriminate against foreign firms, including local ownership requirements.
- Allegations of forced technology transfer if firms are required to transfer technologies to local partners in order to do business in a third country. USTR regularly cites China for this.
- Health regulations that may be interpreted in a manner discriminating against foreign firms.

## Findings

Figure 14.1(a) shows the overall change in the number of countries that PhRMA requested to have listed in the Special 301 Report each year, and the number of *these* countries that were included in the same year's Special 301 Report. The number of countries PhRMA requested to have placed in the Special 301 Report fell by about half between 2009 and 2020, with a big drop in 2016. Figure 14.1(b) shows that USTR has remained responsive to

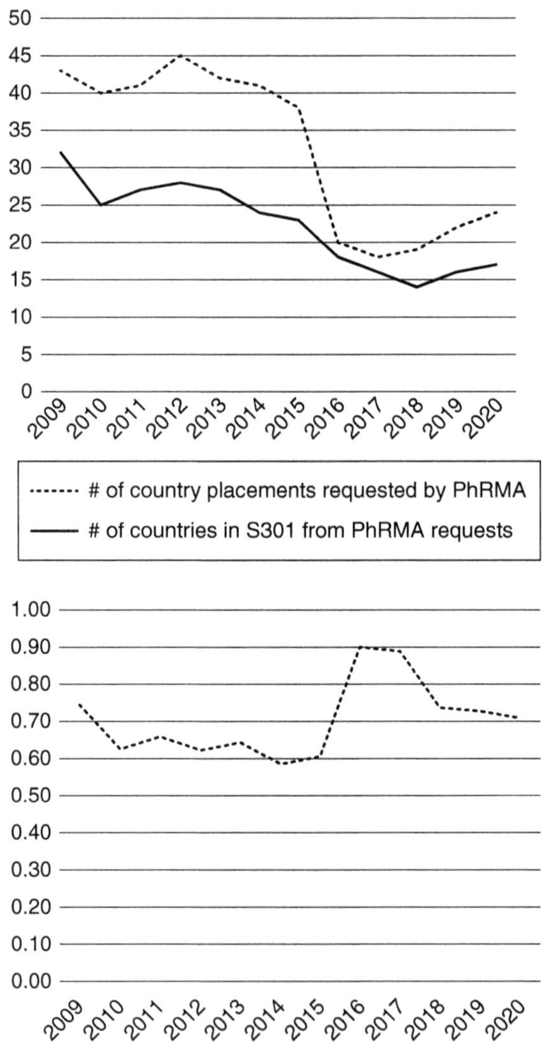


*Figure 14.1 PhRMA and USTR Identify Fewer Countries; USTR's Responsiveness to PhRMA is Consistent* (a) PhRMA country requests & USTR inclusions and (b) PhRMA's inclusion requests in report (%)

PhRMA's requests, becoming more responsive as the number of listing requests by PhRMA has fallen.

a Between 2009 and 2015, USTR listed 64 percent of the countries requested by PhRMA.
b Between 2016 and 2020, USTR listed 79 percent. (Notably, as PhRMA requests the listing of fewer countries in the report, changes in USTR's response yield larger percentage changes in its responsiveness to PhRMA requests.)

Figure 14.2(a) demonstrates a decrease in country requests and country listings that PhRMA prioritized by asking USTR to include the country as a PFC, on the PWL, or to list as a subject of Section 306 monitoring. This represents a subset of the countries from Figure 14.1(a). The countries in Figure 14.2(a) are those that seem to be highly prioritized by PhRMA. In 2009, PhRMA asked USTR to include 24 countries in the report at these levels. In 2020, PhRMA asked USTR to include 17 countries at these levels – a decline of 29 percent.

Figure 14.2(b) shows that USTR has consistently been very responsive to these requests over the 12-year period. On average, 82 percent of the countries prioritized by PhRMA through its listing recommendations were included in the Special 301 Report. The number of countries that USTR added as a PFC, PWL, or Section 306 country varied from a low of 46 percent in 2009 to a high of 65 percent in 2011, and has averaged 54 percent over the 12 years. The figures above show a temporary increase in USTR's responsiveness in 2016 to 2017. All of the countries PhRMA requested to have listed as PFC/PWL/306 were included USTR's report in these years. In 2018, PhRMA unsuccessfully requested the inclusions of South Korea and Japan, causing the bump to recede.

### *PhRMA-identified Special 301 Listings Focus on Middle-income Countries*

Countries identified by PhRMA and then listed in Special 301 Reports tend to be middle-income countries (based on the World Bank classification). Since 2012, over 75 percent of such countries have been middle-income countries each year, and the remainder were high-income countries (*see* Figure 14.3(a)). With the exception of Tajikistan, PhRMA did not ask USTR to list any low-income countries during this period.

The average income per capita in the listed countries has fallen as USTR has listed relatively less wealthy countries. As demonstrated in Figure 14.3(b), the average Gross National Income per capita of countries identified by PhRMA and listed by USTR was above the World Bank's threshold for classification as a high-income country until 2014, after which the average has been below

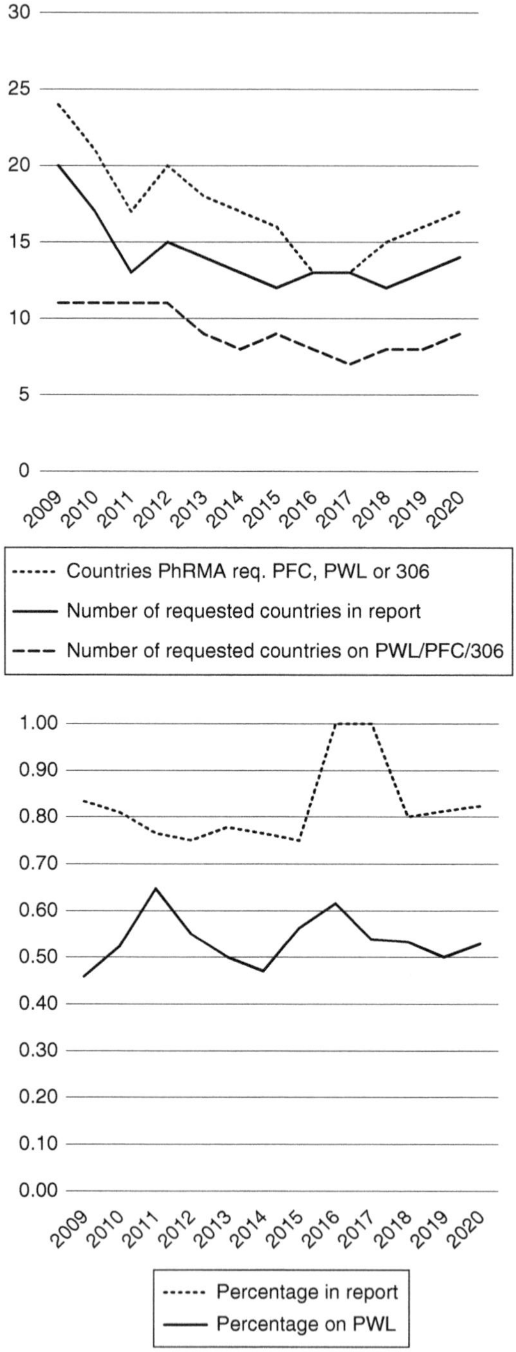


*Figure 14.2* (a) PhRMA requests for PFC/PWL/306 & USTR inclusions and (b) USTR responsiveness to PhRMA req. For PFC/PWL/306 (%)

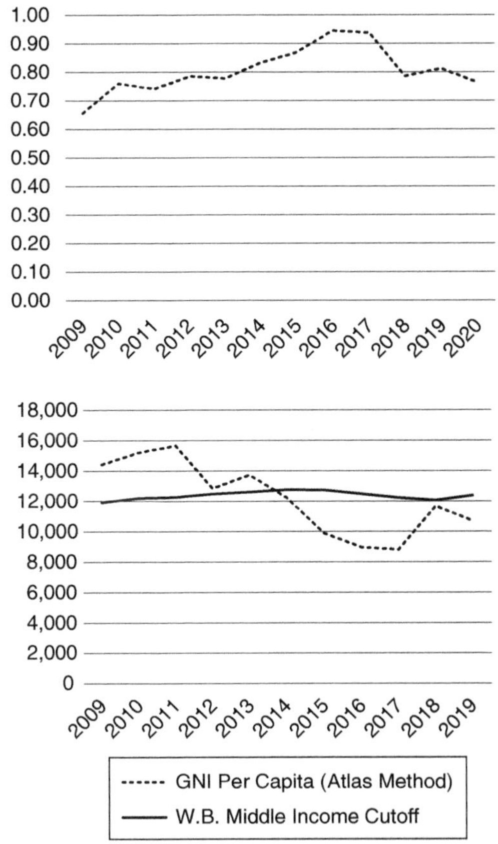


*Figure 14.3* (a) Percentage of countries identified by PhRMA and subsequently listed by USTR that are designated "Middle Income" by World Bank and (b) average income of countries identified by PhRMA and subsequently listed by USTR v. Middle Income Classification (US$)

the threshold.[15] The cutoff changed slightly from year to year, but it remained approximately $12,000 over the period.

## *PhRMA-identified Special 301 Listings Increasingly Focus on More Populous Countries*

The countries included in the Special 301 Report for health reasons tend to be large in terms of population. This is apparent from the annual inclusions

15 *See World Bank Development Indicators*, World Bank, https://datacatalog.worldbank.org/dataset/world-development-indicators (for data on Gross National Income per capita through 2019).

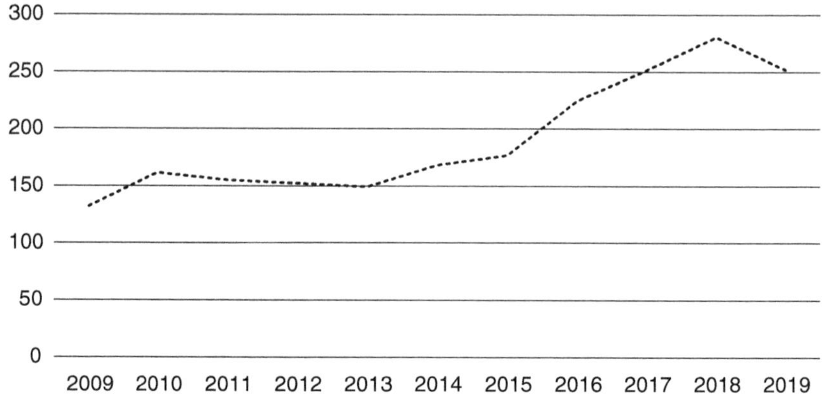


*Figure 14.4* Average population identified by PhRMA and subsequently listed by USTR

of China and India alone, but it bears mentioning that more than half of the world's population resides in countries identified by PhRMA and subsequently listed by USTR in the Special 301 Report.

As shown by Figure 14.4, the average population in countries identified by PhRMA and listed by USTR has increased as the overall number of countries in the report has fallen,[16] indicating a sustained focus on relatively populous countries.

## *Trends in the Reasons Cited for Listing Countries in the Special 301 Report*

This section examines trends in the reasons given by USTR for its listing of the countries that PhRMA had requested to have included in the Special 301 Reports. It shows where the *relative* focus of USTR is as the overall number of countries listed has declined.

Figure 14.5 shows three categories of alleged policy shortcomings cited by USTR in its listings of countries: (a) IP enforcement shortcomings; (b) use of TRIPS flexibilities; and (c) market access barriers for US firms that rely on IP protection. The percentage of complaints about inadequate enforcement of IP and the use of TRIPS flexibilities have been relatively stable as the overall number of countries listed has fallen. However, the percentage of countries cited for market access violations outside of the realm of IP has increased.

There are also many instances where USTR makes vague complaints about unnamed inadequacies of a country's IP landscape. For instance, USTR

16 *Id.*

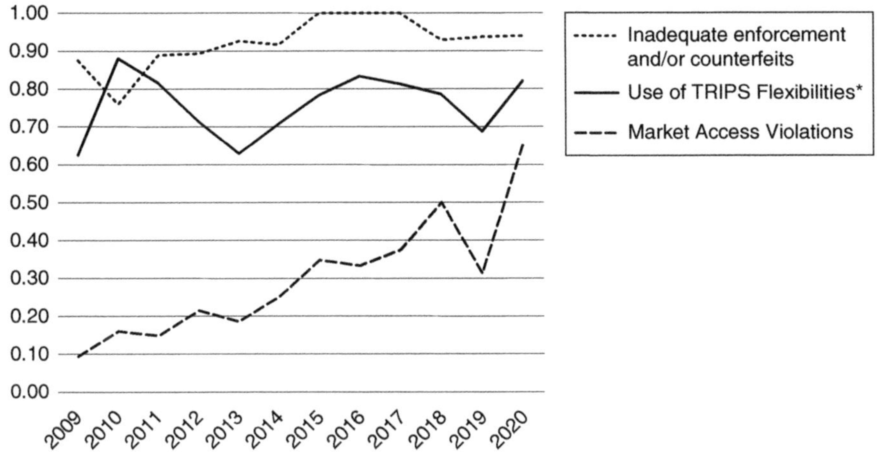


*Figure 14.5* Among countries PhRMA requested to have placed in the Special 301 Report that were included, % of countries cited by USTR

regularly refers to pending patent legislation in Jamaica without indicating what is in the bill. The 2009 Special 301 Report claimed the legislation was "intended to implement Jamaica's obligations under the TRIPS Agreement,"[17] without describing how Jamaica was out of compliance with the TRIPS Agreement or how the legislation would change the standing law. USTR continued to push for passage of the legislation without addressing the specific shortcomings of patent protection in the country: "Jamaica remains on the Watch List in 2019 due to its outdated patent and industrial designs regime."[18] Jamaica was dropped from the WL in the 2020 Special 301 Report, which notes that the legislation passed, but does not indicate how the law changed.[19]

Many individual country listings include a set of specific grievances and close with a statement that USTR is also concerned with other unspecified policies or shortcomings. For instance, after listing a number of problems with IP enforcement in Bolivia, USTR wrote in 2011 that it would monitor Bolivia's progress on these "and other" issues.[20] USTR promised to monitor "other matters" in the Dominican Republic the same year.[21]

17 Office of the U.S. Trade Rep., 2009 Special 301 Report, 27 (2009), https://ustr.gov/ [hereinafter 2009 Special 301 Report].
18 Office of the U.S. Trade Representative, 2019 Special 301 Report, 82 (2019), https://ustr.gov/.
19 2020 Special 301 Report, *supra* note 3, at 31.
20 Office of the U.S. Trade Rep., 2011 Special 301 Report, 32 (2011), https://ustr.gov/.
21 *Id.* at 34.

### *Countries Listed on PhRMA's Request were Criticized for Using TRIPS Flexibilities in 75 Percent of the Listings*

Approximately 75 percent of countries identified by PhRMA and listed by USTR were criticized each year for using TRIPS flexibilities (*see* Figure 14.5). Variation by year ranged from a low of 63 percent in 2009 and 2013, to a high of 88 percent in 2010. In 2020, USTR cited 82 percent of these countries for using TRIPS flexibilities. This finding is based on tallying the instances of four types of TRIPS flexibilities in the country listings – test data protection policies short of data exclusivity; lack of patent linkage; setting the scope of patentability such that certain drugs patentable in the United States were denied patents in the listed country; and compulsory licensing.

Figure 14.6 shows how often each of these alleged violations were cited in the Special 301 Report in countries identified by PhRMA. Inadequacy in test data protection is the alleged shortcoming that USTR cites most frequently. Each year, between 47 percent and 79 percent of the countries listed by PhRMA were cited for having weaknesses in test data protection. This tally includes countries with laws that protect test data with mechanisms other than data exclusivity, such as Argentina, which meets its TRIPS obligation with a law that prohibits dishonest use of test data submitted to health authorities and permits generic pharmaceutical firms to win marketing approval based on foreign regulatory filings.[22]

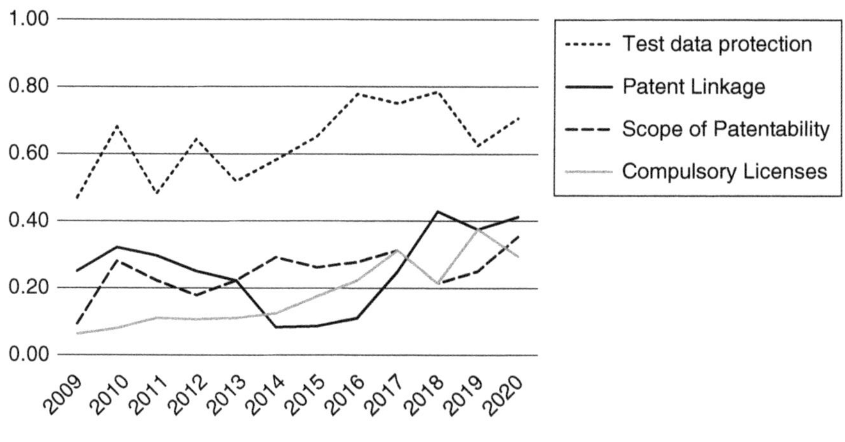


*Figure 14.6* Frequency of TRIPS flexibilities cited in countries identified by PhRMA and listed by USTR (%)

22 The United States challenged this law through the WTO dispute settlement process in 1999, but the countries reached a Mutually Agreed Solution in 2002, which left specifics on data exclusivity open to further negotiation. The Dispute Settlement Panel never issued a Report on the matter. *See Argentina - Certain Measures on the Protection of Patents and test Data* (WT/DS196), https://www.wto.org/english/tratop_e/dispu_e/cases_e/ds196_e.htm.

It also includes countries that have data exclusivity rules that are implemented in ways that do not provide exclusivity for all types of medicine products, such as China, which grants six years of data exclusivity to new pharmaceutical products. In 2016, USTR cited China for inadequate protection of test data, noting a regulation that limited the definition of "new drugs" to "those for which marketing approval is first sought in China."[23]

Listings for lacking patent linkage fell from 32 percent in 2010 to a low of 13 percent in 2014 and have generally risen since then, hitting an all-time high of 43 percent in 2018 (and 42 percent in 2020). Usually, USTR does not use the term "linkage" in the Special 301 Reports but describes the countries as lacking a mechanism to help patent holders block infringing products before they reach the market. For instance, in the 2018 Special 301 Report, USTR cited Egypt for lacking an "effective system for notifying interested parties of applications for marketing approval of follow-on pharmaceuticals in a manner that would allow for the early resolution of potential patent disputes."[24]

Listings for limiting the scope of patentability have averaged 25 percent over the 12-year period, with a gradually increasing trend. In 2020, USTR cited 35 percent of PhRMA-identified countries for issues related to the scope of patentability. These include (a) countries that did not allow patents on new uses of known medical products, such as Colombia;[25] (b) countries that did not allow new versions of existing products, such as Brazil;[26] and (c) countries that provided process patents protection for pharmaceuticals during the pre-TRIPS years, specifically Finland and Norway.[27]

India was regularly included by USTR in the Special 301 Report for allegations that Section 3(d) of India's Patents Act violates the TRIPS Agreement's requirements of patentability. Section 3(d) denies patents for "the mere discovery of a new form of a known substance which does not result in the enhancement of the known efficacy of that substance…" However, as stated above, many countries deny patents for new uses and forms of medicines.[28]

Citations of countries for compulsory licensing have increased over the 12-year period. In 2009 and 2010, countries were rarely cited for compulsory licensing, but 37.5 percent of the countries singled out by PhRMA and included in the 2019 Special 301 Report were criticized for policies related to this flexibility.

23 Office of the U.S. Trade Rep., 2016 Special 301 Report, 36 (2016), https://ustr.gov/.

24 Office of the U.S. Trade Rep., 2018 Special 301 Report, 69 (2018), https://ustr.gov/.

25 Office of the U.S. Trade Rep., 2014 Special 301 Report, 50 (2014), https://ustr.gov/ [hereinafter 2014 Special 301 Report] (vaguely alleging problems with scope of patentability); *see also* PhRMA Special 301 comments in 2014 Special 301 Report, at 186 (asserting that Colombia does not issue "second use" patents).

26 2009 Special 301 Report, *supra* note 17, at 23 (Brazil was cited for not allowing patents on polymorphs).

27 *Id.* at 26 and 29.

28 Clara Ducimetière, *Second Medical Use Patents: Legal Treatment and Public Health Issues*, South Centre Research Paper No. 101 (2019), https://www.southcentre.int/research-paper-101-december-2019/.

This figured dropped to 29 percent in 2020. The countries cited for compulsory licensing include some that have taken a well-known stand on the issue to expand access to medicines for thousands of patients. For instance, Thailand issued CLs on *Efavirenz* and *Lopinavir+Ritonavir*, expanding treatment to 20,000 and 8000 patients, respectively.[29] Other countries have not actually used CLs, but have taken steps needed to issue a license under their domestic laws. The 2019 Special 301 Report complained that Chile passed a health resolution "which declared that there are public health reasons that justify issuing CLs on certain patent-protected drugs used to treat hepatitis C. While Chile has not issued a CL, the resolution satisfies an initial legal requirement after which a third party may then make the request."[30]

From 2009 through 2018, only middle-income countries were cited for compulsory licensing (China, Ecuador, India, Indonesia, and Thailand). USTR cited Chile for its new CL policy in the 2019 and 2020 reports. It did not cite other high-income countries that issued licenses or changed their compulsory licensing laws in March 2020 in response to the coronavirus. These include Israel (which issued a CL for a potential COVID-19 treatment in March);[31] Canada (which amended its law to accelerate the process of compulsory licensing for health reasons);[32] and Germany (which passed a law granting the government more authority to issue CLs in epidemics).[33]

Other alleged IP violations are routinely included in Special 301 Reports, often at the request of PhRMA. These include backlogs of patent applications and problems with patent prosecution. Sometimes, these allegations are paired with calls to extend patent terms (which countries are not required to do under the TRIPS Agreement). Other times, USTR simply criticizes the country for delays. These are not included in Figure 14.4 because the delays are not a TRIPS flexibility – though the right to refuse to extend patent terms beyond 20 years is a flexibility.

### *Special 301 Reports have Focused More on Enforcement of IP Protection Than on Specific Policies*

Allegations of inadequate enforcement of IP were more frequent than allegations of inadequate policies. Almost all countries listed by USTR in the Special

29 Thai Ministry of Public Health and National Health Security Office of Thailand, *Facts and Evidences on the 10 Burning Issues Related to the Government Use of Patents on Three Patented Essential Drugs in Thailand* (2007), http://www.cptech.org/ip/health/c/thailand/thai-cl-white-paper.pdf.

30 2019 Special 301 Report, *supra* note 17, at 65.

31 Hilary Wong, *The Case for Compulsory Licensing During COVID-19*, 10 J. Glob. Health 1 (2020), https://www.ncbi.nlm.nih.gov/pmc/articles/PMC7242884/.

32 *Id.*

33 Christian Dekoninck et al., *COVID-19 and Public Compulsory Licensing of Drugs in Europe*, SYNAPSE: Taylor Wessing (Apr. 17, 2020), https://www.taylorwessing.com/fr/insights-and-events/insights/2020/04/covid-19-and-public-compulsory-licensing-of-drugs-in-europe.

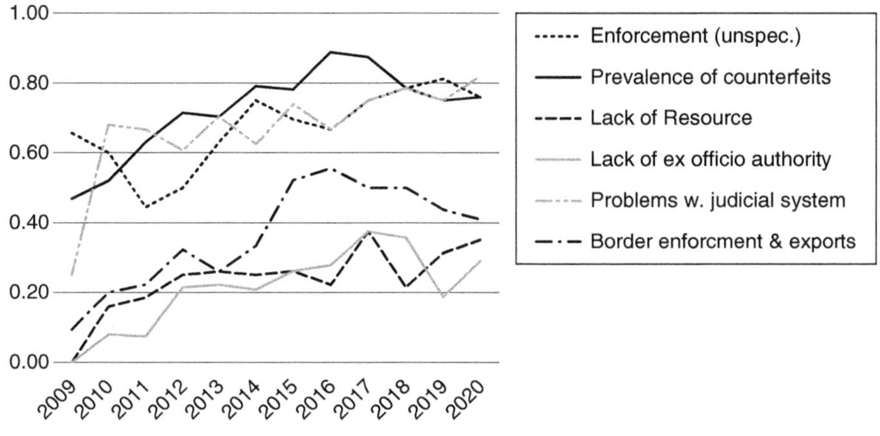


*Figure 14.7* IP enforcement citations in countries identified by PhRMA and listed by USTR (%)

301 Report for IP and healthcare reasons contain some form of allegation that enforcement is lacking.

Figure 14.5 shows that 92% of the countries identified by PhRMA and listed by USTR were cited for IP enforcement concerns between 2009 and 2020. The percentage of such countries being cited for alleged problems with IP enforcement was consistently high, reaching 100% from 2015 through 2017.

Figure 14.7 shows the types of enforcement complaints commonly found in the Special 301 Report. The most common complaint was the prevalence of counterfeits on the market in a given country. Seventy-two percent of the countries recommended by PhRMA and listed by USTR were criticized for this. Other common enforcement shortcomings cited in the Special 301 Report included concerns with the judicial process, including sentences not strong enough to deter future infringement (67 percent); under-resourced enforcement authorities (24 percent); a lack of *ex officio* authority for enforcement authorities (21 percent); and weak border enforcement and/or the export of infringing products (36 percent).

USTR frequently highlights the need to strengthen enforcement generally, usually in addition to other specific allegations. For instance, the 2017 Special 301 Report urges Guatemala to "take clear and effective actions in 2017 to improve the protection and enforcement of IP in Guatemala."[34] Such unspecific criticisms of IP enforcement occurred in 66 percent of the listings of countries identified by PhRMA and included by USTR.

34 Office of the U.S. Trade Rep., 2017 Special 301 Report, 64 (2017), https://ustr.gov/.

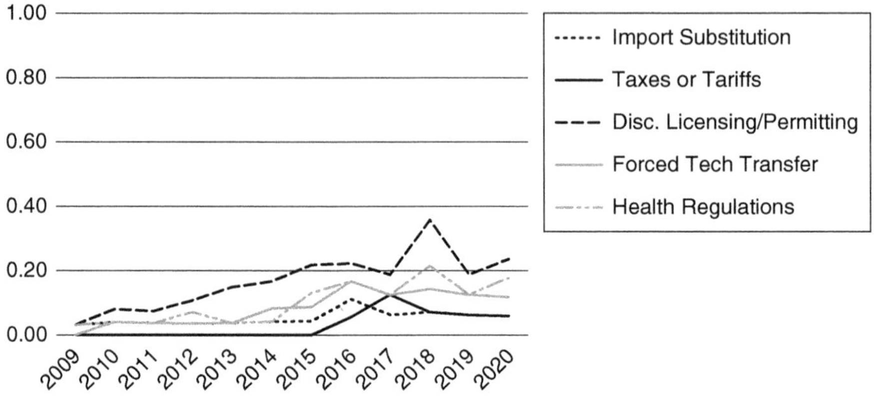


*Figure 14.8* Market access policies (non-IP) cited in countries identified by PhRMA and listed by USTR (%)

### *Countries are Increasingly Listed for Market Access Violations Outside the Intellectual Property Realm*

USTR increasingly uses the Special 301 Report to criticize countries for policies that have nothing to do with IP. These fall under the scope of the Trade Act's instructions to identify countries that deny "fair and equitable market access to United States persons that rely upon intellectual property rights." PhRMA's comments to USTR regularly complain of such market access barriers. Initially, USTR focused more directly on alleged IP shortcomings, but it has increased these types of allegations over time. Figure 14.5 shows that these complaints were in 9 percent of the Special 301 Report listings of countries identified by PhRMA in 2009 and 65 percent in 2020. This finding is based on a tally of allegations of various licensing and permitting policies that discriminate against foreign firms (including local ownership requirements); forced technology transfer; import substitution; tariffs and other taxes on medicines; and allegedly discriminatory health regulations. Figure 14.8 shows how each of these have grown in percentage since 2009.

The percentage of countries identified by PhRMA and listed by USTR that were singled out for discriminatory licensing and permitting policies has grown the most – starting at 3 percent in 2009 and remaining at or above 19 percent since 2015. Allegations of discriminatory use of health regulations applied to 3 percent of the listed countries in 2009, but to 13 percent or higher each year since 2015. There have been smaller increases in citations for policies requiring technology transfer for US firms to operate in listed countries, as well as citations about taxes and tariffs.

## Conclusion

Since its inception, the Special 301 Report has been an instrument used by USTR to pressure foreign nations to change their laws at the behest of American business interests. Policies that allow countries to access lower priced generic medicines feature prominently in USTR's allegations of inadequate and ineffective protection of IP.

This report has reviewed trends over the past 12 years. USTR has reduced the number of countries listed in the Special 301 Report, but it has been consistent in its responsiveness to country listing requests by PhRMA. This is especially true for the countries prioritized by PhRMA. USTR included between 75 percent and 100 percent of these PhRMA-prioritized countries in each year's Special 301 Report over the period studied. It also consistently focused its attention on middle-income countries and populous countries.

USTR has regularly used the report to criticize countries for employing TRIPS flexibilities. There has been an increased number of complaints about (mostly middle-income) countries issuing CLs or adopting pro-compulsory licensing policies. Alleged inadequacies in countries' test data protection, patent linkage, and the scope of patentability have all been criticized in the Special 301 Reports as well. There have been increased complaints against countries for inadequate enforcement of intellectual property, and increased complaints that pharmaceutical firms have been denied fair market access.

The 2020 Special 301 Report did not criticize countries for exploring and expanding TRIPS flexibilities in the face of the COVID-19 pandemic. Indeed, neither the word "coronavirus" nor "COVID-19" appears in the report. The absence of citations for countries seeking to use TRIPS flexibilities to fight the COVID-19 pandemic is notable, especially given press reports that countries were preparing to issue CLs, and in Israel's case, had already issued one. Perhaps the obvious need for access to COVID-19 treatments took precedence over the need to protect pharmaceutical firms' IP. If this is the case, it is fair to ask why the use of TRIPS flexibilities for other urgent health needs (such as HIV/AIDS, hepatitis C, or cancer) does not get the same deference. It may also be that policy inertia and the report's regular focus on health actions by middle-income countries caused the report's authors to overlook the actions of high-income trading partners in this area.

There are many avenues for further research into the Special 301 Report. One could examine the impact that Special 301 listings have on the ground in countries included in the reports. Does inclusion in a report lead policy makers in these countries to change laws and policies in ways favorable to US interests? How directly are Special 301 listings connected to other trade and diplomatic pressures?

Finally, PhRMA is only one of the groups that submit comments and testify in support of pharmaceutical industry interests. Further research could examine how USTR has responded to listing suggestions by other groups such as the Biotechnology Innovation Organization and the Chamber of Commerce's Global Innovation Policy Center. One could also compare USTR's responsiveness to the pharmaceutical industry to its responsiveness to other IP-intensive industries, such as publishing and media.

# Part III

# Global Patterns and Emerging Issues

## Third Generation

# 15 Access to Medicines Activism

## Collaboration, Conflicts, and Complementarities

*Brook K. Baker*

### Introduction and Context

Access-to-medicines (A2M) civil society activists, an informal network of affiliated legal scholars, along with intellectual property (IP) and global health experts have interacted with global health institutions, Indian generic producers, and a vanguard of low- and middle-income countries (LMICs) to achieve remarkable success in lowering the prices of antiretroviral (ARV) medicines in response to the global AIDS pandemic. The steepest price fall worldwide was in 2001, when Indian generic company Cipla offered a triple-dose antiretroviral therapy (ART) for just $350 per year,[1] approximately three percent of the price charged by Big Pharma companies six months earlier: $10,439.[2] Eighteen years later, best in class triple-dose ART *tenofovir disoproxil fumarate* (TDF)/*lamivudine* (3TC) plus *dolutegravir* (DTG) – the equivalent of which (TDF/*emtricitabine*/DTG) can cost as much as $54,876 per person per year in the US[3] – is now available as a single daily pill for as little for $75 per person per year[4] in approximately

1 Donald G. McNeil, Jr., *Indian Company Offers to Supply AIDS Drugs at Low Cost in Africa*, N.Y. Times (Feb. 7, 2001), https://www.nytimes.com/2001/02/07/world/indian-company-offers-to-supply-aids-drugs-at-low-cost-in-africa.html.

2 Carmen Perez-Casas, Cécile Mace, Daniel Berman & Julia Double, *Accessing ARVs: Untangling the Web of Price Reductions for Developing Countries*, Medicins San Frontieres 3 (Sept. 20, 2001), https://msfaccess.org/sites/default/files/MSF_assets/HIV_AIDS/Docs/AIDS_report_UTW1_ENG_2001.pdf. Cipla initially set a price of $800 per person per year for a triple-dose ARV combination which prompted innovators' first substantial ARV price discounts to select low- and middle-income countries.

3 Department of Health and Human Services, *Guidelines for the Use of Antiretroviral Agents in Adults and Adolescents with HIV*, NIH K-27 (Oct. 25, 2018), https://aidsinfo.nih.gov/contentfiles/lvguidelines/adultandadolescentgl.pdf.

4 *New High-Quality Antiretroviral Therapy To Be Launched In South Africa, Kenya and Over 90 Low- and Middle-Income Countries At Reduced Price*, Clinton Health Access Initiative (Sept. 21, 2017), https://clintonhealthaccess.org/new-high-quality-antiretroviral-therapy-launched-south-africa-kenya-90-low-middle-income-countries-reduced-price/.

130 countries covering over 90 percent of people in LMICs living with HIV,[5] largely because of A2M campaigns and actions of key partners. The more affordable generic ARVs were a necessary precondition to increased donor and domestic funding[6] and to what became the largest global response to a pandemic disease killing millions every year – resulting in 24.5 million getting treatment by June 2019, 65 percent of the 37.9 million living with HIV globally.[7]

The need for the global A2M movement germinated from a global IP protection movement started by the World Trade Organization (WTO) Agreement on Trade-Related Aspects of Intellectual Property Rights (TRIPS Agreement).[8] This Agreement, pursued over a 15-year campaign by Big Pharma and 10 years of intensive US trade pressure,[9] instantiated new global minimum standards of IP rights (IPR) for pharmaceuticals. No longer could countries deny patents on pharmaceuticals as over 50 countries had done in the pre-TRIPS era. Instead, WTO member states were required to enact minimum patent terms of 20 years,[10] provide for patents in all fields of technology including medicines, and eliminate discrimination against issuing patents based on foreign ownership or likelihood

5 Although the original announcement referenced coverage under the ViiV dolutegravir ("DTG") license with the Medicines Patent Pool ("MPP"), which then included 92 countries, approximately 39 countries were included later in the "indirect" coverage of the license. *Cf.* Brook K. Baker, *Beyond the Obvious – Direct and Indirect Territorial Coverage of MPP/ViiV Voluntary License Dolutegravir*, IP WATCH (May 24, 2017) (finding 38 countries/territories with indirect coverage) https://www.ip-watch.org/2017/05/24/beyond-obvious-direct-indirect-territorial-coverage-mppviiv-voluntary-license-dolutegravir/; *When Will ViiV, Clinton Health and Partners Officially Repair the Mistake on Missing out 39 Countries from the DTG Pricing Agreement?*, MAKE MEDICINES AFFORDABLE (June 13, 2018) (reporting that Clinton Health Access Initiative, MPP, ViiV will allow at least one licensee, Mylan's decision to honor pricing agreement for public procurement in 39 unnamed countries), http://makemedicinesaffordable.org/en/when-will-viiv-clinton-health-and-partners-officially-repair-the-mistake-on-missing-out-39-countries-from-the-dtg-pricing-agreement/.

6 Between 2000 and 2016, the total LMIC spending on HIV and AIDS increased from $4 billion to $19.9 billion. Annie Haakenstad et al., *Potential for Additional Government Spending On HIV/AIDS in 137 Low-Income and Middle-Income Countries: An Economic Modelling Study*, 6 LANCET HIV (2019).

7 *Fact Sheet – World Aids Day 2019: Global HIV Statistics*, UNAIDS (Dec. 1, 2019), http://www.unaids.org/sites/default/files/media_asset/UNAIDS_FactSheet_en.pdf.

8 TRIPS: Agreement on Trade-Related Aspects of Intellectual Property Rights, Apr. 15, 1994, Marrakesh Agreement Establishing the World Trade Organization, Annex 1C, 1869 U.N.T.S. 299, 33 I.L.M. 1197 (1994) [hereinafter TRIPS Agreement], art. 8(1).

9 *See generally* PETER DRAHOS & JOHN BRAITHWAITE, INFORMATION FEUDALISM: WHO OWNS THE KNOWLEDGE ECONOMY (2003) (history of political and strategic genesis of the TRIPS Agreement as engineered by United States knowledge industries); SUSAN K. SELL, PRIVATE POWER, PUBLIC LAW: THE GLOBALIZATION OF INTELLECTUAL PROPERTY RIGHTS (2003) (arguing that the TRIPS Agreement resulted from the lobbying of powerful IP-based multinational firms in bending intergovernmental decision-makers to their private corporate interests).

10 TRIPS Agreement, *supra* note 8, at art. 33.

of importation.[11] The resulting monopoly right to exclude generic competition guaranteed drug companies the power to charge whatever the market would bear. In LMICs, the income inequality meant that Big Pharma companies could maximize profits by selling at higher prices to economic elites, even as the majority of poor people were denied medicines.[12]

While the TRIPS Agreement protected patent monopolies on medicines, it also included public health flexibilities for countries to bypass or even override monopoly protections. Though not routinely acknowledged, these flexibilities included longer transition periods of least developed countries (LDCs), stringent standards of patentability and disclosure, allowance for opposition procedures challenging patents and patent applications, and exclusions from and exceptions to patent rights, parallel importation, compulsory use patents, and government use patents.

This chapter addresses three phases of A2M advocacy. The first phase ran between the late 1990s and mid-2000s when collaboration between A2M advocates ballooned as they confronted a scourge of HIV compounded by pharmaceutical companies and rich country governments refusing to increase affordability of ART. This led to securing lower prices and gaining access to off-patent generic ARVs.

The second phase, starting in the mid-2000s, focused on strategies to address patents on medicines. Unfortunately, this phase resulted in differences within the A2M movement.

In the third phase, new tensions arose about the impact of delinkage and transparency issues on ensuring equitable access to existing medicines in LMICs. Although the monumental efforts resulted in improvement in access to medicines, the path forward continued to be complicated and contested.

## First Phase: Shared Enemies and International Collaboration

The first phase of the international A2M movement involved intense contestation with Big Pharma alongside a growing solidarity between activists in the Global North and South. Cipla's revolutionary price of $350 per year was achieved during the first wave of global A2M activism, when most LMICs were required under the TRIPS Agreement to abide with international norms for protecting pharmaceutical patents. Although AIDS activists had attacked domestic prices in the United States (US),[13] it was not until the late 1990s and early 2000s that activists focused on the extortionate prices of newer and more

11 *Id.* at art. 27.

12 Sean Flynn et al., *An Economic Justification for Open Access to Medicines Patents in Developing Countries*, 37 J. L. Med. & Ethics 184 (2009).

13 *See* Patricia D. Siplon, AIDS and the Policy Struggle in the United States, 23–25 (2002).

effective ARVs that limited access to ARVs in LMICs to well under 0.1 percent of people infected.[14] Meanwhile, as Big Pharma filed lawsuits against progressive government actions of developing countries, activists filed counteractions in courts and at the WTO.

Despite negligible media coverage of the global HIV/AIDS pandemic in the 1990s, pharmaceutical executives knew of the looming global crisis and how high prices would impact ARVs. In 1991, CEOs of 18 major pharmaceutical companies discussed the magnitude of the AIDS crisis in the developing world and the pricing of new ARVs at the World Health Organization (WHO). Over the next two years, industry would respond to repeated requests for discounted prices in poorer countries by championing its research and development (R&D) mission and questioning Africa's health infrastructure.[15]

Perversely, instead of offering discounted prices, industry and its subservient government supporters, including President Clinton, went on the offensive. In South Africa, 39 US and European drug companies and trade associations – and their South African subsidiaries – sued the South African government over their determination to purchase cheaper generic ARVs under the Medicines and Related Substances Control Amendment Act Number 90 of 1997.[16] Originally filed in 1998, this lawsuit was dismissed on April 18, 2001, after the Treatment Action Campaign (TAC) intervened and after Global Days of Protest challenged it. During this protracted litigation, 400,000 South Africans died of AIDS.

In another example of misused corporate and state power, the Office of the US Trade Representative (USTR) routinely used Section 301 of the Trade Act to threaten trade sanctions against developing countries that "abused" or "threatened to abuse" pharmaceutical patents.[17] Significant pressure was applied – first on Thailand and later on South Africa – to "respect IP rights."[18] This pressure continued until late 1999, when the AIDS Coalition to Unleash Power (ACT-UP) and Health Global Access Coalition's "zaps" actions against Vice President Al Gore[19] forced President Clinton to revise US policy in South

14 *Id.* at 111–34.

15 Barton Gellman, *An Unequal Calculus of Life and Death*, Washington Post (Dec. 27, 2000), https://www.washingtonpost.com/archive/politics/2000/12/27/an-unequal-calculus-of-life-and-death/4f6d22c0-d918-441c-b6e9-e270554bc73b/?utm_term=.a6322191f597.

16 David Barnard, *In the High Court of South Africa, Case No. 4138/98: The Global Politics of Access to Low-Cost AIDS Drugs in Poor Countries*, 12 Kennedy Inst. Ethics J. 159 (2002).

17 Section 301 gives the Trade Office broad discretion to threaten and eventually impose trade sanctions against listed countries. 19 U.S.C. § 2242 (2012).

18 Patrick Bond, *Globalization, Pharmaceutical Pricing and South African Health Policy: Managing Confrontation with U.S. Firms and Politicians*, 29 Int'l J. Health Servs. 765 (1999); Tido von Schoen-Angere & Jiraporn Limpananont, *Correspondence: US Pressure on Less-developed Countries*, 358 Lancet 245 (2001).

19 Mark Milano, *Personal Perspective: Zapping for Drugs*, The Body Pro (Sept. 1, 2016), https://www.thebodypro.com/article/personal-perspective-zapping-drugs.

Africa.[20] This resulted in an executive order in 2000 prohibiting trade pressure against Sub-Saharan African countries using TRIPS-compliant measures to access affordable ARVs.[21] Shortly thereafter, civil society campaigns challenged the US' misguided WTO case against Brazil's provision to compulsorily license medicines not produced locally.[22]

Not only did the A2M movement fight against negative pressures, activists and the WTO Africa Group turned the tables on TRIPS-flexibility denialists to pursue clarification of the TRIPS flexibilities and access to medicines.[23] This resulted in the Doha Declaration on the TRIPS Agreement and Public Health (Doha Declaration).[24] As part of confirming WTO member states' right to advance public health and to promote "access to medicines for all," the Doha Declaration clarified national sovereignty to define grounds for compulsory licenses (CLs) and to allow parallel importation. It further motivated a new transition period for least developed countries (LDCs) to recognize and enforce pharmaceutical patents, while also mandating a new compulsory licensing mechanism to allow manufacture, exportation, and importation of medicines to countries with insufficient domestic manufacturing capacity despite the limitations otherwise expressed in Article 31(f) of the TRIPS Agreement.[25]

Responding to persistent A2M demands for price reductions through generic access, some Big Pharma companies made early price concessions. Bristol Myers Squibb (BMS), the first to respond to the African AIDS pandemic, launched its so-called Secure the Future program in 1999.[26] It promised $100 million over five years to fight AIDS in Africa, initially focused in Botswana but later expanded to 14 countries. On May 11, 2000, a consortium of BMS, Glaxo

20 Siplon, *supra* note 13, at 120–26 (detailing US pressure against South Africa and the activist response).

21 Exec. Order No. 13155, 65 Fed. Reg. 30,521 (May 10, 2000), https://www.govinfo.gov/content/pkg/FR-2000-05-12/pdf/00-12177.pdf; Neil A. Lewis, *Clinton Issues Order to Ease Availability of AIDS Drugs in Africa*, N.Y. Times (May 11, 2000), https://www.nytimes.com/2000/05/11/world/clinton-issues-order-to-ease-availability-of-aids-drugs-in-africa.html.

22 Haroon Ashraf, *USA and Brazil End Dispute Over Essential Drugs*, 357 Lancet 2112 (2001).

23 *See* Brook K. Baker, *Arthritic Flexibilities for Access Medicines: Analysis of WTO Action Regarding Paragraph 6 of the Doha Declaration on the TRIPS Agreement and Public Health*, 14 Ind. Int'l & Comp. L. Rev. 613, 623–28 (2004).

24 World Trade Organization, Declaration on the TRIPS Agreement and Public Health, WTO Doc. WT/MIN(01)/DEC/2 (2001), https://www.wto.org/english/thewto_e/minist_e/min01_e/mindecl_trips_e.htm [hereinafter Doha Declaration]; *see* Frederick M. Abbott, *The Doha Declaration on the TRIPS Agreement and Public Health: Lighting a Dark Corner at the WTO*, J. Int'l Econ. L. 469 (2002).

25 Baker, *supra* note 23, at 627–28. The adoption of a paragraph 6 waiver was long delayed by the United States and the resulting waiver unfortunately contains many unnecessary and labyrinth procedures. *Id.* at 627–55.

26 Bristol-Myers Squibb, *Secure the Future 10th Anniversary Brochure* (2009), http://securethefuture.com/Shared%20Documents/media/2008_STF_media.pdf.

Welcome, Merck, Boehringer Ingelheim, and Hoffman-La Roche, in conjunction with the Joint United Nations Programme on HIV/AIDS (UNAIDS), announced substantial reductions in HIV/AIDS medicine prices in poor countries through the Accelerating Access Initiative (AAI), although these were negotiated on a drug-by-drug and company-by-company basis.[27] As of March 2002, the number of patients accessing ARVs through AAI efforts was only 35,500, but prices had decreased by 80–90 percent with significantly greater transparency on prices.[28]

In September 2000, Dr. Hamied of Cipla offered to sell triple-dose combination ARTs for $800 a day at a European Commission conference.[29] The pharmaceutical participants were stunned; the politicians present had no response. After Jamie Love of the Consumer Project on Technology (now Knowledge Ecology International or KEI) asked for an even lower price, Cipla offered the dollar-a-day price on February 6, 2001.[30] This provoked a new round of price concessions from Big Pharma. On March 14, 2001, and under intense pressure from Médecins sans Frontières (MSF) in South Africa and Yale students protesting patent abuse of a medicine originally developed at Yale,[31] BMS doubled down on Secure the Future by offering to make two AIDS medicines, *didanosine* (ddI) and *stavudine* (d4T), available "below cost" at a dollar per day to sub-Saharan African countries and

27 AAI participants announced five conditions for price reduction: (1) unequivocal political commitment by the recipient countries to a comprehensive HIV/AIDS program; (2) agreement by international agencies to assume responsibility for increasing public health infrastructures; (3) instituting an efficient distribution system to prevent gray markets; (4) acknowledgement that affordability is an issue in developing countries and a commitment to further price reductions; and (5) that developing countries would support adequate IP rights to provide a satisfactory return on investment in the high-risk search for new medicines. Barton Gellman, *A Turning Point That Left Millions Behind*, Washington Post (Dec. 28, 2000), https://www.washingtonpost.com/archive/politics/2000/12/28/a-turning-point-that-left-millions-behind/afe238d9-49a6-4b03-bfff-2ba83c0c4cd7/?utm_term=.68aba8ad39a9.

28 WHO, Accelerating Access Initiative Progress Report, Annex 3 & Annex 4 (2002), https://www.who.int/hiv/pub/prev_care/en/isbn9241210125.pdf?ua=1.

29 Dr. Y.K. Hamied's speech at the European Commission (Sept. 28, 2000), https://www.youtube.com/watch?v=NK7GDpYjGXM. For a description of the conference, *see* Press Release, European Commission, World Health Organization, and Joint United Nations Programme on HIV/AIDS Takes a United Stand Against Killer Diseases (Sept. 28, 2000), http://europa.eu/rapid/press-release_IP-00-1072_en.htm.

30 For a dramatic recounting of this story, see the film, *Fire in the Blood* (2012), or its *Transcript*, 8–11, Media Education Foundation (2013), https://www.mediaed.org/transcripts/Fire-In-The-Blood-Transcript.pdf. For a newspaper account, see Donald G. McNeil, Jr., *Indian Company Offers to Supply AIDS Drugs at Low Cost in Africa*, N.Y. Times (Feb. 7, 2001), https://www.nytimes.com/2001/02/07/world/indian-company-offers-to-supply-aids-drugs-at-low-cost-in-africa.html.

31 Donald G. McNeil, Jr., *Yale Pressed to Help Cut Drug Costs in Africa*, N.Y. Times (Mar. 12, 2001), https://www.nytimes.com/2001/03/12/world/yale-pressed-to-help-cut-drug-costs-in-africa.html.

agreeing not to assert its patent rights to d4T.[32] Ten days later, on March 27, 2001, Abbott Laboratories agreed to sell two ARVs – *Norvir* and *Kaletra* – in Africa at prices covering costs of manufacture, distribution, and import tax, resulting in a price of below $1000 per year per patient for each medication.[33]

Soon the drug donation programs started. Pfizer was put under heavy pressure by AIDS activists over excessive pricing of *fluconazole*, vital for treating fungal infections in HIV patients. Shortly before the International AIDS Conference in 2000, Pfizer announced a planned partnership with the South African Ministry of Health to provide free *fluconazole* to HIV/AIDS patients. Responding to inadequacies in Pfizer's donation program,[34] the TAC launched its Defiance Campaign to import generic *fluconazole* from Thailand and submitted samples to the South African Medicines Control Council for approval. On December 1, 2000, after months of tense negotiations, Pfizer and the South African Department of Health announced an expanded agreement for free distribution of *fluconazole* for two years.[35] Responding to continued demands, Pfizer announced on June 6, 2001, that it would offer free *fluconazole* to five other African countries and all LDCs,[36] later claiming to have donated $1.2 billion worth of *fluconazole* to governments and nongovernment organizations (NGOs) in developing countries with an HIV prevalence rate greater than one percent over an 18-year period.[37] Around the same time, Boehringer Ingelheim announced *nevirapine* donation for five years throughout Africa to prevent mother-to-child transmission.

Beginning in the early 2000s, bowing to AIDS activists' pressure and government threats to issue CLs, several pharmaceutical companies – including BMS, Boehringer Ingelheim, GlaxoSmithKline, and Gilead – offered territorially limited voluntary licenses (VLs) or nonassertion/nonenforcement agreements

32 Melody Petersen & Donald G. McNeil, Jr., *Maker Yielding Patent in Africa for AIDS Drug*, N.Y. Times (Mar. 15, 2001), https://www.nytimes.com/2001/03/15/world/maker-yielding-patent-in-africa-for-aids-drug.html.

33 Melody Petersen, *Abbott to Sell Low-Cost AIDS Drugs in Africa*, N.Y. Times (Mar. 18, 2001), http://www.nytimes.com/2001/03/28/business/28DRUG.html.

34 Pfizer initially limited the donation: (1) the drug would be provided only for treatment of cryptococcal meningitis not oral thrush or life-threatening esophageal candidiasis; (2) only for patients unable to afford the medicine would receive the drug; (3) the donation was structured as a clinical trial with onerous reporting requirements; (4) the donation was time limited to 2.5 years (the remaining term of the patent); and (5) the donation was limited to South Africa.

35 Pfizer estimated the value of the fluconazole donation program at $50 million, presumably based on the wholesale price of the donated medicine, not the $1–$2 million actual cost of production. In addition, it is quite likely that Pfizer will end up with significant tax advantages, exceeding the costs of the program, because of current charitable deduction rules.

36 *Pfizer to Expand Fluconazole Donation Program to More than 50 Developing Nations*, Kaiser Health News (June 7, 2001), https://khn.org/morning-breakout/dr00005040/.

37 *Diflucan Partnership*, Pfizer, https://www.pfizer.com/responsibility/global_health/diflucan_partnership_program (last visited June 5, 2019).

for ARVs.[38] A unique early case was the successful Hazel Tau Competition Commission case brought by the TAC and the AIDS Law Project in South Africa against the price and refusal to license generic ARVs, resulting in multiple VLs.[39] Among the most influential early VLs was one issued by Gilead. Lacking an international presence and facing protests from AIDS activists,[40] Gilead granted VLs to eight generic companies in India in 2006 with several over-restrictive terms.[41] Following a complaint to the Federal Trade Commission,[42] Gilead modified one questionable provision: removing prohibitions against licensees challenging licensed patents.[43]

## Second Phase: Law Reform, Compulsory Licenses, Oppositions, Medicines Patent Pool, TRIPS-plus Trade Agreements, and Intra-coalition Conflict

The second phase of the A2M movement overlapped chronologically with the first but included more aggressive use of TRIPS flexibilities to overcome IP monopolies such as adoption transition periods for LDCs, reliance on CLs, use of patent opposition procedures, and increased VLs negotiated by the Medicines Patent Pool (MPP). Unfortunately, this confluence of strategies caused some contestation and finally, some fracturing in the A2M movement.

38 Tahir Amin, *Voluntary Licensing Practices in the Pharmaceutical Sector: An Acceptable Solution to Improving Access to Affordable Medicines?*, OXFAM 7 (Feb. 28, 2007), https://apps.who.int/medicinedocs/documents/s19793en/s19793en.pdf; Peter Beyer, *Developing Socially Responsible Intellectual Property Licensing Policies: Non-Exclusive Licensing Initiatives in the Pharmaceutical Sector*, *in* RESEARCH HANDBOOK ON INTELLECTUAL PROPERTY LICENSING 227–56 (Jacques de Werra ed., 2013). On July 1, 2001, Bristol Myers also offered "emergency patent relief" to Aspen Pharmacare agreeing not to sue the generic manufacturer for the next five years for production/sale of ddI in South Africa and in 47 other African countries where it did not have a patent.

39 BELINDA BERESFORD, THE PRICE OF LIFE: HAZEL TAU AND OTHERS VS GLAXOSMITHKLINE AND BOEHRINGER INGELHEIM: A REPORT ON THE EXCESSIVE PRICING COMPLAINT TO SOUTH AFRICA'S COMPETITION COMMISSION 35–37 (2003); Mark Heywood, *South Africa's Treatment Action Campaign: Combining Law and Social Mobilization to Realize the Right to Health*, 1 J. HUM. RTS. PRAC. 14, 14–36 (2009).

40 Liz Highleyman, *Activists Protest Gilead*, THE BAY AREA REPORTER (May 17, 2006), https://www.ebar.com/news///236991.

41 Press Release, Gilead, Gilead Announces Licensing Agreements with Eight India-Based Companies for Manufacturing and Distribution of Generic Versions of Viread in the Developing World (Sept. 22, 2006), http://investors.gilead.com/phoenix.zhtml?c=69964&p=irol-newsArticle&ID=908393. The licenses limited sourcing of pharmaceutical ingredients, seeking royalties, and preventing sales in unapproved markets even with non-patented drugs. James Love, *Blog: Gilead Efforts to Control Global Market for Two AIDS Medicines*, HUFFINGTON POST (Feb. 15, 2007, updated May 25, 2011), https://www.huffingtonpost.com/james-love/gilead-efforts-to-control_b_41304.html.

42 *KEI asks FTC to Investigate Gilead Effort to Control Market for AIDS Drugs Ingredients*, KEI BLOG (Feb. 15, 2007), http://keionline.org/content/view/23/1.

43 *Amendment to the Gilead-Ranbaxy License Agreement*, KEI BLOG (June 9, 2008), https://www.keionline.org/?s=Amendment+to+the+Gilead-Ranbaxy+License+Agreement.

This second phase began with A2M activists initiating campaigns to amend patent laws to incorporate TRIPS flexibilities in several countries. Because India was considered "the pharmacy of the developing world," the most important law reform effort occurred in 2004–2005 when the Indian Patent Act was amended to meet minimum TRIPS requirements. Progressive forces in the Indian government along with civil society called for measures to restrict secondary patents and permit TRIPS-compliant public health flexibilities.[44] Although not perfect, especially in preventing evergreening,[45] the amended Act incorporated many safeguards, including robust opposition procedures and generous conditions for issuing CLs.[46]

India's example encouraged many countries to pursue TRIPS flexibilities, with significant reforms in Zanzibar,[47] Philippines,[48] Indonesia,[49] Uganda,[50] Zambia,[51] South Africa,[52] and the African Regional Intellectual Property

44 Julie George et al., *Intellectual Property and Access to Medicines: Development and Civil Society Initiative in India, in* INTELLECTUAL PROPERTY RIGHTS AND ACCESS TO ARV MEDICINES: CIVIL SOCIETY RESISTANCE IN THE GLOBAL SOUTH, 110–25 (Renata Reis et al. eds., 2009).

45 *See* Sudip Chaudhuri et al., *Five Years into the Product Patent Regime: India's Response* (2010); Bhaven N. Sampat & Tahir Amin, *How Do Public Health Safeguards in Indian Patent Law Affect Pharmaceutical Patenting in Practice*, 38 J. POLITICS, POLICY & LAW 735–55 (2013); FEROZ ALI ET AL., PHARMACEUTICAL PATENT GRANTS IN INDIA: HOW OUR SAFEGUARDS AGAINST EVERGREENING HAVE FAILED, AND WHY THE SYSTEM MUST BE REFORMED (2018), https://www.accessibsa.org/media/2018/04/Pharmaceutical-Patent-Grants-in-India.pdf.

46 Amy Kapczynski, *Harmonization and Its Discontents: A Case Study of TRIPS Implementation in India's Pharmaceutical Sector*, 97 COL. L.R. 1571 (2009); Janice M. Mueller, *The Tiger Awake: The Tumultuous Transformation of India's Patent System and the Rise of Indian Pharmaceutical Innovation*, 68 U. PITT. L.R. 491 (2006).

47 Zanzibar Industrial Property Act No. 4 of 2008 (Tanz.).

48 An Act Providing for Cheaper and Quality Medicines, Amending for the Purpose Republic Act No. 8293, or the Intellectual Property Code, Republic Act No. 6675 or the Generics Act of 1988, and Republic Act No. 5921 or the Pharmacy Law, and for other purposes, Rep. Act No. 9502 (2008).

49 Law of the Republic of Indonesia No. 13 of July 28, 2016, on Patents, https://wipolex.wipo.int/en/text/421120 (English translation on file with the author).

50 Uganda Industrial Property Act, 2014, https://www.wipo.int/edocs/lexdocs/laws/en/sc/sc014en.pdf.

51 Patents Act, Cap, 40 (2016) (Zam.).

52 *South African Cabinet Approves New Intellectual Property Policy,* FIX THE PATENT LAWS (May 24, 2018), https://www.fixthepatentlaws.org (last visited June 9, 2019). For a history of Fix the Patent Laws campaign, see Brook K. Baker, *International Collaboration on IP/Access to Medicines: Birth of South Africa's Fix the Patent Laws Campaign*, 60 N.Y.L. SCH. L. REV. 309, 312–14, 317–19, 320–21 (2015–2016) (and sources cited). For the recently adopted South African policy reform, see THE DEPARTMENT OF TRADE AND INDUSTRY, INTELLECTUAL PROPERTY POLICY FOR THE REPUBLIC OF SOUTH AFRICA – PHASE I (2018), https://www.gov.za/sites/default/files/gcis_document/201808/ippolicy2018-phasei.pdf. For recommended legislative changes, see Brook K. Baker & Yousuf Vawda, *Submission by University of KwaZulu Natal Affiliated Academics on the Draft Intellectual Property Policy of the Republic of South Africa Phase 1 2017* (Oct. 23, 2017) http://law.ukzn.ac.za/Libraries/2017-doc/Submission_by_UKZN_Academics_on_SA_Draft_IP_Policy_2017_-_23_October_2017.sflb.ashx.

Organization (ARIPO) region.[53] South African activists, in particular, waged an eight-year campaign to amend South Africa's Patent Law. The United Nations Development Program (UNDP) and the United Nations Conference on Trade and Development (UNCTD) played an important advisory and convening role in many of these efforts, as have NGOs, including the Health Global Access Project (Health GAP), Third World Network (TWN), and South Centre.

From demanding price concessions or donations from Big Pharma to seeking to overcome patent barriers, A2M activists began an entirely new phase of campaigning for CLs focused on fostering generic competition to lower the price of medicines. In Brazil in the early 2000s, activists worked with the government to use the threat of CLs, which resulted in discounted prices on two ARVs, *nelfinavir* and *efavirenz*.[54] Likewise, civil society in Thailand and the Governmental Pharmaceutical Organization unsuccessfully advocated for the issuance of a CL but subsequently succeeded in revoking the patent on ddI.[55]

The push for CLs accelerated in the mid-2000s as funding expanded for treatment and access, and as global health initiatives – including the Global Fund to Fight AIDS and the President's Emergency Plan for AIDS Relief – required non-violation of patent rights as a precondition to procuring quality generic medicines. Researcher Ellen t'Hoen reports as many as 100 formal and informal CL efforts in sub-Saharan Africa and a few Southeast Asian and Latin American countries, 81 of which were implemented.[56]

53 For a description of civil society policy objectives of the ARIPO reform process, see Brook K. Baker, *A Full Description of WTO TRIPS Flexibilities Available to ARIPO Member States and Critique Of ARIPO's Comparative Study Analyzing and Making Recommendations Concerning Those Flexibilities* (Mar. 5, 2019) (addressing national legislation), https://www.kelinkenya.org/wp-content/uploads/2019/05/ARIPO-Member-States-obligations-and-flexibilities-under-the-WTO-TRIPS-Agreement-March-2019.pdf; Civil Society Proposals to Address Policy and Legal Incoherencies in the Harare Protocol that Impact Access to Health Technologies in ARIPO Member States (June 4, 2019) (addressing Harare Protocol reforms), https://www.kelinkenya.org/wp-content/uploads/2019/06/CSO_TRIPSFlexibilitiesProposalsForARIPOFinal-with-sign-ons-4-6-19.pdf.

54 Jane Galvão, *Brazil and Access to HIV/AIDS Drugs: A Question of Human Rights and Public Health*, 95 Am. J. Pub. Health 1110, 1112–13 (2005).

55 *See* Gaëlle Pascale Krikorian, *From AIDS to Free Trade Agreements: Knowledge Activism in Thailand's Movement for Access to Medicines*, 3 Engaging Sci., Tech. & Soc. 154 (2017); Nathan Ford et al., *Challenge and Co-Operation: Civil Society Activism for Access to HIV Treatment in Thailand*, 14 J. Trop. Med. & Int'l Health 258 (2009).

56 Ellen FM 't Hoen et al., *Medicine Procurement and the Use of Flexibilities in the Agreement on Trade-Related Aspects of Intellectual Property Rights, 2001–2016*, 96 Bull. World Health Org. 185–93 (2018) (19 compulsory licensing undertakings were resolved by other means, including price reductions or VLs, or were otherwise abandoned or invalidated). For efforts to track compulsory licenses on medicines, see Reed Beall & Randall Kuhn, *Trends in Compulsory Licensing of Pharmaceuticals Since the Doha Declaration: A Database Analysis*, 9 PLoS Med. e1001154 (2012), https://journals.plos.org/plosmedicine/article/file?id=10.1371/journal.pmed.1001154&type=printable; James Packard Love, *Recent examples of use of compulsory licenses*, KEI Res. Note No. 2 (2007), https://www.keionline.org/misc-docs/recent_cls_8mar07.pdf.

The first government use licenses were issued in Malaysia in 2003,[57] while Indonesia issued a government use license in October 2004 for manufacturing generic versions of *lamivudine* and *nevirapine*, and to cover *efavirenz* in 2007.[58] On September 3, 2012, Indonesia compulsorily licensed seven HIV and hepatitis B medicines.[59] Between 2006 and 2007, Thailand issued government use licenses on three key ARVs and a cardiovascular medicine.[60] Although Thailand meticulously followed TRIPS flexibilities, Abbott Laboratories – the patentee of *ritonavir* and *lopinavir* – retaliated by withdrawing pending registration applications for multiple medicines. Supporting Abbott, USTR threatened to withdraw trade preferences. Undeterred, the Thai government announced additional government use licenses on several cancer medicines in 2008,[61] before a change in government regrettably paused its compulsory licensing activities.

Inspired by Thailand, Brazil compulsorily licensed *efavirenz*.[62] In another influential case, India's Controller General of Patents, Designs and Trademarks issued an order on March 12, 2012, granting a CL on the cancer drug *sorafenib* in *Natco v. Bayer*,[63] which reduced the price by 95 percent. There were other successful

57 Chee Yoke Ling, *Malaysia's Experience in Increasing Access to Antiretroviral Drugs: Exercising the "Government Use" Option*, Third World Network, IPR Series No. 9 (2006).

58 Sinafah Tunsarawuth, *Indonesia Mulls Compulsory Licenses on Three More HIV/AIDS Drugs*, IP Watch (Nov. 26, 2007), https://www.ip-watch.org/2007/11/26/indonesia-mulls-compulsory-licences-on-three-more-hivaids-drugs/.

59 *Indonesia Issues Compulsory Licenses Against Seven HIV, Hepatitis B Drugs*, IHS Market (Oct. 12, 2012), https://ihsmarkit.com/country-industry-forecasting.html?ID=1065972339.

60 *The Campaign for Use of Compulsory Licensing in Thailand*, Make Medicines Affordable (Feb. 15, 2015), http://makemedicinesaffordable.org/en/the-campaign-for-use-of-compulsory-licensing-in-thailand/.

61 Suwit Wibulpolprasert et al., *Government Use Licenses in Thailand: The Power of Evidence, Civil Movement and Political Leadership*, 7 Glob. Health 1 (2011), https://www.ncbi.nlm.nih.gov/pmc/articles/PMC3180369/pdf/1744-8603-7-32.pdf. For a history of compulsory licensing efforts in Thailand, see *Timeline for US-Thailand Compulsory Licensing Dispute*, Program on Information Justice and Intellectual Property (2009) (and sources cited), http://infojustice.org/wp-content/uploads/2012/11/pijip-thailand-timeline.pdf. For Thailand's defense of its government use licenses, see Ministry of Pub. Health & Nat'l Health Sec. Office, Facts and Evidences on the 10 Burning Issue Related to the Government Use of Patents on Three Patented Essential Drugs in Thailand (2007); Ministry of Pub. Health & Nat'l Health Sec. Offfice, Facts and Evidences on the 10 Burning Issue Related to the Government Use of Patents on four anti-cancer drugs in Thailand (2008).

62 Keith Alcorn, *Brazil issues compulsory license on efavirenz*, NAM aidsmap News (May 7, 2007), http://www.aidsmap.com/Brazil-issues-compulsory-license-on-efavirenz/page/1427206/. For a broader description of Brazilian civil society campaigns to access medicines at the time, see Gabriela Costa Chaves et al., *Access to Medicines and Intellectual Property in Brazil: Reflections and Strategies of Civil Society*, 8 Sur Int'l J. Hum. Rights 163 (2008).

63 *Natco v. Bayer*, (2011) 1 C.L.A. (India).

campaigns for CLs in Ecuador,[64] for a hepatitis C (HCV) CL in Malaysia,[65] and for attempted licenses in Colombia,[66] Peru,[67] and Chile.[68] The US has continually pressured countries against issuing CLs, but its bark is much worse than its bite.[69]

Building on the transition periods for LDCs in Article 66.1 of the TRIPS Agreement, A2M activists fought for extensions of transition periods for LDCs.[70] The TWN and other activists sought extensions of the general TRIPS waiver from 2013 to 2021,[71] and of pharmaceutical extension from 2016 to

64 Carlos M. Correa, *The Use of Compulsory Licenses in Latin America*, Agencia Latinoamericana de Infomacion (Apr. 4, 2013), https://www.alainet.org/en/active/63292; Public Citizen, *Ecuador Takes One Step Forward for Health (Issues New Compulsory Licenses) and One Step Back (Signs Harmful Trade Agreement with the EU)* (2014), https://www.citizen.org/wp-content/uploads/ecuador-compulsory-license-eu-fta-summary-english.pdf.

65 Catherine Saez, *Malaysia Grants Compulsory License for Generic Sofosbuvir Despite Gilead License*, IP Watch (Sept. 15, 2017), https://www.ip-watch.org/2017/09/15/malaysia-grants-compulsory-licence-generic-sofosbuvir-despite-gilead-licence/. Lekhya Kintada, *Compulsory Licensing for Hepatitis C Medicines in Malaysia*, Citizenvox (Apr. 10, 2019), https://citizenvox.org/2019/04/10/compulsory-licensing-for-hepatitis-c-medication-in-malaysia/.

66 *Background FAQ on Glivec (imatainib) Compulsory License in Colombia*, Knowledge Ecology International, https://www.keionline.org/book/background-faq-on-glivec-imatinib-compulsory-license-in-colombia (last visited June 13, 2019); Press Release: Compulsory Licensing in Colombia: Leaked Documents Show Aggressive Lobbying by Novartis, Public Eye (Apr. 12, 2017), https://www.publiceye.ch/en/media-corner/press-releases/detail/compulsory-licensing-in-colombia-leaked-documents-show-aggressive-lobbying-by-novartis/; Ed Silverman, *U.S. Trade Rep is Urged to Revamp Trade Deal with Colombia over Compulsory Licensing*, STAT Pharmalot (June 26, 2018) https://www.statnews.com/pharmalot/2018/06/26/trade-rep-colombia-compulsory-licensing/.

67 Ed Silverman, *Peruvian Lawmakers Seek a Compulsory Licenses for a Bristol HIV Drug*, STAT Pharmalot (May 26, 2017), https://www.statnews.com/pharmalot/2017/05/26/peru-compulsory-license-bristol-drug/.

68 *Inside Views: New Health Ministry of Chile Reaffirms Path to Compulsory Licence for Hepatitis C Drug*, IP Watch (Apr. 9, 2018), https://www.ip-watch.org/2018/09/04/new-health-ministry-chile-reaffirms-path-compulsory-licence-hepatitis-c-drugs/.

69 Brook Baker, *Don't Be Afraid of Compulsory Licenses Despite US Threats: Special 301 Reports 1998–2017 – Listing Concerns But Taking Little Action*, infojustice.org (Feb. 20, 2018), http://infojustice.org/archives/39594; Brook Baker, *Lies, Distortions, and False Promise: The U.S. Position on Compulsory Licenses in the 2018 Special 301 Report*, infojustice.org (May 1, 2018), http://infojustice.org/archives/39888; *see* Brook K. Baker, *Will the Modi Government Succumb to US and Industry Pressure to Modify Its Pro-Access Pharmaceutical Patent Policy?*, 25 Expert Opin. Ther. Patents 6, 1–4 (2015) (presenting a more detailed account of United States pressure against India).

70 Ellen FM 't Hoen et al., *Medicine Procurement and the Use of Flexibilities in the Agreement on Trade-Related Aspects of Intellectual Property Rights, 2001–2016*, 96 Bull. World Health Org. 185–93 (2018) (reporting 40 instances of 28 LDCs invoking the TRIPS pharmaceutical waiver).

71 *See* TRIPS Agreement, *supra* note 8, at art. 66.1. Extension of the Transition Period Under Article 66.1 for Least Developed Country Members, World Trade Organization (Nov. 30 2005) http://www.wto.org/english/tratop_e/trips_e/ta_docs_e/7_1_ipc40_e.pdf; Extension of the Transition Period Under Article 66.1 for Least Developed Country Members, World Trade Organization ¶ 1 (June 12, 2013), https://www.wto.org/english/tratop_e/trips_e/ta_docs_e/7_1_ipc64_e.pdf.

2033.[72] Civil society organizations also supported LDC transition demands,[73] provided technical assistance to LDC negotiators, publicized US and European pressure against extended transition periods,[74] garnered letters of support from law professors, legal experts,[75] and from several global health organizations and institutions, including the UNDP and UNAIDS.[76]

A2M activists also created platforms for revoking patents through opposition procedures.[77] The Lawyers' Collective in India, an early sponsor, succeeded along with generic companies in challenging multiple patent applications released from India's backlog of applications held in the TRIPS Article 70 "mailbox."[78] Indian

72 Paragraph 7 of the Doha Declaration on the TRIPS Agreement and Public Health addressed LDC members' need for an extended transition period with respect to pharmaceutical products. Actualizing Paragraph 7, the TRIPS Council first provided a pharmaceutical extension until Jan. 1, 2016. Extension of the Transition Period under Article 66.1 of the TRIPS Agreement for Least-Developed Country Members for Certain Obligations with Respect to Pharmaceutical Products, World Trade Organization (July 1, 2002), http://www.wto.org/english/tratop_e/trips_e/art66_1_e.htm. Thereafter, there was a further and broader extension until 2033. WTO Members Agree to Extend Drug Patent Exemption for Poorest Members, WTO (Nov. 6, 2015), https://www.wto.org/english/news_e/news15_e/trip_06nov15_e.htm; Council for Trade-Related Aspects of Intellectual Property Rights, Extension of the Transition period under Article 66.1 of the TRIPS Agreement for Least Developed Country Members for Certain Obligations with Respect to Pharmaceutical Products, World Trade Organization (Nov. 6, 2015).

73 Civil Society Letter to Members of the World Trade Organization: Request by Least Developed Country Members for an Extension of the Transitional Period with Respect to Pharmaceutical Products and for Waivers from the Obligation of Articles 70.8 and 70.9 of the TRIPS Agreement, http://infojustice.org/wp-content/uploads/2015/06/LDC-extension-letter.pdf.

74 *US Position on LDC Pharmaceutical Extension of TRIPS Transition Period*, Health GAP (Sept. 15, 2015), https://healthgap.org/us-position-on-ldc-pharmaceutical-extension-of-trips-transition-period/.

75 Global Academics' and Expert Letter on LDCs' TRIPS Extension Request to WTO TRIPS Council Members (Apr. 27, 2013), https://d3n8a8pro7vhmx.cloudfront.net/healthgap/pages/102/attachments/original/1406058716/Global_Academics1_Expert_Letter_on_LDC_Extension_(1).pdf?1406058716.

76 UNAIDS & UNDP, Issue Brief: TRIPS Transition Periods for Least Developed Countries (2013), https://www.unaids.org/sites/default/files/media_asset/JC2474_TRIPS-transition-period-extensions_en_0.pdf; TRIPS Article 70, available at: https://www.wto.org/english/res_e/publications_e/ai17_e/trips_art70_jur.pdf.

77 The TRIPS Agreement references the legality of administrative opposition procedures in art. 62.3, requiring only that they be governed by general principles set out in paragraphs 2 and 3 of art. 41. *See* WIPO, *Opposition Systems*, World Intell. Prop. Org., https://www.wipo.int/scp/en/revocation_mechanisms/opposition/index.html (last visited Feb. 15, 2019). Countries with pre-grant opposition systems include Argentina, Colombia, Costa Rica, Egypt, Honduras, India, Mongolia, Pakistan, Portugal, Spain, and Zambia. Countries and regional bodies with post-grant oppositions include Brazil, Denmark, Finland, Germany, India, Japan, Norway, Pakistan, Moldova, Korea, Sweden, Turkey, United States, EAPO, and EPO.

78 *India's Patent Office Rejects Boehringer's Application for Pediatric Antiretroviral*, Kaiser Health News (June 23, 2008) (reporting 13 oppositions against AIDS medicines), https://khn.org/morning-breakout/dr00052881/.

opposition procedures were used to challenge unworthy, time-barred, and secondary or "evergreening" of patents on key medicines, including most famously Novartis' cancer medicine *imatinib* (*Glivec®*).[79] Supported by hard-fought grants from Unitaid[80] and additional funding from the MSF,[81] the Lawyers' Collective – with the Initiative for Medicines Access and Knowledge (I-MAK),[82] International Treatment Preparedness Coalition (ITPC), and their allies[83] – launched oppositions to key ARVs and HCV medicines in India, Argentina, Brazil, Thailand, Ukraine, and other countries.

Since 2006, after it won patent oppositions on four ARVs in India, I-MAK became a major player in opposing patents given its founders' technical expertise. Today, I-MAK's work is significant to 49 countries and 33 therapies for 16 diseases, including HCV, HIV, leukemia, tuberculosis (TB), diabetes, cancer, and blood-related disorders.[84] I-MAK has helped catalyze a coalition of five global partners to work on patent oppositions to key medicines in middle-income countries not typically benefitting from inclusion in VLs: Argentina, Brazil, Thailand, and Ukraine. I-MAK and its partners' opposition efforts have grown with significant estimated cost savings, price negotiations, and policy dialogues.[85]

Under activist pressure, some pharmaceutical companies began to negotiate bilateral VLs with generic companies in the early 2000s. However, some activists – concerned about the slow pace of law reform and the country-by-country and drug-by-drug nature of CLs and opposition procedures – worked toward

79 Chan Park & L. Menghaney, *TRIPS Flexibilities: The Scope of Patentability and Oppositions to Patents in India*, *in* Access to Knowledge in the Age of Intellectual Property (Gaelle Krikorian & Amy Kapczynski, eds. 2010), http://mitpress.mit.edu/books/chapters/189095196Xchap18.pdf.

80 Unitaid supported Lawyers Collective's opposition work in India though the work was prematurely shut down because of actions taken by the government of India against the Lawyers Collective. *See* Unitaids' approach to intellectual property, 27 (2016), http://itpcglobal.org/wp-content/uploads/2018/05/ITPC-Annual-Review-2017.pdf. Unitaid has supported the ITPC-led coalition's opposition work in several countries. *See Blog: Unitaid Investment Expands Our Work on Access to Medicines*, make medicines affordable (Sept. 11, 2018), http://makemedicinesaffordable.org/en/unitaid-investment-expands-our-work-on-access-to-medicines/.

81 In addition to providing financial support for oppositions, MSF also maintains a webpage reporting on and supporting use of oppositions. Patent Opposition Database, https://www.patentoppositions.org.

82 *See Solving the Drug Patent Problem*, I-MAK, https://www.i-mak.org (last visited June 7, 2019) [hereinafter *Solving Drug Patent Problem*].

83 *See* Make Medicines Affordable, http://makemedicinesaffordable.org/en/strategy/patent-challenges/.

84 *See Our Impact*, I-MAK, https://www.i-mak.org/impact/ (last visited June 7, 2019) [hereinafter *Our Impact*].

85 ITPC claims that its past opposition work (seven oppositions in four countries) under its first Unitaid grant produced $472 million in cost savings. ITPC, What Community Activism Can Achieve: Annual Report 2017, 15 (2018), http://itpcglobal.org/wp-content/uploads/2018/05/ITPC-Annual-Review-2017.pdf. I-MAK claims that its opposition work has resulted in $2 billion of cost savings. *Our Impact*, *supra* note 84.

an efficient solution for securing VLs with more pro-access terms: a patent pool for medicines. Jamie Love, the first and leading proponent of a patent pool for medicines, was joined by the MSF and others to push for establishing the MPP under the financial sponsorship of Unitaid.[86] Established in 2010, the early history of the MPP has been chronicled[87] along with the provision of its licenses.[88] It has received multiple statements of high-level support in several international forums.[89]

The MPP's basic approach is to seek VLs from originators and to negotiate multiple out-licenses to qualified generic producers, who are thereby permitted to manufacture and sell single-dose and fixed-dose combination medicines in designated LMIC territories. Besides granting permission to work the patents in the allowed field(s) of use, the licenses frequently allow access to trade secret know-how and bypass rules interfering with registration at national drug regulatory authorities. The licenses mandate that global quality standards be met: prequalification by the WHO, registration by a stringent regulatory authority, or temporary approval by a WHO expert review committee. Also, MPP licenses must represent an improvement over existing agreements and must not interfere with countries' or generic producers' right to oppose or invalidate patents or

86 UNITAID Executive Board, *Resolution No. 7: Memorandum of Understanding Between UNITAID and Medicines Patent Pool Foundation*, Unitaid (June 8–9, 2010), https://unitaid.eu/assets/07_eb12-res7-mou-patent-pool.pdf; World Health Organization, *Memorandum of Understanding Between the World Health Organization and the Medicines Patent Pool Foundation* (Sept. 14, 2010) (on file with the author).

87 *See generally* Jorge Bermudez & Ellen 't Hoen, *The UNITAID Patent Pool Initiative: Bringing Patents Together for the Common Good*, 4 Open AIDS J. 37 (2010), https://www.ncbi.nlm.nih.gov/pmc/articles/PMC2842943/pdf/TOAIDJ-4-37.pdf; Michelle Childs, *Towards a Patent Pool for HIV Medicines*, 4 Open AIDS J. 33 (2010), https://www.ncbi.nlm.nih.gov/pmc/articles/PMC2817875/pdf/TOAIDJ-4-33.pdf; Krista L. Cox, *The Medicines Patent Pool: Promoting Access and Innovation for Life-Saving Medicines Through Voluntary Licenses*, 4 Hastings Sci. & Tech. L. J. 291 (2012).

88 Brook K. Baker, *A Sliver of Hope: Analyzing Voluntary Licenses to Accelerate Affordable Access to Medicines*, 10 Northeastern U. L. Rev. 226, 255–308 (2018).

89 WHO, Global Strategy and Plan of Action on Public Health, Innovation and Intellectual Property (2011) (referencing patent pools for medicines), http://www.who.int/phi/publications/Global_Strategy_Plan_Action.pdf; endorsed in WHO, Consultative Expert Working Grp. on Research & Dev.: Fin. & Coordination, *Research and Development to Meet Health Needs in Developing Countries: Strengthening Global Financing and Coordination*, at 56–57 (Apr. 2012), http://apps.who.int/iris/bitstream/10665/254706/1/9789241503457-eng.pdf?ua=1; and supported by the U.N. Secretary-General's High-Level Panel on Access to Med., *Promoting Innovation and Access to Health Technologies*, 8, 10–11 (Sept. 2016), https://static1.squarespace.com/static/562094dee4b0d00c1a3ef761/t/57d9c6ebf5e231b2f02cd3d4/1473890031320/UNSG+HLP+Report+FINAL+12+Sept+2016.pdf. The Lancet Commission on Essential Medicines recommended that coverage of MPP be expanded to include access to all essential medicines. Veronika J. Wirtz et al., *Essential Medicines for Universal Health Coverage*, 389 Lancet 403, 454–55, 460 (2017), http://www.thelancet.com/pdfs/journals/lancet/PIIS0140-6736(16)31599-9.pdf?code=lancet-site.

to seek or grant CLs. Finally, transparency is assured as the agreements are published on the MPP webpage, and in maintaining the MPP patent licenses database (MedsPaL) that seeks to keep accurate and up-to-date information on the patent status of key AIDS, TB, HCV, and other essential medicines in LMICs.[90]

The geographical scope of MPP licenses included directly and indirectly licensed jurisdictions where there is no blocking patent in the country of use, or alternately, pursuant to marketing permissions allowing production, import, or use of patented medication. A recent MPP license with ViiV Healthcare allows market segmentation – by permitting generic sales to the public, NGOs, and to major global health initiatives – while retaining the private sector for more profitable sales by innovators. These are voluntary government use licenses under Article 31 of the TRIPS Agreement. MPP licenses in LMICs cover TB (100 percent), HIV pediatric medicines (99 percent), HIV (78.9 percent to 90 percent), and HCV (47.5 percent to 65.4 percent) at significantly lower coverage. Despite this, millions with HIV and tens of millions with HCV in certain middle-income countries cannot source low-cost generic equivalents from MPP licensees.[91]

As of December 2018, MPP licenses with nine patent holders covered 13 HIV ARVs, 1 HIV nanotechnology and TB treatment, and 4 HCV antivirals. The MPP also executed sublicenses with 23 generic manufacturers.[92] The public health impact of MPP agreements include access to HIV and HCV treatment totaling 14.6 million treatment years in 125 countries, and a reduction in prices by 89 percent, amounting to $631 million saved through June 2018,[93] with $2.3 billion protected toward HIV medicines through 2028.[94]

Additionally, the MPP has incentivized new pediatric and adult formulations and launched the Paediatric HIV Treatment Initiative[95] and the Drug for

90 *MedsPaL Factsheet*, Meds. Patent Pool (Dec. 7, 2017), https://medicinespatentpool.org/uploads/2017/07/MedsPaL-Flyer_Dec17_FINAL.pdf.

91 *License Overview*, Meds. Patent Pool, *https://medicinespatentpool.org/what-we-do/global-licence-overview/* (last accessed June 13, 2019). To access licenses' direct territorial coverage, see *Products Licensed*, Meds. Patent Pool, https://medicinespatentpool.org/what-we-do/global-licence-overview/licences-in-the-mpp/ (last visited June 13, 2019).

92 *Update on Progress of Sublicenses*, Meds. Patent Pool, https://medicinespatentpool.org/what-we-do/global-licence-overview/update-on-progress-of-mpp-sublicensees/ (last visited June 13, 2019). Details of then current licenses, see *License Overview*, *supra* note 91.

93 *Update on Progress of Sublicenses*, *supra* note 92.

94 Sandeep Juneja et al., *Projected Savings Through Public Health Voluntary Licences of HIV Drugs Negotiated by the Medicines Patent Pool (MPP)*, 12 PLoS One e177770 (2017), http://journals.plos.org/plosone/article/file?id=10.1371/journal.pone.0177770&type=printable.

95 Press Release, Medicines Patent Pool, Paediatric HIV Treatment Initiative (PHTI) to Spur Innovation and Access to Improve the Lives of Children Living with HIV (May 19, 2014), https://medicinespatentpool.org/mpp-media-post/paediatric-hiv-treatment-initiative-phti-to-spur-innovation-and-access-to-improve-the-lives-of-children-living-with-hiv/.

Neglected Diseases initiative (DNDi).[96] For adults, MPP licenses have allowed novel co-formulation of TDF/*lamivudine* (3tC)/*efavirenz* (EFV) and more recently, TAF/3tC/EFV. The MPP's most significant contribution to new adult formulations is a more efficacious, durable, less toxic, and cheaper combination of *dolutegravir* (DTG), 3tC, and TDF, and will be sold in about 92 countries. Also, the MPP development license for new nanotechnologies might eventually result in improved and long-lasting formulations.[97] The MPP has explored expansion of its mandate to other diseases, and GlaxoSmithKline has expressed an intention to license cancer medicines for LMICs.[98]

Multilateral initiatives to expand access to needed medicines have included the efforts of the MSF and the Drugs for Neglected Diseases Working Group's focus on so-called neglected diseases.[99] This campaign pushed the WHO to invest R&D on Type 3 neglected diseases that primarily affect the poorest in tropical regions.[100]

96 Press Release, Drugs for Neglected Diseases Initiative, Child-friendly Formulation of WHO-recommended Treatment Now Approved by the US FDA for Children Living with HIV (June 3, 2015) https://www.dndi.org/2015/media-centre/press-releases/pr-phti-fda-approval-pellets/.

97 E-mail from Esteban Burrone, Head of Policy, Medicines Patent Pool, to author (May 14, 2018, timestamp) (on file with author) (referencing adult TAF/FTC/DTG and pediatric ABC/3tC/EFV); Press Release, Medicines Patent Pool, The Medicines Patent Pool Signs a Collaborative Agreement with the University of Liverpool to Develop HIV Nanomedicines (Dec. 1, 2015), https://medicinespatentpool.org/mpp-media-post/the-medicines-patent-pool-signs-a-collaborative-agreement-with-the-university-of-liverpool-to-develop-hiv-nanomedicines/; Meds. Patent Pool & Unitaid, Intellectual Property Report on Long-Lasting Technologies (2018), https://medicinespatentpool.org/uploads/2018/12/MPP-Unitaid_Intellectual-property-report-on-long-acting-technologies.pdf.

98 *See* Press Release, GlaxoSmithKline, GSK Expands Graduated Approach to Patents and Intellectual Property to Widen Access to Medicines in the World's Poorest Countries (Mar. 31, 2016), https://www.gsk.com/en-gb/media/press-releases/gsk-expands-graduated-approach-to-patents-and-intellectual-property-to-widen-access-to-medicines-in-the-world-s-poorest-countries/.

99 MSF & DND, Fatal Imbalance: The Crisis in Research and Development for Drugs for Neglected Diseases (2001) (reporting that of the 1393 total new drugs approved between 1975 and 1999, only one percent (13 drugs) were specifically indicated for a tropical disease), https://msfaccess.org/sites/default/files/MSF_assets/NegDis/Docs/NEGDIS_report_FatalImbalance_CrisisInR%26D_ENG_2001.pdf.

100 The WHO Commission on Intellectual Property Rights, Innovation and Public Health was established in 2003 and issued its first report, Public health, innovation and intellectual Property Rights in 2006. https://www.who.int/intellectualproperty/documents/thereport/ENPublicHealthReport.pdf?ua=1. Subsequently, as debates within the WHO continued, A Global Strategy and Plan of Action on Public Health, Innovation and Intellectual Property was published in 2011. https://www.who.int/phi/publications/Global_Strategy_Plan_Action.pdf?ua=1. There was as well a Consultative Expert Working Group on Research and Development, which issued its primary report in 2012. Research and Development to Meet Health Needs in Developing Countries: Strengthening Global Financing and Coordination: Report of the Consultative Expert Working Group on Research and Development: Financing and Coordination, https://www.who.int/phi/CEWG_Report_5_April_2012.pdf?ua=1.

This campaign resulted in significant funding[101] resulting in private-public and product development partnerships focusing on investigating new products for treating neglected diseases.[102] One of the most progressive initiatives is the DNDi, which has launched several products to or near to market[103] with significant cost savings in R&D expenses.[104]

Meanwhile, following on the Commission on Macroeconomics and Health's monumental report,[105] the highly influential United Kingdom (UK) Commission on Intellectual Property Rights issued a report criticizing several aspects of the TRIPS regime.[106] Another multilateral effort to increase access to medicines was the development agenda at the World Intellectual Property Organization (WIPO), first initiated by Argentina and Brazil in 2004, and adopted in 2007 after being supported by 12 developing countries with

101 *See* Nick Chapman et al., Neglected Disease Research: Reaching New Heights, G-Finder Policy Cures Research 22, 80 (2018) (reporting R&D investments that increased significantly from 2007 to 2009, followed by a dip in funding but then increases in 2016 and 2017, with 65 percent of funding in 2017 coming from public sources, 19 percent from charitable sources, and on 16 percent from private industry), https://www.policycuresresearch.org/wp-content/uploads/Y11_G-FINDER_Full_report_Reaching_new_heights.pdf.

102 *See* Rachel Kiddell-Monroe et al., Re:Route: A map of the Alternative Biomedical R&D Landscape, Universities Allied for Essential Medicines (2016), ***available at*** http://www.altreroute.com/assets/download/UAEM_Reroute_Report.pdf; *See also* Brook Baker, Background Paper: Existing and prior work, initiatives and proposals to improve innovation and access to health technologies, U.N. Secretary-General's High-Level Panel on Access to Medicines (Mar. 2016), https://static1.squarespace.com/static/562094dee4b0d00c1a3ef761/t/56da11782b8dde9c3d5865b4/1457132156145/DRAFT+Background+Paper+on+Existing+and+prior+work+initiatives+and+propo+++.pdf.

103 DNDi, *R&D Portfolio Updates, February 2019*, https://mailchi.mp/dndi/dndi-rd-portfolio-update-pp0aldai09?e=17b66dfb62.

104 DNDi, An Innovative Approach to R&D for Neglected Patients: Ten Years of Experience and Lessons Learned by DNDi (Jan. 2014) (reporting DNDi's cost of development ranges from EUR 6–20 million for an improved treatment, to EUR 30–40 million for a new chemical entity, but taking risk of failure into account brings the cost range of an improved treatment to EUR 10–40 million, and to EUR 100–50 million for a new chemical entity), https://www.dndi.org/wp-content/uploads/2009/03/DNDi_Modelpaper_2013.pdf.

105 Jeffrey D. Sachs, World Health Org. (WHO), Comm'n on Macroeconomics & Health, Macroeconomics and Health: Investing in Health for Economic Development (2001), http://www3.who.int/whosis/menu.cfm?path=whosis,cmh&language=english.

106 Comm'n on Intellectual Prop. Rights, Integrating Intellectual Property Rights and Development, Report of the Commission on Intellectual Property Rights 29–55 (2002), http://www.iprcommission.org/papers/pdfs/final_report/CIPRfullfinal.pdf.

45 recommendations.[107] However, there have been criticisms of the WIPO's implementation of technical assistance under the development agenda.[108] A more successful initiative was the creation of Unitaid, a Geneva-based organization supported largely with innovative levies on airline tickets and focused on overcoming market barriers to accelerate access to new medicines. Unitaid has had significant public health impacts over its first 13 years of existence.[109]

The second phase of activism continued its long-lasting focus on protecting key LMICs from the IP-maximalist demands of the US and Big Pharma. The US made repeated TRIPS-plus demands in bilateral and regional trade negotiations, including in failed negotiations in the Americas region,[110] with Thailand,[111] and with the Southern Africa Customs Union,[112] all of which failed partly because of protracted civil society opposition.[113] Typically, the US pursued substantive

107 World Intellectual Property Organization (WIPO), *WIPO Development Agenda: Background 2004–2007*, https://www.wipo.int/ip-development/en/agenda/background.html (last visited June 10, 2019).

108 *See* Carolyn D. Birkbeck & Santiago Roca, An External Review of WIPO Technical Assistance in the Area of Cooperation for Development (2011), https://www.wipo.int/edocs/mdocs/mdocs/en/cdip_8/cdip_8_inf_1-annex1.pdf.

109 Unitaid, *Our Impact: Defining and Measuring Impacts is at the Core of Unitaid's Strategic Model*, https://unitaid.org/impact/#enhttps://unitaid.org/impact/#en (last visited June 10, 2019).

110 Kimberly Amadeo, *FTAA Agreement, Its Members, With Its Pros and Cons: Why the World's Largest Trade Zone Failed*, https://www.thebalance.com/ftaa-agreement-member-countries-pros-and-cons-3305577 (last updated Dec. 21, 2018).

111 Office of the U.S. Trade Rep., *Thailand*, https://ustr.gov/countries-regions/southeast-asia-pacific/thailand (last visited Apr. 24, 2019); *see also* Raymond J. Ahearn & Wayne M. Morrison, US-Thai Free Trade Agreement Negotiations, CRS Report for Congress (2006), https://nationalaglawcenter.org/wp-content/uploads/assets/crs/RL32314.pdf; *see generally* Jakkrit Kuanpoth et al., *Public Health at Risk: A US Free Trade Agreement could Threaten Access to Medicines in Thailand*, Oxford Int'l Briefing Paper no. 86 (2006), https://ro.uow.edu.au/cgi/viewcontent.cgi?referer=https://www.google.com/&httpsredir=1&article=1113&context=lawpapers (analyzing the negative impacts of the proposed US-Thai FTA on access to medicines).

112 Jonathan Berger & Achal Prabhala, *Addressing the Impact of TRIPS-Plus Patent Rules in the Proposed US-SACU Free Trade Agreement* (draft 2005), https://www.who.int/hiv/amds/capacity/tza2_oxfamreport_pricing_financing.pdf.

113 *See* Biothai, *Fight FTAs: The Experience in Thailand* (Oct. 2007), https://www.bilaterals.org/IMG/pdf/fightingFTA-en-Hi-2-b-experience-in-thailand.pdf (documenting a long history of Thai opposition to FTAs, including a demonstration on Jan. 11, 2006); Press Release, American Friends Service Committee, Departing from USTR, Portman leaves dead US-Southern Africa negotiation behind (Apr. 18, 2006), https://www.bilaterals.org/?departing-from-ustr-portman-leaves (referencing an international campaign opposing US-SACU free trade negotiations); *Protest Photos*, Citizens Trade Campaign (2003), https://www.citizenstrade.org/ctc/trade-policies/potential-trade-agreements/the-free-trade-area-of-the-americas-ftaa/protest-photos/ (displaying photos of protests against the FTAA in Miami).

TRIPS-plus provisions that lengthen, strengthen, and broaden IPR and enforcement, including eased standards of patentability and disclosure; limitations on allowable exclusions from patentability and limited exceptions to patent rights; patent term extensions; regulatory data exclusivity and patent-registration linkage; and disallowance of opposition procedures.[114]

Simultaneously, the US and Europe sought enhanced enforcement and anti-counterfeiting measures in bilateral and regional trade agreements, including market-price damages, new border measures, criminal enforcement, and investor-state dispute settlement (ISDS) of IP-related claims. The most aggressive enforcement effort was the Anti-Counterfeiting Trade Agreement (ACTA).[115] Although A2M activists raised concerns about the ACTA's impact on access to medicines,[116] especially after illegal seizures of lawful generic medicines-in-transit in Europe in 2008 and 2009,[117] it was European civil society challenging the ACTA's restrictions on internet freedoms that

114 *See generally* Sean Flynn et al., *U.S. Proposal for an Intellectual Property Chapter in the Trans-Pacific Partnership Agreement*, 28 Am. U. Int'l L. Rev. 105–202 (2012).

115 *See generally* Michael Blakeney, Intellectual Property Enforcement: A Commentary on the Anti-Counterfeiting Trade Agreement (ACTA) (2012).

116 *See* Brook K. Baker, *ACTA: Risks of Third-Party Enforcement to Access to Medicines*, 26 Am. U. Int'l L. Rev. 579 (2011), http://www.auilr.org/pdf/26/26.3.3.pdf; Sean Flynn & Bifan Madhani, *ACTA and Access to Medicines*, PIJIP Res. Paper Series, Paper 22 (2011), http://digitalcommons.wcl.american.edu/research/22; Medecins Sans Frontieres, A Blank Check: The Anti-Counterfeiting Trade Agreement (ACTA) and its Impact on Access to Medicines (Feb. 2012), https://msfaccess.org/sites/default/files/MSF_assets/Access/Docs/Access_Briefing_ACTABlankCheque_ENG_2012.pdf.

117 Frederick M. Abbott, *Seizure of Generic Pharmaceuticals in Transit Based on Allegations of Patent Infringement: A Threat to International Trade, Development and Public Welfare*, 1 WIPO J. 43 (2009), (detailing how civil society mobilized to condemn seizures ); *see* William New, *International Health Groups Warn WHO and WTO on Medicines Seizures*, IP Watch (Feb. 21, 2009), https://www.ip-watch.org/2009/02/21/international-health-groups-warn-who-wto-on-medicines-seizures/; William New, *Alarm Escalates Over Delayed Generic Shipments As Action Sought*, IP Watch (June 3, 2009), https://www.ip-watch.org/2009/03/06/alarm-escalates-over-delayed-generic-drug-shipments-as-action-sought/; *see generally* Bryan Mercurio, *'Seizing' Pharmaceuticals in Transit: Analysing the WTO Dispute that Wasn't*, 61 Int'l & Comparative L. Quarterly 389 (2012) (discussing the resulting WTO case and its settlement); Brook K. Baker, *Settlement of India/EU WTO Dispute re Seizures of In-Transit Medicines: Why the Proposed EU Border Regulation Isn't Good Enough*, PIJIP Research Paper Series (2012), http://digitalcommons.wcl.american.edu/cgi/viewcontent.cgi?article=1026&context=research.

ultimately led to its demise.[118] However, A2M activists continued the fight against anti-counterfeiting threats, including the WHO's IMPACT initiative[119] and in Uganda and Kenya.[120]

To achieve IP maximalization, the US and EU deployed an IP ratchet that escalated IP demands in each successive agreement.[121] Although the ratchet ultimately faltered in the US in 2007 as a result of the New Trade

118 James Losey, *The Anti-Counterfeiting Trade Agreement and European Civil Society: A Case Study on Networked Advocacy*, 4 J. INF. POL. 205 (2014), https://www.jstor.org/stable/pdf/10.5325/jinfopoli.4.2014.0205.pdf?refreqid=excelsior%3A064c10c698ba3f7a69b-c8fe8ddd239fa; *see* Torie Bosch, *European Parliaments Rejection of ACTA Demonstrates the Power of Digital Activism*, SLATE (July 4, 2012), https://slate.com/technology/2012/07/acta-defeat-in-european-parliament-inspired-by-anti-sopa-activism.html.

119 *See generally* World Health Organization, *Growing Threat from Counterfeit Medicines*, 88 BULL. WORLD HEALTH ORGAN. 245 (2010), https://www.who.int/bulletin/volumes/88/4/10-020410.pdf?ua=1. (describing IMPACT and responses of critics, *see* World Health Organization & International Medical Products Anti-Counterfeiting Taskforce (IMPACT), IMPACT: FREQUENTLY ASKED QUESTIONS WITH ANSWERS (2010), https://www.who.int/medicines/services/counterfeit/impact-faqwa.pdf; WHO & IMPACT, COUNTERFEIT DRUGS KILL!, https://www.gphf.org/images/downloads/impactbrochure.pdf; Sangeaeta Shashikant, *WHO: Concerns Voiced over IMPACT, Secretariat's Role on "Counterfeits"*, TWN INFO SERVICE ON WTO & TRADE ISSUES (Feb. 2, 2009) (expressing civil society opposition to IMPACT), https://www.twn.my/title2/wto.info/2009/twninfo20090201.htm; South Centre & Center for International Environmental Law, *Counterfeit Medical Products: Need for Caution Against Co-Opting Public Health Concerns for IP Protection and Enforcement*, INTELL. PROP. QUARTERLY UPDATE (2009), https://www.ciel.org/wp-content/uploads/2015/06/IP_Update_1Q09.pdf. For a response to the critique, *see* Sushmi Dey & Khomba Singh, *WHO won't Redefine Fake Drugs*, THE ECONOMIC TIMES (Jan. 27, 2009), https://economictimes.indiatimes.com/industry/healthcare/biotech/pharmaceuticals/who-wont-redefine-fake-drugs/articleshow/4034234.cms?from=mdr.

120 Allan Maleche & Emma Day, *Right to Health Encompasses Right to Access Essential Generic Medicines: Challenging the 2008 Anti-Counterfeit Act in Kenya*, 16 HEALTH & HUM. RIGHTS J. 96 (2014), https://cdn2.sph.harvard.edu/wp-content/uploads/sites/125/2014/12/Maleche-final1.pdf; Center for Health, Human Rights and Development (CEHURD), *Anti-counterfeiting Laws and Access to Essential Medicines in East and Southern Africa*, EQUINET POLICY BRIEF NUMBER 22 (2010), http://www.equinetafrica.org/sites/default/files/uploads/documents/POL_Brief22_counterfeits.pdf; Michael Wambi, *Uganda: New Version of Anti-Counterfeiting Bills Still Problematic*, INTER PRESS SERVICE NEWS AGENCY (May 6, 2010), http://www.ipsnews.net/2010/05/uganda-new-version-of-anti-counterfeiting-bill-still-problematic/.

121 Peter Drahos, The Global Ratchet for Intellectual Property Rights: Why It Fails as Policy and What Should Be Done About It, 1–2 (2003) (unpublished manuscript), http://www.anu.edu.au/fellows/pdrahos/reports/pdfs/2003globalipratchet.pdf (summarizing that the intellectual property ratchet "means that each subsequent bilateral or multilateral agreement can and usually does establish a higher standard of IP protection."); *see* Bryan Mercurio, *TRIPS-Plus Provisions in FTAs: Recent Trends, in* REGIONAL TRADE AGREEMENTS AND THE WTO LEGAL SYSTEM (Lorand Bartels & Federico Ortino eds., 2006); Susan Sell, *The Global IP Upward Ratchet, Anti-Counterfeiting and Piracy Enforcement Efforts: The State of Play*, PIJIP RESEARCH PAPER NO. 15 (2010) (applying the IP-ratchet metaphor to the TRIPS-plus enforcement agenda).

Policy,[122] the temporary retractions or limitations on the most damaging TRIPS-plus demands for developing country trade partners were reversed in Trans-Pacific Partnership Agreement negotiations[123] and more recently in NAFTA 2.0.[124] Additionally, both the US and Europe issued veiled trade threats against countries that failed to accede to their excessive demands or that used TRIPS-compliant public health flexibilities – in the US, via annual Special 301 Reports,[125] and in Europe, via reporting on the protection and enforcement of IPR in third countries and on counterfeiting and piracy.[126] In fact, US Special 301 featured a new demand to cut back on use of price controls, whether in the form of reference pricing or listing and pricing decisions in their therapeutic formularies.[127]

During this second phase, Big Pharma pursued its TRIPS-plus demands in lawsuits, most notably its infamous challenge to India's decision denying a

122 I. M. (Mac) Destler, AMERICAN TRADE POLITICS IN 2007: BUILDING BIPARTISAN COMPROMISE, PETERSON INSTITUTE FOR INTERNATIONAL ECONOMICS NO. PB07-5, Appendix B (May 2007), https://piie.com/sites/default/files/publications/pb/pb07-5.pdf. Such provisions included (1) concurrent period of data exclusivity if trading partner granted marketing approval within six months of application; (2) patent term extensions; (3) elimination of patent linkage required establishment of expeditious adjudication of patent disputes; and (4) textual affirmation to data exclusivity. *Id.* at 25–26. These requirements were incorporated in the U.S.-Peru, U.S.-Panama, U.S.-Columbia, and U.S.-Korea free trade agreements. Brook K. Baker, *Ending Drug Registration Apartheid – Taming Data Exclusivity and Patent/Registration Linkage*, 34 AM. J. LAW & MED. 303, 335–41 (2008), https://journals.sagepub.com/doi/pdf/10.1177/009885880803400209.

123 Sean Flynn et al., *supra* note 114; Brook K. Baker, *Trans-Pacific Partnership Provisions in Intellectual Property, Transparency, and Investment Chapters Threaten Access to Medicines in the US and Elsewhere*, 13 PLoS MED. e1001970 (2016), http://journals.plos.org/plosmedicine/article?id=10.1371/journal.pmed.1001970; Deborah Gleeson et al., *The Trans Pacific Partnership Agreement, Intellectual Property and Medicines: Differential Outcomes for Developed and Developing Countries*, 18 GLOBAL SOCIAL POLICY 7–27 (2017).

124 Burcu Kilic, NAFTA 2.0 CHAPTER 20 PHARMACEUTICAL-RELATED PATENT PROVISIONS (2019), https://www.citizen.org/wp-content/uploads/nafta-2.0-pharmaceutical-related-patent-provisions.pdf.

125 *Special 301*, OFFICE OF THE U.S. TRADE REP., https://ustr.gov/issue-areas/intellectual-property/Special-301 (last visited Apr. 24, 2019); for a critique of the legality of US Special 301 practice, *see* Sean M. Flynn, *Special 301 of the Trade Act of 1974 and Global Access to Medicines*, 7 J. GENERIC MEDS. 309 (2010).

126 *See* European Commission, COMMISSION STAFF WORKING DOCUMENT: REPORT ON THE PROTECTION AND ENFORCEMENT OF INTELLECTUAL PROPERTY RIGHTS IN THIRD COUNTRIES, SWD (2018) 47 final, http://trade.ec.europa.eu/doclib/docs/2018/march/tradoc_156634.pdf; European Commission, Commission Staff Working Document: COUNTERFEIT AND PIRACY WATCH LIST, SWD (2018) 492 final, http://trade.ec.europa.eu/doclib/docs/2018/december/tradoc_157564.pdf.

127 *See* OFFICE OF THE U.S. TRADE REP., 2019 SPECIAL 301 REPORT, 15 (2019), https://ustr.gov/sites/default/files/2019_Special_301_Report.pdf. For a detailed discussion of long-standing United States concerns about foreign price controls, see U.S. Department of Commerce Internal Trade Administration, *Pharmaceutical Price Control in OECD Countries: Implications for U.S. Consumers, Pricing, Research and Development, and Innovation* (2004), https://2016.trade.gov/td/health/DrugPricingStudy.pdf.

patent on Novartis cancer medicine *Glivec*®. Novartis pursued a two-part challenge against India's amended patent law and the decision to deny a secondary patent on the active pharmaceutical ingredient, *imatinib*.[128] In its first lawsuit, Novartis tried to invalidate Section 3(d) of the Amended Indian Patent Act of 2005, alleging that it was both unconstitutional and in violation of the TRIPS Agreement because the section denied patents on variations of known substances unless there was significant new efficacy. This lawsuit was forcefully rejected by the Madras High Court.[129] On appeal, in a momentous decision, the Indian Supreme Court rejected this challenge, upholding a broad anti-evergreening interpretation of Section 3(d) in clarifying that change in efficacy must demonstrate significant *therapeutic* efficacy.[130]

Big Pharma's lawsuit against Argentina's pharmaceutical patent examination guidelines[131] had a chilling effect on countries' willingness to closely examine and reject pharmaceutical patents.[132] More quietly, pharma companies have filed multiple court challenges to patenting, regulatory, and pricing decisions by LMICs. Alarmingly, Big Pharma has recently resorted to pursuing IP-related claims through ISDS mechanisms, whereby private arbitrators are appointed to consider whether government decisions and policies have unfairly or discriminatorily treated the investment return interests of companies intent on maximizing profits from their IP monopolies on medicines. The most notorious case is *Eli Lilly v. Canada*, where Eli Lilly unsuccessfully challenged court decisions

128 *See* Anand Grover, *Analysing the Novartis Story*, XLVIII Lawyers' Collective Newsl. No. 32 (Aug. 10, 2013), https://www.lawyerscollective.org/updates/analysing-the-novartis-story.

129 *Novartis AG v. Union of India*, (2007) AIR 24759 (Madras H.C.); Linda L. Lee, *Trials and TRIPS-ulations: Indian Patent Law and Novartis AG v. Union of India*, 23 Berkeley Tech. L. J. 281, 299–302 (2008).

130 *See* Ravinder Gabble & Jillian Clare Kohler, *To Patent or Not to Patent? The Case of Novartis' Cancer Drug Glivec in India*, 10 Glob. Health (2014), https://globalizationandhealth.biomedcentral.com/track/pdf/10.1186/1744-8603-10-3; Saby Ghoshray, *3(d) View of India's Patent Law: Social Justice Aspiration Meets Property Rights in Novartis v. Union of India & Others*, 13 J. Marshall Rev. Intell. Prop. L. 719 (2014); for a more negative view, *see* Dorothy Du, *Novartis AG v. Union of India: "Evergreening," TRIPS, and "Enhanced Efficacy" Under Section 3(d)*, 21 J. Intell. Prop. L. 223 (2014).

131 "Pautas para el examen de Patentabilidad de las solicitudes de Patentes sobre Invenciones Químico-Farmacéuticas", enacted by a joint regulation of the Ministries of Industry and Health and the Instituto Nacional de la Propiedad Industrial (the Argentine Patent Office), Nos. 118/2012, 546/2012 and 107/2012, issued on May 2, 2012. The official text (in Spanish) can be found at http://www.wipo.int/wipolex/en/details.jsp?id=13007.See *also Argentina Adopts Guidelines to Examine Patent Applications for Pharmaceuticals*, Don't Trade Away Our Lives (May 31, 2012), https://donttradeourlivesaway.wordpress.com/2012/05/31/argentina-adopts-guidelines-to-examine-patent-applications-for-pharmaceuticals/.

132 *Argentina Civil Society Launch Campaign "Big Pharma Drop the Case!"*, Make Medicines Affordable (July 11, 2016), http://makemedicinesaffordable.org/en/argentina-civil-society-launch-campaign-big-pharma-drop-the-case.

invalidating two pharmaceutical patents.[133] Unfortunately, ISDS claims were more successful in Ukraine and Colombia, where governments stopped efforts to allow generic competition to overpriced medicines.[134]

The MPP's first innovator license with Gilead caused serious fractures in the A2M movement, with some seeking revised and better licensing terms.[135] Some activists opined that voluntary licensing empowered pharma companies to dictate covered territories and key licensing terms and would result in coopting generic companies (with some cause[136]) and weakening LMICs' resolve to use TRIPS flexibilities, enact transformative IP reforms, or issue CLs systematically. Proponents of MPP VLs saw VLs as complementary to other A2M strategies, with the added advantage of securing wholesale access for nearly 90 percent of people living with HIV in LMICs.[137] Guaranteed access in a hundred-plus countries decreased the burden of pursuing opposition and compulsory licensing strategies in hostile forums.

Nonetheless, the impact of voluntary licensing remained country-specific and linked to whether a country is included within the direct or indirect territory coverage of the relevant MPP license. Current MPP licenses routinely exclude commercially attractive middle-income countries, always China and Brazil, and usually other so-called pharmerging markets.[138] While the A2M activists' suspicions were understandable, the resulting divisions were regrettable at a time when a fractured A2M movement was the last thing needed.

133 Brook K. Baker & Katrina Geddes, *The Incredible Shrinking Victory: Eli Lilly v. Canada, Success, Judicial Reversal, and Continuing Threats from Pharmaceutical ISDS*, 49 Loy. Chi. L. J. 479 (2017).

134 *Id.* at 508–12.

135 While the Gilead-MPP license has been amended multiple times the controversy about VLs has not died down. Baker, *supra* note 88, at 248–51.

136 The Indian generics industry preferred VLs with commercial potential to costly and time-delayed opposition strategies. *See* Patralekha Chatterjee, *Gilead Sovaldi Case Reveals Patent-Health Fissures in India*, IP Watch (Mar. 3, 2016), http://www.ip-watch.org/2016/03/09/gilead-solvaldi-case-reveals-patent-health-fissures-in-india, (quoting D.G. Shah of Indian Pharmaceutical Alliance: "We support provision for CL [compulsory license] to pre-empt abuse of monopoly. However, the CL route is full of thorns and uncertainties. VL [voluntary licensing] offered the same outcome without pain. We see in it a better solution than confrontation with Big Pharma;" … "It is the most effective way of reducing medicines prices.").

137 *See* Baker, *supra* note 88, at 308–15 (for a discussion of VLs licenses vis-a-vis potential complementarity or conflict with alternative strategies).

138 Twenty-two countries are considered "pharmerging" based on market size and prospects. Murray Aitken et al., *Outlook for Global Medicines Through 2021: Balancing Cost and Value*, QuintilesIMS Inst., 44–49 (2016), https://www.iqvia.com/-/media/iqvia/pdfs/institute-reports/global-outlook-for-medicines-through-2021.pdf?la=en&hash=6EA26BACA0F1D81EA93A 74C50FF60214044C1DAB&_=1517325781735. Since 2011, global expansion in the volume of medicine usage has been driven by pharmerging markets. The pharmaceutical market growth rate in pharmerging countries is projected to be higher than in rich economies: six to nine percent vs. four to seven percent, respectively. *Id.* at 9.

## Third Phase: Expansion and Contraction – Domestic Campaigns in Rich Countries

The third phase of A2M activism has been a strange mixture of expansion and contraction. On the expansion side, A2M focused beyond HIV to other diseases; on alternative incentives for targeted R&D; transparency in drug pricing, R&D expenditures, public financing, and clinical trials; and involvement in new global forums, including the broader UN system, for IP reform. On the contraction side, Northern activists focused inward to challenge the impact of crushing drug prices in high-income countries. These vigorous and headline-grabbing new A2M campaigns are paired with concerns of attention waning from basic access concerns in LMICs.

The recent focus of A2M campaigns has expanded beyond HIV to include most focus on HCV and on direct acting antivirals (DAAs), cancer medicines, insulin, and TB. When Gilead gained Food and Drug Administration marketing approval in 2014 for *sofosbuvir*, a backbone DAA that cured over 90 percent of all major genotypes, and as AbbVie, Merck, and other competitors rushed to bring their DAAs to market, there was increased A2M advocacy to get combo treatments that could cure the 71 million HCV-affected persons worldwide. Although therapeutically much better, the new DAA therapies were high-priced; *sofosbuvir* cost $1,000 per day for a 12-week course of treatment ($84,000). Gilead partially addressed access concerns in LMICs with a VL ultimately covering 105 countries, but a significant percentage of people in middle-income countries were still excluded from coverage and the license had multiple other troubling provisions.[139] Responding to the A2M movement, governments deployed a multitude of strategies[140] to oppose Gilead patents in multiple countries,[141] resulting in a CL on *sofosbuvir* in Malaysia.[142]

139 Brook K. Baker, *Gilead's Hepatitis C Medicines License – Troubling Territorial Exclusions, Illusory Exceptions, and Tiered Pricing Policy Fracture Global Access*, INFOJUSTICE (Sept. 17, 2014), http://infojustice.org/wp-content/uploads/2014/09/brookbaker09172014.pdf; Tahir Amin, *The Dirty Motivation Behind Gilead's Hepatitis C Agreement*, ALJAZEERA AMERICA (Nov. 21, 2014), http://america.aljazeera.com/opinions/2014/11/pharmaceuticals-gileadhepc.html.

140 Caitlin H. Douglass et al., *Pathways to Ensure Universal and Affordable Access to Hepatitis C Treatment*, 16 BMC MED. 175 (2018), https://www.ncbi.nlm.nih.gov/pmc/articles/PMC6176525/pdf/12916_2018_Article_1162.pdf.

141 Catherine Saez, *Collective Efforts by Civil Society Groups Bar the Way to Hepatitis C Patents*, IP WATCH (Oct. 5, 2018), https://www.ip-watch.org/2018/05/10/collective-efforts-civil-society-groups-bar-way-hepatitis-c-patents/; *see Sofosbuvir*, PATENT OPPOSITION DATABASE, https://www.patentoppositions.org/en/drugs/sofosbuvir (last visited June 13, 2019); *Sofosbuvir/Velpatasvir*, PATENT OPPOSITION DATABASE, https://www.patentoppositions.org/en/drugs/sofosbuvir-slash-velpatasvir (last visited June 13, 2019).

142 Fifa Rahman, *Inside Views: Malaysia Inclusion in Gilead Voluntary Licence – A Product of Compulsory Licence Pressure*, IP WATCH (Aug. 24, 2017), https://www.ip-watch.org/2017/08/24/malaysia-inclusion-gilead-voluntary-licence-product-compulsory-licence-pressure/.

Global A2M advocacy moved far beyond HIV and HCV. Recently, cancer price advocacy has expanded greatly, bringing it center stage at the WHO.[143] Meanwhile, A2M advocacy has expanded to address medical innovation systems, not just access. Addressing medical R&D incentive systems and overreliance on patent and data exclusivities, activists focused on delinkage.[144] Under the proposed delinked system, the first step involves setting research priorities, sharing R&D costs,[145] supporting open and collaborative research,[146] and using a mix of push mechanisms (most commonly research grants and[147] subsidies)[148] and pull mechanisms (most commonly prizes)[149] to incentivize innovation.[150]

143 WHO, *Access To Medicines, Vaccines and Pharmaceuticals*, Technical Report: Pricing of Cancer Medicines and Its Impacts (2018), https://apps.who.int/iris/bitstream/handle/10665/277190/9789241515115-eng.pdf?ua=1.

144 *See Mechanics of Delinkage*, Delinkage.Org, https://delinkage.org/mechanics/ (last visited June 10, 2019); James Love, An Economic Perspective on Delinking the Cost of R&D from the Price of Medicines (2016), http://www.unitaid.org/assets/Delinkage_Economic_Perspective_Feb2016.pdf.

145 The process for establishing R&D priorities for sharing costs is complicated. The WHO has established a Global Observatory on Health Research and Development, to keep track of the global epidemiology of disease opportunities in medical preventatives and therapies. *Global Observatory on Health R&D*, World Health Org., https://www.who.int/research-observatory/en/ (last visited June 10, 2019). *See* Marie Paule Kieny et al., *Global Platform to Inform Investments for Health R&D*, 387 Lancet 1157 (2016), https://www.thelancet.com/pdfs/journals/lancet/PIIS0140-6736(16)00705-4.pdf. For sharing R&D costs globally, one of the most promising mechanisms has been the call for an R&D treaty, a discussion of which is in Nicoletta Dentico & Nathan Ford, *The Courage to Change the Rules: A Proposal for an Essential Health R&D Treaty*, 2 PLoS Med. 96 (2005), https://journals.plos.org/plosmedicine/article/file?id=10.1371/journal.pmed.0020014&type=printable; Suerie Moon et al., *Innovation and Access to Medicines for Neglected Populations: Could a Treaty Address a Broken Pharmaceutical R&D System?*, 9 PLoS Med. e1001218 (2012), https://journals.plos.org/plosmedicine/article?id=10.1371/journal.pmed.1001218.2011).

146 Delphine Gallaud, *Collaborative Innovation and Open Innovation*, *in* Encyclopedia of Creativity, Invention, Innovation and Entrepreneurship 239–40 (Elias G. Carayannis ed., 2013).

147 *Direct Funding of R&D by Government*, Delinkage.Org, https://delinkage.org/mechanics/direct-funding/.

148 *Subsidies*, Delinkage.Org, https://delinkage.org/mechanics/subsidies/ (last visited June 10, 2019).

149 James Love & Tim Hubbard, *Prizes for Innovations of New Medicines and Vaccines*, 18 Ann. Health L. 155 (2009), https://lawecommons.luc.edu/cgi/viewcontent.cgi?referer=https://www.google.com/&httpsredir=1&article=1111&context=annals; Kevin Outterson et al., *Delinking Investment in Antibiotic Research and Development from Sales Revenues: The Challenges of Transforming a Promising Idea into Reality*, 13 PLoS Med. e1002043 (2016), https://journals.plos.org/plosmedicine/article/file?id=10.1371/journal.pmed.1002043&type=printable.

150 *Incentives*, Delinkage.Org, https://delinkage.org/mechanics/incentives/ (last visited June 10, 2019).

Thereafter, the second link would be used to produce and market affordable generic medicines without monopoly prices.

For over a decade, the WHO has considered a treaty to fund biomedical R&D based on delinking R&D costs from product prices. More recently, there has been considerable global cooperation on the development of new antibiotic drugs, embracing the principle of delinkage. Several health groups such as KEI, MSF, and Oxfam have proposed additional public-sector R&D funding as an alternative to trade agreements that expand patent rights and raise drug prices, and to address a variety of critical health innovation needs, including public health challenges such as Ebola and Zika.[151]

The cost savings of a delinkage system are projected to be at least $92 billion a year in the US under Senator Sanders' 2017 Medical Innovation Prize Fund bill, and much greater on a global scale.[152] A large number of individuals, governments, and institutions endorse delinkage.[153]

A2M advocacy in the third phase has sought transparency across the entire spectrum of the pharmaceutical life cycle. Transparency advocates have pressed for information on web-based access to clinical trial data, cost of drug development, cost of clinical trials, direct and indirect subsidies paid by public and charitable resources, including tax subsidies, and drug pricing strategies vis-a-vis costs of manufacturing, marketing, and net profits.[154] Although disclosure commitments have been achieved,[155] implementation and enforcement have been relatively weak thus far.[156] In 2019, the World Health Assembly passed a transparency resolution – first proposed by Italy – requiring disclosure of drug

151 *Direct Funding of R&D by Government*, *supra* note 147, at 8.

152 *Savings*, DELINKAGE.ORG, https://delinkage.org/savings/ (last visited June 10, 2019).

153 *Endorsements*, DELINKAGE.ORG, https://delinkage.org/endorsements/ (last visited June 10, 2019).

154 For details of key transparency efforts, see KEI, *Background note on Transparency Norms* (Feb. 11, 2019), https://www.keionline.org/wp-content/uploads/Background-Transparency-15Feb2019.pdf.

155 WHO, JOINT STATEMENT ON PUBLIC DISCLOSURE OF RESULTS FROM CLINICAL TRIALS, https://www.who.int/ictrp/results/ICTRP_JointStatement_2017.pdf?ua=1; Nicolas J. DeVito et al., *Research Letter: Noncommercial Funders' Policies on Trial Registration, Access to Summary Results, and Individual Patient Data Availability*, 319 JAMA 1721 (2018).

156 U.K. House of Commons Science and Technology Committee, *Research in Integrity: Clinical Trials Transparency*, https://publications.parliament.uk/pa/cm201719/cmselect/cmsctech/1480/1480.pdf; Lynn Eaton, *Clinical Trials in Europe: Less Than a Fifth Report Within 12 Months*, 365 BR. MED. J. 1963 (2019); *see Civil Money Penalties Relating to the ClinicalTrials.gov Data Bank; Draft Guidance for Food and Drug Administration Staff, Responsible Parties, and Submitters of Certain Applications and Submissions to the Food and Drug Administration; Availability*, 83 Fed. Reg. 47926 (Sept. 21, 2018); *Who's Sharing Their Clinical Trial Results?*, FDAAA TRIALS TRACKER (showing only 66.5 percent of trials are reported and that the United States government could have imposed fines over $3.4 million), https://fdaaa.trialstracker.net (last visited June 13, 2019).

prices but unfortunately watered down disclosure of R&D cost requirements.[157] Civil society, led by KEI, played a vigorous role in advocating for strengthening and adopting the resolution – to the displeasure of several rich country delegations.[158]

This phase of A2M activism draws on the earlier global institutional work of the Commission on Macroeconomics and Health, the UK Commission on Intellectual Property Rights, and the WHO Commission on Intellectual Property Rights, Innovation, and Public Health. Activists have increasingly turned to international platforms to advance A2M goals, including the Global Commission on HIV and the Law (GCHL), the UN Secretary General's High Level Panel on Access to Health Technologies, and the Lancet Commission on Essential Medicines. The GCHL produced a major report focusing on abuse of IPR, even calling for a moratorium on the enforcement of pharmaceutical patent rights, a cessation of all TRIPS-plus demands, and accelerated adoption of TRIPS public health flexibilities.[159] The 2016 Report of the UN Secretary General's High-Level Panel on Access to Medicines took up the challenge to deeply interrogate defects in the current IP regime and its negative impacts on both innovation and access, calling for new incentives for R&D, greater transparency, and increased use of TRIPS flexibilities.[160] The Lancet Commission on Essential Medicines Policies repeatedly highlighted five areas of work: paying for a basket of essential medicines, making them affordable, assuring quality and safety, promoting quality use of medicines, and developing missing essential medicines.[161]

157 WHO, *Improving the Transparency of Markets for Medicines, Vaccines, and Other Health Products*, A72/A/CONF./2 Rev.1 (May 28, 2019), http://apps.who.int/gb/ebwha/pdf_files/WHA72/A72_ACONF2Rev1-en.pdf; *see* Priti Patnaik, *WHO Transparency Resolutions Seeks to Dispel Opacity Around Drug Prices and Sheds Light on International Policy*, INT'L HEALTH POLICY NEWS (May 31, 2019), https://www.internationalhealthpolicies.org/who-transparency-resolution-seeks-to-dispel-opacity-around-drug-prices-and-sheds-light-on-international-policy-making/; Elaine Ruth Fletcher, *World Health Assembly Approves Milestone Resolution on Price Transparency*, HEALTH POLICY WATCH (May 29, 2019), https://www.healthpolicy-watch.org/world-health-assembly-approves-milestone-resolution-on-price-transparency/.

158 Elaine Ruth Fletcher, *WHO's EB Considers New Ways to Work with NGOS – Some Countries Criticise Activists' Roles at WHA 72*, HEALTH POLICY WATCH (May 30, 2019), https://www.healthpolicy-watch.org/whos-eb-considers-new-ways-to-work-with-ngos-some-countries-criticise-activists-role-at-wha72/; *see* James Love, *KEI Statement on Adoption of the WHA72 Transparency Resolution*, KNOWLEDGE ECOLOGY INTERNATIONAL (May 28, 2019), https://www.keionline.org/30887.

159 UNDP, GLOBAL COMMISSION ON HIV AND THE LAW: RISKS, RIGHTS AND HEALTH, ch. 6 (2012), https://hivlawcommission.org/wp-content/uploads/2017/06/FinalReport-RisksRightsHealth-EN.pdf.

160 PROMOTING INNOVATION AND ACCESS TO MEDICINES (2016), https://static1.squarespace.com/static/562094dee4b0d00c1a3ef761/t/57d9c6ebf5e231b2f02cd3d4/1473890031320/UNSG+HLP+Report+FINAL+12+Sept+2016.pdf.

161 Veronika J. Wirtz et al., *Essential Medicines for Universal Health Coverage*, 389 LANCET 403 (2017), https://www.thelancet.com/pdfs/journals/lancet/PIIS0140-6736(16)31599-9.pdf.

The contraction aspect of the A2M movement's third phase was an inward focus in high-income countries, where price escalations on older on-patent medicines and exorbitant prices on newer medicines threatened to bankrupt rich payers and left the poorly insured or uninsured people bereft of access to medicines. Although escalating drug prices was a concern for some years, Gilead's price of $1000 a pill for *sofosbuvir*, a DAA to cure HCV, precipitated the crisis.[162] Even the US Congress investigated Gilead's pricing practices.[163] Although Gilead's CEO expressed some remorse over *sofosbuvir*'s pricing,[164] Gilead had projected $47 billion on cumulative sales of its HCV medicines from 2015 to 2018.[165]

Gilead's pricing scandal resulted in major campaigns in the US – led by Public Citizen,[166] Families USA,[167] Coalition for Fair Drug Prices,[168] and others – seeking lower drug prices and minimizing abuse of patent monopolies for a host of medical conditions. Consequently, multiple bills in Congress and state legislatures purport to address the drug pricing crisis – with solutions ranging from stopping pay-for-delay deals, transparency about drug prices in advertisements, and more broadly, parallel importation from Canada, Medicare price negotiation, reference pricing, compulsory and government use licenses, government pharmaceutical manufacturing, and many more.[169]

162 Richard Knox, *$1000 Pill for Hepatitis C Spurs Debate over Drug Prices*, Nat'l Public Radio (Dec. 30, 2013), https://www.npr.org/sections/health-shots/2013/12/30/256885858/-1-000-pill-for-hepatitis-c-spurs-debate-over-drug-prices.

163 United States Senate Committee on Finance, *Wyden-Grassley Sovaldi Investigation Finds Revenue-Driven Pricing Strategy Behind $84,000 Hepatitis Drug* (Dec. 1, 2015), https://www.finance.senate.gov/ranking-members-news/wyden-grassley-sovaldi-investigation-finds-revenue-driven-pricing-strategy-behind-84-000-hepatitis-drug.

164 John LaMattina, *Gilead's CEO Admits to 'Failures' in Setting Price of $1000-A-Pill Breakthrough*, Forbes (Dec. 8, 2016), https://www.forbes.com/sites/johnlamattina/2016/12/08/gileads-ceo-apologetic-about-sovaldis-1000-per-pill-price-tag/#707a4b791a97.

165 Ned Pagliarulo, *Brief: Gilead Forecasts Steep Slide in 2018 Hepatitis C Revenues*, Biopharma Dive (Feb. 6, 2018), https://www.biopharmadive.com/news/gilead-hepatitis-c-revenues-slide-fourth-quarter-earnings/516494/.

166 *See* Public Citizens, *Access to Medicines Archives*, https://www.citizen.org/article/access-to-medicine-archives/ (last visited June 11, 2019) (listing multiple domestic drug pricing issues Public Citizens is engaged with).

167 *Prescription Drug Costs*, Families USA, https://familiesusa.org/initiatives/prescription-drug-costs (last visited June 11, 2019).

168 *Coalition for Fair Drug Prices* (listing 12 coalition members), Families USA, https://familiesusa.org/initiatives/coalition-fair-drug-prices (last visited June 11, 2019).

169 *See, e.g.*, Thomas Sullivan, *Aggressive Drug Pricing Proposals Introduced in Congress*, Policy & Medicine, (Jan. 28, 2019), https://www.policymed.com/2019/02/aggressive-drug-pricing-proposals-introduced-in-congress.html; Shefali Luthra, *Drug-Pricing Policies Find New Momentum As 'A 2020 Thing'*, Kaiser Health News (Jan. 25, 2019), https://khn.org/news/drug-pricing-policies-find-new-momentum-as-a-2020-thing/; Claire McAndrew, *Report: 2018 State Legislation on High and Rising Drug Prices*, Families USA (Aug. 2018), https://familiesusa.org/product/2018-state-legislation-high-and-rising-drug-prices; National Academy for State Health Policy, State Legislative Action to Lower Pharmaceutical Costs, https://nashp.org/rx-legislative-tracker-2019/ (last visited June 11, 2019).

Civil society activism and government initiatives against high drug prices have been active in the US, UK, the Netherlands, and Australia, among others. In the UK, a new organization, Just Treatment, is campaigning to lower drug prices and to convince the government to issue government use licenses on overpriced medicines.[170] In the Netherlands, the Pharmaceutical Accountability Foundation is also challenging the unconscionable inflation of drug prices.[171] Swiss NGO Public Eye has likewise asked the Swiss government to compulsorily license Roche's cancer drug *pertuzumab*.[172] The region-wide concerns about drug prices have caused the European Council to undertake a review of incentive mechanisms in the pharmaceutical sector.[173] Similarly, Australia recently used a Netflix model to procure affordable HCV medicines,[174] and Japan instituted cost-containment measures,[175] as did Canada.[176]

This third phase has created new conflicts and fissures in the global A2M movement. Activists who have historically focused on access to existing health technologies in LMICs hope to continue that focus. Delinkage advocates have preferred new incentive systems with resources for targeted R&D. Concurrently, domestic drug pricing advocates argue that reform cannot occur unless people in rich countries, whose governments support IP maximalization, realize the

170 Just Treatment, *Just Treatment is a New Campaign Demanding That Fair Access to Medicines Comes Before Drug Company Profits*, Just Treatment, https://justtreatment.org/about (last visited June 12, 2019).

171 Ellen 't Hoen, *New Dutch Foundation to Address High Medicines Pricing Announces Plan to File Complaint with Competition Authority*, Medicines Law & Policy (Aug. 25, 2019), https://medicineslawandpolicy.org/2018/08/new-dutch-foundation-to-address-high-medicines-pricing-announces-plan-to-file-complaint-with-competition-authority/; Ed Silverman, *From $360 a Year to $179,000: Drug Price Hike in Netherlands Prompts Call for Investigation*, Stat+ Pharmalot (Aug. 27, 2018), https://www.statnews.com/pharmalot/2018/08/27/drug-prices-netherlands-investigation/.

172 Public Eye Letter to Chancellor Alain Berset (Jan. 30, 2019), https://www.publiceye.ch/fileadmin/doc/Medikamente/PublicEye_CL-Request-Perjeta_CH_2019.pdf.

173 Press Release, European Council, Council Conclusions on Strengthening the Balance in the Pharmaceutical Systems in EU and Its Member States (June 17, 2016), https://www.consilium.europa.eu/en/press/press-releases/2016/06/17/epsco-conclusions-balance-pharmaceutical-system/.

174 Tina Rosenberg, *Treat Medicines Like Netflix Treats Shows*, N.Y. Times (Mar. 5, 2019), https://www.nytimes.com/2019/03/05/opinion/can-netflix-show-americans-how-to-cut-the-cost-of-drugs.html; Suerie Moon & Elise Erickson, *Universal Medicines Access Through Lump Sum Remuneration – Australia's Approach to Hepatitis C*, 380 New Engl. J. Med. 607 (2019), https://www.nejm.org/doi/pdf/10.1056/NEJMp1813728?articleTools=true.

175 Takasi Umekawa, *As Medical Costs Mount, Japan to Weigh Cost-Effectiveness in Setting Drug Prices*, Reuters (Feb. 18, 2019), https://www.reuters.com/article/us-japan-drugs/as-medical-costs-mount-japan-to-weigh-cost-effectiveness-in-setting-drug-prices-idUSKCN1Q71ZG.

176 Brittany Humphries & Feng Xie, *Canada's Amendment to Patented Drug Price Regulation: A Prescription for Global Drug Cost Control?*, 321 J. Am. Med. Assoc. 1565 (2009), https://jamanetwork.com/journals/jama/fullarticle/2730014.

deleterious effects of IP maximalization on their own health. LMICs hope that achieving pricing reform in rich countries may result in the citizens in those countries eventually expressing more solidarity for people living with inadequate access to affordable medicines in LMICs.

Paradoxically, the problem of access to affordable medicines is becoming acute in middle-income countries transitioning out of eligibility for donors' health assistance.[177] At the same time, middle-income countries face higher tier prices on medicines and are excluded from MPP licenses. Similarly, while the Northern focus on LMICs fades, key populations are particularly at risk in post-transition settings.[178] In this context, questions from Southern A2M activists are simmering.

## Conclusion

This is far from a complete history of the heroic society struggle for access to medicines; even so, it reveals the breadth of transformative actions undertaken and the shrewd and coordinated strategies deployed. Over a scant 20-year history of concerted activism, the A2M movement – spawned in the depths of the AIDS crisis – has had tremendous impacts on right to health and access to medicines. Fundamental structures in the international IP regime have been challenged and countries have been pushed to adopt TRIPS flexibilities. Human rights proponents and IP experts have worked with and within a social movement led by grassroots activists, many of them living with diseases for which medicines were both available and denied. Through collaborative coalitions, the issue of access

177 *See* Equitable Access Initiative Report (2016) (criticizing inappropriate reliance on World Bank county income categories as the sole measure to establish cut-offs for health aid eligibility), https://www.theglobalfund.org/media/1322/eai_equitableaccessinitiative_report_en.pdf; Rachel Silverman, *Project Health Financing Transitions: Timeline and Magnitude*, Center for Global Development Working Paper 48 (2018), https://www.cgdev.org/sites/default/files/projected-health-financing-transitions-timeline-and-magnitude.pdf; *Beyond Gross National Income: Innovative Methods for Global Health Aid Allocation*, 33 Health Policy and Planning suppl _ 1 (2018); Gavin Yamey et al., *Transitioning from Foreign Aid: Is the Next Cohort of Graduating Countries Ready?*, The Ctr. for Policy Impact in Glob. Health Working Paper (2018), http://centerforpolicyimpact.org/wp-content/uploads/sites/18/2018/03/Transition-from-foreign-aid_DukeCPIGH-Working-Paper-final.pdf; Open Society Foundations Public Health Program, Lost in Transition: three Case Studies of Global Fund Withdrawal in South Eastern Europe (2017), https://www.opensocietyfoundations.org/publications/lost-transition; Mercedes Taty & Els Torreele, *Ensuring Access to Life-saving Medicines as Countries Shift from Global Fund Support*, 97 Bull. World Health Org. 311 (2019) (decrying the risks of rapid transition from Global Fund support with respect to procurement of affordable and quality assured medicines), https://www.who.int/bulletin/volumes/97/5/19-234468.pdf?ua=1.

178 Sara L. M. Davis, *Donors Risk Human Rights Violations When Leaving Middle-Income Countries*, Health & Human Rights J. (April 29, 2019), https://www.hhrjournal.org/2019/04/donors-risk-human-rights-violations-when-leaving-middle-income-countries/.

to affordable medicines is now at the head of policy debates within the UN, at the WHO, in legislative chambers, and in the court of public opinion.

During the three phases of the A2M movement, conflicts have emerged and persisted between key actors about "optimal" access strategies. However, these fractures must be redressed. Clearly, there is no single strategy sufficient for the pressing task of assuring the universal human right of all people to access the affordable health technologies they need, no matter where they live, or how much money they have, or what their health need is.

The biopharmaceutical industry, with enormous economic clout and political leverage, has the support of the rich countries that host it. Industry pays huge amounts to lobby receptive government officials and to influence medical prescribers to steer their practices toward more profitable medicines. Enshrined IP and regulatory systems bind the hands of potential generic producers, and in some instances, the hands of governments themselves. Clearly, more thought is needed on how strategies can be deployed to maximize complementarities rather than conflicts. It is hoped that this chapter contributes to better collaboration, cohesion, and trust in the A2M movement as it continues its virtuous struggle against a trillion dollar Big Pharma industry and its rich government supporters.

# 16 GTPI

## Experiences to Overcome IP Barriers to Increase Access to Medicines

*Felipe de Carvalho Borges da Fonseca, Marcela Fogaça Vieira, and Pedro Villardi*

### Introduction

Since its inception, the access to medicines movement has been a global effort strongly marked by local experiences and their articulation in a common narrative. A clear expression of such dynamic lies in organizations and coalitions created at national levels to apply strategies to actualize the slogan "treatment for all," while at the same time, tackling global debates and sharing experiences in solidarity with groups from other countries. The experience of the Working Group on Intellectual Property (GTPI) of the Brazilian Network for the Integration of Peoples (REBRIP) is worth noting as a case of an independent and active civil society coalition that has preserved, over a long period of time, the skills to address the local access to medicines challenges and to contribute to the global picture.

The GTPI was created in 2003 and currently comprises 19 organizations from different Brazilian states and with a variety of backgrounds, including coalitions of nongovernmental organizations (NGOs) and people living with HIV, health workers, lawyers, and academics. The main criterion for membership is independence from pharmaceutical companies (multinationals and generics), including not receiving resources from these companies or their foundations. The GTPI is the only civil society group exclusively dedicated to promoting the public interest in intellectual property (IP) policies in health in Brazil.

Given its longstanding experience, the GTPI has interacted with many players of the global access to medicines movement, participated in international debates, engaged in global campaigns, and has developed, learned, and applied a variety of strategies that characterize the fight for access to medicines for all. This chapter illustrates the role played by civil society organizations in reaction to the perverse effects of trade policies and the implementation of human rights policies. Also, it hopes to inspire not only organizations in the Global South with a history of fighting back but also fellow activists from the Global North who have long been partners in solidarity and are now increasingly facing the problems posed by the IP system "at home."

## Origins, Principles, and First Steps

The GTPI was created in the congruence of two social agendas: health as a human right and anti-neoliberal movements. This has shaped the composition of the group, its strategies, its actions, its objectives, and its vision of the future.

The shaping of access to medicines as a social agenda in Brazil was a multistep process, from the fight for the recognition of the right to health as a constitutional right in the 1980s to the establishment of an ambitious program of universal access to HIV/AIDS treatment. During the 1980s, while Brazil was going through re-democratization after decades of military dictatorship, civil society groups and social movements started to reorganize themselves.[1] These included the "sanitary reform" movement, pushing for a right to health maximizing agenda, and the emerging HIV/AIDS movement, pushing for an adequate response to the epidemic.

The Constitution approved in 1988 was a victory in many aspects. The new institutional model expanded civil society participation in political decision-making processes and created an enabling environment for social groups dedicated to rights-based agendas.[2] In particular, health became, for the first time, a constitutional right of all citizens and an obligation of the state, and a public health system founded on the principles of universality, equality, integrality, and social participation was created in 1990.

For the HIV/AIDS movement, the creation of a universal public health system was an opportunity to reverse the narrative of fear, exclusion, and death that surrounded the disease. Herbert Daniel termed the concept of loss of rights and citizenship that came along with the HIV/AIDS epidemic as "civil death,"[3] and highlighted free treatment not only as a biomedical approach, but also as a powerful political tool to restore the dignity of people with HIV/AIDS. For Herbert de Souza (Betinho), an HIV/AIDS activist and exponent of Brazil's re-democratization process, solidarity was an essential political principle to make the fight against HIV/AIDS a collective effort to combat stigma, discrimination, and other "ideological viruses."[4] Betinho was also one of the first to articulate the response to HIV/AIDS as a human rights issue. Consequently, access to treatment as a human right became deeply embedded in the origins of the Brazilian Interdisciplinary AIDS Association (ABIA), which he founded in 1987. The ABIA has been acting as the executive secretariat of the GTPI since its creation in 2003.

The fight for access to medicines is thus grounded in the HIV/AIDS and health movement in Brazil and was taken forward in a variety of ways such as

1 O. Cerqueira & Veriano Terto, Jr., *Sobre a construção da agenda de acesso a tratamentos para o HIV/AIDS no movimento social de AIDS no Brasil*, *in* Prêmio GTPI Jacques Bouchara De Produção Acadêmica Voltada Para O Ativismo (2015).

2 Oscar Vilhena Vieira, *Supremocracia*, 4 Revista Direito GV 441–64 (2008).

3 Associação Brasileira Interdisciplinar de AIDS (ABIA), Herbert Daniel, Vida antes da morte, 3a (2018).

4 Herbert de Souza, A cura da AIDS (1994).

in publications aimed at promoting mass treatment education, legal actions demanding access to medicines, and successful advocacy for the approval of a law on universal access to HIV/AIDS treatment (Law 9313/93).[5] This victory focused on maximizing equity inside a neo-liberalizing state. As stated in the literature:

> Despite enormous trade and political pressure from the US and the large pharmaceutical companies Brazil during the first part of the 1990s had played a stalling game (...). With the encouragement of civil society Brazil went down the path of providing free anti-retroviral therapy.[6]

As regards the anti-neoliberal agenda, Brazil pushed back against a free trade agreement proposed by the United States (US) in the late 1990s and early 2000s – the Free Trade Area of the Americas (FTAA). A coalition of 60 NGOs, unions, and social movements organized the first popular plebiscite in the continent about the FTAA in 2002. By 2005, the negotiation was suspended for an undefined period at the 4th Americas Summit in Mar del Plata, Argentina.[7] The experience from the fight against the FTAA resulted in[8] the creation of the REBRIP, which the GTPI is part of. The REBRIP sought to monitor and mitigate social impacts of the international trade agenda and pursue alternative forms of integration that contrast with the logic of trade and financial liberalization prevailing in the economic agreements. The REBRIP's strong role within and outside the FTAA negotiations helped to block the advancement of the agreement.

The successive victories of the early 2000s created synergies among the right to health movement, access to treatment as a human right, and the anti-neoliberal movement against the negative impacts of international trade agreements in the implementation of social policies. But the real convergence came when these movements faced the same threat: patents as a trade rule, introduced to developing countries by the World Trade Organization (WTO) in 1994, and the Agreement on Trade-Related Aspects of Intellectual Property Rights (TRIPS Agreement).[9]

5 Veriano Terto Jr. & Carlos Passarelli, *As organizações não-governamentais e o acesso aos tratamentos anti-retrovirais no Brasil*, 27 Divulgação em Saúde para Debate 122–35 (2003).

6 Peter Drahos & John Braithwaite, Information Feudalism: Who Owns the Knowledge Economy? 9 (2007).

7 G. Berrón, *Identidades e estratégias sociais na arena transnacional: o caso do movimento social contra o livre comércio nas Américas* (2008) http://www.teses.usp.br/teses/disponiveis/8/8131/tde-07042008-102949/ (last visited Aug. 16, 2019)

8 This was a fundamental experience of agenda and movements convergence, and from that experience derived many strategies and alliances.

9 TRIPS: Agreement on Trade-Related Aspects of Intellectual Property Rights, Apr. 15, 1994, Marrakesh Agreement Establishing the World Trade Organization, Annex 1C, 1869 U.N.T.S. 299, 33 I.L.M. 1197 (1994), https://www.wto.org/english/docs_e/legal_e/27-trips_01_e.htm (last visited Feb. 6, 2020) [hereinafter TRIPS Agreement].

At that time, the Brazilian HIV/AIDS movement felt that the response to the epidemic must include universal treatment, made possible through local production of generic medicines by public laboratories.[10] At the same time, international organizations and national governments took too long to start treatment programs, leaving behind people already living with the virus.[11] A remarkable story at the *New York Times* entitled "Look at Brazil" captured this dynamic and highlighted that "activist groups were the keystone" in preventing the World Bank's estimation that by the year 2000, Brazil would have 1.2 million people living with HIV/AIDS. It credited activists working on prevention and providing treatment for all.[12]

However, the TRIPS Agreement would alter the universality dimension dramatically. In 1996, Brazil changed its patent regime to allow the granting of product patents to pharmaceuticals, which endangered the successful AIDS response as patents impeded local production of medicines, threatening the capacity to provide universal treatment.

At the international level, Brazilian negotiators opposed the inclusion of IP rights and insisted on the adoption of measures to protect health in the TRIPS Agreement negotiations.[13] However, the national patent law included TRIPS-plus provisions such as patent term extensions and revalidation of patents granted abroad and did not include many of the TRIPS flexibilities. This contradiction can be explained by the intensive lobby by multinational companies at the Brazilian Congress during the discussion of the patent law. If the signature of the TRIPS Agreement was already a bad result, the national patent law was far worse, as measures strongly opposed during the TRIPS Agreement negotiations were approved in the Brazilian patent law.[14]

In 2000, HIV/AIDS activists were concerned with the risks that the IP regime would bring to treatment policies, and anti-neoliberal activists were concerned with the IP rules imposed by the TRIPS Agreement. Under these circumstances, it was a trade dispute between the US and Brazil that brought the two groups together for the first time. In February 2001, the US acted against Brazil at the WTO Dispute Settlement Body (DSB), challenging a provision

10 Santiago Alcázar, *The Copernican Shift in Global Health* (Glob. Health Programme, Working Paper No. 3, 2008); Maurice Cassier & Marilena Correa, *Patents, Innovation and Public Health: Brazilian Public-sector Laboratories' Experience in Copying AIDS Drugs*, *in* Economics of Aids Aid and Access in Developing Countries 89–107 (2003).

11 *The History of Aids in Africa Black History*, https://www.blackhistorymonth.org.uk/article/section/real-stories/the-history-of-aids-in-africa/ (last visited Feb. 10, 2020).

12 Tina Rosenberg, *Look at Brazil*, N.Y. Times (Jan. 28, 2001), https://www.nytimes.com/2001/01/28/magazine/look-at-brazil.html (last visited Aug. 16, 2019).

13 Drahos & Braithwaite, *supra* note 6.

14 Renata Reis, Redes invisíveis: grupos de pressão na Câmara dos Deputados – o processo de aprovação da Lei de Propriedade Industrial brasileira (2015) (Ph.D. thesis, Universidade Federal de Rio de Janeiro).

of the Brazilian patent law that allowed for compulsory licensing in case of "non-local working."[15]

In response, at the 2001 National Meeting of AIDS NGOs (ENONG), more than 250 activists organized a demonstration in front of the US embassy in Recife, followed by a meeting with the consul in which they expressed the demand to "drop the case" at the DSB. The international NGO community also mobilized to pressure the US. Brazilian civil society and the government were praised as champions in the fight for access to treatment during the Durban International AIDS Conference the year before.[16] As Brazil became vocal in international debates about IP and access to medicines and offered its expertise in transfer of technology and know-how regarding the production of antiretroviral medicines (ARVs), the US complaint was seen as harmful to the country's capacity to maintain its leadership on these issues. This sparked international solidarity around the US-Brazil case at the WTO. One month after the protest in Recife, the US announced that it would withdraw the WTO complaint.[17]

This strengthened the global access to medicines movement, which was already celebrating the success of the drop the case campaign in South Africa just a few months before, and resulted in an unprecedented victory later in 2001, with the adoption of the Doha Declaration at the WTO Ministerial Conference. This was a "Copernican shift in global health" to make health prevail over trade and ensured that the link between human rights and access to medicines was established at the highest level.[18] The 2001 mobilization in Recife and the follow-up of IP as a central issue for HIV/AIDS activism matched the REBRIP's efforts to influence Brazil's position at the WTO Ministerial Conference in Doha. Access to medicines became a common ground that aligned the grassroots-based health movement, a network specialized in trade policy, and a country with remarkable negotiation skills at the international fora.

In 2003, the REBRIP created the GTPI, with its coordination at the ABIA, to resist the trade agenda's influence over health and to propose solutions. From the beginning, the group promoted an interdisciplinary dialogue between different organizations to reveal the political aspects of IP's technical discourse to a broader audience.[19]

15 Ellen t'Hoen, *Pharmaceutical Patents and Access to Essential Medicines: Seattle, Doha and Beyond*, *in* Economics of AIDS and Access to HIV/AIDS Care in Developing Countries: Issues and Challenges 39–68 (2003) http://www.who.int/intellectual-property/topics/ip/tHoen.pdf (last visited Nov. 20, 2018).

16 Cerqueira & Terto Jr., *supra* note 1.

17 Ellen t'Hoen, The Global Politics of Pharmaceutical Monopoly Power: Drug Patents, Access, Innovation and the Application of the WTO Doha Declaration on TRIPS and Public Health (2009).

18 Alcázar, *supra* note 10.

19 Cerqueira & Terto, Jr., *supra* note 1.

## A Historical Overview of Landmark Cases

### *The Long Road Toward a Compulsory License*

The Brazilian government was recognized as a global health leader and a reference in IP and access to medicines, and despite challenges to turn the international discourse into action domestically, there were attempts to use TRIPS flexibilities. For example, between 2001 and 2005, the Ministry of Health repeatedly used the threat of compulsory licensing to push pharmaceutical companies to reduce the price of patented ARVs.[20] However, the next step – the actual issuing of a compulsory license (CL) – only took place with strong civil society pressure. Activists brought the debate of IP and access to medicines to the heart of the HIV/AIDS movement in the ENONG in 2003,[21] leading to a street protest in São Paulo in 2004 using signs about the need for a CL, urging "Lula,[22] break the AIDS drugs patents"[23] or "without breaking patents, the SUS will break." Civil society also strongly criticized the government for not taking the CL threats forward. In May 2005, a letter signed by 150 organizations[24] called the Brazilian government a "toothless tiger" for not acting on the issuance of a CL despite threats and strong discourse defending the use of TRIPS flexibilities at the international level.[25] At this point, authorities from Brazil and the US embassy recognized the pressure:

> Hugueney (…) said Itamaraty [Brazilian MoFA] is following MoH negotiations with the pharmaceutical companies closely and described them as boiling down to issues of pricing or voluntary license/royalty payments. He noted the intense pressure the GoB is under from civil society, particularly NGOs, to issue compulsory licenses.[26]

Later that year, the government declared the ARV *lopinavir/ritonavir* of public interest, which represented the first step toward issuing a CL. Expectations

20 Gabriela Costa Chaves et al., *Strategies for Price Reduction of HIV Medicines Under a Monopoly Situation in Brazil*, 49 Rev. Saúde Pública (2015), http://www.scielo.br/scielo.php?script=sci_abstract&pid=S0034-89102015000100309&lng=en&nrm=iso&tlng=en (last visited Aug. 16, 2019).

21 ENONGs were high-level political events and the Minister of Health attended it in 2003.

22 Lula was the Brazilian president, enjoying very high levels of popularity.

23 Information from GTPI archives.

24 *ONGs cobram do Brasil licença compulsória para medicamentos de aids anunciada em março MSF*, https://www.msf.org.br/noticias/ongs-cobram-do-brasil-licenca-compulsoria-para-medicamentos-de-aids-anunciada-em-marco (last visited Aug. 16, 2019).

25 The letter asked the Minister to fulfill his promise to issue CLs for the drugs *Efavirenz*, *Tenofovir*, *Nelfinavir*, and *Lopinavir/Ritonavir*. These four drugs only consumed 70 percent of the ARVs budget.

26 Ambassador's Meeting with Foreign Ministry U/S Hugueney on Compulsory Licensing Threat and Other Trade Issues, wikileaks (2005), https://wikileaks.org/plusd/cables/05BRASILIA1567_a.html (last visited Aug. 16, 2019).

were that with the CL, public production could start and the price would drop from $1.17 per unit to $0.41.[27]

The GTPI pressed for the actual issuance of a CL and made it a central point of action at the 2005 ENONG in Curitiba. The topic was so high in the agenda that the ENONG's organizing committee refused any kind of resources from pharmaceutical companies to organize the event.[28] In that year, the ENONG gathered more than 700 activists from 500 organizations,[29] and the "toothless tiger" image was again emphasized by activists wearing tiger masks in street actions. At the end of a big street march closing the meeting, a manifesto signed by 500 organizations was read, calling for the interruption of negotiations with multinational companies and the use of compulsory licensing.

In parallel, the National Health Council passed Resolution 352/05, ruling for immediate compulsory licensing not only for *lopinavir/ritonavir*, but also for other ARVs such as *efavirenz* and *tenofovir*, which were also burdening the budget of the Unified Health System (SUS).[30] However, in October 2005, the government announced an agreement signed behind closed doors with Abbott, which reduced the *lopinavir/ritonavir* price but established that there would be no further reductions until 2011 and prohibited the government from granting a CL that could have led to the local production of the medicine.[31] The deal was strongly criticized by the GTPI and other stakeholders and damaged Brazil's image as a CL champion.[32]

In December 2005, the GTPI mobilized the Federal Prosecution Office (PGR) to jointly file a pioneer legal action against the agreement and requesting the CL to be issued.[33] The court ruled against a CL, arguing that it would

27 Renata Reis et al., *Acesso a medicamentos e propriedade intelectual no Brasil: a experiência da sociedade civil*, *in* Direitos de Propriedade Intelectual e Acesso aos Antiretrovirais: resistências da sociedade civil no Sul Global (2011).

28 Liandro Lindner, *ENONGs: de onde vem? Para onde vão?* (2013) https://enong2013.files.wordpress.com/2013/06/artigo-enong-liandro-lindner.pdf.

29 *Coordenador Toni Reis diz que o encontro é um mosaico – Enong em Curitiba Agência AIDS*, GIV (2005) https://www.giv.org.br/Not%C3%ADcias/noticia.php?codigo=1242.

30 Carolinne Thays Scopel & Gabriela Costa Chaves, *Iniciativas de enfrentamento da barreira patentária e a relação com o preço de medicamentos adquiridos pelo Sistema Único de Saúde*, 32 Cad. Saúde Pública e00113815 (2016).

31 Gabriela Chaves et al., *Acesso a medicamentos e propriedade intelectual no Brasil: reflexões e estratégias da sociedade civil*, 8 Sur – Revista Internacional de Direitos Humanos 171–93 (2008).

32 Kenneth C. Shadlen, Coalitions and Compliance: The Political Economy of Pharmaceutical Patents in Latin America (2017), https://www.oxfordscholarship.com/view/10.1093/oso/9780199593903.001.0001/oso-9780199593903 (last visited Aug. 16, 2019).

33 *Litigância estratégica em Direitos Humanos – A atuação da sociedade civil no acesso a medicamentos no Brasil*, *in* Justiça e Direitos Humanos: Experiências de Assessoria Jurídica Popular (2010), http://terradedireitos.org.br/wp- content/uploads/2010/09/Miolo_PB_final.pdf.

cause commercial retaliations.[34] But, as is often the case with strategic litigation, this dispute raised awareness and attracted allies to the cause by reversing the unfavorable narrative of compulsory licensing in the press, which had often termed it as piracy and theft. The dispute highlighted views other than that of the industry in technical and public debates and resulted in the GTPI being recognized as an important stakeholder on the subject. These conditions were essential for the effective issuance of the CL in 2007.

In March 2007, new Health Minister José Gomes Temporão took office and declared the ARV *efavirenz* to be of public interest. The drug was in civil society's priority list for a CL since 2005.[35] The government's negotiations with the patent owner (Merck) for reduction of the drug's price failed, causing President Lula to sign a decree to compulsorily license the drug in an open ceremony attended and celebrated by GTPI representatives.[36]

The GTPI played a major role in this. Importantly, the threats that Brazil would suffer retaliation and judicial actions and that drug companies would avoid registering drugs in Brazil all proved to be false, because the decision had strong legal grounds and social legitimacy. After five years, the CL for *efavirenz* generated a savings of approximately $103.5 million.[37]

This experience showed that the social demand for compulsory licensing is a practice of citizenship, which emerges to reverse a process of social exclusion. It also contributes to the development of the notions of democracy and social justice in the context of the fight against HIV/AIDS. Moreover, compulsory licensing helps to show that IP is not only a technical issue; it is a highly political issue.

### *Correcting a Historical Mistake: The Pipeline Case*

Brazil is generally known as a country that has issued several CLs on medicines, but the reality is that it has used compulsory licensing only once. On the other hand, TRIPS-plus provisions favoring multinational pharmaceutical companies have been frequently applied.[38] One such provision is the "pipeline" mechanism,

34 Justiça Federal do Distrito Federal, Case 0035093-68.2005.4.01.3400. GTPI filed an appeal against the decision, which is still pending decision by the Tribunal Regional Federal da 1a Região.

35 *Brasil declara o Efavirenz de interesse público*, ENSP (2007), http://www.ensp.fiocruz.br/portal-ensp/informe/site/materia/detalhe/3906 (last visited Aug. 17, 2019).

36 Brasil, Decreto No. 6108, de 4 de Maio de 2007, Concede licenciamento compulsório, por interesse público, de patentes referentes ao efavirenz, para fins de uso público não-comercial (2007), http://www.planalto.gov.br/ccivil_03/_Ato2007-2010/2007/Decreto/D6108.htm (last visited Aug. 17, 2019).

37 Francisco Viegas Neves da Silva et al., *Compulsory Licence and Access to Medicines: Economic Savings of Efavirenz in Brazil* (2012), http://pag.aids2012.org/session.aspx?s=228#2.

38 Eduardo Mercadante, Concessão de patentes farmacêuticas no Brasil pós-Acordo TRIPS 10.13140/RG.2.2.31084.00640 (2019) http://www.ie.ufrj.br/images/pos-graducao/ppge/2018/defesas/mestrado/eduardo_mercadante_santino_de_oliveira_93efa.pdf (last visited Aug. 17, 2019).

through which patents that had been granted abroad for alimentary or chemical-pharmaceutical substances, which were excluded from patentability in Brazil prior to 1996, could be revalidated in the country.

Brazil granted 814 patents under the pipeline mechanism. A study conducted by the GTPI identified 259 medicines covered by pipeline patents, out of which 54 are or were distributed in the public health system, including the ARVs *abacavir*, *didanosine*, *fosamprenavir*, *nelfinavir*, *lopinavir/ritonavir*, and *efavirenz*. Among the main patent holders that benefited were Sanofi-Aventis (52 patents), Abbott (33), GlaxoSmithKline (30), Roche (26), Pfizer (22), Novartis (22), BASF (22), Merck (21), Boehringer Ingelheim (16), Eli Lilly (15), Dow Chemicals (14), Monsanto (13), Ajinomoto (12), Otsuka Pharmaceuticals (12), and Bristol Myers Squibb (11).

Most of the patents for HIV/AIDS drugs were already targeted by the GTPI's actions, but by challenging the pipeline mechanism itself, the GTPI could have all these patents and others granted through this mechanism revoked at once. The GTPI then started to raise awareness about the impact caused by pipeline patents by organizing events, hearings at the parliament, studies, publications, and others. These helped to solidify the thesis that pipeline patents are unconstitutional, as the Brazilian Constitution mandates patents to be granted in view of the country's social interest and technological and economic development.[39]

In 2007, the National Federation of Pharmacists, as a member of the GTPI, filed a petition with the PGR, arguing for the unconstitutionality of pipeline patents. In 2009, the PGR used the arguments to propose a Direct Action of Unconstitutionality (ADI 4234) at the Supreme Court.[40,41] The case became the first constitutional action related to IP at the Brazilian Supreme Court and offered a great opportunity to discuss abuses of the IP system and its unacceptable obstacles to access to essential goods, public health, and the right to life, as well as to technological and economic development. The GTPI was accepted as *amici curiae* and allowed to present arguments before the Supreme Court. However, the case is yet to be decided. This inaction by the Brazilian Supreme Court benefits the companies that profit from unconstitutional monopolies.[42]

39 Brazil, 1988 Federal Const., art. 5, XXIX – "the law shall ensure the authors of industrial inventions of a temporary privilege for their use, as well as protection of industrial creations, property of trademarks, names of companies and other distinctive signs, viewing the social interest and the technological and economic development of the country".

40 Notícias STF: STF – Supremo Tribunal Federal Notícias STF (2009) http://www.stf.jus.br/portal/cms/verNoticiaDetalhe.asp?idConteudo=107628&caixaBusca=N (last visited Aug. 17, 2019).

41 Supremo Tribunal Federal – ADI 5529 (processo) (2020) http://portal.stf.jus.br/processos/detalhe.asp?incidente=4984195 (last visited Feb. 10, 2020).

42 Marcela Fogaça Vieira & Pedro Villardi, *Inside Views: Brazilian Supreme Court Refuses to Judge Its Biggest Case on IP and Access to Medicines, and Benefits Big Pharma with Undue Monopolies*, IP Watch (2018) https://www.ip-watch.org/2018/09/13/brazilian-supreme-court-refuses-judge-biggest-case-ip-access-medicines-benefits-big-pharma-undue-monopolies/.

For instance, a study conducted by the GTPI in 2019[43] found that the financial impact of pipeline patents related to only 10 drugs amounted to $1.5 billion.[44]

The GTPI also acted as *amicus curiae* in another case at the Supreme Court[45] questioning the constitutionality of patent term extensions applied to pharmaceutical patents in Brazil. It also participated in a public hearing convened by the Court in 2009 to debate the right to health, showing the impact of IP on drug prices and on public policies as a response to the overall concern of scarce resources for addressing demands for high-cost medicines, pointed out by health managers as their main concern.[46] Throughout this process, the GTPI has been the voice of the people affected by these patents at the Brazilian Supreme Court.

### *Do Not Mess with Our Health Safeguards: The ANVISA Prior Consent Case*

There is a saying among access to treatment activists that goes "if your country is not in the Special 301 list, you are not doing your job right." Having this target as measurement, the GTPI has been doing a good job, as Brazil has been in the US government Special 301 watch list for decades. One item in particular has repeatedly ensured Brazil's presence in the list: the prior consent mechanism of the National Agency for Health Surveillance (ANVISA).

The ANVISA was created in 1999, the same year that an amendment to the Brazilian patent law introduced a new mechanism through Article 229-C: "The grant of patents for pharmaceutical products and processes will depend on the prior consent of ANVISA." This mechanism introduced the participation of the health sector in the examination process of pharmaceutical patent applications, alongside the National Patent Office (*Instituto Nacional de Propriedade Industrial* or INPI) which is under the Ministry of Industry, with the objective that "[t]his joint work between INPI and ANVISA will ensure the best technical standards in the decision-making process over pharmaceutical patents."[47] This innovative measure adopted in Brazil is an important safeguard to avoid granting unmerited patents in the pharmaceutical sector.

Until 2012, 179 (12.5 percent) of 1482 patent applications reviewed by the ANVISA did not receive prior consent, which means that without the ANVISA's participation in the examination process, they would have been granted by the INPI. Also, around 40 percent of the ANVISA-approved patent applications

43 GTPI, *Contestação de patentes* (2017), http://deolhonaspatentes.org/acoes/contestacao-patentes-2/ (last visited Jan. 7, 2017).

44 Exchange rate is $1 = R$4 as of Aug. 17, 2019.

45 Supremo Tribunal Federal, *supra* note 41.

46 Marcelo Vieira & Eloísa Machado, Access to Medications: Public Health Hearings, *in* Aceso a medicamentos : audiência pública sobre saúde (V. Terto Jr. et al. ed., 2009), *available at* http://abiaids.org.br/campanhas (June 13, 2014).

47 Brasil, Medida Provisória No. 2.006, de 14 de Dezembro de 1999 (1999).

had to comply with demands such as improvement of clarity or reduction of scope, leading to an increase in the quality of the patents granted.[48]

However, such efforts to provide better examination in the pharmaceutical sector displeased transnational pharmaceutical companies. From 2001 to 2010, several cases were filed against the ANVISA's decisions, obtaining mixed verdicts from the courts. The GTPI acted to defend this important public health safeguard not only in Brazil, but also in the international arena.

In May 2008, the GTPI filed a case at the Permanent People's Tribunal (TPP)[49] regarding human rights violations by European companies.[50] The case was against the Swiss company Roche, which the GTPI accused of violating the right to health of the Brazilian population and the national sovereignty for its judicial actions against the ANVISA's prior consent mechanism. Roche was found guilty by the TPP for harming access to medicines in Brazil.

The INPI was also not pleased with the prior consent mechanism, as it gave the ANVISA the final word on the grant or rejection of a patent. The INPI interpreted it as a way of removing its authority in the field, and in 2007 sought the intervention of the *Advocacia Geral da União* (AGU), which is the competent authority for settling disputes between public bodies. The AGU's decision issued in January 2011 removed the ANVISA from the analysis of the patentability requirements. In response, the GTPI filed a complaint with the United Nations (UN) Special Rapporteur on the Right to Health against the AGU's decision.[51]

Transnational pharmaceutical companies supported the AGU's decision. The GTPI mobilized other stakeholders, leading to a public hearing in the Parliament in 2011. Soon after, the Federal Prosecution Office (MPF) filed a court case against the AGU's opinion.[52] In response, the interministerial working group created to deal with the case decided to recreate the space for the ANVISA's participation in the examination of the patentability criteria for applications relating to medicines of particular importance to the SUS. This decision was further clarified by an ANVISA internal ruling in 2013 and by a decree from the Ministry of Health in 2014, both converging to give back to the ANVISA the capacity to review patentability criteria. However, the AGU decision was never

48 Newton Lima, *A revisão da Lei de patentes: inovação em prol da competitividade nacional*, Câmara dos Deputados (2013).

49 The People's Permanent Tribunal is an opinion court and does not have any legal jurisdiction. For more information, *see* http://permanentpeoplestribunal.org/?lang=en.

50 Reis et al., *supra* note 27.

51 GTPI, *Atualização do Apelo Urgente – a fim de informar o desenrolar da situação denunciada e solicitar ao Relator Especial das Nações Unidas sobre o direito de toda pessoa de desfrutar o mais elevado atingível padrão de saúde física e mental para responder diante das violações do direito humano à saúde pelo governo brasileiro* (2015), https://www.conectas.org/arquivos/editor/files/atualizacao%20apelo%20urgente_final.pdf.

52 Ação 46656-49.2011.4.01.3400, Justiça Federal – 7a Vara Brasília (2011) https://processual.trf1.jus.br/consultaProcessual/processo.php [hereinafter Justiça Federal].

officially revised and was used in another case initiated by international pharmaceutical companies in the Brazilian courts.

In 2014, the *Associação da Indústria Farmacêutica de Pesquisa* (INTERFARMA), an association that gathers 52 pharmaceutical companies (mostly big transnational ones), filed a case against the ANVISA demanding the end of the prior consent mechanism.[53] The GTPI filed an *amicus curiae* brief and engaged with the MPF to defend the ANVISA's prior consent. The court case is still pending decision.

The GTPI also presented a case in the scope of UN debates on human rights violations by transnational companies, especially in the UN Working Group on the matter. The UN Working Group highlighted in its 2015 report the importance of the ANVISA's prior consent: "without the Agency's involvement, there was the risk of patent monopolies emerging, which would hinder access to medicines."[54] That same year, the GTPI organized a side event about the attacks on the ANVISA at the UN Human Rights Council and launched the international campaign "INTERFARMA drop the case."[55]

However, the executive branch issued a decree reducing the ANVISA's power related to the patentability criteria.[56] In this new framework, the ANVISA's analysis lost its deliberative status and is now seen as a "subsidy to the examination," meaning that the ANVISA can provide elements against the granting of a patent based on failure to meet the patentability criteria, but it will not necessarily define the final result as before. The GTPI publicly denounced this decree and mobilized allies to act for its review, including presenting demands at the MPF, which prompted another court case against such decree that is still ongoing.[57] Currently, the GTPI is seeking to reinforce the ANVISA's prior consent through the Parliament.

## Lessons Learned, Adaptation, and Renovation

As described above, the GTPI adopted a multifaceted approach to occupy "technical spaces" within politics and "political spaces" with technical arguments to

53 *Direito à saúde ameaçado nos tribunais*, Repórter Brasil, https://reporterbrasil.org.br/2016/04/direto-a-saude-ameacado-nos-tribunais/ (last visited Feb. 11, 2020).

54 OHCHR, *Informe del Grupo de Trabajo sobre la cuestión de los derechos humanos y las empresas transnacionales y otras empresas*, 6 (2016), https://acnudh.org/informe-del-grupo-de-trabajo-sobre-la-cuestion-de-los-derechos-humanos-y-las-empresas-transnacionales-y-otras-empresas-mision-al-brasil/ (last visited Feb. 11, 2020).

55 Marcela Fogaça Vieira & Lorena Di Giano, *Taking on the Challenge of Implementing Public Health Safeguards on the Ground: The Experience of Argentina and Brazil from a Civil Society Perspective, in* Routledge Handbook on the Politics of Global Health 332–45 (Richard Parker & Jonathan Garcia eds., 2018).

56 Brasil, Portaria Conjunta No. 1, de 12 de Abril de 2017 – Imprensa Nacional (2017), http://www.in.gov.br/materia (last visited Aug. 17, 2019).

57 Justiça Federal, *supra* note 52. Case 1007660-18.2018.4.01.3400 was attached to Case 46656-49.2011.4.01.3400.

move forward the access to medicines agenda. One such technical space that the GTPI had to occupy was the INPI. Similar to majority of patent offices in the world, the INPI is marked by strong influence from its "clients," the companies.[58] The INPI has also been marked by a lack of transparency and unreceptiveness to civil society participation, with few exceptions. This animosity against civil society expressed both by the INPI and industry translated into several attempts to discredit civil society's voice in the IP debate.

To confront this situation, the GTPI invested in reinforcing its legitimacy and technical capacity. Several articles were published by its members in important publications from fields such as public health, law, economics, and international relations. The GTPI also established partnerships with universities to produce studies with original data that would become references for important national IP debates. This led to increased recognition of the GTPI as a relevant actor in the field, allowing for greater ability to present technical arguments strongly rooted in the public interest and designed to achieve the political goal of increasing access to medicines for all.

For example, the INPI applied a very broad interpretation of patentability requirements, resulting in the granting of low-quality patents. In 2007, a process of revision of the guidelines started but was being carried out in closed doors with strong presence from the pharmaceutical industry.[59] In response, the GTPI prepared a position paper calling for stricter patent examination, emphasizing the impact of patents on health, and demanding a more democratic process. The discussion became so contentious that it went up to the level of the Interministerial Group on Intellectual Property (GIPI), created to address topics of relevance for the national IP policy. After a long process of debate in which the GTPI was very active, the GIPI issued in 2008 a decision aligned with the GTPI's view that some types of secondary patents (namely, second use and polymorph) should not be granted.

Similarly, in 2018, the INPI published new examination guidelines allowing the grant of secondary patents such as combinations and new forms of known substances if they present an "unexpected therapeutic effect." The GTPI is currently developing a strategy to challenge these guidelines, furthering the ongoing debate to reform similar provisions in countries such as India, where they have been shown to favor patent system abuse by companies and increase the grant of low-quality patents.[60]

The GTPI has also actively filed patent oppositions (or "subsidies to the examination"). This strategy has three purposes. The first was to confront the view that only industry has a stake in the patent system. By filing patent oppositions,

58 Peter Drahos, The Global Governance of Knowledge: Patent Offices and their Clients (1st ed. 2010).

59 Reis et al., *supra* note 27.

60 Feroz Ali et al., *Pharmaceuticals Patent Grant in India: How Our Safeguards Against Evergreening Have Failed and Why the System must be Reformed*, accessibsa (2018), https://accessibsa.org/media/2018/04/Pharmaceutical-Patent-Grants-in-India.pdf.

the GTPI helped reinforce the notion that patients are also interested parties in the granting of a patent, bringing up the spirit of Thailand's Supreme Court decision that for the first time accepted patients as plaintiffs in a patent nullification case.[61] The second purpose was to push the INPI to apply stricter standards in its examination for pharmaceuticals, by presenting strong technical arguments showing how patent applications were failing to fulfill patentability requirements. The third purpose was to prevent the granting of poor patents. After years of campaigning for CLs, the GTPI learned that avoiding the granting of a patent in the first place was a more effective solution. Furthermore, patent oppositions, in contrast to CLs, could be done directly by civil society without relying on government action and are less politically contentious.

Filing patent oppositions thus became a major strategy for the GTPI, starting with a patent opposition for the ARV *tenofovir disoproxil fumarate* (TDF) in 2006. It developed this opposition through a partnership with Lawyers Collective from India, which led to the rejection of the patent. The successful pre-grant opposition is emblematic, as it was the first time that a patent challenged by civil society was rejected.[62,63] The outcome inspired confidence among patients and encouraged other oppositions to ARV patents in Brazil. Since then, the GTPI has filed 20 patent oppositions, with major victories leading to generic competition in the cases of TDF, TDF/FTC (*Tenofovir/emtricitabine*), and *sofosbuvir*.[64]

This process has yielded the following lessons. First, high prices are sustained through the strategic weakening of public health safeguards such as patent examination regulations. Second, civil society participation through patent opposition procedures effectively contribute to the quality of the examination. It shows that most of the choices that the INPI claimed as "technical" were actually political options that favored multinational pharmaceutical companies. The GTPI then pushed, through technical arguments, for a more favorable environment for the public interest.

Meanwhile, the GTPI had to adapt to a changing environment in Brazil. After a long cycle of strong mobilization capacity, the global retreat of international donors from HIV/AIDS projects starting around 2010 particularly affected Latin America. In Brazil, many NGOs closed their doors due to lack of funding. The successes of the previous decade led to a misperception that everything was solved, leading to a reduced level of funding from national and international sources.

61 MSF, *Drug Patents Under the Spotlight – Sharing Practical Knowledge About Pharmaceutical Patents* (2003), https://apps.who.int/medicinedocs/pdf/s4913e/s4913e.pdf (last visited Feb. 11, 2020).

62 Pedro Villardi & Carolinne Thays Scopel, *A luta pelo tenoforvir: vitórias e desafios futuros*, *in* Políticas públicas de produção local de medicamentos no Brasil: elementos para o debate 131–58 (2017).

63 It should be noted that Farmanguinhos/Fiocruz, a public laboratory, also filed patent oppositions against TDF patents. For more, *see* Villardi & Scopel, *supra* note 62.

64 GTPI, *Contestação de patentes* (2017), http://deolhonaspatentes.org/acoes/contestacao-patentes-2/ (last visited Jan. 7, 2017).

To rebuild mobilization, the GTPI reenforced its "first steps" workshops aimed at bringing the basics of IP debates and access to medicines advocacy agendas to the basis of the HIV/AIDS movement. Between 2013 and 2019, 15 workshops were organized in 13 different cities throughout the country. By doing so, the GTPI revived the topic in major local and regional HIV/AIDS events and assemblies and engaged new activists in national campaigns either to pressure state parliamentarians or to demand from the national government a specific action toward a given drug. These workshops underscored a key component of GTPI work – the translation of technical knowledge into political action.

One prominent case to illustrate this is the mobilization demanding access to *dolutegravir*. In December 2015, the GTPI held a workshop at the ENONG about IP and access to medicines. At that time, many HIV/AIDS patients were complaining about side effects from the TDF-based first-line regimen used in Brazil, and adherence was a growing issue. The GTPI presented the IP barriers that were preventing the introduction in Brazil of new treatment options already used in other countries, including *dolutegravir*. Since the beginning of 2015, the GTPI had been pressuring the government to incorporate *dolutegravir* in the public health system by sending letters, participating in public consultations, and inviting government officials to events to talk about the case. At a seminar organized by the GTPI in October 2015, a government representative declared that it would be impossible to provide *dolutegravir* in Brazil due to its high price. All these elements were shared at the workshop in December, helping to intensify the demand for *dolutegravir*, and rebuilding the HIV/AIDS movement's interest in the topic of access to medicines and strategies to challenge price and patent barriers. This case was an important trigger for mobilization because it reiterated the injustice of a world divided between a treatment regimen for the rich and that for the poor.

The government had invested in a first-line fixed-dose combination at the time and was reluctant to consider any guideline changes. The workshop organized by the GTPI during the ENONG attracted criticism from both the government and international agencies. As a reaction, the GTPI provided policy recommendations to the Ministry of Health, emphasizing the need to challenge the price of *dolutegravir* using available policy options such as priority examination of the patent application, strategic use of public laboratories to define production price, issuing a CL, and others. The GTPI also provided Ministry of Health staff with technical information about *dolutegravir*'s patents and prices in other countries, which served as background information for the negotiation process. The addition of *dolutegravir* into the guidelines as a first-line regimen and the invocation of TRIPS flexibilities provided leverage for the government to negotiate an 85 percent decrease in the price with the originator company (GSK), from \$3606 to \$548. Finally, in September 2017, the ABIA/GTPI filed a pre-grant opposition[65] to the patent application covering *dolutegravir*'s main

65 *Id.*

compound. The rejection of the patent has the potential to lead to further price reductions, enabling generic competition.

In 2013, the GTPI decided to expand its mandate beyond HIV/AIDS to include comorbidities such as hepatitis C. In 2015, after a GTPI-organized workshop on IP and access to medicines in Joao Pessoa, activists organized a protest at the National HIV/AIDS and Viral Hepatitis Conference calling for "health now, patents out." This demonstration was the first to bring together HIV/AIDS and hepatitis activists in Brazil, in an effort to show that access barriers posed by the IP system affect all diseases. The case of the hepatitis C drug *sofosbuvir* became a major focus of attention for the GTPI, which from 2015 onwards used all its repertory of strategies to make treatment available for all. This included filing patent oppositions, court cases, holding demonstrations, and street actions in front of the INPI and Gilead offices, an intensive media strategy that helped strengthen public debate on high medicine prices and the need for patent rejection to allow generic competition, which reached the 2018 presidential election debate. This case was also essential in rebuilding indignation among Brazilian activists and further connecting the GTPI with global allies, including challenging Gilead's strategies of sustaining its unfair monopoly over *sofosbuvir*.

## Conclusion: Unfinished Business

Over time, the GTPI has acquired expertise in knowledge and data production, capacity building, public campaigns, patent oppositions, strategic litigation at national and international fora, parliamentary advocacy, and policy dialogue. All these strategies have been complementary in dealing with complex cases that last for long periods. Through its innovative thinking, the GTPI has largely influenced the IP debate in Brazil and contributed to global debates.

During these developments, the GTPI has incorporated violations to the right to health caused by abusive patenting practices in the "global campaign to dismantle corporate power." It has also presented a contribution to the High-Level Panel on Access to Medicines convened by the UN Secretary-General in 2016, highlighting the need to support the ongoing UN process for a binding treaty on the violation of human rights by transnational companies.[66]

From its early days to the present, the GTPI remains committed to the mission of removing from pharmaceutical companies the power to use patent monopolies to decide who lives and who dies, or the power to privatize scientific knowledge that can save lives to put it at the service of financial markets. This power flows from an architecture of impunity that enables commercial rules to become

66 Pedro Villardi et al., Políticas de produção local de medicamentos: elementos para o debate (2017).

"politics of death."[67] This is why the GTPI has also been strongly engaged in the call for other regimens of knowledge production and distribution.

At one of its first seminars in 2006, the GTPI issued the "Leme letter," expressing strong criticism to the privatization of knowledge and highlighting that IP rules in different fields "block the sustainability and the right to human, economic, social and cultural development by peoples."[68] Twelve years later, the GTPI helped to draft the health paragraph of the People's Summit declaration in Buenos Aires, which calls for the "suspension of the TRIPS Agreement for health technologies" and demands a "new R&D model that promote free and accessible technologies for all and whose results (data, processes and products) are considered common goods."

Therefore, the GTPI keeps confronting specific monopolies over essential drugs but also seeks to address the underlying causes of a power structure that replicates the access and innovation crisis. Unchecked monopoly powers, unbalanced legislations, and co-opted governments are factors of this fatal equation. Overall, the GTPI believes that to deactivate the central engines used by pharmaceutical companies to gain control over knowledge and the lives of millions is a necessary step in creating proper conditions for the emergence of a new regimen where health technologies are seen as common goods, collectively owned, and equitably shared.

67 Achille Mbembe, Necropolitica (N-1) (2018).
68 *Carta do Leme*, https://www.alainet.org/pt/active/10670 (last visited Aug. 19, 2019).

# 17 Private Sector

## Right to Health Responsibilities of Pharmaceutical Companies

*Emmanuel Kolawole Oke*

### Introduction

Corporations, especially multinational corporations, exert considerable influence in setting the agenda for and shaping the structure of international law.[1] This can be seen in the process that led to the emergence of the World Trade Organization (WTO) Agreement on Trade-Related Aspects of Intellectual Property Rights (TRIPS Agreement).[2] The power wielded by these corporations has motivated some countries to demand for the regulation of their activities under international law, and some countries are currently negotiating a legally binding treaty on business and human rights.[3]

This chapter explores the evolution of corporate responsibility for human rights under international law. It also highlights the implications of these developments for the responsibility of pharmaceutical corporations to respect the right to health. The chapter is structured into three parts. The first examines the role of the pharmaceutical industry in shaping the TRIPS Agreement. The second focuses on the evolution of the human rights responsibilities of corporate actors under international law. The third, forward-looking, explores the possibility of using international investment law as a mechanism for holding corporate actors, including pharmaceutical companies, accountable for their human rights responsibilities.

1 *See* Sharon Beder, Suiting Themselves: How Corporations Drive the Global Agenda ( 2006); Susan K. Sell, Private Power, Public Law: The Globalization of Intellectual Property Rights (2003).

2 TRIPS: Agreement on Trade-Related Aspects of Intellectual Property Rights, Apr. 15, 1994, Marrakesh Agreement Establishing the World Trade Organization, Annex 1C, 1869 U.N.T.S. 299, 33 I.L.M. 1197 (1994) [hereinafter TRIPS Agreement].

3 U.N., Human Rights Council, *Mandate on Open-ended Intergovernmental Working Group [OEIGWG] on Transnational Corporations and Other Business Enterprises with Respect to Human Rights, Chairmanship Revised Draft, Legally Binding Instrument to Regulate, in International Human Rights Law, the Activities of Transnational Corporations and Other Business Enterprises* (July 16, 2019) [hereinafter *OEIGWG*], https://www.ohchr.org/Documents/HRBodies/HRCouncil/WGTransCorp/OEIGWG_RevisedDraft_LBI.pdf.

## The Role of Pharmaceutical Companies in Shaping the TRIPS Agreement

The role of corporate actors – including pharmaceutical companies – in the emergence of the TRIPS Agreement is well documented.[4] The objective here is to provide a brief overview of the role played by corporate actors (including pharmaceutical companies) in shaping the text of the TRIPS Agreement. This provides a backdrop for analysis of the right to health responsibility of pharmaceutical companies. By highlighting the extent of pharmaceutical companies' influence at the global level, the goal is to show why it is crucial to ponder about the human rights responsibilities of these corporate actors under international law.

The origins of the incorporation of intellectual property (IP) into international trade law is traceable to the activities of United States (US) corporate actors that successfully convinced their government to use trade negotiations at both bilateral and multilateral levels as a means of securing IP protection abroad.[5] In this regard, the Advisory Committee for Trade Negotiations (ACTN), set up to provide input from the US business sector into US trade policy, played a very crucial role.[6] As Drahos points out, the ACTN was chaired from 1981 by Edmund Pratt, then CEO of Pfizer, a pharmaceutical company.[7] Drahos notes that "Pratt himself became a leading exemplar of a trade-based approach to IP protection."[8] The ACTN set up a Task Force on Intellectual Property, and its recommendations were crucial to the formation of a US strategy on IP.[9] These recommendations included the use of unilateral and bilateral efforts aimed at improving the protection of US IP rights (IPR) abroad and, ultimately, the inclusion of IP in

4 *See generally* Peter Drahos, *Global Property Rights in Information: The Story of TRIPS at the GATT*, 13 Prometheus 1, 6 (1995); Robert Weissman, *Long, Strange TRIPS: The Pharmaceutical Industry Drive to Harmonize Global Intellectual Property Rules, and the Remaining WTO Legal Alternatives Available to Third World Countries*, 17 U. Penn. J. Econ. L. 1069, 1069 (1996) (noting that the United States pharmaceutical industry "has played a critical role in placing intellectual property protection on the free trade agenda."); Edmund T. Pratt, Jr., *Intellectual Property Rights and International Trade*, Inst. for Agric. Trade & Pol'y (Dec. 21, 1999), https://www.iatp.org/sites/default/files/Intellectual_Property_Rights_and_International.htm; Peter Drahos & John Braithwaite, Information Feudalism: Who Owns the Knowledge Economy (2002); Sell, *supra* note 1; Christopher May & Susan Sell, Intellectual Property Rights: A Critical History (2006) (For a fuller discussion of the history behind the role of the pharmaceutical industry in shaping the TRIPS Agreement, please see the introductory chapter of this book).

5 Drahos, *supra* note 4, at 8–9.

6 *Id.* at 8.

7 *Id.*

8 *Id.*

9 *Id.*

the Uruguay Round of the GATT negotiations,[10] which was set to begin with a Ministerial Conference in Punta del Este in Uruguay in September 1986.[11]

To ensure the objective of including IP in the Uruguay Round, corporate actors in the US had to convince other businesses in Europe, Japan, and Canada about the importance of achieving this crucial objective.[12] In furtherance of this objective, the Intellectual Property Committee (IPC) was set up in March 1986.[13] Composed of companies from various sectors including the pharmaceutical industry, the IPC included companies like Bristol Myers, Merck, and Pfizer.[14] The IPC was tasked with securing a consensus among corporate actors in the US, Europe, Japan, and Canada for the inclusion of IP in the Uruguay Round.[15] After securing this international corporate consensus, the governments of these four countries could be lobbied to support the inclusion of IP in the Uruguay Round.[16] The goals of the IPC toward an international agreement on IP were the adoption of minimum standards of protection, an enforcement mechanism, and a dispute settlement system.[17] The IPC successfully achieved an international corporate consensus prior to the commencement of the Uruguay Round; unsurprisingly, IP was included in the agenda of the Uruguay Round of negotiations.[18]

The IPC remained active after successfully including IP on the agenda of the Uruguay Round. During these negotiations held in June 1988, the IPC (alongside its counterparts in the European Union [EU], i.e. UNICE, and in Japan, i.e. Keidanren) published a text titled *Basic Framework of GATT Provisions on*

10 *Id.* at 9.
11 Drahos & Braithwaite, *supra* note 4, at 118.
12 Drahos, *supra* note 4, at 12; Sell, *supra* note 1, at 102.
13 *Id.*
14 Drahos, *supra* note 4, at 12; Drahos & Braithwaite, *supra* note 4, at 118 (noting that, "The IPC was an ad hoc coalition of 13 major United States corporations: Bristol-Myers, DuPont, FMC Corporation, General Electric, General Motors, Hewlett-Packard, IBM, Johnson & Johnson, Merck, Monsanto, Pfizer, Rockwell International and Warner Communications."); *see also*, Sell, *supra* note 1, at 103 (noting that, "The IPC operated as a committee of the whole, and its streamlined structure was designed to get things done quickly. It represented a broad array of U.S. industries – chemical, computer, creative arts, electronics, heavy and consumer manufacturing, and pharmaceutical industries.").
15 Drahos, *supra* note 4, at 12.
16 *Id.*
17 Sell, *supra* note 1, at 103.
18 Drahos, *supra* note 4, at 13 (As Drahos points out, "Between the time of its formation in March of 1986 and the meeting at Punta del Este in September of 1986 the IPC managed, incredibly, to put in place amongst the giants of the international business community (Europe, Japan, and the United States) a consensus on the GATT and intellectual property. At the Punta del Este conference the group of sovereign nations which made up the Contracting Parties of the GATT agreed to a Ministerial Declaration which included on its agenda GATT rules for intellectual property protection."). *See also* Drahos & Braithwaite, *supra* note 4, at 120; Sell, *supra* note 1, at 106.

*Intellectual Property*,[19] which was circulated to the GATT Secretariat and several states.[20] In their description of the *Basic Framework*, Drahos and Braithwaite note:

> It was not just a statement of goals or objectives, but the prescription of a set of basic principles that would pattern the domestic regulation of knowledge and information by States ... Piracy would have to be eliminated, infringement of IP would have to be criminalized, States would have to set severe limits on public interest exceptions to intellectual property protection and finally, States themselves would have to agree to become the subjects of meaningful enforcement procedures if they did not comply with their obligations to spread the fundamentals of intellectual property.[21]

The *Basic Framework* reflected the targets of the corporate actors involved in this process. For instance, they wanted patent rights to be protected for a term of 20 years, patent protection for agrochemicals and pharmaceuticals, and the weakening of compulsory licensing.[22] The *Basic Framework* eventually became the basis of what is now known as the TRIPS Agreement.[23] Like the TRIPS Agreement, the *Basic Framework*'s text included minimum standards of protection, national enforcement measures, and a dispute settlement mechanism.[24]

However, despite the successful incorporation of IP into international trade law at the Uruguay Round and the eventual adoption of the TRIPS Agreement, some corporate actors were still unsatisfied with the final text of the TRIPS Agreement.[25] Specifically, some actors – such as the pharmaceutical industry – were not happy with the transitional period given to developing countries to

19 *See* Intellectual Prop. Comm. et al., Basic Framework of GATT Provisions on Intellectual Property: Statement of Views of the European, Japanese and United States Business Communities (1988) (UNICE is the Union of Industrial and Employers' Confederations of Europe while Keidanren is the Japan Business Federation).

20 May & Sell, *supra* note 4, at 154.

21 Drahos & Braithwaite, *supra* note 4, at 123.

22 Intellectual Prop. Comm. et al., *supra* note 19, at 34–40; Drahos & Braithwaite, *supra* note 4, at 144.

23 *See* Pratt, *supra* note 4. In this regard, Edmund Pratt notes that, the IPC, UNICE, and Keidanren worked together and "were able to draft intellectual property standards that would be supported by dispute resolution and enforcement mechanisms." *Id.* He further notes that this combined strength enabled them to "establish a global private sector government network which lay the groundwork for what became 'TRIPS.'" *Id. See also* Sell, *supra* note 1, at 107; May & Sell, *supra* note 4, at 154 (stating that "the IPC essentially drafted the TRIPS Agreement, and the actual negotiations fine-tuned the text and made some concessions to developing countries' negotiators").

24 Sell, *supra* note 1, at 107.

25 *E.g.*, Pratt, *supra* note 4 (stating that, "there is still more to be done. The GATT standards, while good, are still inadequate.").

implement the TRIPS Agreement.[26] Nevertheless, the IPC successfully achieved most of its goals in the Uruguay Round.[27]

The success achieved by corporate actors (including pharmaceutical companies) in shaping the current global IP legal framework demonstrates their power and influence.[28] This explains why many countries have pushed for regulating the activities of corporations under international law. In this regard – both prior to and after the adoption of the TRIPS Agreement – efforts have been made to impose human rights responsibilities on corporate actors under international law. These efforts are examined below.

## The Evolution of the Human Rights Responsibilities of Corporate Actors Under International Law[29]

In the 1970s, developing countries attempted to regulate the conduct of transnational corporations at the international level through negotiations on the United Nations Code of Conduct on Transnational Corporations (Code).[30] The negotiations, conducted under the auspices of the United Nations Centre on Transnational Corporations (UNCTC),[31] occurred in a context characterized by the ascendancy of newly independent developing countries and the demands for a New International Economic Order (NIEO).[32] However, the negotiations on this Code failed for various reasons, including the inability of developing countries to maintain a stable coalition, the collapse of the Soviet bloc, and the

26 *See* Drahos & Braithwaite, *supra* note 4 at 147 (noting that, "All the critics were annoyed by the time given to developing countries to bring their laws into line with TRIPS. One or two years to implement TRIPS was more than enough, figured the U.S. pharmaceutical industry.").

27 Sell, *supra* note 1, at 115 (noting that, "The IPC succeeded in getting most of what it wanted in the [TRIPS Agreement] in the Uruguay GATT round ... The IPC was particularly pleased with the enforcement provisions. The industry representatives' demands are reflected clearly in the final agreement.").

28 *See* Sell, *supra* note 1, at 96 (noting that, "The private actors succeeded in getting most of what they wanted from an IP agreement, which now has the status of public international law.").

29 *See generally* Emmanuel Oke, *Defining the Right to Health Responsibilities of Patent-Owning Pharmaceutical Companies*, 1 Intellectual Property quarterly 43, 46–51 (2019).

30 *See generally* Tagi Sagafi-Nejad, The UN and Transnational Corporations: From Code of Conduct to Global Compact (2008); Karl Sauvant, *The Negotiations of the United Nations Code of Conduct on Transnational Corporations: Experience and Lessons Learned*, 16 J. World Inv. & Trade 1, 11 (2015).

31 *See* Khalil Hamdani & Lorraine Ruffing, United Nations Centre on Transnational Corporations: Corporate Conduct and the Public Interest 1 (2015) (noting that, "The United Nations Centre on Transnational Corporations ... was established in 1975 and abolished in 1992. It was an early effort by the UN to address the overlapping issues of national sovereignty, corporate responsibility, and global governance.").

32 Hamdani & Ruffing, at 7; *see also*, Sauvant, *supra* note 30, at 13–6.

emergence of the Washington Consensus.[33] The Code was dropped from the UN agenda by 1996.[34]

In the 1990s, another attempt was made to develop norms toward imposing binding human rights obligations on corporations under the auspices of the UN Sub-Commission on the Promotion and Protection of Human Rights, through its Working Group on the Working Methods and Activities of Transnational Corporations, which was created in 1998.[35] This Working Group's document – "Norms on the Responsibilities of Transnational Corporations and Other Business Enterprises with regard to Human Rights" (Norms) – was approved by the Sub-Commission in 2003.[36]

According to the Norms, states bear the primary responsibility to promote, fulfill, respect, ensure respect for, and protect human rights. However, the Norms further provided that, "[w]ithin their respective spheres of activity and influence, transnational corporations and other business enterprises have the obligation to promote, secure the fulfillment of, respect, ensure respect of and protect human rights."[37] But a number of states and corporations opposed the Norms.[38] The former UN Commission on Human Rights (now the UN Human Rights Council) subsequently noted that the Norms had no legal status,[39] and they were eventually abandoned.[40]

Nevertheless, both states and corporations acknowledged the necessity to clarify the human rights responsibilities of corporate actors.[41] As Ruggie notes, in the face of campaigns from advocacy groups and lawsuits, "business itself felt a need for

33 *See* David Coleman, *The United Nations and Transnational Corporations: From an Internation to a "Beyond-state" Model of Engagement*, 17 GLOBAL SOC'Y 339, 349–50 (2003).

34 *Id.*

35 *See* Pini Pavel Miretski & Sascha-Dominik Bachmann, *The UN "Norms on the Responsibility of Transnational Corporations and Other Business Enterprises with Regard to Human Rights": A Requiem*, 17 DEAKIN L. REV. 5, 6 (2012).

36 U.N. ESCOR, 55th Sess., 22nd mtg. at, U.N. Doc. E/CN.4/Sub.2/2003/12/Rev.2 (Aug. 13, 2003); David Weissbrodt & Muria Kruger, *Norms on the Responsibilities of Transnational Corporations and Other Business Enterprises with Regard to Human Rights*, 97 AM. J. INT'L. L. 901 (2003); David Kinley & Rachel Chambers, *The UN Human Rights Norms for Corporations: The Private Implications of Public International Law*, 6 HUM. RTS. L. REV. 447 (2006).

37 Weissbrodt & Kruger, *supra* note 36.

38 Miretski & Bachmann, *supra* note 35 at 8–9; *see also* JOHN GERARD RUGGIE, JUST BUSINESS: MULTINATIONAL CORPORATIONS AND HUMAN RIGHTS, xvii (2013) (noting that, "The Norms triggered a deeply divisive debate between human rights advocacy organizations and the business community. Advocates were fervently in favor because the Norms proposed making these obligations binding on companies directly under international law. Business vehemently opposed what it described as 'the privatization of human rights,' transferring to companies obligations that they believed belonged to States.").

39 *See*, UN Commission on Human Rights, 60th Sess., at E/CN.4/Dec/2004/116 (20 April 2004) (affirming that the Norms had "not been requested by the Commission and, as a draft proposal, has no legal standing, and that the Sub-Commission should not perform any monitoring function in this regard.").

40 Miretski & Bachmann, *supra* note 35, at 9.

41 RUGGIE, *supra* note 38, at xvii.

greater clarity regarding their human rights responsibilities from some reasonably objective and authoritative source."[42] This eventually led to the UN Commission on Human Rights establishing a special mandate for an individual expert on this issue in 2005,[43] specifically requesting the UN Secretary-General to appoint the expert as a "Special Representative on the issue of human rights and transnational corporations and other business enterprises."[44] The then UN Secretary General Kofi Annan appointed John Ruggie as the Special Representative in July 2005.[45]

Ruggie's objective was not to develop a legally binding instrument but a politically authoritative formula that could form the basis for further legal developments.[46] Ruggie was guided by what he termed "principled pragmatism";[47] in his 2006 interim report, he noted that:

> [T]he Special Representative of the Secretary-General takes his mandate to be primarily evidence-based. But insofar as it involves assessing difficult situations that are themselves in flux, it inevitably will also entail making normative judgments. In the Special Representative's case, the basis for those judgments might best be described as a principled form of pragmatism: an unflinching commitment to the principle of strengthening the promotion and protection of human rights as it relates to business, coupled with a pragmatic attachment to what works best in creating change where it matters most – in the daily lives of people.[48]

In March 2011, Ruggie submitted his final report to the UN Human Rights Council. This report, containing Ruggie's *Guiding Principles on Business and Human Rights: Implementing the United Nations 'Protect, Respect and Remedy' Framework*[49] (Guiding Principles), was endorsed by the UN Human Rights Council in June 2011. Ruggie's Guiding Principles rest on three pillars: the duty of states to respect, protect, and fulfill human rights; the duty of corporate actors to comply with all applicable laws and to respect human rights; and the need to provide appropriate and effective remedies to those whose rights have been breached.[50] Essentially, the Guiding Principles provide that business enterprises should respect human rights, and "this means that they should avoid infringing on the human rights of others and should address the adverse human rights impacts with which they are

42 *Id.* at xvii–xviii.
43 U.N. ESCOR, 61st Sess., 16th mtg., U.N. Doc. E/CN.4/2005/L.87 (Apr. 15, 2005).
44 *Id.*
45 RUGGIE, *supra* note 38, at xviii.
46 *Id.* at xlvi.
47 *Id.* at xlii.
48 U.N. Secretary-General, *Promotion and Protection of Human Rights*, ¶ 81, U.N. Doc. E/CN.4/2006/97 (Feb. 22, 2006).
49 U.N. Secretary-General, Human Rights Council, *Guiding Principles on Business and Human Rights: Implementing the United Nations "Protect, Respect and Remedy" Framework*, U.N. Doc. A/HRC/17/31 (Mar. 21 2011).
50 *Id.* at 6.

involved."[51] It also provides that the responsibility to respect human rights requires that business enterprises "avoid causing or contributing to adverse human rights impacts through their own activities, and address such impacts when they occur."[52]

Thus, Ruggie's Guiding Principles identified the responsibility to respect as the baseline responsibility of corporate actors. Without creating new obligations under international law, the Guiding Principles elaborate on the implications of existing standards and practices for states and corporate actors.[53] Although non-binding, the Guiding Principles have been endorsed by the UN Human Rights Council and can serve as the basis for further legal developments.[54]

Indeed, building on the Ruggie Guiding Principles, there has been an attempt to adopt a binding treaty on business and human rights. In this regard, the negotiations on the draft text of a "Legally Binding Instrument to Regulate the Activities of Transnational Corporations and Other Business Enterprises"[55] (Legally Binding Instrument) is being held under the auspices of the UN Open-ended Intergovernmental Working Group on Transnational Corporations and Other Business Enterprises with respect to Human Rights (OEIGWG). The OEIGWG was created by the UN Human Rights Council in 2014 to "elaborate an internationally legally binding instrument to regulate, in international human rights law, the activities of transnational corporations and other business enterprises."[56]

In its Preamble, the draft Legally Binding Instrument stresses that the primary obligation to respect, protect, fulfill, and promote human rights rests with states. But in line with the Ruggie Guiding Principles, the Preamble underlines that all business enterprises have the responsibility to respect all human rights. Echoing the Ruggie Guiding Principles, the Preamble states that the responsibility of business enterprises to respect human rights includes avoiding causing

51 *Id.* at 13 (Principle 11).
52 *Id.* at 14 (Principle 13(a)).
53 *Id.* at 5, ¶ 14 (noting that, "The Guiding Principles' normative contribution lies not in the creation of new international law obligations but in elaborating the implications of existing standards and practices for States and businesses; integrating them within a single, logically coherent and comprehensive template; and identifying where the current regime falls short and how it should be improved.").
54 *Id.* ¶ 13 (noting that, "Council endorsement of the Guiding Principles, by itself, will not bring business and human rights challenges to an end. But it will mark the end of the beginning: by establishing a common global platform for action, on which cumulative progress can be built, step-by-step, without foreclosing any other promising longer-term developments.").
55 *OEIGWG, supra* note 3. The analysis here is based on the revised version of the draft Legally Binding Instrument that was released by the OEIGWG in July 2019. *Id.* It should be noted that an earlier version of the Legally Binding Instrument was released by the OEIGWG in July 2018. *See*, U.N., Human Rights Council, *Mandate on Open-ended Intergovernmental Working Group [OEIGWG] on Transnational Corporations and Other Business Enterprises with Respect to Human Rights, Chairmanship Revised Draft, Legally Binding Instrument to Regulate, in International Human Rights Law, the Activities of Transnational Corporations and Other Business Enterprises*, Zero Draft, (July 16, 2018), https://www.ohchr.org/Documents/HRBodies/HRCouncil/WGTransCorp/Session3/DraftLBI.pdf.
56 *See* Human Rights Council Res. U.N. Doc. A/HRC/RES/26/9, ¶ 1 (July 14, 2014).

or contributing to adverse human rights impacts through their activities, and addressing such impacts when they occur. This responsibility also includes preventing or mitigating adverse human rights impacts directly connected to the operations, products, or services of business enterprises.

In terms of the scope of application, Article 3(1) of the draft Legally Binding Instrument clarifies that the treaty shall apply to all business activities, including those of a transnational character.[57] Article 3(3) of the draft text further states that the treaty shall cover all human rights.[58] Importantly, in Article 5(1), the draft Legally Binding Instrument imposes a duty on states to effectively regulate the activities of business enterprises in their territories and to ensure that their domestic laws require all persons conducting business activities in their territory to respect human rights.[59]

One cannot accurately predict when this proposed treaty on business and human rights will enter into force as it is still currently being negotiated. The practical usefulness of the proposed treaty is also unclear as the US has expressed opposition to the entire treaty process,[60] and the EU has also raised concerns regarding some provisions in the draft Legally Binding Instrument.[61]

57 *OEIGWG*, *supra* note 3.

58 *Id.*

59 *Id.*

60 See *The United States' Opposition to the Business and Human Rights Treaty Process*, U.S. Mission to Int'l Orgs. in Geneva (Oct. 15, 2018), https://geneva.usmission.gov/2018/10/15/the-united-states-opposition-to-the-business-and-human-rights-treaty-process/ (noting that "it remains opposed to the treaty process and the manner in which it has been pursued. The [OEIGWG] is detracting from the valuable foundation laid by the UN Guiding Principles (GPs), a framework for avoiding and addressing adverse human rights impacts that involve business activity. The international community has spoken clearly on this topic, emphasizing the need for the voluntary, multi-stakeholder, and consensus-based approach developed through the GPs. The [OEIGWG] runs counter to the consensus of the international community.").

61 *See*, EU, OEIGWG, 5th Sess., *Opening Remarks by the European Union,* (Oct. 14, 2019), https://www.ohchr.org/Documents/HRBodies/HRCouncil/WGTransCorp/Session5/IO/EU_General.docx (In relation to its concerns with some of the provisions in the draft Legally Binding Instrument, the European Union notes, inter alia, that "in the scope (Article 3), there is no clear definition of 'all human rights' to which the draft treaty would apply, with otherwise there being only a reference made to them in the preamble … The new draft appears to address a key EU concern about the scope of the Instrument, given that the scope is no longer limited to transnational corporations and activities. However, there is a need for greater clarification on the definition of the scope. The treaty should not distinguish between transnational corporations and other business enterprises. As to another of the EU's key concerns, the consistency with and complementarity to the UN Guiding Principles on Business and Human Rights, the EU notes that the preamble now mentions the role played by the Guiding Principles and paraphrases parts thereof, and the due diligence requirements set out in Article 5 also appear to be better targeted and more in line with the UNGPs. However, there is still scope for the text to be more closely aligned with the UNGPs. While in some respects the document is thus an improvement, further in-depth analysis is needed before a solid conclusion can be drawn as to whether we see it as a workable basis for a legally sound, implementable and enforceable instrument.").

Crucially, a number of the transnational corporations which the draft treaty aims to regulate are headquartered in either the US or the EU; it is thus important that these regional powers be on board to guarantee the effectiveness of this proposed treaty.

Despite the uncertainty regarding the draft Legally Binding Instrument, the baseline responsibility of corporate actors to respect human rights – as espoused by the Ruggie Guiding Principles and endorsed by the UN Human Rights Council – remains unchanged. Thus, there is widespread acceptance of this baseline responsibility to respect human rights by various stakeholders, including states and corporations.[62]

Beyond the Guiding Principles, which deal with corporate actors' responsibility in relation to human rights at a general level, significant work has also been done in defining the specific responsibilities of pharmaceutical companies pertaining to the right to health.[63] In 2008, Paul Hunt, the UN Special Rapporteur on the right to the highest attainable standard of health between 2002 and 2008, presented his report to the UN General Assembly. Hunt's report – *Human Rights Guidelines for Pharmaceutical Companies in Relation to Access to Medicines* (Guidelines) – contains a set of 47 guidelines on the right to health responsibilities of pharmaceutical companies.[64] Opining that merely urging pharmaceutical companies to comply with their right to health responsibility is unhelpful, Hunt's goal in developing the Guidelines was to clarify and explain the human rights responsibility of pharmaceutical companies in relation to access to medicines.[65]

The Hunt Guidelines arose in the context of the drive to find solutions to the problem of access to medicines; it was equally part of the process of developing

62 *See* John Ruggie, *The Social Construction of the UN Guiding Principles on Business and Human Rights* 1–2 (Corp. Resp. Initiative, Harv. Kennedy School, Working Paper No. 67, June 2017) (noting that, although the Guiding Principles do not create new legally binding obligations, they "derive their normative force through their endorsement by states and support from other key stakeholders, including business itself.").

63 The right to health is recognized in Article 25 of the Universal Declaration of Human Rights and in Article 12 of the International Covenant on Economic, Social and Cultural Rights. *See* Universal Declaration of Human Rights art. 25, Dec. 10, 1948, G.A. Res. 217 (III) A, U.N. Doc. A/810 at 71; International Covenant on Economic, Social and Cultural Rights art. 12, Dec. 16, 1966, 993 U.N.T.S. 3, 6 I.L.M. 360.

64 G.A. Dec. 6/29, U.N. Doc. A/63/263 (Aug. 11, 2008); *see also* Paul Hunt & Rajat Khosla, *Are Drug Companies Living up to Their Human Rights Responsibilities? The Perspective of the Former United Nations Special Rapporteur (2002–2008)*, 7 PLoS Med., Sept. 28, 2010, at 1; Joo-Young Lee & Paul Hunt, *Human Rights Responsibilities of Pharmaceutical Companies in Relation to Access to Medicines*, 40 J. L., Med. & Ethics 1, 220, 221 (July 1, 2012).

65 *See*, Rajat Khosla and Paul Hunt, *Human Rights Responsibilities of Pharmaceutical Companies in Relation to Access to Medicines*, *in* Access to Medicines as a Human Right: Implications for Pharmaceutical Industry Responsibility, 37–38 (Lisa Forman & Jillian Clare Kohler eds., 2012).

the idea of access to medicines as a component of the right to health.[66] Khosla and Hunt's report that discusses the context and background of the Guidelines states:

> Medical care in the event of sickness, as well as the prevention, treatment, and control of diseases, are central features of the right of everyone to the enjoyment of the highest attainable standard of physical and [mental] health (in short, the "right to the highest attainable standard of health" or "right to health"). These features depend upon access to medicines. Thus, access to medicines forms an indispensable part of the right to the highest attainable standard of health.[67]

Importantly, however, the immediate impetus behind the development of the Guidelines was Hunt's observation on the lack of clarity regarding the right to health responsibilities of pharmaceutical companies.[68] Hunt noted that the lack of clarity in this regard was in contrast to the right to health responsibilities of states which, prior to that time, had already been explored in great detail.[69] Indeed, in its General Comment Number 14 on the right to health adopted in 2000, the UN Committee on Economic, Social and Cultural Rights (UNCESCR) had elaborated in detail states' responsibilities pertaining to respecting, protecting, and fulfilling the right to health as recognized in article 12 of the International Covenant on Economic, Social and Cultural Rights.[70] While the UNCESR had noted that the private business sector also had "responsibilities regarding the realization of the right to health,"[71] it had

66 In relation to the idea of access to medicines as a component of the right to health, *see generally* Hans Hogerzeil et al., *Is Access to Essential Medicines as part of the Fulfilment of the Right to Health Enforceable through the Courts?*, 368 LANCET 305 (2006); Stephen Marks, *Access to Essential Medicines as a Component of the Right to Health, in* REALIZING THE RIGHT TO HEALTH, 80–99 (Andrew Clapham & Mary Robinson eds., 2009); *see also* U.N. Human Rights Council, *Access to Medicine in the Context of the Right of Everyone to the Enjoyment of the Highest Attainable Standard of Physical and Mental Health*, U.N. Doc., A/HRC/RES/12/24 (June 30, 2016) (recognizing that "access to medicine is one of the fundamental elements in achieving progressively the full realization of the right of everyone to the enjoyment of the highest attainable standard of physical and mental health.").

67 Rajat Khosla & Paul Hunt, *Human Rights Guidelines for Pharmaceutical Companies in Relation to Access to Medicines: The Sexual and Reproductive Health Context*, U. OF ESSEX 2 (2008), http://repository.essex.ac.uk/4425/1/human-rights-guidelines-pharmaceutical-companies-access-medicines.pdf [hereinafter *Human Rights Guidelines Context*].

68 *Id.* at 9 (noting that, "the nature and scope of pharmaceutical companies' human rights responsibilities in relation to access to medicines were not clear").

69 *Id.*

70 *See* U.N. Committee on Economic, Social and Cultural Rights, *General Comment No. 14: The Right to the Highest Attainable Standard of Health (Art. 12)*, U.N. Doc., E/C.12/2000/4 (Aug. 11, 2000).

71 *Id.* ¶ 42.

not elaborated on the nature of the private business sector's responsibilities in this regard.[72]

Moreover, Hunt had been informed by public officials that the "policies and practices of some pharmaceutical companies constitute obstacles to States' implementation of the right to the highest attainable standard of health and, in particular, their endeavors to enhance access to medicines."[73] While these public officials acknowledged the indispensable role of the pharmaceutical sector with regard to access to medicines and equally recognized the "constructive contribution of specific pharmaceutical companies," Hunt was also informed of some practices of pharmaceutical companies that hindered the enjoyment of the right to health and access to medicines.[74] These include "excessively high prices, inadequate attention to research and development concerning diseases that disproportionately impact people in developing counties, inappropriate drug promotion, and problematic clinical trials."[75]

These sets of circumstances led Hunt to prioritize the development of specific guidelines regarding the right to health responsibilities of pharmaceutical companies. As Khosla and Hunt state:

> It became imperative, therefore, to address this situation. How can pharmaceutical companies sensibly be asked to respect their human rights responsibilities in relation to access to medicines without much more specific guidance, as well as the identification of good practices? How can they be monitored, and held to account, if their human rights responsibilities in relation to access to medicines are unclear?[76]

Hunt's draft version of the Guidelines, released in September 2007, was available for comments from the public till May 2008.[77] It was aimed at assisting pharmaceutical companies and actors intending to monitor pharmaceutical companies' performance in relation to access to medicines.[78] Based on the comments received from states, pharmaceutical companies, nongovernmental organizations, and academics, the final version was presented to the UN General Assembly in 2008.[79] Essentially, the Guidelines include responsibilities for "transparency, management, monitoring and accountability, pricing, and

72 *Human Rights Guidelines Context*, *supra* note 67, at 9 (noting that, "While the Committee's general statement of principle is very important, it provides no practical guidance about the human rights responsibilities of pharmaceutical companies in relation to access to medicines.").

73 *Id.*

74 *Id.*

75 *Id.*

76 *Id.*

77 *Id.* at 29.

78 *Id.*

79 *Id.* at 30.

ethical marketing, and against lobbying for more protection in IP laws, applying for patents for trivial modifications of existing medicines, inappropriate drug promotion, and excessive pricing."[80]

While the Guiding Principles emphasize the baseline responsibility of corporate actors to respect human rights, the Hunt Guidelines go beyond this baseline responsibility. In 2012, Joo-Young Lee and Paul Hunt examined the relationship between the Guiding Principles and the Hunt Guidelines and stated that:

> [t]aking into account the right-to-health framework, which is based on the dignity and well-being of individuals and communities, as well as globally recognized standards, the *Guidelines for Pharmaceutical Companies* encompass, but also look beyond, the corporate responsibility to respect. In our view, an examination of human rights responsibilities beyond the duty to respect is critically important because the pharmaceutical sector has highly distinctive functions directly impacting upon the life, health, and prosperity of countless individuals and communities.[81]

The attempt in the Hunt Guidelines to surpass the baseline responsibility of corporate actors to respect human rights led to an overlap in some of the Guidelines between the responsibility of states to respect, protect, and fulfill the right to health, and pharmaceutical corporations' baseline responsibility to respect the right to health as specified in the Guiding Principles. As Suerie Moon rightly contends, "it is useful to distinguish between those guidelines that primarily relate to the responsibility to respect and those that may relate to additional responsibilities."[82] Moon identifies three reasons why it is useful to draw this distinction.

Firstly, "if 'respect' forms the baseline, then it is important to ensure that companies are indeed living up to this most fundamental responsibility"; distinguishing between the responsibility to respect and other responsibilities helps to "focus attention on the most fundamental responsibilities of industry."[83] Secondly, "conflating the responsibilities of State and non-State actors risks detracting attention away from State obligations, making it easier for governments to shirk their own obligations."[84] Thirdly, "the limited resources of civil society organizations, journalists, and other watchdog entities underscore the importance of getting the baseline right, allowing such groups to focus their

80 Hunt & Khosla, *supra* note 64, at 1.
81 Lee & Hunt, *supra* note 64, at 224.
82 Suerie Moon, *Respecting the Right to Access to Medicines: Implications of the UN Guiding Principles on Business and Human Rights for the Pharmaceutical Industry*, 15 HEALTH & HUM. RTS. J., 32, 37 (2013).
83 *Id.*
84 *Id.*

energies on holding companies accountable for at least their most basic human rights responsibilities, and governments for theirs."[85]

This overview (of the evolution of the human rights responsibilities of corporate actors under international law) indicates an emerging consensus based on the Ruggie Guiding Principles that corporate actors have a baseline responsibility to respect human rights. In the present context, this implies that corporate actors, particularly pharmaceutical corporations, have a baseline responsibility to respect the right to health. This further implies that in exercising and enforcing their patent rights, pharmaceutical corporations need to respect the right to health, i.e. the exercise and enforcement of patent rights should not impede access to essential medicines. Nevertheless, as the negotiations on a binding treaty on business and human rights is still ongoing, it is necessary to explore other mechanisms that can be used to hold corporate actors (including pharmaceutical companies) accountable for their human rights responsibilities. One potential mechanism, international investment law, is examined below.

## Is International Investment Law the New Frontier?

International investment law is essentially a body of several investment agreements (i.e. bilateral investment treaties and free trade agreements that include an investment chapter) entered into between states, and the decisions of investment tribunals. It protects foreign investments according to the standards contained in the agreement between the host state and home state of the foreign investor. Investment agreements usually permit foreign investors to sue states before investment tribunals. This method of dispute settlement is known as the investor-state dispute settlement (ISDS) system.

Typically, an international investment agreement contains certain standards of protection such as rules: prohibiting host states from discriminating in favor of domestic investors (national treatment); prohibiting discrimination between foreign investors (most-favored-nation treatment); prohibiting direct and indirect expropriation of investment assets; requiring the fair and equitable treatment of foreign investment (FET standard); and requiring the host state to provide full protection and security to foreign investments.

International investment law has become important to some corporate actors that own IPR because corporate actors cannot sue states before the WTO. Thus, investment law provides an avenue for these corporate actors to challenge national laws and measures relating to IP before investment tribunals, and a number of such cases have been decided in recent years.[86] While this use of

85 *Id.*

86 *See Philip Morris Asia Ltd. v. Australia*, PCA Case No. 2012-12, Award on Jurisdiction and Admissibility (Dec. 17, 2015); *Philip Morris Brands Sarl & Others v. Uruguay*, ICSID Case No. ARB/10/7, Award (July 8, 2016); *Eli Lilly v. Canada*, Case No. UNCT/14/2, Final Award (Mar. 16, 2017); *Bridgestone Licensing Services, Inc., v. Republic of Panama*, ICSID Case No. ARB/16/34, Decision on Expedited Objections (Dec. 13, 2017).

investment law can potentially have a chilling effect on the regulatory powers of states,[87] there is also a possibility of using investment law as a means of holding corporate actors accountable for their human rights responsibilities.[88]

It is, however, difficult to generalize in the context of international investment law due to the lack of a doctrine of binding precedent in investment arbitration. Furthermore, cases being decided pursuant to different investment treaties makes it equally difficult to generalize.[89] Thus, the interpretation and application of the standards of protection highlighted above would depend on the provisions of the investment treaty applicable to a dispute and the specific facts of each case. Nevertheless, previous investment disputes dealing with analogous issues can provide some guidance and indicate how investment tribunals would apply and interpret the standards of protection in future cases.[90]

In this regard, the decision of the tribunal in *Urbaser v. Argentina*[91] demonstrates the crucial role of human rights in the context of international investment law. The case involved a concession for water and sewage services that was subsequently terminated by Argentina. Urbaser claimed that Argentina adopted measures that had a negative impact on its investment; it also alleged that these measures violated the FET standard. Argentina counterclaimed that Urbaser violated its obligation in relation to the right to water by not providing the necessary investment for the concession. The tribunal's decision in this case lays down a framework that other investment tribunals can build on. Importantly, in this case, the tribunal noted that the interpretation of the FET standard is conditioned by international human rights law. It stated:

> The fair and equitable treatment standard is not focused exclusively on interests and expectations of a legal nature. It does include the actual social and economic environment of the host State, which is also part of the expectations the investor has to acknowledge when making its

87 Cynthia Ho, *Sovereignty Under Siege: Corporate Challenges to Domestic Intellectual Property Decisions*, 30 Berkeley Tech. L. J., 213 (2015).

88 *See generally* Markus Krajewski, *A Nightmare or a Noble Dream? Establishing Investor Obligations Through Treaty-Making and Treaty-Application* 5 Bus. Hum. Rights J., 105 (2020); Ludovica Chiussi, *The Role of International Investment Law in the Business and Human Rights Legal Process*, 21 Int'l Community Law Rev., 35 (2019); Ursula Kriebaum, *Human Rights and International Investment Law*, *in* Research Handbook on Human Rights and Investment 13 (Yannick Radi ed., 2018); Eric De Brabandere & Maryse Hazelzet, *Corporate Responsibility and Human Rights: Navigating Between International, Domestic and Self-Regulation*, *in* Research Handbook on Human Rights and Investment 221 (Yannick Radi ed., 2018); Gilles Lhuilier, *MNCs' Obligations in Their 'Sphere of Influence'*, *in* Research Handbook on Human Rights and Investment 244 (Yannick Radi ed., 2018).

89 *See* Benn McGrady, *International Investment Law*, *in* Regulating Tobacco, Alcohol and Unhealthy Foods: The Legal Issues 117 (Tania Voon et al. eds., 2014).

90 *Id.*

91 Urbaser v. Argentina, ICSID Case No. ARB/07/26, Award, (Dec. 8, 2016).

> business decision. In this respect, Respondent rightly recalls that the Province had to guarantee the continuation of the basic water supply to millions of Argentines. The protection of this universal basic human right constitutes the framework within which Claimants should frame their expectations.[92]

Ultimately, the tribunal ruled against Argentina, stating that it violated the relevant bilateral investment treaty in this case by not affording fair and equitable treatment to the claimants in relation to the renegotiation of the concession contract.[93] Nevertheless, in relation to Argentina's counterclaim, the tribunal noted that corporate actors have human rights obligations under international law. Drawing on Ruggie's Guiding Principles, the tribunal noted that corporations are subjects of international law:

> The Tribunal may mention in this respect that international law accepts corporate social responsibility as a standard of crucial importance for companies operating in the field of international commerce. This standard includes commitments to comply with human rights in the framework of those entities' operations conducted in countries other than the country of their seat or incorporation. In light of this more recent development, it can no longer be admitted that companies operating internationally are immune from becoming subjects of international law.[94]

Further noting that corporate actors have a duty not to act in disregard of human rights, the tribunal stated:

> The 1948 Universal Declaration of Human Rights proclaims that "All human beings are born free and equal in dignity and rights" (Art. 1), that "Everyone has the right to equal access to public service in his country" (Art. 21(2)), and that "Everyone has the right to a standard of living adequate for the health and well-being of himself and of his family, including food, clothing, housing and medical care and necessary social service" (Art. 25(1)). It may be said that these and other provisions do not state more than rights pertaining to each individual. Nevertheless, in order to ensure that such rights be enjoyed by each person, it must necessarily also be ensured that no other individual or entity, public or private, may act in disregard of such rights, which then implies a corresponding obligation, as stated in Article 30 of the Declaration: "Nothing in this Declaration may be interpreted as implying for any State, group or person any right to engage in any

92 *Id.* ¶¶ 623–24.
93 *Id.* ¶ 1234.
94 *Id.* ¶ 1195.

> activity or to perform any act aimed at the destruction of any of the rights and freedoms set forth herein." (Art. 30) The Declaration may also address multinational companies.[95]

In other words, the Universal Declaration of Human Rights (Declaration) should not be construed as a document that merely contains the human rights of individuals; it equally implies a corresponding obligation on other actors (including corporate actors) not to act in a manner that disregards the rights recognized in the Declaration. This corresponding obligation is a *sine qua non* for the enjoyment of the rights contained in the Declaration. The tribunal added: "At this juncture, it is, therefore, to be admitted that the human right for everyone's dignity and its right for adequate housing and living conditions are complemented by an obligation on all parts, public and private parties, not to engage in activity aimed at destroying such rights."[96]

Perhaps influenced by the distinction between the obligation of states to respect, protect, and fulfill human rights on the one hand, and the obligation of corporate actors to respect human rights on the other (as recognized in the Ruggie Guiding Principles), the tribunal ultimately ruled that the human right to water does not contain an obligation for performance on the part of any corporate actor[97] and Argentina's counterclaim was ultimately rejected. According to the tribunal:

> While it is thus correct to state that the State's obligation is based on its obligation to enforce the human right to water of all individuals under its jurisdiction, this is not the case for the investors who pursue, it is true, the same goal, but on the basis of the Concession, and not under an obligation derived from the human right to water. Indeed, the enforcement of the human right to water represents an obligation to perform. Such obligation is imposed upon States. It cannot be imposed on any company knowledgeable in the field of provision of water and sanitation services. In order to have such an obligation to perform applicable to a particular investor, a contract or similar legal relationship of civil and commercial law is required. In such a case, the investor's obligation to perform has as its source domestic law; it does not find its legal ground in general international law. The situation would be different in case an obligation to abstain, like a prohibition to commit acts violating human rights, would be at stake. Such an obligation can be of immediate application, not only upon States, but equally to individuals and other private parties. This is not a matter for concern in the instant case.[98]

95 *Id.* ¶ 1196.
96 *Id.* ¶ 1199.
97 *Id.* ¶ 1208.
98 *Id.* ¶ 1210.

The key point here is that certain measures that states can implement – for instance, with regard to the regulation of patent rights owned by corporate actors for the purposes of protecting the right to health – would arguably fall under an obligation to abstain, not an obligation to perform a specific action. In this regard, one can think of provisions prohibiting the grant of patents on trivial modifications of existing inventions,[99] and provisions permitting the grant of a compulsory license on the grounds of failure to make a patented invention available to the public at a reasonably affordable price.[100] Such provisions require pharmaceutical companies that own patent rights to abstain from certain practices that can hinder access to medicines and could therefore be construed as a means of ensuring respect for the right to health. Thus, it could be argued that, following the tribunal's approach in *Urbaser*, international investment law permits states to regulate IPR for the purpose of holding corporate actors accountable for human rights.

## Conclusion

In summary, the success achieved by corporate actors (including pharmaceutical companies) with regard to shaping the current global IP legal framework demonstrates the power and influence of these actors. Considering the power and influence wielded by these corporate actors at the global level, one can appreciate why a number of countries have pushed for the regulation of their activities under international law. While the Ruggie Guiding Principles have been endorsed by both states and corporate actors, there is still no binding legal framework regulating the activities of corporate actors under international human rights law. Nevertheless, while acknowledging that international investment law can potentially weaken the regulatory powers of states, this chapter also explored the possibility of using investment law for holding corporate actors accountable for their human rights responsibilities.

99 *See e.g.*, The Patent Act, No. 39 of 1970, INDIA CODE § 3(d) (1998).
100 *See e.g.*, *Id.* § 84(1)(b).

# 18 Competition

## Can Excessive Pricing be Fixed Through Abuse of Dominant Position?

*Shirin Syed*

### Introduction

Since the adoption of the Agreement on Trade-Related Aspects of Intellectual Property Rights (TRIPS Agreement) in 1995,[1] all members of the World Trade Organization (WTO) other than least developed ones are obligated to provide product patent protection to pharmaceutical inventions. While the obligation is justified as a tool to spur innovation in the pharmaceutical sector, the major concern is the high prices of patented medicines. The absence of competition in patented medicines allows the patent owner to fix an exorbitantly high price. For example, the cost of *sofosbuvir* – a patented medicine for treating hepatitis C – is around $84,000 per patient. In the absence of patents, the price for the same medicine is less than $72.[2] The use of TRIPS flexibilities is the best way to address issues such as lack of access to medicines due to high prices.[3] These flexibilities, such as compulsory licenses (CLs) and government use, are provided to lessen the impact of the TRIPS Agreement on medicine access. The Doha Declaration on the TRIPS Agreement and Public Health (Doha Declaration), which was adopted at the WTO Ministerial Conference of 2001, confirmed the members' right to use these flexibilities.[4] However, certain remedies outside patent law can also be used to address the issue of access to medicines.

Competition law is one of the options outside the patent regime that can be an effective tool to address public policy concerns on patent protection. Article 40

1 TRIPS: Agreement on Trade-Related Aspects of Intellectual Property Rights, Apr. 15, 1994, Marrakesh Agreement Establishing the World Trade Organization, Annex 1C, 1869 U.N.T.S. 299, 33 I.L.M. 1197 (1994) [hereinafter TRIPS Agreement].

2 Andrew Hill, *Prices versus Costs of Medicines in the WHO Essential Medicines List* (Sept. 2, 2020), https://www.who.int/phi/1-AndrewHill.pdf.

3 Matthias Lamping et al., *Declaration on Patent Protection: Regulatory Sovereignty Under TRIPS*, Max Planck Inst. for Innovation & Competition Res. (Apr. 15, 2014), https://www.mpg.de/8132986/Patent-Declaration.pdf.

4 TRIPS Agreement, *supra* note 1.

of the TRIPS Agreement provides the flexibility to use competition law to mitigate the abuse of patent rights.[5]

In the absence of any international law or treaty at the multilateral level that spells out common standards, there is much more freedom for WTO member states to shape their competition law and policy.[6] The United Nations (UN) Secretary-General's High-Level Panel on Access to Medicines[7] highlighted the importance of using competition law to address the high prices of medicines: "Competition policies are important levers that governments can employ to ensure that health technology markets operate competitively and that the public benefits from low prices and innovation. Should governments pay closer attention to competition law, it could serve as an important policy tool for increasing access to health technologies."[8]

Although competition law can be used to address various forms of abuse of intellectual property (IP), such as restrictive provisions in licensing agreements, payment for delaying the introduction of generic medicines and abuse of patent procedures to extend patent monopoly, this chapter focuses on the competition law remedy to excessive medicine prices. It discusses the scope of competition law–related flexibilities within the TRIPS Agreement and subsequently analyzes the conceptual framework of competition law to address the issue of excessive medicine prices, with a focus on patented medicines. The chapter then examines the South African experience of using competition law to address the problem of excessive medicine prices. It also outlines the major challenges, especially in the context of developing countries, in using competition law to address this problem.

## TRIPS Agreement Provisions on Competition Law

Articles 8, 31, and 40 of the TRIPS Agreement refer to the regulation of anticompetitive practices concerning IP protection. Article 8 states the principles of the TRIPS Agreement, which stress the need for a balanced perspective on IP

5 *Id.* at art. 40.2 ("Nothing in this Agreement shall prevent Members from specifying in their legislation licensing practices or conditions that may in particular cases constitute an abuse of intellectual property rights having an adverse effect on competition in the relevant market. As provided above, a Member may adopt, consistently with the other provisions of this Agreement, appropriate measures to prevent or control such practices, which may include, for example, exclusive grant back conditions, conditions preventing challenges to validity and coercive package licensing, in the light of the relevant laws and regulations of that Member.").

6 Shirin Syed, *Incorporation of Competition-Related TRIPS Flexibilities in the Domestic Law: A Case Study of India*, 23 J. World Intellect. Prop. 2 (Nov. 15, 2019).

7 *See generally* U.N. Secretary General, *Report of the United Nations Secretary-General's High-Level Panel on Access to Medicines* (Sept. 2016), https://static1.squarespace.com/static/562094dee4b0d00c1a3ef761/t/57d9c6ebf5e231b2f02cd3d4/1473890031320/UNSG+HLP+Report+FINAL+12+Sept+2016.pdf.

8 *Id.* at 24.

protection and enforcement and socioeconomic welfare. It also gives member states the freedom to take measures to protect public health, promote public interest in the crucial areas of socioeconomic and technological development, and prevent the abuse of IP rights (IPR), including practices restraining international technology transfer. According to Article 8.2, "appropriate measures, provided that they are consistent with the provisions of this Agreement, may be needed to prevent the abuse of intellectual property rights by right holders or the resort to practices which unreasonably restrain trade or adversely affect the international transfer of technology." Thus, the principles of the TRIPS Agreement recognize that there could be abuses of IPR and allow member states to address such abuses within the framework of competition law or IP law, including patent law.

Article 31K of the TRIPS Agreement provides the following exceptions to the procedures and norms for the issuance of a CL as a remedy to anti-competitive practices: (1) no requirement to attempt to obtain a voluntary license; (2) no requirement of supply predominantly to the domestic market; (3) royalty payment for the use of the CL can be waived by petition authorities; or (4) termination of the CL can be refused if and when the conditions that led to such authorization are likely to recur.

Article 40 of the TRIPS Agreement enables member states to take steps to curb certain licensing practices or conditions that would adversely affect trade, transfer, and dissemination of technology. It covers all forms of IP mentioned in part II of the TRIPS Agreement. For example, the general terms of licensing practices or conditions in the provision refer to all such conduct for the grant and execution of licenses. Thus, refusal to license, discriminatory grant of licenses, discriminatory license terms, and restrictive clauses in general, all fall within the scope of this provision.[9] It should be noted that refusal to deal, that is, denying licensing would result in a restriction in market competition and is also treated as a ground for granting a CL in many jurisdictions.

Although the TRIPS Agreement recognizes the anticompetitive implications of IP, it does not set any minimum standards for competition law. It allows for the possibility of addressing this issue within the IP law framework of competition law or both. In the absence of multilateral standards on competition law, WTO member states are free to set normative standards and to remedy anti-competitive practices within the competition law framework. This allows WTO member states, especially developing countries, to address the issue of excessive prices of patented medicines without necessarily following the approaches of developed country's competition law authorities.

9 F. Abbott et al., *UNDP, Using Competition Law To Promote Access To Health Technologies: A Guidebook For Low- and Middle-Income Countries*, 556, PAPERS.SSRN.COM (2020), https://hivlawcommission.org/wp-content/uploads/2017/06/UNDP-Using-Competition-Law-to-Promote-Access-to-Medicine-05-14-2014-1.pdf.

The TRIPS Agreement provisions do not make any direct reference to "access," "affordability," or "excessive prices" but the flexibilities therein, such as compulsory or government use licenses and parallel importation, can be used to address the issue of excessive prices. Article 31 deals with compulsory or government licenses but does not limit the grounds for granting such licenses. The Doha Declaration states that "[e]ach member has the right to grant compulsory licenses and the freedom to determine the grounds upon which such licenses are granted."[10] There is nothing in the TRIPS Agreement to prevent WTO member states from providing a remedy for excessive prices under competition law, and this remedy would generally include patented and non-patented products. Consequently, the Indian Patents Act has made unaffordable prices a ground for granting a CL. Under Section 84 of the Indian Patents Act, a CL can be sought if "the patented invention is not available to the public at a reasonably affordable price."

Competition law or its predecessor, monopoly-controlling legislations, identified excessive pricing as a form of monopoly abuse and as actionable conduct. Many developing countries had monopoly restrictive laws which prohibited excessive pricing prior to the adoption of competition laws.

The TRIPS Agreement thus allows countries to provide remedies under both patent and competition laws. India provides such a remedy under its competition law to address the issue of excessive prices, particularly in Section 4(1)(a)(ii) of the Competition Act of 2002: "There shall be an abuse of dominant position if an enterprise or a group directly or indirectly, imposes unfair or discriminatory price in purchase or sale (including predatory price) of goods or service."

## Relevant Competition Law Principles

### *In General*

As mentioned above, excessive prices are treated as an abuse of dominant position under the competition laws of various countries (including India). When excessive prices are charged by a dominant firm, it attracts action under competition law. Excessive prices charged by a firm that is not dominant in that market falls outside the scope of competition law.

When a dominant player uses its position to charge an excessive price for a product, this results in exploitation of the consumer. The excessive price is treated as part of the exploitative abuse of the dominant position[11] as such it compromises consumer welfare – one of the key objectives of competition law.

10 World Trade Organization, Ministerial Declaration of 14 November 2001 WTO Doc. WT/MIN(01)/DEC/1, 41 ILM 746 (2002) [hereinafter Doha Declaration].

11 M.A.H Schrijen, *Excessive Prices in the Pharmaceutical Sector: Is Competition Law the Best Remedy?*, Utret U. 26 (June 29, 2018), https://congresmededingingsrecht.nl/public/thesis_maureen_schrijen.pdf.

However, the issue of excessive price is a controversial topic in competition law circles despite the adverse impact on consumer welfare.[12] Competition authorities in developed countries follow a very cautious approach to intervening on issues of excessive pricing.[13] As the Chicago School notion of the self-correcting market resulted in a noninterventionist approach on such issues,[14] competition authorities of the United States (US) and the European Union (EU) under the influence of liberal economic theory and the Chicago School generally maintain a safe distance from the issue of excessive prices.[15]

According to the noninterventionist approach, high prices are a temporary phenomenon that is corrected by the market itself through competition from other firms.[16] New firms would enter the market to exploit the opportunities of unmet demand, i.e. failure to meet consumer needs due to high prices and other supply constraints and potential profit. Interfering with excessive pricing may benefit consumer welfare in the short term but will deter potential competitors from entering the market.[17] It would also hinder the dominant firm's ability to make investments to achieve maximum efficiency.[18] The noninterventionist school also argues that fixing excessive prices makes competition authorities and courts – who are not up to speed in understanding market dynamics – the de facto regulators.[19]

On the other hand, the interventionist approach posits that exclusionary excessive prices harm consumer welfare and there is a need for intervention.[20] High prices are not a temporary phenomenon as held by the noninterventionist school, and the likelihood that the dominant firm will reduce the price after the entry of a new firm is real. The potential competitor would consider this fact and enter only if it can compete with the reduced price through efficiency in production.[21] Thus, it is efficiency and not high prices that is the real deciding factor.

12 Liyang Hou, *Excessive Price Within EU Competition Law*, 7 Eur. Competition J. 47 (2011).
13 *Id.*
14 *See* Richard A. Posner, *The Chicago School of Antitrust Analysis*, 127 U. Pa. L. Rev. 925 (1979).
15 *See* Behrang Kiazad, *Excessive Pharmaceutical Prices as an Anticompetitive Practice in TRIPS and European Competition Law*, *in* New Developments in Competition Law and Economics 197–220 (7th Law and Economics Conference in Lucerne, Lucerne, Switzerland, 7th ed. 2018).
16 Frederick M. Abbott, *Excessive Pharmaceutical Prices and Competition Law: Doctrinal Development to Protect Public Health*, 6 U.C. Irvine L. Rev. 281, 286 (2016).
17 Liyang Hou, *Excessive Price Within EU Competition Law*, 7 Eur. Competition J. 47, 48 (2011).
18 Massimo Motta & Alexandre de Streel, *Exploitative and Exclusionary Excessive Prices in EU Law*, *in* European Competition Law Annual 2003: What Is an Abuse of a Dominant Position? 91 (Claus-Dieter Ehlermann & Isabela Atanasiu eds., 2006).
19 Hou, *supra* note 17, at 49.
20 *Id.* at 50.
21 *Id.*

The interventionist school also points out that the noninterventionist argument ignores the existence of high entry barriers that are often not temporary. Such a situation demands intervention.[22] Interventionists also argue that the remedy for excessive pricing is not always price regulation as there are other remedies that would facilitate competition by eliminating entry barriers.

The assumption behind the noninterventionist approach to excessive prices does not hold true in the case of medicines. Unlike other products, there is a little price elasticity when it comes to medicines.[23] Consumers cannot change from one product to another at will merely as a result of high prices. Similarly, the decision concerning medicine purchase is often taken by the doctors, not the consumers, and the doctor's decision is not guided by price alone. In developed countries, it is often the exchequer or insurance companies that pay the price, not the doctor or the patient. Therefore, prescriptions are not based on the price of the product.[24] Alternative products may not be available in the market to allow patients to switch to a cheaper version.

The situation gets more complicated when it comes to patented medicines. Due to patent protection, there is no possibility of introducing the generic version in the market. If the patented medicine offers high therapeutic advantages and efficacy compared to existing medicines or treatment, it becomes the dominant product irrespective of the price. New medicines in the market are often patent-protected, and the patent prevents the entry of competitors during the lifetime of the patent. In such situations, the assumptions of the noninterventionist approach do not hold true. One has to wait until the expiry of the patent for the reduction of the price.

The main objection to the excessive price action against patented medicines is that their high prices are a mechanism to recover research and development (R&D) costs, including the R&D cost of failed attempts and future R&D cost. Therefore, terming the high price of medicines as excessive and acting pursuant to competition law would affect future investment in R&D. High prices provide dynamic efficiency and consumer welfare in the long run. According to the noninterventionist, acting against excessive pricing is tantamount to killing the goose that lays the golden egg.

However, this approach fully ignores the opaque nature of R&D expenditure and the range of activities related to product development in the pharmaceutical sector. There is no verifiable data available that would support the veracity of R&D expenditure claims. Further, the early stages of product development are often funded by public money; thus, the entire expenditure for product

22 *Id.*

23 Chris Fonteijn et al., *ACM Working Paper—Reconciling Competition and IP Law: The Case of Patented Pharmaceuticals and Dominance Abuse*, Aurtoriteit Consument & Markt 12 (2017), https://www.acm.nl/sites/default/files/documents/2018-03/mededingings-recht-ook-van-toepassing-op-medicijnen-onder-patent-2018-03-07.pdf.

24 *Id.* at 12.

development is not solely from the pharmaceutical company. Although there is not much transparency concerning R&D expenditure, it is not impossible to find out the R&D cost.[25]

Patented products are largely created with the aim of recouping R&D expenditure at the earliest by charging very high prices. As a result, people in poor countries spend a larger part of their income in accessing the product. Moreover, due to the sharp rich-poor divide in least developed and developing countries, the monopolist tries to capture only the wealthy section of the population, leaving large parts of the poor population devoid of access to medicines. Nearly 67 percent of the pharmaceutical market is in developed countries.[26] Therefore, a developing country's pharmaceutical market is not necessary to recoup the so-called R&D expenditure. The inaction on excessive prices, especially in developing country markets, means that nonintervention until the expiry of the patent often comes at the cost of peoples' lives.

Another important argument against intervention is that a patent is a statutory monopoly, thus the remedy should be within patent law and competition authorities should keep a safe distance. This approach assumes that the action under competition law undermines patent law. However, the action under competition law is permitted only when there is an abuse of patent rights. As competition law does not consider a patent per se as dominant or anticompetitive, the action under competition law does not undermine the objectives of patent law. The TRIPS Agreement itself recognizes this and allows for remedies against abuse of patent rights.

## *Essential Facilities Doctrine*

When a patented medicine turns out to be the only efficacious way to cure or better manage the conditions of a disease, it becomes an essential product. Competition law recognizes the principle of essentiality and allows for CLs in certain areas of the economy. The "essential facilities doctrine" (EFD) originated in the commentary on US antitrust case law and now has multiple meanings, each having to do with mandating access to something by those who do not otherwise have access. The EFD specifies when the owner(s) of an "essential" or "bottleneck" facility is mandated to provide access to that facility at a "reasonable" price. For example, it may specify when a railroad must be made available on "reasonable" terms to a rival rail company, or an electricity transmission grid to a rival electricity generator.

Although the EFD informed a few earlier cases, it was explicitly mentioned by the Seventh Circuit Court's opinion in the case of *MCI Communications Corp.*

25 *See* Abbott, *supra* note 16, at 309.

26 Matej Mikulic, *Share of Pharmaceutical Revenue Worldwide in 2017, By Country*, TEX. A&M U. (Aug. 9, 2019), https://www.statista.com/statistics/784420/share-of-worldwide-pharma-revenue-by-country/.

*v. AT&T Co.*[27] According to the Seventh Circuit, four elements are necessary to establish liability under the EFD: (1) control of the essential facility by a monopolist; (2) a competitor's inability to practically or reasonably duplicate the essential facility; (3) denial of the use of the facility to a competitor; and (4) feasibility of providing the facility.[28] The EFD with contextual changes was applied in US cases such as *Aspen Skiing Co. v. Aspen Highlands Skiing Corp.*[29] and *Microsoft Corp. v. Commission.*[30] In *Microsoft*, the court observed that as Windows has become the de facto operating system standard for personal computers and is a critical link for complements, a decision by Microsoft to deny interoperability of information to program developers, which can have significant anticompetitive effects.[31] As a result, in the final settlement worked out under the court's supervision, Microsoft was required to license interoperability of information to producers of non-Microsoft servers. This was a reasoned move to encourage "open access" with the hope that it would encourage continuing innovation.

The EU recognizes the EFD as a principle associated with the abuse of dominant position,[32] so much so that recent European guidelines on abuse of dominance consciously endorse the doctrine. The first case within the EU on the EFD was *Commercial Solvents Corp. v. Commission of the European Communities.*[33] The 1974 judgment notes that a dominant supplier of an input abused its dominant position when it refused to supply the input to a customer, the supplier's competitors in the downstream derivative market, "with the object of reserving such raw materials for manufacturing its own derivatives, and therefore risks eliminating all competition" from that competitor.[34] Over time, the European Commission has imposed liability on owners of ports, harbors, tunnels, and others who prevented downstream competition through their control of the infrastructure.

The application of the EFD in India is intimately linked with infrastructure provision (in addition to the Indian Patents Act's compulsory licensing regime), albeit not as a doctrine upheld by Indian courts. It is in regulatory statutes associated with certain infrastructure goods, such as the Telecom Regulatory Authority of India Act of 1997, the Electricity Act of 2003, and the Petroleum and Natural Gas Regulatory Board Act of 2006. The concept of the EFD can be inferred as inherent in the Indian Patents Act, particularly in the CL provision in Section 84(1)(a) read with relevant clauses of Section 84(7),

27 *MCI Commc'n Corp. v. AT&T Co.*, 708 F.2d 1081 (7th Cir. 1983).

28 *Id.*

29 *Aspen Skiing Co. v. Aspen Highlands Skiing Corp.*, 472 U.S. 585 (1985).

30 Case T-201/04, *Microsoft Corp. v. Commission* (2007) E.C.R. II-3601.

31 *Id.*

32 Treaty of Rome: Treaty Establishing the European Economic Community, 25 March 1957, 298 U.N.T.S. 3, 4 Eur. Y.B. 412, art. 82.

33 Cases 6 and 7/73, *Istituto Chemioterapico Italiano S.p.A. and Commercial Solvents Corporation v. Commission* (1974) E.C.R. 223.

34 *Id.* at para. 25.

among other provisions. The message is that if the patent holder's "refusal to deal" is "trade-restrictive" or amounts to an "entry barrier," particularly (but not only) concerning goods not protected by the patent, then it can be a ground for a CL. This goes with the basic facets of the EFD.

The Competition Act of 2002 has sufficient structure for the judiciary to invoke the EFD if needed. Although the doctrine is not mentioned in the law, it has clauses that prohibit the abuse of a dominant position, similar to European legislation that appears to have inspired it. Section 4(c) of the Competition Act of 2002 asserts that denial of market access to others by a dominant player would be an abuse of dominant position, while Sections 18 and 19 states that the Commission must abolish practices that have an adverse effect on competition. Sections 19(3) and 19(4) deal with determining factors that restrict the emergence of competition, such as the creation of barriers to new entrants and driving existing competitors out of the market, as well as the criteria for ascertaining dominant position (such as market share of the firm, size, and importance of competitors).

The EFD provides a good ground for competition authorities to intervene and address the issue of excessive pricing of patented medicines in the absence of alternative efficacious remedies to a disease's condition. Often medicine is the backbone of the health-care infrastructure and should be treated as an essential facility. If competition authorities apply the EFD, the reasoning would be simpler. First, they should find out whether the medicine in question is efficacious compared to existing medicines or interventions for the same condition. In the event of an affirmative finding, the next step is to find out whether there is an unmet demand, and whether the price of the product is the main reason for such unmet demand. This approach demands an intervention from competition authorities when "a dominant supplier of medicine does not make the benefit of the patented invention available at reasonably affordable prices to the public."[35] In case of a positive finding, competition authorities should intervene to enhance competition and access.

## Approaches of Competition Authorities

As mentioned above, competition authorities rarely intervene in the issue of excessive prices. In its submission to the Organization for Economic Cooperation and Development (OECD) Round Table on excessive prices, the US stated that its antitrust law "does not prescribe excessive pricing as an independent antitrust violation, although high prices may be indicative of other anticompetitive

35 Fredrick Abbott et al., *Using Competition Law to Promote Access to Health Technologies*, United Nations Development Programme (UNDP) 146 (2014), https://hivlawcommission.org/wp-content/uploads/2017/06/UNDP-Using-Competition-Law-to-Promote-Access-to-Medicine-05-14-2014-1.pdf.

activities."[36] This position is articulated in the following judgment of the US Supreme Court:

> The mere possession of monopoly power and the concomitant charging of monopoly prices is not only not unlawful; it is an important element of the free-market system. The opportunity to charge monopoly prices-at least for a short period-is what attracts "business acumen" in the first place; it induces risk-taking that produces innovation and economic growth. To safeguard the incentive to innovate, the possession of monopoly power will not be found unlawful unless it is accompanied by an element of anticompetitive conduct.[37]

Thus, the US competition authorities do not recognize excessive prices as an independent ground for cause of action. It becomes actionable only when accompanied by the other three pillars of competition law, agreements, abuse of dominant position, or mergers and acquisitions.

On the other hand, Article 102 of the Treaty on the Functioning of the EU states:

> Any abuse by one or more undertakings of a dominant position within the internal market or in a substantial part of it shall be prohibited as incompatible with the internal market in so far as it may affect trade between the Member States. Such abuse may, in particular, consist in (a) directly or indirectly imposing unfair purchase or selling prices or other unfair trading conditions...

Since the establishment of the EU, the European Court has only found excessive prices twice.[38] However, several EU member states have initiated actions against pharmaceutical companies on excessive prices in the past decade. For example, the Italian Competition Authority (AGCM) announced an investigation in 2017 against the pharmaceutical company Aspen for excessive prices of generic anticancer medicines.[39]

In *United Brands Company and United Brands Continental B.V. v. Commission of the European Communities*,[40] the European Court developed specific questions and a two-step test to find out whether there is excessive pricing. The questions, according to the European Court, are to determine "whether the

36 *Directorate for Financial and Enterprise Affairs Competition Committee: Excessive Prices*, OECD (Feb. 7, 2012), https://www.oecd.org/daf/competition/abuse/49604207.pdf (emphasis added).

37 *Verizon Commc'ns Inc. v. Law Offices of Curtis V. Trinko*, LLP, 540 U.S. 398, 407 (2004).

38 Hou, *supra* note 12, at 47.

39 Judgment of Lazio Regional Administrative Court (TAR) No. 8945 of July 26, 2017.

40 Case 27/76, *United Brands Co. & United Brands Cont'l B.V. v. Comm'n of the European Cmtys.* (1978) E.C.R. I-207.

difference between the costs actually incurred and the price actually charged is excessive, and, if the answer to this question is in the affirmative, whether a price has been imposed which is either unfair in itself or when compared to competing products." In answering the questions, the following steps are applied. The first step is to find out the actual cost of making the product and then compare it with the price charged to the consumers. The second step is to find out whether the charged price is unfair in itself. Alternatively, the findings on excessive pricing can be done by comparing with the price of competing products.

A few EU member states initiating recent actions on excessive medicine prices have used the above steps. These actions show that there is a change in the approaches of competition authorities on the issue of excessive prices. Cases were reported from Italy, the United Kingdom (UK), and Denmark. Apart from the EU, South African competition authorities also announced investigations in 2017 against Aspen, Pfizer, and Roche for excessive prices of certain cancer medicines.[41]

### *The Italian Aspen Case*[42]

In 2009, Aspen purchased in Italy the marketing rights for off-patent cancer medicines *Leukeran*, *Alkeran*, *Purinethol*, and *Tioguanine* from the originator GlaxoSmithKline (GSK). The AGCM found that Aspen abused its dominant position in Italy by imposing price increases of between 300 percent and 1500 percent, and by applying particularly aggressive tactics in negotiating these prices with the Italian Medicines Agency. The Italian National Competent Authority imposed a €5.2 million fine and ordered Aspen to put in place measures aimed at, among other things, setting new fair prices for the medicines concerned. An appeal against this judgment is currently pending before the Italian State Council.

### *UK Case*[43]

In December 2016, the UK Competition and Markets Authority (CMA) found that Pfizer and Flynn had abused their respective dominant position by imposing unfair prices for an epilepsy medicine *Epanutin* (*phenytoin sodium* capsules) manufactured by Pfizer in the UK. In 2012, Pfizer and Flynn had entered into agreements under which Pfizer transferred its marketing authorizations for *Epanutin* to Flynn but continued to manufacture and supply the product to Flynn for distribution in the UK. However, the supply prices to Flynn were

41 https://www.reuters.com/article/us-safrica-pharmaceuticals/pfizer-roche-and-aspen-face-south-african-probe-into-cancer-drug-prices-idUSKBN1941HG.

42 https://one.oecd.org/document/DAF/COMP/WD(2018)106/en/pdf.

43 *The Competition and Market Authority v. Flynn Pharma & Ors* (2017) EWCA (Civ) 1631 (Eng.).

between 780 percent and 1600 percent higher than what Pfizer had previously charged distributors. Following the transfer, Flynn genericized *Epanutin* (it started selling the medicine under its generic name *phenytoin sodium*, without the brand name), taking advantage of a loophole in the law at that time which did not subject generic medicines to any price limits (contrary to branded medicines). Flynn hiked up prices to distributors by up to 2600 percent, compared to previous price levels when the medicine was sold. The CMA fined Pfizer £84.2 million (€103 million) and Flynn £5.16 million (€6.32 million).

### *The Danish Case*[44]

On January 31, 2018, the Danish Competition Council (DCC) ruled in a case concerning pharmaceutical distributor CD Pharma's abuse of dominant position by charging unfair prices for the drug *Syntocinon*, which contains *oxytocin*, an active substance given to pregnant women in connection with childbirth. The DCC fined CD Pharma for supplying *Syntocinon* (*oxytocin*) at 2000 percent and submitted the case to the Danish State Prosecutor for Serious Economic and International Crime.

### *South Africa Case*[45]

In September 2002, Hazel Tau – a woman living openly with HIV – and her fellow activists in the South Africa Treatment Action Campaign filed a complaint against GSK and Boehringer Ingelheim (BI), suppliers of the first-line antiretroviral (ARV) medicines *zidovudine* and *lamivudine*. The ARV medicines under patent were three to ten times more expensive than the generic versions at the time. There had been requests for licenses by the generic pharmaceutical producer Cipla and from the medical services humanitarian organization Médecins Sans Frontières. The respondents refused licenses for generic supply of their products, resulting in high prices, which were unaffordable for at least 80 percent of all South Africans. The South African Competition Commission held that the high prices and refusal to license to Indian generic manufacturers constituted three cases of abuse of dominance under Section 8 of the South

44 *Excessive Pricing in Pharmaceutical Markets – Note by Denmark*, OECD (Oct. 25, 2018), https://one.oecd.org/document/DAF/COMP/WD(2018)104/en/pdf.

45 *Hazel Tau et al. v. GlaxoSmithKline, Boehringer Ingelheim, et al. & Aids Healthcare Foundation et al. v. GlaxoSmithKline, Boehringer Ingelheim, et al.*, Case Nos. 2002sep226 & 2002jan357, http://www.section27.org.za/wp-content/uploads/2010/10/TauvGSKevidenceAndLegalSubmissions.pdf. The Commission initiated complaints against GSK and BI in 2002 after identical complaints were lodged by a number of complainants, among them Ms. Hazel Tau and the Treatment Action Campaign (TAC). After conducting the investigation, the Commission concluded that GSK and BI had both abused their dominance and contravened Sections 8(a) (excessive pricing), 8(b) (refusing a competitor access to an essential facility), and 8(c) (an exclusionary act) of the Act. This was denied by both GSK and BI.

African Competition Act: (1) excessive pricing; (2) refusing to give a competitor access to an essential facility when it is economically feasible to do so; and (3) engaging in exclusionary conduct if the anticompetitive effect of that act outweighs its technological, efficiency, or other procompetitive gains.[46]

Upon investigation, the South African Competition Commission found sufficient evidence to support the referral based on prohibited excessive pricing and on two additional grounds, both of which dealt with the failure of GSK and BI to license generic manufacturers under the circumstances. To remedy this, the Competition Commission requested the Competition Tribunal to issue an order authorizing any person to market generic versions of the respondents' patented medicines or fixed dose combinations that require these patents, in return for payment of a reasonable royalty.

In December 2003, two months after the Competition Commission's announcement, GSK and BI entered into separate settlement agreements with the complainants and the Competition Commission, effectively agreeing to open up the market for these drugs to four generic competitors.

It was also in this case where the issue of market definition came up, particularly the identification of relevant geographic and product markets where the respondent companies allegedly abused their dominant positions. This was overcome by the complainant's statement that clarified that the relevant geographical market for each ARV subject of the complaint is the national market. This follows from the fact that the registration of and authorization to use and sell medicines in South Africa rest exclusively with the South African Medicines Control Council. Moreover, the complainant asserted that South Africa is the relevant market under the competition law because both agencies involved in the ARV market are operating within South Africa, i.e. the agency responsible for financing ARV procurement and the patent office responsible for patent protection of ARVs.[47]

The complaint explained the impact of patent protection in the following words:

> As a result of the respondents' reliance on patent protection, none of the ARVs that are the subject of this complaint can at present be sold in the South African market in the form of generics. In other words, the respondents' branded ARVs are not substitutable by equivalent products in South Africa. To establish whether the respondents are dominant in a relevant market the remaining question is whether other ARVs that are available in South Africa can be substituted for the particular ARVs which are the subject of this complaint. In other words, for example, can a patient whose proper and effective treatment require the use of

46 Section 8 of the Competition Act of South Africa 1998.

47 Para. 53. The statement of complaint is available at http://www.section27.org.za/wp-content/uploads/2010/10/TauvGSKevidenceAndLegalSubmissions.pdf.

zidovudine be satisfactorily treated by the substitution of another ARV available in South Africa.[48]

In a submission to the OECD, the South African Competition Commission stated that the decision resulted in "an estimated cost saving of $887 million, which had been realized over the period (from 2000 to 2015) and much of which accrued directly to the state."[49] Further, there was an expansion of treatment programs at a reasonable cost. In 2004, during the introduction of the South African government's ARV treatment program, only 47,500 people received treatment. By 2016, this figure had increased to 3407,336, the largest in the world.[50] Further, the license has resulted in 32 producers of commercial ARVs in South Africa.[51]

## Barriers in Using Competition Law

Though excessive prices of patented medicines conceptually and practically fall well within the domain of abuse of dominant position, there could be several challenges to using competition law option to ensure access to medicines. These include the question of the relevant market and sufficiency of data.

### *Relevant Market*

Market definition plays an important role in the determination of anticompetitive conduct. As the competition authority determines the market where the anticompetitive conduct is taking place, it is important to identify the relevant geographical market and product market.

The relevant geographical market includes both the national and subnational markets on a case-to-case basis. Identification of the geographical market is easy and often confined to the principal jurisdiction of the competition authority. On the other hand, determining the relevant product market is tricky. If the relevant product market is defined broadly, it would be difficult to prove dominance and abuse of a dominant position through excessive prices. In determining abuse of dominant position, defining the market enables a determination of whether the firm in question is indeed dominant and, therefore, subject to the law's regulation. The broader the definition, the more difficult it is to establish dominance. This translates into complainants seeking to define the market narrowly, with firms, the conduct of which is under investigation seeking to define the market as broadly as is reasonably possible.

48 *Id.* at para. 54 (emphasis added).

49 *Excessive Pricing in Pharmaceutical Markets – Note by South Africa*, 8, OECD (Nov. 19, 2018), https://one.oecd.org/document/DAF/COMP/WD(2018)117/en/pdf.

50 *Id.* at 9.

51 *Id.* at 10.

The definition of the relevant market depends on various factors that are likely to be case-specific, including the extent to which the products or medicines are interchangeable from a treatment standpoint.[52] In the field of medicine, substitutability has a peculiar character as consumers are unable to switch to other products in case of an increase in prices. For example, even a substantial increase in the price of a drug to treat blood cancer will not make patients switch to breast cancer medicines, unlike in the case of an increase in the price of Pepsi consumers, which may lead to a switch to Coke. This also makes the determination of the relevant market easy in the case of medicines. The relevant market should be defined at the product level using the Anatomical Therapeutic Chemical (ATC) classification system, which divides active substances into different groups according to the organ or system on which they act and their therapeutic, pharmacological, and chemical properties.[53] Drugs are classified in groups at five different levels. ATC level 5 gives more product-specific segments. Using the ATC level with scientific information about the efficacy of medicines can help define the relevant market. In this regard, the UN Development Programme (UNDP) recommends as follows:

> It is ordinarily appropriate to start the assessment with the lowest ATC level and move upward to identify potential substitutes, there may be cases where the starting point of the market definition should be even more specific than the ATC level 5 – that is by first considering the galenic form of the drug. The galenic form refers to the pharmaceutical dosage form of medicine – whether oral (tablet, capsule, solution or other), topical or for intravenous injection. It may be appropriate to use the galenic form as a starting point, for example, when dealing with a drug used to treat young children. In other cases, it may even be appropriate to distinguish between prescription and OTC markets involving the same active ingredient medicine.[54]

The burden of proof on defining the relevant market generally falls on the complainant. UNDP recommends that such burden should be on the entity alleged of abusing a dominant position.[55]

52 "Market definition is about determining the size of the playing field, as well as the number and type of players on it. The size of the field refers to the relevant geographic market; the number and type of players refer to the relevant product market. Field, a third-team playing on a second field cannot complain about the conduct of any particular team on the first field. But if the market is defined more broadly, to include all teams in the relevant league, then the third team would be able to pursue a complaint that relates to the impact of the result of the match between teams one and two on its league prospects." Abbot et al., *supra* note 9, at 96–97.

53 *See Anatomical Therapeutic Chemical (ATC) Classification*, World Health Org., https://www.who.int/medicines/regulation/medicines-safety/toolkit_atc/en/ (last visited Feb. 16, 2020).

54 Abbot et al., *supra* note 35, at 143 (defining the relevant product market in access to medicines cases in Model 2.1).

55 *Id.*

The dominant position is established where consumers or patients may not have any alternative (here, due to patent protection), especially when the medicine is unique in its therapeutic class. In such a situation of monopoly due to patents, consumers are left with no choice but to purchase the product regardless of the price. This monopolistic behavior of the manufacturer (patent holder) enables him/her to set prices without a concern for direct competition in the absence of an identical or equivalent product. These elements constitute an abuse of dominant position. Competition authorities can act against a pharmaceutical patent holder when they conclude that there is no reasonable relationship between the price being charged for the medicine and the expenses of the patent holder in developing and supplying it. Further, the high price prevents the dissemination of the benefits of the patented invention to the public.

### *Data Requirements*

In making their decisions, competition authorities rely on facts and figures about the company and its products or services in question. It is important to build up a case using public health indicators such as the prevalence of a disease condition and the number of people requiring access to the patented medicine. For instance, the Indian Patents Office rejected a CL application for diabetic medicine *Saxagliptin* due to, among other reasons, the lack of evidence to prove that the medicine is available at an affordable price. The decision states that "in the absence of exact quantum of *Saxagliptin* required and the number of patients vis-a-vis doctor's prescriptions as against the other options existing in the market, the question of accessibility and affordability cannot be determined."[56]

The related information should be provided in the complaint to the competition authorities; however, there is no central mechanism or platform in the public domain to access such data. This poses a major hurdle in approaching competition laws. In the context of developing countries, it is often difficult to determine the real number of people who require the medicine and those who access it at a given time. In the absence of such data, it would be difficult to find information regarding unmet demand. The insistence of accurate data by competition authorities can neutralize the use of competition law to address the issue of excessive prices.

The South African Competition Authority's submission to OECD also mentions the difficulties in obtaining data: "One particular challenge noted concerning the pursuit of competition enforcement in pharmaceutical markets is access to information required to conduct a thorough analysis."[57]

Another difficulty that would be faced by competition authorities would be the lack of transparency concerning R&D expenditure. In the absence of

56 *Lee Pharma Ltd v. AstraZeneca AB* (C.L.A No, 1 of 2015).
57 DAF/COMP/WD (2018)117, para. 50, 14, http://www.oecd.org/officialdocuments/publicdisplaydocumentpdf/?cote=DAF/COMP/WD(2018)117&docLanguage=En.

verifiable data, the estimation of the real expenditure for the development cost of medicines would be difficult. However, competition authorities should look into the actual turnover of the medicine globally while making such an assessment.

## Conclusions

The pharmaceutical and health-care sectors, in general, are of particular societal and economic importance. Being healthy and having access to affordable and innovative medicines are important to people and their human rights. The past enforcement record provides a solid basis for competition authorities to continue their commitment to rigorously enforce competition law in the pharmaceutical sector. Ensuring that effective competition law enforcement helps patients and health-care systems access affordable and innovative medicines is a priority.

The compulsory product patent regime eliminates the possibility of competition and compromises access to medicines. Though the flexibilities in the TRIPS Agreement, such as CL or government use, can address the situation, such licenses can be issued either against the application of a generic company or at the discretion of the government. Affected parties such as patient groups or civil society organizations often have little say in the invocation of such licenses. The decision of generic companies to apply for CLs is primarily guided by commercial interest and their business models. Similarly, governments may be reluctant to issue a government use license for fear of backlash from developed countries. The remedy against excessive prices under competition law offers an opportunity to initiate such actions.

Compared to the remedies available under the patents law such as CL, competition law-based remedies thus offer an advantage, of individual and public interest groups to seek remedy against excessive pricing of patented medicines. The approaches of the competition authorities in defining the relevant market and the absence of critical information hamper the use of competition law in developing countries. Competition authorities should proceed under the assumption that "an excessive price of a needed medicine may be presumed where the price maintained by a dominant supplier of medicine does not make the benefits of the patented invention available at reasonably affordable prices to the public."[58] Further, while taking the R&D cost, competition authorities should look at the global sales turnover of the product and the purchasing power of the people. They should examine the unmet demand due to the price of the medicine. Such an approach would make competition law sensitive to addressing human rights.

58 https://hivlawcommission.org/wp-content/uploads/2017/06/UNDP-Using-Competition-Law-to-Promote-Access-to-Medicine-05-14-2014-1.pdf&sa=D&source=hangouts&ust=1585667395630000&usg=AFQjCNHaCYYDWBlfVCbcW-g28qV9flArw5A, 146.

# 19 The Unique World of Pharmaceutical Intellectual Property Rights

*Emily Michiko Morris*

## Introduction

While several factors determine access to medicines, one of the most commonly cited – and criticized – is pharmaceutical patent protection.[1] Considering that they provide the right to exclude others from making, using, selling, or importing a drug, pharmaceutical patents can have marked effects on drug pricing, with obvious implications for patient access.[2] However, patents are neither the only factor nor the only intellectual property (IP) rights that affect a patient's ability to obtain medication. Further, to the extent that they do have an effect, patents and other IP rights (IPR) in pharmaceuticals operate in a *sui generis* legal framework that in highly convoluted ways both increase and decrease access to medicines. Whether this framework effects the correct balance is a matter of much debate, as drug prices continue to be higher than many in the United States (US) and elsewhere can afford.[3] The purpose here is not to criticize or defend the IP practices in the pharmaceutical industry but rather to illustrate how much pharmaceutical IPR differ from other industries because of the law's emphasis on access to medicines.

To review the unique world of pharmaceutical innovation, the discussion will focus on the legal framework in the US, although analogs of the US framework

1 *See, e.g.*, FEROZ ALI, THE ACCESS REGIME: PATENT LAW REFORMS FOR AFFORDABLE MEDICINES, xxvii–xxix (2016); Tahir Amin, *The Problem with High Drug Prices Isn't "Foreign Freeloading," It's the Patent System*, CNBC.COM (June 27, 2018), https://www.cnbc.com/2018/06/25/high-drug-prices-caused-by-us-patent-system.html; *see also* Hannah Brennan, *The Cost of Confusion: The Paradox of Trademarked Pharmaceuticals*, 22 MICH. TELECOMM. & TECH. L. REV. 1, 2–3 (2015) (stating that patents are not the only cause of high drug prices); Michael A. Carrier & Steve D. Shadowen, *Product Hopping: A New Framework*, 92 NOTRE DAME L. REV. 167, 181 (2016).

2 PHILIP W. GRUBB ET AL., PATENTS FOR CHEMICALS, PHARMACEUTICALS, AND BIOTECHNOLOGY: FUNDAMENTALS OF GLOBAL LAW, PRACTICE, AND STRATEGY 3.57–3.59 (6th ed. 2016) (noting, however, that patents cannot guarantee higher prices); Rebecca Eisenberg, *The Role of The FDA in Innovation Policy*, 13 MICH. TELECOMM. TECH. L. REV. 345, 373 (2007).

3 THE NAT'L ACADS. OF SCIS., ENG'G, & MED., MAKING MEDICINES AFFORDABLE: A NATIONAL IMPERATIVE, xi–xii (Norman R. Augustine et al. eds., 2018).

have now been exported to almost all developed countries through the Agreement on Trade-Related Aspects of Intellectual Property Rights (TRIPS Agreement) and later trade agreements.[4] This discussion provides only a basic outline of the topic and necessarily omits some of its more arcane intricacies. It should nevertheless offer a striking view into the unusual, and unusually complex, statutory and regulatory schemata that govern pharmaceuticals.

## Regulation and the Drug Development Process

The pharmaceutical industry is one of the most highly regulated on the market, which significantly increases the cost of developing, manufacturing, and marketing drugs.[5] Companies must obtain governmental approval to market their drugs, and collecting the data necessary for such approval can greatly increase overall drug development costs. To prove that a drug is safe and effective enough to sell, pharmaceutical companies typically must conduct multiphase clinical trials of the drug on human subjects, which is an expensive process. The exact amount of this and other expenses necessary to develop a new drug is highly contentious, with estimates ranging anywhere from tens of millions to well over a billion US dollars per drug on average, but the clinical stage of development clearly constitutes a sizeable portion of overall costs.[6] The recent regulatory trend in the US, moreover, has also been to call for ongoing post-marketing data collection as a condition for continued permission to market.[7] The cumulative costs of regulatory approval thus serve as a market barrier, limiting market entrants to those companies willing to commit the requisite financial and other resources.[8]

For this reason, the pharma industry relies heavily on IPR – primarily patents and trade secrecy – to help recoup the investment necessary for drug development.[9] The US government heavily subsidizes pharma through federal tax deductions and credits for research and development (R&D) expenditures,

4 *See generally* Cynthia M. Ho, Access to Medicine in the Global Economy: International Agreements About Patents and Related Rights, 55–88, 223–51 (2011) (referring to the spread of pro-pharma protections through TRIPs and subsequent "TRIPS-plus" agreements); Richard D. Smith et al., *Trade, TRIPS, and Pharmaceuticals*, 373 Lancet 684, 685 (2009).

5 Eisenberg, *supra* note 2, *passim* (noting that the FDA's heavy regulation can simultaneously increase both costs and profits); Lee G. Branstetter et al., *Regulation and Welfare: Evidence from Paragraph IV Generic Entry in the Pharmaceutical Industry*, 47 RAND J. Econ. 857, 859–60 (2016).

6 Mark A. Lemley, *Industry-Specific Antitrust Policy for Innovation*, 2011 Colum. Bus. L. Rev. 637, 641–2 & n.18 (2011) (noting dissension over development costs but stating "there is no doubt that R&D is extremely expensive in the pharmaceutical industry").

7 Eisenberg, *supra* note 2, at 376.

8 *Id.* at 356.

9 James Bessen & Michael J. Meurer, Patent Failure: How Judges, Bureaucrats, and Lawyers Put Innovators at Risk, 88–89 (2008).

federal grants supporting upstream research, and other resources.[10] Nonetheless, without the prospect of earning supra-competitive returns through IP exclusivities, economic theory suggests that the pharma industry would be less motivated to invest in drug development.[11] Regardless of the debate over how much it actually costs to develop pharmaceuticals, it is clear that development costs are higher for pharma than for other technologies and that IP protections can help to recoup those costs. From a long-term dynamic efficiency point of view, IPR can be seen as helping to increase access to medicines by supporting the production of new therapeutics.[12] From a more immediate static efficiency point of view, IPR decrease access to medicines by blocking price-lowering competitors from entering the market.[13] Maintaining robust access to medicines thus relies on constraining patent and trade secrecy rights without unduly undermining incentives for development.[14]

## Safety and Efficacy Data, Trade Secrecy, and Data Exclusivities

Prior to 1984, trade secrecy over clinical trial data was in many respects more powerful than patents in keeping less expensive generic forms of brand-name drugs off the US market. The US Food and Drug Administration (FDA) would not authorize a generic drug for marketing unless the manufacturer could submit clinical trial data showing that it was safe and effective. However, brand-name drug companies protect their clinical trial data as trade secrets so that generics could not rely on that data to gain regulatory approval. Generating their own safety and efficacy data was often cost-prohibitive (and likely unethical), so relatively few generics could enter the market. In this manner, many brand-name manufacturers used trade secrecy to create what was effectively indefinite exclusivity over their drugs, long after any patents on them might have expired.[15]

10 Ho, *supra* note 4, at 8.

11 Lemley, *supra* note 46, at 6; *see also* C. Scott Hemphill & Bhaven N. Sampat, *When Do Generics Challenge Drug Patents?*, 8 J. Empirical L. Stud. 613, 614 (2011) ("Effective patent protection has provided a critical stimulus to that life-saving research. Patents are widely thought to have a unique role in stimulating drug research and development, compared to other industries.").

12 The Nat'l Acads. of Scis., Eng'g, & Med., *supra* note 3, at xviii; Lemley, *supra* note 6, at 642. Notwithstanding, patents on basic scientific research, genomics, and other tools of research and development can obstruct pharmaceutical innovation. *See, e.g.*, Arti K. Rai, *The Information Revolution Reaches Pharmaceuticals: Balancing Innovation Incentives, Cost, and Access in the Post-Genomics Era*, 2001 U. Ill. L. Rev. 173, 192–94; Peter Lee, *Toward a Distributive Commons in Patent Law*, 2009 Wis. L. Rev. 917, 935–37.

13 Lee, *supra* note 12, at 937.

14 *See generally* Janet A. Gongola, *Prescriptions for Change: The Hatch-Waxman Act and New Legislation to Increase Availability of Generic Drugs to Consumers*, 36 Ind. L. Rev. 787 (2003).

15 Ho, *supra* note 4, at 260.

The US removed this obstacle for generic market entry by passing the Drug Price Competition and Patent Term Restoration Act (Hatch-Waxman Act).[16] The Hatch-Waxman Act allows a generic manufacturer to file an abbreviated new drug application (ANDA) for marketing approval that relies on the brand name's previously submitted data, as long as the generic proves that its version has the same active ingredient, route of administration, dosage form, strength, and labeling as the previously approved brand name.[17] The brand name's clinical trial data itself remains a trade secret, but the generic can refer to the data to show that the drug as formulated is safe and effective.[18]

The generic manufacturer's right of reference to the data is not immediate, however. It must wait five years before relying on data submitted to the FDA in support of a new active ingredient (new chemical entities),[19] and three years before relying on data submitted in support of new therapeutic uses or formulations for already approved drugs (new clinical indications).[20] The Hatch-Waxman Act nonetheless shortened what were potentially infinite *de facto* waiting periods for rights of reference to safety and efficacy data to the now comparatively brief "regulatory" or "data" exclusivity periods that allow generics to enter the US market more easily.[21] As a consequence, generic market entry in the US rose from less than 20 percent in the early 1980s to now more than 90 percent of all prescriptions.[22] Given that generic manufacturers market their drugs at as little as 20 or 30 percent of brand-name prices, the effect of the Hatch-Waxman Act's data provisions on access to medicines within the US has been dramatic.[23]

## Pharmaceutical Patent Rights

In conjunction with curbing the effect of trade secrecy on generic market entry, the Hatch-Waxman Act also altered pharmaceutical patent protections. This is particularly noteworthy given that, after the removal of trade secrecy as an impediment to approval of generics, patents now stand as the most salient barrier to generic market entry. Now that lower priced generics can readily enter the market, a drug's price can drop significantly as soon as the drug "goes off patent."[24]

16 The Drug Price Competition and Patent Term Restoration Act of 1984, Pub. L. No. 98-417, 98 Stat. 1585 (1984).
17 21 U.S.C § 355(j) (2006).
18 Eisenberg, *supra* note 2, at 380.
19 21 U.S.C. § 355(j)(5)(F)(ii).
20 *Id.* at § 355(j)(5)(F)(iii).
21 Ho, *supra* note 4, at 262.
22 The Nat'l Acads. of Scis., Eng'g, & Med., *supra* note 3, at 77.
23 Aaron S. Kesselheim & Jonathan J. Darrow, *Hatch-Waxman Turns 30: Do We Need A Re-Designed Approach for the Modern Era?*, 15 Yale J. Health Pol'y, L. & Ethics 293, 314 (2015).
24 The Nat'l Acads. of Scis., Eng'g, & Med., *supra* note 3, at 122.

Pharma companies customarily apply for patent protection on the active ingredients for new drugs before commencing clinical trials.[25] Because a patent's 20-year term begins when the patent application is filed, much of that patent term will have ticked away long before the drug can be marketed, which can take from four to 14 years of development. As a result, the average effective patent life – the term during which the patented invention can actually be marketed – formerly was several years shorter on average for pharmaceuticals than the average patent term of 17 years.[26] To compensate, the Hatch-Waxman Act now allows for restoration of a single patent term per drug with an addition of time equal to one-half of the time spent on clinical trials and all of the time spent on the FDA approval process. New pharmaceutical active ingredients can receive an extension of up to five years of term restoration, for a maximum 14 years from the date of marketing approval.[27] No other technology receives such patent term extensions. Still, the average patent term in pharmaceuticals remains around 11–12 years, even after patent term restoration.[28] Whether such extensions are necessary or sufficient to provide pharmaceuticals with average effective patent lives adequate to recoup R&D costs is another highly disputed issue.[29]

Another provision that has strengthened pharmaceutical patents is patent linkage, which bars the FDA from granting generic marketing approval for a patented drug unless the applicant either owns the drug's patent rights or has given the owner an opportunity to resolve any possible infringement claims. This effectively gives the patent owner automatic agency enforcement of its patent rights, a nother benefit that no other industry enjoys.[30] Patent linkage thus imposes the responsibility on the regulatory agency to track the patent status of all approved drugs and monitor for potential patent infringement, even though the agency has no expertise in patent law and must simply trust in the validity of patents alleged to cover a given drug. In this fashion, patent linkage may unduly delay generic market entry, especially if the patents at issue are ultimately held to be invalid or the generic is held not to infringe them.[31]

On the other hand, patent linkage also gives generic manufacturers a chance to resolve any infringement claims before they incur any liability for damages

25 Eisenberg, *supra* note 2, at 348.

26 Ho, *supra* note 4, at 23–24; Kesselheim & Darrow, *supra* note 23, at 307–08.

27 35 U.S.C. § 156.

28 Ho, *supra* note 4, at 23–24; Kesselheim & Darrow, *supra* note 23, at 307–08.

29 *Compare, e.g.*, Henry G. Grabowski & John M. Vernon, *Effective Patent Life in Pharmaceuticals*, 19 Int'l J. Tech. Mgmt. 98, 100–01 (2000) (presenting data that new drugs need at least 16 years of exclusivity) *with* Kesselheim & Darrow, *supra* note 23, at 327–28 (suggesting that five to eight years of exclusivity is adequate); *see also* Hemphill & Sampat, *supra* note 11, at 643–44 ("Accordingly, even if [pharmaceutical patent] challenges were saving purchasers significant sums or improving access to drugs, we cannot say definitively whether reining in the patent term via challenges would be good or bad, since we do not know the dynamic effect on innovation.").

30 Ho, *supra* note 4, at 273–74, 277–78.

31 *Id.* at 274–76.

by going on the market. Patent linkage may thereby lower risk and enhance certainty in ways that may encourage greater generic market entry.[32] Because the FDA obliges new drug manufacturers to disclose any patents they believe protect their drugs, it has notice of what patents may force it to withhold approval of a later generic drug application.[33] In the US, the FDA makes this list public through the "Orange Book,"[34] notifying generic manufacturers of the patents they might infringe and thereby eliminating their patent search costs. In contrast, identifying and analyzing the breadth of non-pharmaceutical patents, particularly in fields that depend on cumulative or complementary technologies, entail much higher clearance costs compared to small-molecule drugs, which are single-chemical entities that can usually be covered by a single patent with easily defined boundaries.[35]

Laws like the Hatch-Waxman Act arguably bolster drug patents further by placing an automatic 30-month stay on generic approval should the parties at issue commence litigation over any patents that might still be in force at the time. This stay is premised on the fact that FDA review of generic applications takes an average of 25 months even without patent linkage or infringement litigation. Thus, generics must wait at least two years before being able to enter the market, regardless of whether this delay is due to the 30-month stay or simply to regulatory approval, Many nonetheless say that the 30-month litigation stay functions like an automatic preliminary injunction, in contrast to the usual requirement that a patent holder show a likelihood of success on the merits as well as irreparable harm in order to secure a preliminary injunction.[36]

While the Hatch-Waxman Act and other such laws thus have strengthened pharmaceutical patent rights, they also offset any benefits by simultaneously weakening those rights in several ways as well.

The most direct manner in which the law constricts pharmaceutical patent exclusivity is through experimental use exemptions, which do not meaningfully exist in US patent law outside of the pharmaceutical context. The exceptions allow competitors to make and use a drug, even while it is still under patent protection, if they do so for the purpose of submitting information requested under federal regulatory law. Generics as a result can file ANDAs well before patent expiration so that they can be approved for market launch the moment

32 Press Release, Office of the U.S. Trade Rep., Trade Enhancing Access to Medicines 1 (Sept. 2011), https://ustr.gov/about-us/policy-offices/press-office/press-releases/2011/september/trade-enhancing-access-medicines.

33 21 U.S.C. § 355(b)(1).

34 FDA, Orange Book: Approved Drug Products with Therapeutic Equivalence Evaluations, https://www.accessdata.fda.gov/Scripts/cder/ob/index.cfm.

35 *See* Bessen & Meurer, *supra* note 9, at 89 (Patents on methods of producing or using the drug or on variations of the drug are also possible.); Kevin J. Hickey et al., Cong. Research Serv., R45666, Drug Pricing and Intellectual Property: A Legal Overview for the 166th Congress, 10 (2019).

36 Michael A. Carrier, *Unsettling Drug Patent Settlements: A Framework for Presumptive Illegality*, 108 Mich. L. Rev. 37, 44–48 (2009); Ho, *supra* note 4, at 274.

that the relevant patents expire. No other technology can do this. Permitting generics this regulatory review exception to patent infringement thus shortens the effective patent life for pharmaceuticals and expedites lower-priced generic market entry.[37]

A more indirect and complex mechanism for curbing pharmaceutical patents to expedite generic market entry lies in the Hatch-Waxman Act's procedures for challenging pharmaceutical patents. Per the law's patent linkage provisions, the FDA cannot approve an ANDA on a drug that still has unexpired patents listed for it. To mitigate the effects of patent linkage, however, the law provides that simply filing an ANDA constitutes a constructive act of infringement so that the generic applicant has immediate standing to challenge the patents as invalid, uninfringed, or both in federal court.[38]

Constructive infringement shifts patent litigation in a couple of critical ways. First, courts can adjudicate infringement claims before the generic defendant even enters the market, which, in combination with the regulatory review exception, effectively shields the generic defendant from any liability for damages should the patents at issue be found not invalid and infringed. To create a justiciable case of patent infringement in other technologies, the alleged infringer would have to invest in some sort of allegedly infringing activity, thereby risking not only that investment but also liability for any consequent damages should the patent at issue be found not invalid and infringed. Generic manufacturers hoping to enter the market before patent expiration, by contrast, can challenge pharmaceutical patents while risking only the cost of litigation, thereby facilitating such challenges.[39] Second, and more importantly, this odd risk allocation has created some perverse incentives not only for brand-name patent holders but also for their generic challengers, as discussed below.[40]

Perhaps the most significant means through which the Hatch-Waxman Act cabins pharmaceutical patents is by incentivizing generics to challenge pharmaceutical patents by granting them 180 days of exclusivity as the only generic on the market if they are the first to file and maintain ANDAs for drugs covered under unexpired patents. The first-to-file generic could earn hundreds of millions of US dollars in supra-competitive profits on their products during that 180-day period, depending on how many other ANDA applicants are also

37 *See generally* Joshua D. Sarnoff & Christopher M. Holman, *Recent Developments Affecting the Enforcement, Procurement, and Licensing of Research Tool Patents*, 23 Berkeley Tech. L.J. 1299 (2008) (describing how experimental-use exceptions to patent rights apply only to pharmaceuticals).

38 21 U.S.C. § 355(j)(2)(A)(vii)(IV) (allowing certification that any unexpired patents are invalid or uninfringed); 35 U.S.C. § 271(e)(2)(a) (establishing such certifications as constructive infringement); *see also* Ho, *supra* note 4, at 277 (describing Hatch-Waxman's patent litigation procedures as limiting the harm of patent linkage).

39 C. Scott Hemphill, *Paying for Delay: Pharmaceutical Patent Settlement as a Regulatory Design Problem*, 81 N.Y.U. L. Rev. 1553, 1577–78 (2006).

40 *Id.*; *see also infra* text accompanying notes 57–65.

deemed to be "first-to-file."[41] The Hatch-Waxman Act created this bounty on the premise that a generic would not invest in such (often costly) litigation if other generic manufacturers would be able later to free ride on that investment in invalidating brand-name patents, although the profits from this exclusivity can be so substantial as to more than compensate for litigation costs.[42]

The goal of these provisions is to eliminate "weak" patents that either are too broad in scope or erroneously granted. Critics of the pharma industry point particularly to patents on incremental or "secondary" innovations, such as new doses, formulations, metabolites, or therapeutic uses of existing drugs, which have proliferated under the Hatch-Waxman Act.[43] Because they claim subject matter that is necessarily similar to what was already known in the art, secondary innovation patents are more prone to invalidity for lack of novelty or nonobviousness, although because they are necessarily narrower in scope than the existing technology on which they build, they are also easier to "design around" to avoid infringement.[44] In some cases, secondary patents are clearly underhanded attempts to "evergreen" drug exclusivity. The most obvious example is when a patentee alleges that a generic cannot produce an earlier patented version of a drug without infringing a patent on a later, sequential version of it, which courts have held falls well afoul of patent law principles against double patenting and anticipation.[45] However, it is not clear whether these and other invalidity problems plague pharmaceuticals more than other technologies. While some who research the matter cite high rates of patent invalidation in pharma,[46] others cite low rates.[47] The question may ultimately be difficult to resolve with certainty

41 Hemphill, *supra* note 39, at 1579–80. Because of Hatch-Waxman's regulatory exclusivities, generics must wait exactly four years to the day after the brand-name first markets a drug before filing their ANDA applications to market generic versions of the drug. This often leads to multiple first ANDA applicants filing on the same day, and under a 2003 change to the law, all first-filers now share the entitlement to the 180-day generic exclusivity. *Id.* at 1583.

42 C. Scott Hemphill & Mark A. Lemley, *Earning Exclusivity: Generic Drug Incentives and the Hatch-Waxman Act*, 77 Antitrust L.J. 947, 953–55 (2011).

43 *E.g.*, Hemphill & Sampat, *supra* note 11, at 617, 621, 629.

44 *Id.*

45 *See, e.g.*, *Schering Corp. v. Geneva Pharma. Corp.*, 339 F.3d 1373 (Fed. Cir. 2003); *Smithkline Beecham Corp. v. Apotex Corp.*, 403 F.3d 1331 (Fed. Cir. 2005); *see also* Lars Noah, *Product Hopping 2.0: Getting the FDA to Yank Your Original License Beats Stacking Patents*, 19 Marq. Intellectual Property L. Rev. 161, 166 & n.5 (2015).

46 *E.g.*, Fed. Trade Comm'n, Generic Drug Entry Prior to Patent Expiration: An FTC Study, 20 (2002), http://www.ftc.gov/os/2002/07/genericdrugstudy.pdf); C. Scott Hemphill & Bhaven Sampat, *Drug Patents at the Supreme Court*, 339 Science 386, 386 (2013).

47 *E.g.*, Kent S. Bernard & Willard K. Tom, *Antitrust Treatment of Pharmaceutical Patent Settlements: The Need for Context and Fidelity to First Principles*, 15 Fed. Cir. B.J. 617, 627 (2006); Williams & Connolly LLP, *Inter Partes Review in the Life Sciences Industry*, IAM (May 13, 2019), https://www.iam-media.com/inter-partes-review-life-sciences-industry.

because of the immense heterogeneity of sequential pharmaceutical patenting and the limited sample size of those whose validity has been fully adjudicated.[48]

For secondary pharmaceutical patents, moreover, the concern seems to be less about correcting problems with in validity and more about the patents' capacity to block off "commercially interesting markets" and to do so as late in time as possible.[49] Critics argue that by sequentially acquiring patents on variations of or new use for a previously patented drug, secondary pharmaceutical patents effect prolong patent exclusivity over the drug.[50] Some point to the fact that sequential patents have significantly lengthened "nominal patent life," or the total time between a drug's launch and expiration of its last related patent.[51] Others point out, however, that sequential patenting in fact has not lengthened the total "market exclusivity period" for new drugs, or the period between the drugs' launch and first generic market entry, which has in fact been shrinking over time.[52] Only the latter affects generic market entry, the marked growth in sequential patenting notwithstanding.[53] It is also worth noting that nothing prevents physicians from prescribing generics for new indications on an "off-label" basis, even if this technically may infringe sequential patents on new therapeutic uses.[54]

Although generics increasingly challenge sequential patents, moreover, use of the Hatch-Waxman Act's patent challenge mechanism has not been confined to sequential innovation patents, particularly when the drug in question is highly profitable.[55] Without some basis for believing that pharmaceutical patents as a whole are more suspect than in other technological fields, the fact that the law has erected a special mechanism to screen out potentially invalid pharmaceutical patents instead highlights the threat they pose to access to medicines. The only other such system in the US is that for challenging the validity of

48 Eur. Comm'n Compet. Directorate-Gen., Pharmaceutical Sector Inquiry Final Report, 191 (July 8, 2009), https://ec.europa.eu/competition/sectors/pharmaceuticals/inquiry/staff_working_paper_part1.pdf; Henry Grabowski et al., *Pharmaceutical Patent Challenges: Company Strategies and Litigation Outcomes*, 3 Am. J. Health Econ. 33, 34, 51–52 (2017).

49 *See* Cynthia M. Ho, *Should All Drugs Be Patentable? A Comparative Perspective*, 17 Vand. J. Ent. & Tech. L. 295, 314 (2015) (differentiating "sequential" patents as later expiring secondary patents that incrementally improve upon existing technologies).

50 Hans Ullrich, *Strategic Patenting by the Pharmaceutical Industry: Towards a Concept of Abusive Practices of Protection*, *in* Pharmaceutical Innovation, Competition, and Patent Law, 241, 245–46 (Josef Drexl & Nari Lee eds., 2013); *see also* Ho, *supra* note 49, at 314 (differentiating "sequential" patents as later expiring secondary patents that incrementally improve upon existing technologies).

51 Hemphill & Sampat, *supra* note 11, at 622.

52 Grabowski et al., *supra* note 48, *passim*.

53 *Id.* at 37; Hemphill & Sampat, *supra* note 11, at 643.

54 Eisenberg, *supra* note 2, at 360–61.

55 Grabowski et al., *supra* note 48, at 47; *see also* Hemphill & Sampat, *supra* note 11 (noting that, although they increasingly focus on sequential patents, patent challenges also involve basic compound, or active ingredient, patents).

so-called business method patents through a specifically instituted but temporary post-issuance administrative review program.[56] This latter system was established because business methods as a category raise "special problems in terms of vagueness and validity."[57] Pharmaceutical patents, by contrast, are presumably targeted principally for their potentially negative effects on access to medicines.

Unfortunately for access to medicines, how much the legal framework for pharmaceuticals diverges from all other industries is highlighted yet further by the unanticipated consequences of the Hatch-Waxman Act's unusual modification of pharma IPR. One of these unintended consequences has been the allegedly anticompetitive "reverse payment" settlements of Hatch-Waxman patent litigation.[58] In non-pharmaceuticals, any payments made as part of the settlement of an infringement case often flow from the alleged infringer to the patent owner, based on lost profits or other damages that the patent owner might have been able to demand and the odds of the owner prevailing had there been a trial.[59] In infringement suits under the Hatch-Waxman Act, however, the trend has been the opposite: settlement agreements have often involved enormous transfers of money, patent licenses, or other consideration from the patent holders – typically brand-name drug manufacturers – to generic challengers. The reversed direction of these transfers stems in part from the marked reshaping of each party's risk calculus under the Hatch-Waxman Act, as noted above. Pharmaceutical patent owners do not have the threat of potential damages to induce the generic defendant to settle. Instead, because the only thing at risk in Hatch-Waxman infringement cases is invalidation of the underlying patent, patent owners have an incentive to offer payment to their generic challengers.[60]

What has prompted intense scrutiny from the Federal Trade Commission (FTC) and others is the unusual size of these reverse settlement payments. Critics contend that the size of these transfers indicate a purpose to pay the generic challengers to delay market entry and protect weak pharmaceutical patents from invalidation. Whether this is true is a highly disputed question well beyond the scope of the discussion here.[61] What can be said with certainty, however, is that

56 37 C.F.R. § 42.300.

57 *Bilski v. Kappos*, 130 S. CT. 3218, 3229 (2010).

58 Carrier, *supra* note 36, *passim*; Hemphill, *supra* note 39, *passim*.

59 Carrier, *supra* note 36, at 37.

60 Hemphill, *supra* note 39, at 1577–81.

61 For more on this debate, *compare, e.g.*, Carrier, *supra* note 36 (arguing that reverse-payment settlements should be presumptively illegal), Hemphill, *supra* note 39 (same), and Herbert Hovenkamp et al., *Anticompetitive Settlement of Intellectual Property Disputes*, 87 MINN. L. REV. 1719 (2003) (same), *with, e.g.*, Daniel A. Crane, *Ease over Accuracy in Assessing Patent Settlements*, 88 MINN. L. REV. 698 (2004) (arguing that reverse payment settlements can be procompetitive), Christopher M. Holman, *Do Reverse Payment Settlements Violate the Antitrust Laws?*, 23 SANTA CLARA COMP. & HIGH TECH. L.J. 489 (2007) (same), and Marc G. Schildkraut, *Patent-Splitting Settlements and the Reverse Payment Fallacy*, 71 ANTITRUST L.J. 1033 (2004) (same).

although these reverse payment settlements benefit both brand-name patentees and their generic challengers, to the extent that settlement also prevents courts from eliminating invalid patents, patients will likely be subject to continued higher prices in the meantime, lowering their access to medicines.[62] The FTC therefore mandates that all such settlements be submitted for its review,[63] and the US Supreme Court has now held that, although these settlements are not per se antitrust violations, they are highly suspect when they involve any significant transfers of value.[64]

Another unanticipated consequence of the Hatch-Waxman Act has been abuse of its 180-day generic exclusivity and 30-month stay provisions. Prior to 2003, some generics would settle infringement cases by agreeing to use their 180-day exclusivity periods to block other generics from applying for approval. At that time, the 180-day exclusivity period did not commence until a generic began marketing or until a court ruled that the underlying patents were invalid or uninfringed. If a generic and brand name settled their infringement case and agreed that the generic would stay off the market, the generic's 180-day exclusivity would never commence, blocking other generics from being approved for market entry. Moreover, at that time only one generic could be the first-to-file and entitled to the 180-day exclusivity period, giving a single generic complete control over when to trigger the 180-day period and in this sense, complete control over whether any other generic could obtain FDA approval, to the detriment of patient access.[65] The US amended the Hatch-Waxman Act in 2003, however, not only to allow multiple generics to share the 180-day exclusivity but also to make the exclusivity subject to rescission if the generic effectively fails to market in due time.[66]

Similarly, brand-names sometimes abused the Hatch-Waxman Act's 30-month stays before the 2003 amendments. Brand-name patent holders could delay the approval of a generic's application for years by adding patents one by one to the FDA's patent records, filing suit on each one, and seeking successive 30-month stays. The 2003 amendments ended this practice by restricting patent holders for the most part to a single 30-month stay per generic approval application.[67] These adjustments thus have constrained abuse of not only the 180-day

62 *FTC v. Actavis, Inc.*, 133 S. CT. 2223, 2234–35 (2013). Even patented drugs may face some price-lowering competition, however, from "me-too" drugs with the same mechanism of action or from other drugs in the same therapeutic class. *See infra* text accompanying notes 156–65.

63 Medicare Prescription Drug, Improvement, and Modernization Act of 2003 (MMA), Pub. L. No. 108-173, § 1112, 117 Stat. 2066, 2461–63.

64 *Actavis*, 133 S. Ct. at 2237–38.

65 *See* Hemphill, *supra* note 39, at 1586–88; Hemphill & Lemley, *supra* note 42, at 962–95.

66 C. Scott Hemphill, *An Aggregate Approach to Antitrust: Using New Data and Rulemaking to Preserve Drug Competition*, 109 Colum. L. Rev. 629, 659–61 (2009).

67 *See* Hemphill & Lemley, *supra* note 42, at 959–60.

exclusivity but also 30-month stay provisions and their impact on access to medicines, although substantial delays are still possible.[68]

Some studies indicate that the Hatch-Waxman Act's patent challenge procedures nonetheless have shortened average brand-name market exclusivity by as much as one to two years, especially for the most profitable drugs.[69] However, its limitations on patent exclusivity have been at most a qualified success and not nearly as effective as its ANDA right of reference provisions in increasing access to medicines. Even without reverse payment settlements and regulatory gaming, other less recognized concerns likely reduce the impact of its patent provisions on aiding access to medicines. For example, economists agree that generics tend to focus on the most profitable drugs[70] and not necessarily those with the most social value or urgent patient need, and in any event eliminating patents through litigation is both costly and protracted.[71] Other mechanisms, such as compulsory licensing, may be more efficient in increasing access to medicines and can be consciously targeted at the most needed drugs. However, the US has remained adamantly opposed to compulsory patent licensing.[72] Alternatively, many advocates have called for the development and application of more stringent patentability standards for pharmaceuticals, especially for sequential innovations, to preclude patent exclusivity altogether in many cases.[73] Like compulsory licensing, however, more stringent patentability standards face vehement objections on the grounds that they would unduly undermine patent incentives.[74]

## Further Regulatory Exclusivities

Additional legislation has set pharmaceuticals even further apart from other technologies, particularly by expanding the use of regulatory exclusivities. Unlike the Hatch-Waxman data exclusivities, many of the newer regulatory exclusivities

68 Carrier, *supra* note 36, at 48–49; Hemphill, *supra* note 66, at 659–61.

69 *See, e.g.*, Grabowski et al., *supra* note 48; Hemphill & Sampat, *supra* note 11, at 643.

70 *E.g.*, Grabowski et al., *supra* note 48; Hemphill & Sampat, *supra* note 11.

71 Hemphill & Sampat, *supra* note 11, at 644.

72 *See generally* Ali, *supra* note 1.

73 *E.g.*, Carlos M. Correa, Guidelines for the Examination of Pharmaceutical Patents: Developing a Public Health Perspective (U.N. Dev't Prog. 2016), http://www.undp.org/content/undp/en/home/librarypage/hiv-aids/guidelines-for-the-examination-of-patent-applications-relating-t.html (calling for several changes to patentability standards for pharmaceuticals); Mark A. Lemley, *Expecting the Unexpected*, 92 Notre Dame L. Rev. 1369 (2017) (proposing heightened nonobviousness standard most likely to affect pharmaceutical and chemical industries).

74 *E.g.*, *Copy or Compete? How India's Patent Law Harms Its Own Drug Industry's Ability to Innovate*, Geneva Network (Nov. 2018), https://geneva-network.com/wp-content/uploads/2019/07/WP-Copy-or-Compete-JULY-2019.pdf (concluding that India's heightened utility standard discourages Indian pharmaceuticals from innovating domestically); Christopher M. Holman et al., *Patentability Standards for Follow-On Pharmaceutical Innovation*, 37 Biotech. L. Rep. 131 (2018).

create exclusions from the market where none previously existed. For example US law has now added market exclusivities, such as "orphan" drug exclusivity barring the FDA from approving generic versions of a drug for a designated rare disease or condition for seven years, regardless of whether the generic submits its own clinical trial data.[75] Thus, while the *data* exclusivities under the Hatch-Waxman Act are designed to shorten potentially infinite trade secrecy protection over safety and efficacy data, the seven-year *market* exclusivities granted to orphan drugs – and the 180-day market exclusivity granted to generic challengers to brand-name patents – do not shorten existing IP exclusivities but instead create new exclusivities that keep all second-comers off the market, regardless of data rights.[76] These newer regulatory exclusivities are much like IPR in this way.[77] In fact, some of the newest regulatory exclusivities, such as those for new antibiotics for serious infectious diseases or for clinical studies in children, are malleable and can be used to extend a variety of exclusivities, including patent, data, or marketing exclusivities.[78]

This profusion in number and type of regulatory exclusivities complicates analysis of their ultimate effect on access to medicines.[79] Like IPR, the exclusivities for orphan drugs, antibiotics, and pediatric studies are designed to incentivize investments in new drugs and drug uses by providing additional opportunities for earning returns on those investments.[80] Regulatory exclusivities in this way can step in to provide incentives to develop therapeutics that are unpatentable or whose patents have expired.[81] Although the hope is that these new exclusivities will yield more investment in new drugs, formulations, and uses in the long term, thereby ultimately improving access to a wider variety of medicines and therapies, the additional returns these exclusivities provide of course reduce access to medicines in the near term, much like IPR.[82]

One final commonality between the changes to pharmaceutical IPR and the newer regulatory exclusivities is the ways in which they have allegedly been abused. Orphan drug exclusivity, for example, has raised questions over whether drugs purported to treat rare diseases or conditions are in fact used for a variety of diseases and conditions, such that demand for the drug already earns enough profit

75 Orphan Drug Act, Pub. L. No. 97-414, 96 Stat. 2049 (1983).

76 *See* Daniel J. Gervais, *The Patent Option*, 20 N.C. J.L. & TECH. 357, 367–69, 384–95 (2019).

77 *Id.* at 380; Robin Feldman, *Regulatory Property: The New IP*, 40 COLUM. J.L. & ARTS 53, 60–61 (2016).

78 Feldman, *supra* note 77, at 85–87.

79 *Id.* at 54–56.

80 Noah, *supra* note 45, at 167.

81 Eisenberg, *supra* note 2, at 379; Benjamin N. Roin, *Unpatentable Drugs and the Standards of Patentability*, 87 TEX. L. REV. 503 (2009).

82 Brook K. Baker, *Ending Drug Registration Apartheid: Taming Data Exclusivity and Patent/Registration Linkage*, 34 AM. J.L. & MED. 303 (2008).

without the need for additional exclusivity.[83] It is this susceptibility to misuse has the most worrisome implications for drug pricing and access to medicines.

## The Biologics Price Competition and Innovation Act

Despite the lack of evidence on whether the Hatch-Waxman Act struck a good balance between lowering drug prices and maintaining incentives to invent new drugs, the US and other jurisdictions have devised additional *sui generis* statutory regimes to modify pharmaceutical IPR. The US enacted the Biologics Price Competition and Innovation Act (BPCIA) in 2009 to address the new generation of biologic therapeutics such as antibodies, gene therapies, and colony-stimulating factors.[84] Although the BPCIA was loosely patterned after the Hatch-Waxman Act to constrain trade secrecy and patent rights to lower prices,[85] however, some suggest that the current state of technology presents a greater barrier to market entry than does IP or other legal concerns.[86]

The Hatch-Waxman Act addresses small-molecule compounds, which are relatively simple chemical compounds manufacturable through standard chemistry techniques. The new wave of therapeutics governed by the BPCIA, by contrast, is produced through biological processes, such as cell cultures or isolation from natural resources. Biologics also tend to be more unstable and thousands of times larger and more difficult to characterize chemically than small-molecule drugs. As a result, reproducing another's biologics is much more difficult than copying a small-molecule drug. Biologic production processes are highly sensitive to the slightest alterations, and even small adjustments in structure can cause considerable differences in function and immunogenicity. Indeed, the goal in biologics is not production of exact "generic" copies but rather "follow-on" versions that, even though not identical to the original "reference" biologic, are nonetheless sufficiently similar so as to have no clinically significant differences (biosimilars) or to be substitutable without consulting the prescribing health-care provider (interchangeables). Demonstrating such similarity requires competitors to conduct studies on human pharmacodynamics and the clinical effects of substitution, raising estimated overall development costs to \$100–\$200 million per

83 *See, e.g.*, Feldman, *supra* note 77, at 78–80; Sarah Jane Tribble, *FDA Commissioner: Are the Incentives Right for Orphan Drugs?*, NPR (Dec. 22, 2017), https://www.npr.org/sections/health-shots/2017/12/22/572673636/fda-commissioner-are-the-incentives-right-for-orphan-drugs.

84 Patient Protection and Affordable Care Act, Pub. L. No. 111-148, Title VII, Subtitle A, 124 Stat. 119, 804–21 (2010).

85 Erika Lietzan, *The Uncharted Waters of Competition and Innovation in Biological Medicines*, 44 Fla. St. U. L. Rev. 883, 888–89 (2017).

86 *See, e.g.*, David E. Adelman & Christopher M. Holman, *Misplaced Fears in the Legislative Battle over Affordable Biotech Drugs*, 50 IDEA 565 (2010); John R. Thomas, *Follow-On Biologics: The Law and Intellectual Property Issues*, Cong. Research Serv., 13–14 (Jan. 15, 2014), https://fas.org/sgp/crs/misc/R41483.pdf.

follow-on biologic. As a result, follow-on biologics sell at much higher prices – only 15–20 percent lower than reference product prices – than generic versions of small-molecule drugs.[87] As with small-molecule drugs, however, advances in technology are hoped eventually to reduce the time and cost of the preclinical stages of both new and follow-on therapeutics.[88]

Furthermore, altering how IPR operate for biologics may not be as productive in spurring creation of lower priced options as it is for small-molecule drugs, although the BPCIA does differ from the Hatch-Waxman Act in how it modifies IPR.

First, biologics are highly complex molecules, derived from naturally occurring organisms and made of thousands of interconnected parts, and inventors can patent only the human-made parts of the biologic molecule or the processes for isolating, producing, or using it.[89] Patents on biologics therefore tend to be both more numerous and narrower in scope. Because of the number of patents per biologic, the BPCIA does not compel the FDA to list applicable patents or apply patent linkage. Unlike the Hatch-Waxman Act, moreover, the BPCIA does not offer any exclusivity or other benefits for the first biosimilar to challenge the reference drug's patents, nor does it grant reference biologics any stays of approval during such patent challenges.[90] While the BPCIA does establish very complex procedures for notice and resolution of such disputes,[91] recent case law indicates that adherence to these procedures is difficult to enforce.[92]

Second, the data exclusivities under the BPCIA are inherently different from those under the Hatch-Waxman Act. The BPCIA's data exclusivity for new therapeutics is for an initial period of four years, during which no follow-on biologic may apply for FDA approval, followed by another eight years before the FDA may grant such approval (during which the follow-on and reference product manufacturers can resolve any patent infringement issues).[93] The first follow-on biologic to qualify as "interchangeable" for a given reference

87 Lietzan, *supra* note 85, at 890–92, 894–96; Thomas, *supra* note 86, at 12–18.

88 Jeremiah J. Kelly & Michael David, *No Longer "If," but "When": The Coming Abbreviated Approval Pathway for Follow-on Biologics*, 64 Food Drug L.J. 115, 120 (2009) (noting possible advances in biologic characterization); Rai, *supra* note 12, at 190 (noting advances in ultra-high throughput screening technology to identify candidate compounds).

89 Adelman & Holman, *supra* note 86, at 571–79; Yaniv Heled, *Patents vs. Statutory Exclusivities in Biological Pharmaceuticals – Do We Really Need Both?*, 18 Mich. Telecomm. Tech. L. Rev. 419, 456–61 (2012).

90 Lietzan, *supra* note 85, at 932–36.

91 42 U.S.C. § 262(l); *see also* Thomas, *supra* note 86, at 8–12, 20 (describing complexity of procedures).

92 *See* Alison Inserro, *Bipartisan House Bill Seeks to Amend Patent Dance with Limit on Some Types of Patents*, Ctr. Biosimilars (July 31, 2019), https://www.centerforbiosimilars.com/news/bipartisan-house-bill-seeks-to-amend-patent-dance-with-limit-on-some-types-of-patents (describing proposed bill to streamline procedure).

93 The BPCIA's criteria for new biologic exclusivity also differ from those for New Chemical Entity exclusivity under Hatch-Waxman. Lietzan, *supra* note 85, at 928–31.

biologic may also receive a year or more of market exclusivity. Given the complexity of patenting patterns and the technological obstacles and costs of developing both reference and follow-on biologics, however, it is unclear whether these data exclusivities are too long, too short, or simply irrelevant in terms of their effect on access to medicines.[94] Because of the vagueness of the standards for follow-on biologics, reference biologic manufacturers are also expected to disagree over whether putative follow-on biologics actually qualify as biosimilars or interchangeables, posing further difficulties in introducing lower priced alternatives to the market.[95]

## Effects on Trademark and Copyright Protections

Other less frequently discussed changes in the law have also had collateral effects on the pharma industry's IPR, particularly those involving marketing. Many criticize brand-name pharma its for expenditures on marketing as merely rent-seeking efforts to sway patient and physician choices.[96] It is true that pharma spends significant amounts on direct-to-consumer marketing and branding, which does little to nothing to improve access to medicines.[97] However, it is also true that a large portion of marketing funds go toward socially beneficial free drug samples, continuing medical education, and "detailing" to educate physicians, hospital formularies, pharmacies, and insurers about a drug's indications, dosage, benefits, and risks.[98] How the public may view their appropriateness in the pharma industry notwithstanding, these branding and advertising investments are protected indirectly under trademark law, which prohibits the use of a mark that is misleadingly or even confusingly similar to another's mark.[99] Trademarks are

94 Adelman & Holman, *supra* note 86 (prices for follow-on biologics will be so high that delays due to data exclusivity will be irrelevant in determining access to medicine); Heled, *supra* note 89 (data exclusivity performs better than patents in incentivizing biologic R&D); Lietzan, *supra* note 85, at 937–38 (BPCIA exclusivity may be inadequate to incentivize development of new formulations and indications for existing biologics).

95 Lietzan, *supra* note 85, at 897–98, 905, 924–27 (noting complexities and uncertainties of biosimilarity and interchangeability standards and great inter-product variation in evidence necessary to meet those standards).

96 *E.g.*, Brennan, *supra* note 1, *passim*; Eugene McCarthy, *The Pharma Barons: Corporate Law's Dangerous New Race to the Bottom in the Pharma*, 8 MICH. BUS. & ENTREPRENEURIAL L. REV. 29, 51–59 (2018).

97 Direct-to-consumer (DTC) advertising typically targets the most profitable drugs. Carolyn B. Sufrin & Joseph S. Ross, *Pharmaceutical Industry Marketing: Understanding Its Impact on Women's Health*, 63 OBSTETRICAL & GYNECOLOGICAL SURVEY 585, 586 (2008).

98 *See, e.g.*, Jun Ma et al., *A Statistical Analysis of the Magnitude and Composition of Drug Promotion in the United States in 1998*, 25 CLIN. THERA. 1503 (2003); Pew Charitable Trusts, *Persuading the Prescribers: Pharmaceutical Industry Marketing and Its Influence on Physicians and Patients* (Nov. 11, 2013), https://www.pewtrusts.org/en/research-and-analysis/fact-sheets/2013/11/11/persuading-the-prescribers-pharmaceutical-industry-marketing-and-its-influence-on-physicians-and-patients (measuring 2012 expenditures).

99 William M. Landes & Richard A. Posner, *Trademark Law: An Economic Perspective*, 30 J. L. & ECON. 265, 270 (1987).

protected to help the public identify the source, and the reputation and expected quality associated with that source, of marked goods or services.[100]

Starting from just before the Hatch-Waxman Act was enacted, however, both state law and insurers shifted from discouraging or prohibiting substitution of generics for brand-name drugs to encouraging or outright requiring automatic substitution.[101] For follow-on biologics, only interchangeables can typically be substituted without consulting the prescribing caregiver,[102] but under these newer laws for small-molecule drugs, substitution can happen without the physician or patient's permission. Unless the patient or physician affirmatively refuses, automatic substitution occurs regardless of whether the branded version was prescribed.[103] Substitution laws and policies thus increase access to medicines by switching patients to lower priced generics.[104]

But automatic substitution also effectively allows generics to free ride on brand-name marketing to save the cost of doing so themselves.[105] Although brand names typically stop investing in advertising for a drug once its generic enters the market,[106] the effects of marketing are thought to linger and in fact to expand the market for the generic once it becomes available.[107] At least one commentator has argued that state substitution laws in this way effectively treat pharmaceutical trademarks as if they were unprotectable generic descriptions of the underlying drug rather than its source.[108] Of course, pharmaceutical trademarks are otherwise still fully enforceable; for example, trademarking drugs allows much more severe liabilities and penalties to be imposed

100 *Id.* at 269.

101 Jeremy A. Greene & Aaron S. Kesselheim, *Why Do the Same Drugs Look Different? Pills, Trade Dress, and Public Health*, 365 N. ENG. J. MED. 83, 85 (2011); Joanna Shepherd, *Deterring Innovation:* New York v. Actavis *and the Duty to Subsidize Competitors' Market Entry*, 17 MINN. J. L. SCI. & TECH. 663, 686–87 (2016).

102 Michael Gabay, *Biosimilar Substitution Laws*, 52 HOSP. PHARM. 544, 544 (2017).

103 Carrier & Shadowen, *supra* note 1, at 175; Yan Song & Douglas Barthold, *The Effects of State-Level Pharmacist Regulations on Generic Substitution of Prescription Drugs*, 27 HEALTH ECON. 1717, 1718 (2018).

104 Greene & Kesselheim, *supra* note 101, at 85.

105 *New York ex rel. Schneiderman v. Actavis PLC*, 787 F.3d 638, 657 (2d Cir. 2015) (referring to generic substitution as "'free-riding' … authorized" by state law); Shepherd, *supra* note at 101, at 666 (similar); *see also Mylan Pharm., Inc. v. Warner Chilcott Pub. Co.*, No. CIV. 12-3824, 2013 WL 5692880, at *2 (E.D. Pa. June 12, 2013) (finding description of substitution laws as "forced 'free-riding'" to be "compelling"); Steve D. Shadowen et al., *Anticompetitive Product Changes in the Pharmaceutical Industry,* 41 RUTGERS L.J. 1, 46 (2009) (noting that generics have no incentive to promote their products due to potential of free riding by other generics).

106 Shadowen et al., *supra* note 105, at 15.

107 *See, e.g.*, Jayanta Bhattacharya & William B. Vogt, *A Simple Model of Pharmaceutical Price Dynamics*, 46 J.L. & ECON. 599 (2003); Fiona Scott Morton, *Barriers to Entry, Brand Advertising, and Generic Entry in the US Pharmaceutical Industry*, 18 INT'L J. INDUS. ORG. 1085, 1087 (2000).

108 Alfred B. Engelberg, *Have Prescription Drug Brand Names Become Generic?*, 20 AM. J. MANAGED CARE 867, 867–68 (2014).

on counterfeiters.[109] Still, state substitution laws create a notable exception to the general rule that competitors cannot be compelled to permit others to free ride on their marketing investments.[110] This interplay between automatic substitution and trademark rights thus represents another unique way in which the law limits pharmaceutical IPR to facilitate access to medicines.[111]

These industry-specific laws come with good reason. Studies show that brand names have been able to use trademarks and branding to protect market share by influencing both physicians and patients. Patients often perceive brand-name drugs as being of higher quality than generics, and physicians often defer to their patients' inclinations.[112] This may also be due to journalists and other commentators expressing concerns about generic manufacturing and quality standards, especially for generics manufactured overseas.[113] However, the pharmaceutical industry differs from others in that drug quality is closely monitored.[114] The FDA recently published a statement to combat these popular perceptions of generic drugs, explaining that it closely evaluates foreign and domestic manufacturers for adherence to both bioequivalence standards and Current Good Manufacturing Practices.[115] Complaints that automatic substitution devalues investments in trademarks and branding are also belied by brand-name marketing of "authorized generics" – that is, unbranded versions of their own drugs – once other generics enter the market.[116] Preferences for brand-name

109 Sandra L. Rierson, *Pharmaceutical Counterfeiting and the Puzzle of Remedies*, 8 Wake Forest Intell. Prop. L.J. 433 (2008).

110 *Olympia Equip. Leasing Co. v. W. Union Tel. Co.*, 797 F.2d 370, 377–78 (7th Cir. 1986).

111 Dmitry Karshtedt, *The More Things Change: Improvement Patents, Drug Modifications, and the FDA*, 104 Iowa L. Rev. 1129, 1150 (2019); Bruce N. Kuhlik, *The Assault on Pharmaceutical Intellectual Property*, 71 U. Chi. L. Rev. 93, 95 (2004) (similar).

112 *E.g.*, William H. Shrank et al., *Patients' Perceptions of Generic Medications*, 28 Health Affairs 546, 553–54 (2009); Thomas Chen, *Authorized Generics: A Prescription for Hatch-Waxman Reform*, 93 Va. L. Rev. 459, 473 (2007) (and sources cited therein).

113 *E.g.*, Katherine Eban, *Americans Need Generic Drugs. But Can They Trust Them?*, N.Y. Times (May 11, 2019), https://www.nytimes.com/2019/05/11/opinion/sunday/generic-drugs-safety.html; C. Michael White, *Generics Are Cheap and Popular, But Some Might Not Be as Safe as You'd Expect*, Wash. Post (Dec. 8, 2019), https://www.washingtonpost.com/health/generics-are-cheap-and-popular-but-some-might-not-be-as-safe-as-youd-expect/2019/12/06/40059b6e-16e5-11ea-a659-7d69641c6ff7_story.html; *see also* Landes & Posner, *supra* note 99, at 275 (noting that chemically identical products can differ in manufacturing quality).

114 *Id.* at 23; Carrier & Shadowen, *supra* note 1, at 184–90 (referring to this effect as market failure based on "price disconnect").

115 U.S. Food & Drug Admin., Statement from FDA Commissioner Scott Gottlieb, M.D., and Director of FDA's Center for Drug Evaluation and Research Janet Woodcock, M.D., on the FDA's Continuing Efforts to Maintain Its Strong Oversight of Generic Drug Quality Issues Domestically and Abroad (Feb. 22, 2019), https://www.fda.gov/news-events/press-announcements/statement-fda-commissioner-scott-gottlieb-md-and-director-fdas-center-drug-evaluation-and-research-0.

116 Engelberg, *supra* note 108, at 868.

over generic drugs are therefore likely meritless and even irrational.[117] Such irrationality characterizes trademark and branding effects in many industries,[118] but pharmaceuticals is one market in which irrational choices can be harmful, especially given that patients do not have the expertise to make fully informed choices and often do not bear the full cost of their choices anyway.[119]

Likewise, the law has even changed the pharma industry's copyright rights. Brand-name manufacturers must create a wide range of packaging and informational materials to advise both patients and care providers on the proper use of their drugs.[120] Drug labeling and marketing materials are closely regulated, and gaining government approval of drug packaging, package inserts, detailing, and advertising can consume sizable outlays of time and money.[121] These materials are only minimally protectable under copyright law – the vast majority of pharmaceutical labeling is necessarily information-intensive, and copyright law protects only original "expression," not facts and information – but whatever is original and expressive in the selection and arrangement of that information can be grounds for a copyright infringement suit if substantially copied.[122] To enable generics to avoid the costs and delays of creating and seeking approval of their own labeling and promotional materials, however, the Hatch-Waxman Act requires generics to copy from the brand names, thereby placing the generics at risk of copyright infringement.[123] The US mandates that any written or graphic matter designed to accompany a generic drug be "the same" as the brand-name versions, a standard that has been interpreted as requiring near identity.[124]

117 *E.g.*, Brennan, *supra* note 1, *passim*.

118 *See, e.g.*, Brennan, *supra* note 1, at 10–15; Mark A. Lemley, *The Modern Lanham Act and the Death of Common Sense*, 108 YALE L.J. 1687, 1689–92 (1999).

119 Carrier & Shadowen, *supra* note 1, at 175.

120 21 U.S.C. § 355(b)(1)(F); *see also* Kristin E. Behrendt, *The Hatch-Waxman Act: Balancing Competing Interests or Survival of the Fittest?*, 57 FOOD & DRUG L.J. 247, 261 (2002).

121 U.S. Food & Drug Admin., Prescription Drug Labeling Resources (last visited May 12, 2020), https://www.fda.gov/drugs/laws-acts-and-rules/prescription-drug-labeling-resources (collecting over fifty documents physician and patient labeling requirements); U.S. Food & Drug Admin., The Office of Prescription Drug Promotion (OPDP) (last visited May 12, 2020), https://www.fda.gov/about-fda/center-drug-evaluation-and-research-cder/office-prescription-drug-promotion-opdp (offering resources on promotional labeling rules).

122 *See Feist Publications, Inc. v. Rural Tel. Serv. Co.*, 499 U.S. 340, 345–48 (1991) (noting that most factual compilations are copyrightable because only minimal creativity is required); *SmithKline Beecham Consumer Healthcare, L.P. v. Watson Pharm., Inc.*, 211 F.3d 21, 27 n.2 (2d Cir. 2000) (noting that most commercial labeling is information-intensive and only thinly copyrightable). Copyrights protect original written and graphic works, among others, by providing their creators with exclusive rights of reproduction, distribution, and so on. 17 U.S.C. §§ 102 & 106.

123 *SmithKline Beecham*, 211 F.3d at 25; Behrendt, *supra* note 120, at 259, 261.

124 21 U.S.C. §§ 355(j)(2)(A)(v) & (j)(4)(G); 21 CFR §§ 314.94(a)(8) & 314.127(a)(7).

Unlike potential patent infringement, however, the Hatch-Waxman Act is silent as to how to resolve any consequent copyright infringement claims.

The US Court of Appeals for the Second Circuit ultimately took up the issue in its 2000 decision in *SmithKline Beacham Consumer Healthcare v. Watson Pharmaceuticals* and held that the Hatch-Waxman Act outright preempts copyright law, regardless of whether a drug's labeling and promotional materials are otherwise copyrightable.[125] SmithKline had invested almost three years in creating and seeking FDA approval for a user's guide and audiotape for its over-the-counter version of a *Nicorette* gum smoking cessation aid and had registered for federal copyright rights in the guide and the audiotape's script and music.[126] The FDA thereafter required that Watson's generic version of the nicotine gum be accompanied by a user's guide and audiotape that were "virtually identical" to SmithKline's, but when SmithKline sued for copyright infringement, the Second Circuit denied SmithKline's claim.[127] The court reasoned that the Hatch-Waxman Act's requirement that generic labeling be "the same" as the brand-name reference drug's labeling effectively preempted copyright infringement claims.[128] Otherwise, infringement litigation over even the little that is copyrightable in these materials could delay generic regulatory approval and increase generic entry costs. These costs would ultimately be passed down to patients, decreasing access to generics and undermining the main purpose of the Hatch-Waxman Act.[129] (For much the same reasons, the US Supreme Court also held that generics are exempt from liability under both federal and state law for failure to warn of possible dangers from their drugs, although this latter point is an issue of product liability law, not IP law.)[130]

Only the Hatch-Waxman Act has been held to preempt the Copyright Act in this way.[131] Producing copyrightable content is hardly a main line of business for the pharmaceutical industry, and whether brand names can assert copyright rights over that content is certainly a minor point. Nonetheless, *SmithKline Beacham* shows again how the need to promote access to medicines has led to IPR in the pharmaceutical industry being treated differently than in others.[132]

125 *SmithKline Beecham*, *supra* note 123, at 25–29.
126 *Id.* at 23.
127 *Id.*
128 *Id.* at 25.
129 *Id.* at 28; *see also* Behrendt, *supra* note 120, at 261.
130 *PLIVA, Inc. v. Mensing*, 131 S. Ct. 2567 (2011).
131 *See, e.g.*, *Schwarz Pharma, Inc. v. Breckenridge Pharm., Inc.*, 388 F. Supp. 2d 967, 979 (E.D. Wis. 2005) (copyright preemption applies only to drug approved under Hatch-Waxman); *Int'l Swaps & Derivatives Ass'n, Inc. v. Socratek*, L.L.C., 712 F. Supp. 2d 96, 100-01 (S.D.N.Y. 2010) (copyright claim actionable even if it conflicted with acts authorized under Securities Exchange Act); *FMC Corp. v. Control Sols., Inc.*, 369 F. Supp. 2d 539, 568 (E.D. Pa. 2005) (copyright claims not preempted by EPA labeling statute).
132 Behrendt, *supra* note 120, at 259.

## Criticisms of Other Alleged Pharmaceutical IPR Abuse

Other criticisms of the way in which the pharma industry uses IPR further highlight its dissimilarity with other industries. Critics have been quite skeptical about secondary patents on known drugs, as noted above, and for reasons beyond just suspected invalidity.[133]

Secondary innovation on existing technology is routine in all areas of science and technology, given that cumulative R&D on existing technology is by far the most common mode of innovation,[134] but some assume that the incremental nature of innovations protected under secondary patents necessarily makes them less socially valuable.[135] Many also question whether too many patents on incremental innovation could hinder future innovation.[136] However, such secondary and cumulative innovation can yield significant benefits; for example, secondary pharmaceutical patents typically cover new forms of and uses for existing therapeutics that can improve patient outcomes, improve drug usability, and provide treatment alternatives.[137] Nevertheless, as mentioned above, many commentators criticize sequential pharmaceutical patenting, not so much for their use in blocking later innovation, but for their use in allegedly "evergreening" patent exclusivity.[138]

A further variation on this theme is the use of sequential pharmaceutical reformulations for "product hopping." This is a tactic in which brand names attempt to circumvent automatic substitution laws and policies by introducing new formulations of existing products for which no generics yet exist and then heavily marketing the newer reformulations. Prescriptions for and sales of the new reformulation then flow solely to the brand name, as pharmacists have no generic equivalent to substitute for these prescriptions.[139] Although product hopping technically does not require the use of trademarks, branding facilitates the practice in what can be seen as an abusive manner.[140] Effective product hopping also does not depend on trademarks or patent and regulatory exclusivities, as the time necessary for generics to develop and obtain authorization for generic copies of new formulations gives brand names a first-mover advantage.[141]

133 *See supra* text accompanying notes 43–55.

134 Ho, *supra* note 49, at 317; Suzanne Scotchmer, *Standing on the Shoulders of Giants: Cumulative Research and the Patent Law*, 5 J. Econ. Persp. 29, 30 (1991).

135 *See, e.g.*, Hemphill & Sampat, *supra* note 11, at 644.

136 *See, e.g.*, Dan L. Burk & Mark A. Lemley, *Policy Levers in Patent Law*, 89 Va. L. Rev. 1575, 1612–13 (2003); Richard R. Nelson, *The Market Economy, and the Scientific Commons*, 33 Res. Pol'y 455, 464 (2004).

137 *Walgreen Co. v. AstraZeneca Pharm. L.P.*, 534 F. Supp. 2d 146, 151 (D.D.C. 2008); Noah, *supra* note 45, at 165, 172–73.

138 *See supra* text accompanying notes 43–48.

139 Ho, *supra* note 49, at 317–21; Carrier & Shadowen, *supra* note 1, at 171, 177–78.

140 P. Sean Morris, *Trademarks as Sources of Market Power: Drugs, Beers and Product Differentiation*, 35 J.L. & Com. 163, 250 (2017) (referring to branded product hopping as "predatory brand proliferation").

141 Carrier & Shadowen, *supra* note 1, at 176 (detailing many steps necessary for generics to market reformulated drugs).

(However, patent and regulatory exclusivities can prolong the term during which automatic substitution for the reformulation is blocked.) Many brand names further their goals by withdrawing their earlier formulations from a given market or by launching new reformulations just before generics are approved, so that there are no longer prescriptions for which generics can be substituted.[142]

Brand names justify both the withdrawal of the older formulation and introduction of the newer, often patented reformulation by arguing that the latter is better for patients, and empirical data analyses have shown that most new drug reformulations do in fact offer genuine advantages over earlier ones and are unconnected to imminent generic competition.[143] However, critics argue that a subset of these reformulations represent only trivial variations and are intended solely to thwart generic substitution.[144] This carries particular weight with regard to brand names that withdraw the earlier versions of their reformulated drugs only when a generic is about to enter the market.[145] It also adds evidence that reformulations are not just secondary but also intentionally sequential and that the motivation of brand names that do this is to preserve their market share, not to bring better versions of their drug to patients.[146] Nevertheless, this practice does not distinguish pharma from other industries, as product hopping is endemic in many.[147] Indeed, courts usually express some skepticism about claims that a company's product changes harmed competition, even when that company has a dominant market position.[148] Competition and the desire to beat out one's competitors is often thought to be a desirable incentive for innovation.[149] On the other hand, no other industry has automatic substitution laws that would be frustrated by such product hopping.

Even though product hopping undoubtedly impedes automatic generic substitution, however, generics are still capable of garnering sales. Nothing prevents them from continuing to sell and physicians continuing to prescribe generic

142 Carrier & Shadowen, *supra* note 1, at 176–77; Karshtedt, *supra* note 111, at 1134; Noah, *supra* note 45, at 167–70.

143 Noah, *supra* note 45, at 165, 172–73; Shadowen et al., *supra* note 105, at 2, 27, 78 (2009).

144 *E.g.*, Carrier & Shadowen, *supra* note 1, at 176–80.

145 *Id.* at 202.

146 *Id.*; *see also supra* text accompanying notes 49–50 (discussing the distinction between secondary and sequential drug changes).

147 Noah, *supra* note 45, at 171 (describing product hopping with repeatedly updated editions of law casebooks). Product hopping affects only small-molecule drugs, not biologics, however. Michael A. Carrier & Carl J. Minniti III, *Biologics: The New Antitrust Frontier*, 2018 U. Ill. L. Rev. 1, 28–31 (2018); Lietzan, *supra* note 85, at 941 (2017).

148 *Foremost Pro Color, Inc. v. Eastman Kodak Co.*, 703 F.2d 534, 544–45 (9th Cir.1983) (no anticompetitive harm from introduction of photographic equipment incompatible with other competitors' equipment).

149 *United States v. Microsoft Corp.*, 253 F.3d 34, 65 (D.C. Cir. 2001) (even if innovations are incompatible with competitors' goods); *In re Suboxone (Buprenorphine Hydrochloride & Naloxone) Antitrust Litig.*, 64 F. Supp. 3d 665, 679 (E.D. Pa. 2014).

versions of older formulations.[150] Although some suggest that physicians are not motivated to prescribe lower priced generics because they do not bear the costs of their prescribing decisions,[151] physicians do keep drug costs in mind. For example, physicians will frequently respond to elevated drug prices by switching their patients to lower priced choices within the same therapeutic class.[152] And even if a generic had not yet entered the market by the time a brand-name older formulation was withdrawn, the generic can still seek approval to enter the market with its own less expensive version.[153] That generics typically do not seek approval in such cases reflects the fact that, without the possibility of automatic substitution, generics would not be able to ride on the coattails of brand-name advertising and promotion. As one federal court described it, a product hopping claim is simply a complaint that a generic has become "a 'victim' of its own business strategy, not Defendants' 'predatory' conduct."[154] Nevertheless, the problem with expecting generics to bear the costs of doing their own advertising is that, again, those costs would have to be passed on to patients in the form of higher drug prices.[155] Criticisms of product hopping thus reflect not so much anticompetitive concerns as a sense that social welfare and access to medicines should take precedence over profit, a sentiment that also underlies how the law has reshaped pharmaceutical IPR.

Even pharmaceutical innovations such as "me-too" drugs have faced criticism. Me-too drugs are identical in basic chemical structure, mechanism of action, and use to existing drugs but differ in attached subgroups, geometry, and so on.[156] Although they pose some price-lowering competition for other drugs in their therapeutic class, they are typically priced much higher than generic drugs.[157] Even if me-too drugs do not impede generic market entry or substitution, they are thought to distract physicians away from prescribing

150 Daniel A. Crane, Provigil: *A Commentary*, 3 Hastings Sci. & Tech. L.J. 453, 454–5 (2011); Noah, *supra* note 45, at 170–71 (noting that many critics erroneously overlook this point).

151 Carrier & Shadowen, *supra* note 1, at 168.

152 Crane, *supra* note 150, at 454–55.

153 *See, e.g.*, *Abbott Labs. v. Teva Pharm. USA, Inc.*, 432 F. Supp. 2d 408, 423 (D. Del. 2006). Only once marketing approval for a specific drug formulation has been rescinded will the FDA refuse to approve a generic abbreviated approval application. This occurs very infrequently. *See also* Noah, *supra* note 45, at 176–77 & n.54.

154 *Mylan Pharm., Inc. v. Warner Chilcott Pub. Co.*, No. CIV. 12-3824, 2015 WL 1736957, at *13 (E.D. Pa. Apr. 16, 2015), aff'd, 838 F.3d 421 (3d Cir. 2016).

155 *See* Carrier & Shadowen, *supra* note 1, at 204; Eric L. Cramer & Daniel Berger, *The Superiority of Direct Proof of Monopoly Power and Anticompetitive Effects in Antitrust Cases Involving Delayed Entry of Generic Drugs*, 39 U.S.F. L. Rev. 81, 133 (2004).

156 Ron A. Bouchard, *Qualifying Intellectual Property I: Harmonized Measurement of New and Follow-on Drug Approvals, Patents and Chemical Components*, 18 B.U. J. Sci. & Tech. L. 38, 51 (2012); Carrier & Shadowen, *supra* note 1, at 183.

157 Carrier & Shadowen, *supra* note 1, at 183–84; Joshua J. Gagne & Niteesh Chaudhry, *How Many "Me-Too" Drugs Is Too Many?*, 305 JAMA 711, 711 (2011).

generics.[158] They thus are often perceived as merely free riding on commercially successful drugs and a waste of R&D resources for little or no patient benefit.[159] Some of the most famous examples of me-too drugs are analogues of drugs such as *Prozac*, which led to an entire panoply of serotonin-specific reuptake inhibitors to treat depression and anxiety, and *Lipitor*, which gave way to a long line of HMG-CoA reductase inhibitors (statins) to treat hypercholesterolemia.[160]

However, producing me-too drugs does not necessarily lower drug development costs as most me-too drugs are not in fact knockoffs but drugs that were in development at the same time as the first-in-class therapeutic but that happened to be second or third on the market.[161] The degree of heterogeneity within therapeutic classes also varies, such that many me-too drugs actually differ in clinically significant characteristics, including expected efficacy, potency, and side-effect profiles, and can offer patients more alternatives and physicians more flexibility in tailoring treatment according to how patients individually react to particular therapeutics.[162] This latter point may be of particular relevance for personalized medicine.[163] Moreover, me-too drugs in less differentiated classes of drugs limit brand-name market power, albeit to a limited extent, and in any event provide consumer choices that are generally seen as desirable in any other market.[164] In the pharmaceutical market, however, critics clearly views competition and consumer choice based on variation as less important than competition and consumer choice based on price, once again underscoring how the need for access to medicines alters what the law views as optimal market structure.

## Pharmaceutical IPR Outside the US

Since the Hatch-Waxman Act was first put into law in the US, several countries have enacted similar laws modifying pharmaceutical IP protections.[165] Either of their own accord or in response to (mostly US-negotiated) free trade agreements,

158 Gagne & Chaudhry, *supra* note 157, at 711; Neel U. Sukhatme & M. Gregg Bloche, *Health Care Costs and the Arc of Innovation*, 104 Minn. L. Rev. 955, 976 (2019).

159 Marcia Angell, The Truth About the Drug Companies: How They Deceive Us and What to Do About It, 75 (2004); Yaniv Heled et al., *Why Healthcare Companies Should Be(Come) Benefit Corporations*, 60 B.C. L. Rev. 73, 88–89 (2019).

160 Heled et al., *supra* note 159, at 88; Rai, *supra* note 12, at 205 (2001) (listing also oral antihistamines and anti-ulcerants).

161 Cong. Budget Off., Research and Development in the Pharmaceutical Industry, 12 (2006).

162 *Id.* at 13; Gagne & Chaudhry, *supra* note 157, at 711.

163 Dov Greenbaum, *Regulation and the Fate of Personalized Medicine?*, 14 AMA J. Ethics 645, 648 (2012).

164 Cong. Budget Off., *supra* note 161, at 12–13; Frank A. Sloan & Chee-Ruey Hsieh, *Introduction*, *in* Pharmaceutical Innovation: Incentives, Competition, and Cost-Benefit Analysis in International Perspective, 1, 9 (Frank A. Sloan & Chee-Ruey Hsieh eds., 2007).

165 *See, e.g.*, Ho, *supra* note 4, at 223–51.

these other jurisdictions have implemented their own renditions of regulatory exclusivities, generic substitution or prescription laws, patent linkage, regulatory use exceptions, and patent term extensions, *inter alia* (although none seem to have adopted anything analogous to the Hatch-Waxman Act's 180-day exclusivity period to encourage generic manufacturers to challenge brand-name patents).[166] To say that these laws and regulations have been controversial is an understatement, particularly among developing countries.[167] Although the Hatch-Waxman Act and similar legislative enactments were designed to increase access to medicines while simultaneously maintaining incentives to generate new medicines, the result in many developing countries has likely been to decrease access to medicines without appreciable growth in pharmaceutical development.[168]

To understand this point, it is important to note that, historically, neither patent nor trade secrecy rights did much to protect pharmaceuticals in many developing countries and posed few obstacles to generic market entry. For example, prior to the signing of the TRIPS Agreement by World Trade Organization member states in 1995, countries such as India and China held pharmaceutical products to be unpatentable subject matter, and it is this historical lack of pharmaceutical product patents that allowed India to become the generic manufacturing powerhouse that it continues to be today.[169] Requiring these countries to moderate patent or trade secrecy rights in fact required creating these rights, a move that created particularly harmful barriers to generic availability.[170] Advocates for including these pharma-specific provisions in trade agreements nevertheless argued that they were necessary to protect pharmaceutical R&D investments and to attract investments in domestic pharmaceutical R&D in less developed countries.[171] Critics counter that pharmaceutical firms in developed countries already earn sufficient returns from those markets and that, because less developed countries are net importers of drug innovation, there are few gains to be had from trying to use IP law to attract investment in domestic drug development.[172] Given that developing countries typically do not possess the financial resources to pay supra-competitive prices, much less to invest in pharmaceutical R&D, exporting the developed world's pharma-specific IP scheme would seem to be neither necessary nor desirable.[173]

166 *Id.* at 223–52, 275; ALI, *supra* note 1, at 42–46.

167 *See, e.g.*, Baker, *supra* note 82.

168 *See, e.g.*, ALI, *supra* note 1, at 207; HO, *supra* note 4, at 243–44.

169 Avery K. Hason & Jean E. Shimotake, *Recent Developments in Patent Rights for Pharmaceuticals in China and India*, 18 PACE INT'L L. REV 303 (2006); Janice M. Mueller, *The Tiger Awakens: The Tumultuous Transformation of India's Patent System and the Rise of Indian Pharmaceutical Innovation*, 68 U. PITT. L. REV. 491, 495 (2007).

170 *See, e.g.*, ALI, *supra* note 1, *passim*; HO, *supra* note 4, at 245–50.

171 *See, e.g.*, Press Release, *supra* note 32.

172 *See, e.g.*, ALI, *supra* note 1, *passim*.

173 HO, *supra* note 4, at 250.

## Conclusion

The notable divergence between IPR in the pharmaceutical industry and those in every other industry affects not only patents but also trade secrecy, copyright, and even trademark law to some degree. The need to cabin pharmaceutical IPR is understandable, given the need for expanding access to medicines through the availability of lower cost generic medications. Of course, IPR are already designed to be limited in scope or duration to avoid prolonging any consequent supra-competitive pricing and the deadweight losses it can cause, but such losses are particularly concerning when it comes to pharmaceuticals and health care. On balance, the modifications to pharmaceutical IPR have favored generics, and generic market entry has risen markedly as a result.

This rise in generic market entry has been mostly due to the replacement of potentially infinite trade secrecy protections with more time-limited data exclusivity periods for clinical trial data. Several of the other pharma-specific changes, however, strengthen pharmaceutical patent protections to preserve incentives to invest in drug development. Having so many changes happening in so many different directions has led to many unintended consequences, most of which implicate the existing tensions between IP and antitrust law.[174] Pharmaceutical IPR and regulatory exclusivities have created further conflicts between these two bodies of law and muddied the question of how best to resolve them, as exemplified by the debate over reverse payment settlements.[175] This is not entirely surprising, given that antitrust law, despite its focus on market power and competition, ultimately targets the power to raise consumer prices and reduce consumer choice.[176] Nevertheless, the US government has continued to enact even further variations on these themes, particularly regulatory exclusivities of both the data and market variety, and appears ready to consider proposals that might also further affect IPR.[177] What these continuing changes portend for access to medicines is a question that remains.

174 Michael A. Carrier, *Three Challenges for Pharmaceutical Antitrust*, 59 Santa Clara L. Rev. 615 (2020).

175 Rebecca S. Eisenberg & David A. Crane, *Patent Punting: How FDA and Antitrust Courts Undermine the Hatch-Waxman Act to Avoid Dealing with Patents*, 21 Mich. Telecomm. & Tech. L. Rev. 197 (2015).

176 Carrier & Shadowen, *supra* note 1, at 190–91.

177 Yaniv Heled, *Regulatory Competitive Shelters*, 76 Ohio St. L.J. 299 (2015).

# 20 Innovation Policies

## Roadblocks to Establishing Sustainable Pharmaceutical Innovation Policies

*Doris Estelle Long**

Twenty-five plus years ago, the Agreement on Trade-Related Aspects of Intellectual Property Rights (TRIPS Agreement)[1] changed the norms in international protections for pharmaceutical innovations[2] by assuring that such protections would not only be increased, but would also be established as part of a country's *trade* policy. The stronger protections required by the TRIPS Agreement under both patent[3] and data exclusivity[4] regimes have become

* I would like to thank Srividhya Ragavan and Amaka Vanni for allowing me to share my views on some practical efforts that I believe can help make public access to medicine a reality. I would also like to thank all those individuals who have graciously given their time to discuss and debate these issues with me.

1 TRIPS: Agreement on Trade-Related Aspects of Intellectual Property Rights, Apr. 15, 1994, Marrakesh Agreement Establishing the World Trade Organization, Annex 1C, 1869 U.N.T.S. 299, 33 I.L.M. 1197 (1994) [hereinafter TRIPS Agreement].

2 Michael Lanthier et al., *An Improved Approach to Measuring Drug Innovation Finds Steady Rates of First-in-Class Pharmaceuticals, 1987–2011*, 32 Health Affairs 1433 (2013). I believe that the three-tier innovation classification set forth by Lanthier *et al.* in their article may be useful in determining the appropriate level/type of competitive regulation to assure adequate public access. It divides new molecular entities ("NMEs") into three innovation categories – "(1) whether an NME was the first drug approved in its class; (2) whether it was a therapeutic advance within an existing drug class; or (3) whether it was an addition to a drug class, providing only modest additional benefit relative to other drugs." But for purposes of this chapter, unless specifically identified to the contrary, I am using the term "innovation" and its variants to include all three Lanthier classification categories.

3 TRIPS Agreement, *supra* note 1, at art. 27 (1) ("patents shall be available for any inventions, whether products or processes, *in all fields of technology*, provided that they are new, involve an inventive step and are capable of industrial application") (emphasis added).

4 *Id.* at art. 39(3) (requiring protection against the "unfair commercial use" of data, including clinical test data, for "pharmaceutical and agricultural chemical products which utilize new chemical entities" where such data is required to be submitted to the government to secure marketing approval). For a detailed exploration of the interrelationship between intellectual property, including patents, trade secrets (data exclusivity), and trademarks, and access to medicine, *see* World Health Org., World Trade Org., & World Intellectual Prop. Org., Promoting Access to Medical Technologies and Innovations: Intersections Between Public Health, Intellectual Property and Trade Second Edition (World Trade Organization, World Health Organization and World Intellectual Property Organization 2020) [hereinafter second Trilateral Report on Access to Medical Technologies].

subjects of increasing concern over their adverse impact on the fundamental human right to reasonable access to medicines for all.[5] In 2000, less than *six* years after the TRIPS Agreement was established, the United Nations Sub-Commission on the Promotion and Protection of Human Rights specifically identified patent protection for pharmaceuticals as creating "apparent conflicts between the intellectual property rights (IPR) regime embodied in the TRIPS Agreement, on the one hand, and international human rights law, [specifically the right to health] on the other."[6] Unfortunately, while the trade policies of the TRIPS Agreement – in particular, its strong protection for intellectual property (IP) rights (IPR) in the pharmaceutical sector – continue to drive health costs upwards,[7] potential regulatory doctrines aimed at reducing those costs often remain underutilized or ineffective despite the recognition in Article 8(2) that "appropriate measures" can be taken "to prevent the abuse of IPR by right holders … or the resort to practices which unreasonably restrain trade."[8] The need to resolve this issue, to assure both rapid innovation and reasonable access on a socially just basis to the treatments that result from such innovation, has become even more pressing as deaths at the time of publication of this chapter continue to soar from the COVID-19 global pandemic.

This chapter will briefly examine seven "roadblocks" that hinder the creation of effective competitive regulatory mechanisms for controlling pharmaceutical prices, and ultimately capping global pharmaceutical profits in a manner supporting socially just and sustainable innovation. I use the term "competitive regulatory mechanisms" in its broadest sense – to include all attempts to regulate price and access, allowing either greater price competition within the pharmaceutical sector and/or greater access to affordable medicines. For purposes of this chapter, these competitive mechanisms include reducing the likelihood of improvidently granting patents covering innovations that lack the requisite

5 *See, e.g.*, International Covenant on Economic, Social and Cultural Rights, art. 12(1), Jan. 3, 1976, S. Treaty Doc. No. 95–19, 993 U.N.T.S. 3 ("The States Parties to the present Covenant recognize the right of everyone to the enjoyment of the ***highest attainable standard*** of physical and mental health.") (emphasis added); UN Resolution Adopted by the General Assembly on Sept. 25, 2015, The 2030 Agenda for Sustainable Development, A/Res/ 70/1, Goal 3.8 (Oct. 21, 2015) ("Achieve universal health coverage, including … access to quality essential health-care services and access to safe, effective, quality and ***affordable*** essential medicines and vaccines for all.") (emphasis added).

6 Sub-Commission on Human Rights Res. 2000/7, ***Intellectual Property Rights and Human Rights***, ESCOR, Commission on Human Rights, Sub-Commission on the Promotion and Protection of Human Rights, 52nd Sess., 25th mtg,, U.N. Doc. E/CN.4/Sub.2/Res/2000/7, ¶2 (2000).

7 *See infra* notes 37–43 and accompanying text regarding abuses of the TRIPS protection regime.

8 TRIPS Agreement, *supra* note 1, at art. 8(2); *see also id.* at art. 40 (2) ("Nothing in this Agreement shall prevent Members from specifying in their legislation licensing practices *or conditions* that may in particular cases constitute an abuse of intellectual property rights having an adverse effect on competition in the relevant market.") (emphasis added).

inventiveness,[9] establishing limitations on a patent holder's exclusive rights,[10] such as through compulsory licenses (CLs)[11] granted when protected drugs are not "reasonably available" on the domestic market,[12] and efforts to increase competition by removing competitive access barriers for generics, biosimilars, and gray market imports.[13] This chapter explores seven currently existing "roadblocks" in efforts to create such mechanisms and suggests potential avenues to overcome them to create *sustainable* innovation with a strong social justice component to strengthen access to medicines, while still providing the necessary research and development (R&D) support that *rational* protection of IPR in pharmaco-medical innovations can provide.[14]

Although the apparently easiest policy solution to combatting high drug costs would be some form of price control achieved through direct price control

9 *See, Mayo Collaborative Servs. v. Prometheus Labs., Inc.*, 566 U.S. 66 (2012), and discussion *infra* notes 49–56 and accompanying text regarding recalibration of the patent system to reduce improvidently granted patents,

10 TRIPS Agreement, *supra* note 1, at arts. 28(1)(c) and art. 28(1)(b) (these rights include the right to prevent unauthorized third parties from "making, using, offering for sale, selling, or importing" a patented product, and from "using, offering for sale, selling or importing," products "attained directly by" a patented process).

11 *See id.* at art. 31(f) (allowing compulsory licenses where the use is "authorized predominantly for the supply of the domestic market of the Member authorizing such use"); *Id.* at art. 31*bis* (allowing compulsory licenses for export to "eligible countries" that lack sufficient manufacturing capacity to supply their domestic needs).

12 *See* The Patent Act § 84(1), No. 39 of 1970, India Code (1998) (requiring "enhancement of a known efficacy" for new use patents) and discussion *infra* notes 49–56 and accompanying text regarding patent law recalibrations for "new uses."

13 *See* Medicines and Related Substances Act 90 of 1997 § 15C (S. Afr.) (providing for gray market imports for pharmaceuticals) and discussion *infra* notes 69–79 and accompanying text regarding gray market reform.

14 I believe patents remain a viable component of a sustainable innovation system, subject to recalibration. They have served a historic and important source for encouraging private sector pharmaceutical innovation. *See, e.g.*, Jayashree Watal & Rong Dai, WTO Staff Working Paper on Product Patents and Access to Innovative Medicines in a Post-TRIPS-Era 1 (WTO, Staff Working Paper ERSD-2019-05, Apr. 4, 2019) [hereinafter WTO Staff Working Paper] ("Using launch data from 1980 to 2017 covering 70 markets, the study finds that introduction of product patent for pharmaceuticals in the patent law has a positive effect on launch likelihood, especially for innovative pharmaceuticals. However, this effect is quite limited in low-income markets. Also, innovative pharmaceuticals are launched sooner than non-innovative ones, irrespective of the patent regime in the local market."); Karin Timmermans & Togi Hutadjulu, The TRIPS Agreement and Pharmaceuticals: Report of an ASEAN Workshop on the TRIPS Agreement and Its Impact on Pharmaceuticals 8, World Health Org. (2000), https://apps.who.int/medicinedocs/pdf/h1459e/h1459e.pdf [hereinafter ASEAN Workshop Report] ("Patents may have positive 'dynamic effects' so far as they foster the development of new products that benefit society."). For a discussion of the required recalibration, *see infra* notes 49–56 regarding suggested patent law recalibrations.

regulations – caps on patient costs under health-care plans or low-cost CLs[15] – price regulation alone is not enough. On the contrary, price regulation without regard to its impact on future R&D funding is a recipe for disaster. Shorn of rhetorical flourishes, the real issue is to determine the level of return on investment (ROI) sufficient to encourage future innovation by private enterprises, while allowing for reasonably priced deliverables to the public.

As the World Health Organization (WHO) recognized, such regulatory mechanisms are only part of a total strategy for resolving the growing global health-care crisis.[16] Yet I believe that unless we create regulatory models for sustainable innovative development – ones that assure both reasonable access to current medical treatments *and* R&D support for future innovations, including, but not limited to, *rational* IP protection for the results of such innovation – we will not be able to craft a global health system post-TRIPS that meets the critical present *and future* health needs of all peoples. This chapter is a modest effort to provide some potential pathways toward that goal.

In the first section, I explore the confluence of factors that has created consistent and pernicious barriers to reasonable access to medicines. Although there are many such barriers, including under-resourced health systems, I focus on those created as a result of skyrocketing prices in the pharmaco-medical sector because of their persistence and the growing recognition that such barriers are not merely a result of socioeconomic disparities, but threaten public health policies of even the most developed countries. I contend that the mandatory patent protection of pharmaceuticals required as a result of accession to the TRIPS Agreement forced countries *as a question of trade policy* to adopt a system that has proven readily subject to industry abuse. This abuse has ultimately resulted in the extension of patent monopolies far beyond the 20-year term required by the TRIPS Agreement. I explore the scope and practices of abuses that impede price-reductive competition, including evergreening, patent thickets, litigation excesses, and nontransparent pricing methodologies, and contend that these abuses can be curtailed through effective competitive regulatory mechanisms that include new models for sustainable innovation, with a strong social justice component that reduces or seriously erodes existing access barriers.

15 *See* TRIPS Agreement, *supra* note 1, at arts. 31, 31*bis*; Jerome Reichman, *Compulsory Licensing of Patented Pharmaceutical Inventions: Evaluating the Options*, 37 J. Law Med. Ethics 247 (2009); WTO Staff Working Paper, *supra* note 14; Roger Kampf, *Special Compulsory Licenses for Export of Medicines: Key Features of WTO Members' Implementing Legislation*, RSD-2015-07 (July 31, 2015).

16 *See also* World Health Org., Overall Programme Review of the Global Strategy and Plan of Action on Public Health, Innovation and Intellectual Property, Review Panel Report (Nov. 2017), https://www.who.int/medicines/innovation/gspa-review/en/; U.N. Secretary General, Report of the United Nations Secretary-General's High-Level Panel on Access to Medicines: Promoting Innovation and Access to Health Technologies (Sept. 14, 2016), http://apps.who.int/medicinedocs/documents/s23068en/s23068en.pdf.

In the second section, I explore the challenge of creating effective regulatory mechanisms that meet the dual goals of supporting sustainable innovation while reducing existing access barriers. I identify seven overlooked or frequently underappreciated roadblocks that often hamper reform efforts and explore potential solutions or workarounds tried by diverse countries to combat them. These seven roadblocks are (1) the natural hesitation to start the daunting process of reform for such a complex issue, including patent law recalibration; (2) the adoption of "quick fixes," such as CLs and gray market imports, without safeguards to ensure necessary continued innovation; (3) lack of transparency in drug pricing methodologies; (4) hidden competitive barriers from unaffiliated regulations, such as those governing school health, that impede accessibility even in the face of patent-based reforms; (5) an unrequited romance with technology that ignores the need to assure that artificial intelligence (AI) does not raise new accessibility barriers; (6) failing to act because purported industry voluntary self-regulation gives rise to an illusion that no further steps are necessary; and (7) the mirage that differential pricing resolves all accessibility challenges. I conclude by stressing the need to begin addressing these seven roadblocks so that access to medicines for all can be ensured as quickly as possible. Removing these roadblocks may not fully remove all access barriers, but it is undeniably a critical first step.

## Access Barriers in Innovation

### *The Rising Cost of Pharmaceuticals*

Undoubtedly, the costs of pharmaceuticals, including biosimilars and digital health delivery technologies, have been rising. Since 2012, in the United States (US) alone, the prices of the 12 top-selling patented drugs[17] have risen 68 percent.[18] These same drugs have been the subject of at least 71 granted patents *per drug*.[19] *Herceptin*®, patented since 1985, has a pending application that could extend its patent protection to 2033 – a potential 48-year monopoly.[20] Patents for *Herceptin*® have been the subject of diverse lawsuits in the US over efforts

17 The 12 top-selling drugs were, in descending order, – *Humira*® (*adalimumab*); *Rituxan*® (also sold as *MabThera*; *rituximab*); *Revlimid*® (*lenalidomide*); *Enbrel*® (*etanercept*); *Herceptin*® (Trastuzumab); *Eliquis*® (Apixaban); *Remicade*® (*infliximab*); *Avastin*® (Bevacizumab); *Xarelto*® (*trivaroxaban*); *Eylea*® (*afibercept*); *Lantus*® (*insulin glargine*); and *Lyrica*® (*pregabalin*). I-MAK, *Overpatented, Overpriced: How Excessive Pharmaceutical Patenting is Extending Monopolies and Driving Up Drug Prices* 7 (2018), https://www.i-mak.org/wp-content/uploads/2018/08/I-MAK-Overpatented-Overpriced-Report.pdf.

18 *Id.* at 6.

19 *Id.*

20 *Id.* at 3.

by competitors to market biosimilar equivalents. Although five *Herceptin®* biosimilar equivalents have been approved for marketing by the US Food and Drug Administration (FDA) since 2016, when the first request was filed,[21] only two have actually been marketed in the US as of February 2020.[22] The delay is largely due to ongoing litigation over potential patent infringement caused by the anticipated marketing of the approved biosimilars. Many of the disputed patents are not product patents per se, but related to delivery and manufacturing processes.[23]

No single factor is responsible for the challenge to global access to medicines that these high prices and related industry practices pose. To the contrary, "[m]any reasons exist why people do not get the healthcare they need, ranging from: under-resourced health systems, a lack of sufficiently qualified and skilled healthcare workers, and inequalities between and within countries."[24] Other weaknesses of public health systems include "regulatory obstacles for both originator and generic products [which] reflect weaknesses of public health systems overall, especially in poor countries."[25]

Significantly, there is growing recognition that access to medicines is not merely a concern of developing and least developed countries. To the contrary, even the US Congress has held hearings to examine the reasons behind

21 The first biosimilar for *Herceptin* for which United States marketing approval was sought, *Ogivri*, was filed in 2016. It was approved in December 2017. Due to patent litigation between the parties, Mylan/Biocron did not begin to market Ogivri until December 2019. *See* Kelly Davio, *Mylan and Biocon Launch Biosimilar Trastuzumab, Ogivri in the United States*, The Center for Biosimilars (Dec. 2, 2019), https://www.centerforbiosimilars.com/news/mylan-and-biocon-launch-biosimilar-trastuzumab-ogivri-in-the-united-states.

22 These two are *Ogivri* marketed by Myland/Biocon and *Kanjinti*, marketed by Amgen/Alletgan. *See generally* Robert Browne, *Analysis of the Trastuzumab Biosimilar Market as Herceptin Exclusivity Nears an End* (Apr. 23, 2019), https://www.biosimilardevelopment.com/doc/analysis-of-the-trastuzumab-biosimilarmarket-as-herceptin-exclusivity-nears-anend-0001. *See also Biosimilar Approval Status*, Biosimilars Review and Report (Jan. 15, 2020), https://biosimilarsrr.com/us-biosimilar-filings (containing chart and data regarding current approval and marketing status for biosimilars for *Herceptin*, *Trastuzumab*).

23 *See generally* Mike Zhai et al., *Why Are Biosimilars Not Living up to their Promise in the US?*, 8 AMA J. Ethics E669-678 (Aug. 2019), https://journalofethics.ama-assn.org/article/why-are-biosimilars-not-living-their-promise-us/2019-08 (discussing adverse impact of biosimilar availability as a result of patent litigation, including patent settlements that delay entry of biosimilars). For examples of filed patent complaints in the *Herceptin* biosimilar litigations, *see, e.g.*, *Genentech, Inc. v. Celltrion, Inc.*, Complaint (D. Del. July 11, 2018) (claiming infringement of 40 different patents related to intended launch of *Herceptin®* biosimilar), https://www.biosimilarsip.com/wp-content/uploads/2018/07/ded-1-99-cvde822-1_Genentech-Celltrion-Herceptin-Complaint.pdf; *Genentech, Inc. v. Pfizer, Inc.*, Complaint (D. Del Nov. 11, 2017) (similar), https://www.fdanews.com/ext/resources/files/2017/11/11-21-17-Genentech.pdf?1512743476.

24 U.N. Secretary-General, *supra* note 16, at 15.

25 *Id.*

skyrocketing drug prices and regulatory measures to reduce such costs in the future.[26]

## *TRIPS, Pharmaceuticals, and Trade Policy*

In 1994, with the creation of the TRIPS Agreement, trade policy became inextricably linked to the critical problem of providing accessible medicines to the public. Before the TRIPS Agreement, the decision to establish patent laws, and the scope of protection under those laws, was "the preserve of sovereign decision-making."[27] Forty-nine countries at the time did not provide patent protection for pharmaceutical products, 44 did not patent methods of treatment, and 10 countries did not patent pharmaceutical processes.[28]

Despite many countries' reluctance to surrender their sovereignty over the issue of patent protection for pharmaceuticals, they nonetheless accepted the stronger IP protections required under the TRIPS Agreement to gain *perceived trade benefits* provided under other World Trade Organization (WTO) agreements. IP protection "was expressly linked to trade concessions in non-intellectual property related areas such as agriculture and textile standards."[29] The developing countries' arguable abandonment of their insistence on welfare-enhancing protections in prior IPR treaty negotiations "appears to have been based in part on the perceived trade benefits obtained in other agreements simultaneously enacted with TRIPS."[30] I believe this trade-off was a predictable result of the "take it or leave it" nature of package *trade* deals that the TRIPS Agreement represented.[31] This package approach was repeated in numerous free trade agreements

26 *See* Examining the Actions of Drug Companies in Raising Prescription Drug Prices: Hearing Before the U.S. H. Comm. on Oversight and Reform, 116th Cong., 1st Sess. (Jan. 29, 2019), https://oversight.house.gov/legislation/hearings/examining-the-actions-of-drug-companies-in-raising-prescription-drug-prices; Drug Pricing in America: A Prescription for Change: Hearing Before the S. Comm. on Finance, 116 Cong., 1st Sess. (Jan. 29 and Feb. 26, 2019), https://www.finance.senate.gov/hearings/drug-pricing-in-america-a-prescription-for-change-part-i; https://www.finance.senate.gov/hearings/drug-pricing-in-america-a-prescription-for-change-part-ii.

27 WTO Staff Working Paper, *supra* note 14, at 3.

28 Negotiating Group on Trade-Related Aspects of Intellectual Property Rights, including Trade in Counterfeit Goods, Existence, Scope and Form of Generally Internationally Accepted and Applied Standards/Norms for the Protection of Intellectual Property, WTO Doc. MTN.GNG/NG11/W/24, 47–49 (May 5, 1988).

29 Doris Estelle Long, *"Democratizing" Globalization: Practicing the Policies of Cultural Inclusion*, 10 Cardozo J. Int'l & Comp. L. 217 (2002); *see also* ASEAN Workshop Report, *supra* note 14, at 29–30 ("While it is true that some countries put particular emphasis on TRIPS matters in the Uruguay Round negotiations, it is also true that other countries attached great importance to other areas, for example textiles and agriculture.").

30 Long, *supra* note 29.

31 *See, e.g.*, Michael Ryan, Knowledge Diplomacy: Global Competition and the Politics of Intellectual Property 12–13, 18, 92–93 (1998) (describing the impact of "bargain linkage diplomacy" during the Uruguay Round negotiations).

post-TRIPS, including, most recently, the Trans-Pacific Partnership[32] and the free trade agreement between the US, Mexico, and Canada (USMCA).[33] Similar to the TRIPS Agreement, the trade benefits offered in these package deals often overcome individual country reluctance to expand IPR in the pharmaceutical sector as a matter of domestic innovation policy. They also usually result in increasingly higher levels of protection under IP law ("TRIPS-plus"). Thus, in the recently negotiated USMCA, the TRIPS-plus provisions include the obligation to provide patents for "at least one of the following: new uses of a known product, new methods of using a known product, or new processes of using a known product"[34] and to provide data exclusivity protection for "biologics" for 10 years.[35] Although many of these TRIPS-plus provisions were ultimately rejected by the US Congress in its implementation of the USMCA,[36] strong patent protection reemerged in the subsequently negotiated US-China Trade Agreement (Phase 1).[37]

### *"Abuses" of the TRIPS Protection Regime*

As IP-based protections for pharmaceutical innovations increased post-TRIPS, drug companies relied increasingly on a variety of patent-based competition policies to enhance their position in the marketplace. Applications and grants

32 Trans-Pacific Partnership (Feb. 4, 2016), https://ustr.gov/sites/default/files/TPP-Final-Text-Intellectual-Property.pdf [hereinafter TPP]. Notably, however, many of the strong IPR provisions contained in the TPP, including in particular TRIPS-plus protections for data exclusivity and for patent protection for new uses and biosimilars, were suspended under the "replacement TPP," negotiated by the remaining parties after the United States withdrawal. The Comprehensive and Progressive Agreement for the TransPacific Partnership (2018), https://www.international.gc.ca/trade-commerce/trade-agreements-accords-commerciaux/agr-acc/cptpp-ptpgp/text-texte/cptpp-ptpgp.aspx?lang=eng.

33 Office of the U.S. Trade Rep., US-Mexico-Canada Free Trade Agreement [USMCA], https://ustr.gov/trade-agreements/free-trade-agreements/united-states-mexico-canada-agreement/agreement-between (last visited Feb.18, 2020).

34 *Id.* at art. 20.36(2). Interestingly, however, when the United States Congress finally ratified the USMCA, it expressly removed many of the TRIPS-plus provisions protecting pharmaceuticals, including the protection for new uses. *See infra* note 37. Unfortunately, it is too soon to tell if this is an aberration or a reflection of future developments given the inclusion of facially stronger patent protection in the subsequently negotiated US-China Trade Agreement (Phase I). *See infra* note 38.

35 *Id.* at art. 20.49. The provision regarding stronger protection for data exclusivity for biologics has similarly been removed by Congress in the USMCA Implementation Act. *See infra* note 37.

36 *See* USMCA Implementation Act, Public Law No. 116-113, sec. 101 (including the Protocol Amendment to the USMCA which expressly eliminated patent new uses and data exclusivity for biologics).

37 *See* Economic and Trade Agreement Between the Government of the United States of America and the Government of the People's Republic of China, ch. 1, sec. C (Dec. 13, 2019).

for pharmaceutical-related patents skyrocketed as companies developed patent portfolios designed to reduce the chances of a successful validity challenge to key patents and to block the entry of competing products. These portfolios included "evergreen patents," where companies extend their patent protection for a particular drug by seeking patent protection for new uses, new formulations to increase effectiveness, new delivery methods, and other post-grant improvements. For example, Abbott Laboratories lowered the dosage for its cholesterol treatment *Prilosec* and changed it from a tablet to a capsule to obtain a new patent.[38] Forest Laboratories similarly received a patent for its Alzheimer drug *Namenda* by reformulating it as *Namenda XR*; the "enhancement" was a changed dosage from twice to once daily.[39] Forest Laboratories also product-hopped patients to the new formulation by removing the originator drug *Namenda* from the market. A class action challenging such product-hopping as an unlawful attempt to avoid competition from generic versions of the parent drug was eventually settled for $750 million.[40]

Pharmaceutical companies also build "patent thickets," where patents are secured on a variety of related technologies to block others from developing potentially competitive products. Although there is a presumption that patent protection for a particular drug consists of a single patent,[41] the reality is that most drugs in the US have generally been protected by two to five patents.[42] Two to five patents may not qualify as an impressive "thicket." Yet there is ample evidence that pharmaceutical companies are building much larger thickets around key drug patents. These can include evergreen patents, manufacturing, dosage delivery, and monitoring technologies. Although patent thickets (often called "patent fences") are generally associated with technology-focused products such as smartphones, the pharmaceutical industry has increasingly adopted such techniques to protect key originator drugs from generics and biosimilars. Large defensive patent portfolios are often used to threaten counterclaims against any challenger's patent with the problematic result that improvidently granted patents remain unchallenged and retain their power to be used to prevent third party entries into the market. The use of these patent thickets will undoubtedly

38 Sarah Jane Tribble, *Drugmakers Play the Patent Game to Lock in Prices, Block Competitors*, Kaiser Health News (Oct. 2, 2018), https://khn.org/news/drugmakers-play-the-patent-game-to-lock-in-prices-block-competitors/.

39 *Id.*

40 Jonathan Stempel, *Allergan Signs $750 Million Settlement with Purchasers of Alzheimer's Drug Namenda*, Reuters (Dec. 24, 2019), https://www.reuters.com/article/us-allergan-namenda-settlement/allergan-signs-750-million-settlement-with-purchasers-of-alzheimers-drug-namenda-idUSKBN1YS1C4. The settlement was finally approved by the court in May 2020.

41 Lisa Larrimore Ouellette, *How Many Patents Does It Take To Make A Drug? Follow-On Pharmaceutical Patents and University Licensing*, 17 Mich. Telecomm. Tech. L. Rev. 299, 300 (2010) ("Although many have repeated this one-patent, one-drug assumption, there has been little empirical analysis of how many patents actually protect each drug.").

42 *Id.*

become more prevalent as more patents are issued for biologics which rely more heavily on new technologies for their creation and delivery. For example, AbbVie's rheumatoid arthritis drug *Humira*®, a biologic, is currently covered by more than 100 patents.[43]

### *Combatting Patent Abuses*

These and other post-TRIPS abuses of the patent system have undoubtedly contributed to the high cost of health care globally. Suggested alternatives to patent protection include: creating a nonprofit global entity to source R&D grants for biomedical research; patent "prizes" that dedicate a new innovation to the public in exchange for various monetary rewards, including graduated license fees to provide a reasonable ROI; and innovation processes that assure fewer proprietary rights, at least in the initial research phase.[44] These suggestions, and many others, provide excellent potential policy levers to enable sustainable innovation. However, I also agree with the WHO's assessment: "The evolving state of the global disease burden creates a constant demand for new and adapted technologies, so innovation and access are inevitably intertwined."[45]

In order to meet this demand, countries and international organizations such as the WHO have often supported a mix of private and public sector inputs because "innovation in the field … differs from innovation in general due to the ethical dimension of medical research, a rigorous regulatory framework, liability questions, and the high cost and high risk of failure."[46] Current evidence indicates that the reported "rising expenditure for medical research has not been matched by a proportionate increase in new products entering the market."[47] This failure, however, does not necessarily require abandonment of this public-private coordination. But it does open that door to what the WHO called "new models of innovation and for financing R&D."[48]

43 Cynthia Koons, *This Shield of Patents Protects the World's Best-Selling Drug*, BLOOMBERG (Sept. 7, 2017), https://www.bloomberg.com/news/articles/2017-09-07/this-shield-of-patents-protects-the-world-s-best-selling-drug.

44 *See, e.g.*, Doris Estelle Long, *Big Pharma Initiative Required to Avoid Price Controls*, CHICAGO DAILY LAW BULLETIN (Apr. 17, 2019); World Health Organization, WHO GUIDELINE ON COUNTRY PHARMACEUTICAL PRICING POLICIES (2015), https://apps.who.int/medicinedocs/documents/s21016en/s21016en.pdf.

45 WORLD HEALTH ORG., WORLD TRADE ORG., & WORLD INTELLECTUAL PROP. ORG., PROMOTING ACCESS TO MEDICAL TECHNOLOGIES AND INNOVATIONS: INTERSECTIONS BETWEEN PUBLIC HEALTH, INTELLECTUAL PROPERTY AND TRADE FIRST EDITION at 7 (World Trade Organization, World Health Organization and World Intellectual Property Organization 2013). Accord SECOND TRILATERAL REPORT ON ACCESS TO MEDICAL TECHNOLOGIES *supra* note 4, at 16 ("recognizing that innovation and access are inevitably intertwined – both are indispensable to meeting an evolving global disease burden.")

46 *Id.*

47 *Id.* at 12.

48 *Id.*

## Seven Roadblocks to Sustainable Innovation

Attempting to craft new models for sustainable innovation, which also includes recalibrating existing patent systems, is a daunting task. It is often made more difficult by overlooked or frequently underappreciated roadblocks hampering the beginning or successful completion of the creation of new policy levers to support such new models. Recognizing those potential roadblocks, and crafting workarounds to avoid them, or at least to reduce their adverse impact, can help countries develop socially just and sustainable innovation policies that meet domestic market needs.

This section outlines seven such roadblocks and provides suggestions for removing them or reducing the barrier they pose. They are (1) taking the first step, (2) "quick fixes," (3) transparency 101, (4) hidden competitive barriers, (5) the unrequited romance with technology, (6) the illusion of calm, and (7) the mirage of differential pricing.

### *Roadblock One: Taking the First Step*

The sheer magnitude of creating new models for assuring reasonable access to drugs while promoting sustainable development can be overwhelming. Among the first steps to take while considering other alternatives is to recalibrate the existing patent system to reduce identified abuses. Recalibration may not require an entire reconstruction of domestic patent laws, but it does require modifications that impose more robust regulatory mechanisms to counteract the numerous anticompetitive uses of current domestic patent regimes made by some companies. Fortunately, useful examples of such mechanisms already exist.

Many countries, including the US, are already undertaking a recalibration of subject matter eligibility to assure that pharmaceutical patents are only granted for *inventions,* not for simple discoveries of naturally occurring elements. In *Mayo Collaborative Servs. v. Prometheus Labs., Inc.*,[49] the US Supreme Court found that a process for determining the metabolization rate – and therefore the efficacy – of thiopurine drugs to treat autoimmune diseases lacked patentable subject matter *because* it did not sufficiently transform a law of nature into a potentially patent-eligible invention. In reaching this conclusion, the Court recognized the problematic impact of improvidently granted patents that essentially grant protection to "phenomena of nature, though just discovered, mental processes, and abstract intellectual concepts"[50] which it described as "the basic tools of scientific and technological work."[51] However, the Court also recognized that "too broad an interpretation of this exclusionary principle could eviscerate

49 566 U.S. 66 (2012).
50 *Id.* at 71.
51 *Id.*

patent law [because] all inventions at some level embody, use, reflect, rest upon, or apply laws of nature, natural phenomena, or abstract ideas."[52]

To prevent overprotection of inventions based on or related to natural phenomena, the Supreme Court established a two-part test. The first part requires a determination that the invention is directed to patent-ineligible categories. The second part requires that an applied-for process "focuses upon the use of a natural law also contain other elements or a combination of elements, sometimes referred to as an 'inventive concept,' sufficient to ensure that the patent in practice amounts to significantly more than a patent upon the natural law itself."[53]

This patent eligibility test has not always been easy to apply or predictable, but it represents an effort to assure that only those inventions in the biomedical field that are truly inventive are granted the 20-year term monopoly required under the TRIPS Agreement.[54] Unless an applied-for invention leaps the eligibility barrier of *Mayo* and its progeny,[55] it is not subject to an even more searching analysis under US patent inventiveness standards.

Other countries have applied similarly exacting tests to limit the grant of new use patents. For example, Section 3(d) of the Indian Patent Act provides that:

> The mere discovery of a new form of a known substance which does not result in the enhancement of the known efficacy of that substance is not a patentable invention … For the purposes of this clause, salts, esters, ethers, polymorphs, metabolites, pure form, particle size, isomers, mixtures of isomers, complexes, combinations, and other derivatives of known substance shall be considered to be the same substance, unless they differ significantly in properties with regard to efficacy.[56]

Similar to the subject matter eligibility test in the US under *Mayo*, Section 3(d) attempts to assure that only truly inventive new uses may be patented. Like *Mayo*, it has also been criticized for its lack of predictability, but I believe both of these efforts are necessary to recalibrate the patent system to begin reducing its abuse by drug companies.

By assuring that only innovations of sufficient inventiveness are rewarded with a 20-year monopoly under patent law, patent thickets can be reduced, and the building blocks of future innovation can remain available for all to use.

52 *Id.*

53 *Id.* at 72–3.

54 TRIPS Agreement, *supra* note 1, at art. 33.

55 *See, e.g.*, *Alice Corp. Pty. Ltd. v. CLS Bank Int'l*, 134 S. Ct. 2347 (2014) (discussing the latest Supreme Court explanation of this one-size-fits-all gateway barrier for patent ineligible subject matter; this decision addressed abstract ideas, as opposed to natural occurring phenomenon).

56 The Patent Act § 3(d), No. 39 of 1970, India Code (1998).

### *Roadblock Two: Quick Fixes*

Two of the most important "flexibilities"[57] recognized under the TRIPS Agreement relating to public health policy are CLs[58] and the importation of gray market versions of patented drugs.[59] Each can serve as a powerful counterbalance to high drug prices. But they are also among the most difficult competitive mechanisms to calibrate for creating a sustainable innovation system. As the Trilateral Report on *Promoting Access to Medical Technologies and Innovation* recognized: "Many medical technologies are expensive to develop but are relatively cheap to reproduce. In such instances, it would be unsustainable for companies to invest capital in product development and regulatory approval if their competitors were in a position to immediately introduce replica products."[60] This requires a delicate balance between access and profits, which ultimately requires a level of transparency from drug companies regarding issues such as R&D costs, pricing mechanisms, and global returns on investment – information that such companies are reluctant, at best, to disclose.[61] Although neither CLs nor gray market imports are "quick fixes" to the long-term problem of sustainable innovation, they can nevertheless serve as powerful components to a recalibrated patent system so long as appropriate steps are taken to assure their effectiveness.

#### *Compulsory License Reform*

CLs can fill gaps in health coverage when a patented drug is not "reasonably available" in the domestic market. Such "availability" can include consideration

57 Although the term "flexibility" does not appear in the TRIPS text, the concept has always been allowed for domestic variations in protection. *See, e.g.*, World Trade Organization, Ministerial Declaration of 14 November 2001, ¶ 4, WTO Doc. WT/MIN(01)/DEC/1, 41 ILM 746 (2002) [hereinafter Doha Declaration] ("[W]e affirm that the [TRIPS] Agreement can and should be interpreted and implemented in a manner supportive of WTO members' right to protect public health and, in particular, to promote access to medicines for all. In this connection, we reaffirm the right of WTO members to use, to the full, the provisions in the TRIPS Agreement, which provide *flexibility* for this purpose.") (emphasis added); *see also* TRIPS Agreement, *supra* note 1, at art. 8 ("Members may, in formulating or amending their laws and regulations, ***adopt measures necessary to protect public health*** and nutrition, and to promote the public interest in sectors of vital importance to their socio-economic and technological development, provided that such measures are consistent with the provisions of this Agreement.").

58 TRIPS Agreement, *supra* note 1, at arts. 31 and 31*bis*.

59 Although there is no express provision allowing gray market imports, exhaustion of intellectual property rights is excluded from enforcement under WTO dispute settlement, TRIPS Agreement, *supra* note 1, at art. 6, and was specifically strengthened by the Doha Declaration. Doha Declaration, *supra* note 57, at art. 5(d) ("The effect of the provisions in the TRIPS Agreement that are relevant to the exhaustion of intellectual property rights is to leave each Member free to establish its own regime for such exhaustion without challenge…").

60 Second Trilateral Report on Access to Medical Technologies, *supra* note 4, at 63.

61 *See infra* notes 85–89 and accompanying text regarding transparency.

of high prices resulting in patients' inability to afford the drug. For example, under Section 84 of the Indian Patent Law, a CL can be issued at any time three years after the patent grant on the grounds that the (1) ***reasonable requirements of the public*** with respect to the patented invention have not been satisfied; or (2) the patented invention is not ***available*** to the public ***at a reasonably affordable price***.[62]

In *Natco Pharma Ltd.*,[63] involving the grant of a CL for the manufacture and sale of Bayer's patented drug *Nexavar* for treating advanced-stage liver and kidney cancer, the Controller found that Bayer had satisfied neither "the reasonable requirements of the public" nor the obligation to provide the invention at a "reasonably affordable price." In establishing Bayer's failure to meet public needs, the Controller relied, in part, on the limited amount of the drug Bayer sold in light of patient need. He stated,

> During the last four years the sales of the drug by the Patentee at a price of about Rs.2,80,000/(for a therapy of one month) constitute a fraction of the requirement of the public. ***It stands to common logic that a patented article like the drug in this case was not bought by the public due to only one reason, i.e. its price was not reasonably affordable to them***.[64]

*Natco* is notable, because the Controller found that Bayer's use of a single "global" price for the drug did not assure its reasonable availability under the statute. To the contrary, he agreed with Bayer's argument that affordability had to be considered with regard to different classes and sections of the public: "I only wonder why the Patentee did not execute this concept by offering differential pricing for different classes/sections of public in India."[65]

The Controller further acknowledged, albeit indirectly, that ascertaining what qualified as a "reasonable price" would include some consideration of the costs of development and a reasonable ROI. Although he admitted, "***I do not fully agree*** with the submission of Patentee that reasonably affordable price has to be construed with reference to the public as well as patentee,"[66] he also underscored that consideration of the public need was only a "predominant" factor in the analysis, not the sole basis for establishing the need for a CL or its terms.[67] He also considered "the costs of development"[68] in setting the royalty rate. This implicit recognition that a reasonable price must include recovery of reasonable R&D costs and some reasonable profit (on a global basis),

62 The Patent Act § 84, No. 39 of 1970, INDIA CODE (1998) (emphasis added).

63 In re Natco Pharma Ltd, Application for a Compulsory License (Mumbai Controller of Patents 2012), https://patentdocs.typepad.com/files/compulsory-license-application.pdf.

64 *Id.* at 36 (emphasis added).

65 *Id.* at 35.

66 *Id.* at 36 (emphasis added).

67 *Id.*

68 *Id.* at 60.

I believe, assures that such licenses fulfill the critical goal of promoting sustainable, socially just innovation. Unfortunately, the Controller could not further analyze how to apply these elements in connection with a globally distributed product, because Bayer declined to provide information about its R&D costs or its global profits.

### *Gray Market Reforms*

Gray market imports can play a valuable role in assuring adequate access to reasonably priced drugs. For example, South Africa has provided for the importation of gray market versions of patented drugs without the permission of the patent holder since 1997. Section 15C(b) of the South African Medicines and Related Substances Act, subtitled "Measures to ensure supply of more affordable medicines," provides that the Minister of Health can allow the importation of "any medicine which is identical in composition, meets the same quality standard and is intended to have the same proprietary name as that of another medicine already registered in the Republic."[69] It further provides that gray market goods can be imported "notwithstanding anything to the contrary contained in the Patents Act."[70]

The South African Minister of Health currently requires importers to receive permits whose grant requires evidence that the importer can "comply with good manufacturing and distribution practices as determined by the Authority" and an "undertaking to ensure the continued safety, efficacy and quality of the medicine."[71] The purpose of these provisions is to allow South Africa to earn the benefit of lower prices for the drugs in other countries, including by importing generic versions. An initial challenge to the legislation by the Pharmaceutical Manufacturers' Association (PMA) and 39 pharmaceutical companies for patent infringement[72] was eventually discontinued as a result of the public outcry against it. This lawsuit ultimately led to a voluntary reduction in prices charged by pharmaceutical companies.[73]

69 Medicines and Related Substances Act 90 of 1997 § 15C (b) (S. Afr.).

70 *Id.* at § 15C (a).

71 *Id.* at § 5.

72 *Pharmaceutical Manufacturers Association of South Africa v. the President of the Republic of South Africa* (Case No. 4183/98, High Court of South Africa (Transvaal Provincial Division)).

73 William W. Fisher III & Cyrill Rogamonti, *The South Africa AIDS Controversy: A Case Study in Patent Law and Policy* 48, Harv. L. School: L. & Bus. of Patents (Feb. 10, 2005), https://cyber.harvard.edu/people/tfisher/South%20Africa.pdf. The case was also a "key factor leading to global dialogue around the potentially negative impact of IPRs on public health, culminating in the Doha Declaration on TRIPS and Public Health." Int'l Trade & Dev., Intellectual Property Policy of the Republic of South Africa Phase I, 14 (2018), https://www.gov.za/sites/default/files/gcis_document/201808/ippolicy2018-phasei.pdf.

Among the greatest challenges posed by gray market imports is the need to maintain quality control of such imports in light of the growing threat of counterfeit drugs.[74] This threat is not new,[75] and not caused solely by the importation of gray market drugs.[76] But such importation, without adequate controls,[77] undoubtedly adds to the problem. Among possible controls is limiting avenues through which gray market drugs can be imported, including prohibition of online marketing of such drugs except through licensed or authorized websites, and limiting unauthorized entry points for imported pharmaceuticals. For example, Nigeria has attempted to combat the problem of counterfeit drugs by limiting authorized importation to two national points of entry.[78]

Further limitations could include limiting importation to exporters and importers whose ability to provide safe non-counterfeit versions of the relevant drug is proven *before* such licenses are issued.[79] Finally, some method of enforcement, including tracking and monitoring such licensed shipments, combined with severe penalties for trafficking in counterfeit drugs, including potential prison sentences, must be established to assure public safety.

74 Trends in Trade in Counterfeit and Pirated Goods, OECD (2018) (estimating that trade in counterfeit goods is now 3.3 percent of global trade a threat to consumer health and safety); Kristina Acri, *Pharmaceutical Counterfeiting: Endangering Public Health and Safety,* Fraser Institute 30 (2018), https://www.fraserinstitute.org/sites/default/files/pharmaceutical-counterfeiting-endangering-public-health-society-and-the-economy.pdf ("Pharmaceutical counterfeiting is a pervasive problem, impacting nations of every size and income level, and drugs of every class and description. Since pharmaceutical treatments and cures are very high value products relative to their bulk, and demand is mostly price-inelastic over a wide price range, pharmaceutical counterfeiting has assumed enormous proportions. The immense size of the global pharmaceutical market and the margin between manufacturing costs and market price create a substantial economic incentive.").

75 World Health Organization, *Guidelines for the Development of Measures to Combat Counterfeit Drugs*, WHO/DM/QSM/9.1 (1999), https://apps.who.int/medicinedocs/pdf/h1456e/h1456e.pdf.

76 Kristina Lybecker, Illicit Trade in Counterfeit Medicines in Illicit Trade: Converging Criminal Networks (2016); Robin Cartwright & Ana Baric, *The Rise of Counterfeit Pharmaceuticals in Africa*, Enact (Nov. 2018), https://enactafrica.org/research/policy-briefs/the-rise-of-counterfeit-pharmaceuticals-in-africa.

77 *See Combatting Substandard and Falsified Medicines*, Usp (2017), https://www.usp.org/sites/default/files/usp/document/about/public-policy/combatting-substandard-and-falsified-medicines-policy-position.pdf (outlining various steps countries can take to protect their domestic and global supply chains from fake medicines); *Standards Development for Prescription Drug Supply Security,* U.S. Food & Drug Admin., https://www.fda.gov/drugs/drug-safety-and-availability/standards-development-prescription-drug-supply-chain-security (last visited Feb. 16, 2020) (listing diverse FDA reports accessible online for supply chain protections, including standardized numerical identification, validation and track and trace techniques).

78 Cartwright & Baric, *supra* note 76, at 30.

79 *See, e.g.*, Medicines and Related Substances Act 90 of 1997 (S. Afr.).

### *Roadblock Three: Transparency 101*

There is no consensus on what particular mechanism could best establish reasonable accessible prices for pharmaceuticals. Some have argued that pricing should be delinked from the cost of R&D. This principle is "based on the premise that costs and risks associated with R&D should be rewarded, and incentives for R&D provided, other than through the price of the product."[80] Such delinking can be facilitated through various mechanisms – including grants and tax credits for R&D investment, and milestone or end prizes granted for the outcomes of R&D – which could provide partial or complete funding for R&D.[81]

Other delinking alternatives include basing prices on the social value of the treatments. One methodology is to estimate the medical costs incurred if the treatments were not available. For example, for *Sovaldi®*, a breakthrough treatment to cure hepatitis C, the price would be based on the cost of a ($600,000) transplant – the end result if such treatment were unavailable.[82] Another methodology, "QALY," considers the effectiveness of a given drug in extending life for one year, providing a monetary value for such extensions over the course of treatment to establish a cap for drug prices.[83]

Unless complete public funding is available for all stages of R&D "from discovery to late stage and post approval clinical testing,"[84] delinking could ultimately undermine sustainable innovation. On an individual per treatment or per drug basis, such complete public funding might be possible. But given the current limited budgets even for developed countries, pricing considerations must reflect a reasonable ROI to assure adequate private participation. But to create such pricing methodologies, pharmaceutical companies must be transparent about the methods used to establish drug prices, including the basis on

80 Second Trilateral Report on Access to Medical Technologies, *supra* note 4, at 156.

81 *See generally An Economic Perspective on Delinking the Cost of R&D from the Price of Medicines*, Unitaids (2016), http://www.unitaid.org/assets/Delinkage_Economic_Perspective_Feb2016.pdf; second Trilateral Report on Access to Medical Technologies, *supra* note 4, at ch. III.

82 Sarah Kliff, *Each of These Hepatitis C Pills Cost $1,000. That's a Great Deal*, Vox (July 16, 2004, 4:30 PM), https://www.vox.com/2014/7/16/5902271/hepatitis-c-drug-sovaldi-price; Catherine Saenz, *UN High-Level Panel on Access to Medicines Takes Next Step at Human Rights Council*, IP-Watch 4 (Sept. 3, 2017), https://www.ip-watch.org/2017/03/09/un-high-level-panel-access-medicines-takes-next-step-human-rights-council/ ("The price of hepatitis C medicines was based on the price of a liver transplant.").

83 Denise Roland, *Obscure Model Puts a Price on Good Health – and Drives Down Drug Costs*, Wall St. J. (Nov. 4, 2019), https://www.wsj.com/articles/obscure-model-puts-a-price-on-good-healthand-drives-down-drug-costs-11572885123.

84 UNITAIDS, *supra* note 81, at 17.

which differential prices are established.[85] Part of this necessary transparency must include transparency on R&D costs, the recoupment of which is being sought through the pricing mechanism at issue, as well as the ROI such price is intended to earn and/or has already earned.

As *Natco*[86] amply demonstrates, such transparency is generally not provided without compulsion from government officials.[87] For example, although *Sovaldi* was undeniably a breakthrough discovery that cured hepatitis C, members of the US Congress considered its $84,000 price suspiciously high. The report of their findings provides troubling insights into pharmaceutical pricing methodologies:

> Gilead's own documents and correspondence show its pricing strategy was focused on maximizing revenue—even as the company's analysis showed a lower price would allow more patients to be treated … Over the eight months Gilead spent determining the price of Sovaldi, the company repeatedly made clear its primary focus was outmaneuvering potential competitors to ensure its drugs had the greatest share of the market, for the highest price, for the longest period of time … During its pricing process, Gilead also considered what price it could set without risking "external factors," such as public outrage, media attention, and congressional inquiries—potentially diminishing the drug's reputation or revenue potential … Review of company documents reveals that the ROI for acquiring Pharmasset and additional research and development were not key considerations in determining the pricing of these drugs.
>
> The $84,000 price tag significantly affected patient access. At least 27 state Medicaid [healthcare] programs—including Iowa and Oregon—restricted Sovaldi's use to only the sickest patients because of the drug's price and the cumulative cost of treating HCV patients. Likewise, private insurers instituted strict access controls for the drug.[88]

Such information calls into question the use of "value" alone as a basis for pricing formulations. It also suggests that actual R&D figures may be lower

85 For a further discussion of additional challenges to assuring effective differential pricing regimes, *see* notes 116 -119 and accompanying text. For the most recent international resolution on drug transparency, *see Italy Draft Resolution, Involving the Transparency of Markets for Drugs, Vaccines and Other Related Technologies,* Knowledge Ecology Int'l (Feb. 16, 2019), https://www.keionline.org/29721.

86 In re Natco Pharma Ltd, *supra* note 63.

87 *See* discussion regarding refusal of Bayer to provide R&D and pricing data, In re Natco, *supra* note 63, at 59–60.

88 U.S. Senate Committee on Finance, Executive Summary, The Price of Sovaldi and Its Impact on the U.S. Health Care System, 124th Cong. 1st Sess., S. Prt.114-20 (Dec. 20, 2015) [hereinafter Sovaldi Pricing Report].

than drug companies claim,[89] so that even if recovery of such costs is included in pricing methodologies, prices would still be markedly reduced. But to secure the necessary information to support such policy choices, transparency must be mandated, supported by stringent legal penalties to assure compliance, even the award of a CL for noncompliance.

### *Roadblock Four: Hidden Competitive Barriers*

In addition to the impact of the TRIPS Agreement on global pricing regimes for medicines, there are other competitive barriers in the pharmaceutical sector unrelated to such protections which can have an equally deleterious effect on accessibility. Among the most problematic drug pricing issues in the US is the 700 percent price increase for *EpiPen*®, an off-patent automatic injector system for *epinephrine* used to treat various allergies. This price increase is not due to the greater efficacy of the *EpiPen*® over other delivery systems, or even due to the brand loyalty that often keeps branded originator drugs competitive even when markedly cheaper generics enter the field. It is due, in significant part, to local regulations that have identified required medicines to be kept at educational institutions for student health emergencies *by name* or in a manner that allows only *EpiPen*® injectors to be used.[90]

When dealing with the critical issue of assuring adequate health care for all, an inventory of existing regulatory systems is a critical step in assuring that such unintended regulatory barriers are eliminated. Removing these school health regulations may not be at the top of the government's to-do list for reducing public health-care costs, but should certainly be included. In creating new domestic accessibility and innovation policies, it is critical to conduct a regulatory audit beyond obvious competition and IP rules to ensure that the benefits secured through their competitive regulation are not lost through other farcical (ineffective and impractical) unrelated "patches."

### *Roadblock Five: The Unrequited Romance with Technology*

While recalibrating patent law to reduce present competitive abuses by the pharmaceutical industry, we must carefully avoid overprotection for new technologies

89 Written Statement, Gerald F. Anderson, U.S. House Representatives Committee on Oversight and Reform, Hearing on What We Know and Don't Know About Drug Pricing 3–5 (Jan. 29, 2019) (discussing potential overestimation of research costs by pharmaceutical companies).

90 *See, e.g.*, Darrell Hulisz, *The Soaring Price of EpiPen®*, AMN Healthcare Educ. Services, https://www.rn.com/featured-stories/the-soaring-price-of-epipen/ (last visited Feb. 15, 2020); Jayne O'Donnell, *Family Matters: EpiPens had High-Level Help Getting into Schools*, USA Today (Sept. 21, 2016, 12:46 PM), http://www.usatoday.com/story/news/politics/2016/09/20/family-matters-epipens-had-help-getting-schools-manchin-bresch/90435218/.

that can result in loss of benefits from the recalibration. In short, we need to deal effectively with our romance with technology.

There is little doubt that AI innovations will have a positive impact in reducing R&D costs, including the cost of conducting clinical trials, as well as general access and delivery of medical treatment and advice.[91] Those benefits, however, could be undermined if companies are allowed to snarl this critical new technology in improvidently granted patents that allow companies to continue the abusive patent acquisition strategies currently employed to restrict competition in pharmaceuticals.[92] Companies are already securing rights to critical AI processes for improving drug design and effectiveness, while key issues about inventorship have yet to be fully addressed.[93] Similar to the debates over copyright and AI authorship,[94] there are emerging disagreements about inventorship.[95] Despite the relative newness of AI technology, however, the question of nonhuman inventorship is not new. In fact, one of the first reported US patents granted for an AI-related invention in 1998 was for "a neutral network based prototyping system and method."[96] The listed inventor, Stephen L. Thaler, admitted that the system was invented by the Creativity Machine, an early AI application, but he did not raise the issue before the US Patent and Trademark Office (USPTO)

91 Int'l Telecomm. Union, *Report of Focus Group on Artificial Intelligence for Health*, at 1 (2018), https://www.itu.int/en/ITU-T/focusgroups/ai4h/Documents/FG-AI4H_Whitepaper.pdf ("The potential for AI assistance in the health domain and advancing the field of digital health is immense, because AI can support medical and public health decision making at reduced costs, everywhere."); Shailendra Sinhasane, *Artificial Intelligence in the Pharmaceutical Industry: An Overview of Innovations*, MOBISOFT (Oct. 4, 2019), https://mobisoftinfotech.com/resources/blog/artificial-intelligence-in-the-pharmaceutical-industry; Bianca Nogrady, *Artifical Intelligence Shakes Up Drug Discovery,* THE SCIENTIST (May 1, 2019), https://www.the-scientist.com/bio-business/artificial-intelligence-shakes-up-drug-discovery-65787#:~:targetText=Australia's%20government%20drug%20safety,antifungal%20agent%20terbinafine%20in%201996.&targetText=Louis%20hit%20upon%20a%20way,is%20metabolized%20by%20the%20liver.

92 *See supra notes* 41–43 and accompanying text regarding patent thickets.

93 *See, e.g.*, Doris Estelle Long, *AI and Big Data Get Bigger, Will Nonhuman Inventors be Next?*, 165(253) CHI. DAILY L. BULL. 4 (Dec. 30, 2019); Doris Estelle Long, *Using Databases, Now and in the Future, is Critical for All,* 165(254) CHI. DAILY L. BULL. 2 (Dec. 31, 2019); *Artificial Intelligence Collides with Patent Law*, WORLD ECON. FORUM (2018), http://www3.weforum.org/docs/WEF_48540_WP_End_of_Innovation_Protecting_Patent_Law.pdf.

94 Doris Estelle Long, *Protecting Artificial Intelligence with Some Old Fashioned Know-How*, CHI. DAILY L. BULLETIN (May 23, 2018), http://www.dlnnews.com/editorial/20165.

95 *Compare* Ryan Abbott, *I Think, Therefore I Invent: Creative Computers and the Future of Patent Law*, 57 B.C. L. REV. 1079 (2016) (advocating for inventorship for computers), *with* AIPLA/AIPPI/FICPI, AI Colloquium Primer (Feb. 2019) (exploring current requirements for human authorship internationally).

96 U.S. Patent No. 5,852,815 (filed May 5, 1998) (issued Dec. 22, 1998).

because he was concerned his patent application would be denied.[97] Similar non-human inventorship applications continue to be filed without disclosure of their true nature,[98] powerful evidence that potentially improvidently granted patents may exist in this field.

In addition to inventorship, other critical issues include inventiveness based on randomness; the level of algorithmic transparency required to adequately disclose an AI invention; whether inventiveness should be judged against the skill level of an AI-enabled program/process; and who is liable for patent infringement by an AI program. These issues, among others,[99] should be addressed now to avoid the inevitable onslaught of patent applications and their predictable adverse impact on pharmaceutical costs that any overprotection might cause. Without considering the unique issues posed by AI, improvidently granted patents could adversely impact the price-reducing benefits AI and big data could otherwise bring to R&D costs, and ultimately to drug pricing.

Fortunately, many developed countries are already taking steps to address the challenges raised by AI patents. These efforts provide a useful basis for others to follow without "reinventing the wheel" and allow for a range of choices in approaches. For example, the Japanese Patent Office issued specific AI-related examples to cover a wider variety of AI-based inventions in 2018.[100] In 2019, the European Patent Office issued new guidelines specifically addressing AI and machine learning inventions.[101] In 2019, the USPTO similarly published revised guidelines to deal with software patents that also indirectly addressed some issues raised in patenting software[102] and added a new example in its Examination Guidelines to cover an AI-specific invention – a Method for Training a Neural

97 Ryan Abbott, *Patenting the Output of Autonomously Inventive Machines*, LANDLINES: A.B.A. (Sept./Oct. 2017), https://www.americanbar.org/groups/intellectual_property_law/publications/landslide/2017-18/september-october/patenting-output-autonomously-inventive-machines/.

98 *See* U.S. Patent No. 5,852,815, *supra* note 96.

99 These additional issues include a wide variety of legal personality and liability questions that must be decided before any form of AI-inventorship can or should be established effectively. *See, e.g.*, Kay Firth-Butterfield & Yoon Chae, *Robot Inventors Are on The Rise. But Are They Welcomed by The Patent System?*, WORLD ECO. FORUM (Apr. 20, 2018), https://www.weforum.org/agenda/2018/04/robot-inventors-on-rise-patent-system-US; Stuart Meyer, *A Looming AI War: Transparency and IP Rights*, JD SUPRA (Aug. 25, 2019), https://www.jdsupra.com/legalnews/a-looming-ai-war-transparency-v-ip-34524.

100 *Newly Added Case Examples for AI-Related Technologies*, JAPAN PATENT OFF. (Jan. 30, 2019), https://www.jpo.go.jp/e/system/laws/rule/guideline/patent/document/ai_jirei_e/jirei_tsuika_e.pdf (including Example 48, an autonomous vehicle, and Example 50, Method for Estimating Allergy Incidence Rate of Test Substance).

101 *See Revised Guidelines for Examination Section 3.3.31 Artificial Intelligence and Machine Learning*, EURO. PATENT OFF. (Sept. 17, 2018), https://www.epo.org/law-practice/legal-texts/html/guidelines2018/e/g_ii_3_3_1.htm.

102 2019 Revised Patent Subject Matter Eligibility Guidance (2019 PEG) published on Jan. 7, 2019 (84 Fed. Reg. 50), updated by Oct. 2019 PEG, 84 Fed. Reg. 55943 (Oct. 18, 2019).

Network for Facial Detection.[103] The German, US, and United Kingdom Patent Offices have also conducted specific studies on AI or held conferences to discuss diverse patent issues raised by AI innovations.[104]

These represent an excellent beginning, but the race to blanket AI technology with patents is already well underway and could stifle innovation if not carefully regulated. According to the 2019 WIPO Tech Study Report on AI, over 339,828 patents related to AI have been filed globally since 1980,[105] with 53 percent being filed since 2013.[106] The most marked increases in patenting activity between 2013 and 2016 "features a machine learning technique, deep learning,"[107] a critical component in AI technology. According to the WIPO Report, deep learning patents had an average annual growth rate of 175 percent; both robotics and control methods had an average 55 percent annual growth rate.[108]

On one hand, AI patents should be subject to appropriate refinements such that only sufficiently unique innovations are granted patents in the pharmaceutical sector; on the other hand, we must be careful not to lose the race to patent truly novel AI innovations. As we learned from the US patenting of biomedical innovations, business methods, and computer software, it is easy to confuse non-patentable building blocks – such as mathematical processes, algorithms, and data analysis (abstract ideas) – with patentable subject matter, simply because the applications of those building blocks appear new. For example, when the human genome was finally mapped in 2000, the ability to use such groundbreaking information was already restrained by over 1000 US patents covering DNA-related inventions.[109] In keeping with the US' historic romance with new

103 Method for Training a Neutral Network for Facial Detection, *supra* note 97.

104 *See, e.g.*, *"Smart IP" Conference at the DPMA*, German Patent & Trademark Off. (Feb. 22, 2019), https://www.dpma.de/english/our_office/publications/background/ai/smartip-konferenzimdpma/index.html (summarizing diverse issues raised at conference on AI); *Artificial Intelligence: Intellectual Property Policy Considerations*, U.S. Patent & Trademark Off. (Jan. 31, 2019), https://www.uspto.gov/about-us/events/artificial-intelligence-intellectual-property-policy-considerations (listing the various issues to be addressed at the conference); *Artificial Intelligence: A Worldwide Overview of AI Patents and Patenting by the UK AI Sector*, U.K. Intell. Prop. Off. (June 18 2019), https://www.gov.uk/government/publications/artificial-intelligence-a-worldwide-overview-of-ai-patents. For a good overview of international patent issues related to AI inventions, *see* AIPLA/AIPPI/FICPI, AI Colloquium Primer (Feb. 2019), https://ficpi.org/_/uploads/files/AIPLA-AIPPI-FICPI_Artificial_Intelligence_Colloquium_Patent_ONLY_Primer.pdf.

105 World Intellectual Property Organization, Technology Trends 2019: Artificial Intelligence 23 (2019), https://www.wipo.int/edocs/pubdocs/en/wipo_pub_1055.pdf.

106 *Id.* at 39.

107 *Id.*

108 *Id.* at 40.

109 Andrew Pollack, *U.S. Hopes to Stem Rush Toward Patenting of Genes*, N.Y. Times (June 28, 2000), https://archive.nytimes.com/www.nytimes.com/library/national/science/062800sci-genome-patents.html.

technologies, patent protection in the biomedical field was eventually refined once that technology was fully understood by the courts.[110] But we can ill afford such delay for an advance as critical as AI.

### *Roadblock Six: The Illusion of Calm*

This may be the most significant roadblock countries have to face. This illusion arises from actions by industry that make such regulations seem unnecessary, such as offers of differential pricing in-country to assure access to low-income patients, self-regulation, and even voluntary licenses that support entry by generic competitors.[111] Such illusions of calm can even arise from the pharmaceutical industry's settling litigation to avoid the award of CLs, as was the case with the South African HIV/AIDS gray market challenge.[112]

Such actions reduce the possibility of lower prices being imposed through governmental action. But even more problematically, they conceal necessary information about pharmaceutical pricing practices, which makes it difficult to establish properly calibrated future regulatory mechanisms.

I am not advocating that offers to reduce pharmaceutical prices should be rejected. To the contrary, although regulation to assure *continued* availability of reasonably priced access remains a critical goal, temporary reductions can be helpful in at least beginning the reduction of prices. South Africa has successfully used its Competition Commission to investigate such anticompetitive actions as a coordinated refusal to license generic drug manufacturers, price-fixing, and geographic market divisions to maintain high prices. Many of these cases have been settled through voluntary agreements, which have helped increase access to medicines. They have also encouraged even more prosecutions – an undeniably positive outcome.[113]

South Africa demonstrates the appropriate use of industry settlements to encourage greater scrutiny. Because offers of industry self-regulation in the form

110 *See Ass'n for Molecular Pathology v. Myriad Genetics, Inc.*, 569 U.S. 576 (2013) (rejecting patent protection for mapping and isolating the BRCA 1&2 genes). "Myriad's principal contribution was uncovering the precise location and genetic sequence of the BRCA1 and BRCA2 genes within chromosomes 17 and 13 … Groundbreaking, innovative, or even brilliant discovery does not by itself satisfy the §101 inquiry [for patentability]…" *Id.* at 590–91.

111 *See infra* note 116.

112 *See* Medicines and Related Substances Act 90 of 1997 § 5 (S. Afr.); *Pharmaceutical Manufacturers Association of South Africa v. the President of the Republic of South Africa* (Case No. 4183/98, High Court of South Africa [Transvaal Provincial Division]), and the accompanying text regarding pharmaceutical companies' challenge to South African laws allowing the importation of patented gray market goods without the patent holder's permission.

113 Catherine Saez, *Use Competition Law For Wider Access To Cheap Medicines?*, IP Watch (Sept. 29, 2017), https://www.ip-watch.org/2017/09/27/use-competition-law-wider-access-cheap-medicines/.

of discounts or differential pricing – without adequate transparency or sufficient guarantees of continuity – are not the solution they purport to be. In the US, to counter the public outcry against the $84,000 price tag for *Sovaldi®*, Gilead ultimately provided a 10 percent discount. However, the impact of such discount was limited, since only 2.4 percent of all patients could afford the treatment even with the discount.[114]

Offers of self-regulation by industry have proven equally problematic. In a notorious example, the CEO of Johnson & Johnson said that the pharmaceutical industry needed to self-police on pricing. Three days later, Johnson & Johnson raised the prices of hundreds of its drugs, "including drugs that account for billions in Medicare [US health care] spending."[115]

Voluntary licenses, discounts, and dispute settlement agreements are undeniably useful in resolving current competitive abuses. But they should ***not*** be used to excuse or pause ongoing efforts to craft the competitive regulatory solutions necessary to create an effective sustainable innovation policy across all drugs and all patients – nor should they be used to shield critical information about pharmaceutical pricing practices.

### *Roadblock Seven: The Mirage of Differential Pricing*

International trends are often cyclical. Differential pricing was the prevalent global pricing response to the South African HIV/AIDS dispute in 1998[116] and the intended result of Article 31*bis* of the TRIPS Agreement, which expressly tied the rate of authorized CLs to the "economic value to the importing member" of the authorized use.[117] Yet there is evidence that drug companies have once again adopted global pricing as their primary price mechanism despite the clear pushback in favor of differential pricing as a critical regulatory technique.

Differential pricing, also referred to as "tiered pricing," is not limited to the range of prices available for authorized, essentially generic, or gray market imports. To the contrary, it can be applied across a wide range of locally sourced drugs and can be based on a variety of factors, including per capita differences in

114 Sovaldi Pricing Report, *supra* note 88.

115 *Wyden Statement at Finance Committee Hearing on Drug Prices with Pharma CEOs*, U.S. Senate Comm. On Fin. (Feb. 26, 2019), https://www.finance.senate.gov/wyden-statement-at-finance-committee-hearing-on-drug-prices-with-pharma-ceos.

116 *See* discussion *supra* notes 69–73 and accompanying text regarding South Africa's use of gray market imports to combat domestic HIV/AIDS pandemic.

117 TRIPS Agreement, *supra* note 1, at art. 31*bis* (2) ("Where a compulsory license is granted by an exporting Member under the system set out in this Article and the Annex to this Agreement, adequate remuneration pursuant to Article 31(h) shall be paid in that Member *taking into account the economic value to the importing Member of the use that has been authorized in the exporting Member.*") (emphasis added).

intended geographic markets or among intended patients, value-based pricing, ethical pricing, and scarcity.[118]

Although there is a strong presumption that differential pricing necessarily results in lower domestic drug prices, there are numerous challenges to ensuring that patients are actually the beneficiaries of such differential pricing. Diversion of lower priced drugs to unintended recipients, including transborder diversions, was expressly recognized as a threat to the goals of enhanced access under Article 31*bis*. The Annex to the TRIPS Agreement (TRIPS Annex) requires specific markings to identify the drug "as being produced under the system."[119] Among the allowed "markings" are specific labeling, special packaging, and "special coloring or shaping" of the covered products so long as such marking "does not have a significant impact on price."[120]

In addition to labels and markings designed to distinguish in-country-use-only imports, the TRIPS Annex also requires both "reasonable" and "proportionate" administrative measures to prevent reexportation of covered drugs,[121] and "effective" enforcement measures "to prevent the importation into, and sale in, their territories of products produced under the system and diverted to their markets."[122] These types of enforcement provisions are the minimum that should be available to assure that the patients designed to receive the benefits of the lower cost actually receive the drugs.

Although the focus of these provisions seems to be preventive border control measures, such measures may not be sufficient to keep differential prices an effective economic reality for domestic patients. To the contrary, anti-diversion protections should be extended to include domestic diversions of lower priced goods into the secondary gray market. There is disturbing evidence of a growing international secondary gray market that not only diverts imported gray market drugs to other countries, but also sells the drugs at *higher* costs in order to profit from domestic shortages.[123] In some cases, markups have been reported as high as 3000 percent–4000 percent of their typical price.[124] Such prices are usually charged for diverted drugs already in short supply in the regular market.[125]

118 Patricia Danzon, *Differential Pricing of Pharmaceuticals: Theory, Evidence and Emerging Issues*, 36 PHARMACOECONOMICS 12 (2018).

119 TRIPS Agreement, *supra* note 1, at Annex to the TRIPS Agreement § 2(b)(ii).

120 *Id.*

121 *Id.* at Annex to the TRIPS Agreement § 3.

122 *Id.*

123 U.S. HOUSE COMM. ON OVERSIGHT & REFORM, SHINING LIGHT ON THE GRAY MARKET: AN EXAMINATION OF WHY HOSPITALS ARE FORCED TO PAY EXORBITANT PRICES FOR PRESCRIPTION DRUGS FACING CRITICAL SHORTAGES, sec. II B (July 25, 2012), https://oversight.house.gov/sites/democrats.oversight.house.gov/files/documents/7.25.12%20Staff%20Report%20Shining%20Light%20on%20the%20Gray%20Market.pdf.

124 *Id.* at 5.

125 *Id.*

Perhaps even more problematic, widespread diversion into the gray market can actually contribute to drug shortages.[126]

There is little doubt that differential pricing can be a valuable tool in assuring adequate access to pharmaceuticals. But to ensure that such differential pricing is more than a mirage, it is critical to take appropriate steps to trace, monitor, and track such lower priced drugs to confirm they are not diverted. Enhancing regular procedures for protecting the drug supply to track such diversions is a good first step. So is creating both civil and criminal liability for those engaging in such unauthorized diversions. Without these additional enforcement steps, the benefits of differential pricing could well become a mirage rather than reality.

## Conclusion

There are no "quick fixes" to the challenge of combatting high drug prices that make access so problematic globally. Each country's policies to meet those challenges must necessarily be reflective of its own unique situation. But the ultimate goal should be the same: to create policies in favor of socially just and sustainable innovation. This chapter has identified seven often overlooked roadblocks that hinder the creation of such policies. There are undoubtedly many more. Current competition policies that intersect with health or IP issues may present unfortunate barriers to sustainable innovation if their adverse impact is not fully appreciated. For example, the US still considers agreements between competitors to delay or abandon the market entry of generics and biosimilar equivalents potentially lawful so long as they survive the "rule of reason" test under US antitrust law,[127] even in the current environment where the adverse impact of delaying competitive drug entries seem particularly hard to justify. Similarly, laws regarding the scope of permissible disclosure by the government of confidential business information submitted to it might prevent the disclosure of necessary data on pricing transparency to relevant governmental organizations.[128] An ongoing audit of potentially related laws can help assure that domestic innovation policies are not undercut by local "roadblocks," but such audits should not take the place of, or unduly delay, other actions to support sustainable innovation. Creating socially just innovation policies serves everyone's interest. The secret is to start the journey toward creating those policies. NOW.

126 *Id. See also Drug Shortages: Root Causes and Potential Solutions*, Food & Drug Admin. (2019), https://www.fda.gov/media/131130/download.

127 *See, e.g., Fed. Trade Comm. v. Actavis*, 133 S. Ct. 2223 (2013).

128 *See, e.g., Food Mktg. Inst. v. Argus Leader*, 139 S. Ct. 2356 (2019) (broadening the basis on which the disclosure of government-held confidential business information can be denied).

# 21 Not Just Patents and Data Exclusivity

## The Role of Trademarks in Integrated IP Strategy – Where Lies the Public Interest?

*Graham Dutfield**

## Introduction

In the past few years, there has been much controversy about the life-cycle management practices of drug companies. These practices include extending the market power of a given medicine beyond the lifetime of the first patent covering the active pharmaceutical ingredient ('evergreening'), or shifting that power over to a follow-on product that may or may not be much different from, or better than, the previous one ('producing line extensions'). The latter case may sometimes entail withdrawing the initial brand-name product so as not to undermine the market for the second one, while – in some cases – carrying over other protectable 'signs' like shape and color to the newer product. Such practices are enabled by intellectual property (IP) protection and by regulations dealing with approval, naming, and pricing that concern or otherwise impact the medical products trade. Further enablement arises from the recent expansion in the subject matter of IP beyond its traditional remits, including trademarks.

* This article benefited from conversations with Uma Suthersanen, Cesar Ramirez-Montes, Joshua Sarnoff, and attendees at the University of Technology Sydney's Law and History seminar on 1 July 2019, and at the Innovation, Justice, and Globalization – A Celebration of J.H. Reichman Conference at Harvard Law School in September 2019, at which earlier versions of this article were presented. I am grateful to Ruth Okediji and Margo Bagley for their encouraging reactions, to Ruth and Isabella Alexander (UTS) for their respective invitations, and to Sri Ragavan and Amaka Vanni for inviting my participation in their collection, and for reviewing an earlier draft. The article constitutes part of a broader investigation with Uma Suthersanen on the competition law aspects of pharmaceutical branding.

Numerous reports from intergovernmental[1] and nongovernmental organizations concerning these practices and their impacts on pricing, access, and competition have contributed to critical debates.

However, current concerns about pharmaceutical pricing, access, and competition issues understandably have tended to focus largely, if not exclusively, on patents. The scholarly contribution of this article is that it diverges from the entirely understandable, but ahistorical and somewhat reductive, tendency to narrow critiques down to patents, or else to discuss each IP right (IPR) in isolation.[2,3] Using patents and trademarks together is fundamental to how actors in this sector have always done their business, as historical researchers in the

1 European Commission (DG Competition), Pharmaceutical Sector Inquiry – Final Report (2009); European Commission, Report from the Commission to the Council and the European Parliament, Competition Enforcement in the Pharmaceutical Sector (2009–2017): European Competition Authorities Working Together for Affordable and Innovative Medicines (2019); OECD, Directorate for Financial and Enterprise Affairs – Competition Committee, *Excessive Prices in Pharmaceutical Markets. Background Note by the Secretariat*, DAF/COMP(2018)12 (2018); United Nations Secretary-General's High-Level Panel on Access to Medicines, *Promoting Innovation and Access to Health Technologies* (2016). The latter report does acknowledge the need for what the present article investigates: 'The panel's deliberations focused on patent law, and understandably so. But trademarks and copyright can exert monopolistic effects in the market that rival those associated with patents and with a far greater duration. The Report is silent on these issues, but there is much work that should be done to tackle the combined effects of different IP rights and other non-IP factors on the cost, distribution accessibility of medicines and health technologies.'

2 *E.g.* T. Amin & A. Kesselheim, *Secondary Patenting of Branded Pharmaceuticals: A Case Study of How Patents on Two HIV Drugs could be Extended for Decades*, 31(10) Health Aff. 2286–94 (2012); G. Dutfield, *Healthcare Innovation and Patent Law's 'Pharmaceutical Privilege': Is There a Pharmaceutical Privilege? And If so, Should We Remove It?*, 12(4) Health Econ. Policy Law 453–70 (2017); O. Gurgula, *Strategic Accumulation of Patents in the Pharmaceutical Industry and Patent Thickets in Complex Technologies – Two Different Concepts Sharing Similar Features*, 48(4) IIC Int. Rev. Int. Prop. Comp. Law 385–404 (2017); I-MAK, *Overpatented, Overpriced: How Excessive Pharmaceutical Patenting is Extending Monopolies and Driving up Drug Prices* (2018), http://www.i-mak.org/wp-content/uploads/2018/08/I-MAK-Overpatented-Overpriced-Report.pdf. There is also the phenomenon of 'tertiary patenting,' whereby a medicine's use or administration is tied to a patented medical device. R.F. Beall & A.S. Kesselheim, *Tertiary Patenting on Drug-Device Combination Products in the United States*, 36(2) Nat. Biotechnol. 142–45 (2018).

3 Two book-length exceptions, both of which mainly cover the United States, are J.M. Gabriel, Medical Monopoly: Intellectual Property Rights and the Origins of the Modern Pharmaceutical Industry (2014) and J.A. Greene, Generic: The Unbranding of Modern Medicine (2014).

area have shown, and so they need to be analyzed together.[4] This alternative approach forms the article's main claim to originality.

More specifically, in this article, we consider the role of trademarks and trademark expansionism in countering free competition beyond the lifetime of patents, and – in some cases – assisting the transfer of value to related products from the same company. We consider whether this extends the scope of legal or regulatory monopolies too far in the direction of originator companies' interests by encouraging opportunistic behaviors that are detrimental to consumers' ability to choose in their best interests (thus running counter to a fundamental justification of trademarks), and that also unduly restrict healthy competition.

This critique requires that we consider the meaning of branding and assess its relationship with trademarks. The conditions that make branding an effective means to secure and maintain a strong market position are briefly explained. This leads to a discussion on the appeal of branding strategy for this industry, considering the specificities of pharmaceuticals and of the industry. It is important in this context to understand that the constraints and opportunities of regulatory frameworks concerning safety, efficacy, and pricing have affected pharmaceutical branding and the drugs market as a whole. Whereas only brand names and logos were protected by trademarks in the past, product differentiation and trademark coverage are now also applied to the shapes and colors of medicines. We show through some recent case studies how the industry increasingly looks beyond patents and product names to these nontraditional trademarks with the aim of further extending and reinforcing market power on products when patents alone can no longer do the job.

One intriguing issue concerns the possible link between branding covering names of products and their visual appeal and placebo responses that may arise. Placebo responses can affect the extent to which the same chemical substances used for the same medical issues are interchangeable. There are serious questions as to the public interest in trademark extension, to the extent that trademarks, especially covering the appearance of medicines, can cause or increase placebo phenomena that trademark protection prevents from being extendable to generic alternatives containing the same active ingredient.

4 *See* G. Dutfield, That High Design of Purest Gold: A Critical History of the Pharmaceutical Industry, 1880–2020 109–10 (2020). Beyond patents and trademarks are regulations restricting disclosure or use of clinical trials and other data needing to be submitted to regulators as a condition for acquiring marketing authorization, as is provided under Article 39.3 of the TRIPS Agreement: 'Members, when requiring, as a condition of approving the marketing of pharmaceutical or of agricultural chemical products which utilize new chemical entities, the submission of undisclosed test or other data, the origination of which involves a considerable effort, shall protect such data against unfair commercial use. In addition, Members shall protect such data against disclosure, except where necessary to protect the public, or unless steps are taken to ensure that the data are protected against unfair commercial use.'

We consider these practices in the light of regulatory systems that help shape business practice and we reflect upon the consequences. In doing so, we aim to provoke debate about whether there are negative implications for the public, and what should be done legally to alleviate them.

## Pharmaceutical Branding and Trademarks

### *Branding and Trademarks*

Central to any marketing strategy is to have a good name for the product, one which directs those purchasing drugs to that product and not to alternative ones. The wider regulatory environment on the naming of chemicals and active ingredients of drugs is the context that makes strategic naming effective in the marketplace. Names can be surprisingly fluid, as we will see.

Trademark law is what helps to make branding work for sellers, manufacturers, and distributors. Much of the value of the mark lies in its ability to distinguish a good from similar ones made or sold by competitors that are otherwise substitutable. Often, the most valuable marks are those used with products that *lack* novelty or else are very similar, if not identical, to goods already on the market. If the mark attracts customers willing to pay a higher price than similar equivalent products, it is a valuable asset. This was understood by the pharmaceutical industry from the beginning. When companies file a patent on a drug, they need to make the case that it had no prior existence until they brought it into the world. Trademarks make no such claim. The sign may be new but the product, whether as such or as a specific chemical substance, does not have to be. Of course, all invented drugs are exposed to *the possibility of* competition once patents expire, and this is where trademarks become especially important. The patent monopoly is at an end and the market should fall open for others who have their own version of the product hitherto protected by the patent.

We should not be surprised by the industry's huge ongoing reliance on trademarks as their subject matter scope and market functions keep on expanding. Indeed, this expansion is arguably a defining feature. Like a Van Gogh painting which now sells for millions but is made of nothing more – in the material sense – than an old canvas, a frame, and some old paint, there is a huge difference between the manufacturing costs of drugs (especially branded prescription ones), including their constituent chemicals, and their price. The Van Gogh brand, whose market power is vastly bigger more than a century after his death, guarantees the acquired prestige of the works associated with it that makes people willing to pay vast prices for a picture depicting a landscape or a bunch of flowers in a vase, knowing that it can probably be sold for a profit. Whether we talk of esthetic creations or functional objects, this price effect is obviously something that any company would find highly desirable.

In a sense, there is only one of everything. There are countless numbers of $H_2O$ molecules in the Atlantic Ocean, as there are of hydrogen atoms in the universe. Every one of those is the same (in that they are all identical to each other) so that one can stand for another without any difference whatsoever. But often there is a degree of variability among a class of things that many would still assume to be identical to each other. Is a form or variant of a chemical the same thing as that chemical? Or is it something else entirely? It is important to remember that a pill is not just a package comprising multiple numbers of the specified active ingredient, but a collection of those plus various additional chemicals, formulated to enhance the effectiveness of the drug product after it has entered the body. Paradoxically, it is both a pure substance and a mixture.

There are two ways to market a 'new' product. You can advertise a truly new product that is better than anything we have seen before, or you can convey a false impression that it is new and better than what we have now. The industry employs both methods. To make such strategies possible, it helps if the legal and regulatory regimes provide an effective, whether or not intended, 'zone of exclusion' to keep out usurpers, that is, rival companies with products that are in competition or that could compete if permitted to approach this zone.

Commercially, there is much at stake in the ability of a company to control the borderlines between sameness and difference, and much effort is made to 'impose' differentiation in various ways. According to Greene:

> Over the past few decades, critics of generic drugs have repeatedly sought new forms of information to differentiate the manufacturing processes of generic drugs from their brand-name counterparts. As controversies over brands and generics have continued, the number of proofs of difference – and protocols for proving similarity – have continued to expand.

An originator firm seeks as far as the rules allow to achieve a demarcation of the same/different border so that whatever the generic producer would seek to market is either on the wrong side and is therefore significantly different, or else is perceived as being so. The intention is for the generic drug to be deemed a poor substitute or not a substitute at all. The originator firm will also try to present its follow-on product, which might be very similar chemically, as being a wholly different thing for marketing and patenting purposes, but it might want to present it as something similar for the benefit of the regulators. For a generic firm's part, it would seek to oppose any move to prevent its equivalent product from being regarded as different in any substantive sense from the original product (except for the lower price). However, and here things get even more interesting, a generic seller might see an advantage in marketing its own drugs as being different from identical competing products in order to charge higher prices. Hence, in the United Kingdom, we have generic *ibuprofen* sold as '*Ibuprofen*' and as the pricier '*Nurofen*.'

Some over-the-counter branded products muddy the waters of clarity as far as content goes. We tend to think of *Alka-Seltzer* as a single product, appealingly effervescent, good for hangovers, and containing three active ingredients including *aspirin*. In fact, the name *Alka-Seltzer* is applied to a diverse range of formulations aimed at relieving the various symptoms of colds, headaches, upset stomachs, general body aches and pains, and so on. But at least in every *Alka-Seltzer* container, you will find the same active contents, albeit in different forms and combinations. *Anadin* (or *Anacin* in North America), an analgesic launched in Britain in 1932 and currently sold by Pfizer, is far more diverse in terms of what the products contain. Different *Anadin* products may consist of *aspirin* and caffeine, *paracetamol*,[5] or *ibuprofen*. At least the contents are clearly labeled and the product range tends to be distinguished by additional words and phrases, often separately trademarked. For example, Bayer has recently been selling *Alka-Seltzer* products specifically for treating hangovers: *Alka-Seltzer Morning Relief* and *Alka-Seltzer Wake-Up Call*!

This discussion needs to be understood in the context of regulation concerning the naming of chemicals and products. Policy and law concerning naming of drug products is very specific, goes back many decades, and has had a huge influence on how the industry does its business, and can thus be seen as part of what makes the industry special and unique. There is a whole framework of rules concerning the naming of chemicals and products which partially operates in conjunction with trademark law (and to a lesser but still very important extent, patent law). These rules have enormous repercussions for business strategy, industrial structure, research and development decisions, and the interests of the public. Pertinent in this context is the way that product regulation enabling differentiation between different types of therapeutic entities effectively sets boundaries around the industry and thus helps to define not just the pharmaceutical product but also the company *and* the industry itself.

International efforts to standardize the naming of drugs took a much longer time in coming than for chemicals generally, and only really began from the late 1940s, a period that also saw the foundation of the United Nations and the Bretton Woods institutions, and the proclamation of the Universal Declaration of Human Rights. The standardization of pharmaceutical nomenclature was largely initiated by the World Health Organization (WHO) and the American Medical Association. The outcome is the WHO-administered list of nonproprietary names. These are generic names that are simplified and systematized and are no one's property: they cannot be registered as trademarks.

Without knowing any better, it might seem logical that as brand X denotes active ingredient chemical x, Y should be for y, and Z for z. Accordingly, *Aspirin* is *acetyl salicylic acid* (ASA), and nothing but ASA. ASA is *Aspirin*, ASA is nothing else, *Aspirin* is nothing else, and that is the end of it. However, reality is so often different. To consider some examples, *ibuprofen* may be sold as *Advil* by some manufacturers, *Nurofen* by others, and alternatively as just plain *Ibuprofen*. *Losec*, *Prilosec*, and *Nexium* are all used for the same active ingredient. *Sildenafil* may be marketed as *sildenafil* or as *Viagra*, or even as *Revatio*, depending on what it is used for, as will be discussed later.

5 In the United States, the generic name for *para-acetylaminophenol* is not *paracetamol* but *acetaminophen*.

*Zantac* is an interesting case in this context. Similar to *Tagamet*, which was the first medicine of its kind and, in terms of its medical use, *Losec* and *Nexium*, *Zantac* was a blockbuster-status drug dealing with gastric and digestive tract complaints, such as peptic (stomach and duodenal) ulcers and acid reflux. In 1978, Glaxo came up with a powerful $H_2$ receptor antagonist, the second medicine of this type after the aforementioned *Tagamet*. For several years, *ranitidine* sold as *Zantac* was the world's top selling drug, with its predecessor (chemically, *cimetidine*) as number two. However, now that *ranitidine* is a generic drug and GlaxoSmithKline has much less need for the name, *Zantac* is no longer what it was. Now called *Zantac 75*, it continues to be applied to *ranitidine*. But the use of *Zantac* is now also associated with a quite different medicine, albeit targeted at the same health problems as the original *Zantac* product, i.e. digestive tract disorders. This second medicine is called *Rapidol Express*, whose active ingredient is not *ranitidine* but an extract of brown algae, which itself is marketed under the name of *Phycodol*, a registered word mark. This time, *Zantac* is not the name of the product (which is in fact classed as a medical device) but serves instead as an indicator of the product's use. Thus, it is marketed as *Rapidol™ Express by Zantac™*.

### *From Names to Colors and Shapes*

If we return to the Van Gogh painting analogy discussed earlier, a drug is obviously not a painting. Its consumption is literal, entailing its own *physical* destruction. Furthermore, it is a rather undistinguished-looking object, and there are limits as to how to make a pill's appearance communicate information, desirability, or distinction. There really is not much information that such an object can communicate. Of course, there is a brand name and its useful properties are indicated on the label. But its appearance *by itself* tells you nothing about what it is or can do. As historian Antoine Lentacker puts it, 'since drugs both contain and conceal their special powers against disease, they cannot circulate unless supplemented by some set of signs, whether textual or visual, that informs consumers or prescribers of their effects on the body.' There is thus a need for companies to imaginatively consider how to brand these boring looking and inherently uninformative goods.

As a result, companies – in Lentacker's words – make 'uncommon investments…in building credit, gaining recognition, or accumulating *symbolic capital*,' the latter being embodied in brands such that the names of drugs form 'the basic currency' of this form of capital. But branding in this industry goes beyond a distinctive name for the product. What is important to note is that there is a whole political economy of sameness and difference, and companies use trademarks to manage boundaries in ways that can render drug products as unstable things whose names may confuse you as to whether products with different names are or are not the same *and* thus interchangeable.

Tablet form, including visual appearance, and function are hardly separate considerations. Tablet design must consider such factors as therapeutic efficacy, ease of swallowing, and practicality from a manufacturing perspective. But with imagination, the appearance of a medicine itself *can* be made to tell you what it is and is supposed to do, and what its origin is. The industry can be creative in its use of trademark law and the expansion to nontraditional marks can be very helpful in this regard, such as to help turn a single product into two separate ones in a very recognizable visual sense. To give an example from Jackson:

> '*Prozac*, an antidepressant, was about to lose its patent protection. Its manufacturer, Eli Lilly, rebranded the active ingredient – *fluoxetine* – by producing pink and lavender pills (*Prozac* was green and white), naming it *Sarafem*, and marketing it for the treatment of premenstrual dysphoric disorder.'

## *Viagra*

*Viagra*'s 1998 market entry became a global social phenomenon. What is *Viagra*? It cannot be adequately defined by what it is made of, what it is for, or by what it does when the human body absorbs it. In fact, what *Viagra* is, and is not, is determined not just by the regulatory regimes controlling its use, but by the IPR used to protect it, the scope of these rights, and their boundaries with the rights, duties, and freedoms of others, and with the public domain.

*Viagra*, like medicines other than mixtures, is a highly specific product in pill form containing a single active ingredient and other substances called excipients, the typical functions of which are to protect it on its journey through the body, control the active ingredient's rate of absorption, and enhance palatability. The active ingredient can scientifically be identified as either: (i) the tongue-twisting *1-[[3-(6,7-dihydro-1-methyl7-oxo-3-propyl-1H-pyrazolo[4,3-d] pyrimidin-5-yl)4-ethoxyphenyl]sulphonyl]-4-methylpiperazine*, as (ii) the somewhat simpler $C_{22}H_{30}N_6O_4S$, or as (iii) *sildenafil citrate*, or its nonproprietary generic name of *sildenafil*. For obvious reasons, we will settle for the latter name.

To say that *Viagra* is *sildenafil citrate* is surely a statement of fact. However, Pfizer stakes its ownership claims in far more subtle ways than that. This is why it is more accurate to say that *Viagra* has – rather than is – *sildenafil citrate*. Even then, this does not mean that only *Viagra* has *sildenafil citrate*. Pfizer's management of its IP surrounding *Viagra* does not make things that simple. Indeed, the boundaries secured and guarded by the patent and trademark rights around *Viagra* or, to be absolutely specific, as to what it really is – 'a *sildenafil*-containing Erectile Dysfunction treatment called *Viagra*' – are much broader than the active ingredient alone, albeit not as broad as Pfizer would have liked.

*Sildenafil citrate* was discovered with the aim of producing cardiovascular benefits to patients. More specifically, it purposely disrupts a naturally occurring enzyme called *phosphodiesterase type 5* (PDE5) to deal with disorders like hypertension and angina. However, a group of people given the substance described increased incidences of erections. It turned out that PDE5 inhibition enables the flow of blood into the penis by relaxing certain muscles in the erectile tissue.

Medicines must be *for* something. What was *Viagra* for? Aphrodisiacs are not medicines. Consequently, erectile dysfunction had to be 'invented' in order for *sildenafil* to become the prescription medicine *Viagra* rather than a recreational drug like *Ecstasy*. Pfizer did not invent erectile dysfunction as such, but it invested huge sums in promoting the medicalization of the condition, one previously thought either to be too trivial or inherently psychological to 'deserve' its own drug. This of course suited numerous men who could point to their 'condition' as a medical problem that they should not be blamed for.

*Viagra* as a product name has been hugely successful, generating vast sums of money for Pfizer. Registration of the word mark is of course the first step in protecting the name of your drug (or any other product). Being ready to guard the mark through enforcement actions and opposition to the registration of similar marks is essential. Doing so has ensured that there is no such thing as 'Natural *Viagra*,' at least in law, notwithstanding attempts still made to use the term for herbal products of varying levels of dubiety. Keeping control over the use of '*Viagra*' in the marketplace helped prevent it becoming a genericized synonym of 'aphrodisiac,' something that was assisted by Pfizer's own educational program to enhance public awareness of erectile dysfunction as a condition. Here, trademark and patent strategy supported each other. Until Pfizer informs us otherwise, *Viagra* must consist of *sildenafil citrate*, a substance patented in the early 1990s (these patents have now mostly expired). As such, this remains a defining quality. On the other hand, when *sildenafil citrate* is prescribed for pulmonary arterial hypertension, it is not *Viagra*™ but *Revatio*™, the only differences other than name and appearance being that the therapeutic effect and side effect have been reversed. All *Viagra* is *sildenafil citrate*, but not all *sildenafil citrate* in the form of a pill is *Viagra*. In this sense, we can say that Pfizer is narrowing the boundaries of its monopoly to accommodate another one, so that it is *sildenafil citrate* only when indicated for erectile dysfunction. But, in a sense, it is even more specific than this. Pfizer has numerous trademarks relating to *Viagra*, including ones covering the blue-colored and diamond-shaped appearance of the tablet, and even a European design right. Thus, in the minds of the consumer and indeed the general public, *Viagra* is that 'little blue pill.' In this case, the specificity of *Viagra*'s look will prevent generic firms selling *sildenafil* – its nonproprietary name – from making their copies look like Pfizer's original product.

### *Branding and the Placebo Effect: Help or Hindrance?*

A few drugs are guaranteed lifesavers that cure serious diseases, keep alive people who would otherwise be dead, or otherwise provide substantial relief from suffering, and are therefore essential. But most are not such high-stakes products. They may be much better than alternative treatments, just a bit better, or they may be inferior. What of generic medicines? Are they functionally equivalent to originator drugs to the extent that they are completely interchangeable? This had been a hugely contested issue for decades, although presumably, this is a settled matter. If generic medicines are granted marketing authorization, it is because they have been found to be functionally equivalent to the extent that they are interchangeable. Accordingly, by dint of regulation, the active ingredient is commodified in the sense that there can be more than one source of the same thing.

But do branded and unbranded versions always function equally? First, are the 'same' products sold under different names precisely interchangeable? Second, are equivalent products with the same active ingredients, but that are differently named, also interchangeable? The first matter concerns whether the brand name and the generic name point to the same thing, neither more nor less. The answer is 'not necessarily.' The generic name is for the active ingredient, not the specific formulation. Tablets contain other chemicals selected, mixed, and processed in certain physical forms and proportions with a view to effective admission into the body, transport to its place of dissolution and action, potency, speed and duration of therapeutic effect, and stability. Indeed, the active pharmaceutical ingredient typically comprises less than 10 percent of the drug. So, in a sense, the generic name and the brand name may not be referring to precisely the same thing: the generic name refers to active ingredient A, whereas the brand name coined (and normally trademarked) actually covers not A alone, but A + B + C, and so forth, in prescribed proportions. This leads to the second matter. The generic may also contain B + C, and so forth, and in the same proportions. But this is by no means certain. For example, it might be that the formulation is under patent after the patent on the active molecule has expired. If so, the generic maker cannot offer the drug in the same formulation. Accordingly, it is possible that the patient experience will vary to some extent whether she takes the brand name drug or the generic equivalent as a consequence of the active ingredient being mixed with other chemicals that are not the same. Nonetheless, drug regulatory requirements for generic drugs stipulate that they not be just chemically equivalent to the original drug, but that their interaction with the human body is sufficiently equivalent that they are effectively adequate substitutes. Thanks to the regulators, notwithstanding the possibility of certain regulator market exclusivities available to the second comer, first-time grant of marketing authorization to a generic product turns the active ingredient into a commodity, albeit not necessary one whose price drops markedly in response to competing products increasingly become available. Often, few competitors actually emerge.

But that is not quite the end of it. Branding, including naming and visual features such as shape and color, can do much to build goodwill in a particular product. Can the goodwill protected or conferred by branding translate into placebo effects whereby patients perceive positive health benefits from taking something even if what is consumed contains no superior qualities to the generic version? Scientific research suggests that positive views about a branded drug (and perhaps branded drugs generally) seem likely to increase the possibility of placebo effects, at least in some therapeutic areas.[6]

6 K. Faase et al., *The Effect of an Apparent Change to a Branded or Generic Medication on Drug Effectiveness and Side Effects*, 75(1) Psychosom. Med. 90–96 (2013). Placebo responses have been observed in a range of product types, not just pharmaceuticals, suggesting in many cases that pricing and branding can influence consumers' expectations, which in turn affects their consumption experience. There is thus nothing remarkable about finding that placebo responses do occur among users of pharmaceutical products. D. Borsook & L. Becerra, *Placebo: From Pain and Analgesia to Preferences and Products*, 42 J. Mark. Res. 394–98 (2005); B. Shiv et al., *Placebo Effects of Marketing Actions*, 42 J. Mark. Res. 383–93 (2005).

What does this imply for the industry and for the public? For the industry, the science of placebo effects suggests both opportunities and threats. Discussion on their implications for public health raises numerous issues. From a *commercial* perspective, placebo effects may be highly significant in how marketing can benefit firms or not. One experiment reported by Waber et al. found that some people responded better to a dummy pill said to cost $2.50 than to the same pill costing, as they were informed, only $0.10. Similarly, some patients report poorer health when switched from a brand-name drug to a generic version. It is important to note here that such is the psychological power of 'the drug' itself that offering a placebo 'packaged' as a tablet, as was reported by Kaptchuk et al., has been proven to have positive health effects in an experiment giving some people no treatment for irritable bowel syndrome and others the placebo. This was even when patients were informed they were getting 'placebo pills made of an inert substance, like sugar pills, that have been shown in clinical studies to produce significant improvement in IBS symptoms through mind-body self-healing processes.' The fact that a useless pill for something or other can be 'better' than nothing, and that a branded expensive pill with no inherent superiority over cheaper unbranded alternatives can obtain higher patient satisfaction is of course good for business. It incentivizes both brand-based marketing and the pharmaceuticalization of society.[7] These placebo effect studies are quite recent, but they merely confirm what marketing people have assumed to be true anyway, probably for as long as the industry has existed, hence the priority given to marketing strategy from the start. Marketing is about so much more than just bringing new products to the attention of customers. It is also about persuasion: the art of 'talking up' products, making people believe they *should* buy them, that they should accept no substitutes, and that they are better than they really are. The pharmaceutical industry is no less dedicated to the art of persuasion than other business sectors, if not more so in many cases.

This is not to say the industry always has it easy in this regard. Placebo phenomena can affect consumer behavior, potentially in both positive[8] and negative ways. Indeed, they are a two-edged sword. Experimental evidence using clinical trial data from 1990 to 2013 has shown that for painkillers, placebo effects are stronger, and actually getting stronger still, in the United States (US) than in European and Asian countries. At the same time, actual drug responses have

7 This is well exemplified by *Ritalin* in the United States. R. DeGrandpre, The Cult of Pharmacology: How America Became the World's Most Troubled Drug Culture 4–12 (2006).

8 One study found evidence of potential placebo responses due to color: 'green and blue may have more sedative effects and red and orange may have more stimulant effects'. A.M.J. de Craen et al., *Effect of Colour of Drugs: Systematic Review of Perceived Effect of Drugs and of Their Effectiveness*, 313 Br. Med. J. 1624–26 (1996). Similar findings have been reported, *see* K. Schapira et al., *Study on the Effects of Tablet Colour in the Treatment of Anxiety States*, 2 Br. Med. J. 446–49 (1970); L.W. Buckalew & K.A. Coffeld, *An Investigation of Drug Expectancy as a Function of Capsule Color and Size and Preparation Form*, 2 J. Clin. Psychopharmacol. 4, 245–48 (1982).

not improved during the period surveyed. A plausible explanation is that the US is one of the few countries that allows companies to advertise their prescription drugs directly to consumers. So far so good for the industry apparently; but perhaps not so good. As Dahl suggests: 'So it's possible that hearing the lofty promises pledged by pharmaceutical firms in these ads may have increased consumer expectation of the potential efficacy of any old drug handed to them by a person in a lab coat.' Strong placebo effects have also been identified with antidepressants, though how these effects are manifested is somewhat confusing. One Harvard study reported by Kirsch on antidepressants found marginal differences in effect between the taking of a placebo and the actual drug. Both helped a significant number of people, but the latter was not helping them a great deal more than the former. An Oxford University study reported by Cipriani et al., using a different methodology, however, found a big difference in response between the antidepressant and the placebo, in favor of the former.

This situation is of course something of a headache for the industry. Perhaps the industry is falling into its own trap as it were – over-advertising plus the placebo effect leading ironically to a *reduced* difference in response to the real drug and the fake. If so, perhaps the solution for the industry would be a bigger commitment to radical innovation and a reduced one to marketing. On the other hand, one public health expert in a news report by Marchant suggests an approach that, if widely acted upon, would be even less convenient for the industry: 'If the major component of a drug in any particular condition is its placebo component, we need to develop non-pharmacological interventions as a first-line response.' Nonetheless, like all addictions, drug-taking alongside the 'epidemics' of mass-scale prescription and health-care interventionism have not been contained in the US.

As for the public, placebo responses on their face are good so anything that triggers such an effect must be a good thing. If the mere appearance of pills produces placebo effects, one could argue, surely there is nothing to criticize in allowing their protection under trademark law. Two questions arise: do the social gains of any arising placebo effect outweigh the social costs of the originator product's persistent market domination, including its likely higher price, due to continued preference for the branded product even when it is more expensive than the alternatives? And second, if there is a placebo effect, would it not be better for the public – on both therapeutic and informational clarity grounds – to allow the relevant placebo-inducing features to be shifted to all equivalent medical products? In other words, why do we not allow the generic *sildenafil* pills to look just like Pfizer's *Viagra*? There is of course a counterargument: trademark-owning companies did not just come up with those visual features, but probably invested in maintaining goodwill in them. Nonetheless, it makes little sense from a public interest perspective to give a company a permanent monopoly on features of a pill that produce placebo effects. If one were to disagree with this argument, forbidding a generic company from using the same shape and color marks is at least confusing to those patients who are not interested in the identity of the trademark owner but just want, chemically speaking, the same thing.

Nontraditional trademarks take us beyond words, phrases, and figurative marks to embrace such subject matters as the full range of visual and other perceptible aspects of products and the packaging they are 'dressed up' in. The trend to extend trademark protection this way has proved to be useful for many pharmaceutical companies. However, some examples show us that trademarks are not necessarily there to *reduce* confusion.

### *Prilosec and Nexium: The Purple Pills*

In 1979, the Swedish company Astra, later merged with Zeneca, came up with a first-in-class treatment for stomach disorders such as heartburn. This was *omeprazole*, the first proton pump inhibitor whose effect was to reduce stomach acid production. It was a huge commercial success. It was sold as *Prilosec* in the US, or *Losec* in most other countries. With attempts to evergreen its monopoly in a number of countries thwarted, the company sought to switch users to *esomeprazole*, branded as *Nexium*, a product that was both chemically and therapeutically virtually identical to *Prilosec* but was 10 times more expensive than the former drug. They did this by deploying aggressive marketing tactics, claiming that it was both newer and better. Admittedly, the fact that it comprises optically pure salts of *omeprazole* enabled it to pass the novelty test in the key patent jurisdictions. But novelty in this context is of course a legal fiction. Like more than half of the drugs currently on the market, the active ingredient of *Prilosec/Losec* is a racemic mixture: a 50-50 mix of molecules that are mirror images of each other. *Nexium* is the so-called (S) enantiomer of *omeprazole*, the one that is therapeutically active. Therefore, *esomeprazole* was part of the contents of *omeprazole*.

This effort cost hundreds of million dollars in marketing but resulted in a hugely successful line extension that is hard to justify from a public interest perspective. According to Manners, 'about 40 percent of *Prilosec* users made the switch to *Nexium* earning the drug over $3 billion in 2003 and almost $5 billion in 2004.'[9] So was *Nexium* any better than *Losec* to which it is chemically very closely related? It appears that the improvement was modest to say the least, apart from needing less of it to have the same therapeutic effect by dint of the fact that the other enantiomer is inactive.[10]

9 In Europe, the company also sought to delay generic competition with *Losec*. However, the means of doing so was found by the European Commission in June 2005 to be an abuse of its dominant position, and AstraZeneca was fined €60 million.

10 The similarity between the two goes beyond this. Both *Losec* and *Nexium* are prodrugs. Prodrugs are those which are converted by the human body into the substance which is the real active ingredient. Both *Losec* and *Nexium* are converted into the same compound, *sulfenic acid*, which only has a single-handed form: it is achiral, not chiral. Therefore, whether *omeprazole* or *esomeprazole* is taken, an optically and pharmacologically identical active pharmaceutical ingredient is formed *in vivo*, which goes about its business in a way that does not depend on which of the two products it is derived from.

However, by giving them two very different names, it became possible to mask this similarity to impressive commercial effect. And yet, in the US at least, AstraZeneca chose to exploit the goodwill it has built up in the purple coloring of *Prilosec* pills by making *Nexium* the same color and virtually identical in appearance. This seems ironic. Differentiation has been accentuated by the choice of names but has been blurred by the strategy of blending the appearance of the pills themselves.

In 2015, the company submitted a complaint to the US district court for Delaware, alleging trademark infringement and other offenses by Indian pharmaceutical company Dr. Reddy's Laboratories (DRL) selling purple colored generic *esomeprazole* without licenses to use the 'The Purple Pill' and any of the purple coloring trademarks covering 'preparations and substances for the treatment of gastrointestinal diseases.'[11] The court responded with a temporary injunction. At the very least, this testifies to the extent of the company's determination to protect its investments in associating AstraZeneca with purple-colored capsules for treating certain digestive tract ailments and its commercial success in doing so. One presumes that the company was convinced that the commercial advantages of transferring the goodwill outweighed the risk of the public assuming *Nexium*, by its visual similarity to *Losec*, as being nothing more than the latter by another name. But perhaps we should not be too surprised by this or see any contradiction. Empirical research, including by Wan et al. suggests that people make assumptions about what their experience of a drug will be by its physical appearance, including its shape and color. This merely confirms what AstraZeneca knew anyway, hence 'The Purple Pill®.' If just looking at it evokes a warm feeling in the gut, why squander that goodwill so expensively acquired with a different-looking pill?

On the face of it, the impacts of making DRL change the color of its pills seem unlikely to have much effect on the public. Teva and Mylan also sell *esomeprazole* using other colors so there is competition, and *esomeprazole* is not expensive. However, in what sense did DRL's purple coloring cause the consumer confusion which trademarks are supposed to prevent? As long as consumers have visual access to the packaging, they will be aware that the source is DRL and not AstraZeneca, but that it is still *esomeprazole*. So, there is little or no confusion as far as they are concerned from making the pills look the same. On the other hand, preventing other producers from using the same color arguably causes confusion by blurring the chemically equivalent and substitutable relationship between brand name and generic medication. This could matter a great deal in the market for a medicine where there is little competition and the original market entrant has been able to keep prices high.

As we have seen, patents and trademarks function together to secure and maintain market power. Patents on medical products will eventually expire, but this does not of itself turn a medicine into a commodity whose economic value

11 *AstraZenica v. Dr. Reddy's Lab*, 209 F. Supp. 3d 744 (D. Del. 2016).

plunges toward little more than marginal cost. Trademarks are part of the reason. But it is fair so say that they are not wholly responsible. Lack of competition is a very serious matter, perhaps more than many people realize. Most medicines markets contain few competing products: 'approximately 40% of generics' markets are supplied by a single manufacturer'[12] in the US, suggesting price drops due to competition may be less steep than is commonly supposed. Aside from IP, a range of entry barriers exist, including the necessary regulatory ones that prevent the marketing of falsified and unsafe medicines. Originator firms may also benefit from distribution networks that restrict the availability of samples for would-be competitors who need them for the testing necessary to secure their own marketing authorization.

## Conclusions

In this article, we have found that trademarks, which function strategically alongside patents and data exclusivity regimes, can unduly extend – in part or in full – the lifetimes of monopolies and increase and sustain market power to the detriment of the public and to fair competition. In addition, branding based on trademark registration covering product names can actually generate confusion when their use blurs the essence of the product to the advantage of owners, and potentially has anticompetitive consequences. The expansion of trademark subject matter to colors and shapes can produce additional confusion or even *mis*information. As we have seen, branding strategy can exploit placebo effects, and this is true even with the pitfalls. But is there not a concern that using trademarks to protect the visual features of a medical product to exploit placebo effects make these features functional and therefore not capable of trademark protection?

Leaving that question to one side, I argue that competition law in this context may be difficult to apply to what is in effect common practice in the pharmaceutical industry. Instead, it would be preferable either not to permit trademark protection for shape and color in this market or else to make them unenforceable against authorized generic products for the same indications. Of course, there is a bigger picture here that such legal 'tweaks' can hardly fully resolve: the pharmaceuticals market is hugely flawed from a public interest perspective. More ambitious legal and regulatory solutions will need to be devised and put in place.

12 In OECD, *supra* note 1, at 29, citing several sources.

# 22 Indigenous Knowledge

## Bridging with Modern Medicine

*Anthony C. K. Kakooza*

## Introduction: The Value-chain in Access to Medicine

Traditional Medical Knowledge (TMK), simply defined, is an aspect of medicinal practice that relies on herbal remedies and other concoctions derived out of nature, as well as – in some instances – on sacred rituals in the treatment of body ailments. In many respects, TMK is closely related to modern forms of medicine, many of which evolved from years of research and development (R&D) tied to or derived from TMK. This chapter expounds on the relationship between TMK and modern medicine in supporting the argument that the ultimate objective of both practices is the prevention of ailments or treatment of a person. As such, it is essential to appreciate the synergy in both types of medicinal practices and the value chain that results in granting access to medicine to those that need it.

This chapter highlights that medical practice, premised on the foundation of the pharmaceutical industry, evolved and grew during a vibrant tenure of traditional medical practice. However, although modern medical practice appears to override and marginalize TMK, there are many synergies between the two that emphasize the significance of their coexistence.

I examine the practice of TMK before the growth of the pharmaceutical industry, then address the rise of the pharmaceutical industry and the marginalization of TMK, especially in the developed world as the need for patent protection grew. I draw out the differences and similarities between TMK and patents by highlighting the perceptions of TMK in less industrialized countries and by presenting case studies on how modern access to medicine has exploited TMK. In doing this, I also present the concerns of different stakeholders and the global efforts being undertaken to bridge the gap between TMK and modern medicine before making my conclusion.

## Down History Lane: From the Early Practice of TMK to the Growth of the Pharmaceutical Industry

Flora and fauna have always played a central role in the prevention and treatment of diseases. The traditional concept of treating common ailments in India, for instance, mainly involved indigenous plants, though animal remedies (such as the milk of various animals, bones, and gallstones) were also utilized.[1] The Chinese are also historically known to have relied on about 1000 different famous herbal remedies as part of a vast amount of traditional medicine that included vegetable, animal, and mineral remedies.[2] Codified Traditional Chinese Medicine (TCM) dates back to 1100 BC during the West Zhou era in which natural products – majorly derived from plants – were used in disease therapy, ulcer therapy, diet therapy, and as veterinary medicine.[3] It is postulated that the slow transition from traditional to modern medicine first occurred in Greece, though the "Greek" influences were drawn from Babylonia, Egypt, India, and China.[4] Even then, the Greek physician Hippocrates (born 460 BC) – regarded as the father of medicine – appealed more toward the healing power of nature over diseases and advocated for dieting as well as the use of less drugs.[5]

Greek medical tradition also greatly influenced Roman medicine. This was mainly attributed to vast conquests that saw the expansion of the Roman Empire all over Europe and North Africa. These conquered territories had Greek medical practitioners and libraries with vast volumes of ancient Greek medical information, thus paving the way for the influence of Greek traditional medical practice all over the Roman Empire.[6] After the collapse of the Roman Empire, the development of modern medicine slowed down through the Middle Ages, until the Christian church and Arab scholars brought about its revival.[7] It is noteworthy that in the medieval period, the practice of childbirth was left to midwives who relied on folklore and traditional knowledge (TK).[8] In Africa, Christian missionaries played a strong role in introducing modern medicinal practice among ethnic communities, slowly starting a process in which community mindsets were diverted from traditional medicine to the Western mode of medical treatment.[9] Although introduced in the 16th century in China, Western medicine

1 William Archibald Robin Thomas et al., *History of Medicine, the Development of the Prevention and Treatment of Disease From Prehistoric and Ancient Times to the 21st Century,* Encyclopaedia Britannica https://www.britannica.com/science/history-of-medicine (last visited May 2, 2019).
2 *Id.*
3 Xuan Li & Weiwei Li, *Inadequacy of Patent Regime on Traditional Medicinal Knowledge*, 10 J. World Intell. Prop., 125, 126 (Apr. 10, 2007).
4 Thomas et al., *supra* note 1.
5 *Id.*
6 Vivian Nutton, Ancient Medicine 163 (2 ed., 2012).
7 The strength and influence of the Catholic Church in Europe was fueled by its dominance over political leadership as well as earnings from tithes which were never taxed; while in the Middle East, the spread of Islam was heavily orchestrated by the writings of scholars, giving a foundation for the vibrant intellectual and cultural life that influenced growing curiosity for knowledge and sparked off various inventions. *See Middle Ages*, History (Apr. 22, 2019), https://www.history.com/topics/middle-ages/middle-ages.
8 Thomas et al., *supra* note 1.
9 Yolana Pringle, *Crossing the Divide: Medical Missionaries and Government Service in Uganda, 1897–1940,* in Beyond the State: The Colonial Medical Service in British Africa 19–38 (Anna Greenwood ed. 2016).

did not take significant root until the 19th century – yet TCM continued to play a relevant role long after that.[10] The Medieval and Renaissance periods thus witnessed the slow growth of medical schools across Europe and parts of the Middle East, many of which became points of reference before people could be allowed to practice medicine.

The 17th century was the period of Enlightenment, with the first impact of medical schools coming about through thinkers such as Francis Bacon, Rene Descartes, Sir Isaac Newton, and William Harvey, but it was not until the 19th century that the world started witnessing the rise of scientific medicine.[11] This was partly due to the research and writings of the great physicists and medical practitioners in the preceding years, which led to the full understanding of the human body by the beginning of the 19th century. The rise of scientific knowledge during this time revolutionized and expanded medicinal practice.[12] It also marked a proportionate increase in the grant of patents in the pharmaceutical industry, as the great thinkers of modern medicine rushed to protect their inventions, thus creating a justification for property rights in the field of medicine. In the United States (US), as is highlighted elsewhere in this chapter, this trend was mainly influenced by the monopolist John D. Rockefeller, who sought to gain economic control of access to medicines by discouraging the use of traditional medicines.

This trajectory of modern medicine shows how man has always relied on nature in the treatment of ailments from time immemorial. Over the years, this reliance went through a transformation in some parts of the world with knowledge building, until modern laboratories came into the picture, thus changing perspectives in the drug industry. Nonetheless, the origins still link back to nature.

## The Pharmaceutical Industry, Patent Protection, and the Marginalization of Traditional Medicine

In the 17th century, English philosopher and physician John Locke penned down the *Second Treatise* on government, stating[13]:

> Though the Earth, and all inferior Creatures be common to all Men, yet every Man has Property in his own Person. This no Body has any Right to but himself. The Labour of his Body, and the Work of his Hands, we may say, are properly his. Whatsoever he then removes out of the State that

10 Haidan Yuan et al., *The Traditional Medicine and Modern Medicine from Natural Products*, 21 MOLECULES 5, 559 (Apr. 29, 2016), https://pubmed.ncbi.nlm.nih.gov/27136524/ (last visited Feb. 26, 2021).

11 Thomas et al., *supra* note 1.

12 *Id.*

13 Patrick J. Connolly, *John Locke (1632–1704)*, INTERNET ENCYCLOPEDIA OF PHILOSOPHY, https://www.iep.utm.edu/locke/#SH4a (last visited Aug. 6, 2019).

> Nature hath provided, and left it in, he hath mixed his Labour with, and joined to it something that is his own, and thereby makes it his Property ... [I]t hath by this labour something annexed to it, that excludes the common right of other Men. For this Labour being the unquestionable Property of the Labourer, no Man but he can have a right to what that is once joined to, at least where there is enough, and as good left in common for others.[14]

The Lockean theory thus clearly supports the pharmaceutical industry in establishing patent protection over modern medicines. Extensive costs go into research, clinical testing, and the production of pharmaceutical products primarily meant for the developed countries in which they are produced.[15] The pharmaceutical industry is said to be one of the biggest spenders in R&D, with up to 17 percent of revenues poured into the R&D departments.[16] This justifies the high market costs for such drugs in free market economies of the developed world. According to a compilation of studies by Ranjan Gupta and others, modern Western medicine disregards the significance of traditional medicine, although its connection with traditional herbal remedies cannot be denied. It was reported that "60% of the anticancer drugs and 75% of the anti-infectious disease drugs approved from 1981–2002 could be traced to natural origins."[17]

Chris Kanthan highlights how John D. Rockefeller, the US' first billionaire, proposed to undermine the popularity of natural and herbal medicines in the US in the early-20th century. The intention was to increase commercial support for his petrochemicals, which could be patented and sold for high profits in the pharmaceutical industry.[18] Rockefeller enjoyed 90 percent control of the US oil industry by the turn of the 20th century, at the time when it was discovered that various pharmaceutical drugs could be made out of crude oil and patented. In outwitting competition from traditional medicine, Rockefeller's plan was to financially divert medical colleges and hospitals away from following traditional medicines to following patented drugs.[19] Kanthan reports further that, "Scientists received huge grants to study how plants cured diseases, but their

14 Book II, ch. V (1690), adapted from JULIE E. COHEN ET AL., COPYRIGHT IN A GLOBAL INFORMATION ECONOMY 4 (3rd ed. 2010).

15 Bruce Lehman, *The Pharmaceutical Industry and the Patent System*, WAKE FOREST U. (2003), https://users.wfu.edu/mcfallta/DIR0/pharma_patents.pdf.

16 *How Much of a Drug Company' Spending is Allocated to Research and Development on Average?*, INVESTOPEDIA, https://www.investopedia.com/ask/answers/060115/how-much-drug-companys-spending-allocated-research-and-development-average.asp (last updated Oct. 15, 2018).

17 Rajan Gupta et al., *Nature's Medicines: Traditional Knowledge and Intellectual Property Management: Case studies from the National Institutes of Health (NIH)*, USA, 2 CURR. DRUG DISCOV. TECHNOL., 203 (Dec. 2005).

18 Chris Kanthan, *How Rockefeller Founded Modern Medicine & Killed Natural Cures*, DEFEND DEMOCRACY PRESS (Oct. 20, 2015), http://www.defenddemocracy.press/how-rockefeller-founded-modern-medicine-and-killed-natural-cures/.

19 *Id.*

goal was to first identify which chemicals in the plant were effective, and then recreate similar – but not identical – chemicals in the lab that could be patented."[20] The rest, as they say, is history. Today, the same medical colleges and hospitals, whose perspectives have international appeal and influence, continue to train medical practitioners who believe more in lab-created drugs than in the benefits of traditional medicine or herbal remedies.

The growth of the pharmaceutical industry and the drive toward patent protection is therefore understandable in light of the transactional costs involved in keeping such an industry afloat and the need to recoup such costs through business profits. But the link between modern medicine and TMK continues and should not be ignored. For instance, Boots, a leading pharmaceutical health and beauty retailer in the United Kingdom, started operations in 1849 by selling herbal remedies concocted by the mother of its founder, John Boots. John had always desired to make medicine affordable and accessible to the poor. With the same principle, his son Jesse transformed and expanded the family business using the slogan "Health for a Shilling."[21] The transition of Boots, from a retailer of herbal medicine to the big contributor in the pharmaceutical industry that it is today, does not belie the underlying principle in its establishment: providing access to medicine for all.

Unfortunately, manufacturing processes in the pharmaceutical industry are normally easy to replicate by persons conversant in the field. Furthermore, market demand for drugs is quite high, both in developing and least developed countries (LDCs) that cannot afford them. This ultimately created an increase in counterfeits and illegally replicated versions of the same drugs. The Agreement on Trade-Related Aspects of Intellectual Property Rights (TRIPS Agreement) envisaged such scenarios arising and thus attempted to effectively provide for them. Article 31 of the TRIPS Agreement provides for special compulsory licensing by stipulating situations within which a patent can be used through exceptions to the rights of the patent owner. Such situations pertain to use by the government or third parties authorized by the government and would normally fall in settings wherein the patentee and the ones desirous of using the patent are in the same country, including developed countries. However, all members of the World Trade Organization (WTO) – including LDCs – are eligible to import medicines under this special compulsory licensing mechanism.

Article 31(f) of the TRIPS Agreement limits the amount of medicine a country can export under a compulsory license arrangement, since it provides that the medicine should be "predominantly for domestic market." Initially, therefore, exporting such medicines to other countries was not possible. The position was reversed through what came to be known as "Paragraph 6" of the Doha Declaration of the TRIPS Agreement and Public Health, which recognized the

20 *Id.*
21 Jenny Lovell, *Jesse Boot*, Royal Society of Chemistry (Dec. 2014), http://www.rsc.org/diversity/175-faces/all-faces/jesse-boot/.

limited capacity of LDCs in the pharmaceutical sector to effectively use compulsory licensing. It thus makes it possible for LDCs to import pharmaceutical products under compulsory licensing even if a medicine is patent-protected.

On the issue of affordability of modern medicine, LDCs are also particularly catered for under Article 66 of the TRIPS Agreement. Paragraph 1 of this article provides that, in view of the "special needs and requirements of LDC Members, their economic, financial and administrative constraints," they are not required to have patent protection in certain categories for a given period of time. On November 6, 2015, the WTO's Council for TRIPS extended until January 2033 the period during which key provisions of the TRIPS Agreement do not apply to pharmaceutical products in LDCs.[22] This means that LDCs have until 2033 to decide whether or not to protect pharmaceutical patents and clinical trial data. Article 66 of the TRIPS Agreement is thus meant to further guarantee easy access to medicine for LDCs.

As articulated through the Lockean theory, patent protection in the pharmaceutical industry is premised on labor and effort, which justifies the need for creating a monopoly of ownership during the life of the patent to control production and profit. The pillars upon which the creation of patent rights stand are self-centered to the extent that the position of monopoly in the production of patented products has to be controlled from the center, so as to guarantee a given quality and a good run of profit generated from royalties. The TRIPS Agreement thus supports such objectives through the minimum standards of protection given for inventions that are new, involve an inventive step (nonobvious), and are capable of industrial application (useful).[23] Access to medicines coming under this protective regime is thus determined by the patent owner and is a complete contrast in practice from the way accessibility to medicine is controlled in the context of TMK. However, this raises questions as to how the argument for the need for pharmaceutical patents can be sustained. This is especially so where the knowledge base is facilitated by the knowledge of traditional communities' utilization of natural resources to prevent and cure ailments. The next part of this chapter explores the intricacies in the operation of TMK and how this is a matter of concern for the pharmaceutical industry.

## Perceptions of TMK in Less Industrialized Countries

As explained, the history of the practice of traditional medicine is as old as many ethnic communities, most of which still exist today in developing and LDCs. Such communities have grown through centuries, practicing the same kind of

22 *WTO Members Agree to Extend Drug Patent Exemption for Poorest Members*, World Trade Org. (Nov. 6, 2015), https://www.wto.org/english/news_e/news15_e/trip_06nov15_e.htm [hereinafter *WTO Members Agree*].

23 *See* TRIPS: Agreement on Trade-Related Aspects of Intellectual Property Rights, Apr. 15, 1994, Marrakesh Agreement Establishing the World Trade Organization, Art. 27(1), 1869 U.N.T.S. 299, 33 I.L.M. 1197 (1994) [hereinafter TRIPS Agreement].

TK, to the extent that it is embedded within their cultural setup and, as such, part of their cultural heritage. In this sense, TK should not be perceived as relating to something ancient, but to knowledge that is developed, sustained, and passed on from generation to generation, forming part of the community's cultural and spiritual identity.[24] According to the World Health Organization (WHO), it is estimated that in most nonindustrialized countries, the majority of the population – between 80 and 90 percent – still relies on traditional forms of medicine for their everyday health care.[25]

TMK is therefore a subset of TK. On the whole, TK is a living body of knowledge that integrates the technical know-how, skills, innovations, and practices that are part of the living embodiments of indigenous and local communities who are considered the custodians of such knowledge.[26] Apart from medical knowledge, other aspects of TK include agricultural and environmental knowledge.[27] Between 1998 and 1999, the World Intellectual Property Organization (WIPO) conducted a fact-finding study on the needs and expectations of TK holders.[28] The studies revealed a number of challenges unique to TK, which cuts across different custodial communities all over the world. These are summarized below:

a *Inadequate documentation*: Most TK holders do not have documentation concerning their TK. This comes across as natural, considering that the knowledge is passed on from one generation to another over an undefined number of years. In some respects, documentation is considered taboo because the TK is of a spiritual or sacred nature and its documentation may risk making it open to the public. TK custodians are therefore normally leery of creating any commercial value out of TK that has an attached spiritual element. This places them at cross-purposes with the IP practice that attaches trade and commerce to medicinal practice.

b *Un-authored works*: For lack of documentation, most TK cannot be easily attributed to any individual or clan. It is taken as general knowledge within

24 *Traditional Knowledge and Intellectual Property*, World Intell. Prop. Org. (2015), https://www.wipo.int/edocs/pubdocs/en/wipo_pub_tk_1.pdf.

25 Gerard Bodeker, *Indigenous Medical Knowledge: The Law & Politics of Protection*, Institute for Agriculture & Trade Policy 2 (Jan. 25, 2000) https://www.iatp.org/sites/default/files/Indigenous_Medical_Knowledge_The_Law_and_Po_2.pdf.

26 World Intellectual Property Organization, Intellectual Property and Genetic Resources, Traditional Knowledge and Traditional Cultural Expressions (2017). https://www.wipo.int/edocs/pubdocs/en/tk/933/wipo_pub_933.pdf (last visited Jan. 27, 2020).

27 *Id.*

28 World Intellectual Property Organization, Intellectual Property Needs and Expectations of Traditional Knowledge Holders, WIPO Report on Fact-finding Missions on Intellectual Property and Traditional Knowledge (1998–1999)(2001) https://www.wipo.int/edocs/pubdocs/en/tk/768/wipo_pub_768.pdf (last visited Jan. 27, 2020) [hereinafter WIPO Report on Fact-finding Missions].

a given community whose members have been practicing certain aspects of their TK indefinitely, but it is rare for them to single out the origin of such practices, or which person may have created such innovation or skill. Duration of protection is therefore not considered (nor desirable) an element of TK, as opposed to the patent regime, which assigns 20 years of protection for the grant of a patent.

c *Unrestricted ownership*: Since TK ownership is attributed to a given indigenous or local community, the TK – by its very nature – is part and parcel of the culture of that community. It has no individual owner; neither can it be said that the cultural head of the community is the sole owner of the TK. As such, every member of that community is considered an owner of the TK as part of his or her culture. In the absence of a legal representative of the community, negotiated usage and practical measures toward sharing of benefits becomes a challenge. Whom do you compensate, and in what form should such compensation entail?

d *Cross-border communities*: Many indigenous and local communities transcend two or more countries as a result of state borders being drawn by former colonial governments without consulting indigenous communities on the ground. This is true for many communities in Asia and Africa. For instance, during the Berlin Conference of 1884–1885 concerning the regulation of European colonization and trade in Africa, the British Prime Minister Lord Salisbury remarked cynically: "We have been giving away mountains and rivers and lakes to each other, only hindered by the small impediment that we never knew exactly where they were."[29] As a result of that oversight, over 10,000 African ethnic communities were haphazardly divided into 40 European colonies and protectorates.[30] Having the same communities cutting across different national boundaries results in having the same TK shared by different countries, which also makes negotiated use much more complicated, especially in the absence of a regional or domestic regulatory framework. This is also at odds with the IP registration and protection framework, which is territorial in nature.

Since 2001, there have been long-standing debates and negotiations at the WIPO's Inter-Governmental Committee of Intellectual Property and Genetic Resources, Traditional Knowledge and Folklore (IGC) for the creation of an international instrument(s) to regulate this area. It is not the purpose of this chapter to discuss such policy and regulatory issues in detail. However, there are two key areas of protection germane to TK holders over the appropriation of their TK: *defensive* and *positive* protection. In the former, external persons are completely excluded from acquiring any IP rights (IPR) out of the community's

29 Martin Meredith, The State of Africa: A History of Fifty Years of Independence 2 (2005).

30 *Id.*

TK; in the latter, the community controls the means within which access can be granted for use of their TK, including controlling prior informed consent (PIC) as well as access and benefit sharing (ABS).

Nonetheless, it is mainly based on the abovementioned challenges that patent holders within the pharmaceutical industry can easily exploit loopholes in appropriating TMK during the process of generating IPR. The IP system has, to a large extent, always been deemed as inadequate in protecting TK and handling the needs and interests of custodial communities, generally on the credo that the "IP system and the needs of indigenous peoples are too distinct."[31]

These challenges highlight the distinctiveness of patent rights from TK rights. A patent, by its very nature, is documented to bring out the ingredients or disclosures that are necessary in generating its grant. The documentation creates an inviolable record as to who the owner of the patent is, so as to generate the grant of the patent over a defined 20-year period. On the other hand, the absence of such a criterion for TK places such knowledge, in the perspective of IP, as public domain works and therefore free for all. TK custodians disagree to such qualification of their TK, insisting that their cultural heritage cannot be free for all. Another challenge is that TK, which is spread across communities in different countries, can be easily appropriated by the pharmaceutical industry due to weaknesses in checks and balances in the countries of origin. A number of case studies highlighting this situation are portrayed elsewhere in this chapter. It is noteworthy, however, that the granting of a patent is heavily reliant on the efficiency and due diligence of the patent examiner in ensuring that the patent application qualifies for novelty. It is quite difficult for the patent examiner or prosecutor to fulfill this requirement, especially where the TMK related to the patent application is tucked away and jealously guarded by an indigenous community in some remote part of the world.

## Exploring the Similarities: Any Possibilities of Synergies?

The historical analysis given at the beginning highlights how the growth and evolution of the pharmaceutical industry marginalized the practice of TMK. However, the overriding axiom is that the two cannot be completely severed. The case studies below describe a variety of approaches currently employed in utilizing the relationship between TMK and the pharmaceutical industry – categorized as good, not-so-good, and bad – based on their impact on the indigenous or local communities that are the custodians of the TMK in each case study.

31 WIPO Report on Fact-finding Missions, *supra* note 28, at 72 (citing comments from an interviewee at a roundtable discussion, Sydney, Australia, June 18, 1998).

## Case Studies

### *The Good News*

#### *The Yao Community of China*

For thousands of years, the Yao ethnic community of Jinping County, Yunnan Province in Southwest China has been known for its strong resistance to illnesses and understanding of medicinal herbs.[32] The harsh terrain and living conditions in that area forced them to depend on Mother Nature to survive, hence coming up with traditionally innovative ways of relying on medicinal baths in the treatment of ailments such as rheumatic diseases, skin diseases, and injuries from falls. In 2006, Yang Xianhui founded a health-care company called Jiangshen Yao Health Products Co. Ltd. or Guizhou Congjiang Shenyao, in the southeastern Guizhou's Congjiang County. The health-care company partners with the local Yao community in the production of herbal products, including bath powder, foot powder, soap, shampoo, and body wash. The locals are given seedlings and trained in modern planting techniques that suit the company's business projections; in turn, the farmers utilize their own lands and provide labor. The produce is sold to Yang's company, earning the farmers a favorable and stable source of income. This initiative was hailed as a means for the local Yao community to move away from poverty.[33] According to Yang Xianhui, since the establishment of the company in 2006, its output value increased from ¥500,000 ($79,807) to more than ¥16 million ($2360,960), maintaining an average growth rate of 30 percent.[34] In 2014, Jiangshen Yao Health Products Co. Ltd. was ranked as a leading poverty alleviation enterprise in Southeastern China.[35]

The economic transformation of the Yao community that has benefitted from partnering with the Jiangshen Yao Health Products Co. can therefore be considered as good news for both TMK and the pharmaceutical industry, especially in terms of boosting access to medicine. However, one concern is about the practicality of the sharing of benefits between the company and the local community. The Yao community, as migrants, are spread out across Southeastern China in

32 Sumei Li et al., *Herbs for Medicinal Baths Among the Traditional Yao Communities of China,* 108 J. Ethnopharmacol. 59 (Nov. 2006), https://www.researchgate.net/publication/7047952_Herbs_for_medicinal_baths_among_the_traditional_Yao_communities_of_China (last visited Jan. 27, 2020).

33 Liang Zhengfen & Liang Yu, *Yang Xianhui: Developing the Yao Medicated Bath Industry to Lead the Masses to Become Rich*, People's Network (Oct. 13, 2018), http://www.sohu.com/a/259220990_114731.

34 Zhao Yandi, *Qiandongnan Prefecture to Promote Health Industry*, http://www.eguizhou.gov.cn/2018-04/20/content_36066326.htm (last updated Apr. 4, 2018).

35 Zhengfen & Yu, *supra* note 33.

the provinces of Guangxi, Guangdong, Guizhou, and Hunan.[36] Although the TMK is attributed to the Yao people, it is not the whole ethnic community that has gained economically from the partnership with the pharmaceutical company. As for the company itself, it has found a way of cementing its hold using IPR protection out of the resources gained from the TMK. Four trademarks were registered – FROM YAO, SHEN YAO, CUN XI YAUN, and JIANG JIANG YAO – and four patents granted for the medicated bath.[37]

### *The Kani Community of India*

The Kani is a relatively small traditionally nomadic tribe inhabiting the tropical forests of the Agasthyamalai hills of the Western Ghats, a mountain range in Kerala State in India.[38] In December 1987, Dr. Palpu Pushpangadan, then Director of the Jawaharlal Nehru Tropical Botanical Garden and Research Institute (JNTBGRI) in Kerala, was carrying out an ethnobotanical expedition in these mountain ranges and had employed a few Kani men as guides. A few hours into the expedition, he realized that although he and his team were tired, the Kani guides showed no sign of fatigue; this was soon attributed to black fruits that the guides had been eating during the walk.[39] Plant researchers at the JNTBGRI worked with pharmaceutical company Arya Vaidya Pharmacy to investigate the plant, called *Aarogyappacha* by the Kani people. The researchers were able to devise a tonic formula, which was granted a patent and named *Jeevani* – meaning "source of life" or "giver of life."[40]

After Arya Vaidya Pharmacy commercialized *Jeevani*, a trust fund was established to share the benefits with the Kani people for their TMK.[41] The first payment, based on a benefit-sharing agreement, was given to the Kani people for an equivalent of $12,500, and further payments were to follow on an annual basis.[42] To establish a sustainable supply of leaves from the *Aarogyappacha* plant without destroying it, the JNTBGRI also paid $40 to fifty Kani families to cultivate the plant, thus providing the Institute a steady supply of leaves per month and, in turn, a guaranteed source of income for the Kani people.[43] Dr. Pushpangadan was thus able to combine the interests of the JNTBGRI with those of the Kani

36 Rachel Deason, *An Introduction to China's Yao People*, Culture Trip, https://theculturetrip.com/asia/china/articles/an-introduction-to-chinas-yao-people/ (last updated Apr. 25, 2018).

37 Zhengfen & Yu, *supra* note 33.

38 *Using Traditional Knowledge to Revive the Body & a Community*, World Intell. Prop. Org., https://www.wipo.int/ipadvantage/en/details.jsp?id=2599 (last updated Oct. 26, 2015) [hereinafter *Using Traditional Knowledge*].

39 *Id.*

40 *Jeevani: The Source of Life*, Med. Hunter (July 2010), http://www.medicinehunter.com/jeevani-source-life.

41 *Id.*

42 *Id.*

43 *Id., Using Traditional Knowledge, supra* note 38.

people through IP protection, by using the commercial success of the R&D to also create financial rewards for the Kani people.

### *The Not-so-good News*

#### *The Use of* Sangre de drago *in Peru*

A local community in Peru has been drawing its TMK from a tropical plant called *Sangre de drago.* The local community was approached by California-based company Shaman Pharmaceuticals Inc. (Shaman) for the use of the TMK. A three-stage benefit-sharing agreement was executed with the company, the local community, and the local government.[44] The first stage of the agreement covered provision of the indigenous peoples' immediate needs such as health care and forest conservation. The second stage covered mid-term benefits such as educational material and related resources. The last stage covered long-term benefits such as a share of the profits from the commercial success of the patent.[45] Shaman made payments for potable water, roads, and health care for the local community after filing for two patents derived from the TMK: one for a pediatric respiratory disease, another for herpes. Unfortunately, Shaman went bankrupt shortly thereafter, and the local community was never able to fully benefit from the commercial utilization of their TMK.[46] Having started the commercial exploitation of *Sangre de drago* and then not being able to see it through to a fruitful conclusion implies that the local community's TMK is now out in the open with no protective measures of control. Any entity can therefore utilize it as it deems fit without recourse to the local community from Peru, which is an erosion of their cultural heritage. It also destroyed their hopes of economic gain from their TMK.

#### *The San Community in Southern Africa*

The San indigenous people of Southern Africa have been using the hoodia plant as an energizer and hunger-depressant for hundreds of years.[47] Although this community is spread out in most South African countries, it is the San people

44 Srividya Ragavan, *Protection of Traditional Knowledge*, 2 Minn. Intell. Prop. Rev. 1, 22–23, (citing Donald E. Bierer et al., *Shaman Pharmaceuticals: Integrating Indigenous Knowledge, Tropical Medicinal Plants, Medicine, Modern Science and Reciprocity into a Novel Drug Discovery Approach*, http://www.retreatayahuasca.com/Ethnobotanique/feature11.html (last visited Feb. 19, 2001).

45 *Id.*

46 John Reid, *Biopiracy: The Struggle for Traditional Knowledge Rights*, 34 Am. Indian L. Rev. 77, 95 (2009) (citing Murray Lee Eiland, *Patenting Traditional Medicine*, 89 J. Pat. & Trademark Off. Soc'y 45, 55–56 (2007).

47 World Intellectual Property Organization, *Intellectual Property as a Lever For Economic Growth: The African Experience, Part II*, WIPO Magazine (Nov.–Dec. 2003), https://www.wipo.int/export/sites/www/pct/en/inventions/hoodia/african_experience.pdf.

of the Republic of South Africa that brought the benefits of using hoodia to light. The South African research institute Council for Scientific and Industrial Research (CSIR) studied the San people's use of hoodia and obtained a patent in 1995 after isolating the active ingredient in the plant.[48] The CSIR then gave a license to British biotech company Phytopharm, which entered into a sublicensing agreement with Pfizer for $21 million. Almost simultaneously, the San people realized that their TMK in the hoodia plant was being exploited, thus pushing the CSIR to enter into a benefit-sharing agreement with the South African San Council – a representative body of the San community – in 2002.[49] The benefit-sharing agreement took three years to negotiate, though unfortunately, Pfizer lost interest in the patent and pulled out of the lucrative sublicensing arrangement with Phytopharm in 2003.[50] As a result, the San people, earlier on the verge of benefiting commercially from their TMK through the use of the CSIR's patent, now suffered a loss.

This case study resonates with that of the local community in Peru. A pharmaceutical company takes up a strong interest in an indigenous community's TMK and discloses it to the public, opening up the local community's cultural heritage to third parties, then abandons the community's culture to the vultures. In such instances, traditional practices – having lost the cultural protective mechanisms that previously kept it intact and under control – can only suffer ruin.

### *The Bad News*

#### *The Oubli Berry from Local Communities in Gabon*

The Oubli berry is a West African fruit with a protein 2000 times sweeter than sugar.[51] Ethnic communities in Gabon discovered and nurtured the plant, using it as TMK to help nursing infants in accepting substitutes for mother's milk.[52] When a researcher from the University of Wisconsin (UW) caught on to the idea, the UW sought and was granted three US patents and one European patent for isolating and reproducing the protein Brazzein in a laboratory. The UW averred that Brazzein was "an invention of a UW-Madison researcher."[53] As such, no recognition or benefit-sharing agreement was ever undertaken with the

48 *See* Case Study 4: The San People and the Hoodia Plant, Glob. F. on Bioethics in Res., http://gfbr.global/wp-content/uploads/2015/09/Fifth_Casestudy4.pdf.

49 *Id.*

50 *Id.*

51 World Intellectual Property Organization, *Key Questions on Patent Disclosure Requirements for Genetic Resources and Traditional Knowledge*, 1, 10, (2017) [hereinafter *Key Questions on Patent*].

52 *Id. Pentadiplandra Brazzeana*, World Heritage Encyclopedia, http://worldheritage.org/Find/Pentadiplandra%20brazzeana.

53 House of Commons, Select Committee on Environmental Audit Appendices to the Minutes of Evidence (Nov. 1999), www.publications.parliament.uk/pa/cm199900/cmselect/cmenvaud/45/4502.htm#evidence.

local community in Gabon. What worsened the situation was that due to the low market price of the UW's synthetic substitute, many women from the local community in Gabon who used to harvest the fruit have since lost their source of income. The annual global market for artificial and high-intensity sweeteners, on the other hand, is projected to be worth around $3 billion.[54]

This case study closely resembles the measures undertaken by John D. Rockefeller in ensuring that pharmaceutical industries usurped the position of TMK in generating access to medicine to create profits for pharmaceutical companies. It portrays a position taken up by pharmaceutical companies that is diametrically different from what was highlighted in the previous case studies: choosing not to partner with custodians of TMK after establishing how the TMK works. Unfortunately, in taking up this approach, the livelihood and cultural heritage of the local community are negatively affected.

## What are the Concerns?

The above case studies from South America, Asia, and Africa clearly show that the provision of access to medicine – as contested between the pharmaceutical industry and custodians of TMK – is a global issue. Although the WTO is set up with membership from developed, developing, and least developed nations, LDCs lack the capacity to apply the TRIPS obligation of providing patent protection for pharmaceutical products. The WTO has acted on this by revising Articles 31(f) and 66 of the TRIPS Agreement as discussed above. Apart from LDCs lacking the capabilities to enforce such protective measures, another factor is that TMK is still the preferred means of accessing medicine in most developing countries and LDCs.[55] As such, regardless of the extension up to 2033 granted by the WTO Council for TRIPS,[56] LDCs may be least interested in instituting such measures as long as they have alternative means of accessing medicine through TMK. The key concern, however, is where pharmaceutical companies continue marginalizing the practice of TMK by establishing alternative and cheaper ways in which such medicine can be accessed and exploited. As evidenced by the case study from Gabon, pharmaceutical companies do not necessarily have to set up their bases within the same jurisdiction as the indigenous community practicing the TMK. All they need is to establish how the TMK works, then employ their own R&D to create substitute products.

The Gabon case study also raises concerns because it shows that pharmaceutical companies can negatively affect the practice of TMK, ultimately eroding cultural practices, regardless of whether this is done in good faith or otherwise.

54 Scheherazade Daneshkhu, *Health Drive Whets Drink Industry's Thirst For Sugar Alternative*, Financial Times (Apr. 5, 2015).

55 *See* Dr. Margaret Chan, *Opening Remarks at the International Forum on Traditional Medicine*, World Health Org. (Aug. 19, 2015), https://www.who.int/dg/speeches/2015/traditional-medicine/en/.

56 *WTO Members Agree*, *supra* note 22.

Another major concern is that developing countries and LDCs following the trend of prioritizing TMK over modern medicine could completely discourage genuine research into using modern medicine to combat new diseases. This is due to the absence of protective mechanisms for patents as well as the concretized mindset toward reliance on TMK in such countries.

Many scholars also oppose or challenge the use of unique or *sui generis* legislation over TK and folklore. They argue that extending protections to intangibles is problematic as it requires governments to go "beyond the default position that information is in the public domain, to protect information for an indefinite, potentially infinite time."[57]

Other questions reflecting global concern, due to the inadequate answers given so far, relate to the principles of ABS and PIC. The ABS principle relates to the position that local communities – from which TMK is appropriated and used in the research and establishment of patentable medicine – are deserving of a share of the pie. This is in the sense that they ought to enjoy a right of attribution as the community from which the knowledge emanates; they are entitled to easier access to the patented medicines; and they are entitled to a share in the royalties that accrue with enjoyment of the patent. The PIC principle relates to the position that the local communities that own the TMK are entitled to a sort of licensing arrangement which spells out the key terms which an entity seeking to rely on their TMK to develop a patentable product would be obliged to follow. Considering that TMK is part of the cultural heritage of indigenous communities, the challenges in handling ABS agreements and initiating negotiations over PIC always raise questions as to who speaks for the communities, and as to how benefit sharing is executed over communities.

It is therefore necessary to explore and embrace new initiatives through which the concerns and interests of the pharmaceutical industry and those of the custodians of TMK are jointly addressed in order to create a unified approach necessary for sustaining both groups' long-term interests. The last part of the chapter discusses such initiatives.

## Global Efforts in Bridging the Gap between TK and Modern Medicine

Most custodians of TK agree that the IPR legal framework under the TRIPS Agreement is not the ideal or suitable method for the protection of TK.[58] The TRIPS Agreement was created to primarily promote efficient and effective international trade through an adequate IP regulatory system.[59] There are other

57 Dennis S. Karjala & Robert K. Paterson, *The Failed Case for Property Rights in Intangible Indigenous Cultural* Property, *in* INTELLECTUAL PROPERTY, CULTURAL PROPERTY AND INTANGIBLE CULTURAL HERITAGE, 89 (Christoph Antons & William Logan eds., 1st ed. 2018).

58 WIPO REPORT ON FACT-FINDING MISSIONS, *supra* note 28.

59 *See* TRIPS Agreement, *supra* note 23, at Preamble.

ways of creating a policy and regulatory bridge between the practice of TMK and the pharmaceutical industry, premised on the fact that TMK led to the birth of the latter. A number of measures explored at the international level are discussed below.

### *International Instruments*

The 1992 Convention on Biological Diversity (CBD) recognizes the sovereign right of states over their natural resources and affirms that governments have the authority, subject to their national legislation, to determine access to genetic resources.[60] Under Article 2 of the CBD, genetic resources can be interpreted to mean parts of biological material that contain genetic information of value and are capable of reproducing or being reproduced. Although genetic resources are encountered in nature (therefore not creations of the mind and not worth IP protection), TMK falls in the category of genetic resources associated with TK and is covered under the CBD. The CBD is considered the only major international instrument that ascribes ownership of biodiversity to indigenous peoples and individuals, and affirms their right to protect such knowledge.[61] The 2010 Nagoya Protocol,[62] as a supplement to the CBD, sets out the rules and mechanisms for ABS. It generally provides for a legal framework for the effective implementation of the fair and equitable sharing of benefits arising out of the utilization of genetic resources associated with TMK.

The CBD and, more especially, the Nagoya Protocol therefore step in to cover the position that the TRIPS Agreement entirely left out, by providing the international minimum standards that state parties are obliged to adhere to by creating legal certainty and transparency for both custodians and providers of TMK and its users. The Nagoya Protocol adequately caters for issues such as fair and equitable benefit sharing (Article 5); access to TK associated with genetic resources (Articles 7 and 12); the controversy of transboundary ownership of TK (Article 11); creation of government agencies or national authorities that can be used as liaisons between custodial communities and the users of their TMK (Article 13); and capacity development and support in the utilization of genetic resources and TK (Articles 22 and 23).

The WIPO has also ramped up measures to address the issue of granting erroneous patents associated with existing TMK. The WIPO seeks to encourage member states to improve their disclosure requirements under their patent

60 *See* U.N., Convention on Biological Diversity, Article 15: Access to Genetic Resources (1992), https://www.cbd.int/doc/legal/cbd-en.pdf.

61 Gerard Bodeker, *supra* note 25, at 3.

62 Secretariat of the Convention on Biological Diversity Montreal, Nagoya Protocol on Access to Genetic Resources and the Fair and Equitable Sharing of Benefits Arising from Their Utilization to the Convention on Biological Diversity (2010), https://www.cbd.int/abs/doc/protocol/nagoya-protocol-en.pdf.

application systems *and* to include ABS system implementation within their domestic laws.[63]

### *State Initiatives*

A number of WIPO member states have already undertaken initiatives to bridge the gap between TMK and the pharmaceutical industry, ensuring that TMK is given due recognition during patent applications. In China, for instance, the Law of the People's Republic of China on TCM,[64] which came into effect in 2017, strongly advocates for the protection of TCM alongside advancement of modern science. Article 3 states: "The State shall encourage the mutual learning from each other between, mutual supplementation, and coordinated development of TCM and Western medicine, maximize their advantages, and promote the integration of TCM and Western medicine."[65]

In Europe, Belgium was among the first countries to amend its patent laws to incorporate full disclosure requirements and avoid the grant of erroneous patents. Article 15, Section 1, 6 of the Belgium Patent Law states that "patent applications must contain the geographic source of the plant or animal material, if known, that formed the basis for the development of the invention."[66]

In the same vein, Section 21(8) of Uganda's Industrial Property Act[67] stipulates that an application's description for grant of patent should contain an identification of the origin of genetic or biological resources collected in the territory of Uganda and used in the making of the claimed invention as well as any element of TK, associated or not with those resources, used in the making of the claimed invention.

Such patent disclosure requirements (PDRs) worldwide are the WIPO's new measures to address what is considered as wrongful access by pharmaceutical industry researchers into genetic resources and TMK that is closely intertwined with the cultural heritage of indigenous persons. Where an application for grant of patent fulfills these PDRs, it ensures legal acquisitions through PIC and mutually agreed terms over ABS.[68] Furthermore, by avoiding the grant of erroneous patents, PDRs simplify the patent examiner's job of investigating

63 *See* Intergovernmental Committee on Intellectual Property and Genetic Resources, Traditional Knowledge and Folklore, *Proposal for the Terms of Reference for the Study by the WIPO Secretariat on Measures Related to the Avoidance of the Erroneous Grant of Patents and Compliance with Existing Access and Benefit-Sharing Systems*, World Intell. Prop. Org. (Aug. 27–31, 2018), https://www.wipo.int/edocs/mdocs/tk/en/wipo_grtkf_ic_37/wipo_grtkf_ic_37_14.pdf.

64 Order 59 of the President of the People's Republic of China, Standing Comm. Nat'l People's Cong. Gaz. (Dec. 25, 2016), http://en.pkulaw.cn/display.aspx?cgid=287286&lib=law.

65 *Id.*

66 Directive 98/44/EC of the European Parliament and of the Council of July 6, 1998 on the legal protection of biotechnological inventions, Official J. Eur. Comm.

67 Cited as The Industrial Property Act, No. 3 of 2014.

68 *Key Questions on Patent*, *supra* note 51.

the requirement of novelty by virtue of the full disclosure of related genetic resources and TMK.

Furthermore, PDRs facilitate and guarantee a legally protected practice of ABS agreements between custodians of TMK and patent holders. ABS agreements are technically another form of licenses that inevitably make access to medicine easier by building bridges between TMK and the pharmaceutical industry. As long as these agreements safely cover the interests of all parties concerned, the pharmaceutical industry can utilize the patents obtained while the TMK custodial communities also keep their cultural heritage intact without any possible erosions.

## Conclusion

The TRIPS Agreement was never drafted with any consideration for TMK. This is totally understandable, because the TRIPS Agreement is a trade initiative that sprang out of the WTO to boost trade and make it more worthwhile by protecting the IP interests of trading partners. But as observed in this chapter, TMK is not premised on trade and is not IP due to its divergent characteristics. This does not negate the fact that there are a number of patentable products and processes in the pharmaceutical industry that have been drawn from TMK. Yet one cannot focus on the TRIPS Agreement to provide answers toward a future integration of TMK interests with those of patent protection, as this would be like trying to fit a square peg in a round hole. Lessons should therefore be drawn from other international instruments such as the CBD and Nagoya Protocol and how their underlying principles can help create minimum domestic standards to guarantee access to medicine while protecting the mutual interests of all stakeholders.

# 23 Digital Divide and Access to Medicines

## The Debate

*Swaraj Paul Barooah**

## Introduction

The fierce backlash that followed the World Trade Organization (WTO) Agreement on Trade-Related Aspects of Intellectual Property Rights (TRIPS Agreement) resulted in some significant victories for the access to medicines (A2M) movement – from the global response to the HIV/AIDS crisis, to the relatively recent Indian Supreme Court decision restricting the patenting of 'me-too' drugs. Much of the momentum of the A2M movement has been made possible by the coming together of a number of actors around a particular set of historical circumstances. However, despite the simultaneous breakout of the digital revolution, there is a relative absence of notable and accessible accounts, scholarship, and analysis by actors from the Global South in the digital sphere. This chapter aims to discuss some of the reasons for this digital gap, noting especially how this relatively overlooked aspect may be leading to delegitimization of knowledge from the Global South. This is observed to be of particular significance as (a) the historical circumstances that catalyzed and drove the movement are quickly changing, thus requiring new contexts and ideas to drive the debate forward; and (b) the current arc of the digital arena, increasingly acting as a networked public sphere, carries the danger of normalizing the invisibilization of voices from the Global South in this networked public sphere. The chapter then goes on to look at the implications this has on the narratives created and used in the A2M debate. Finally, the chapter concludes by considering examples of how narrative building in the digital sphere can more effectively take place, especially given the new concerns brought about by new technologies.

* As described in the chapter, there is a relative dearth of documented and accessible research on the current topic. In light of this paucity of documented information, he has drawn significantly upon his experiences, interactions, and observations for the purposes of this chapter. The author would like to thank Kumar Panda and Shashank Venkat for their invaluable research assistance. Mistakes, if any, remain attributable to the author alone.

### *Old and New Beginnings: Initial Framings and the A2M Resistance*

Three decades ago, the world saw the formalization of a new international political economy for knowledge production and the information society through the TRIPS Agreement. Piggybacking on the desperation of countries to partake in international trade,[1] the TRIPS Agreement created the first ever set of global minimum standards for exclusion rights over different forms of information. As has been well documented, these 'minimum standards' were mostly anchored by a few Northern countries,[2] most of which had already greatly benefited from mass transfers of wealth through colonization.[3] More specifically, this whole process had been driven by some of the industrial elite from these Northern countries, through a combination of corporate lobbying as well as regulatory and policy capture at the highest levels.[4] The 50 plus countries that had earlier not allowed exclusion rights over food and medicines[5] suddenly found that they needed to allow private companies these exclusion rights if they wanted to be part of the global trading regime. The relative inexperience that many countries had with 'strong' intellectual property (IP) standards, combined with the long-standing desire to be part of a global trading regime, led to very insufficient scrutiny of the TRIPS Agreement provisions from those that would go on to bear the brunt of it.

Fast forward 25 years to the present and we see much more awareness, knowledge, and discussion about IP rights, but perhaps just as little agreement on how to justify them, calibrate them, and what exactly their effects are.[6] There has been a host of economic and empirical studies[7] on the effects of IP in the last few decades, and yet the evidence connecting the patent system with net social benefit, or even innovation, is still far from conclusive.

Meanwhile, aside from policy makers themselves, the last couple of decades have also seen a tremendous amount of discussion and debate around IP issues

1 Susan K. Sell, Private Power, Public Law: The Globalization of Intellectual Property Rights 108–20 (2003).

2 Through this article, countries have been referred to as 'developed/developing', 'northern/southern', 'western/eastern'. For the purposes of this article, these labels have been used approximately and interchangeably, unless otherwise specified. Each set of terms has its own drawbacks and politics, which will not be discussed here.

3 Different levels of IP protection affect countries differently, depending on the level of industrialization they are currently in. *See* Shamnad Basheer & Annalisa Primi, *The WIPO Development Agenda: Factoring in the 'Technologically Proficient' Developing Countries*, *in* Implementing WIPO's Development Agenda 100–10 (Jeremy DeBeer ed., 2008).

4 Sell, *supra* note 1, at 96–120.

5 Carlos Correa, Integrating Public Health Concerns into Patent Legislation in Developing Countries 11 (2001).

6 Mark A. Lemley, *Faith-Based Intellectual Property*, 62 UCLA L. Rev. 1328, 1334–38 (2015).

7 Though most of these have been done in western countries, where access to data is more readily available.

within the extended policy-influencing space – i.e. activists and advocacy groups, academia, and civil society. This has been in no small part due to the increased access to resources, knowledge, and skill, as well as increased networking, all of which has, in turn, been greatly helped by the simultaneous advent of the digital revolution. With respect to pharmaceutical innovation and A2M, arguably the most controversial TRIPS-related sector,[8] this has manifested in several activists and patient groups having access to forums to share ideas, experiences, and perspectives, as well as platforms to mobilize with their counterparts in their own countries and around the world.

Soon after the TRIPS Agreement, the A2M movement coalesced to successfully reframe TRIPS concerns from a trade issue to a public health issue. This lent more power and flexibility to the movement, bringing in new advocacy groups from various countries (such as developing countries undergoing HIV/AIDS crises), humanitarian nongovernmental organizations (NGOs), and scholars from various disciplines. It also allowed for new institutions such as the World Health Organization (WHO) to be co-opted on the international level.[9]

## *The Changing Landscape*

However, as some scholars have pointed out, it was a particular set of historical circumstances that fueled the A2M movement to many of its current successes; circumstances that seem unlikely to repeat, or to help continue or grow the movement's momentum.[10] There is good reason to take note of this. The circumstances around the HIV/AIDS crisis led to the building up of a 'moral imperative' that had become difficult to sideline, especially as certain crucial actors started taking radical actions that could not be ignored. This combination of strong moral imperative with compelling narrative and actionable alternatives[11] brought different actors together and fueled the A2M movement. The various transnational networks of influence that contributed to the A2M

8 While the debate is often shorthanded as an Access to Medicines debate, it would perhaps be more accurately described as a contestation between a 'market-innovation' framework and a 'right to health' framework, i.e. a contestation between providing incentives claimed necessary for innovation of pharmaceutical products and providing access to patients for those pharmaceutical products.

9 Susan K. Sell, *A Comparison of A2K Movements from Farmers to Medicines*, *in* Access to Knowledge in the Age of Intellectual Property 391 (Gaëlle Krikorian & Amy Kapczynski eds., 2010).

10 Eduard Grebe & Marcus Low, *Transnational Mobilisation on Access to Medicines: The Global Movement Around the Imatinib Mesylate Case and Its Roots in the AIDS Movement*, ResearchGate (Dec. 2, 2014); *see also* Joe Karaganis, Keynote Address at 2nd Global Congress on IP and the Public Interest (2012) (presentation on file with author).

11 Solutions were made possible due to the triple combination of (a) major donors (such as the Global Fund, PEPFAR, and the Clinton Health Action Initiative), (b) the exponentially cheaper antiretrovirals (ARVs) made possible by generic pharmaceutical company Cipla and others, and (c) the changing international landscape of TRIPS.

movement included academics, civil society, patient communities, bureaucrats, politicians, lawyers, businessmen, celebrities, and religious and community leaders.[12]

While the moral imperative may have fueled the coming together of these various networks of influence over a common cause in the past, there is no longer a simple crux to build a moral consensus around. Earlier, the narrative had been simple to weave together, as a focus on (a) the sheer number of people dying in non-Western countries from HIV/AIDS (a viral disease that carried fear even in its name), (b) an existing treatment already being on the market, and (c) Cipla's revolutionary offer to provide those medicines for 1/30th of the branded drug price, together acted as a strong lynchpin around which the movement could be built and guided. However, now, the narrative is not so straightforward.[13]

It is still true that patents allow pharmaceutical companies to exercise monopolistic rights over patented pharmaceuticals. However, other significant factors are changing. There is a global shift of disease burden from communicable to noncommunicable diseases (NCDs) as countries improve their performance on socio-development indices, and all countries have decreased their communicable disease burden in the last few decades. However, in terms of coalitions and country priorities, 'developing nations' and groups within them have lesser incentive to act as one bloc, as their states' problems grow further apart. This is especially important to note in light of the differing political prowess that countries have as they become more economically advanced.

NCDs, also known as 'lifestyle diseases', are driven by globalization of unhealthy lifestyles, physical inactivity, and tobacco and alcohol use.[14] While communicable diseases like AIDS and tuberculosis led to earlier deaths in the affected populace, several NCDs worsen the quality of life as life spans increase. In fact, though life expectancy has increased across all groups of countries, the increase in number of years of 'healthy' life has not kept pace – resulting in an increase in number of years lived in poor health.[15] While health informatics have numerically quantified disease burden in terms of 'Disease Adjusted Live

12 Stefano Villa & David Wilson, *Access to Medicines: Lessons from the HIV Response*, 4 LANCET 147 (2017).

13 While 'cancer' does carry the aura of fear around it today that HIV-AIDS did in the 1990s, it is actually an umbrella term, as there are over 100 types of cancer, with several different types of treatment depending on the patient, the severity, etc. Unlike the relatively straightforward ARV approach in HIV/AIDS, there is no simple solution, much less a simple narrative, to build consensus around.

14 *Non Communicable Diseases*, WORLD HEALTH ORG. (June 1, 2018), https://www.who.int/news-room/fact-sheets/detail/noncommunicable-diseases.

15 *See* GBD 2017 DALYs and HALE Collaborators, *Global, Regional, and National Disability-Adjusted Life-Years (DALYs) for 359 Diseases and Injuries and Healthy Life Expectancy (HALE) for 195 Countries and Territories, 1990–2017: A Systematic Analysis for the Global Burden of Disease Study 2017*, 392 GLOBAL HEALTH METRICS 1859, 1869 (*"Figure 1, Trends of HALE at birth and years in poor health from birth by SDI quintile and sex, 1990–2017"*) (2018).

Years' (DALYs) to include a combination of total years lost to disability and death, there is no getting around the fact that early death has a higher emotional impact when one is trying to build advocacy narratives. In other words, it is harder to build as powerful advocacy narratives around 'years lived in poor health' than it has been to build advocacy narratives around 'years lost to death'.

On top of this, the novelty and shock factor of the price differential between generics and branded drugs is no longer as impactful, as extreme health-care costs are becoming increasingly normalized. Even the WHO has noted that expenditure on national health is growing faster than the rest of the national economy, currently accounting for 10 percent of the global gross domestic product.[16] The new type and distribution of the disease burden therefore necessitates a change in rhetoric and strategy when it comes to how the A2M movement approaches it.

Additionally, changing circumstances and power dynamics do not lend themselves to continuing the same type of momentum. For example, Indian generic pharmaceuticals earlier had their interests more obviously aligned with the A2M movement, as their primary market consisted of patients with lower purchasing power than the Western markets that benefitted from Big Pharma's focus. However, with the opening of international trade and development of capabilities and markets over the last decade, many generic companies are finding that the bigger Western markets are now more viable for them. Meanwhile, Big Pharma companies are also finding that emerging economies like China represent areas of interest for them.[17] These changing priorities reduce the area of interest overlap that was earlier more apparent between generic pharmaceuticals and the A2M movement. Regulatory and market forces are also pushing pharmaceutical companies to engage in new behavior such as partnerships[18] and in-licensing[19] to reduce risk and increase revenue. These types of partnerships are

16 The WHO also note that health spending in low- and middle-income countries is growing on average at 6 percent annually, compared to 4 percent in high-income countries. *See Countries are Spending More on Health, But People Are Still Paying Too Much Out of Their Own Pockets*, World Health Org. (Feb. 20, 2019), https://www.who.int/news-room/detail/20-02-2019-countries-are-spending-more-on-health-but-people-are-still-paying-too-much-out-of-their-own-pockets.

17 *See, e.g.*, Ajay Gautam & Xiaogang Pan, *The Changing Model of Big Pharma: Impact of Key Trends*, 21 Drug Discov. Today 3, 379–84 (2016).

18 More partnerships are also seen between Big Pharma and generics, with Big Pharma also buying out some generic companies. Certain experts also predict that Big Pharma's struggle with revenues are directing them toward buying generics as that is where a lot of growth is coming from. *See Drug Wars: Pharma Firms Battle over Brazil's Generics*, Knowledge@Wharton (Feb. 23, 2011), https://knowledge.wharton.upenn.edu/article/drug-wars-pharma-firms-battle-over-brazils-generics/.

19 Isha Trivedi, *Hurt By Competition, Price Caps, Drug Firms Turn to In-licencing*, Live Mint, (Apr. 11, 2017), https://www.livemint.com/Companies/gejhDiYvDZ9osjBUyZz4oL/Hurt-by-competition-price-caps-drug-firms-turn-to-inlicen.html.

also bound to affect how these players act on the market and with each other, as new considerations are now in the picture.

Next is the issue of rising of costs involved, lowering the potential of low prices. While most pharmaceutical drugs have been chemical products till now, the future is increasingly moving toward therapeutic biological products[20] ('biologics') for treatment. In comparison to chemical drugs that tend to be small molecules with well-known structures, biologics have a more complex manufacturing process. They are large-molecule drugs produced in living organisms, making the manufacturing process more complicated. And as compared to generic versions of chemical drugs (which are exact duplicates of the original compound), generic versions of biologics ('biosimilars') are only 'highly similar' to the original reference product.[21] Biosimilars thus tend to be more expensive to create, while also requiring a higher regulatory burden than chemical generics.[22] This combination reduces the potential of price differential, as well as of accessible prices per se, that may even be impossible regardless of patents.[23]

Finally, as it becomes harder to weave a simple and hard-hitting narrative for methods to increase A2M, there may be a sort of activism fatigue or staleness that surrounds the field of public health. While it is widely recognized that fundamental areas such as public health and education are vital for a society's development, it is a bit harder to generate a moral imperative once a problem does not have a simple narrative around which that moral imperative can be built. This is especially so when 'trendier' fundamental problems like climate change and global socioeconomic systems occupy the mind-space of those who may have otherwise been persuaded to participate in the A2M movement.

20 *See* Gautam & Pan, *supra* note 17.

21 For more on the differences, *see* Erwin A. Blackstone & P. Fuhr Joseph Jr., *The Economics of Biosimilars*, 6 Am. Health Drug Benefits 8, 469–78 (2013).

22 WHO guidelines list out certain mandatory regulatory submissions including quality, purity, potency, immunogenicity, stability, biosimilarity, comparability, interchangeability, preclinical and abbreviated clinical testing, as compared to the relatively simple requirements of quality, purity, and stability, for chemical generics. *See generally* Anita Krishnan et al., *Global Regulatory Landscape of Biosimilars: Emerging and Established Market Perspectives. Biosimilars*, 5 DovePress: Biosimilars 19–32 (2015).

23 *See generally Generic Competition and Drug Prices*, U.S. Food & Drug Admin., https://www.fda.gov/about-fda/center-drug-evaluation-and-research/generic-competition-and-drug-prices (last visited Jan. 15, 2020) (showing that an FDA study in the US shows that on average, generic entry can reduce the price by 80 percent or more than that of the equivalent patented product); *but see* Andrew W. Mulcahy et al., *The Cost Savings Potential of Biosimilar Drugs in the United States*, Rand Corp. (2014), https://pdfs.semanticscholar.org/42d0/665cb73c416ad0124d3b477ab199a4f165b0.pdf (showing, however, that estimates for price reductions with the entry of (usually much more expensive) biologic products are between 10 and 30 percent. Thus, biologic treatments tend to have a higher baseline price, as well as lower cost reduction potential); *see also* Katelijne van de Vooren et al., *Biosimilar Versus Generic Drugs: Same But Different?*, 13 Appl. Health Econ. Health Policy 2, 125–27 (Feb. 5, 2015), https://link.springer.com/content/pdf/10.1007%2Fs40258-015-0154-9.pdf.

## The Networked Public Sphere

### *In General*

While significant, the TRIPS Agreement was not the most important technology-related milestone to take place in the 1990s: that position surely goes to the commercial popularization of the Internet. As the revolutionary impact of the Internet started making its presence felt, many Internet scholars started predicting that the Internet and other network forms of communication would create a fundamentally new social formation for human society.[24] The dramatically reduced costs of the creation, production, and distribution of information, as well as the changing methods of distribution, have led to greater democratization of access to information. It was posited that, in combination with the relatively more accessible communication made possible through the networked era, this would allow for greater political participation, especially by communities and people who did not earlier have the ability to make their voices heard.[25] However, it soon became clear that the Internet is not a flat medium. While it may represent a redistribution of power over who can create, modify, and distribute information, it cannot guarantee equal or fair redistribution over what type of information is seen, consumed, or even created. This, as it turns out, is now in the hands of a few search engines and social media platforms that make decisions on what type of information is shown to users and what type of information can be ignored.

As of 2017, thanks to fast-moving technological advancements in the digital communication sphere, nearly half of the world's population has been estimated to be 'internet users'.[26] While it is not yet clear whether the Internet is the great democratizer that Benklar and others theorized it to be, it is certainly clear that the digitally connected world is playing a heavy role in countries all around the world, be it in creating new social movements or for purposes of elections.[27] This change is noteworthy in the context of collective action problems that sociologists

24 *See generally* 12 Manuel Castells, The Rise of the Network Society (2011).

25 *See generally* Yochai Benkler, The Wealth of Networks: How Social Production Transforms Markets and Freedom 25 (2006) (stating, 'This new freedom holds great practical promise: As a dimension of individual freedom; as a platform for better democratic participation; as a medium to foster a more critical and self-reflective culture; and, in an increasingly information-dependent global economy, as a mechanism to achieve improvements in human development everywhere'.).

26 *See* Global ICT Developments, ITU Statistics, https://www.itu.int/en/ITU-D/Statistics/Pages/stat/default.aspx (last visited Jan. 15, 2020) (estimating that nearly 52 percent of the world will be internet users by 2019).

27 *See generally* Anita Gurumurthy & Deepti Bharthur, *Democracy and the Algorithmic Turn – Issues, Challenges and the Way Forward*, 15(27) Sur Int. J. Hum. Rights 39–50 (July 2018), https://www.researchgate.net/publication/328760413_Democracy_and_the_algorithmic_turn-_Issues_challenges_and_the_way_forward.

have been pointing out since the 1960s,[28] i.e. the systematic disadvantage that large diffused collectives face due to high organizational costs and difficulties with effective resource mobilization. This has often been pointed out as a significant reason for why corporate interests, when mobilized, have had more success in trumping 'public interest' concerns in lobbying governments, policy matters, and others.

### *Missing Voices or Invisibilization?*

Coming back to the context of the A2M movement, an often-underappreciated fact is that the digital sphere has been, and will continue to act as, a window and a point of entry into the access to knowledge (A2K) and A2M debates at large. In this context, it is important to note that even though the A2M movement has had a fair amount of success over the last two decades, there seems to have been proportionately very little institutional memory recorded regarding the actors and actions on the ground that have made it possible, especially when the actors and actions are based in the Global South. Even where information has been recorded, the plethora of information (and misinformation) available online means that this can easily be lost in a sea of other information. This obfuscation, in the attention economy[29] of today, has nearly the same effect as censorship. If material is not thrown up in the first few pages of popular search engines, or if material has not managed to garner attention on popular platforms, it is, for all practical purposes, invisible.

If one is to examine the global disease burden database,[30] developing countries (here, low-income and lower middle-income countries) carry a higher portion of the global health burden. The greatest rate of improvement of DALYs over the last three decades also comes from these countries. There is also ample evidence of tremendous effort coming from various developing countries in achieving the A2M goals, be it the usage of TRIPS flexibilities in India,[31] public

28 *See* Mancur Olson, The Logic of Collective Action: Public Goods and the Theory of Groups (1965); For contemporary analysis of this issue and its application to IP advocacy, see *generally* Amy Kapczynski, *The Access to Knowledge Mobilization and the New Politics of Intellectual Property*, 117 Yale L. J. 804 (2008).

29 *See* Herbert A. Simon, Designing Organizations for an Information-rich World 70, 187–202 ( Jan. 1996). H. Simon pointed out in 1971 that in an attention-rich world, the real scarcity is attention, and a key question becomes figuring out how to allocate attention efficiently.

30 GBD 2017 DALYs and HALE Collaborators, *supra* note 15.

31 *See* Shamnad Basheer, *India's Tryst with TRIPS: The Patents (Amendment) Act, 2005*, 1 Indian J. Law Technol., 15 (2005); *see also* Swaraj Paul Barooah, *India's Pharmaceutical Innovation Policy: Developing Strategies for Developing Country Needs*, 5 Trade L. & Dev. 150–197 (2013).

health programs in Brazil,[32] or widespread efforts that led to 39 pharmaceutical companies dropping their lawsuit against the South African government regarding a law to make medicines more affordable.[33] Given all of this activity from the Global South, one might be forgiven for assuming that voices from the Global South have made their presence felt online as well.

However, if one goes to Google Scholar, a popular and accessible search engine for academic works, and searches for 'Access to Medicines in Developing Countries', one might find, as I did when I searched in June 2019, that nearly 90 percent of the top 50 search results are by authors not based in developing countries.[34] In fact, nearly any search phrase that an interested beginner might enter seems to result in similar findings.[35] Similarly, one may find that nearly all, if not all, rankings of IP, patent, or pharmaceutical patent blogs rarely contain more than two websites from a developing country in their 'top 10' lists.

In fact, it would likely appear to a casual Internet user[36] that the most number, if not the most valued voices, in the A2M debates are coming from Northern countries. Given that there is significant cause, as described above, to believe that the ground reality is very different, it would appear that the promise of digital democracy has not materialized in any significant form in the A2M context.

32 *See* Jane Galvão, *Brazil and Access to HIV/AIDS Drugs: A Question of Human Rights and Public Health*, 95 Am. J. Public Health 7, 1110 (Oct. 10, 2011), https://doi.org/10.2105/AJPH.2004.044313; *see also* Kenneth C. Shadlen, *The Politics of Patents and Drugs in Brazil and Mexico: The Industrial Bases of Health Policies*, 42 Comp. Polit. 41 (Oct. 2009), http://eprints.lse.ac.uk/27051/1/politics_of_patents_and_drugs_in_Brazil_and_Mexico_(LSERO).pdf.

33 Toby Kasper, *South Africa's Victory for the Developing World*, MSF Access (June 30, 2001), https://msfaccess.org/south-africas-victory-developing-world.

34 This is merely indicative and not meant to be precise, as the exact number may change based on when the search is conducted and how the search algorithm may account for one's preferences. However, the broader point remains the same. Paid research services have not been used so as to get a more realistic idea of the type of search results the average internet user may get. Results indicating the same broader issue are seen when using a regular Google search (controlling for IGO publications) or DuckDuckGo, another common search engine.

35 For example, 'Access to medicines', 'Public Health and IP', and 'Patents and Public Health'.

36 The assumption here is that a casual user would look into major search engines and reputed sources such as Wikipedia. While the Wikipedia page for 'access to medicines' appears to be more balanced in the sourcing of its citations, the overall quality of the page is very underwhelming, with insufficient information, as well as incorrect information on the page, making it a dead-end for moving further. For example, it says India 'reintroduced patent law for drugs' in 2015. It also states three main causes for deaths in developing countries, with each having apparently claimed more than 85 percent of the total deaths! There are many more such errors as of Sept. 1, 2019. *See* https://en.wikipedia.org/wiki/Access_to_medicines.

The question is whether there has been an invisibilization of online voices from the Global South in this vital A2M debate. Why has the networked economy not contributed toward the amplification of these voices? Is it the case that, despite having platforms available, they are not using them?[37] Or are these voices not being seen as legitimate? This is not to say that accounts from the Global South are not available online. However, it is not enough that a voice has some digital presence, it must be able to catch the attention of an audience by easily showing up on searches or in research. It is difficult to answer these questions without rigorous research into the various causes that may be contributing to this gap or invisibilization. However, the broader point remains that the A2M debate does not seem to have proportionately benefited from the digital revolution. The following section looks into some possible reasons for this and why it matters.

## Digital Inequality and Narrative Building

### *The Digital Divide*

Those looking at digital inequality earlier focused primarily on 'access' from a technological perspective,[38] i.e. that it was available only to those who had access to stable electricity, basic literacy, and access to these connected technologies. The updated perspective on the digital divide, however, started looking beyond those who had basic 'access' and looked at political, sociological, and economic factors that acted as censors and gatekeepers not just to the Internet per se, but also to activity on the Internet. This raised two questions: first, who had the resources (such as time and energy) to effectively avail of this access, and second, whether people are restrained in the scope of their online activities due to their offline circumstances.

In the context of advocacy efforts, the fact that the 'online' cannot exist independent of the 'offline' means that there are a number of sociopolitical factors that govern how 'online' mobilization can function. Indicatively, a recent study has shown that within the United States (US), there exists a massive race and

37 *See generally The 5th Global Congress Polis.*, American Assembly Columbia Univ. (June 13, 2019), http://www.civic-assembly.org/the-5th-global-congress-polis/#Else (noting for example the usage of the online collaborative discussion tool 'pol.is' which had been in use during the 2018 Global Congress on IP and the Public Interest). Despite the group consisting of perhaps one of the largest and most international civil society groupings that work on the intersection of IP and the Public Interest, a nearly negligible percentage of its members used the online tool to discuss A2M.

38 Paul DiMaggio & Eszter Hargittai, *From the 'Digital Divide' to 'Digital Inequality': Studying Internet Use as Penetration Increases*, 4 Center for Arts and Cultural Policy Studies, Woodrow Wilson School, Princeton U. 1, —2–4 (2001).

class-based chasm in digital activism.[39] Reasons include the working-class activists not having time to be online, not feeling empowered to act online, and fear of real-world retaliation (in workplaces and otherwise) for their online activity.[40]

In the world of activism and advocacy, the unfortunate truth is that there are often several actors who have valid reasons to fear retaliation, be it through indirect bullying that may make their work life more difficult or through more direct methods which give people reasons to fear for their physical safety.[41] After all, the power and money that people have riding on various positions in the pharmaceutical world can be quite staggering.[42] For various practical reasons, much of this type of danger is often kept out of the public eye and is rarely documented. Aside from firsthand knowledge of fellow writers who have been on the receiving end of such treatment, many activists and advocates from the A2M movement are quite aware of the power dynamics which can easily place them in direct danger, be it legal, professional, or even personal. It is also not uncommon for activists, advocates, and scholars (especially in developing countries) to be concerned that their funding will be affected if they actively contradict a government position on a controversial topic. These too are often not documented. While many in the field know of such examples, the unfortunate truth is that the only way such examples could be exposed would be if an organization or actor has already had their funding cut and is also willing to risk potential future funding. Any external 'transparency' on their hidden threats would otherwise risk aggravating those who could have influence over their already reduced chances of funding.

While it is therefore difficult to formally record what informed actors in the field may already know, it is possible to write about extraneous circumstances that may or may not be linked, depending on one's risk appetite for defamation claims, reduced funding, or other pressure tactics. At the time of writing this chapter, there are criminal proceedings being conducted on Lawyers Collective,[43] an NGO based in New Delhi, India. The National Human Rights Commission is currently hearing petitions that allege that Lawyers Collective is facing retaliation for its humanitarian work. Anand Grover, co-founder of Lawyers Collective, was the United Nations (UN) Special Rapporteur for Health from 2008 to 2014 and also a vital part of the A2M movement, including in landmark cases.[44] There are reports, as well as Lawyers Collective's own

39 Jen Schradie, *The Digital Activism Gap: How Class and Costs Shape Online Collective Action*, 65 Soc. Probl. 51, 65 (2018).

40 *Id.*

41 *Id.*

42 Richard Anderson, *Pharmaceutical Industry Gets High on Fat Profits*, BBC (Nov. 6, 2014), https://www.bbc.com/news/business-28212223.

43 Lawyers Collective, https://lawyerscollective.org (last visited Jan. 15, 2020).

44 *NHRC Seeks Report from CBI on Probe Against Lawyers Collective*, Hindu (June 21, 2019), https://www.thehindu.com/news/national/nhrc-seeks-report-from-cbi-on-probe-against-lawyers-collective/article28103038.ece.

response,[45] that openly theorize that they are being targeted for their work in various human rights–related contexts.

An unfortunate side effect of these experiences not being documented and perspectives being hidden is that priceless on-ground knowledge does not form part of the larger discourse. This is also leading to the inevitable reduction in diversity of perspectives that contribute to the dominant discourse. With this reduced ability of Global South movements to share institutional memory in writing, they tend to be limited to the ability of individuals to spread them orally. In India, the very recent past saw the unfortunate passing of Prof. Shamnad Basheer, Dr. Amit Sengupta, and Mr. DG Shah.[46] All three were giants in their respective areas (academia, activism, and industry) in terms of their contributions to the A2M movement globally. Their deep inside knowledge and understanding of the systems, actors, and ecosystem will be supremely hard to replicate given the lack of documented evidence of the barriers, successes, and dynamics on how the A2M movement actually progressed on the ground. The spirit of this is very well captured in a tribute message left by a researcher from the University of British Columbia for Dr. Amit Sengupta after his unfortunate demise: 'I was researching my book on AIDS activism... My interview with him ... was the single most insightful meeting of that year'.[47] Yet, it is hard to find his voice as part of the mainstream voice on the A2M conversations.

### *Digitally Enabled Divide (DED)*

While these explorations of the digital divide are useful in understanding digital inequality, relying on it alone ignores the digitally 'enabled' divide that is being created. This digitally enabled divide (DED) refers to the increased disempowerment that occurs as the benefits of the networked era accrue disproportionately toward the more privileged participants. Thus, operating under the belief that the Internet always has an equalizing power disregards the fact that in certain

45 *Lawyers Collective Being Targeted for Work On Human Rights, Says Indira Jaising*, BLOOMBERGQUINT (Jul. 11, 2019), https://www.bloombergquint.com/politics/lawyers-collective-being-targeted-for-its-work-on-human-rights-says-indira-jaising; *see also Statement in Support of the Lawyers Collective and Denouncing the CBI Raids at the Office and Homes of Ms. Indira Jaising and Mr. Anand Grover of Lawyers Collective: From Public Health Experts, AIDS Activists, People Living with HIV and Representatives of Marginalised Communities* (July 12, 2019), https://lawyerscollective.org/2019/07/18/statement-in-support-of-the-lawyers-collective-and-denouncing-the-cbi-raids-at-the-office-andhomes-of-ms-indira-jaising-and-mr-anand-grover-of-lawyers-collective-from-public-health-experts-aids-ac/.

46 Jyothi Datta, *Shamnad Basheer, The Man Who Made IP a Lot Less Intimidating, Passes Away*, THE HINDU BUSINESSLINE (Aug. 9, 2019), https://www.thehindubusinessline.com/news/shamnad-basheer-the-man-who-made-ip-a-lot-less-intimidating-passes-away/article28934848.ece.

47 *Write Your Tributes for Dr. Amit Sengupta*, P.H. MOVEMENT, Aug. 27, 2009, https://phmovement.org/write-your-tributes-to-dr-amit-sengupta/.

circumstances, the disproportionate benefits of digitalization are directly contributing to increasing and exacerbating the inequality. The digital divide is an insidious danger to watch out for. This 'enablement' can take place via more recognizable forms such as oppressive hegemonization of perspectives (for example, by elite Western academia which tends to disproportionally invest into one side of the conversation with an effect of indirectly drowning other voices) or via less recognizable forms such as the harms caused by the misattribution of truth-value to new technologies. As the historical circumstances for the A2M movement's successes start giving way to new momentum triggers, it is important to note how this DED can contribute to narrative building.

While Western hegemonization of political, social, and economic thought is nothing new, how the digital sphere has exacerbated these issues should be considered, if for no other reason than that the way to counter these issues seem to arise more naturally from the digital terrain than the non-digital. Regardless of the realities of how the digital has been harnessed thus far,[48] it remains the most cost-effective and accessible method of widespread communication and mobilization.[49]

Irrespective of how insightful digital communication, information, and materials may be, it remains true that when actors are able to be physically present at important venues, their work is more likely to be looked at and noticed. This requires time and funding, especially when the 'global' meetings tend to take place in expensive Western locales.[50] In many developing countries, this also often means that when activists or scholars are funded, it is by foreign (often Western) donors. These donors then also play an important role in deciding which venues are worth funding. This does not necessitate ill intentions or biased interests on the part of donors (though that can also be a concern), but even the mere optics of having foreign donors can affect an actor's options.[51]

Funding trends have also changed significantly over the last two decades. As Joe Karaganis has noted,[52] the 'boom' phase of funding that helped give rise to public interest IP research and advocacy lasted from around 2000 to 2010 – around the same time that activism momentum reached its highest. After that,

48 Jen Schradie, *The Digital Activism Gap: How Class and Costs Shape Online Collective Action*, 65 Soc. Probl. 51–74 (2008).

49 Of course, there are also dangers and drawbacks to this relying on these methods for advocacy efforts. *See generally* Zeynep Tufecki, Twitter and Tear Gas: The power and Fragility of Networked Protest (2017).

50 For example, while WHO, WTO, and WIPO do have meetings in other locations, they are all headquartered in Geneva, Switzerland.

51 For more on reduced funding for civil society, *see State of Civil Society Report*, Civicus (2015), https://www.civicus.org/images/StateOfCivilSocietyFullReport2015.pdf.

52 Karaganis, *supra* note 10. In this presentation, he also notes that two major reasons for the reduced donor interest include the perceived untenability of tackling corporate interests, and that IP portfolios in these funding organizations remained person-centric rather than institutional, with most of the entire public interest IP funding hinging on perhaps four to five individuals, leading to it eventually falling apart.

however, it has been on the decline, despite the entrance of new funders like Google. He observed the danger this posed to developing country voices, noting:

> Collectively, we are at a moment of great promise but also great fragility. With so few funders in the field, there is some risk of a funding monoculture... There is some risk that the resource crisis of the field could force a retreat to the few well-resourced law schools and non-profits that have some independent staying power. That would also be a serious problem, first because few of those institutions are outside the US and Europe and second because both research and public interest advocacy have benefitted enormously from the diversification of the field in recent years.

Aside from funding, in-kind resources become more available to those with the privilege of physically attending such meetings. These include A2K, time, and skill, all of which act as differentiating factors for how people from different classes are able to subsequently mobilize themselves and their resources.[53]

Finally, the way in which people from different classes or geopolitical regions experience power and entitlement also affects inputs and outputs. For example, when members from the Global South give their perspective on a policy, their perspective tends to be labeled as 'a Global South perspective', while contributions from their Global North counterparts are simply taken as part of the larger narrative. While problematic on its own, this framing also nudges participants to stay within those categories, thus reducing their direct contributions to the larger narrative.

### *Embedded Power Imbalances in Narratives*

As authors have pointed out, it is crucial to look into the underlying assumptions of the narratives or frames that have been successfully mobilized in international relations, as these are good indicators of the power dynamics and imbalances inherent in global and local governance.[54] The A2M movement has been largely reactive to the public health concerns generated from the 'international IP and trade' narrative that gave birth to the TRIPS Agreement and subsequent free trade agreements. The institutional norms and values set forth by these agreements are posited as objective and universally beneficial.

This simultaneously creates two axes of difficulty that competing narratives must scale. The first is the onus of successfully reframing narratives using different lenses, such as that of public health, to relocate policy priorities. This involves strategizing about the ways in which concerns with the dominant narrative can be co-opted within different but equally powerful frames, such as

53 Schradie, *supra* note 48, at 53.

54 Denisse Albornoz et al., *Framing Power: Tracing Key Discourses in Open Science Policies*, ELPUB (June 2018).

bringing patent price–related concerns within a human rights framework. The second axis of difficulty is subtler and perhaps more controversial: ensuring that the 'anchor' provided by the dominant narrative does not determine the boundaries for competing narratives. That is to say, in its attempts to address perceived harms caused by the dominant narrative, it is a challenge to ensure that an alternate narrative is not simply a 'counter' narrative but also one that can disrupt the logic that gave rise to the dominant narrative. In the context of human rights in the age of neoliberalism, Kapczynski articulates this challenge in the following way:

> A right to medicines imbricated into this regime is plausibly regressive: it places significant strain on healthcare budgets, redistributes upwards, and provides medicines on terms largely dictated by one of the most profitable industries in the world. This right to medicines, in short, reflects and even intensifies a neoliberal approach to medicines. It mandates discrete individual relief, but rarely sees, much less disrupts, the underlying legal logics and structures that help produce radical health inequities.[55]

While that broader example may be subject to some debate, one does not need to look at such a theoretical level to see this failure in action. For example, when 80 percent of the world uses some form of traditional medicine,[56] why is the A2M debate primarily thought of in terms of allopathic medicine? To what extent have holistic healing practices been integrated into the A2M debate? While some may have hesitations about these methods, the stark absence of these issues from debates appears to be a demonstration of a form of epistemic governance, where the counter-narrative is only reacting to the harms caused by the dominant narrative rather than looking at larger public health goals, even if only to rule them out as options. No doubt, there are other debates that focus on traditional knowledge and medicine – but these seem to be insufficiently brought up in the context of the A2M debate. Following this logic, it can be argued that the de facto importance placed by the A2M movement on accessibility of allopathic patent protected medicines has reduced the value placed on solutions outside of this patent product innovation framework altogether,[57] or

55 Amy Kapczynski, *The Right to Medicines in an Age of Neoliberalism*, HUMANITY J. (Apr. 26, 2019), http://humanityjournal.org/issue10-1/the-right-to-medicines-in-an-age-of-neoliberalism/.

56 Martins Ekor, *The Growing Use of Herbal Medicines: Issues Relating to Adverse Reactions and Challenges in Monitoring Safety*, FRONTIERSIN (Jan. 10, 2014), https://www.ncbi.nlm.nih.gov/pmc/articles/PMC3887317/.

57 Note the 'humble checklist' example in the following paper. *See* Amy Kapczynski & Talha Syed, *The Continuum of Excludability and the Limits of Patents*, 122 YALE L.J. 1900–02 (2013), https://digitalcommons.law.yale.edu/cgi/viewcontent.cgi?article=5699&context=fss_papers.

solution mechanisms that may, in fact, be more suitable for the anthropological and geographical specificities of the developing world.

## Realizing Digital Narratives

The simplistic narrative of 'strong' IP being an absolute necessity is no longer nearly as dominant as it was two decades ago. Part of that change is owed to the A2M movement, which has successfully countered by highlighting the flaws of the dominant narrative. Nonetheless, the A2M movement will need to account for the changing circumstances to keep pace with the neoliberal juggernaut as it continues forward. The tremendous coordination and efforts that brought victories to the A2M movement will require new impetus and narratives to be continued in these new circumstances. And, in light of the ever-increasing pervasiveness of the digital sphere in our lives, there is an urgent need to remedy the problem of missing voices from the A2M movement. Not just for correcting the record, but to effectively lay the groundwork for new mobilization.

Indeed, there is already a glaring example of failure to use the digital to mobilize support around a crucial A2M development even though the development also existed on the digital sphere! An important concern raised by the A2M movement was that of disproportionate research vis-a-vis developing country diseases.[58] One significant attempt to address this issue was the Indian government's CSIR Open Source Drug Discovery (OSDD) program to work on treatments for neglected tropical diseases.[59] Despite a few hiccups,[60] the project seems to have been running smoothly. Through its online platform, it can decentralize costs to a great extent,[61] and through its mission of staying patent-free, it is able to price drugs very affordably.[62] Despite being a direct solution to the questions posed by the counter-narrative, the OSDD project is relatively underemphasized in the A2M movement, and even in the general public's consciousness.[63] While the reasons for this may be varied, one hopes that the A2M

58 Martina Casenghi et al., *New Approaches to Filling the Gap in Tuberculosis Drug Discovery*, 4 PLoS Med. 11, 1722 (2007), https://journals.plos.org/plosmedicine/article/file?id=10.1371/journal.pmed.0040293&type=printable.

59 Nisha Chandran & Samir K. Brahmachari, *A Decade of OSDD for TB: Role and Outcomes*, 115 Curr. Sci. 1858–64 (2018), doi: 10.18520/cs/v115/i10/1858-1864.

60 Thomas J. Vallianeth, *Spicyip Tidbit: Bureaucracy may Cost the OSDD a Year of Funding*, Spicyip (Apr. 3, 2014), https://spicyip.com/2014/04/spicyip-tidbit-bureaucracy-may-cause-the-osdd-a-year-of-funding.html.

61 Its budget of $12 million for a treatment for tuberculosis is almost a negligible fraction of the estimated $2.6 billion that a new drug generally is estimated to cost.

62 Casenghi et al., *supra* note 58.

63 *The Missing Discovery: CSIR's Open Source Drug Development Making Waves Everywhere Except India*, Economic Times Bureau (update Sept. 9, 2015, 3:18 PM), https://economictimes.indiatimes.com/industry/healthcare/biotech/pharmaceuticals/the-missing-discovery-csirs-open-source-drug-development-making-waves-everywhere-except-india/articleshow/48180990.cms.

movement absorbs these lessons as they form new digital (and non-digital) strategies moving forward.

In an interesting turn, one of the biggest lessons for advocacy movements could come from the global right-wing turn of the sociopolitical world. Several countries have seen new political struggles at their national level, with more 'right-wing' parties or candidates gaining favor with voters, such as Donald Trump in the US, Narendra Modi in India, or Jair Bolsonaro in Brazil. A novel factor that they all have in common is the extraordinary use of social media in their elections.[64] A masterful use of social media to build or rebuild narratives of nationalistic fervor, often laced with messages of returning to a period of rich traditional history, has not only helped them gain supporters but by hitting upon the right spots, has ensured that their narrative is evangelized passionately as well. Understanding how these frames work and how to effectively use frame overlays is crucial, as it not only allows for effective norm setting but also allows for the creation of positive and not just reactive agendas. In India, for example, the 'glorious past' narrative has led to the creation of a ministry[65] dedicated to certain types of traditional medicine. This may or may not have had anything to do with the A2M movement, but regardless, it is potentially a development which the A2M movement could strongly co-opt and utilize in framing new narratives.

With the digital sphere playing an ever-increasing role in social interactions and therefore, movement building, its importance in reframing narratives cannot be emphasized enough. At the same time, it must be recognized that there are certain digital health narratives already at play that have already come with their own embedded biases. The more immediate past has seen the ever-increasing pervasiveness of technology in our lives, adding words that would have formerly been categorized as technobabble, into our daily vocabulary – 'AI', 'facial recognition', 'blockchain', and others. Artificial intelligence (AI) in health care, for example, is predicted to set up a paradigm shift.[66] It is important to not automatically ascribe a high 'truth-value', as what tends to happen to these new digital based technologies. For example, the automated nature of AI-based health-care solutions will tend to make them be seen as more 'accessible' or 'cheap' health-care resources. However, it should be realized that they can also suffer from limitations such as bias, lack of accountability, and limited or incomplete

64 Ralph Schroeder, Social Theory After the Internet: Media, Technology, and Globalization 60–81 (2018).

65 Ministry of Ayurveda, Yoga & Naturopathy, Unani, Siddha and Homoeopathy (AYUSH), http://ayush.gov.in/ (last visited Jan. 15, 2020).

66 *See, e.g.*, Fei Jiang et al., *Artificial Intelligence in Healthcare: Past, Present and Future*, 2 Stroke Vasc. Neurol. 230–43 (2017), doi:10.1136/svn-2017-000101.

datasets from which conclusions are drawn.[67] The increased efficiency or convenience, combined with the perceived objectivity of these technology-based solutions, is very likely to thrust such solutions forward as immediately attractive options in addressing health-care issues. It will be increasingly important for A2M advocacy to include narratives that highlight the requirement for appropriate safeguards to preempt and negate the illusion of 'complete objectivity' of these technology-based solutions.

## Conclusion

As it currently stands, there are two definite steps that activists can use with the digital – reclaiming and repairing the DED and using the digital to promote alternative frames that help push the movement forward. The A2M movement of the next two decades will most certainly unravel in a very different way from that of the last two decades. What will be interesting to see is whether it can finally drive the dominant narrative as well!

67 'It's possible that similar racial biases could inadvertently be built into health-care algorithms. Health-care delivery already varies by race. An algorithm designed to predict outcomes from genetic findings will be biased if there have been few (or no) genetic studies in certain populations'. Danton S., M. D., Nigam H. Shah, M. B. B. S., Ph. D., and David Magnus, Ph. D., *Implementing Machine Learning in Health Care – Addressing Ethical Challenges*, 378 N. Engl. J. Med. 11, 981–83 (2018); *see also* Dave Gershgorn, *If AI is Going to be the World's Doctor, It Needs Better Textbooks*, Quartz (Sept. 6, 2018), https://qz.com/1367177/if-ai-is-going-to-be-the-worlds-doctor-it-needs-better-textbooks/.

# Part IV

# COVID-19 and Access to Medicines

# Lessons from COVID-19 for Medicines Access

*Amaka Vanni*

## Introduction

Cases of COVID-19 first emerged in late 2019, when a mysterious illness was first reported in the city of Wuhan in China's Hubei Province. The cause of the disease was soon confirmed as a new kind of coronavirus. Later named severe acute respiratory syndrome (SARS)-CoV-2, this form of coronavirus can cause mild flu-like symptoms (or even be asymptomatic) that can progress to acute pneumonia-like respiratory illness called novel coronavirus-infected pneumonia (NCIP). On March 11, 2020, the World Health Organization (WHO) officially announced that COVID-19[1] is a global pandemic.[2] The magnitude and impact of COVID-19 is staggering. It has crashed economies, caused thousands of deaths, crippled national health systems, separated families and coworkers, emptied public spaces, and disrupted our world as we know it. At the time of writing, the number of infections worldwide has crossed over 3.5 million while more than 245,000 people have died. (Un)surprisingly, Europe and the United States (US) are the hardest hit and projections estimate the number will swell to hundreds of thousands in the coming months.

This concluding chapter undertakes two tasks. First, the magnitude and urgency of COVID-19 has forced us to revisit the present system of patents, and intellectual property (IP) more generally, and to see more clearly the ways that it is not the model for delivering the products now needed to respond to global health emergencies. The second task addresses the issue of research and development (R&D) of new treatments for infectious diseases without the whims of the market such that we can be best prepared for future pandemics.

1 This is not the formal name for the virus. The International Committee on Taxonomy of Viruses (ICTV) calls it the "severe acute respiratory syndrome coronavirus 2," or SARS-CoV-2. *See* A.E. Gorbalenya et al., *The Species Severe Acute Respiratory Syndrome-Related Coronavirus: Classifying 2019-nCoV and Naming it SARS-CoV-2*, 5 Nat. Microbiol. 536–44 (2020), https://doi.org/10.1038/s41564-020-0695-z.

2 Peng Zhou et al., *A Pneumonia Outbreak Associated with a New Coronavirus of Probable Bat Origin*, 579 Nature 270–73 (2020).

## Global Patent Regime and Structural Violence

The public health impact of the COVID-19 pandemic has resurfaced the importance of pharmaceuticals on everyday lives and the need to de-link the costs of R&D from the prices of products.[3] It has also highlighted another issue that was always actively present within the global IP regime – the structural violence[4] embedded within our world order, which manifests in our treatified global economic structure, including the Agreement on Trade-Related Aspects of Intellectual Property Rights (TRIPS Agreement) and other free trade agreements (FTAs).

### *Understanding Structural Violence*

Our concept of structural violence builds on the work of Johan Galtung, who defines it as "forms of harm or violence built in the systems (social, economic, biological) and shows up as unequal power and consequently as unequal life chances."[5] According to Galtung, it is the avoidable "impairment of fundamental human needs or human life, which lowers the actual degree to which someone is able to meet their needs below that which would otherwise be possible."[6] These structures – tying in with the theoretical framework explicated in our introduction to mean the modern global capitalist framework – by their very nature (and history) churn out harm, generate or perpetuate poverty and inequality, and cause basic human needs deficits.[7] This form of violence is indirect because there may not be any person who directly harms another in the structure, and yet harm is done because this form of violence is embedded and enabled in our social and economic systems. For example, Galtung explains, if a "person died from tuberculosis in the 18th century, it would be hard to conceive this as violence since it might have been quite unavoidable, but if he dies from it today, despite all the medical resources in the world, then violence is present according to our definition."[8] In a similar vein, he continues, "life expectancy of thirty years during the Neolithic period was not an expression of violence but the same life-expectancy today (whether due to wars, or social injustice, or both) would be seen as violence according to our definition."[9] Thus for Galtung, if people are dying or starving when such death or starvation is objectively

3 James Love, *Discussion Paper: An Economic Perspective on Delinking the Cost of R&D from the Price of Medicines*, Knowledge Ecology International (2016), https://www.keionline.org/wp-content/uploads/Delinkage_economic-perspective_Feb2016.pdf.

4 Johan Galtung, *Violence, Peace, and Peace Research*, 6 J. Peace Res. 167–91 (1969).

5 *Id.* at 171; *see also* Johan Galtung & Dietrich Fischer, *Violence: Direct, Structural and Cultural, in* 5 SpringerBriefs on Pioneers in Science and Practice 35 (Hans Günter Brauch ed., 2013).

6 Johan Galtung, *Violence, Peace and Peace Research*, 6 J. Peace Res. 167–91 (1969).

7 Galtung & Fischer, *supra* note 5.

8 *Id.* at 168.

9 *Id.* at 168.

avoidable, then violence is being committed regardless "of whether there is a clear subject-action-object relation, as during a siege or no such clear relation, as in the way world economic relations are organized today."[10]

Paul Farmer expands this theory further and draws it into the field of public health and anthropology to show how structural violence is embodied in epidemic diseases, violation of human rights, and genocide.[11] For Farmer, while structural violence manifests in the ways violence is exerted systematically and indirectly by everyone who belongs to a certain social order, it is also about power – the power to decide over the distribution of and access to resources, including (but not limited to) health care, education, food, and water quality.

### *Global IP Regime and Structural Violence*

The current global property law regime exported by the developed countries, particularly the US and embodied in the TRIPS Agreement and other TRIPS-plus FTAs exemplifies a form of *structural violence.* As analyses in this book have shown, the avoidable deaths from HIV/AIDS as a result of lack of medicines access due to high prices caused by patent monopoly, and despite pharmaceutical developments and availability of required medications, illustrate this. The growing practice of patent thickets and exclusivities in domestic IP regimes, exported in trade agreement, and adds years of monopoly protection underscores how violence is built into IP structures. This allows pharmaceutical companies to increase prices at whim, subsequently deepening unequal access and unequal life chances. Thus, to the extent that there is an increasing presence of society divided only by the ability to access medication ("privileged-to-access-medicine" or PTAM), it is possible to critique the international and domestic IP regimes in terms of *structural violence* because it facilitates the conditions for global health inequities and continues to inflict harm by systematically disadvantaging certain groups of people from access to lifesaving medicines. In this view, the structural violence of the patent regimes continues to play itself out in the daily injury and deaths it causes – the inequity and inequality in access as a result of high prices caused by patent monopoly. It goes without saying there are other factors that inhibit equitable medicines access such a poor, underfunded healthcare systems and corruption to state failure. While these are valid factors, it is also important to recognize the role of law in maximizing the profitability of particular forms of property, regardless of the human cost.

Of course, many could argue (and have already argued) that pharmaceutical companies are to be explicitly blamed for the deaths as a result of exorbitant costs

10 *Id.* at 171.

11 Paul Farmer, *An Anthropology of Structural Violence*, 45 CURR. ANTHROPOL. 305–25 (2004). Paul Famer built on the work of Galtung to define structural violence as "violence exerted systematically—that is, indirectly—by everyone who belongs to a certain social order."

attached to essential lifesaving medicines, which are priced out of reach for the poor[12] and thus directly responsible for those pernicious avoidable deaths. While such analysis is valid, it ignores the complex factors that expanded the scope of protection and introduced novel patent-related rights such as market and data exclusivities, thereby allowing pharmaceutical companies to exploit global and national IP regimes. In fact, a historical examination of the contemporary patent regime shows how colonialism,[13] racism,[14] and inequality[15] became deeply sedimented into the international IP law, particularly patents, to enforce a particular type of property rights and to protect the economic interest of the transnational capitalist class.

Furthermore, the TRIPS Agreement – in harmonizing IP rules across regions – disregards wealth disparities, disease burdens, and asymmetrical levels of development within and across countries. It also created "exclusivity" that set the stage for a systematic model of harm in the production of inequitable access to medicines and health technologies. This exclusivity gives rise to scarcity as right owners decide who is allowed to use an innovative drug, at what cost, and who is excluded. The outcome and potency of this scarcity is not only in the lack of access but also in the normalization of the attendant morbidity and deaths. Monopoly, as a result of patents, has turned medicines and access to them into strategic assets that shape life so precariously. Thus, by its very nature, the contemporary patent regime primarily and irrevocably perpetuates violence, especially at a time when scientific research continues to yield miraculous outcomes.

Although there are exceptions and flexibilities within the global patent regime to remedy the harm caused, it still does not make it less so. If anything, it increases the scope for structural inequality by expanding a patentee's control of an unjust system. For instance, a government can issue a compulsory license (CL) but it also has to pay royalties to a patent holder, who usually benefits

12 David Barnard, *In the High Court of South Africa, Case No. 4138/98: The Global Politics of Access to Low-Cost AIDS Drugs in Poor Countries*, 12 Kennedy Inst. Ethics J. 159–74 (2002).

13 Amaka Vanni, 1 Patent Games in the Global South: Pharmaceutical Patent Law-Making in Brazil, India and Nigeria 37–51 (2020). On the introduction of patent law through colonialism, *see* Edith Penrose, *International Patenting and the Less-Developed Countries*, 83 Econ. J. 768 (1973); Constantine Vaitsos, *Patents Revisited: Their Function in Developing Countries*, 9 J. Dev. Stud. 71–97 (1972).

14 Natsu T. Saito, *From Slavery and Seminoles to AIDS in South Africa: An Essay on Race and Property in International Law*, 45 Villanova Law Rev. (2000). In fact, it has been argued that an analytic omission and erasure of these histories in analysis of public health policies and interventions (I will also add IP laws in general and patent regimes in particular) is a form of structural violence. *See* Farmer, *supra* note 11, at 1690.

15 B.S. Chimni, *Political Economy of the Uruguay Round of Negotiations: A Perspective*, 29 Int. Stud. 135–58 (1992); Antony Anghie, *Time Present and Time Past: Globalization, International Financial Institutions, and the Third World*, 32 N.Y. Univ. J. Int. Law Polit. (2000); Antony Anghie, *Imperialism, Sovereignty, and the Making of International Law*, Cambridge Studies in International and Comparative Law (2005).

from government subsidies.[16] And even at that, CLs are insufficient measures to remedy the harm caused by patent policies because they require a capable manufacturing exporter who can successfully produce the emergency medicines. In fact, the chapters on Brazil and Thailand in this volume succinctly illustrate this. Other commentators also highlight voluntary license (VL)[17] practices as an acceptable solution to overcome the market effect of patents and to increase access to lower cost generic medicines, especially in low- and middle-income countries. While a VL does bring down the price of newer expensive drugs, its role as a remedy remains fragile as long as its success depends on the willingness and benevolence of pharmaceutical companies. This is because individualistic benevolence is not a substitute for systemic change. In fact, the VL deal Gilead issued for *remdesivir* underscores this.[18] Though this agreement allows generic manufacturers to produce the medicine for 127 countries, it excludes key lower middle–income countries with high COVID-19 infections such as Brazil, China, and Mexico. In this regard, the Gilead monopoly still holds and it gets to decide who lives and who dies.

## *COVID-19, Patents, and the Revolving Door of Structural Violence*

The COVID-19 pandemic has underscored the continued harm caused by {abusive} patents and the politico-economic systems that maintain them. The global high demand, limited supply, and the risk that pharmaceutical companies will exploit the patent regime for financial benefits bring attention to this structural violence – the life and death significance, and the way in which health and medical resources will be allocated and experienced, especially at a time when the world could ill-afford such.[19]

16 According to the National Institute of Health (NIH), it invests about $41.7 billion annually in medical research for the American people. *See also* Mariana Mazzucato & Azzi Momenghalibaf, *Drug Companies Will Make a Killing from Coronavirus*, N.Y. Times (Mar. 18, 2020), https://www.nytimes.com/2020/03/18/opinion/coronavirus-vaccine-cost.html. According to Mariana Mazzucato and Azzi Momenghalibaf, the NIH funding contributed to every one of the 210 new drugs approved by the Federal Drug Administration from 2010 to 2016.

17 Voluntary license refers to a practice where IP owners voluntarily grant licenses to their patents to generic manufactures against the payment of royalties. *See* Jorge Bermudez & Ellen 't Hoen, *The UNITAID Patent Pool Initiative: Bringing Patents Together for the Common Good*, 4 Open AIDS J. 37–40 (2010); Reed Beall & Randall Kuhn, *Trends in Compulsory Licensing of Pharmaceuticals Since the Doha Declaration: A Database Analysis*, 9 PLoS Med. 4–6 (2012).

18 *Voluntary Licensing Agreements for Remdesivir*, Gilead, https://www.gilead.com/purpose/advancing-global-health/covid-19/voluntary-licensing-agreements-for-remdesivir (last visited July 3, 2020).

19 Not there is ever a time violence of any sort is warranted. However, with such an invisible enemy such as coronavirus and its history-shattering impact, any sort of avoidable violence is needed.

Around $8 billion of public, philanthropic, and private funding has already been poured into R&D efforts to detect, treat, and prevent COVID-19.[20] Yet, because of patent monopoly ensuing as a result of possibly developing the innovative drug for its treatment, pharmaceutical companies will most likely determine its market price. A report has emerged that investment banks are urging pharmaceutical companies to raise their prices and to create a business out of products currently under development.[21] Meanwhile, some companies are already employing age-old patent barrier practices in the production and provision of vital coronavirus drugs. In March 2020, Gilead applied to the US Food and Drug Administration (FDA) for orphan drug status for the drug *remdesivir* when it was reported that the drug could be used in COVID-19 treatment.[22] Orphan drug status is designated for the treatment of rare diseases affecting less than 200,000 to allow the drug maker to recoup development costs because the drug serves a relatively small patient population. It also gives the manufacturer tax breaks and a seven-year marketing exclusivity period, which would allow Gilead to charge high monopoly prices and block the market entry of lower cost generic versions. In fact, what was most glaring about Gilead's attempt was that, at the time of its application and approval by the FDA, there were already more than 40,000 confirmed COVID-19 cases in the US, and an estimation that the number will grow exponentially in the coming weeks.[23] After much criticism from the press and public, Gilead rescinded its application.

20 Matina Stevis-Gridneff & Lara Jakes, *World Leaders Join to Pledge $8 Billion for Vaccine as U.S. Goes it Alone*, N.Y. Times, https://www.nytimes.com/2020/05/04/world/europe/eu-coronavirus-vaccine.html (last visited May 18, 2020).

21 Lee Fang, *Banks Pressure Health Care Firms to Raise Prices on Critical Drugs, Medical Supplies for Coronavirus*, Intercept, https://theintercept.com/2020/03/19/coronavirus-vaccine-medical-supplies-price-gouging/ (last visited May 7, 2020).

22 Lee Fang & Sharon Lerner, *Coronavirus Treatment Developed by Gilead Sciences Granted "Rare Disease" Status, Potentially Limiting Affordability*, Intercept, https://theintercept.com/2020/03/23/gilead-sciences-coronavirus-treatment-orphan-drug-status/ (last visited May 8, 2020).

23 *Id. See also* Manas Mishra & Michael Erman, *Gilead Asks FDA to Take Back Lucrative Orphan Drug Status on Possible Coronavirus Treatment U.S.*, Reuters, https://www.reuters.com/article/us-health-coronavirus-gilead-sciences/gilead-asks-fda-to-take-back-lucrative-orphan-drug-status-on-possible-coronavirus-treatment-idUSKBN21C3MG (last visited May 8, 2020). A study by the pharmaceutical advocacy groups, Knowledge Ecology International (KEI) and Public Citizen, shows that *remdesivir* benefited at every stage of development from public funding through federal grants and clinical trials. From KEI, *see* Kathryn Ardizzone, *KEI Briefing Note 2020: 1 Role of the Federal Government in the Development of GS-5734/Remdesivir*, Knowledge Ecology International, https://www.keionline.org/wp-content/uploads/KEI-Briefing-Note-2020_1GS-5734-Remdesivir.pdf (last visited May 8, 2020). From Public Citizen, *see* Public Citizen, *The Public Already Has Paid for Remdesivir*, Public Citizen, https://www.citizen.org/news/the-public-already-has-paid-for-remdesivir/ (last visited May 8, 2020).

In addition, protective equipment and diagnostic test tools have become the other focal points in the coronavirus pandemic. Makers of the 3M respiratory masks filed multiple patents between March 3 and April 7,[24] preventing generic competitors from manufacturing the respiratory masks. Meanwhile, countries such as the Netherlands were unable to scale up testing for COVID-19 because of shortage of chemical apparatus needed for testing, particularly the lysis buffer solution, which breaks down cells in the molecular analysis of the coronavirus. This is because the Swiss manufacturer Roche, the original maker of the lysis buffer, "refused to reveal the formula and technical specifications needed to ensure compatibility with Roche's hardware."[25] Hiding access to life-saving knowledge behind thickets of patents (or over-patenting) not only slows progress but is also at variance with the objective of the TRIPS Agreement.[26] Over-patenting, many scholars acknowledge, is now a growing business strategy to "avoid competition in order to earn outsized profits on medicines for many years beyond what was intended."[27] According to I-Mak, patent thickets increase the price of branded drugs by an average of 68 percent in six years, and stall generic competition by an average of 38 years.[28] Doris Long in her chapter illustrates this scenario with the case of 12 top-selling patented drugs in the US, which have at least 71 granted patents per drug.[29] This shows how the present patent regime is ill-suited to respond to global public health needs as private profits continue to take precedence over human life. Again, we see how the current neoliberal capitalist structure, made legitimate through shifts in patent rules that promote exclusivity, monopoly, and predatory value extraction over human life, continues to wreak violence on the lives and bodies of the "have-nots" by denying access to lifesaving medicines. These events reveal just how structural violence, at the root of the patent regime, takes up new forms in every era.[30]

24 Alexander Zaitchik, *No Vaccine in Sight*, New Republic, https://newrepublic.com/amp/article/157594/no-coronavirus-vaccine-big-pharma-drug-patent-system (last visited May 14, 2020).

25 Ed Silverman, *Roche Backpedals on Providing Liquid for Covid-19 Tests in the Netherlands*, Stat, https://www.statnews.com/pharmalot/2020/03/27/roche-covid19-coronavirus-netherlands/ (last visited May 14, 2020). *See also* Ellen 't Hoen, *Protect Against Market Exclusivity in the Fight Against COVID-19*, Nat. Med. 813 (2020).

26 Article 7, TRIPS Agreement states that the objective of the agreement is to contribute to the promotion of technological innovation, the transfer and dissemination of technology in a mutually advantageous way to producers and users of technological knowledge.

27 I-MAK, *Overpatented, Overpriced: How Excessive Pharmaceutical Patenting is Extending Monopolies and Driving up Drug Prices*, http://www.i-mak.org/wp-content/uploads/2018/08/I-MAK-Overpatented-Overpriced-Report.pdf (last visited Apr. 3, 2020).

28 *Id.* at 11.

29 *See* Doris Long, Part III, chapter 6.

30 Farmer, *supra* note 11, at 315.

## Post-COVID-19 and Addressing Infectious Diseases

While many nations are rightly focused on the COVID-19 pandemic, the issues of lack of access to medicines and treatment for other infectious diseases still remain. Commentators, for example, estimate that in a typical year, the influenza virus causes as many as five million cases of severe illness in humans and 500,000 deaths.[31] Meanwhile, infectious disease incidents in the early 2000s such as the SARS in 2003, the H5N1 avian influenza in 2005, the H1N1 influenza in 2009, and the Ebola outbreak in 2013 underscored the global inability to address the problem of preparedness for serious disease events. For example, in reviewing the global response to the 2009 H1N1 influenza that killed over 100,000 people,[32] Harvey V. Fineberg notes that the inability to distribute enough influenza vaccines in a timely way was the most serious operational shortcoming in the global response to the outbreak. Furthermore, though "78 million doses of vaccine were sent to 77 countries, it was mainly long after they would have done the most good."[33] Other commentators note how high-income governments stockpiled most of the world's vaccine supply through early purchase commitments, leaving many poor and lower income countries out in the cold.[34] The same failure was seen during the Ebola outbreak.[35] These failures highlight the critical importance of global vigilance for infectious diseases. Yet, the severity of and the damages caused by COVID-19 shows how the world is nowhere close to being prepared to handle a pandemic. Importantly, the difficulties experienced with the coronavirus response demonstrate the multifaceted failure of the drug development system and the market framework that props it up, and how we cannot abandon the treatment of infectious diseases to the whims of the market such that we can be best prepared for future pandemics.

As COVID-19 continues to spread, companies, institutes, and researchers race to find a cure or at least a vaccine. To shorten the timeline from development to market entry, pharmaceutical companies are "repurposing" medicines normally indicated for other diseases to treat COVID-19. For instance,

31 Harvey V. Fineberg, *Pandemic Preparedness and Response – Lessons from the H1N1 Influenza of 2009*, 370 New Eng. J. Med. 1335–42 (2014).

32 Estimates ranges of 123,000–203,000 deaths and 105,700–395,600 deaths. *See* Lone Simonsen et al., *Global Mortality Estimates for the 2009 Influenza Pandemic from the GLaMOR Project: A Modeling Study*, 10 PLoS Med. e1001558 (Nov. 2013); Fatimah S. Dawood et al., *Estimated Global Mortality Associated with the first 12 Months of 2009 Pandemic Influenza A H1N1 Virus Circulation: A Modelling Study*, 12 Lancet Infect. Dis. 687–95 (2012).

33 *Id.*

34 Gavin Yamey et al., *Ensuring Global Access to COVID-19 Vaccines*, 395 Lancet 1405–06 (May 2, 2020); Surie Moon, *The Vaccine Race: Will Public Health Prevail over Geopolitics?* (June 2020), https://globalchallenges.ch/issue/special_1/the-vaccine-race-will-public-health-prevail-over-geopolitics/.

35 Alexander Zaitchik narrates this failure in the case of Ebola vaccine development. *See* Alexander Zaitchik, *No Vaccine in Sight*, The New Republic (May 11, 2020), https://newrepublic.com/amp/article/157594/no-coronavirus-vaccine-big-pharma-drug-patent-system.

*remdesivir* – which is one of the leading candidates for COVID-19 treatment – was initially developed and approved for the treatment of Ebola. This practice of repurposing is particularly expedient in a pandemic in two ways. First, it helps reduce the cost of developing new drugs because approved methodologies and safety profiles have already been established, decreasing the need for costly clinical trials.[36] Second, it facilitates a rapid upscale of production of the most promising drugs within a shortened timeframe, thereby quickening market entry.[37] However, repurposing highlights a consequential failure of the current patent system to encourage the R&D of new drugs and vaccines for diseases which it sees as unprofitable – the so-called neglected diseases – because they primarily affect populations with little purchasing power, and therefore offer an insufficient market for attracting investment from the pharmaceutical industry.[38]

Meanwhile, many pharmaceutical companies have stopped investing in the development of new antibiotics or in general antibiotic research and innovation because there is no lucrative market for them.[39] Instead, these companies are focused on the development of blockbuster drugs with guaranteed high financial returns and on other shareholder obligations such as stock buybacks.[40] In 2018, 12 of the largest pharmaceutical companies in the US spent more money buying back their stock than on drug R&D.[41] The 2019 report by the Global Funding of Innovation for Neglected Diseases (G-Finder) also noted that while the global funding for neglected disease R&D rose to $4 billion in 2018, funding for neglected tropical diseases (NTDs) has gone backwards in the last decade, dropping by $34 million.[42] This highlights a broken patent system that encourages

36 Andrew Hill et al., *Minimum Costs to Manufacture New Treatments for COVID-19*, J. Virus Erad. 61–63 (Apr. 2020), http://viruseradication.com/journal-details/Minimum_costs_to_manufacture_new_treatments_for_COVID-19/.

37 *Id.*

38 Suerie Moon et al., *Innovation and Access to Medicines for Neglected Populations: Could a Treaty Address a Broken Pharmaceutical R&D System?*, 9 PLoS Med. e1001218 (2012).

39 Sarah Boseley, *Big Pharma Failing to Invest in New Antibiotics, Says WHO*, The Guardian Jan. 17, 2020, https://www.theguardian.com/business/2020/jan/17/big-pharma-failing-to-invest-in-new-antibiotics-says-who.

40 Bob Herman, *Big Pharma is on a Stock Buyback Spree*, Axios Mar. 5, 2020, https://www.axios.com/big-pharma-stock-buybacks-research-123f10f1-79d0-44be-a515-a6603fbcfd9a.html.

41 *Id.* According to the author, these companies repurchased $69.1 billion of their stock in 2018, while spending $65.9 billion on researching new medicines. Specifically, Amgen and Biogen spent more on stock buybacks for the entire period than they spent on R&D. Amgen's stock repurchases ($31.6 billion) were more than twice as much as research ($15.3 billion).

42 Nick Chapman et al., *Neglected Disease Research and Development: Uneven Progress*, Policy Cures Research (2019), https://s3-ap-southeast-2.amazonaws.com/policy-cures-website-assets/app/uploads/2020/02/11150341/G-Finder2019.pdf. *See also* Médecins Sans Frontières, *Fatal Imbalance: The Crisis in Research and Development for Drugs for Neglected Diseases*, MSF Access to Essential Medicines Campaign (Sept. 2001), https://msfaccess.org/fatal-imbalance-crisis-research-and-development-drugs-neglected-diseases.

private monetary compensation over innovation at the expense of those who cannot purchase these expensive medicines or are afflicted by diseases of the poor.

The current system for the R&D of new medicines is inadequate to meet the needs of modern times, especially for medicines for new and more virulent pathogens and infections. This is crucial for preparedness and response to future crises,[43] which public health experts warn are likely to become more frequent due to zoonotic spillovers.[44] In fact, many of the problems that have emerged in response to COVID-19 are issues that have emphasized the inability of the market to deal with infectious diseases, particularly access to sufficient medical and health resources (such as drugs, vaccines, diagnostics, and other medical products), equitable delivery of health products, and emergency outbreak response and preparedness. Moreover, the scant efforts by the few pharmaceutical companies involved in drug development for infectious diseases remain ad hoc, fragmented, and lack a reliable sustainable mechanism to generate sufficient funding for research, while relying heavily on donor financing and priorities, and covering a limited set of diseases.[45] Thus, it has become a matter of existential urgency for the development of new technologies to extenuate the vast challenges posed by these infectious diseases, and to also mend the fragile global system for outbreak prevention and prepare for future pandemics.

### *Looking Ahead – When This is Over, What Next?*

Advances in medical science and public health practices have vastly improved our understanding of these illnesses. However, without equitable access, these medical breakthroughs and innovations are futile. The current coronavirus pandemic presents an opportunity for us to not only fundamentally rethink the present patent framework and drug development system, but also dismantle other forms of exclusivities that have been employed to prop up monopolies and have not necessarily led to the health-needed innovations they were meant to incentivize. The bluff of the pharmaceutical industry for the high patent regime and prices for R&D must be called out. Likewise, the era of numerous anticompetitive practices, relying on market forces to deliver on infectious diseases while extracting maximum value from the most expensive drugs for as long as possible, must end. We need to build a new paradigm on vaccine R&D and scale up new models if global efforts are going to tackle problems of new infectious outbreaks.

43 Bill Gates, *The Next Epidemic – Lessons from Ebola*, 372 New Eng. J. Med. 1381–4 (2015); Laurie Garrett, *The Next Pandemic?*, Foreign Affairs (2005), https://www.foreignaffairs.com/articles/2005-07-01/next-pandemic; Michael T. Osterholm, *Preparing for the Next Pandemic*, 84 Foreign Aff. 24–37 (2005).

44 Sonia Shah, *Think Exotic Animals Are to Blame for the Coronavirus? Think Again*, The Nation (Feb. 18, 2020), https://www.thenation.com/article/environment/coronavirus-habitat-loss/.

45 Moon et al., *supra* note 38.

While many alternatives have been offered by various commentators,[46] two key ideas stand out. First, open-source system, which – as the name denotes – is a structure of accessible and transparent development process and licenses. It involves scientists, creators, and inventors publicly sharing procedures and methods in the development of an invention to catalyze new research.[47] It also enables a culture of collaboration and inclusivity, thereby providing a genuinely new competing model for the discovery of new medicines. For instance, in the early days of the COVID-19 pandemic, researchers in countries, including China, Germany, the United Kingdom, and the US, shared information on the genome sequence for COVID-19.[48] This allowed researchers and laboratories around the world to collaboratively work to reveal the structures of key coronavirus proteins. As a result, a team of structural biologists at Shanghai Tech University in China was able to reveal the structure of a key enzyme, *Mpro*, that the virus needs to replicate.[49]

In analyzing the open-source model for influenza, Amy Kapczynski notes how the Global Influenza Surveillance and Response Network produced data, analysis, and research that proved crucial in the discovery and development of new vaccines and diagnostics[50] – none of it could have happened in the closed proprietary black boxes of IP. Such information-sharing initiatives are required to prepare for and tackle future pandemics. Though a number of platforms have been designed to facilitate the free exchange of pharmaceutical technologies and epidemiological and research data on COVID-19 (such as the WHO COVID-19 Technology Access Pool or C-TAP),[51] there are no overarching legal frameworks or regimes in place today to ensure knowledge, data sharing, and scientific

46 James Love, *Discussion Paper: An Economic Perspective on Delinking the Cost of R&D from the Price of Medicines*, Unitaid (2016), https://www.keionline.org/wp-content/uploads/Delinkage_economic-perspective_Feb2016.pdf; Jorge Bermudez & Ellen 't Hoen, *The UNITAID Patent Pool Initiative: Bringing Patents Together for the Common Good*, 4 The Open AIDS J. 37–40 (2010); World Health Organization, World Intellectual Property Organization, World Trade Organization, *Promoting Access to Medical Technologies and Innovation – Intersections between Public Health, Intellectual Property and Trade* (2013), https://www.wipo.int/publications/en/details.jsp?id=305&plang=EN (last visited Jun 22, 2020).

47 Amy Kapczynski, *Order without Intellectual Property Law: Open Science in Influenza*, 102 Cornell L. Rev. 1544–46 (Sept. 2017), https://scholarship.law.cornell.edu/cgi/viewcontent.cgi?article=4738&context=clr.

48 *Coronavirus: Everyone Wins When Patents are Pooled*, Editorials, 581 Nature 240 (2020).

49 *Id.*

50 Kapczynski, *supra* note 47, at 1591–95.

51 Coronavirus Treatment Acceleration Program (C-TAP) was first proposed by was first proposed by Costa Rica and aims to accelerate the development of vaccines and medicines through the sharing of research and information and to increase manufacturing capacity for any products that are developed. *See* COVID-19 Technology Access Pool, *Live: Launch of the COVID-19 Technology Access Pool*, World Health Org. (May 29, 2020), https://www.who.int/emergencies/diseases/novel-coronavirus-2019/global-research-on-novel-coronavirus-2019-ncov/covid-19-technology-access-pool.

cooperation. If we are to prepare for the next pandemic, rapid knowledge production and dissemination are essential. Limits to accelerating scientific research and understanding must be removed to ensure the production and sharing of data, knowledge, and technology.[52] This would not only avert long delays from laboratories to market, but would help expedite rapid scale-up and manufacture of new treatment for future epidemics.

Second, in addition to the open-source model, a move back to publicly funded research and innovation as well as the strengthening of health systems, including laboratories, are essential. The chaos and unraveling of public health facilities by the COVID-19 crisis, even in developed countries, has accentuated how severely unprepared many countries are in dealing with the emergence of deadly viruses. Years of defunding health systems and publicly funded research and surveillance structures have severely weakened coordinated national responses to manage new risks and dangers. As we have seen, without a functioning health system, it is very hard for a country to deal with epidemics. A robust investment in health facilities and sustainable financing of public research laboratories capable of developing and manufacturing drugs and vaccines on their own would ensure that the public interest and not market forces drive innovation.

## Conclusion: TRIPS Agreement and Medicines Access

The myriad issues explored in this book, as we have seen, address distinct shifts and *ruptures* within the medicines access debates and global pharmaceutical patent regime. In focusing on these issues, the chapters in this book have interrogated the substantive concerns and crises of the global pharmaceutical patent regime. The COVID-19 pandemic redoubles these crises, further generating unforeseen chaos globally, which has both short- and long-term implications. Auspiciously, the current crisis presents an opportunity for change and creates space for new beginnings. The world has a chance for an enduring systemic reform of IP rights, pharmaceutical industry practices, and the global system for responding to outbreaks and other infectious diseases. Let us not waste a "good" crisis so that the catastrophe of the coronavirus pandemic and the unnecessary deaths will never be repeated.

52 Katrina Perehudoff & Jennifer Sellin, *COVID-19 Technology Access Pool (C-TAP): A Promising Human Rights Approach*, Medicines Law & Policy (June 18, 2020), https://medicineslawandpolicy.org/2020/06/covid-19-technology-access-pool-c-tap-a-promising-human-rights-approach/.

# Index

For Product Safety Concerns and Information please contact our EU
representative GPSR@taylorandfrancis.com
Taylor & Francis Verlag GmbH, Kaufingerstraße 24, 80331 München, Germany

www.ingramcontent.com/pod-product-compliance
Ingram Content Group UK Ltd.
Pitfield, Milton Keynes, MK11 3LW, UK
UKHW020024200926
475702UK00014B/2055
* 9 7 8 1 0 3 2 0 0 9 7 0 4 *